Lecture Notes in Artificial Intelligence 3192

Edited by J. G. Carbonell and J. Siekmann

Subseries of Lecture Notes in Computer Science

T0255325

Christoph Bussler   Dieter Fensel (Eds.)

Artificial Intelligence: Methodology, Systems, and Applications

11th International Conference, AIMSA 2004
Varna, Bulgaria, September 2-4, 2004
Proceedings

 Springer

Series Editors

Jaime G. Carbonell, Carnegie Mellon University, Pittsburgh, PA, USA
Jörg Siekmann, University of Saarland, Saarbrücken, Germany

Volume Editors

Christoph Bussler
Digital Enterprise Research Institute (DERI)
National University of Ireland
University Road, Galway, Ireland
E-mail: chris.bussler@deri.org

Dieter Fensel
Digital Enterprise Research Institute (DERI)
University of Innsbruck
Technikerstr. 13, 6020 Innsbruck, Austria
E-mail: dieter.fensel@deri.org

This work relates to the Department of Navy Grant N00014-04-11116 issued by the
Office of Naval Research International Field Office. The United States Government
has a royalty-free license for any governmental purpose in all material and proceedings
of this conference.

Library of Congress Control Number: 2004110972

CR Subject Classification (1998): I.2, H.4, F.1, H.3, I.5

ISSN 0302-9743
ISBN 3-540-22959-0 Springer Berlin Heidelberg New York

Springer is a part of Springer Science+Business Media

springeronline.com

© Springer-Verlag Berlin Heidelberg 2004
Printed in Germany

Typesetting: Camera-ready by author, data conversion by PTP-Berlin, Protago-TeX-Production GmbH
Printed on acid-free paper   SPIN: 11317104   06/3142   5 4 3 2 1 0

Preface

The 11th Conference "Artificial Intelligence: Methodology, Systems, Applications – Semantic Web Challenges" (AIMSA 2004) continued successfully pursuing the main aim of the AIMSA series of conferences – to foster the multidisciplinary community of artificial intelligence researchers, embracing both the theoretic underpinnings of the field and the practical issues involved in development, deployment, and maintenance of systems with intelligent behavior. Since the first conference in 1984 AIMSA has provided an ideal forum for international scientific exchange between Central/Eastern Europe and the rest of the world and it is even more important nowadays in the unifying Europe.

The current AIMSA edition is focused on Semantic Web methods and technologies. The Internet is changing the everyday services landscape, and the way we do things in almost every domain of our life. Web services are rapidly becoming the enabling technology of today's e-business and e-commerce systems, and will soon transform the Web as it is now into a distributed computation and application framework. The emerging Semantic Web paradigm promises to annotate Web artefacts to enable automated reasoning about them. When applied to e-services, the paradigm hopes to provide substantial automation for activities such as discovery, invocation, assembly, and monitoring of e-services.

One hundred and seventy-six interesting papers were submitted to the conference. Each paper was reviewed by at least three independent reviewers. The programme committee selected for the conference program 56 high-quality contributions. 52 of them were prepared in time to form the current volume. These papers concern a wide spectrum of artificial intelligence areas, e.g., ontology engineering, Semantic Web tools and services, but also some traditional AI topics, e.g., knowledge representation, machine learning and data mining, natural language processing, soft computing, multi-agent systems, e-learning Systems, intelligent decision making, and intelligent information retrieval.

AIMSA 2004 invited two keynote speakers: Jeffrey T. Pollock from Network Inference for his contributions to AI business applications, and Darina Dicheva for her work on Semantic Web approaches to e-learning.

We would like to thank the AIMSA program committee and the additional reviewers for their hard work in helping make this conference a success.

July 2004

Christoph Bussler
Dieter Fensel

Conference Chair

Dieter Fensel
Digital Enterprise Research Institute
Innsbruck, Austria

Program Committee Chair

Christoph Bussler
Digital Enterprise Research Institute
Galway, Ireland

Program Committee

Karl Aberer (Switzerland)
Nabil Adam (USA)
Sudhir Agarwal (Germany)
Gennady Agre (Bulgaria)
Marco Aiello (Italy)
Yuan An (Canada)
Anupriya Ankolekar (USA)
Budak Arpina (USA)
Boualem Benatallah (Australia)
Bettina Berendt (Germany)
Sonia Bergamaschi (Italy)
Abraham Bernstein (Switzerland)
Elisa Bertino (Italy)
Omar Boucelma (France)
Paolo Bresciani (Italy)
Diego Calvanese (Italy)
Fabio Casati (USA)
Tiziana Catarci (Italy)
Edward Chang (USA)
Vincenzo D'Andrea (Italy)
Veleria de Antonellis (Italy)
Maarten de Rijke (The Netherlands)
Stefan Decker (Ireland)
Christo Dichev (USA)
Ying Ding (Austria)
Danail Dochev (Bulgaria)
Asuman Dogac (Turkey)
Jerome Euzenat (France)
Martin Frank (USA)
Martin Gaedke (Germany)
Jonathan Gelati (Italy)
Carole Goble (UK)
Asun Gomez-Perez (Spain)
Sergio Greco (Italy)
William Grosso (USA)
Francesco Guerra (Italy)
Siegfried Handschuh (Germany)
Andreas Hotho (Germany)

Zachary Ives (USA)
Paul Johannesson (Sweden)
Gerti Kappel (Austria)
Vipul Kashyap (USA)
Alfons Kemper (Germany)
Rania Khalaf (USA)
Roger King (USA)
Atanas Kiryakov (Bulgaria)
Mauel Kolp (Belgium)
Irena Korpinska (Australia)
Manolis Koubarakis (Greece)
Winfried Lamersdorf (Germany)
Doug Lea (USA)
Alain Leger (France)
Qing Li (Hong Kong)
Xuemin Lin (Australia)
Chengfei Liu (Australia)
Jianguo Lu (Canada)
Raphael Malyankar (USA)
Ioana Manolescu (France)
Maurizio Marchese (Italy)
Massimo Marchiori (Italy)
David Martin (USA)
Pat Martin (Canada)
Brian McBride (UK)
Massimo Mecella (Italy)
Sergey Melnik (Germany)
Michele Missikoff (Italy)
Pavlos Moraitis (Cyprus)
Boris Motik (Germany)
Enrico Motta (UK)
Haralambos Mouratidis (UK)
Claire Nedellec (France)
Natasha Noy (USA)
Borys Omelayenko (The Netherlands)
Maria Orlowska (Australia)
Massimo Paolucci (USA)
Mike Papazoglou (The Netherlands)

Loris Penserini (Italy)
Giacomo Piccinelli (UK)
Dimitris Plexousakis (Greece)
Christoph Quix (Germany)
Zbigniew Ras (USA)
Michael Rosemann (Australia)
Michael Rys (USA)

Shazia Sadiq (Australia)
Wasim Sadiq (Australia)
Monica Scannapieco (Italy)
Guus Schreiber (The Netherlands)
Karsten Schulz (Australia)
Ming-Chien Shan (USA)
Keng Siau (USA)

Additional Reviewers

David Ahn
Ferda N. Alpaslan
Nedjem Ayat
Kartik Babu
Shahram Bahadori
Toby Baier
Roberta Benassi
Marco Benedetti
D. Beneventano
Daniela Berardi
Stephan Bloehdorn
George Boukeas
Lars Braubach
Andrea Calì
Malu Castellanos
Jean Caussanel
S. Sze-Man Chan
Jing Chen
Philipp Cimiano
Dana Cobzas
Ahmet Cosar
Simon Cox
Gregory Craske
P. Cudre-Mauroux
Arun D. Qamra
Agnieszka Dardzinska
Anwitaman Datta
Luigi Dragone
Ludger van Elst
Peter Fankhauser
Alain Ferrarini
Rudi Freund
Alfredo Garro
Gionata Gelati
Rosella Gennari

Georgi Gluhchev
Daniel Gmach
Ozgur Gulderen
Chris Halaschek
Nadim Haque
Dau Hoang
Bodo Huesemann
Prasad Jayaweera
Andrew Jennings
Esther Kaufmann
Markus Keidl
Shailesh Kelkar
Christoph Kiefer
Stephen Kimani
Fabius Klemm
Jacek Kopecky
Iris Kösters
Richard Kuntschke
Brian Lam
Alexander Lazovik
Jens Lechtenboerger
Yuangui Lei
Elvis Leung
Sonia Lippe
Riccardo Maroglia
F. Martin-Recuerda
Eric Max Meisner
Michele Melchiori
Diego Milano
Willie Milnor
Daniele Miselli
Vladimir Monov
Daniele Montanari
Kemal Oflazer
Emanuele Olivetti

Navneet Panda
Markus Peters
Eleftheria Petraki
Alexander Pokahr
George Potamias
Jean-Francois Puget
Maurizio Rafanelli
Dnyanesh Rajpathak
Andreas Rauber
Martin Reczko
Robert Richardson
Mark Riding
Jean-Claude Saghbini
Nora Sanchez
Federica Schiappelli
Christoph Schmitz
Ron Van Schyndel
Zhe Shan
Spiros Skiadopoulos
Gleb Skobeltsyn
Diego Sona
Nikolaos Spanoudakis
Peter Stuckey
Yannis Stylianou
Andrea Tagarelli
Francesco Taglino
Julien Tane
Ismail Hakki Toroslu
F. Toumani
Erwan Tranvouez
Irina Trubitsyna
Vassil Vassilev
S. Veeramachaneni
Kunal Verma
Peter Vorburger

Wei-Jen Wang
Peter Westerkamp
Alicja Wieczorkowska
Gang Wu

Jie Wu
Yi Wu
Murat Yukselen
Massimo Zancanaro

Bernhard Zeller
Ning Zhang
Yuting Zhao
Anna Zhdanova

Local Organizers

Danail Dochev (Chair)
Gennady Agre

Violeta Magerska
Ivo Marinchev

Kamenka Staykova

Table of Contents

Knowledge Presentation and Processing

Machine Learning and Data Mining

Natural Language Processing

Soft Computing

Neural Networks

E-learning Systems

Multi-agent Systems

Pattern Recognition

Intelligent Decisionmaking

Information Retrieval

Adoption of the Classical Theory of Definition to Ontology Modeling

Patryk Burek

Onto-Med Research Group, University of Leipzig, Germany
burek@informatik.uni-leipzig.de

Abstract. Ontology modeling requires modeling languages expressive enough to represent various definition types. A definition type which seems to be of particular significance is that provided by the Classical Theory of Definition. In this paper we investigate if and how far the Classical Theory of Definition is adopted by some of the ontology modeling formalisms, namely by UML, ORM and DL. Moreover, we provide a means for representing some crucial issues in the context of the Classical Theory of Definition which seem to have no representation in the formalisms discussed. Among them are the identification of essential, peculiar and incidental predications and the representation of subsumption in the manner of the genus-differentia definition.

Keywords: Knowledge Representation, Ontology Engineering, Knowledge Modeling.

1 Introduction

The backbone of ontology modeling is the construction of a taxonomy of concepts founded on subsumption links. It seems so far that there is no agreement on the nature of subsumption [2], [17] and on the rules of taxonomy evaluation [5]. Moreover, one can observe that the definitional status of the concepts in most of the domains is not equal. There are various techniques used for defining concepts and there are tacit assumptions often lost during the ontology engineering/knowledge modeling process. The development of data models/ontologies not suffering from deformation of the input knowledge is still a difficult task. Of some help here may be the theories of concepts, definitions and categorization developed across philosophy, linguistics and cognitive science. Here we concentrate on the oldest of these theories, namely on the Classical Theory of Definition. The Classical Theory of Definition seems especially promising for modeling taxonomies, since it provides an interesting genus-differentia pattern for representing subsumption and permits making more explicit some of the tacit assumptions underlying the concept definitions.

In this paper we examine how far the Classical Theory of Definition is adopted by some of the languages proposed for ontology modeling. The formalisms investigated include Unified Modeling Language (UML), Object Role Modeling (ORM) and Description Logic (DL). Arguments for adopting UML, which was developed for soft

C. Bussler and D. Fensel (Eds.): AIMSA 2004, LNAI 3192, pp. 1–10, 2004.

ware engineering, in ontology engineering are proposed in [4], [7]. It seems that ORM, which is, like UML, a commonly used software engineering technique, may be of some use in ontology engineering for the same reasons. DL has recently become a prime candidate for ontology modeling especially in the context of the Semantic Web.

The purpose of this work is not to provide a comparison or a ranking of the formalisms discussed: our work concentrates only on the following issue: how far the Classical Approach is adopted in each of these formalisms and what consequences it may have on ontology modeling.

For those aspects of the Classical Theory of Definition that are not reflected in the formalisms discussed we propose a framework of definitional tags. Our framework of tags is not intended as a new formalism for ontology modeling but rather as the general extension pattern of the formalisms discussed. Among the issues supported by the framework introduced are the identification of essential, peculiar and incidental predications and the representation of subsumption in the manner of the genus-differentia definition.

In the case of UML, only class diagrams will be investigated and only classes will be interpreted as *ontological* concepts. The notions of concept, UML class and ORM entity type are used here as equivalent.

We use the notions of concept extension and intension as they are generally accepted in the literature. By concept extension we understand the set of all objects for which a concept can be truly predicated. By concept intension we understand a set of its *defining characteristics* [15].

Section 2 discusses the basic tenets of the Classical Theory of Definition. In section 3 the distinction between essential, peculiar and incidental components of definitions is discussed. In section 4 the genus-differentia definition is analyzed, and in section 5 conclusions are presented. The overall structure of sections 2, 3 and 4 is as follows: first the preliminaries are presented, secondly DL, UML and ORM are analyzed with respect to the given issues and finally our proposal is introduced.

2 Basic Tenets of the Classical Theory of Definition

We consider here the Classical Theory of Definition in a broad sense dating back to ancient Greek philosophy. The following two fragments encode the Classical Theory of Definition: [1]

> Most concepts (esp. lexical concepts) are structured mental representations that encode a set of necessary and sufficient conditions for their application. [8]

> The Classical Theory of Definition has two principal tenets: that there are intensional definitions for each of the class terms which we use; and that a 'proper' intensional

---

[1] The first paragraph refers to the Classical Theory of Definition, concerned with the structure of definition, while the second refers to the Classical Theory of Concepts concerned with the structure of concepts. For our purposes this distinction is not relevant so we treat both theories as aspects of the same approach, called later the Classical Approach or the Classical Theory of Definition.

definition states in the definiens the logically necessary and sufficient conditions for the application of the definiendum. [15]

Both fragments have in common the optimistic assumption that concepts are definable by the necessary and sufficient conditions of concept application.

Furthermore, both fragments reveal the second tenet of the Classical Approach concerning the definition's structure: the definition is a compound of sufficient and necessary conditions for the concept application. The definition consists of the definiendum, the definiens and the copula jointing them. The definiendum contains the concept to be defined. Of interest for our purposes here are the definitions where the definiendum contains only the defined term – explicit definitions.

The definiens defines the definiendum and is understood here as the conjunction of the true predications about the definiendum, although other functional patterns of the definiens [10] may be investigated in the future. The definiens and the definiendum are linked by the copula being the equivalence functor, which indicates that the definiens provides both sufficient and necessary conditions.

2.1 Analysis: Basic Tenets in DL, UML, and ORM

Generally in knowledge modeling the first tenet of the Classical Approach is commonly accepted - knowledge is definable and presentable in the form of intensional definitions. The second tenet seems to be accepted too. We will see that the classical structure of the definition is adopted in UML, ORM and DL.

In DL concepts are defined in the Terminology Box (TBox) by explicit definitions in the classical manner. The definitions can be equivalences with only the defined concept in the definiendum [1].

In UML definitions have a graphical form. Each class is represented by a rectangle divided into compartments separated by horizontal lines (Fig.1) [12]. The top compartment containing only a class name can be interpreted as the definiendum. The middle list compartment holds the list of attributes, the bottom one the list of operations. Together with associations assigned to the class they provide the intension specification and can be interpreted as the definiens.

In UML classes are defined by necessary and sufficient conditions. The full list of class attributes, operations and associations delimits precisely the direct class extension. Hence we see that UML meets also the second tenet of the Classical Approach.

In ORM concepts, called entity types, are also defined in a graphical form (Fig 2) [6]. Each entity type is presented as an oval with a name of the entity type in it. The oval with the name can be interpreted as the definiendum. Entity types play roles in facts. Facts are depicted as rectangles divided into named boxes. Each box represents the role of the entity linked with it by an arc. The list of all roles played by an object provides the necessary and sufficient conditions for instantiation of the entity.

We see then that all three formalisms permit the definitions of the classical structure. UML and ORM moreover seem to restrict the definition types to only the classical one, while DL allows also another, less restrictive, definition type in form of the inclusion axiom.

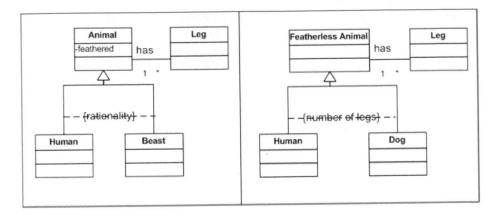

Fig. 1. An UML diagram with a discriminator

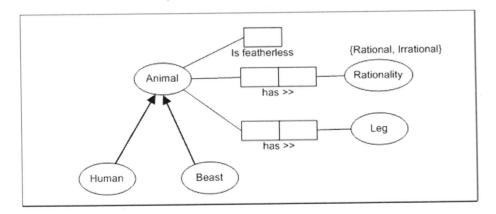

Fig. 2. An ORM diagram

3 Account of Essence

Originally, the classical definition not only provided necessary and sufficient conditions, but according to Aristotle it was the account of essence [9], [13]. An account of essence is the answer to the question "what makes a thing what it is?". The sentence "a human is an animal" tells something which is fundamental (essential) for *human*, but on the other hand saying that "human is civilized" is not fundamental for *human* but rather something that merely happens to be universally true for *human* and only for him. The second predication, in contrast to the essential, is called peculiar. The predication reflecting nonessential features that are not shared by all referents of the concept is called incidental [9], [13].

It is questionable whether one can reveal the essence of things, and whether such a demand is not the result of the excessively high ambitions of some philosophers. This question is, however, outside the scope of our interest here. The point here is to distinguish statements that are true parts of definitions from those which only happen to be true. Hence we understand an essence in a "lite" version, not as the true objective nature of things, but as the intentions of a definition's author. The essence of a concept is what an author of the concept's definition believes is fundamental for an object to be understood as a member of the concept's extension.

3.1 Analysis: Account of Essence in DL, UML, and ORM

The distinction between essential, peculiar and incidental predications is partially adopted in systems performing classification, where the properties that are true parts of definitions are separated from those nonessential. The nonessential properties are shared by all members of the concept's extension but are not considered as parts of the concept's definition. The classification algorithm requires that the position of a concept in a taxonomy does not depend on contingent facts, even those which are universally true. In CLASSIC [3] nonessential properties are modeled not as parts of a concept's definition but as rules that do not take part in the classification. Brachman suggests in [1] to model nonessential properties in DL not as parts of definitions in TBox but in ABox. Nonessential properties are treated then not as definitional knowledge but as assertional knowledge.

Here one may raise the question of whether the assertion that "Socrates is a human" and the assertion that "a human is civilized" have the same relevance for the definition of the human. It seems that the second statement although not essential for humans still plays a definitional role while the first does not. The ABox does not provide any means to separate the assertions involved, even non-essentially, in definitions, from those not involved in definitions at all. The definitional relevance of nonessential predication seems to be of particular importance in cases where revealing the essence of concepts is problematic. In many domains, including scientific and technical domains, definitions are not intended to provide an account of the essence. It seems that authors of those definitions do not intend to point at any fundamental features of concept referents. In such cases, if we strictly follow the above suggestion many concepts would lack definitions in TBox completely and all knowledge stated about them would be contained only in ABox, where nonessential but definitional knowledge would be mixed with purely assertional knowledge.

We observe then that the explicit representation of the distinction between essential, peculiar and incidental properties in DL runs into some problems. Neither in UML nor ORM do we find a means to represent it.

3.2 Proposal: Definitional Tags

The essential, peculiar and incidental properties can be introduced by the definitional tags. The following tags can be introduced: [essential], [peculiar], and [incidental]. These tags can be assigned to any predication present in the definiens, for example:

human ≡ [essential]animal ∧ [essential]rational;
human ≡ [essential]animal ∧ [peculiar]rational.

In both examples the extension of *human* is the same. The intentions seem to be equal as well, since both definitions use the same, *animal* and *rational,* predications.

What distinguishes these two definitions is the relevance of the predication *rational*. In the first definition *humans* are essentially rational animals (*humans* are essentially *animals* and essentially *rational*). In the second example *humans* are essentially *animals* but the fact that that they are *rational* is not essential, although common to all *humans*. It seems that although both definitions have the same extension and intension the assumptions and the intents behind them are different. The definitional tags [essential], [peculiar], [incidental] permit us to grasp these differences.

4 Genus-Differentia Definition

A well-known representative of the Classical Approach is the genus-differentia definition. It was introduced by Aristotle and later elaborated by medieval philosophers [9], [14]. It has a peculiar structure, where the definiens is composed of two elements: the genus and the differentia. The genus subsumes the defined concept and its extension should be possibly the closest to the extension of the defined concept, thus the genus should be the nearest (genus proximum). The differentia specifies the features distinguishing the referents of the defined concept from the referents of other concepts subsumed by the same genus. An example of the genus-differentia definition is the Aristotelian definition of a human: "a human is a rational animal". Here an *animal* is the genus and *rational* is the differentia which distinguishes *humans* from *beasts*.

4.1 Analysis: Genus-Differentia Definition in DL, UML, and ORM

DL permits definitions of the form: *human* ≡ *animal* ∧ *rational*. However the elements of the conjunction are not recognizable in any way as the genus and the differentia. Hence we see that DL does not permit us to explicitly identify the roles played by the components of the genus-differentia definition.

In UML, a generalization with a discriminator can be interpreted as the genus-differentia definition. The generalization associates the class to its parent class. The parent class can thus be interpreted as the nearest genus. The discriminator names the partition of the parent class. The discriminator joins the generalization arc with other generalization arcs taking part in the same partition. In our example on the left-hand side of Fig.1, *rationality* is a discriminator.

The discriminator name must be unique among the attributes and association roles of the parent class. Multiple occurrences of the same discriminator name are permitted and indicate that the children belong to the same partition. Hence one could say that the discriminator names the feature to which the differentia refers. However, it does not name the differentia itself nor does any other element of UML. All attributes, operations and associations of the child class distinguish it form the parent. However, they can not all be treated as the differentia, since some of them may be shared with other children in the same partition.

In ORM subtype entities are introduced by subtype links which are directed line segments from subtypes to supertypes and by the definitions written under the diagram. The following two definitions specify the subtype entity *human* on Fig. 2: Each *human* is an *animal* which is *rational*; Each *human* is an *animal* which is *featherless* and has two *legs*. The first example in the context of the diagram presented in Fig. 2 can be read: Each *human* is an *animal* who has *rationality* of level "rational". "Rational" is a value of a reference mode of the entity type *rationality* related to the supertype a*nimal*. It plays the role of the differentia in the definition of *human*. In the second example, the differentia is a conjunction of two conditions. The first one is a unary fact *featherless* related to the supertype a*nimal*, the second is the number restriction on the *has (legs)* fact.

The above examples show that the definition pattern adopted in ORM allows every diagram element to play the role of the differentia. However, in ORM the differentia is not marked out in the diagram, and is present only in the additional definition below the diagram. Neither the value *rational,* the fact *featherless* nor the number restriction 2 on the fact *has (legs)* are marked in any way on the diagram as the differentia. Their application in the definition of an entity type *human* cannot be read from the diagram. Moreover, we can observe that the discriminator is not present in ORM at all.

4.2 Proposal

We propose to decompose the notion of differentia to the notions of relationally interpreted differencing principle and difference. Then we introduce the definitional tags for representing subsumption by the pattern of the genus-differentia definitions.

4.2.1 Differencing Principle

The notion of the genus is present in all three formalisms discussed and is crucial for ontology modeling. However, the notion of the differentia is not so popular. Two different aspects seem to be of importance in the context of the differentia.

The first one is the discriminator present in UML. The discriminator can be interpreted as the principle of the class partition. Hence we call the discriminator the *differencing principle* applied to the parent class. A close look to the differencing principle shows that it could be understood as the attribute or the role of the parent class. This corresponds to the UML requirements for the uniqueness of the discriminator name among the parent class attributes and roles.

Furthermore we can observe that the discriminator refers to some other element of the class model. In the right-hand side of Fig. 1 the discriminator *number of legs* refers to the multiplicity of the association ending. UML, however, does not in any way point to the model element that is used as the discriminator. The discriminator in UML is independent from all other model elements.

Instead of treating the discriminator as independent from other model elements we suggest interpreting it as a relational entity. We interpret the discriminator as the role of some model element in the partition of the given parent class. We say that some model element is applied to the given class as a differencing principle. In this case the multiplicity of the association end *number of legs* plays the role of the differencing principle applied to the class *animal*.

The differencing principle is the ground on which subclasses of the class to which it is applied are distinguished. In other words the differencing principle is a branching point of an ontology or an ontological choice. By applying differencing principles to categories, the hierarchical structure of the ontology is built.

The differencing principle can be interpreted as the attribute of the class it is applied to or as a question grounding the partition of that class. *Is rational?* and *how many legs does it have?* are both questions underlying the partition of the class *animal*. The differencing principle presented in the form of the question may be particularly fruitful. A linguistic analysis of the question structure can provide the additional properties of differencing principles and can help in further analysis of subsumption links based on them.

4.2.2 Difference

The second relevant aspect of the differentia, in addition to the differencing principle, is the differentia itself, which is the difference distinguishing the child class. It justifies the introduction of a child class in the context of a given partition. The differentia cannot be identified explicitly in UML or DL but only in ORM's subtypes definitions. The differentia can be interpreted as the value of the differencing principle or the answer to the question stated in the differencing principle. In the Aristotelian definition of human being, *rationality* is the differencing principle and the value *rational* is the differentia.

The differentia firstly distinguishes the child class from the parent class. *Human* is distinct from *animal* since it is *rational*. Secondly, the differentia distinguishes a class from other children classes in the given partition (with the same underlying differencing principle). This, however, only holds for the classification, while in the case of a typology the children concepts may overlap.

4.2.3 Genus-Differentia Tags

We propose to interpret the hierarchical structure based on the genus-differentia definition as the application of a differencing principle to a parent class, where the differencing principle is the role of some element of the model or has the references extending the model. We propose a genus-differentia subsumption pattern based not on a binary subsumption relation, graphically presented by the arrowed edge linking the parent class with the child class, eventually with a discriminator, but as a relation with the following four arguments:

1. Genus as the supertype;
2. Species as the subtype;
3. Differencing principle as the role of some other model element or as the external reference;
4. Differentia - the property of the species interpreted as the corresponding value of the differencing principle or as the answer to the question stated by it.

These four elements of the subsumption can be identified by the following three tags: [gen], [spec], [diff ref=""]. The tags [gen] and [spec] identify, respectively, the supertype and the subtype; the differentia is tagged with [diff ref=""] where ref="" refers to the element playing the role of the differencing principle. For example the definition "A human is a rational animal" annotated with the tags would have the following form:

$$[\text{spec}]\text{human} \equiv [\text{gen}]\text{animal} \wedge [\text{diff ref="rationality"}]\text{rational};$$

where [spec]human and [gen]animal state, respectively, that *human* is a species and *animal* is a genus. [diff ref="rationality"]rational states that *rational* is the differentia with the underlying differencing principle *rationality* which is present in the model or refers to an external source.

5 Conclusions

In the current paper we analyzed how far the Classical Theory of Definition is adopted by the selected ontology modeling languages. We analyzed UML, ORM and DL with respect to the issues relevant for the Classical Theory of Definition. We have observed that some of the tenets of the Classical Approach are accepted in all three formalisms discussed, for example the optimistic assumption of definability of knowledge by both sufficient and necessary conditions. However, we have found that some of the issues of the Classical Approach are not supported by any of the formalisms discussed, like the distinction between essential, peculiar and incidental predications, and some are supported only partially, like the genus-differentia definition. To enable the representation of these issues we have proposed a framework of the definitional tags.

We believe that the Classical Approach adopted by the tags offers several advantages for modeling the taxonomical structures of concepts. Among them the following:
1. Tags [essential], [peculiar], [incidental] identify the tacit intuitions of the author of a definition; separate the essential knowledge from the nonessential; and permit concepts to be distinguished even if their intension and extension are equal.
2. Tags [spec], [gen], [diff ref=""] bind a parent concept and a child concept with the principle of partition and make the subsumption more explicit:
   - [ref=""] identifies the differencing principle, which is a branching point of the taxonomy and serves as the principle of partition. It seems particularly useful in the case of multiple partitions of parent concept;
   - [diff ref=""] labels the characteristics that distinguish the concept in the given partition and that makes the concept a member of that partition. In the case of the multiple subsumption it enables us to state the features by which a concept is assigned to each partition;
   - [ref=""] reduces redundancy in the case of UML and ORM. Instead of adding a new independent model element, one already present in the model is identified as the differencing principle;
   - [ref=""] permits the definitional dependencies in UML and ORM to be traced. It enables one to identify which concepts are suitable as the foundations for the definitions of other concepts. In our second example, we observe that for defining the concept *human,* the concept of *rationality* is needed;
   - [ref=""] identifies the borderlines of the model. In some cases the differencing principle may refer to a concept that is not present in a model. By treating a dif-

ferencing principle as the relational entity, we can state explicitly that the model refers at this point to the external source.

The tags introduced are not intended as a new ontology modeling formalism but rather as a general modeling pattern that could be embodied as an extension to the formalisms discussed. The framework is not intended to be a normative theory of taxonomy evaluation either as it is in the OntoClean approach [5]. Nevertheless, the important task which exceeds the scope of this paper, however, is to compare the tags presented with the meta-properties of OntoClean.

Acknowledgments. I am indebted to Professor Heinrich Herre, Rafał Grabo , Frank Loebe, Hannes Michalek for fruitful discussions and to Hesham Khalil, Evan Mellander and the anonymous reviewers for feedback on earlier versions of this paper.

References

1. Baader, F., et al. (eds.): Description Logic Handbook. Cambridge University Press (2002)
2. Brachman, R.: What isa is and isn't: an analysis of taxonomic links in semantic networks. IEEE Computer, 16(10) (1983)
3. Brachman, R. et al.: Living with CLASSIC: When and how to use a KL-ONE-like language. In Sowa J (ed.): Principles of Semantic Networks. Morgan Kaufmann (1991)
4. Cranefield S., Purvis M.: UML as an ontology modeling language. Proc. IJCAI-99 (1999)
5. Guarino, N., Welty C.: Ontological Analysis of Taxonomic Relationships. In Leander, A., Storey, V. (eds.): Proc. ER-2000. Springer-Verlag LNCS (2000)
6. Halpin, T.: Object-Role Modeling. In Bernus, P., Mertins, K., Schmidt, G. (eds.): Handbook on Architectures of Information Systems. Springer-Verlag, Berlin (1998)
7. Kogut P., et al.: UML for Ontology Development. http://www.sandsoft.com/docs/ker4.pdf
8. Laurence, S., Margolis. E. Concepts and Cognitive Science. In Laurence, S., Margolis. E. (eds.): Concepts Core Reading. MIT Press (1999)
9. Kotarbi ski, T.: Wykłady z Dziejów Logiki. PWN. Warszawa (1985)
10. Rickert, H.: The Theory of Definition. In Seger J., C.: Essays on Definition. John Benjamins Publishing Company. Amsterdam / Philadelphia (2000)
11. Robinson, R.: Definition. Oxford University Press (1963)
12. Rumbaugh, J., Jacobsson, I., Booch, G.: The Unified Modeling Language Reference Manual. Addison Wesley Longman Inc. (1999)
13. Smith, R.: Aristotle's Logic. In Edward N. Zalta (ed.): The Stanford Encyclopedia of Philosophy. URL = http://plato.stanford.edu/archives/fall2003/entries/aristotle-logic. (2003)
14. Sowa J.: Knowledge Representation. Brooks/Cole (2000)
15. Swartz, N.: Definitions, Dictionaries, and Meaning. URL=http://www.sfu.ca/philosophy/swartz/definitions.htm#part2.1 (1997)
16. Temmerman, R.: Towards New Ways of Terminology Description. John Benjamins Publishing Company. Amsterdam / Philadelphia (2000)
17. Woods, W.: Understanding subsumption and taxonomy: A framework for progress. in Sowa, J.F. (ed.) Principles of Semantic Networks. Morgan Kaufmann, San Mateo, CA (1991)

An Approach to Evaluate Existing Ontologies for Indexing a Document Corpus

Nathalie Hernandez[1,2] and Josiane Mothe[1,2]

[1] IRIT, 118 route de Narbonne,
31040 Toulouse, France
{hernandez, mothe}@irit.fr
[2] IUFM, 56 av. de l'URSS,
31078 Toulouse cedex, France

Abstract. Using ontologies for IR is one of the key issues for indexing. It is not always easy to decide which ontology to use for the corpus to index. We propose to define measures reflecting the adequacy of an ontology to a corpus. The goal of these measures is to evaluate if an ontology suits a corpus, but also to compare the adequacy of two or more ontologies to the same corpus. The measures are based on a lexical and a conceptual analysis of the corpus and the ontology. We have carried out a first validation of these measures on a corpus and samples of the ontologies. The results are encouraging.

Keywords: ontology, information retrieval, indexing, adequacy

1 Introduction

As defined in [12], "the semantic web is an extension of the current Web in which information is given well-defined meaning… It is based on the idea of having data on the web defined and linked such that it can be used for more effective discovery, automation, integration, and **reuse** across various applications". In order to be able to add semantics to the current web, ontologies are used as a mechanism for representing such formal and shared domain descriptions. Many newly developed techniques require and enable the specification of ontologies [25]. Thanks to the growing interest in ontologies in the field of information systems, freely accessible ontologies are emerging. Nowadays a key issue in Information Retrieval (IR) is to develop search engines capable of taking into account the knowledge represented by these ontologies. Indexing documents using ontologies makes it possible to define descriptors represented by concepts instead of keywords which are often ambiguous [7]. It also gives a structure to the information [1]. The first step in such processes is to find which domain ontology will contain the right knowledge to improve the indexing of a document corpus. One solution is to create an ontology from the corpus that is indexed either manually or through techniques based on natural language processing. This solution is costly and does not take into consideration the existence of resources that could be reused. The aim of the study presented in this article is thus to define measures capable of identifying if an existing ontology is appropriate to index a

C. Bussler and D. Fensel (Eds.): AIMSA 2004, LNAI 3192, pp. 11–21, 2004.

document corpus and also in the case when several ontologies exist which one is the most suited. The application field is astronomy. In this field, two freely accessible ontologies exist [8] [14]. Both contain more than a thousand concepts. Building a new ontology from an astronomy corpus is a challenging task as in this domain a huge number of notions or concepts can be found.

This paper is organized as follows. We will first present a state of the art on ontologies and IR. We will then propose measures which aim to evaluate the adequacy of an ontology to a document corpus. Finally, we will present a first validation of these measures taking examples from a document corpus linked to the field of astronomy and ontologies freely accessible in this field.

2   Ontology and IR

2.1   Definitions

The term " ontology " has been borrowed from the field of philosophy in which it means "the essence of the essential". In the field of knowledge management, its meaning is different. Gruber [11] introduces the concept of ontology as "an explicit specification of a conceptualisation". This definition has been modified slightly by Borst [4] and the combination of their two definitions is commonly summarized as "an explicit and formal specification of a shared conceptualisation". An ontology provides a sound base for communication between machines and also between humans and machines by defining the meaning of objects first through the symbols (words and phrases) that represent and characterize them and secondly through the structured or formal representation of their role in the domain. Different semiotic levels must be taken into consideration in an ontology [18]. The *lexical level* covers all the terms used to transcribe the meaning of concepts. The *conceptual level* represents the concepts and the conceptual relationships between them. Numerous types of knowledge structures lie behind the word ontology (taxonomy, thesaurus …). These data structures may be both terminological (containing a set of terms), and conceptual (defining concepts). However, these structures may differ in their content (general knowledge: WordNet, Cycl; knowledge of a specific domain: MeSH…), in the type of semantic relations between the concepts (taxonomical, meronymical …) and in the level of formalisation (logical representation, representation in a Semantic Web language such as DAML+OIL, OWL …).

2.2   Use of Ontologies in IR

More and more research is being devoted to the formulation of queries and the indexation of documents using ontologies. Such a semantic approach in IR systems seems particularly promising for improving their performance [19]. An ontology should thus lead to a refining of a system based on a traditional indexing process by increasing the likelihood of a query being formulated with terms or descriptors which best represent the information needed. The query can be expanded, and recall[1] [24] increased, thanks to the relations between the concepts present in the query and those present in the ontology. In OntoBroker and $(Ka)^2$ [2] [9] for example, web pages are manually annotated according to the concepts of the ontology. For any given query, all the concepts related to the concept found in the query are inferred and added to the query. In the same way, the terms used in the query will be disambiguized when referred to the definitions and the relations between the concepts present in the ontology, thus improving precision[2][24].

An ontology can also be used to index documents. In this case, the descriptors of the documents are no longer taken directly from the documents but from the ontology itself. The texts are therefore indexed by concepts which reflect their meaning rather than by words which are frequently ambiguous. It is necessary in this case to use an ontology which reflects the domain(s) of knowledge treated in the document collection.

Moreover, indexing collections using an ontology presents the following advantages: [1].

- It helps the user formulate the query. By presenting the user with the ontology, it is possible to guide him/her in his/her choice of terms used in the query. Several interfaces for the visualisation and exploration of ontologies have been proposed, for example KAON [5], Graphlet [13].

- It facilitates IR in heterogeneous collections by indexing all types of documents according to the same concepts.

In the IR context, an ontology is not usually represented logically. The formalism used generally facilitates the management of concepts as objects, their classification, the comparison of their properties and navigation within the ontology by accessing a concept and those related with it.

3 Ontology Adequacy to a Corpus

This study concerns the use of an ontology to index and explore a corpus linked to a specific domain. Rather than aim at generating a new ontology to cover a particular domain, we have focused on evaluating the link between the information and an existing ontology or ontologies. Measuring adequacy will enable us to evaluate the relevance of the choice of the starting ontology and then its shortcomings and the

---

[1] recall refers to the proportion of correctly retrieved documents among the pertinent documents in the collection

[2] precision refers the proportion of correctly retrieved documents among the documents retrieved by the system

modifications needed when it is updated in function of the corpus to be treated. It will also make it possible to evaluate over a period of time the evolution of the terms and concepts of a domain in function of the updating required. We propose to evaluate the adequacy between an ontology and a corpus independently of information retrieval results. The model and the mechanism chosen for retrieval influence the performance of the system. We want the measures to be system independent. We consider that an ontology is appropriate for a corpus if the knowledge stated in the ontology reflects the knowledge stated in the corpus. Therefore the evaluation of the adequacy is based on different levels of analysis used in the domain of Knowledge Management (section 3.1)and on similarity measures defined in the domain on Information Theory (section 3.2). The ontologies considered in this study are composed of concepts (defined by one or eventually several terms or labels) and by taxonomical and non-taxonomical relations between concepts whose nature is specified (transitive, symmetric…). They are written in OWL-Lite.

3.1   Levels of Analysis

Two levels of analysis must be defined [18]: lexical analysis and conceptual analysis. Our approach therefore studies these two levels.

3.1.1   Lexical Analysis

Lexical analysis consists in comparing the list of terms in the ontology and the list of terms in the collection. This analysis is based on two steps.

The percentage of terms in the ontology also present in the corpus is calculated so as to evaluate the extent to which the ontology covers the corpus. If the number of terms of an ontology found in the collection is limited, the ontology is not considered adapted to the collection.

The terms which are representative of a collection are extracted using the measure tf.idf [24] which is frequently used in IR and which also indicates that a term is all the more representative if it occurs frequently in the text but is not frequent in the collection of texts. The percentage of these terms found in the collection is calculated. It is therefore possible to evaluate whether the important terms of the collection can be found in the ontology. An ontology formed from a list of terms covering that of the collection but not containing the representative terms must be updated. The terms can be added to the ontology by becoming labels of existing concepts or by defining new concepts.

3.1.2   Conceptual Analysis

This level of analysis determines whether the organisation of concepts within the ontology reflects the knowledge present in the document collection. This analysis is based on the following principle: "a concept is representative of a domain if it is related to other concepts of the domain"[7]. All the concepts of the ontology present in the corpus are extracted in order to calculate their representative power. One way to calculate this power would be to consider the number of relations involving the concept in the ontology regardless of the type of relation; this would give a basic evaluation of the principle. However, the relations present in an ontology are in fact of several types (taxonomical, meronymical, causal, functional, or with no logical property). Not taking the type into consideration would mean ignoring part of the semantic content of the ontology. We thus propose a solution based on semantic similarity between concepts taking into acount the type of relation. It is presented in the next section.

3.2 Measures of Adequacy

We propose to evaluate the representative power of a concept within an ontology according to a given corpus thanks to semantic similarity measures defined in the field of information theories.

3.2.1 Similarity Between Concepts Within an Ontology

The evaluation of the semantic link between two concepts based on network representations has long been a problem in the fields of artificial intelligence and psychology. Semantic similarity is an evaluation of the semantic link which aims at estimating the degree to which two concepts are close in meaning [22]. Lin's definition of semantic similarity draws on three suppositions [16]. The similarity of two concepts is linked to the characteristics the concepts have in common (the more there are, the more similar they will be), and to their differences (the more two concepts are different, the less similar they will be). Maximum similarity is obtained when two concepts are identical.

There exists several measures of similarity between concepts linked by the relation "is a" The relation "is a" is a transitive, asymmetrical relation. The measures presented in [21] and [28] are calculated from the depth of each concept in the ontology. The measure proposed in [28] is more pertinent than the former as it takes into account the structure of the hierarchy by considering the depth of the subsuming (or generalising) concept of the two concepts in question. However, it accepts that the semantic distance between two concepts linked by the relation "is a" is equal whereas this is not necessarily the case. For example, astronomy is a science, as is cosmology, but astronomy is a more general science than cosmology. The semantic power of the relation "is a" is due to the choices made during the construction of the taxonomy. The drawbacks of the measures described above can be overcome by different measures which take into account the information content of the concepts. These measures are based on the following principle : the concepts are weighted by the function $IC(c) = -\log (p(c))$ corresponding to the information content of a concept. The probability of a concept c is calculated on the probability of obtaining this concept (and the concepts which subsume it) in a document collection in the domain.

$$\text{Freq(c)}= \sum_{n \in word(c)} count(n) \qquad p(c)= \frac{freq(c)}{N}$$

where word(c) represents all the terms representing the concept c and the concepts subsumed by c, count(n) the number of occurrences of n in the corpus, and N the total number of concepts found in the corpus.

Several similarity measures [22] [15] [16] have been defined considering that

$$pms(c1,c2)= \min_{c \in S(c1,c2)}\{p(c)\}$$

where S(c1,c2) is the set of concepts which subsume c1 and c2.

The probability of obtaining a concept takes into account the probability of obtaining this concept and all the concepts subsuming it, pms (or $_{u \setminus / ,}$) leads to taking the probability of the most specific subsumer of c1 and c2. The measure we have adopted (1) is that of [16]. This measure takes into account the information content of the most specific concept subsuming c1 and c2 but also that of c1and c2, which differentiates the similarity between several pairs of concepts with the same subsumer. This measure takes the values in [0,1] (0 corresponding to the concepts which are not similar and 1 to those which are identical). This measure has been recognized as giving good results in numerous works on calculating similarity between concepts [16] [6] [17].

$$sim(c1,c2)= \frac{2*log(pms(c1,c2)}{log(p(c1)+log(p(c2))} \tag{1}$$

Our aim in considering information content is to use the probability of obtaining a concept in a document corpus to counteract subjectivity in the choice of relations in the ontology. It is appropriate to use this measure in the context of evaluating a correlation between an ontology and a corpus as the evaluation is based on both the terms of the corpus and the organisation of the concepts in the ontology. Since the two ontologies of the astronomy domain were developed manually and therefore subjectively, the semantic distance represented by the relations must be measured. The measure (1) is also used to evaluate the similarity of concepts related by other transitive relations.

Ontologies generally use semantic relations other than the relation "is a". The ontologies of astronomy also includes the relation "part of" and "is related to". Mereology, which studies the relations "part of" and "whole of" plays an important role in ontologies. Studies generally recognized that these relations were transitive. However, Winston et al [26] have shown that this is not always the case as these relations do not represent a type of relation but a family of relations: component-object (pedal-bicycle), member-collection (tree-forest), portion-mass (slice-cake) matter-object (steel-bicycle), characteristic-object (pay-go shopping), place-region (oasis-desert). The ontologies used treat different aspects of the domain of astronomy which can call on different elements of the family of mereological relations (for example sun-solar system or core-earth). In this study, the relation "part of" is thus considered as non-transitive. The same is true for the relation "is related to". It is in fact intuitive to consider that three concepts linked by two relations "is related to" are not systematically related to each other. However unlike the relation "part of", the relation "is related to" is symmetric which means that the relation can be considered in both ways (if c1 is related to c2 by this relation, c2 is also related to c1).

The similarity measure (1) is then also used to evaluate the similarity between concepts related by non-transitive relations in so far as the path relating these two concepts contains other concepts related by this type of relation only once. In the opposite case, similarity is equal to 0. The possibility of having a symmetric relation is also taken into account by considering the relation both ways.

3.2.2 Representative Power of a Concept and Representative Power of an Ontology

The representative power of a concept in an ontology is then calculated as follows:

$$\text{Power}(c) = \sum_{ci \in C} sim(c, ci),$$

c being the set of concepts of the ontology found in the documents.

Very often, an ontology contains at least several hundred concepts, in which case it seems impossible to analyse each of the concepts individually. We propose therefore to define the representative power of the ontology O (result of the conceptual analysis) which is calculated by:

$$\text{Power}(O) = \sum_{c \in C} power(c)$$

c being the set of concepts of the ontology found in the documents.

4   Validation

A validation of the measures presented in the previous section has been carried out on an astronomy corpus and the two existing ontologies. In order to validate our result by astronomers, we have limited the domain considered to the field of "X RAY". A corpus containing 134 abstracts of articles related to this theme (published in the journal A&A in 1995) and a sample of the two ontologies [14] [8] have been considered. In figure 1, the samples of the ontologies (called A and B) are presented. The concepts are represented by the name of the concept and if necessary other labels describing the concept. All the concepts are subconcepts of a concept *top_astronomy* (not represented in the figure). The concepts with a dark border are the ones found in the corpus.

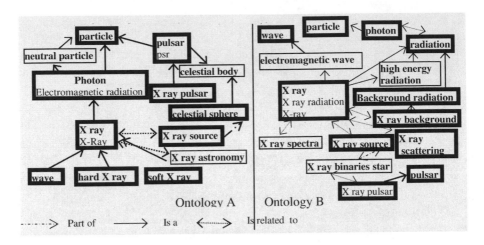

Fig. 1. Ontology A and Ontology B of X ray

To illustrate the measures presented in 3.2, here is how the representative power of the concept wave in ontology B is calculated.

p(wave)= $\frac{17+206}{343}$ as the concept wave appears 17 times in the corpus, its unique subsumer X ray 206 times and the total number of terms describing concepts form ontology B found in the corpus is 342

Power(wave)=sim(wave,x ray) +sim(wave,x ray source) + sim(wave,x ray scattering) + sim(wave, x ray background) + sim(wave, background radiation) + sim(wave,radiation) + sim(wave,photon) + sim(wave,particle) = 0,914+0,29+0,136+0,198+0,075+0,002+0,0022=1,6172

The concepts X ray pulsar and pulsar are also found in the corpus, but their similarity to wave is not calculated as more than one non-transitive relation links wave to this concept.

Sim(wave,x ray)= $\frac{2*\log(p(wave))}{\log(p(wave))+\log(p(xray))}$ =0,914,   as wave is the most specific sub-

sumer of wave and x ray

Sim(wave,particle)= $\frac{2*\log(p(top))}{\log(p(wave))+\log(p(xray))}$ =0,0022, as top is the most specific sub-

sumer of wave and particle. The probability of the top_astronomy concept is calculated by dividing the number of terms describing concepts found in the corpus minus 1 by the number of terms describing concepts found in the corpus. This enables its IC to be very low but the similarity can still be calculated.

The value of the concept wave power is for the most part due to its similarity to its subsumer x ray but the similarity to other concepts still influences the value. The values of the similarity to concepts related to wave through a non transitive relation (e.g. background relation) are higher than the values of similarity to concepts whose subsumer is top_astronomy concept (e.g. Particle). This is coherent as a concept is more similar to one that is related to it than to a concept of the domain not directly linked to it. This also shows that is it beneficial to take into consideration the other relations than 'is a'.

We have considered several power measure results to evaluate if this measure was likely to reflect the adequacy of a concept to a corpus and to compare concepts found in the two ontologies.

First, we considered the concept celestial body in ontology A. The power value of this concept in ontology A is 0,8. This value is lower than the average value obtained for the other concepts in this ontology. This is explained by the fact that this concept is only related to one concept found in the corpus. The term celestial body obtains a high score with the tf.idf measure. According to astronomers this concept is representative of the corpus. Its presence in the ontology is then justified but the value of the power indicates that its representation in the ontology is probably not appropriate (not correctly classified in the ontology). We are evaluating the power measure on other corpus and we aim to fix a threshold that will be able to tell if the representation of a concept is likely to be appropriate or not for a corpus.

Secondly, we considered the concept wave in ontology A The value of the power of this concept in ontology A is 1,7. This value is higher than the one obtained for this concept in ontology B (1,6). This is linked to the fact that in ontology A, the concept wave shares its super class X-ray with two concepts (hard x ray and soft x ray) considered by astronomers to be representative of the corpus that are not in ontology B. However, the power of wave in ontology A remains at the same scale as in ontology B, as it is linked to two representative concepts (x ray scattering and x ray background) not present in ontology A. Thus we can see that the measure of the representative power gives more importance to similarity with concepts that are related by the 'is a' relation than to concepts related by non transitive relations. This seems fair.

5 Conclusion

The use of ontologies is one of the key issues in IR. Deciding which ontology is most appropriate for indexing a corpus, however, is not evident. A solution followed in [27] among others, is to acquire automatically a domain ontology from the corpus. In the application field of our study (astronomy) two domain ontologies exist. Our solution is thus to reuse these existing resources which is also one of the aims of the semantic web. We have chosen to define measures reflecting the adequacy of an ontology to a corpus. The goal of these measures is to evaluate if an ontology suits a corpus, but also to compare the adequacy of two or more ontologies to the same corpus. The measures are based on a lexical and a conceptual analysis of the corpus and the ontology. Measures concerning ontologies have been defined in the literature.

Contrary to [18] that proposes to evaluate similarity between existing ontologies, our aim is to find the most suited to the corpus. [7] and [23] propose to evaluate adequacy between ontology and corpus but the ontologies considered were taxonomies. The measures presented in this article are defined for all transitive, non transitive and symmetric relations. We have carried out a first validation of these measures on a corpus and samples of the ontologies. The results are encouraging. An interface that enables a user to evaluate the results of the measures on two ontologies in OWL according to the same corpus is being developed. The concepts are presented in function of the results of the measures.

Future works will consist in carrying out other evaluations with astronomers as this study is part of a project on large scale data in astronomy. We also plan to take into consideration in the measures the data properties (according to OWL specifications), this will make the evaluation more accurate. A future step will also be to propose an ontology updating mechanism according to the measure results.

References

[1]   Aussenac-Gilles N., Mothe J., Ontologies as Background Knowledge to Explore Document Collections, RIAO, pp 129-142 2004.

[2]   Benjamins R., Fensel D., Decker D., Gomez Perez A., *(KA)2 : building ontologies for the internet : a mid-term report*, International Workshop on ontological engineering on the global information infrastructure, pp 1-24, 1999.

[3]   Bourigault D., Fabre C., " Approche linguistique pour l'analyse syntaxique de corpus ", *Cahiers de Grammaires,* n° 25, 2000, Université Toulouse - Le Mirail, p. 131-151

[4]   Borst P., Construction of Engineering Ontologies for Knowledge Sharing and Reuse, Ph.D Dissertation, Twente University, 1997.

[5]   Bozsak E., Ehrig M., Handschuh S., Hotho A., Maedche A., Motik B., Oberle D., Schmitz C., Staab S., Stojanovic L., Stojanovic N., Studer R., Stumme G., Sure Y., Tane J., Volz R., Zacharias V., KAON - Towards a Large Scale Semantic Web, EC-Web 2002, pp 304-313, 2002.

[6]   Budanitsky A., Hirst G., Semantic distance in WordNet: An experimental, application-oriented evaluation of five measures, Workshop on WordNet and Other Lexical Resources, ACL, 2001.

[7]   Desmontils E., Jaquin C., *Indexing a web site with a terminology oriented ontology*, The Emerging Semantic Web, I.F. Cruz S. Decker J. Euzenat and D. L. McGuinness Ed., IOS Press, pp 181-197, 2002 (ISBN 1-58603-255-0).

[8]   http://www.site.uottawa.ca:4321/astronomy/index.html

[9]   Fensel D., Ontologies: a silver bullet for Knowledge Management and Electronic Commerce, Berlin, Springer Verlag, 2001.

[10]   Guarino N., Masolo C., Vetere G., *OntoSeek: Content-Based Access to the Web*, IEEE Intelligent Systems, 14 (3), pp 70-80, 1999.

[11]   Gruber R. T., *A Translation Approach to Portable Ontology Specification,* Knowledge Acquisition (5), pp 199-220, 1993.

[12]   Hendler, J., Berners-Lee,T., Miller E.: Integrating Applications on the semantic Web. (2002)

[13]   Himsolt M., *The graphlet system*, Graph Drawing, volume 1190 of Lecture Notes in Cornputer Science, Springer- Verlag, pp 233-240, 1996.

[14] http://msowww.anu.edu.au/library/thesaurus/
[15] Jiand J.J., Conrath D.W, Semantic similarity based on corpus statistics and lexical terminology, ICCL, 1998.
[16] Lin D., *An information-theoretic definition of similarity*, 15th international conference on Machine Learning, pp 296-304, 1998.
[17] Lord P.W., Stevens R.D., Brass A., Goble C.A, *Semantic similarity measures as tools for exploring the Gene Ontology*, Pacific Symposium on Biocomputing, pp 601-612, 2003.
[18] Maedche A., Staab S., Measuring similarity between ontologies, EKAW, pp 251-263, 2002
[19] Masolo C., *Ontology driven Information retrieval: Stato dell'arte*, Rapport de IKF (Information and Knowledge Fusion) Eureka Project E!2235. LADSEB-Cnr, Padova (I), 2001.
[21] Rada R., Mili H., Bickel E., *Developement and application of a metric on semantic nets*, IEEE transaction on systems, 19(1), pp 17-30, 1989.
[22] Resnik P., *Semantic similarity in a taxonomy : an information based measure and its application to problems of ambiguity in natural langage*, Journal of Artificial Intelligence Research, pp 95-130, 1999.
[23] Rothenburger B., *A Differential Approach for Knowledge Management*, ECAI, Workshop on Machine Learning and Natural Language Processing for Ontology Engineering, 2002
[24] Salton G., The Smart retrieval system, Prentice Hall, Englewood Cliffs, NJ, 1971
[25] S. Staab, R.Studer (eds.): Handbook on Ontologies, Springer Series on Handbooks in Information Systems, ISBN 3540408347, (2004)
[26] Winston M., Chaffin R., Herramann D., *A taxonomy of Part-Whole relations*, Cognitive Science, 11:417-444, 1987.
[27] Wu SH, Tsai TH, Hsu WL, Domain Event Extraction and Representation with Domain Ontology, in proceedings of the IJCAI-03 Workshop on Information Integration on the Web, Acapulco, Mexico, pp. 33-38, 2003.
[28] Wu Z., Palmer M., *Verb semantics and lexical selection*, 32nd annual meeting of the Association for Computational Linguistics, 1994.

Capturing Semantics Towards Automatic Coordination of Domain Ontologies

Konstantinos Kotis, George A. Vouros, and Kostas Stergiou

Dept. of Information & Communications Systems Engineering,
University of the Aegean,
Karlovassi, Samos,
83100, Greece
{kkot,georgev,konsterg}

Abstract. Existing efforts on ontology mapping, alignment and merging vary from methodological and theoretical frameworks, to methods and tools that support the semi-automatic coordination of ontologies. However, only latest research efforts "touch" on the *mapping /merging* of ontologies using the whole breadth of available knowledge. Addressing this issue, the work presented in this paper is based on the HCONE-merge approach that makes use of the intended informal interpretations of concepts by mapping them to WordNet senses using lexical semantic indexing (LSI). Our aim is to explore the level of human involvement required for mapping concepts of the source ontologies to their intended interpretations. We propose a series of methods for ontology mapping/merging with varying degrees of human involvement and evaluate them experimentally. We conclude that, although an effective fully automated process is not attainable, we can reach a point where the process of ontology mapping/merging can be carried out efficiently with minimum human involvement.

Keywords: Ontology mapping, Ontology merging, Latent Semantic Indexing

1 Introduction

Ontologies have been realized as the key technology to shaping and exploiting information for the effective management of knowledge and for the evolution of the Semantic Web and its applications. In such a distributed setting, ontologies establish a common vocabulary for community members to interlink, combine, and communicate knowledge shaped through practice and interaction, binding the knowledge processes of creating, importing, capturing, retrieving, and using knowledge. However, it seems that there will always be more than one ontology even for the same domain [1]. In such a setting where different conceptualizations of the same domain exist, information services must effectively answer queries bridging the gaps between their formal ontologies and users' own conceptualizations. Towards this target, networks of semantically related information must be created at-request. Therefore, coordination (i.e. mapping, alignment, merging) of ontologies is a major challenge for bridging the gaps between agents (software and human) with different conceptualizations.

C. Bussler and D. Fensel (Eds.): AIMSA 2004, LNAI 3192, pp. 22–32, 2004.
© Springer-Verlag Berlin Heidelberg 2004

There are many works towards coordinating ontologies. These works exploit linguistic, structural, domain knowledge and matching heuristics (e.g [3], [4]). Recent approaches aim to exploit all these types of knowledge and further capture the intended meanings of terms by means of heuristic rules [5]. The HCONE (Human Centered ONtology Eng.)-merge [6] approach to merging ontologies exploits all the above-mentioned types of knowledge. In a greater extent than existing approaches to coordinating ontologies, this approach gives much emphasis on "uncovering" the intended informal interpretations of concepts specified in an ontology. Linguistic and structural knowledge about ontologies are exploited by the Latent Semantics Indexing method (LSI) [7] for associating concepts to their informal, human-oriented intended interpretations realized by WordNet senses. Using concepts' intended interpretations, the proposed merging method translates formal concept definitions to a common vocabulary and exploits the translated definitions by means of description logics' reasoning services.

The HCONE-merge approach requires humans to validate the intended interpretations suggested by LSI for every term in the ontology. Since this process is quite frustrating and error-prone even for small ontologies, we need to investigate the required human involvement for mapping concepts to their intended interpretations efficiently. The ultimate achievement would be to fully automate this mapping, and also to fully automate the merging of ontologies. Towards this goal, the paper investigates a series of novel techniques and heuristics for ontology mapping and merging, with varying human involvement. The paper concludes that a fully automated ontology mapping/merging process is far from realistic, since there must always be a minimum set of human decisions present, at least when the LSI method is employed.

2   HCONE-Merge Approach to Ontology Merging

According to [5], an ontology is considered to be a pair O=(S, A), where S is the ontological signature describing the vocabulary (i.e. the terms that lexicalize concepts and relations between concepts) and A is a set of ontological axioms, restricting the intended interpretations of the terms included in the signature. In other words, A includes the formal definitions of concepts and relations that are lexicalized by natural language terms in S. This is a slight variation of the definition given in [5], where S is also equipped with a partial order based on the inclusion relation between concepts. In our definition, conforming to description logics' terminological axioms, inclusion relations are ontological axioms included in A. It must be noticed that in this paper we only deal with inclusion and equivalence relations among concepts.

Ontology mapping from ontology $O_1 = (S_1, A_1)$ to $O_2 = (S_2, A_2)$ is considered to be a morphism $f:S_1 \rightarrow S_2$ of ontological signatures such that $A_2 \models f(A_1)$, i.e. all interpretations that satisfy O_2's axioms also satisfy O_1's translated axioms. Consider for instance the ontologies depicted in Figure 1. Given the morphism f such that f(Infrastructure)=Facility and f(Transportation)=Transportation System, it is true that $A_2 \models \{f(\text{Transportation}) \sqsubseteq f(\text{Infrastructure})\}$, therefore f is a mapping. Given the morphism f', such that f'(Infrastructure)=Transportation System and f'(Transportation)= Transportation Means, it is not true that $A_2 \models \{f'(\text{Transportation}) \sqsubseteq f'(\text{Infrastructure})\}$, therefore f' is not a mapping.

However, instead of a function, we may articulate a set of binary relations between the ontological signatures. Such relations can be the inclusion ($\sqsubseteq$) and the equivalence ($\equiv$) relations. For instance, given the ontologies in Figure 1, we can say that Transportation$\equiv$Transportation System, Installation$\equiv$Facility and Infrastructure $\sqsubseteq$ Facility. Then we have indicated an alignment of the two ontologies and we can merge them. Based on the alignment, the merged ontology will be ontology O_3 in Figure 1. It holds that $A_3 \vDash A_2$ and $A_3 \vDash A_1$.

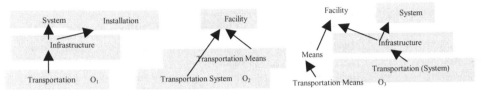

Fig. 1. Example Ontologies

Looking at Figure 1 in an other way, we can consider O_3 to be part of a larger intermediary ontology and define the alignment of ontologies O_1 and O_2 by means of morphisms $f_1: S_1 \rightarrow S_3$ and $f_2: S_2 \rightarrow S_3$. Then, the merging of the two ontologies is the minimal union of ontological vocabularies and axioms with respect to the intermediate ontology where ontologies have been mapped. Therefore, the ontologies merging problem (OMP) can be stated as follows: Given two ontologies find an alignment between these two ontologies, and then, get the minimal union of their (translated) vocabularies and axioms with respect to their alignment.

The HCONE-merge approach, as already pointed, maps concepts to word senses in WordNet. Each sense in a WordNet synset describes a concept. WordNet senses are related among themselves via the inclusion (hyponym – hyperonym) relation. Terms that lexicalize the same concept (sense) are considered to be equivalent through the synonym relation.Note that we do not consider WordNet to include any intermediate ontology, as this would be very restrictive for the specification of the original ontologies (i.e. the method would work only for those ontologies that preserve the inclusion relations among WordNet senses).

We now briefly describe the HCONE-merge method. A detailed description can be found in [6]. The method constructs an intermediate ontology including a vocabulary with the lexicalizations of the specific senses of WordNet synsets corresponding to the ontologies' concepts, and axioms that are the translated axioms of the original ontologies. We call this ontology hidden intermediate. Initially, the method finds a semantic morphism between the original ontologies and a hidden intermediate ontology. To do this, we use the semantic morphism (s-morphism, symbolized by *fs*), which is based on the lexical semantic indexing (LSI) method. LSI [7] is a vector space technique for information retrieval and indexing. It assumes that there is an underlying latent semantic structure that it estimates using statistical techniques. Lexical Semantic Analysis (LSA) allows the arrangement of the semantic space to reflect the major associative patterns in the data. As a result, terms that did not actually appear in a sense may still end up close to the sense, if this is consistent with the major patterns of association in the data [7]. Therefore, it must be emphasized that although LSI exploits structural information of ontologies and WordNet, it ends up with semantic associations between terms. Given a query (a concept description), retrieval aims to locate a point in space that is close to the WordNet sense that expresses the intended meaning of this concept.

The semantic space is constructed by terms in the vicinity of the senses S1, S2...Sm that are the senses of a WordNet lexical entry C', where C' is a linguistic variation of a concept C [6]. Therefore, we have to decide what constitutes the vicinity of a sense for the calculation of the semantic space. The query to the retrieval mechanism is constructed by the concept names of all concepts in the vicinity of the given concept. In an analogous way we have to decide what constitutes the vicinity of an ontology concept for the calculation of the query string. The goal is to provide LSI with the necessary information without distracting it with "noise". Experiments using various ontologies have shown that we can achieve 70% precision in mapping concepts to WordNet senses, if the vicinity of the senses that are in the focus of the algorithm includes the following information:

S1.   The term C' that corresponds to C. C' is a lexical entry in WordNet
S2.   Terms that appear in C' WordNet senses
S3.   Terms that constitute hyperonyms / hyponyms of each C' sense.

The vicinity of the ontology concept should include the following:

Q1.   Concept's C primitive super-concepts
Q2.   Concepts that are immediate sub-concepts of C (subsumed by C)
Q3.   Concepts that are related to C via domain specific relations

Using this method, each ontology concept is associated with a set of graded WordNet senses. For instance, the concept "facility" is associated with the five senses that WordNet assigns to the term "facility", whose meaning range from "something created to provide a service" to "a room equipped with washing and toilet facilities". The highest graded sense expresses the most possible informal meaning of the corresponding concept. This sense can be further validated by a human. In case the human indicates another sense to be the most preferable, then this sense is considered to capture the informal intended meaning of the formal ontology concept. Otherwise, the method considers the highest graded sense as the concept's intended interpretation.

Using the intended meanings of the formal concepts, we construct an ontology $O^n=(S^n, A^n)$, $n=1,2$, where, S^n includes the lexicalizations of the senses associated to the concepts[1] of the ontology $O_n=(S_n, A_n)$, $n=1,2$, and A^n contain the translated inclusion and equivalence relations between the corresponding concepts. Then, it holds that $A^n \models f_s(A_n)$ and the ontology $O^n=(S^n, A^n)$ with the corresponding associations from O_n to O^n, is a model of $O_n=(S_n, A_n)$, $n=1,2....$ These associations define a mapping from O_n to O^n.

Having found the mappings with the hidden intermediate ontology, the translated ontologies can be merged, taking into account the axioms A^1 and A^2 (which are the translated axioms of A_1 and A_2). The merging decisions are summarized in Table 1. We must emphasize that, as shown in Table 1, the semantic information concerning ontology concepts is exploited by the description logics reasoner during merging.

---

[1] Future work concerns mapping domain relations to WordNet senses as well.

Table 1. HCONE-Merge Algorithm table summary

Concept & Role Names[2]	Concept Mapping to WordNet Senses[3]	Action
Match	No match	Rename concepts
Match	Match	Merge concept definitions
No match	Match	Merge concept definitions
No match	No match	Classify Concepts

The HCONE-merge approach requires users to be involved in every concept mapping in order to validate the LSI-suggested WordNet sense. For a small ontology, this may not be considered a major hindrance. However, in real environments with hundreds of concepts, one can guess the frustration when validating the suggested mappings. This problem has led us to investigate the amount in which ontology mapping and merging can be automated. In other words, the question to be answered concerns "how much, if any, human involvement is required for ontology mapping and merging and in which stages of the merging process".

3   On Automating the Mapping of Ontologies

Given the crucial role of uncovering the intended semantics of concepts to the merging process, we aim at automating the following two major steps for the merging of two ontologies O_1 and O_2: a) The mapping of O_1 to WordNet senses, and b) The mapping of O_2 to the senses corresponding to the concepts of O_1. The motivation for step (b) is that LSI must consider senses that are "close" to the meaning of the concepts in the hidden intermediate ontology. Therefore, for the merging of O_2 with O_1, the concepts in O_2 must be mapped to the intended interpretations of concepts in O_1.

3.1   On Automating the Computations of the s-Morphism of O_1

In the following we present three methods towards automating the mapping process. Each method differs from the others in the level of human involvement. All the experiments we have conducted involve ontologies between 10 and 100 concepts. For presentation reasons, we discuss here the results of experiments conducted with a 10-concept ontology taken from the Transportation domain:

$O_1 = ($ {Airplane, Boat, Car, Craft, Motor Vehicle, Ship, Transport, Truck, Vehicle, Vessel},

{Vehicle ⊑Transport, Motor Vehicle ⊑Vehicle, Craft ⊑Vehicle, Vessel ⊑ Vehicle, Car ⊑Motor Vehicle, Truck ⊑Motor Vehicle, Airplane ⊑Craft, Boat ⊑Vessel, Ship ⊑Vessel}).

---

[2] Match in this case means linguistic match of the concept names from the two ontologies.
[3] Match means that both concepts have been mapped to the same WordNet sense

3.1.1 Fully Automated Mapping

Fully automated mapping is achieved by running the mapping algorithm described previously without any human intervention. That is, we simply map each concept of the given ontology to the best-ranked sense returned by the algorithm. This approach to computing the s-morphism for the O_1 ontology, gives the results shown in the "Automated 1st iteration" column of Table 2.

A mapping is considered to be "correct" when the concept is associated with the interpretation intended by the ontology developer. To compute the mappings, the semantic space and the query string are constructed as it is specified in Section 2. In order to increase the mapping precision by taking advantage of the correct mappings produced, we also investigated the following method: Given the computed mappings of concepts to WordNet senses, the algorithm re-computes the s-morphism. Although the semantic space is computed in the same way as in the first iteration, the query string for the 2nd iteration is constructed by taking into account the most frequent terms of the WordNet senses associated with the ontology concepts. The key point here is that the query string is re-computed in the 2nd iteration by using the new concept mappings produced. Thus, if the mapping for a concept C has been changed during the 2nd iteration, then the new associated sense will be used for the computation of the query string for every concept that is related to C via an inclusion relation. Concerning our example, the mapping of the concept Vehicle has been changed in the second iteration of the mapping algorithm since the query string for this concept has been changed due to the corrections made in the mappings of the concepts Craft and Car. The latter concepts are related to the concept Vehicle via inclusion relations. Column "Automated 2nd iteration" of Table 2 shows the results of this method.

Table 2. Results of the proposed methods for mapping ontologies to WordNet sense

Concept	Automated 1st iteration	Automated 2nd iteration	User-based	Semi-Automated
Airplane	✓	✓	✓	✓
Boat	✓	✓	✓	✓
Car		✓	✓	✓
Craft		✓	✓	✓
Motor Vehicle	✓	✓	✓	✓
Ship	✓	✓	✓	✓
Transport	✓	✓	✓	✓
Truck				
Vehicle	✓		✓	✓
Vessel	✓	✓	✓	✓
Precision	70%	80%	90%	90%

A problem with this method is that, due to changes in the mappings of other concepts, some correct mappings from the first run did change to wrong mappings. So, even if the precision of the mapping has been improved, the problem raised here is the computation of wrong mappings, which were computed correctly in the first run. The inability to correct the mapping of some concepts is due to the fact that the mappings of their related concepts have not been changed. Concerning our example, the inability to correct the mapping of concept Truck is explained as follows: the query string remains the same since it is computed by considering only the concept Motor Vehicle, whose mapping has been left unchanged.

3.1.2 User-Based Mapping

To overcome the above problem, we can insist that the "correct" mappings of the 1st run are preserved. We can achieve this by requesting users' feedback on the results of the first run. The user is provided with a list of all the concepts of the ontology, and he/she can choose the concepts that are not mapped to their correct senses. Doing so in the example ontology one can choose to improve the mappings of the three concepts Car, Craft, and Truck. The mapping of the concept Truck remains unchanged (for the reasons described before), but the mappings of the other two concepts are corrected, as the "User-based" column of Table 2 demonstrates.

Although we have achieved 90% precision with this method, the user must check all the returned mappings one-by-one and validate them manually against the intended concept interpretations. Thus, because of this overhead, we are simply back where we started i.e. to the HCONE-merge approach to mapping.

3.1.3 Semi-automated Mapping

To minimize the time spent for the validation of mappings and thus minimize user involvement, we explored methods for the automatic computation of the mappings that need user validation. Along this line we implemented a method that locates inconsistencies between the translated axioms A_1 of ontology O_1 and WordNet inclusion relations. An inconsistency occurs when the mapping to WordNet senses of two concepts related via an inclusion relation is not a morphism. It must be pointed that although we do not insist that mappings of original ontologies must preserve inclusion relations between WordNet senses, the consistency-checking heuristic rule provides useful suggestions for improving the mapping. A similar technique is used in the mapping algorithm proposed in [4].

Concerning our example, the method suggested 4 concept pairs whose mapping is inconsistent to WordNet corresponding senses' relations. For example, the pair Craft/Vehicle is inconsistent since (a) Craft is mapped to the sense of "craft, craftsmanship, workmanship -- (skill in an occupation or trade)", (b) Vehicle is mapped to the sense "vehicle -- (a conveyance that transports people or objects)" and (c) their mapping to these WordNet senses does not preserve their inclusion relation specified in the ontology.

Each suggested pair must be checked to identify which of the two concepts causes the inconsistency. In our example it is the Craft concept that is not mapped correctly. By running the mapping algorithm for this concept, the mapping becomes consistent. However, making mappings consistent does not ensure that mappings become "correct", since a consistent mapping does not necessarily reflect the intended interpretation of the concept.

To achieve a higher mapping precision we have employed the following heuristic: In case the mapping is still wrong or produces an inconsistency then the mappings of the concepts that are semantically related to the suggested concepts are further validated. For instance, the mapping of the pair Craft/Vehicle produces an inconsistency. Then their immediate super-concept's mapping, i.e. the mapping of the concept Transport, is validated. Since the mapping of Transport is wrong, the user runs the mapping algorithm again only for the concept Transport. Having the mapping of Transport corrected, the user re-runs the mapping algorithm for Craft, resulting in a "correct" and consistent mapping. The precision percentage of this method is depicted in the "Semi-automated" column of Table 2.

3.1.4 Comparison of the Methods

Based on the basic algorithm for computing the s-morphism, we have shaped an approach to ontology mapping, where human inspection and validation has been reduced down to the number of algorithm runs needed to correct the suggested inconsistent concept pairs. We have compared the proposed methods according to the amount of automation they achieve and their mapping precision:

The fully automated method, requires the minimum number of user actions, but at the same time it achieves the lowest precision (80% correct mappings). On the other hand, the user-based method achieves higher precision percentage (90%), but the actions that are required by the user imply considerable effort, since the user has to validate the mapping of each ontology concept. It must be pointed that this case requires also a considerable number of additional algorithm runs, equal to the percentage of wrong mappings. The semi-automated method however, in addition to the high percentage of precision (90%) can significantly reduce the number of concepts that need validation by the user. However, in the worst case where each concept is involved in at least one inconsistency, validation of all concepts is required.

3.2 Map Ontology B to Ontology A

Having reached the point where O_1 has been mapped to the hidden intermediate ontology, there is one more step prior to merging: the mapping of O_2. The first step is to repeat the mapping process described in Section 2 for the O_2 ontology. Having mapped the concepts of O_2 to WordNet, definitions of the concepts that have been mapped to the same WordNet sense, as already shown in section 2, can readily be merged. However, in order to increase the precision of the method for those pairs of concepts C_1 and C_2 that are not mapped to the same WordNet sense, C_2 from the ontology O_2 is mapped to the translated O_1 ontology, rather than to WordNet.
The mapping method is as follows:

For each concept C_1 of O_1 and each concept C_2 of O_2 for which either (a) or (b) happens:

(a) Both $fs(C_1)$ and $fs(C_2)$ correspond to the same WordNet lexical entry and belong to the same synset

(b) C_1 and C_2 correspond to a different WordNet lexical entry and either $fs(C_1)$ or $fs(C_2)$ belong to C_1's or C_2's corresponding WordNet sysnset

Run the mapping algorithm for the concept C_2:

- The query string is constructed by taking into account the most frequent terms of $fs(C)$, for every concept C that has a corresponding concept (via fs) to a concept of O_1 and is related to C_2 via an inclusion relation.
- The semantic space is constructed by taking into account the senses of C_2 that have been computed by mapping O_2 to WordNet.

Using the example ontologies of Section 2 and the proposed semi-automated method for mapping, the algorithm produced the mapping of the concept "Transportation" to the concept "Transportation System", and of the concept "Facility" to the concept "Installation".

Although current experiments have shown that additional mappings can be identified through this technique, further investigation is needed in order to identify the amount of information that is necessary to further improve the initial mappings as well as to reduce the impact of reversing the order of the ontologies that have to be mapped.

3.3   Evaluating Semi-automated Ontology Merging with Real-Life Ontologies

Initial experiments showed that the semi-automated ontology mapping/merging process described in Section 3.1.3 achieves high accuracy with little human involvement. To further investigate this, we conducted experiments with real-life ontologies taken from the DAML ontology library[4]. These experiments followed the requirements of similar experiments conducted with PROMPT [13]. We have measured the recall and precision of the suggested merging actions. Generally, *recall* is defined as the fraction of correct matches that the algorithm identifies, and *precision* is defined as the fraction of correct matches among the matches that the algorithm identifies. We have also measured the distance to a manually produced gold-standard ontology that is the merging result of two ontologies widely used in other experiments and taken from the Academia domain.

We compared the results of mappings produced by the HCONE-merge and the Semi-automated merge methods (Section 3.1.3). The recall that both methods return is 97%, which means that there is a high percentage of correspondence of ontology concepts to terms in the WordNet database. The precision that the two methods return is 69% and 79% respectively, when the user is not involved at the validation of mappings. The two methods are different in their design principles as described previously, and therefore result in different percentages of correct mappings. Semi-automated merge returns the higher percentage since this method takes advantage of the LSI runs that make use of previously automatically corrected mappings to the computation of the vicinity for further mappings. HCONE-merge cannot make use of the same advantage since it is a step-by-step assignment of WordNet senses to ontology concepts. For instance, concepts "Visiting Scholar" and "Visiting Staff" are assigned a correct mapping in the Semi-automated merge method whereas in the HCONE-merge they are not. However, when the user is involved (with manually assignment of the correct mappings), as expected, the standard HCONE-merge method

---

[4] DAML. DAML ontology library 2004,

reaches the highest precision percentage (97%). The precision of semi-automated method on the other hand, even user involvement (by re-running LSI for selected mappings) was expected to positively influence the result, in this experiment it had no impact at all.

It is difficult to compare recall and precision percentages of HCONE-oriented approaches with results of other approaches such as GLUE (66-97% precision [12]) and C_{TX}-MATCH (60-76% precision [9]). The trade-off between precision percentages and time/human involvement spent during mapping must be carefully examined when doing such comparisons, as well as the input requirements (kind of knowledge used) of the approach i.e. use of instances or additional information sources such as lexicons or corpus. However, a comparison based on the distance to the "gold-standard" ontology has shown that HCONE-oriented approaches are closer than other approaches (for instance, PROMPT) due to their capability of uncovering semantic similarity between nodes. To our knowledge, the only similar to our mapping approach is S-Match [4], which computes semi-automatic matching with a high overall estimation (90%) using semantic similarity measures but works only for those ontologies that preserve the relations among WordNet senses.

4   Concluding Remarks

In this paper we presented a number of methods dealing with the mapping of concepts to their intended interpretations, with the aim to identify the minimum user interventions required during the mapping and merging of ontologies. From our results we can conclude that a precision of around 80% with a variable number of validations can be achieved with a semi-automated method of mapping.

On automating the mapping and merging processes we conjecture that in real environments such as the Semantic Web humans' intended interpretations of concepts must always be captured. The aim of our research is to reduce human involvement for capturing the intended interpretations of concepts. Existing efforts [10][12][11], place this involvement after the mapping between sources ontologies has been produced, as well as during, or at the end of the merging method. The user is usually asked to decide upon merging strategies or to guide the process in case of inconsistency. Some other efforts head towards automatic mapping techniques [9], [8], [5] but they have not shown that a consistent and automatic merging will follow. The HCONE-merge approach places human involvement at the early stages of the mapping/merging process. If this involvement leads to capturing the intended interpretation of conceptualizations, then the rest is a consistent, error-free merging process, whose results are subject to further human evaluation. The new methods proposed in this paper show that human involvement is necessary to produce valid mappings between ontologies, however they can be reduced significantly.

Finally, we have identified that apart from [9][4][12] all efforts do not consult significant domain knowledge. However, to make use of such knowledge, additional information must be specified in the ontology. WordNet is a potential source of such information [9][4].

Future work concerns mapping relations of concepts too.

References

1. Uschold M. and Gruninger M.: Creating Semantically Integrated Communities on the World Wide Web. Invited Talk, Semantic Web Workshop, WWW 2002 Conference, May, (2002)
2. Uschold M.: Where are the Semantics in the Semantic Web? AI Magazine, Volume 24, No.3, Fall (2003)
3. Madhavan J., Bern-stein P. A., Domingos P., and Halevy A. Y.: Representing and reasoning about mappings between domain models. Proc. of the 18th AAAI, (2002) 80–86
4. Giunchiglia F. and Shvaiko P., Yatskevich M.: S–Match: An Algorithm and Implementation of Semantic Matching. The Semantic Web: Research and Applications, Lecture Notes in Computer Science, Vol. 3053, Springer-Verlag, (2004) 61-75
5. Kalfoglou Y. and Schorlemmer M.: Ontology mapping: the state of the art. The Knowledge Engineering Review 18(1):1-31 (2003)
6. Kotis K. and Vouros G. A.: HCONE approach to Ontology Merging. The Semantic Web: Research and Applications, Lecture Notes in Computer Science, Vol. 3053, Springer-Verlag, (2004) 137-151
7. Deerwester S., Dumais S. T., Furnas G. W., Landauer T. K., Harshman R.: Indexing by Latent Semantic Analysis. Journal of the American Society of Information Science (1990)
8. Madhavan J., Bernstein P. A., and Rahm E.: Generic schema matching with Cupid. VLDB Journal (2001) 49-58
9. Serafini L., Bouquet P., Magnini B., and Zanobini S.: An Algorithm for Matching Contextualized Schemas via SAT. In Proc.of CONTEX (2003)
10. Gangemi A., Pisanelli D. M., Steve G.: An Overview of the ONIONS Project: Applying Ontologies to the Integration of Medical Terminologies. Data and Knowledge Engineering, 1999, vol. 31, (1999) 183-220
11. Stumme G., Mädche A.: FCA-Merge: Bottom-Up Merging of Ontologies. In: B. Nebel (Ed.): Proc. 17th Intl. Conf. on Artificial Intelligence (IJCAI '01). Seattle (2001) 225-230
12. Doan A., Madhavan J., Domingos P., and Halvey A.: Learning to map between ontologies on the semantic web. In Proc. Of WWW-02, 11th InternationalWWW Conf., Hawaii (2002)
13. Noy N. and Musen M.: A. M.: PROMPT: Algorithm and tool for automated ontology merging and alignment. In Proceedings of 7th National Conference on AI, Austin (2000)

Towards a Semantic Representation of Documents by Ontology-Document Mapping

Mustapha Baziz

IRIT, Campus universitaire ToulouseIII
118 rte de Narbonne,
F-31062 Toulouse Cedex 4, France
baziz@irit.fr

Abstract... This paper deals with the use of ontologies in Information Retrieval field. It introduces an approach for document content representation by ontology-document matching. The approach consists in concepts (mono and multiword) detection from a document via a general purpose ontology, namely WordNet. Two criterions are then used: co-occurrence for identifying important concepts in a document, and semantic similarity to compute semantic relatedness between these concepts and then to disambiguate them. The result is a set of scored concepts-senses (nodes) with weighted links called *semantic core of document* which best represents the semantic content of the document. We regard the proposed and evaluated approach as a short but strong step toward the long term goal of Intelligent Indexing and Semantic Retrieval.

Keywords: Information Retrieval, Semantic representation of documents, ontologies, WordNet.

1 Introduction

Ontology-based information retrieval (IR) approaches promise to increase the quality of responses since they aim at capturing within computer systems some part of the semantics of documents, allowing for better information retrieval. Two key contributions can then be distinguished: query reengineering and document representation. In both oh these two cases, the expected advantage is to get a richer and more precise meaning representation in order to obtain a more powerful identification of relevant documents meeting the query. Concepts from an ontology which are semantically related to the query can be added in order to select more documents, namely those using a different vocabulary but dealing with the same topic [1], [2], [3], [4]. In document representation, known as semantic indexing and defined for example by [2] and [5], the key issue is to identify appropriate concepts that describe and characterize the document content. The challenge is to make sure that irrelevant concepts will not be kept, and that relevant concepts will not be discarded. In this paper, we propose an automatic mechanism for the selection of these concepts from documents using a general purpose ontology, namely the WordNet lexical database [6].

C. Bussler and D. Fensel (Eds.): AIMSA 2004, LNAI 3192, pp. 33–43, 2004.

We propose to build a semantic network for representing the semantic content of a document. The semantic network to which we refer here is one as defined by [7]: "*semantic network is broadly described as any representation interlinking nodes with arcs, where the nodes are concepts and the links are various kinds of relationships between concepts*". The resulted scored concepts could be used in indexing and then searching phases of an Information Retrieval System (IRS).

The paper is organized as follows: section 2 gives a brief overview on semantic-based information retrieval and semantic relatedness measures between concepts using semantic representations. Section 3 describes the proposed approach of matching an ontology with a document. The steps include: concept extraction (3.1), concept weighting (3.2), computing semantic relatedness between concepts (3.4) and building and scoring a document's semantic core (3.5). Section 4 presents the evaluation of the approach. Conclusions and prospects are drawn in section 5.

2   Related Works on the Use of Semantics in Information Retrieval

Recently, some approaches have been proposed to use semantics in IR. In semantic-based IR, sets of words, names, noun phrases are mapped into the concepts they encode [8]. By this model a document is represented as a set of concepts: to this aim a crucial component is a semantic structure for mapping document representations to concepts. A semantic structure can be represented using distinct data structures: trees, semantic networks, conceptual graphs, etc. Such structures may be dictionaries, thesauri and ontologies [3]. They can be either manually or automatically generated or they may pre-exist. WordNet and EuroWordNet are examples of (thesaurus-based) lexical data-based including a semantic network. As such, they are close toontologies. They are widely employed to improve the effectiveness of IR system. In [9], the authors propose an indexing method based on WordNet synsets: the vector space model is employed, by using synsets as indexing space instead of word forms. In [2] and [10] concepts from an ontology ("regions" for the first paper) are connected to those in documents (text for the first and xml data for the second). Both authors propose a method for measuring the similarity between concepts via the semantic network of an ontology. [11] proposed in their system (OntoLearn) a method called structural semantic interconnection to disambiguate WordNet glosses (definitions).
   Similarity between concepts in semantic networks is already in the scope of various research works. Several methods and metrics are proposed. The principles of path based measures are presented in [12]; [13] use Information Content measure (similarity between two given concepts is based on the most specific concept, i.e. the least common upper node, in the hierarchy which subsumes both of them) and [14]'s approach uses an adapted Lesk [15] algorithm based on gloss overlaps between concepts for disambiguating words in text. In our case, the finality is not especially Word Sense Disambiguation (WSD) —for a complete survey of WSD, the interested reader may refer to the Senseval home page (http://www.senseval.org) —. However, we were inspired by the Pederson's and colleagues approach described in [14] for computing semantic similarity between concepts in our semantic core building

process. We will explain further on (section 3.3) the interest of using semantic relations for a more efficient concept comparison.

3 Matching a Document with an Ontology

Roughly, the approach consists in 3 steps. At the first step, being given a document, terms (mono and multiwords) corresponding to entries in the ontology are extracted. At step 2, the ontology semantic network is used, first to identify the different senses of each extracted concept and then to compute relatedness measures between these senses (concept-senses). Finally at step 3, a document's semantic core is built up. It is formed by the best group of concepts from the document which can best cover the topic expressed in this document.

3.1   Concepts Extraction

Before any document processing, in particular before pruning stop words, an important process for the next steps consists in extracting mono and multiword concepts from texts that correspond to nodes in the ontology. The recognized concepts can be named entities like *united_kingdom_of great_britain_and_northern_ireland* or phrases like *pull_one's_weight*. For this purpose, we use an ad hoc technique that relies solely on concatenation of adjacent words to identify ontology compound concepts. In this technique, two alternative ways can be distinguished. The first one consists in projecting the ontology on the document by extracting all multiword concepts (compound terms) from the ontology and then identifying those occurring in the document. This method has the advantage of being speedy and makes it possible to have a reusable resource even if the corpus changes. Its drawback is the possibility to omit some concepts which appear in the source text and in the ontology with different forms. For example if the ontology recognizes a compound concept *solar battery*, a simple comparison do not recognizes in the text the same concept appearing in its plural form *solar batteries*. The second way, which we adopt in this paper, follows the reverse path, projecting the document onto the ontology: for each multiword candidate concept trained by combining adjacent words in the text, we first question the ontology using these words just as they are, and then we use their base forms if necessary.

Concerning word combination, we select the longest term for which a concept is detected. If we consider the example shown on Figure1, the sentence contains three (3) different concepts: *external oblique muscle, abdominal muscle* and *abdominal external oblique muscle*.

The first concept *abdominal muscle* is not identified because its words are not adjacent. The second one *external oblique muscle* and the third one *abdominal external oblique muscle* are synonyms, their definition is:

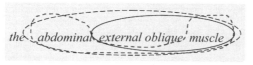

Fig. 1. Example of text with different concepts

The noun external oblique muscle has 1 sense

1. external oblique muscle, musculus obliquus externus abdominis, abdominal external oblique muscle, oblique -- (a diagonally arranged abdominal muscle on either side of the torso)

The selected concept is associated to the longest multiword *abdominal external oblique muscle* which corresponds to the correct sense in the sentence. Remind that in word combination, the order must be respected (left to right) otherwise we could be confronted to the syntactic variation problem (*science library* is different from *library science*).

The extraction of multiword concepts in plain text is important to reduce ambiguity. These concepts generally are monosemous even thought the words they contain can be individually several times ambiguous. For example, when taking each word separately in the concept *ear_nose_and_throat_doctor,* we have to disambiguate between 5 senses for the word *ear*, 13 senses (7 for the noun *nose* and 6 for the verb *nose*) for the word *nose*, 3 senses for *throat* (*and* is not used because it is a stop-word) and 7 senses (4 for the noun and 3 for the verb) for the word *doctor*. So, we would have a number of 5x13x3x7= 1365 possible combinations of candidate senses. But when considering all the words forming a single multiword concept (of course, the multiword concept must be recognized in the ontology), we only will have one sense.

In the case of this example, the full concept and its definition (gloss in WordNet) are as follows:

The noun ear-nose-and-throat doctor has 1 sense

1. ENT man, ear-nose-and-throat doctor, otolaryngologist, otorhinolaryngologist, rhinolaryngologist -- (a specialist in the disorders of the ear or nose or throat.)

In WordNet2.0, there are a total of 63,218 multiword concepts (composed of 2-9 words). 56,286 (89%) of these are monosemous, 6,238 have 2 senses (9.867%) and only 694 (0.01) of multiword concepts have more than 2 senses. Thus, the more there are multiword concepts in a document to be analyzed, the easier is their disambiguation.

3.2   Weighting Concepts

The extracted concepts are then weighted according to a kind of tf.idf that we called cf.idf. For a concept *c* composed of n words, its frequency in a document equals to the number of occurrences of a concept itself, and the one of all its sub-concepts. Formally:

$$cf(c) = count(c) + \sum_{sc \in sub\_concepts(c)} \frac{Length(sc)}{Length(c)} \cdot count(sc) \tag{1}$$

Where *Length(c)* represents the number of words and *sub_concepts(c)* is the set of all possible sub-concepts which can be derived from *c*: concepts of n-1 words from *c*, concepts of n-2, and all single words of *c*. For example, if we consider a concept *"elastic potential energy"* composed of 3 words its frequency is computed as:

f("elastic potential energy") = *count("elastic potential energy")* + *2/3 count("potential energy")* + *1/3 count("elastic")* + *1/3 count("potential")* + *1/3 count("energy")*.

Knowing that *potential energy* is itself also a multiword concept and here, it is a question of adding the number of occurrences of *potential energy* and not its frequency.

Other methods for concept frequencies are proposed in the literature, they use in general statistical and/or syntactical analysis [16], [17]. Roughly, they add single words frequencies, multiply them or multiply the number of concept occurrences by the number of single words forming this concept (equation 2):

$$cf(c) = count\ (c).Length\ (sc) \tag{2}$$

The global frequency *idf(C)* of a concept in a collection is:

$$idf(c) = f(c).\ln(N/df) \tag{3}$$

Where N is the total number of documents and df (document frequency) is the number of documents a concept occurred in. If the concept occurs in all the documents, its frequency is null. We have used 2 as a frequency threshold value.

Once the most important concepts are extracted from a document, they are used to build up the semantic core of this document. The link between two nodes is a condensed value resulting from a comparison of the two concept-senses (nodes) using several semantic relations. It has no precise meaning but expresses the semantic closeness of the two concept meanings. In the next section, we introduce the method of computing semantic relatedness between concepts using a semantic network of ontology.

3.3   Computing Semantic Relatedness Between Concepts

Being given a set of n relations from an ontology $R=\{R_1, R_2, ...R_n\}$, and two concepts, C_k and C_l with affected senses j_1 and j_2: S_{j1}^{k} and S_{j2}^{l}. The semantic relatedness (overlaps) between S_{j1}^{k} and S_{j2}^{l}, noted $P_{kl}(S_{j1}^{k}, S_{j2}^{l})$ or *overlaps*(S_{j1}^{k}, S_{j2}^{l}) is defined as follows:

$$P_{kl}(S_{j1}^{k}, S_{j2}^{l}) = \sum_{(i,j) \in \{1,...,n\}} R_i(S_{j1}^{k}) \cap R_j(S_{j2}^{l}) \tag{4}$$

It represents the adapted Lesk intersection (number of common words which is squared in the case of successive words) between the strings corresponding to the information returned by all relations from R, when applied to the concept senses S_{j1}^{k} and S_{j2}^{l}. For example: if we suppose S_{j1}^{k}= *applied_science#n#1*, a sense1 of the concept *applied_science* and S_{j2}^{l}= *information_ science#n#1*, a sense1 of the concept *information_science*, and R_1= gloss, R_2=holonym-gloss as known relations (gloss and holonymy definitions are given below), Relatedness applied for R1 and R2 between the two concepts equals to 11:

$\mathcal{R}_1$ (applied_science#n#1)= (the discipline dealing with the art or science of applying scientific knowledge to practical problems; "he had trouble deciding which branch of engineering to study")

$\mathcal{R}_2$ (information science#n#1)= (the branch of engineering science that studies (with the aid of computers) computable processes and structures).

Overlaps (applied_science#n#1)=1x "science" +1x "branch of engineering" + 1x "study"

$$= 1 + 3^2 + 1 \ = 11$$

The $\mathcal{R}_i$ relations depend on those available in theontology. In our case (WordNet), we used the following WordNet relations:

- *gloss* which represents the definition of a concept with possibly specific example(s) from the real world. For example, the gloss of sense1 of noun car (car#n#1) is:

(*4-wheeled motor vehicle; usually propelled by an internal combustion engine; "he needs a car to get to work"*). The real world example is given between quotes mark.

- *hypernymy* for the *is-a* relation (physics *is-a* natural science) and *hyponymy* its reverse relation,
- *meronymy* for the *has-a* relation (car *has-a* {accelerator, pedal, car seat}) and *holonymy* (its reverse relation),
- *domain relations:* domain specific relations may be relevant to assess semantic relatedness between concepts. [18] have used domain relations extracted using a supervised method. In our case we used an automatic method since these relations have recently been added to WordNet (Wn2.0 version).

We used six domain relations: domain–category (*dmnc*: for example *acropetal*→ *botany,phytology*), domain–usage (*dmnu: bloody* → *intensifier),* domain–region (*dmnr: sumo* → *Japan*). And the domain member relations are: member of domain-category for nouns (*dmtc: matrix_algebra* → *diagonalization, diagonalisation*), member of domain-usage for nouns (*dmtu: idiom* → *euphonious, spang*), member of domain-region for nouns (*dmtr: Manchuria* → *Chino-Japanese_War, Port Arthur*).

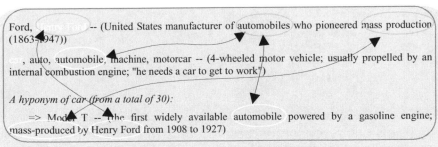

Fig. 2. Use of gloss information for detecting "hidden" semantic links between concepts.

Among all the above relations, we manly used the *gloss* one. It is a cross-categorial "relation". It is not in itself a relation [15] but rather than a concept definition. It is used for exploiting the entire semantic nets of WordNet regardless of parts of speech[1] and for detecting "hidden" relatedness between concepts. To illustrate this, let us consider as an example the two concepts *Henry Ford* and *car*. In WordNet, there is no, explicit semantic relation between these two concepts. But if we consider their gloss information, we find some word overlaps which are indicative of the strong relation between the 2 concepts: as shown in Figure2, there is one overlap between the gloss of the first concept (*Henry Ford*) and the synset of the second (*car*); which is the term *automobile*. And there is a very interesting overlap between, in one hand, the synset of *Henry Ford* and the gloss of the hyponym of the concept *car* which is the compound *Henry Ford*; and between the gloss of *Henry Ford* and the gloss of a hyponym of *car* which are *automobile* and *mass product* in other hand. The hyponym is what comes after the symbol "=>" and it is given in the example of Figure2 only one hyponym between the 30 returned by WordNet to the sense 1 of the concept (*car*).

3.4   Building a Semantic Network

Let

$$D_c = \{C_1, C_2, ..., C_m\} \tag{5}$$

be the set   of the selected concepts from a document D following the extraction method described in section 3.2. Concepts should be mono or multiword and each C_i has a certain number of senses represented by WordNet synsets noted S_i:

$$S_i = \{S_1^i, S_2^i, ..., S_n^i\} \tag{6}$$

Concept C_i has $|S_i| = n$ senses.

If we choose one sense for each concept from D_c, we will always have a set $SN(j)$ of m elements, because we are sure that each concept from D_c has at least one sense, being given that it belongs to the ontology semantic network.

We define a semantic net $SN(j)$ as:

$$SN(j) = (S_{j1}^1, S_{j2}^2, S_{j3}^3, ..., S_{jm}^m) \tag{7}$$

It represents a jth configuration of concepts senses from D_c. $j_1, j_2, .., j_m$ are sense indexes between one and all possible senses for respectively concepts $C_1, C_{2...} C_m$.

For the m concepts of D_c, different semantic networks could be constructed using all sense combinations. The number of possible semantic networks Nb_SN depends on the number of senses of the different concepts from D_c:

$$Nb\_SN = |S_1| . |S_2| .... |S_m| \tag{8}$$

---

[1]   WordNet is designed into four non-interacting semantic nets — one for each open word class (nouns, verbs, adjectives and adverbs). This separation is based on the fact that the appropriate semantic relations between the concepts represented by the synsets in the different parts of speech are incompatible.

For example, Figure3 represents a possible semantic network (S_2^1, S_7^2, S_1^3, S_1^4, S_4^5, S_2^m) resulting from a combination of the 2nd sense of the first concept, the 7th sense of C_2, the 2nd sense of C_m (we suppose that null links are not represented). Links between concepts senses (P_{ij}) in Figure3 are computed as defined in the previous section.

To build the best semantic network representing a document, the selection of each of its nodes (concept senses) relies on the computation of a score (C_score) for every concept sense. The score of a concept sense equals to the sum of semantic relatedness computed for all couples where it belongs to. For a concept C_i, the score of its sense number k is computed as:

$$C\_score(S_k^i) = \sum_{l \neq i} \rho_{i,l} \qquad (9)$$

And then, the best concept sense to retain is the one which maximizes C_score:

$$Best\_score(C_i) = \underset{k=1..n}{Max}\ C\_score(S_k^i) \qquad (10)$$

Let be n is the number of possible senses of the concept C_i. By doing so, we have disambiguated the concept C_i which will be a node in the semantic core. The final semantic core of a document is (S_{j1}^1, S_{j2}^2, S_{j3}^3,..., S_{jm}^m) where nodes correspond respectively to (*Best_Score(C₁)*, *Best_Score(C₂)*, *Best_Score(C₃)*, *Best_Score(Cₘ)*).

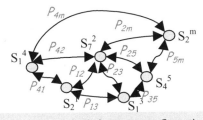

Fig. 3. A semantic network built from one configuration of concepts

4   Evaluation

4.1   Evaluation Method

We evaluated our approach in Information Retrieval (IR). The semantic cores of documents are used for semantic indexing. We compared searching results to those returned when using a classical keywords indexing. In keywords indexing, no compound concepts are used and all frequencies are computed by tf/idf formula both for documents and queries. In semantic indexing, *cf/idf(c)* formula with 2 as a threshold is used to select concepts. Links values between concepts in the resulted semantic core of each document are not used. The values of *c_scores* are used for weighting concepts in documents and queries. However, they are passed to log in order to attenuate too large variations. All other terms, ie those which do not belong to semantic cores of documents in which they appear, are indexed using simple keyword indexing. We have used in our experiments the Mercure search engine[19] for

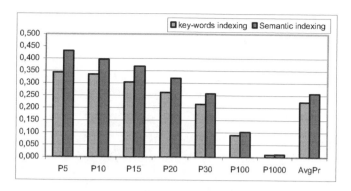

Pn: *Precision for the first n selected documents*
Avg_Pr: *Average precision*

Fig. 4. Search results for key-words versus semantic indexing

which we add some modifications namelly to support multiword concept indexing and the proposed *cf/idf(c)* weighting. The test collection is taken from the MuchMore project [20]. This collection includes 7823 documents with 25 topics from which the queries are extracted and a relevance judgement file done by domain experts. Documents deal with the medical domain, however, the vocabulary is rather general and is roughly covered by WordNet. Our experimental method follows the one used in Trec's campaigns [21]. For each query, the top 1000 retrieved documents are returned by the search engine and precisions are computed at different points (top 5, 10, 15, 20, 30, 100 and 1000 retrieved documents). We have choosen to use a small collection because of the computing complexity: the building of semantic cores for the overall documents of the collection takes about one week (1 minute per document in average).

4.2   Experimental Results

In Figure4, results of search precision are given at different points: 5, 10, 15, 20, 30, 100 and 1000 top selected documents and the average at the last. At each point, the average precision for the 25 queries is given for the two cases of keyword-based indexing and semantic indexing. Results clearly show the advantage of using semantic indexing compared to a simple indexing for enhancing system accuracy.

To sum up, Precision is higher in the case of semantic indexing for all the precision points and especially when considering only the first selected documents. For example, the precision for the 5 top selected documents is 0,3440 with keyword indexing. It goes up to 0,432 (+20%) when semantic indexing is used. And the average precision equals 0,2581 in the case of semantic indexing and only 0,2230 when classical key-word indexing is used.

We can also remark that the gap between semantic and keyword indexing falls when the number of selected documents increases. This can be explained by the total number of relevant documents which is relatively small (even if it may vary from one topic to another) being given the size of the collection.

5 Conclusion

The work developed in this paper lies within the scope of the use of ontologies in the information retrieval field. We have introduced an approach for representing the semantic content of documents. The result is a semantic network where nodes represent disambiguated and scored concepts and edges are materialized by the value of semantic similarity between nodes. This similarity is calculated on the basis of different WordNe semantic relationst. These scored concepts can be considered as a document semantic index. Tests show that the retrieval accuracy is higher thatn with simple keyword indexing. This approach could be generalized to any ontology including a semantic network as defined by [7]: a set of concepts and semantic relations between these concepts.

One possible prospect is to take advantage of the *C_score* measure of nodes for detecting sub-topics in documents. Admitting the hypothesis that nodes (disambiguated concepts) belonging to the same "scale" of scores, belong to the same topic. In the same manner, at inter-document level, semantic cores of documents could be compared for thematization. Documents with closest semantic cores could be regarded as covering the same subject.

References

1.   OntoQuery project net site: http://www.ontoquery.dk
2.   Khan, L., and Luo, F.: Ontology Construction for Information Selection In Proc. of 14th IEEE International Conference on Tools with Artificial Intelligence, pp. 122-127, Washington DC, November 2002.
3.   Guarino, N., Masolo, C., and Vetere, G. "OntoSeek : content-based access to the web". IEEE Intelligent Systems, 14:70-80, (1999).
4.   Baziz, M ., Aussenac-Gilles, N. et Boughanem M.: Désambiguïsation et Expansion de Requêtes dans un SRI : Etude de l'apport des liens sémantiques. Revue des Sciences et Technologies de l'Information (RSTI) série ISI, Ed. Hermes, V. 8, N. 4/2003, p. 113-136, déc. 2003.
5.   Mihalcea, R. and Moldovan, D.: Semantic indexing using WordNet senses. In Proceedings of ACL Workshop on IR & NLP, Hong Kong, October 2000.
6.   Miller, G. *Wordnet: A lexical database*. Communication of the ACM, 38(11):39--41, (1995).
7.   Joon Ho Lee, Myong Ho Kim, and Yoon Joon Lee. "Information retrieval based on conceptual distance in IS-A hierarchies". Journal of Documentation, 49(2):188{207, June 1993.
8.   Haav, H. M., Lubi, T.-L.: A Survey of Concept-based Information Retrieval Tools on the Web. In Proc. of 5th East-European Conference ADBIS*2001, Vol 2., Vilnius "Technika", pp 29-41.
9.   Gonzalo, J., Verdejo, F., Chugur I., Cigarrán J.: Indexing with WordNet synsets can improve text retrieval, in Proc. the COLING/ACL '98 Workshop on Usage of WordNet for Natural Language Processing, 1998.
10. Zarg Ayouna, H., Salotti, S.: Mesure de similarité dans une ontologie pour l'indexation sémantique de documents XML. Dans Ing. des Connais, IC'2004, Lyon Mai 2004. P 249-260.

11. Cucchiarelli, R. Navigli, F. Neri, P. Velardi. Extending and Enriching WordNet with OntoLearn, Proc. of The Second Global Wordnet Conference 2004 (GWC 2004), Brno, Czech Republic, January 20-23rd, 2004
12. Hirst, G., and St. Onge, D.: Lexical chains as representations of context for the detection and correction of malapropisms. In C. Fellbaum, editor, WordNet: An electronic lexical database, pages 305–332. MIT Press, 1998.
13. Resnik, P., "Semantic Similarity in a Taxonomy: An Information-Based Measure and its Application to Problems of Ambiguity in Natural Language", Journal of Artificial Intelligence Research (JAIR), 11, pp. 95-130, 1999.
14. Banerjee, S. and Pedersen, T.: An adapted Lesk algorithm for word sense disambiguation using Word-Net. In Proc. of the Third International Conference on Intelligent Text Processing and Computational Linguistics, Mexico City, February 2002.
15. Lesk, M.: Automatic sense disambiguation using machine readable dictionaries: How to tell a pine cone from a ice cream cone. In *Proc. of SIGDOC '86*, 1986.
16. Croft, W. B., Turtle, H. R. & Lewis, D. D. (1991). The Use of Phrases and Structured Queries in Information Retrieval. In Proceedings of the Fourteenth Annual International ACM/SIGIR Conference on Research and Development in Information Retrieval, A. Bookstein, Y. Chiaramella, G. Salton, & V. V. Raghavan (Eds.), Chicago, Illinois: pp. 32-45.
17. Huang, X. and Robertson, S.E. "Comparisons of Probabilistic Compound Unit Weighting Methods", Proc. of the ICDM'01 Workshop on Text Mining, San Jose, USA, Nov. 2001.
18. Magnini, B. and Cavaglia, G.: Integrating Subject Field Codes into WordNet. In Proc. of the 2nd International Conference on Language resources and Evaluation, LREC2000, Atenas.
19. M. BOUGHANEM, T. DKAKI, J. MOTHE ET C. SOULÉ-DUPUY "*Mercure at TREC-7*". In Proceeding of Trec-7, (1998).
20. Paul Buitelaar, Diana Steffen, Martin Volk, Dominic Widdows, Bogdan Sacaleanu, Spela Vintar, Stanley Peters, Hans Uszkoreit. Evaluation Resources for Concept-based Cross-Lingual IR in the Medical Domain In Proc. of LREC2004, Lissabon, Portugal, May 2004.
21. The Sixth Text REtrieval Conference (TREC{6). Edited by E.M. Voorhees and D.K. Harman. Gaithersburg, MD: NIST, 1998.

Using an Aligned Ontology to Process User Queries

Kleber Xavier Sampaio de Souza[1,2,3] and Joseph Davis[2]

[1]Embrapa Information Technology, Cx. Postal 6041, 13.083-886 Campinas SP, Brazil
[2]School of Information Technologies, Madsen Building F09, University of Sydney, NSW
2006 Australia
[3]Research supported by Capes grant BEX0687/03-0

{kleber,jdavis}@it.usyd.edu.au

Abstract. Ontologies have been developed for a number of knowledge domains as diverse as clinical terminology, photo camera parts and micro-array gene expression data. However, processing user queries over a set of overlapping ontologies is not straightforward because they have often been created by independent groups of expertise, each of them adopting different configurations for ontology concepts. A project being carried out at the Brazilian Corporation of Agricultural Research has produced ontologies in sub-domains such as beef cattle, dairy cattle, sheep and beans, among others. This paper focuses on an alignment method for these ontologies based on Formal Concept Analysis, a data analysis technique founded on lattice theory, and a strategy for processing user queries.

1 Introduction

Ontologies, knowledge specifications of conceptualizations [9], play an important role in knowledge sharing because they establish a common terminology to be used by the members of a community. They have been used in knowledge-based systems to represent objects of a universe of discourse, such as: agreements about objects and messages (requests, queries, assertions etc.) agents exchange with each other, conceptual schemas of database systems, and business objects in a software engineering project.

Differences in terminology and structure of the ontologies may occur even when one constructs them for sub-domains of a specific domain. This is precisely what happened in Embrapa's Information Agency Project that we worked on, which produced separate but overlapping ontologies in sub-domains of the agricultural domain such as: beef cattle, dairy cattle, sheep and beans, among others. The necessity of integrating these various sources of information led to the search for a method of integration. The method proposed in this paper is the alignment of sub-domain ontologies with an upper-ontology based on Agrovoc [7]. The alignment process also uses Formal Concept Analysis (FCA) [8,27], a data analysis technique based on lattice theory. Although the examples are developed in agricultural domain, the results are general and can be applied to any domain.

C. Bussler and D. Fensel (Eds.): AIMSA 2004, LNAI 3192, pp. 44–53, 2004.

The remainder of the paper is as follows. In the next section, we comment on related work. Next, the formalism associated to Formal Concept Analysis and Lattice Theory is introduced. This formalism is associated with an upper-merged ontology in an alignment method in the subsequent section. Then, the result of the aligning process is used for processing queries. Finally, conclusions are drawn.

2 Related Work

Ontology Mapping, which encompasses integration, merging, alignment, articulation and fusion of ontologies, has received much attention recently. For an excellent review on the subject we refer to the work of Kalfoglou and Schorlemmer [11]. One of their conclusions is that the process of production of a fully automated method for ontology mapping has not been achieved by any of the proposed approaches. Moreover, full automation in the actual mapping methods would lead to combinatorial explosion. That is one of the reasons why we favor the alignment strategy anchored on a thesaurus, instead of trying to come up with a merged ontology for the whole agricultural domain.

The difference between merge and alignment is that in the merge process one ontology is produced as a result of a fusion process, whereas the alignment is a pair of ontological mappings between an intermediate ontology (called *articulation of two ontologies* in [11]) and the source ontologies. This articulation, which we call **aligned ontology**, is used as a reference for the comparison of the source ontologies.

Ontology Merging: The design and integration of ontologies have been addressed by many papers [1,2,5,12,13,15,18,19]. They typically use heuristic rules to find appropriate matches among nodes in corresponding source ontologies. They have powerful features to support the user in the task of finding the best matches for a given node, some of them including similarity measures [5]. However, there still remains a lot of work that the user must carry out in order to produce a merged ontology.

Distributed Data and Ontologies: There are several initiatives describing the use of ontologies in integration of information [26]. OBSERVER system [16], for example, explores syntactic relations among elements in ontologies (formalized in Description Logics) to translate a query across multiple related ontologies. Our approach differs from the syntactic ones, because the alignment of ontologies anchored on a thesaurus provides a structural rather syntactical comparison between ontologies (details in Section 4).

Ontology Merging and FCA: Formal Concept Analysis has also been applied to ontology merging [22,23]. The FCA-Merge method uses a set of documents related to the two ontologies to be merged and processes them through natural language processing techniques, producing a pruned concept lattice. That lattice is then used for the generation of the final merged ontology. In our approach, the documents linked to the source ontologies are not reprocessed to find their best classification in the aligned ontology. As of their original classification, they were already linked to the appropriate terms in the thesaurus and were associated to the nodes in the corresponding ontology [21].

FCA and Thesaurus: The formalization of botanical taxonomies with Formal Concept Analysis was studied in [20]. Thesaurus applied organization structuring of medical discharge summaries was reported in [4]. None of these approaches addressed the alignment of ontologies anchored on thesaurus, however.

3   Formal Concept Analysis and Lattice Theory

Formal Concept Analysis (FCA), or Galois Lattice, is a method for data analysis based on Lattice Theory and Propositional Calculus. It has been applied in many domains: from structuring information systems [10], to knowledge discovery in databases [24], political science, understanding building regulations and psychology [4]. For space limitation reasons, we will assume that the reader has familiarity with the Formal Concept Analysis theoretical background. Please, refer to [8] for a detailed explanation.

FCA analyses which subsets $(E \subset O)$ share the same subsets $(I \subset A)$, viz. subsets of objects with the same attributes. E' represents the projection of the set E into A (see Figure 1), as determined by the binary relation R $(R \subseteq O \times A)$. Similarly, I' represents the projection of I into O. Formally, the projection (E,I), with $E \subseteq O$, $I \subseteq A$ is a **formal concept** if, and only if, $E'=\{a \in A \mid \forall o \in E:(o,a) \in R\}$ and $I'=\{o \in O \mid \forall a \in I:(o,a) \in R\}$. The set of all formal concepts is called a **formal context**, denoted by (O,A,R).

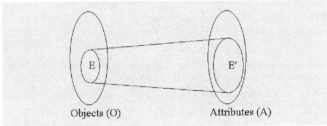

Fig. 1. Galois Connection between O and A

E is called the **extent** and I the **intent** of the formal concept (E,I). It can be seen from the definition above that E is the set of all objects that share the same attributes in I. Similarly, I is the set of all attributes that are shared by the same objects in E. The duality between E and I, or **Galois Connection**, establishes a **subconcept-superconcept** relation, such that:

$$(E_1;I_1) \leq \qquad (E_2;I_2) \Leftrightarrow E_1 \subseteq E_2 \qquad (1)$$

$$(E_1;I_1) \leq \qquad (E_2;I_2) \Leftrightarrow I_1 \supseteq I_2 \qquad (2)$$

This partial ordering results in a complete ordering among all elements of the formal context (O,A,R), with corresponding *infimum (or meet)* and *supremun (or join)*. Moreover, this ordered set is a lattice, called **concept lattice** [8].

Theorem 1 (The basic theorem on concept lattices (adapted from [8])). *The concept lattice $B(O, A, R)$ is a complete lattice in which infimum and supremum are given by:*

$$\bigvee_{j \in J} (E_j, I_j) = ((\bigcup_{j \in J} E_j)'' , \bigcap_{j \in J} I_j) \tag{3}$$

$$\bigwedge_{j \in J} (E_j, I_j) = (\bigcap_{j \in J} E_j , (\bigcup_{j \in J} I_j)'') \tag{4}$$

4 Applying Formal Concept Analysis to the Alignment of Ontologies

Using a direct merge of the concepts in the source ontologies to process a query was discarded because the same concept had been used with different meaning (almost always unreconcilable ones). Moreover, the partial orderings of terms were very dissimilar. For this reason, there was a need to refer to a unified view of the two source ontologies anchored in a common partial ordering. Such view and ordering was provided by a thesaurus, namely Agrovoc.

4.1 Alignment of Ontologies Anchored on Agrovoc

Agrovoc [7] is a multilingual agricultural thesaurus. The terms it contains are supposed to cover the majority of objects, events and processes that occur in agricultural domain. Moreover, a thesaurus is a **partially ordered set (poset)** of terms [10,6], which are organized into many sub-trees. Each sub-tree contains the term's definition, its super-concept and sub-concepts, and related terms. The formal definition of a thesaurus used in this paper is as follows:

Definition 1. A thesaurus $\langle E, \succeq \rangle$ is a set of terms $t_i \in T$ organized in accordance to a partial order $\succeq$.

The Embedding of the thesaurus in the lattice is realized in the following way: initially, each term $t_i \in T$ is transformed into one attribute $a_i \in A$ of the formal context (O,A,R). Then, the partial order $\succeq$ is guaranteed by requiring that the inclusion of a term implies the inclusion of all of its predecessors. This embedding is stated formally in Theorem 2.

Theorem 2. *Let $\underline{B}(O,A,R)$ be a concept lattice and the partial order $\langle T, \succeq \rangle$ of a thesaurus of terms T embedded in B be expressed as $\forall (o,a) \in R, a_1 \succeq a \Rightarrow (o,a_1) \in R$. Then, $\forall o \in E_1, E_2$ such that $a_1 \in I_1, a_2 \in I_2, a_1 \succeq a_2$ implies $a_1 \in I_2$.*

Proof. From the embedding procedure $(o, a_2) \in R, a_1 \succeq a \Rightarrow (o,a_1) \in R$. So, (o,a_1) must exist as a relation. From (2) above: $(E_1, I_1) \geq (E_2, I_2) \Rightarrow I_2 \supseteq I_1$. Therefore, if $a_1 \in I_1$ and $a_2 \in I_2$, then $a_1 \in I_2$ $\square$

The fact that $a_1 \in I_2$ confirms that or a_1 and a_2 are in the same node of the lattice, or a_1 must come from a node above. This result is confirmed when three nodes are compared, as it can be seen in the following corollary.

Corollary 1. *For all $o_1 \in E_1, o_2 \in E_2, o_3 \in E_3$, such that $a_1 \in I_1, a_2 \in I_2, a_3 \in I_3$, with $a_1 \succeq a_2$ and $a_1 \succeq a_3$, then $a_1 \in ((E_2, I_2) \vee (E_3, I_3))$*

Proof. From Theorem 1, $((E_2, I_2) \vee (E_3, I_3)) = ((E_2 \cup E_3)'', (I_2 \cap I_3))$. If $a_1 \in I_2$ and $a_1 \in I_3$, then $a_1 \in (I_2 \cap I_3)$ $\square$

The preceding corollary shows that if the term a_1 is a common attribute between two nodes and it precedes terms a_2 and a_3 in the thesaurus ordering, then it is an element of the least upper bound (or join) of these nodes. This means that the in the lattice a_1 is in a position nearest to the top than a_2 and a_3.

Having established the common ordering through which ontological similarities and differences can be observed, the alignment of ontologies can now be defined:

Definition 2. *Let O_1, O_2, A_1, A_2 and R_1, R_2 be the set of objects, attributes and relations of ontologies O_1 and O_2, respectively. The formal context representing the aligned ontology is defined by $O_M = ((O_1 \cup O_2), (A_1 \cup A_2), (R_1 \cup R_2))$.*

Table 1 shows the formal concept containing part of the ontologies of Beef Cattle and Dairy Cattle. The Objects correspond to rows in the table and Attributes, to columns. Whenever there is a relation between an object and an attribute, the intersection is marked in the table with an X. Objects relating to Beef Cattle ontology are marked with an A before the name, and to Dairy Cattle ontology with a B.

Naturally, the tool used to construct the lattice (Galicia[1]) does not consider ordering among attributes because that is not the standard approach. This is constructed manually by putting a sign ($\rightarrow$) to remind the ontology designer that whenever she or he marks the intersection, the other one must be marked because it corresponds to a predecessor concept in the thesaurus. For example, BeefCattle→Cattle⊔ means that Cattle⊔ is marked whenever BeefCattle⊔ is marked.

5   Processing User Queries

The Hasse diagram corresponding to the formal context displayed in Table 1 is displayed in Figure 2. The names near each node correspond to thesaurus terms and the names in boxes are objects of ontologies A and B, respectively. The objects

[1] Galicia: Galois Lattice Interactive Constructor. http://www.iro.umontreal.ca/galicia/

positioned in a certain node of the diagram inherit all the attributes of the nodes in the path from it to the top node. The object A pasture usage, for example, is linked in its context to grazing systems, feeding systems, growth, developmental stages, continuous grazing, intensive husbandry␣and beef cattle.

That diagram also confirms the correct positioning of thesaurus concepts predicted by Theorem 2. An example is the node developmental stages␣ that is a parent node to the nodes post-weaning, pre-weaning␣and growth.

There are cases in which two concepts, one being the predecessor of the other, were collapsed into a single node. This occurred because there are no other nodes with that same predecessor, viz. the nodes Brachiaria␣ and Brachiaria Decumbens were collapsed because there are no other kinds of Brachiaria␣in the context. However, the predecessor of Brachiaria␣ in its turn, which is poaceae, was represented in a separate node because it is also a predecessor of Pennisetum, another type of grass.

Regarding the result of the alignment, the objects corresponding to ontology A␣are concentrated in the right side of the diagram, whereas those of ontology B␣are on the left side. In the middle there are the linking nodes, i.e. whenever a concept is common to both ontologies, it is dragged to the middle of the diagram.

The queries formulated by the user have currently the form of a set of terms and AND/OR connectors. This matches perfectly with the *join* and *meet* operations that can be performed over the concept lattice. As Chaudron observed in [3], the concept lattice **corresponds** to a zero order logical language. This logical language arises naturally from Galois Connection among subsets of objects and attributes.

Theorem 1 proves how the infimum and supremum between every pair of objects is defined in terms of the usual set operators ($\cup \Leftrightarrow \cap \Leftrightarrow \supset \Leftrightarrow \subset$). For example, in Figure 2, the objects B calves␣and A feeding system2␣have in common the attributes (*join*) developmental stages␣ and feeding systems, because the concept corresponding the supremum of the former has these attributes as intents.

The concept pasture usage, in the example given previously, is a *meet* of grazing systems, feeding systems, growth, developmental stages, continuous grazing, intensive husbandry␣and beef cattle.

Whenever the user submits a query, the processing engine accesses directly the aligned ontology (see Figure 3) and executes the search. It identifies in the lattice the set of servers that contain objects satisfying this query. If the result shows that there is only one ontology, the query can be redirected to the server containing that ontology.

If the user searches for documents relating to intensive husbandry␣ **and** feeding systems, the only nodes that satisfy the query are those below the intersection (meet) in the lattice (see Figure 2) are B elephant grass, B intensive, A brachiaria2, A feeding systems2␣and A pasture usage. If the user further restricts the query, adding growth␣ to it, then only the latter two nodes satisfy it. In this case, it means that the system contains the requested information only in the domain of beef cattle.

If the query were Brachiaria **or** Pennisetum, the **join** node would be the one identified by poaceae. The result of the query would be all the objects below poaceae, namely B elephant grass, B intensive, A Brachiaria2 and A Brachiaria.

Table 1. Alignment formal context for Beef Cattle (A) and Dairy Cattle (B) Ontologies

	Production	AnimalProduction→Production	AnimalHusbandryMethods	IntensiveHusbandry→AnimalHusbandryMethods	Fattening→AnimalFeeding	Growth→DevelopmentalStages	Male→Sex	BrachiariaDecumbens→Brachiaria	Poaceae	FeedingSystems	ContinuosGrazing→GrazingSystems	BeefCattle→Cattle	DairyCattle→Cattle	Postweaning→DevelopmentalStage	Preweaning→DevelopmentalStage	Penisetum→Poaceae	PenisetumPurpureum→Pennisetum	AnimalFeeding	DevelopmentalStages	Sex	Braquiaria→Poaceae	GrazingSystem→FeedingSystems
A production	X	X										X										
A processes	X	X										X										
A prod systems	X	X										X										
A intensive	X	X	X	X								X										
A fattening	X	X	X	X	X							X						X				
A growth	X	X	X	X		X						X							X			
A feeding system	X	X	X	X	X							X						X				
A males	X	X	X	X	X		X					X						X		X		
A brachiaria	X	X	X	X	X			X	X	X	X	X						X		X	X	X
A pasture usage	X	X	X	X		X				X	X	X							X			X
A brachiaria2	X	X	X	X		X		X	X	X	X	X							X		X	X
A feeding system2	X	X	X	X		X				X		X							X			
B production	X	X											X									
B production systems	X	X											X									
B feeding	X	X								X			X									
B concentrate food	X	X								X			X									
B calves	X	X								X			X						X			
B postweaning	X	X											X	X					X			
B preweaning	X	X											X		X				X			
B elephantGrass	X	X	X	X						X	X		X			X	X					X
B intensive	X	X	X	X						X	X		X			X	X					X

It is interesting to note that the alignment provides a means of analysis of the whole set of objects. In the latter result, we showed that nodes satisfying `intensive husbandry`, `feeding systems⎵` and `growth⎵` exist only in the context of `beef cattle`. This fact may serve as an alert to the system managers, in the sense that there might be some information relating these three concepts in `dairy cattle⎵` as well, and that information is not in the system.

5.1 Complexity Issues

The problem of generating the set of all concepts (E,I) in an concept lattice has been addressed by many works. For a review, please refer to the work of Kuznetsov and Obiedkov [14]. In their work, they compared the performance of several of the existing algorithms, except for Titanic [24], which had just been published. They have pointed out that although the number of concepts can be exponential in size of the input context, many algorithms perform reasonably well, provided the formal contexts have a reasonable size. In their experiment, they went up to 900 objects and 100 attributes.

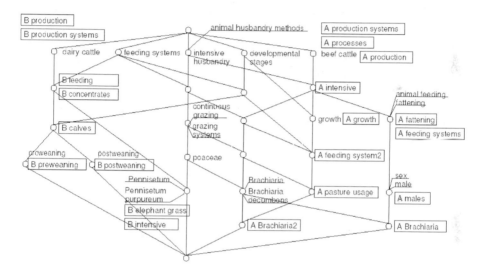

Fig. 2. Hasse Diagram corresponding to the formal context of Table 1.

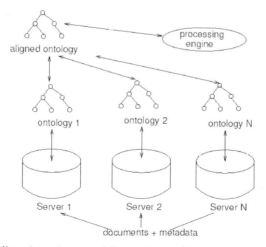

Fig. 3. Aligned ontology providing common view to the search engine

Titanic [24] also performed well for ontologies containing up to 10,000 objects and 141 attributes, generating 124,574 concepts.

It is interesting to note that, the computation of the lattice is performed just once, and can be done when processing demands are lower. After that, the resulting lattice is used in the processing of user queries, which can be done very efficiently, because they involve only the evaluation of join and meet points.

6 Conclusion

This article presented a method for processing user queries based on an alignment method for ontologies. This method is based on Formal Concept Analysis, or Galois Lattices, a data analysis technique grounded on Lattice Theory and Propositional Calculus.

The results showed that anchoring two ontologies in a common partial ordering, provided by a lattice of terms (thesaurus), provides an excellent view of a set of objects existing in a database. Based on this analysis, one can evaluate and decide which set of objects is the best answer for a given query. Actually, a complete logical system can be constructed using lattice terms as first order predicates [3]. As a result, a complex logical system can be built over the lattice, enabling the system to process elaborate queries involving logical operators.

References

1. Fernandez-Breis, J. Martinez-Bejar, R.: A Cooperative Framework for Integrating Ontologies. International Journal of Human-Computer Studies (56) (2002) 665-720
2. Chalupsky, H.: OntoMorph: A Translation System for Symbolic Knowledge. Principles of Knowledge Representation and Reasoning In: Proceedings of the Seventh International Conference on Knowledge Representation and Reasoning (KR-2000), Breckenridge, Colorado, USA. (2000)
3. Chaudron, L., Maille, N., Boyer, M.: The cube lattice model and its applications. Applied Artificial Intelligence **17** (2003) 207-242
4. Cole, R. and Eklund, P.: Application of Formal Concept Analysis to Information Retrieval using a Hierarchically Structured Thesaurus. In: Proceedings of the International Conference on Conceptual Graphs (ICCS96), University of New South Wales, Sydney, (1996) 1-12
5. Doan, A., Madhavan, J., Domingos, P. ,Halevy, A.: Learning to Map Between Ontologies on the Semantic Web. In: Proceedings of the Eleventh International WWW Conference, Hawaii, US (2002) 662-673
6. Dyvik, H.: Translations as Semantic Mirrors. In: Proceedings of Workshop W13: Multilinguality in the Lexicon II, The 13th Biennial European Conference on Artificial Intelligence (ECAI98), Brighton, UK (1998) 24-44
7. FAO (Food and Agriculture Organization of the United Nations): AGROVOC: multilingual agricultural thesaurus. FAO. Rome (1995) 612p. http://www.fao.org/agrovoc/
8. Ganter B., Wille R.: Formal Concept Analysis. Springer (1998)
9. Gruber, T.R.: Translation Approach to Portable Ontology Specifications. Knowledge Acquisition, **5** (2) (1993) 199-220
10. Groh, B., Strahringer S. and Wille, R.: TOSCANA-Systems Based on Thesauri. In: M.-L. Mugnier and M. Chein (Editors), Conceptual Structures: Theory, Tools and Applications, LNAI 1453, Springer-Verlag, (1998) 127-138

11. Kalfoglou, Y., Schorlemmer, M.: Ontology mapping: the state of the art. The Knowledge Engineering Review, **18**(1) (2003) 131

12. Kalfoglou, Y. Schorlemmer, M.: Information-flow-based ontology mapping. In: On the Move to Meaningful Internet Systems 2002 LNLS 2519, Springer (2002) 11321151

13. Kay, J., Holden, S.: Automatic Extraction of Ontologies from Teaching Document Metadata. In: Proceedings of the International Conference on Computers in Education (ICCE 2002). Auckland, New Zealand. (2002) 1555-1556

14. Kuznetsov, S.O., Obiedkov, S.A.: Comparing performance of algorithms for generating concept lattices. Journal Exp. Theor. Artif. Intell. 14(2-3)(2002) 189-216

15. McGuiness, D.L., Fikes, R., Rice, J., Wilder, S.: An Environment for Merging and Testing Large Ontologies. In: Proceedings of Seventh International Conference on Principles of Knowledge Representation and Reasoning (KR2000), Breckenridge, Colorado, USA. (2000)

16. Mena, E., Kashyap, V., Illarramendi, A., Sheth, A.: Domain Specific Ontologies for Semantic Information Brokering on the Global Information Infrastructure. In: Proceedings of the 1st International Conference on Formal Ontology in Information Systems (FOIS98) (1998) 269283

17. Mitra, P., Wiederhold, G.: An Algebra for the Composition of Ontologies. In: Proceedings of the Workshop on Knowledge Transformation for the Semantic Web. Lyon, France (2002)

18. Noy N. F., Musen M.A.: PROMPT: Algorithm and Tool for Automated Ontology Merging and Alignment. In: Seventeenth National Conference on Artificial Intelligence (AAAI-2000), Austin, TX (2000)

19. Park, J., Hunting, S.: XML Topic Maps - Creating and Using Topic Maps for the Web. Addison-Wesley (2002) 544p.

20. Priss, U.: Formalizing Botanical Taxonomies In: De Moor; Lex; Ganter (eds.), Conceptual Structures for Knowledge Creation and Communication. Proceedings of the 11th International Conference on Conceptual Structures, Springer Verlag, LNAI 2746 (2003) 309-322

21. Souza, K.X.S., Davis, J., Souza, M.I.F.: Organizing Information for the Agribusiness Sector: Embrapa's Information Agency In: Proceedings of 2004 International Conference on Digital Archive Technologies. Taipei: Institute of Information Science - Academia Sinica (2004) 159 - 169.

22. Stumme, G., Madche, A.: FCA-Merge: Bottom-up merging of ontologies. In: Proceedings of the 7th Intl. Conf. on Artificial Intelligence (IJCAI '01), Seattle, WA (2001) 225-230

23. Stumme, G., Studer, R., Sure, Y. Towards and Order-Theoretical Foundation for Maintaining and Merging Ontologies In: Proceedings of Referenzmodellierung 2000. Siegen, Germany. (2000)

24. Stumme, G., Taouil, R., Bastide, Y., Pasquier, N., Lakhal, L.: Computing iceberg concept lattices with Titanic. Data & Knowledge Engineering 42(2002) 189-222

25. Valtchev, P., Hacene, M. R., Huchard, M., Roume, C.: Extracting Formal Concepts out of Relational Data In: Proceedings of the 4th Intl. Conference Journes de l'Informatique Messine (JIM'03): "Knowledge Discovery and Discrete Mathematics", Metz, France (2003) 37-49

26. Wache, H.; Vogele, T.; Visscr, U.; Stuckenschmidt, H.; Schuster, G.; Neumann, H.; and Hubner, S. Ontology-based integration of information - a survey of existing approaches. In: Stuckenschmidt, H., ed., IJCAI-01 Workshop: Ontologies and Information Sharing (2001) 108-117

27. Wille, R.: Restructuring Lattice Theory: an Approach Based on Hierarchies of Concepts. In: Rival, I. (ed.), Ordered Sets. Reidel, Dordrecht Boston (1982) 445-470

An Experiment on Modelling Agents and Knowledge for the Semantic Web

Alvaro E. Arenas and Brian M. Matthews

CCLRC Rutherford Appleton Laboratory
Business and Information Technology Department
Oxfordshire, OX11 0QX, UK
{A.E.Arenas, B.M.Matthews}@rl.ac.uk

Abstract. This paper contributes to the area of software engineering for Semantic Web development. We describe how to apply MAS-CommonKADS, an agent-oriented extension of CommonKADS, to the development of the ITtalks Web Portal. Domain-specific knowledge is modelled by reusing well-known ontologies such as FOAF and RDFiCal. We also describe how to specify CommonKADS problem-solving methods as web services, expressed using the OWL-S language.

Keywords: Semantic Web, Knowledge Modelling, CommonKADS, Problem-Solving Methods, Web Services.

1 Introduction

Realising the Semantic Web vision calls for the development and support of intelligent agents as well as the ontologies for sharing knowledge. Several methodologies have been proposed for developing agent-based system [19] and ontologies [6] as well as knowledge-based systems [1, 18]. How to combine these different modelling techniques and adapt them for the semantic web have been identified as an open research question that requires urgent attention [13, pp. 24].

This paper contributes to solve this research question by studying the application of MAS-CommonKADS [16], an agent-oriented extension of the knowledge-based methodology CommonKADS [18], to the design of the ITtalks Web Portal [7]. ITtalks is a case study developed as part of the DAML project at the University of Maryland, USA. It offers access to information about talks, seminars, colloquia and other information technology (IT) related events, making use of DAML+OIL ontologies for knowledge base representation, reasoning, and agent communication.

Section 2 summarises the MAS-CommonKAD methodology. Section 3 describes how to model agents and tasks for ITtalks. Section 4 presents the knowledge modelling. We show how domain-specific knowledge can be defined by making reuse of widely-used ontologies such as FOAF and RDFiCal. Further, CommonKADS problem-solving methods are modelled as web services using the OWL-S language. Section 5 relates our work with that of others while section 6 presents our conclusions and highlights future work.

C. Bussler and D. Fensel (Eds.): AIMSA 2004, LNAI 3192, pp. 54–64, 2004.
© Springer-Verlag Berlin Heidelberg 2004

2   The MAS-CommonKADS Methodology

Many agent-oriented methodologies have evolved from object-oriented technologies, for instance Burmeister [2] and INGENIAS [14] among others. By contrast, other methodologies have evolved from the knowledge engineering community, for example MAS-CommonKADS [16], or from a pure perspective of agent theory, for example Vowel Engineering [11] and Gaia [20]. In this paper we apply MAS-CommonKADS, an agent-oriented extension of the knowledge-based methodology CommonKADS [18], to developing semantic web applications. We have selected MAS-CommonKADS for its emphasis on identifying and modelling the knowledge to be used by the agents, an important characteristic of agents in the Semantic Web arena.

MAS-CommonKADS is based on a set of models covering specific aspects of the development process. The *agent model* specifies agents' characteristics such as reasoning capabilities, sensor/effectors, and services. The *task model* describes the tasks that the agents can carry out. The *knowledge model* defines the knowledge needed by the agents to achieve their goals. The *organisation model* describes the social organisation of the agent society. The *coordination model* illustrates the conversation between agents. The *communication model* details the human-software agent interactions. Finally, the *design model* includes, in addition to the typical action of the design phase, the design of relevant aspects of the agent network, selecting the most suitable agent architecture and the agent development platform.

The application of the methodology consists in developing the different models. Due to space limitation, we concentrate here on the agent, tasks and knowledge models.

3   Modelling Agents and Tasks

ITtalks is organised around domains, which correspond to event-hosting organisations such as universities, research labs or professional groups. Each domain is represented by a separate web domain. Users can access the system through the web or through agents acting on her/his behalf. The web portal includes features such as registration, search, and domain administration. ITtalks users can view information such as location, speaker, hosting organisation and talk topic.

3.1   The Model Agent

For ITtalks, we have identified four agents:

- **User Agent**: Interface agent representing a user. It interacts with the system by servicing particular requests from users and by managing user profiles.
- **Talk Agent**: software agent that discovers the talks in a particular domain according to requests received from the User agent. There is one agent per domain. For instance, three possible domains in the Oxford area are CCLRC, University of Ox-

ford and Oxford Brookes University. There will be an agent for each domain, managing the information about talks in these places.

- **Calendar Agent**: software agent that manages the calendar of the users of a particular domain. There is one agent per domain.
- **Location Agent**: software agent that provides the service of locating places near to a particular location.

The outcome of the agent model is a set of textual templates, one for each agent, which shows information such as agent description, role, etc. For instance, Table 1 presents the template for *Talk Agent*.

Table 1. Textual Template for *Talk Agent*

Talk Agent	
Type:	Software agent
Role:	Information provider
Location:	Within each participating domain
Description:	This agent determines the talks that satisfy the criteria provided by the user. It contacts the *Location Agent* to determine the places within a predetermined number of miles of the location provided by the user. Then, it contacts the *Talk Agents* in other places to get the talks on the requested topic within the defined date range. It also searches its local talk database to get information on local talks. Once it has collected all talks in relevant places, it consults the local *Calendar Agent* to check the user availability on the talk dates. Finally, it notifies the user with the list of talks, including information whether the user is available for such talks.
Coordination:	Talk Agent, Calendar Agent, Location Agent
Resources:	Talk ontology

Similar templates are defined for the other three agents.

3.2   The Task Model

This model describes the tasks each agent can carry out. Use cases are useful for this activity. We have defined the following tasks to be performed for each agent:

- **User Agent**: introduce user profile; update user profile; request talk; confirm talk in user calendar; delete talk from user calendar.
- **Talk Agent**: search talk; contrast talk timing with user availability; notify users about new talk.
- **Calendar Agent**: include talk in user calendar; delete talk from user calendar; check availability for user.
- **Location Agent**: provide distance between two locations; provide nearby locations.

Tasks can be split into subtasks. UML activity diagrams can be used for representing the subtasks involved in realising a task. For instance, the *Search Talk* task realises the request "*give me talks in area X on topic Y during period Z*". This task involves subtasks such as selecting domains in area X; requesting talks on topic Y to all domains in the area; or qualifying a talk according to user's interest and speaker reputation. Figure 1 shows the subtask flow for *Search Talk* task.

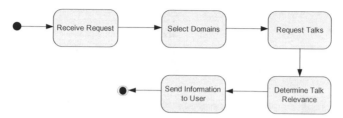

Fig. 1. Subtasks involved in *Search Talk* Task

The methodology also offers templates for describing tasks. Table 2 describes subtask *Determine Talk Relevance*.

Table 2. Template for task *Determine Talk Relevance*

Task Determine Talk Relevance	
Objective:	Determine the relevance of a talk
Description:	This task assesses the relevance of the talk according to user's profiles (for instance, following user's topic of interests). It may include contacting a service such as CiteSeer to determine speaker reputation. It combines these two values to determine the talk relevance.
Dependency/Flow:	See Figure 1
Input:	Talk information; User Profile
Output:	An indicator of the relevance of the talk

4 Knowledge Modelling

The more relevant model for this paper is the knowledge model. It describes the reasoning capabilities of the agents needed to carry our specific tasks and achieve their goals. This model includes the specification of domain knowledge, modelled as concepts, properties, and relationships. The methodology provides a semi-formal language for such modelling, called the Conceptual Modelling Language (CML) [18]. Instead of using CML, we have opted for a UML-based graphical language to represent domain knowledge, then expressing this model in Semantic Web languages such as RDF and OWL. This change has been motivated for the existence of automatic tools for processing knowledge represented in RDF/OWL [15].

4.1 Modelling Domain-Specific Knowledge

In this part we model specific aspects of the ITtalks domain. One of the important characteristics of the semantic web is the use of common ontologies. There are several simple ontologies available for modelling domains such as people and their interests, e.g. FOAF [3], and calendars, e.g. RDFiCal [17]. We have reused these ontologies for defining our main elements. Figure 2 illustrates the domain knowledge.

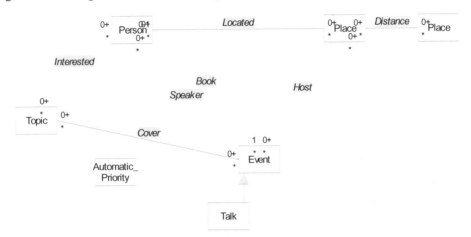

Fig. 2. Domain Knowledge for ITtalks

A domain-knowledge description typically consists of two types of ingredients: one or more domain schemas, and one or more knowledge bases. In our case, domain schemas are given by general ontologies such as FOAF and RDFiCal. The knowledge bases correspond to instances of the ontologies. For example, the concept Person can be defined as follows.

```
<foaf:Person rdf:ID=Arenas>
  <foaf:name>Alvaro Arenas</foaf:name>
  <foaf:mbox rdf:resource=mailto:A.E.Arenas@rl.ac.uk/>
  <foaf:homeAddress>Oxford, OX4</foaf:homeAddress>
  <foaf:interest rdf:resource=http://www.w3.org/2001/sw/>
</foaf:Person>
```

4.2 Modelling Problem-Solving Methods

Problem-Solving Methods (PSMs) are software components that can be assembled with domain knowledge bases to create application systems. The knowledge-engineering community has identified and developed PSMs of general usefulness or for specific high-level tasks such as diagnosis, assessment, planning, etc. Knowledge-based methodologies such as CommonKADS [18] or MIKE [1] consider PSMs as essential structures for controlling the methodological activities that must be carried out to build expertise models. Here, we define PSMs as services described using semantic web technologies.

Let us first consider the *Assessment* PSM as described in CommonKADS. This method aims at finding a *decision category* for a *case* based on a set of domain-specific *norms*. For instance, determining the relevance of a talk can be seen as applying an assessment method, where the case corresponds to information about the talk to be qualified; the norms are the set of rules for qualifying a talk according to the user's profile and the importance of the speaker; and the decision category corresponds to the qualification of the talk. The usual solution involves steps such as abstracting information from the input case data; finding the norms that can be used for the case, this information is normally domain-specific; and evaluating the norm with respect to the case data.

We can represent PSMs as services using the mark-up language OWL-S. This has advantages associated to web services such as facilitating automatic composition and interoperability through their semantic description. Our goal here is interoperability and reuse though semantic description, aiming at providing a library of PSMs that can be used in the implementation of knowledge-intensive tasks for the web. We use OWL-S Processes to describe the functionalities of the method.

We give the process description for the assessment method as a subclass of OWL-S Process. It receives two parameters: a *Case*, which corresponds to a list of things - domain-specific objects that constitute the case to be assessed; and *Norms*, which corresponds to a list of things denoting the norms (evaluation guide) to assess the case. The output is *Decision*, a thing indicating a decision category. We define classes for each parameter data type.

```
<owl:Class rdf:ID="Case" />
<owl:Class rdf:ID="Norms"/>
<owl:Class rdf:ID="Decision"/>
```

To make it easier to express, we also give classes to define the input and output parameters (i.e. the parameters as opposed to the parameter values). We give only *CaseInput* for brevity

```
<owl:Class rdf:ID="CaseInput>
    <rdfs:subClassOf rdf:resource="&process;Input">
    <rdfs:subClassOf>
        <owl:Restriction>
            <owl:onProperty rdf:resource="&process;parameterType"/>
            <owl:hasClass rdf:resource="#Case" />
        </owl:Restriction>
    </rdfs:subClassOf>
</owl:Class>
```

Finally we define the new PSM Assessment. It is a subclass of the generic atomic process class.

```
<owl:Class rdf:ID="Assessment" >
    <rdfs:subClassOf rdf:resource="&process;AtomicProcess">
```

```
<!-- at least one input is a Case -->
  <rdfs:subClassOf>
      <owl:Restriction>
          <owl:onProperty rdf:resource="&process;:hasInput" />
          <owl:someValuesFrom rdf:resource="#CaseInput" />
      </owl:Restriction>
  </rdfs:subClassOf>

  <!-- at least one input is Norms -->
  <rdfs:subClassOf>
      <owl:Restriction>
          <owl:onProperty rdf:resource="&process;hasInput" />
          <owl:someValuesFrom rdf:resource="#NormsInput" />
      </owl:Restriction>
  </rdfs:subClassOf>

  <!-- Only one output available -->
  <rdfs:subClassOf>
      <owl:Restriction>
          <owl:onProperty rdf:resource="&process;hasOutput" />
          <owl:cardinality rdf:datatype=
"&xsd;:nonNegativeInteger">1</owl:cardinality>
      </owl:Restriction>
  </rdfs:subClassOf>
  <!-- that output is a Decision -->
  <rdfs:subClassOf>
      <owl:Restriction>
          <owl:onProperty rdf:resource="&process;hasOutput" />
          <owl:hasClass rdf:resource="#DecisionOutput"/>
      </owl:Restriction>
  </rdfs:subClassOf>
</owl:Class>
```

4.3   Linking Tasks and Problem Solving Methods

This part describes the invocation of the service specified in the previous subsection for the case of task *Determine Talk Relevance*. The input *Case* corresponds to a list including two elements: the grade that the user has giving to the topic of the talk (domain-specific information that is part of the user profile, corresponding a value between 0 –less relevant- and 1 –very relevant-) and the ranking of the speaker according to services such as CiteSeer (we supposed here that in a previous subtask, the number of times that the speaker is cited was requested, corresponding to an integer in the range of 0 to 1000, we assume relevance 0 in case is not in the first 1000 authors).

The input *Norms* corresponds to the rule for determining the relevance of the talk: it is a method indicating that the relevance is obtained by giving 70% of value to the user interest and 30% value to the speaker reputation. The output category decision in this case is a real between 0 and 1 indicating the relevance of the talk.

To define the specific instance of the process for the task Determine Talk Relevance, we provide an instance of the Assessment class, with appropriate new datatypes. This is defined as follows. First we provide new classes for the specific types of the input and outputs.

```
<owl:Class rdf:ID="ITTalksCase" >
  <rdfs:subClassOf rdf:resource="Case" />
</owl:Class>
```

Then add properties for the two values given in the *Case*.

```
<owl:DatatypeProperty rdf:ID="TopicGrade" >
  <rdfs:domain rdf:resource="#ITTalksCase" />
  <rdfs:range rdf:resource="&xsd;#nonNegativeInteger" />
</owl:DatatypeProperty>
<owl:DatatypeProperty rdf:ID="SpeakerRanking" >
  <rdfs:domain rdf:resource="#ITTalksCaseData" />
  <rdfs:range rdf:resource="&xsd;#nonNegativeInteger" />
</owl:DatatypeProperty>
```

Similar definitions are provided for *Norms* and *Decision*. Now for the specific service we give the following instance of the *Assessment* class which we have defined. We bind the input and output parameters to the specific ITtalks types.

```
<Assessment rdf:ID="ITTalksAssessment" >
  <process:hasInput>
    <process:Input ref:ID="UserCase">
      <process:parameterType rdf:resource="#ITTalksCaseData"/>
    </process:Input>
  </process:hasInput>
  <process:hasInput>
    <process:Input ref:ID="ITTalksNorms">
      <process:parameterType rdf:resource="#ITTalksNormsDefn"/>
    </process:Input>
  </process:hasInput>
  <process:hasOutput>
    <process:Output ref:ID="DecisionValue">
      <process:parameterType rdf:resource="#ITTalksDecisionType"/>
    </process:Output>
  </process:hasOutput>
</Assessment>
```

5 Related Work

Our work has been inspired by works in the agent and ontology communities. There has been a fresh interest in studying the application of agent-oriented methodologies for Semantic Web applications. In [4], it is presented an agent-oriented approach to build Semantic Web applications. A web service is seen as an agent itself or as part of an agent – an extension that the agent can incorporate into itself once it finds and chooses to adopt a service. Behaviour-Oriented Design (BOD) methodology is employed, extended with DAML-S to mark up services. The Nuin agent platform [12] is designed for Semantic Web applications around the belief-desire-intension (BDI) principles. Nuin agents are deliberative reasoners in the tradition of first-order logic-based inference, implemented on top of the Jena toolkit [15]. The Agentcities initiative has been also studying the interaction between agents and Semantic Web applications through web services. In [10], it is explored the access of services by agents, when services are represented using the DAML-S model. They are interested in the automatic discovery of services and their composition rather than methodological aspects related to the development of agent-oriented applications.

Our work has been also influenced by research on ontologies. In [8], Crubezy and Musen analyses the relation between problem-solving methods and ontologies. They propose a methodology in which domain knowledge bases and problem-solving methods are described as ontologies that can be reused in different applications. Their approach has been further applied to the Internet Reasoning Service [9], a web-based front-end which provides online problem-solving resources. They have influenced our work, although our interest has been in analysing the use of problem solving methods within the context of agent-oriented methodologies for the case of semantic web applications. Close-related is the topic of knowledge-based service composition [5], in which domain-specific knowledge is exploited to compose Web/Grid services into a workflow specification. They also exploit mark up languages as DAML-S for providing semantic characterisation of available services for discovery and appropriate utilisation.

6 Conclusions

This paper presents our experience in using MAS-CommonKADS for modelling semantic web applications. The methodology's emphasis on the identification and modelling of knowledge has made it suitable for designing agents for the Semantic Web. This is an important characteristic that does not feature in other methodologies such as Gaia [20] or INGENIAS [14].

Another central feature of our work is the representation of problem-solving methods using the OWL-S language. By contrast to traditional web-service discovery, we show how tasks (services) can be determined when modelling a system based on the involved knowledge, so that the development of the service profile can be derived from the development process.

This work is part of an ongoing project aimed at generating a library of problem-solving methods using semantic web technologies. Many issues still remain and will necessitate further research. In particular, we plan to combine OWL-S with other languages such as RuleML in order to gain more expressive power in the description of some method components.

Acknowledgments. This work was carried out as part of the Semantic Web Advanced Development for Europe project --- SWAD-Europe and supported by the IST Programme of the European Commission.

References

1.   J. Angele, D. Fensel, D. Landes, and R. Studer. Developing Knowledge-Based Systems with MIKE. Journal of Automated Software Engineering, 5(4):389–419, 1998.
2.   B. Burmeister. Models and Methodologies for Agent-Oriented Analysis and Design. In Working Notes of the KI'96 Workshop on Agent-Oriented Programming and Distributed Systems, 1996.
3.   D. Brickley. Friend of a Friend RDF Vocabulary. http://xmlns.com/foaf/0.1/, 2001.
4.   J. J. Bryson, D. L. Martin, S. A. McIltraith, and L. A. Stein. Toward Behavioural Intelligence in the Semantic Web. IEEE Computer, pages 48–54, November 2002.
5.   L. Chen, N. R. Shadbolt, C. Goble, F. Tao, S. J. Cox, C. Puleston, and P. R. Smart. Towards a Knowledge-Based Approach to Semantic Service Composition. 2nd International Semantic Web Conference. Lecture Notes in Computer Science, vol. 2870, 2003.
6.   O. Corcho, M. Fernández-López, and A. Gómez-Pérez. Methodologies, Tools and Languages for Building Ontologies. Where is Their Meeting Point? Data & Knowledge Engineering, 46(1):41–64, 2003.
7.   R. Scott Cost, T. Finin, A. Joshi, Y. Peng, C. Nicholas, I. Soboroff, H. Chen, L. Kagal, F. Perich, Y. Zou, and S. Tolia. ITtalks: A Case Study in the Semantic Web and DAML+OIL. IEEE Intelligent Systems, pages 40–47, January/February 2002.
8.   M. Crubezy and M. A.Musen. Ontologies in Support of Problem Solving. Handbook on Ontologies, pages 321–341, 2003.
9.   M. Crubezy, E. Motta, W. Lu, and M. A. Musen. Configuring Online Problem-Solving Resources with the Internet Reasoning Service. IEEE Intelligent Systems, 18:34–42, 2003.
10. J. Dale, and L. Ceccaroni. Pizza and a Movie: A Case Study in Advanced Web Services. In: Agentcities: Challenges in Open Agent Environments Workshop, Autonomous Agents and Multi-Agent Systems Conference 2002, Bologna, Italy, 2002.
11. Y. Demazeau. From Cognitive Interactions to Collective Behaviour in AgentBased Systems. In European Conference on Cognitive Science, 1995.
12. I. Dickinson and M. Wooldrige. Towards Practical Reasoning Agents for the Semantic Web. In Second International Conference on Autonomous Agents and Multiagent Systems, Lecture Notes in Artificial Intelligence, 2003.
13. J. Euzenat. Research Challenges and Perspectives of the Semantic Web. Report of the EU-NSF Strategic Workshop, Sophia-Antipolis, France. 2002.
14. J. J. Gómez-Sanz and R. Fuentes. Agent Oriented Software Engineering with INGENIAS. In IBERAGENTS 2002, 4th Iberoamerican Workshop on Multi-Agent Systems, 2002.
15. HP Labs. The Jena Semantic Web Toolkit. http://www.hpl.hp.com/semweb/jena-top.html. 2002.
16. C. A. Iglesias, M. Garijo, J. Centeno-Gonzalez, and J. R. Velasco. Analysis and Design of Multiagent Systems using MAS-CommonKADS. In Agent Theories, Architectures, and Languages, Lecture Notes in Artificial Intelligence, pages 313–327, 1997.

17. L. Miller and D. Connolly. RDFiCal: iCalendar in RDF.
    http://sw1.iltr.org/discovery/2003/11/rdfical/final.html, 2004.
18. G. Schreiber, H. Akkermans, A. Anjewierden, R. de Hoog, N. Shadbolt, W. Vand de
    Velde, and B. Wielinga. Knowledge Engineering and Management: The CommonKADS
    Methodology. The MIT Press, 2000.
19. A. Tveit. A Survey of Agent-Oriented Software Engineering. In NTNU Computer Science
    Graduate Student Conference, Norwegian University of Science and Technology, 2001.
20. F. Zambonelli, N. Jennings and M. Wooldridge. Developing Multiagent Systems: the Gaia
    Methodology. ACM Transactions on Software Engineering and Methodology, Vol. 12,
    No. 3, 2003.

Automatic Creation and Monitoring of Semantic Metadata in a Dynamic Knowledge Portal

Diana Maynard, Milena Yankova, Niraj Aswani, and Hamish Cunningham

Dept of Computer Science, University of Sheffield, Sheffield, UK
{diana,milena,niraj,hamish}@dcs.shef.ac.uk

Abstract. The h-TechSight Knowledge Management Portal enables support for knowledge intensive industries in monitoring information resources on the Web, as an important factor in business competitiveness. Users can be automatically notified when a change occurs in their domain of interest. As part of this knowledge management platform, we have developed an ontology-based information extraction system to identify instances of concepts relevant to the user's interests and to monitor them over time. The application has initially been implemented in the Employment domain, and is currently being extended to other areas in the Chemical Engineering field. The information extraction system has been evaluated over a test set of 38 documents and achieves 97% Precision and 92% Recall.

Keywords: semantic metadata, ontologies, dynamic knowledge management

1 Introduction

The h-TechSight project integrates a variety of next generation knowledge management (NGKM) technologies in order to observe information resources automatically on the internet and notify users about changes occurring in their domain of interest. In this paper we describe one part of the knowledge management portal, which aims at creating semantic metadata automatically from web-mined documents, and monitoring concepts and instances extracted over time. By tracking their usage and dynamics automatically, a user can be informed about new developments and other topics of interest in their field. We have developed a sample application in the employment domain, and are currently integrating other domains into the system.

1.1 Motivation

Employment is a general domain into which a great deal of effort in terms of knowledge management has been placed, because it is a generic domain that every company, organization and business unit has to come across. Many Human Resources departments have an eye open for knowledge management to monitor their environment in the best way. Many Recruitment Consultant companies

C. Bussler and D. Fensel (Eds.): AIMSA 2004, LNAI 3192, pp. 65–74, 2004.

have watchdogs to monitor and alert them to changes. A number of job search engines (portals) have been launched using knowledge management extensively to link employees and employers[1] [2].

The employment domain contains many generic kinds of concepts. First this means that an existing Information Extraction system can more easily be adapted to this domain (because it does not require too many modifications), and second, it does not require a domain expert to understand the terms and concepts involved, so the system can easily be created by a developer without special domain skills. These two considerations are very important in the fast development of a system.

1.2   Knowledge Management Platform

The Knowledge Management Platform is a dynamic knowledge portal consisting of several different applications, which can be used in series or independently. These can be divided into two parts: tools for generic search (MASH) and tools for targeted search (ToolBox, WebQL and GATE). We shall concentrate here on the GATE tool.

GATE is used to enable the ontology-based semantic annotation of web mined documents. It is run as a web service which takes as input a URL and an ontology, and produces a set of annotations. The web service performs information extraction on the documents, and outputs an HTML page with instances of concepts highlighted. These results are stored in GATE's database and can be reused from another sub-module of GATE for statistical analysis.

2   Semantic Metadata Creation

There are several existing tools for semantic metadata creation, both semi-automatic and fully automatic.

Semi-automatic methods are generally more reliable, but require human intervention at some stage in the process. Usually this involves the user annotating data manually in order to provide training material for the system, which then takes over the annotation process. Examples of this kind of approach are MnM [10], S-CREAM[5] and AeroDAML[6]. These systems can usually be adapted to new domains and ontologies, but will need retraining by the user. This means that they are generally best suited to annotating large volumes of data within a single domain, and in situations where the user has an interest in investing some initial time and effort in the application. They are less suitable for the casual user who wants a ready-made tool to provide instant annotations for his data.

Automatic methods of annotation tend to be less reliable, but they can be suitable for large volumes of text where very high performance is not as paramount as having some kind of result. Because they require no human intervention, they are much more suitable for the casual user who wants a fast result,

---

[1] http://www.job-search.com/
[2] http://www.aspanet.org/solutionstemp/jobport.html

but does not want to invest time and effort in ensuring a very high quality output. Automatic methods tend to be more dynamic in that they can be adapted to new ontologies with no intervention. Ontology modification may also be a part of the process, thereby ensuring that a lifecycle is created by enabling feedback from the modified ontology to reflect in the application. Examples of automated tools are SemTag[4] and KIM[11]. Both of these systems find instances in the text using a large ontology, and perform disambiguation where instances are present in more than one place in the ontology. While SemTag aims more for accuracy of classification, KIM aims more for high recall.

3   Ontology-Based Information Extraction

3.1   GATE

GATE is an architecture for language-engineering developed at the University of Sheffield [2], which contains a suite of tools for language processing, and in particular, a vanilla Information Extraction (IE) system. In traditional IE applications, GATE is run over a corpus of texts to produce a set of annotated texts in XML format. In this case, however, the input to GATE takes the form of a set of URLs of target webpages, and an ontology of the domain. Its output comprises annotated instances of the concepts from the ontology. The ontology sets the domain structure and priorities with respect to relevant concepts with which the application is concerned.

GATE's IE system is rule-based, which means that unlike machine-learning based approaches, it requires no training data (see e.g. [9]). On the other hand, it requires a developer to manually create rules, so it is not totally dynamic. The architecture consists of a pipeline of processing resources which run in series. Many of these processing resources are language and domain-independent, so that they do not need to be adapted to new applications [8]. Pre-processing stages include word tokenisation, sentence splitting, and part-of-speech tagging, while the main processing is carried out by a gazetteer and a set of grammar rules. These generally need to be modified for each domain and application, though the extent to which they need to be modified depends on the complexity and generality of the domain. The gazetteer contains a set of lists which help identify instances in the text. Traditionally, this is a flat structure, but in an ontology-based information extraction (OBIE) application, these lists can be linked directly to an ontology, such that instances found in the text can then be related back to the ontology.

3.2   Employment Ontology

For the employment domain in h-TechSight, a domain-specific OBIE application has been created, which searches for instances of concepts present in a sample Employment ontology. The ontology can be submitted as DAML+OIL or RDF, both of which are handled in GATE. The employment ontology has 9 Concepts:

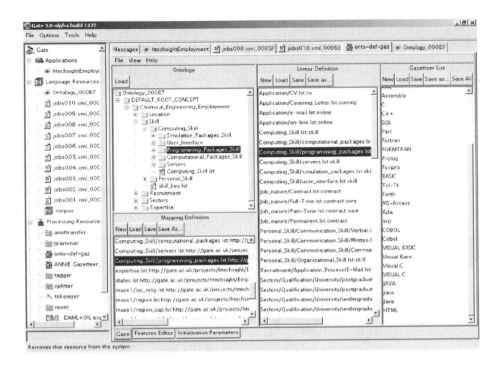

Fig. 1. Section of Employment Ontology in GATE

Location, Organisation, Sectors, JobTitle, Salary, Expertise, Person and Skill. Each concept in the ontology has a set of gazetteer lists associated with it. Some of these (default lists) are reused from previous applications, while others (domain-specific lists) need to be created from scratch. The default lists are quite large and contain common entities such as first names of persons, locations, abbreviations etc. Collection of these lists is done through corpus analysis (examining the texts manually and/or performing statistical analysis to spot important instances and concepts), unless a set of texts has been manually annotated by a user (in which case, the list collection process can be automatic [7]). Grammar rules for recognition of new types of entities mainly use these lists. However, there are also other lists collected for recognition purposes that contain keywords and are used to assist contextually-based rules. Some of the keyword lists are also attached to the ontology, because they clearly show the class to which the identified entity belongs. All lists that correspond to the ontology are ordered in a hierarchy similar to the class hierarchy in the ontology. A sample screenshot of a section of the ontology, the mappings from the lists to the ontology, and the contents of a list is shown in Figure 1.

The concepts (and corresponding instances) in which we are interested can be separated into 3 major groups. The first group consists of classic named entities which are general kinds of concepts such as Person, Location , Organisation. The second group is more specific to the chosen domain of employment, and consists of the following types:

- JobId - shows the ID of posted job advertisements;
- Reference - shows the reference code of the job position;
- Status - shows the employment/position type;
- Application - shows the documents necessary and the method of job application (e.g. by email, letter, whether a CV should be sent, etc.);
- Salary - shows the information available in the text about salary rates, bonus packages, compensations, benefits etc.;
- Qualification - shows the qualifications required for the advertised position, mainly a University degree;
- Citizenship - shows restrictions about the applicant's citizenship and work allowance;
- Expertise - shows the required expertise / skills for the job;

For both groups, the grammar rules check if instances found in the text belong to a class in the ontology and if so, they link the recognised instance to that same class and add the following features:

```
EntityType.ontology = ontology url,
EntityType.class = class name
```

The third group presents instances already annotated with HTML or XML tags (if such exist), and consists of the following:

- Company - contains the name of the organisation advertising the job;
- Date_Posted - shows the date when the job advertisement was posted;
- Title - shows the job title;
- Sector - shows the sector of the job that is advertised;

If these are not already annotated in the texts, they are identified using further rules.

3.3   Grammar Rules

The grammar rules for creating annotations are written in a language called JAPE (Java Annotations Pattern Language) [3].The rules are implemented in a set of finite-state transducers, each transducer usually containing rules of a different type, and are based on pattern-matching. In traditional IE applications, the rules find a pattern on the LHS, in the form of annotations, and on the RHS an action such as creating a new annotation for the pattern. In OBIE applications such as this, the rules also add information about the class and ontology on the RHS of the rule. So for example the string "PhD" found in the text might be annotated with the features:

```
{class = Postgraduate}
{ontology = http://gate.ac.uk/projects/htechsight/Employment}
```

This information is taken from the gazetteer, which is mapped to an ontology, as described earlier. The rules do not just match instances from the ontology with their occurrences in the text, but also find new instances in the text which do not exist in the ontology, through use of contextual patterns, part-of-speech tags, and other indicators.

In total the application contains 33 grammars, which run sequentially over the text. Each grammar contains anything from 1 to about 20 rules, depending on the complexity of the annotation type.

4   Export and Presentation of Results

The GATE application for the employment domain has been implemented in the h-TechSight portal as a web service. Here a user may input a URL and choose the concepts for the ontology. A new web page is created from the selected URL, with highlighted annotations. The result can be saved as an XML file.

Not only is the presentation of instances useful in itself, but furthermore, the occurrence of such instances over time is even more interesting. As well as the visual presentation, the results are also stored dynamically in a database and their statistical analysis is presented inside the hTechSight knowledge management portal. Results currently span January to June 2004. They have been collected by dynamically populating a Microsoft Access database with the following structure:

- Concepts: the concept which the record set of the database is about;
- Annotations: the instance of the record set annotated inside a document;
- Document _ID: a unique ID for the document;
- Time_Stamp: a time stamp found inside the document.

5   Monitoring Instance-Based Dynamics

One of the most primitive dimensions of ontologies is the display of data as concrete representations of abstract concepts, i.e. as instances. Gate leads the data driven analysis in hTechSight, as it is responsible for extracting from the text instances represented in the ontology. These results are stored in a database and statistical analysis is invoked to present instance-based dynamics.

In the h-TechSight platform, we try to monitor the dynamics of ontologies using two approaches: dynamics of concepts and dynamics of instances. Users may not only annotate their own websites according to their ontology, but may also see the results of a dynamic analysis of the respective domain. They may see tabular results of statistical data about how many annotations each concept had in the previous months, as well as seeing the progress of each instance in previous time intervals (months). Following this analysis, end users may also see the dynamics of instances with an elasticity metric that indicates the trend of each individual instance. Developments in the GATE results analysis have eliminated human intervention, as the results are created automatically in a dynamic way.

The two approaches to the monitoring of dynamics are described in more detail in the following sections.

5.1 Dynamics of Concepts

Dynamic metrics of concepts are calculated by counting the total occurrences of annotated instances over time intervals (per month). A visual representation of this analysis follows is shown in Table 1.

Table 1. Visualising Concept Dynamics

Concept	Count of instances for Jan	Count of instances for Feb
Application	4	46
Citizenship	0	9
Email	0	15
Expertise	0	1798
JobTitle	20	513
Location	0	13
Money	0	42
Organisation	0	420
Period	20	553
Qualification	4	51
Salary	12	200
Skills	74	1044

This analysis is dynamic in that counts of months are calculated automatically and new columns are added without human intervention. This automatic process is extremely useful, as a record of the performance of concepts is stored in a log file and may lead experts to useful conclusions and quick, wiser decisions. Occurrences per month may also help experts to monitor dynamics of specific concepts, groups of concepts or even the whole ontology. This analysis may help the decision making of stakeholders, by directing their resources according to the trends of the market of their domain.

5.2 Dynamics of Instances

By clicking on the concepts, a user may see the instances related to a concept. Instances are presented in a time series where the total occurrences per month and a calculation of an elasticity metric of instances are presented in tabular form. The elasticity metric (Dynamic Factor) counts the differences between the total occurrences of every instance over time intervals (per month) taking into consideration the volume of data of each time period (documents annotated per month). Table 2 shows the dynamic factor (DF) and frequency of instances for the concept Organisation from January to March 2004. The higher the DF, the greater the upward trend. Looking at only 3 months of data does not give sufficient results for any conclusions to be drawn, but inferences can clearly be made from results over a longer period of time. Looking at the instances for the concept "Organisation" can monitor which companies are looking for new employees and track the recruitment trends for different companies. Monitoring instances for concepts such as Skills and Expertise can show which kinds of skills are becoming more or less in demand.

Table 2. Visualising the Dynamics of Instances

Instance	DF	Jan	Feb	Mar
ARC	145	-1	12	6
Archimedia SA	-1	0	1	0
Army	23	0	2	1
AT&T	-1	0	2	0
BA	23	0	3	1
BMI British Midland	-335	1	3	0

6   Evaluation

We conducted an initial evaluation of the IE application on a small set of 38 documents containing job advertisements in the Chemical Engineering domain, mined from the website `http://www.jobserve.com`. The web portal is mined dynamically using a web content agent written in a commercial web crawling software [1]. We manually annotated these documents with the concepts used in the application, and used the evaluation tools provided in GATE to compare the system results with the gold standard. Overall, the system achieved 97% Precision and 92% Recall. Table 3 shows the results obtained in more detail. The first column shows the annotation type. The next 4 columns show the numbers of correct, partially correct, missing and spurious annotations found. The last 3 columns show the figures for Precision, Recall and F-measure.

Some of the concepts show figure s of 100% Precision and Recall because they were taken directly from the original markup of the document (i.e. this information was already encoded in the HTML). The lowest performance was for concepts such as Skills and Expertise. This is unsurprising because this kind of information can be encoded in many different ways, and is hard to identify (not only for a rule-based system, but also for a learning-based one). We relied on contextual information and use of keywords to identify such concepts, but

Table 3. Results of Annotating Sample Employment Corpus

Concept	Cor	Par	Miss	Spur	P	R	F
Person	7	1	1	0	93.75	83.34	88.24
Location	289	15	4	3	96.58	96.27	96.42
Organization	126	13	22	10	88.93	82.30	85.48
JobId	38	0	0	0	100	100	100
Reference	31	1	0	0	98.44	98.44	98.44
Status	42	1	0	0	98.84	98.84	98.84
Application	32	3	6	0	95.71	81.71	88.16
Salary	48	10	6	3	86.89	82.81	84.80
Qualification	57	15	9	5	83.77	79.63	81.65
Citizenship	19	2	0	0	95.24	95.24	95.24
Expertise	172	29	33	11	87.97	79.70	83.63
Skills	88	19	37	4	87.84	67.71	76.47
Willingness	4	0	0	0	100	100	100
Company	38	0	0	0	100	100	100
Date_Posted	38	0	0	0	100	100	100
Sector	38	0	0	0	100	100	100
Title	38	0	0	0	100	100	100

the rules could be improved further. Overall, the results are very encouraging, however.

7   Conclusions

In this paper we have presented an application for automatic creation of semantic metadata from webpages in the Chemical Engineering domain. This is incorporated into a dynamic Knowledge Management Platform which also enables the monitoring of instances found and modification of the ontologies used. The application has been tested in the Employment sector with ecxcellent results, and is currently being ported to other genres of text such as news items and company reports. This involves adaptation of some of the rules, and integration of a new ontology more specific to the domain.

There are some problems still to resolved. For example, the system currently only adds class information to the instances found when the instances are already present in the ontology. It is still an open question how to decide whcre to link new instances, or where to link instances found in more than one place in the ontology. Currently we are investigating the use of coreference information and machine learning techniques to solve these problems.

References

1. Caesius. WebQL User's Guide: Introduction to WebQL. http://www.webql.com

2. H. Cunningham, D. Maynard, K. Bontcheva, and V. Tablan. GATE: A Framework and Graphical Development Environment for Robust NLP Tools and Applications. In *Proceedings of the 40th Anniversary Meeting of the Association for Computational Linguistics (ACL'02)*, 2002.

3. H. Cunningham, D. Maynard, and V. Tablan. JAPE: a Java Annotation Patterns Engine (Second Edition). Research Memorandum CS-00-10, Department of Computer Science, University of Sheffield, November 2000.

4. S. Dill, N. Eiron, D. Gibson, D. Gruhl, R. Guha, A. Jhingran, T. Kanungo, S. Rajagopalan, A. Tomkins, J. A. Tomlin, and J. Y. Zien. SemTag and Seeker: Bootstrapping the semantic web via automated semantic annotation. In *Proceedings of WWW'03*, 2003.

5. S. Handschuh, S. Staab, and F. Ciravegna. S-CREAM – Semi-automatic CREAtion of Metadata. In *13th International Conference on Knowledge Engineering and Knowledge Management (EKAW02)*, pages 358–372, Siguenza, Spain, 2002.

6. P. Kogut and W. Holmes. AeroDAML: Applying Information Extraction to Generate DAML Annotations from Web Pages. In *First International Conference on Knowledge Capture (K-CAP 2001), Workshop on Knowledge Markup and Semantic Annotation*, Victoria, B.C., 2001.

7. D. Maynard, K. Bontcheva, and H. Cunningham. Automatic Language-Independent Induction of Gazetteer Lists. In *Fourth International Conference on Language Resources and Evaluation (LREC 2004)*, Lisbon, Portugal, 2004.

8. D. Maynard and H. Cunningham. Multilingual Adaptations of a Reusable Information Extraction Tool. In *Proceedings of the Demo Sessions of EACL'03*, Budapest, Hungary, 2003.

9. D. Maynard, V. Tablan, and H. Cunningham. NE recognition without training data on a language you don't speak. In *ACL Workshop on Multilingual and Mixed-language Named Entity Recognition: Combining Statistical and Symbolic Models*, Sapporo, Japan, 2003.

10. E. Motta, M. Vargas-Vera, J. Domingue, M. Lanzoni, A. Stutt, and F. Ciravegna. MnM: Ontology Driven Semi-Automatic and Automatic Support for Semantic Markup. In *13th International Conference on Knowledge Engineering and Knowledge Management (EKAW02)*, pages 379–391, Siguenza, Spain, 2002.

11. B. Popov, A. Kiryakov, A. Kirilov, D. Manov, D. Ognyano., and M. Goranov. KIM – Semantic Annotation Platform. *Natural Language Engineering*, 2004. To appear.

Coordinating Semantic Peers

P. Bouquet[1], L. Serafini[2], and S. Zanobini[1]

[1] Department of Information and Communication Technology – University of Trento
Via Sommarive, 10 – 38050 Trento (Italy)
[2] ITC – IRST
Via Sommarive, 15 – 38050 Trento (Italy)
{bouquet,zanobini}@dit.unitn.it, serafini@itc.it

Abstract. The problem of finding an agreement on the meaning of heterogeneous schemas is one of the key issues in the development of the Semantic Web. In this paper, we propose a new algorithm for discovering semantic mappings across hierarchical classifications based on a new approach to semantic coordination. This approach shifts the problem of semantic coordination from the problem of computing linguistic or structural similarities (what most other proposed approaches do) to the problem of deducing relations between sets of logical formulas that represent the meaning of nodes belonging to different schemas. We show how to apply the approach and the algorithm to an interesting family of schemas, namely hierarchical classifications. Finally, we argue why this is a significant improvement on previous approaches.

Keywords: Semantic Web, Semantic Interoperability, Information retrieval, Automated Reasoning

1 Introduction and Approach

One of the key challenges in the development of open distributed systems is enabling the exchange of meaningful information across applications which (i) may use autonomously developed schemas for organizing locally available data, and (ii) need to discover mappings between schema elements to achieve their users' goals. Typical examples are databases using different schemas, and document repositories using different classification structures. In restricted environments, like a small corporate Intranet, this problem is typically addressed by introducing shared models (e.g., ontologies) throughout the entire organization. However, in open environments (like the Web), this approach can't work for several reasons, including the difficulty of 'negotiating' a shared model of data that suits the needs of all parties involved, and the practical impossibility of maintaining such a shared model in a highly dynamic environment. In this kind of scenarios, a more dynamic and flexible method is needed, where no shared model can be assumed to exist, and mappings between elements belonging to different schemas must be discovered on-the-fly.

The method we propose assumes that we deal with a network of *semantic peers*, namely physically connected entities which can autonomously decide how to organize locally available data (in a sense, are semantically autonomous agents). Each peer organizes its data using one or more abstract schemas (e.g., database schemas, directories in

C. Bussler and D. Fensel (Eds.): AIMSA 2004, LNAI 3192, pp. 75–84, 2004.

a file system, classification schemas, taxonomies, and so on). Different peers may use different schemas to organize the same data collection, and conversely the same schemas can be used to organize different data collections. We assume to deal with schemas with meaningful labels, where 'meaningful' means that their interpretation is not arbitrary, but is constrained by the conventions of some community of speakers/users[1]. We also assume that semantic peers need to compute mappings between its local schema and other peers' schemas in order to exchange data.

The first idea behind our approach is that *mappings must express semantic relations*, namely relations with a well-defined model-theoretic interpretation[2]. For example, we want to state that the two elements of the schema are equivalent, or that one is more/less general, or that they are mutually exclusive. As we will argue, this gives us many advantages, essentially related to the consequences we can infer from the discovery of such a relation.

Fig. 1. Mapping abstract structures

The second idea is that, to discover such semantic relations, one must *make explicit the meaning* implicit in each element of a schema. Our claim is that addressing the problem of discovering semantic relations across schemas, where meaningful labels are used, as a problem of matching abstract graphs is conceptually wrong.

To illustrate this point, consider the difference between the problem of mapping abstract schemas (like those in Figure 1) and the problem of mapping schemas with meaningful labels (like those in Figure 2). Nodes in abstract schemas do not have an implicit meaning, and therefore, whatever technique we use to map them, we will find that there is some relation between the two nodes D in the two schemas which depends only on the abstract form of the two schemas. The situation is completely different for schemas with meaningful labels. Intuitively, the semantic relations between the two nodes MOUNTAIN and the two nodes FLORENCE of structures in Figure 2 are different, despite the fact that the two pairs of schemas are structurally equivalent between them,

---

[1] In the following we show how this problem is extremely different from the problem of determining the similarity across different graphs.

[2] This is an important difference with respect to approaches based on matching techniques, where a mapping is a measure of (linguistic, structural, ...) similarity between schemas (e.g., a real number between 0 and 1). The main problem with such techniques is that the interpretation of their results is an open problem: should we interpret a 0.9 similarity as the fact that one concept is slightly more general or slightly less general than the other one, or that their meaning 90% overlaps? See [1] for a more detailed discussion.

and both are structurally isomorphic with the pair of abstract schemas in Figure 1[3]. This why we can make explicit a lot of information that we have about the terms which appear in the graph, and their relations (e.g., that Tuscany is part of Italy, that Florence is in Tuscany, and so on).

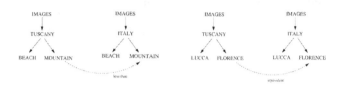

Fig. 2. Mapping schemas with meaningful labels

Using such an information, human reasoners (i) understand the meanings expressed by nodes: e.g., 'images of Tuscan mountains' (say P_1), 'images of Italian mountains' (say P_2), 'images of Florence in Tuscany' (say P_3) and 'images of Florence in Italy' (say P_4); and finally (ii) determine the semantic relations between nodes comparing the meanings, namely that $P_1 \subset P_2$ and $P_3 \equiv P_4$.

In [2], we claim that, for extracting such meanings and for comparing them, we need at least of three kinds of informations:

Lexical knowledge: knowledge about the words used in the labels. For example, the fact that the word 'Florence' can be used to indicate 'a city in Italy' or 'a city in the South Carolina', and, conversely, to handle the synonymy;

World knowledge: knowledge about the relation between the concepts expressed by words. For example, the fact that Tuscany is part of Italy, or that Florence is in Italy;

Structural knowledge: knowledge deriving from how labeled nodes are arranged in a given schema. For example, the fact that the node labeled MOUNTAIN is below a node IMAGES tells us that it classifies images of mountains, and not, say, books about mountains.

Summarizing, the process of discovering semantic relations across meaningful labeled schemas can take advantage of exploiting the complex degree of semantic coordination implicit in the way a community uses the language from which the labels are taken[4]. The method is based on a procedure for explicitating the meaning associated to

---

[3] Indeed, for the first pair of nodes, the set of documents we would classify under the node MOUNTAIN on the left hand side is a subset of the documents we would classify under the node MOUNTAIN on the right; whereas the set of documents which we would classify under the node FLORENCE in the left schema is exactly the same as the set of documents we would classify under the node FLORENCE on the right hand side.

[4] Notice that the status of this linguistic coordination at a given time is already 'codified' in artifacts (e.g., dictionaries, but today also ontologies and other formalized models), which provide senses for words and more complex expressions, relations between senses, and other important knowledge about them. Our aim is to exploit these artifacts as an essential source of constraints on possible/acceptable mappings across structures.

each node in a schema (notice that schemas such as the two classifications in Figure 2 are not semantic models themselves, as they do not have the purpose of defining the meaning of terms they contain; however, they presuppose a semantic model, and indeed that's the only reason why we humans can read them quite easily) and for comparing them. As we clearly show in the next section, this approach shifts the problem of semantic coordination from the problem of computing linguistic or structural similarities (what most other proposed approaches do) to the problem of deducing relations between sets of logical formulas representing the meaning of nodes belonging to different schemas.

2   The Algorithm: CTXMATCH

In this section we show how to apply the general approach described in the previous section to the problem of coordinating *Hierarchical Classifications* (hereafter HCs), namely concept hierarchies [3] used for grouping documents in categories[5].

In our approach, we assume the presence of a network of semantic peers, where each peer is defined as a triple $\langle \mathcal{D}, \mathcal{S}, \langle L, O \rangle \rangle$, where: $\mathcal{D}$ is a set of documents; $\mathcal{S}$ represents the set of schemas used by the peer for organizing its data; and $\langle L, O \rangle$ is defined as a pair composed by a lexicon L and a world knowledge representation O. The structure of the semantic peer reflects the three levels of knowledge we showed before: $\mathcal{S}$ represents structural knowledge, L contains lexical knowledge, and O is world knowledge. Formally, L is a repository of pairs $\langle w, C \rangle$, where w is a word and C is a set of concepts. Each pair $\langle w, C \rangle$ represents the set of concepts C denoted by a word w. For example, a possible entry for a lexicon should express that the word 'fish' can denote at least two concepts: 'an aquatic vertebrate' and 'the twelfth sign of zodiac'. An important example of this kind of repository is represented by WORDNET [4]. A world knowledge O expresses the set of relations holding between different concepts. For example, a world knowledge O should express that the concept 'an aquatic vertebrate' denoted by the word 'fish' stays in a *IsA* relation with the concept of 'animal' ('fish is an animal') and that the concept 'the twelfth sign of zodiac' denoted by the same word 'fish' stays in a *IsA* relations with a geometrical shape ('fish is a geometrical shape'). Formally, world knowledge is a logical theory written is a specific language, as for example Prolog clauses, RDF triples, DAML/OIL, OWL.

Our method is designed for the following scenario: a peer A (called the *seeker*) needs to find new documents relative to some category in one of its HCs, S. Imagine that peer A knew that peer B (the provider) owns interesting documents, and imagine that B classify its documents by means of a HC S'. This problem can be solved in a standard way coordinating the two HCs. Formally, we define the problem of coordinating S and S' as the problem of discovering a mapping $\mathcal{M} = \{\langle m, n, R \rangle \mid m \in S, n \in S'\}$, where R is a semantic relation between m and n. Five relations are allowed between nodes of different HCs: $m \supset n$ (m is more general than n); $m \subset n$ (m is less general than n);

---

[5] Some well-known examples of HCs are web directories (see e.g. the Google[TM] Directory or the Yahoo![TM] Directory), file systems and document databases in content/knowledge management systems.

$m \equiv n$ (m is equivalent to n); $m \cap n$ (m is compatible with n); $m \perp n$ (m is disjoint from n).

Algorithm 1.1 CTXMATCH($S,S'L,O$)

    ▷ *Hierarchical classifications S, S'*

    ▷ *Lexicon L*

    ▷ *World knowledge O*

VarDeclaration:

    contextualized concept $\langle \phi, \Theta \rangle$, $\langle \psi, \Upsilon \rangle$

    relation R

    mapping M

1   **for** each pair of nodes $m, n, m \in S$ and $n \in S'$ **do**

2      $\langle \phi, \Theta \rangle \leftarrow$ SEMANTIC–EXPLICITATION(m, S, L, O);

3      $\langle \psi, \Upsilon \rangle \leftarrow$ SEMANTIC–EXPLICITATION(n, S', L, O);

4      $R \leftarrow$ SEMANTIC–COMPARISON($\langle \phi, \Theta \rangle$, $\langle \psi, \Upsilon \rangle$, O);

5      $M \leftarrow M \cup \langle m, n, R \rangle$;

6   **return** M;

The algorithm CTXMATCH takes as **inputs** the HC S of the seeker and the HC S', the lexicon L and the world knowledge O of the provider[6]. As we will show in the following, the lexicon L and the world knowledge O play a major part in determining the mapping between schemas. But, from the definition of semantic peer follows that each peer has its own lexicon and world knowledge. A consequence of this consideration is that the mapping returned by the algorithm expresses the point of view (regarding the mapping) of the provider, and, consequently, is directional: the seeker, *mutata mutandis*, can find a different mapping.

The **output** of the algorithm will be a set M of triples $\langle m, n, R \rangle$, where R is the semantic relation holding between the nodes m and n.

The algorithm has essentially the following two main macro steps.

Steps 2–3: in this phase, called *Semantic explicitation*, the algorithm tries to interpret pair of nodes m, n in the respective HCs S and S' by means of the lexicon L and the world knowledge O. The idea is trying to generate a formula approximating the meaning expressed by a node in a structure (ϕ), and a set of axioms formalizing the suitable world knowledge (Θ). Consider, for example, the node FLORENCE in left lower HC of Figure 2: steps 2–3 will generate a formula approximating the statement 'Images of Florence in Tuscany' (ϕ) and an axiom approximating the statement 'Florence is in Tuscany' (Θ). The pair $\langle \phi, \Theta \rangle$, called *contextualized concept*, expresses, in our opinion, the meaning of a node in a structure.

Step 4: in this phase, called *Semantic comparison*, the problem of finding the semantic relation between two nodes m and n is encoded as the problem of finding the semantic relation holding between two contextualized concepts, $\langle \phi, \Theta \rangle$ and $\langle \psi, \Upsilon \rangle$.

Finally, step 5 generates the mapping simply by reiteration of the same process over all the possible pair of nodes $m \in S$ $n \in S'$ and step 6 returns the mapping.

---

[6] In the version of the algorithm presented here, we use WORDNET as a source of both lexical and world knowledge. However, WORDNET could be replaced by another combination of a linguistic resource and a world knowledge resource.

The two following sections describe in detail these two top-level operations, implemented by the functions SEMANTIC–EXPLICITATION and SEMANTIC–COMPARISON.

2.1   Semantic Explicitation

In this phase we make explicit in a logical formula[7] the meaning of a node into a structure, by means of a lexical and a world knowledge. In steps 1 and 2, the function EXTRACT–CANDIDATE–CONCEPTS uses lexical knowledge to associate to each word occurring in the nodes of an HC all the possible concepts denoted by the word itself. Consider the lower left structure of Figure 2. The label 'Florence' is associated with two concepts, provided by the lexicon (WORDNET), corresponding to 'a city in central Italy on the Arno' (florence#1) or a 'a town in northeast South Carolina' (florence#2). In order to maximize the possibility of finding an entry into the Lexicon, we use both a postagger and a lemmatizator over the labels.

In the step 3, the function EXTRACT–LOCAL–AXIOMS tries to define the ontological relations existing between the concepts in a structure. Consider again the left lower structure of Figure 2. Imagine that the concept 'a region in central Italy' (tuscany#1) has been associated to the node TUSCANY. The function EXTRACT–LOCAL–AXIOMS has the aim to discover if it exists some kind of relation between the concepts tuscany#1, florence#1 and florence#2 (associated to node FLORENCE). Exploiting world knowledge resource we can discover, for example, that 'florence#1 PartOf tuscany#1', i.e. that exists a 'part of' relation between the first sense of 'Florence' and the first sense of Tuscany.

Algorithm 1.2 SEMANTIC–EXPLICITATION(t, S, L, O)

    ▷ *t is a node in S*
    ▷ *structure S*
    ▷ *lexicon L*
    ▷ *world knowledge O*

VarDeclaration:
    single concept $con[][]$
    set of formulas Σ
    formula δ

```
1   for each node n in S do
2       con[n] ← EXTRACT–CANDIDATE–CONCEPTS(n, L);
3   Σ ← EXTRACT–LOCAL-AXIOMS(t, S, con[], O);
4   con[] ← FILTER–CONCEPTS(S, Σ, con[]);
5   δ ← BUILD–COMPLEX–CONCEPT(t, S, con[]);
6   return ⟨δ, Σ⟩;
```

---

[7] The choice of the logics depends on how expressive one wants to be in the approximation of the meaning of nodes, and on the complexity of the NLP techniques used to process labels. In our first implementation we adopted propositional logic, where each propositional letter corresponds to a concept (synset) provided by WORDNET.

World knowledge relations are translated into logical axioms, according to Table 1. So, the relation 'florence#1 PartOf tuscany#1' is encoded as 'florence#1 → tuscany#1'[8].

Table 1. WORDNET relations and their axioms.

WORDNET relation	axiom
s#k synonym t#h	s#k ≡ t#h
s#k { hyponym | PartOf }t#h	s#k → t#h
s#k { hypernym | HasPart }t#h	t#h → s#k
s#k contradiction t#h	¬(t#k ∧ s#h)

Step 4 has the goal of filtering out unlikely senses associated to each node. Going back to the previous example, we try to discard one of the senses associated to node FLORENCE. Intuitively, the sense 2 of 'Florence', as 'a town in northeast South Carolina' (florence#2), can be discarded, because the node FLORENCE refers clearly to the city in Tuscany. We reach this result by analyzing the extracted local axioms: the presence of an axiom such as 'florence#1 PartOf tuscany#1' is used to make the conjecture that the contextually relevant sense of Florence is the city in Tuscany, and not the city in USA. When ambiguity persists (axioms related to different senses or no axioms at all), all the possible senses are left and encoded as a disjunction.

Step 5 has the objective of building a complex concept (i.e., the meaning of a node label when it occurs in a specific position in a schema) for nodes in HCs. As described in [2], node labels are *singularly* processed by means of NLP techniques and translated into a logical formula[9]. The result of this first process is that each node has a preliminary interpretation, called *simple concept*, which doesn't consider the position of the node in the structure. For example, the simple concept associated to the node FLORENCE of the lower left hand structure of Figure 2 is trivially the atom florence#1 (i.e. one of the two senses provided by WORDNET and not discarded by the filtering). Then, these results are combined for generating a formula approximating the meaning expressed by a node *into a structure*. In this version of the algorithm, we choose to express the meaning of a node n as the conjunction of the simple concepts associated to the nodes lying in the path from root to n. So, the formula approximating the meaning expressed by the same node FLORENCE *into the HC* is (image#1 ∨ ... ∨ image#8) ∧ tuscany#1 ∧ florence#1.

Step 6 returns the formula expressing the meaning of the node and the set of local axioms founded by step 3.

---

[8] For heuristic reasons – see [2] – we consider only relations between concepts on the same path of a HC and their siblings.

[9] Although in this paper we present very simple examples, the NLP techniques exploited in this phase allow us to handle labels containing complex expressions, as conjunctions, commas, prepositions, expressions denoting exclusion, like 'except' or 'but not', multiwords and so on.

2.2 Semantic Comparison

This phase has the goal of finding the semantic relation holding between two contextualized concepts (associated to two nodes in different HCs).

Algorithm 1.3 SEM–COMP($\langle\phi,\Theta\rangle,\langle\psi,\Upsilon\rangle,O$)

    ▷ *contextualized concept* $\langle\phi,\Theta\rangle$, $\langle\psi,\Upsilon\rangle$
    ▷ *world knowledge O*

    VarDeclaration:
        set of formulas Γ
        semantic relation R

1    $\Gamma \leftarrow$ EXTRACT–RELATIONAL–AXIOMS(ϕ,ψ,O);
2   **if** $\Theta,\Upsilon,\Gamma \models \neg(\phi \wedge \psi)$ **then** $R \leftarrow \bot$;
3   **else if** $\Theta,\Upsilon,\Gamma \models (\phi \equiv \psi)$ **then** $R \leftarrow \equiv$;
4   **else if** $\Theta,\Upsilon,\Gamma \models (\phi \rightarrow \psi)$ **then** $R \leftarrow \subset$;
5   **else if** $\Theta,\Upsilon,\Gamma \models (\psi \rightarrow \phi)$ **then** $R \leftarrow \supset$;
6   **else** $R \leftarrow \cap$;
7   **return** R;

In Step 1, the function EXTRACT–RELATIONAL–AXIOMS tries to find axioms which connect concepts belonging to different HCs. The process is the same as that of function EXTRACT–LOCAL–AXIOMS, described above. Consider, for example, the senses `italy#1` and `tuscany#1` associated respectively to nodes ITALY and TUSCANY of Figure 2: the relational axioms express the fact that, for example, 'Tuscany PartOf Italy' (`tuscany#1 → italy#1`).

In steps 2–6, the problem of finding the semantic relation between two nodes n and m (line 2) is encoded into a satisfiability problem involving both the contextualized concepts associated to the nodes and the relational axioms extracted in the previous phases. So, to prove whether the two nodes labeled FLORENCE in Figure 2 are equivalent, we check the logical equivalence between the formulas approximating the meaning of the two nodes, given the local and the relational axioms. Formally, we have the following satisfiability problem:

Θ	`florence#1 → tuscany#1`
ϕ	`(image#1 ∨ ... ∨ image#8) ∧ tuscany#1 ∧ florence#1`
Δ	`florence#1 → italy#1`
ψ	`(image#1 ∨ ... ∨ image#8) ∧ italy#1 ∧ florence#1`
Γ	`tuscany#1 → italy#1`

It is simple to see that the returned relation is '$\equiv$'. Note that the satisfiability problem for finding the semantic relation between the nodes MOUNTAIN of Figure 2 is the following:

Θ	$\emptyset$
ϕ	`(image#1 ∨ ... ∨ image#8) ∧ tuscany#1 ∧ mountain#1`
Δ	$\emptyset$
ψ	`(image#1 ∨ ... ∨ image#8) ∧ italy#1 ∧ mountain#1`
Γ	`tuscany#1 → italy#1`

The returned relation is '$\subset$'.

3   Conclusions and Related Work

In this paper we presented a new approach to semantic coordination in open and distributed environments, and an algorithm that implements this method for hierarchical classifications. The algorithm, already used in a peer-to-peer application for distributed knowledge management (the application is described in [5]), has been tested on real HCs (i.e., pre-existing classifications used in real applications) and the results are described in [6].

CTXMATCH faces the problem of semantic coordination deducing semantic relations between sets of logical formulas. Under this respect, to the best of our knowledge, there are no other works to which we can compare ours. However, there are three other families of approaches that we want to compare to: graph matching, automatic schema matching and semi-automatic schema matching. For each of them, we will discuss the proposal that, in our opinion, is more significant. The comparison is based on the following dimensions: (i) if and how structural, lexical and world knowledges are used; (ii) the type of returned relation. The general results of our comparison are reported in Table 2.

Table 2. Comparing CTXMATCH with other methods

	graph matching	CUPID	MOMIS	CTXMATCH
Struct. knowl.	●	●	●	●
Lex. knowl.		●	●	●
Dom. knowl.				●
Relation returned	id of nodes	Value in $[0,1]$	Value in $[0,1]$	Semantic relation

In graph matching techniques, a concept hierarchy is viewed as a labeled tree, but the semantic information associated to labels is substantially ignored. Matching two graphs G and G' means finding an isomorphic sub-graph of G' w.r.t. G. Some examples of this approach are described in [7,8]. CUPID [9] is a completely automatic algorithm for schema matching. Lexical knowledge is exploited for discovering linguistic similarity between labels (e.g., using synonyms), while the schema structure is used as a matching constraint. That is, the more the structure of the subtree of a node s is similar to the structure of a subtree of a node t, the more s is similar to t. In case of equivalent concepts occurring in completely different structures, and completely independent concepts that belong to isomorphic structures, the match fails. MOMIS [10] is a set of semi–automatic tools for information integration of (semi-)structured data sources, whose main objective is to define a global schema that allows an uniform and transparent access to the data stored in a set of semantically heterogeneous sources. This integration is performed by exploiting knowledge in a Common Thesaurus together with a combination of clustering techniques and Description Logics. The approach is very similar to CUPID and presents the same drawbacks in matching hierarchical classifications.

References

1. Giunchiglia, F., Pavel, S.: Semantic matching. Proceedings of the workshop on Semantic Integration Sanibel Island (Florida, USA) (2003)
2. Bouquet, P., Serafini, L., Zanobini, S.: Semantic coordination: a new approach and an application. In Sycara, K., ed.: Second International Semantic Web Conference (ISWC-03). Lecture Notes in Computer Science (LNCS), Sanibel Island (Florida, USA) (2003)
3. Büchner, A., Ranta, M., Hughes, J., Mäntylä, M.: Semantic information mediation among multiple product ontologies. In: Proc. 4th World Conference on Integrated Design & Process Technology. (1999)
4. Fellbaum, C., ed.: WordNet: An Electronic Lexical Database. The MIT Press, Cambridge, US (1998)
5. Bonifacio, M., Bouquet, P., Mameli, G., Nori, M.: Kex: a peer-to-peer solution for distributed knowledge management. In Karagiannis, D., Reimer, U., eds.: 4th Intern. Conf. on Practical Aspects of Knowledge Management (PAKM-2002), Vienna (Austria) (2002)
6. Magnini, B.M., Serafini, L., Doná, A., Gatti, L., Girardi, C., , Speranza, M.: Large–scale evaluation of context matching. Technical Report 0301–07, ITC–IRST, Trento, Italy (2003)
7. Zhang, K., Wang, J.T.L., Shasha, D.: On the editing distance between undirected acyclic graphs and related problems. In Galil, Z., Ukkonen, E., eds.: Proc. of 6th Symposium on Combinatorial Pattern Matching. Volume 937., Finland, Springer-Verlag, Berlin (1995)
8. Pelillo, M., Siddiqi, K., Zucker, S.W.: Matching hierarchical structures using association graphs. Lecture Notes in Computer Science **1407** (1998)
9. Madhavan, J., Bernstein, P.A., Rahm, E.: Generic schema matching with cupid. In: The VLDB Journal. (2001) 49–58
10. Bergamaschi, S., Castano, S., Vincini, M.: Semantic integration of semistructured and structured data sources. SIGMOD Record **28** (1999) 54–59

Identification of Communities of Peers by Trust and Reputation

Alessandro Agostini[1] and Gianluca Moro[2]

[1] ITC-IRST Trento
Via Sommarive 18, 38050 Povo, Trento
agostini@irst.itc.it
[2] DEIS - University of Bologna
Via Venezia 52, I-47023 Cesena (FC)
gmoro@deis.unibo.it

Abstract. We present a new model and a partial solution to the problem of semantic routing in peer-to-peer networks. When a peer receives a query, an attempt to solve the query by using both *linguistic* and *contextual* knowledge is made. In our proposal, each peer analyzes the result of its queries and increases the trust of those peers who reply with more appropriate semantic contents. In this respect, our approach is adaptive. As queries are resolved, the routing strategy of each peer becomes more and more trust-based, namely, based on the semantics of contents rather than on a mere syntactic matching of keywords. This leads to the emergence of communities of peers semantically related, which in turn corresponds to a peer-to-peer network clustered by contents, capable to resolve queries with a reduced number of hops.

Keywords: Peer-to-peer systems, peer-to-peer communities, information retrieval, semantic routing, trust and reputation.

1   Introduction

Peer-to-peer systems and communities (see for instance [11,17,22,32,12]), are often established dynamically with peers that are unrelated and unknown to each other. This is also true in cooperative conversations [15] and, sometimes, in query-answering systems [10,20,14,30,6], where knowledge "seekers" connect to unknown "providers" by means of query propagation and information retrieval.

Deployed peer-to-peer (P2P) systems such as Gnutella, FreeNet and others [16] give rise to unstructured P2P networks, where contents spread over the network are localized by flooding messages. Several P2P proposals in literature [23,29] structure P2P networks by distributing resources according to a priori hash function common to all peers. These proposals adopt a routing mechanism based on the idea of representing data with a "distributed hash table" (DHT) [24]. Any searching procedure carried out by DHT routing mechanisms conceptually corresponds to looking up the keyword of the target record in the hash table, which is distributed across the peers; each peer connecting to the P2P network assumes responsibility to manage a certain range of keywords.

C. Bussler and D. Fensel (Eds.): AIMSA 2004, LNAI 3192, pp. 85–95, 2004.

Peers have identifiers taken from the same addressing space of the keywords—usually this being strings of digits of some fixed length. Each peer maintains a local routing table consisting of a small subset of nodes of the network. When a peer receives a query for a keyword in the local table, an attempt to solve the query locally is made. Otherwise, when the peer receives a query for a keyword for which it is not responsible, the peer routes the query to the neighbor peer in the network that makes the most progress towards solving the query.

With regard to the definition of "progress" and the way to assign relevance to query answering, algorithms differ. Existing DHT routing algorithms are based on linguistic, or *syntactic* matching of the search keyword with a single attribute of the hash table. Syntactic matching arises when keywords are compared by using simple prefixes and linguistic analysis. They do not allow, for instance, similarity search based on data contents. These existing DHT mechanisms provide *syntactic routing*. Moreover, they assume a data space structured according to the distributed hash table, whose schema must be known a priori to each peer in the system. On the one hand, the use of a homogeneous distributed table limits the possibility of representing and querying unstructured and semi-structured data. On the other hand, the use of a common hash function forces each peer to use a priori hard-coded mechanism to classify data. In fact, the hash function may be thought of as a *static* classification procedure.

In this paper, we propose an approach to resource routing that provides syntactic and *structural* matching of a search keyword with a peer's identifier. We call it *semantic routing*. Structural matching arises when keywords are compared by using their content, or semantics, with respect to the local knowledge of each peer. Local knowledge is organized in structures, each called a "context," which represent the main data structure in our framework. By constructing structural matching on top of syntactic matching, the low-level routing mechanism of our approach, which runs at the beginning of system evolution until the end of a learning phase, can be any DHT existing solution. In contrast to the static classification procedure provided by the hash function in DHT approaches, semantic routing concerns with the *dynamic* classification of peers knowledge.

Semantic routing offers the following advantages to existing DHT approaches:

(1) similarity search based on data contents;

(2) reduction of the number of hops needed to find relevant resources;

(3) absence of an a priori hard-coded mechanism in the peers to classify data;

(4) higher query expressivity and complex data modeling than what provided by existing DHT approaches.

We define semantic routing by using an adaptive approach (Section 2, see also [5,3]) to logically cluster the P2P network by its semantic contents, each forming a community of peers with similar semantics (Section 3). The network clustering is not imposed, but rather it emerges gradually by point-to-point interaction among the peers with the highest reputation [19,1,34,32]. In the selection of trustworthy peers, which forms the basis of our routing procedure, reputation becomes significant. You can think of reputation as the expectation about a peer's future behavior based on information about the peer's past behavior.

2   Adaptive Query Interaction Game

We image that peers in the system build their communication language in an adaptive process. Adaptation is fundamental, as we model a system of peers, by its nature highly dynamic and open to new peers' entry. Each peer uses the same text retrieval and linguistic analysis techniques. In particular, given a document d, we denote by $\mathsf{Text}\,(d)$ the set of keywords that result from text retrieval.[1]

Peers build their classifications of documents by using "contexts" and conceptualize the world by using features from the same set of features. Moreover, peers have preferences over the meaning of their language, language success and usage, as well as a lexicon, where each peer stores and updates words according to preferences' evolution. A context is a simplified version of a concept hierarchy (see for instance [9]). We rely on the following definition.

Definition 1. A **context** is a concept hierarchy $\langle\, C\,, E\,\rangle$ such that (a) each node in C is labelled by a label from language L_C, (b) each node is (or "classifies") documents from a set $\mathcal{D}$, and (c) E induces a tree structure over C.

Intuitively, a context is created and managed according to the needs of each peer, for example by using a special editor, see [8,7]. For simplicity, given a document d in a context $\mathcal{C}$, a peer (p) uses an unique set of features for d, namely, the set of pairs of the form (w, v), where w is a "keyword in d" extracted by using retrieval technique $\mathsf{Text}\,(\cdot)$—that is, $w \in \mathsf{Text}\,(d)$, and $v = \mathsf{W}_p[w, d, \mathcal{C}]$ is w's weight, or preference with respect to the context $\mathcal{C}$ in which d is classified. Note that a word has the same weight in the same context for each peer in the system.

2.1   Query-Answering Protocol: Routing

In introducing this paper, we have compared the problem of resource routing in a P2P network with query-answering. We continue along the same way.

Suppose that a user, in the role of a seeker, selects one or more providers as the target peers for a query. Such query may be thought of as the keyword to match, in a routing problem, with the identifier of a node of the P2P network, namely, an attribute of the distributed hash table. There is no minimal requirement about the peers' capability to provide information in order to solve a query. The user (u), the seeker (s) and the target provider(s)—say, the "players," (p)—continuously go through a loop performing the following actions ("game rules"):

Step 0.   (Before the game starts - **Lexicons initialization**) Each concept node (C) in every context of each peer (p) in the system is labelled by the system itself with a linguistic expression w in the peer's language. Such linguistic expression is formed by the conjunction of terms w_i with

---

[1] For space limitations, we refer to [5,3] for a detailed description of text retrieval and linguistic analysis. Our presentation is self-contained, although, and basic terminology is introduced along the course of the paper.

maximum weight ($\mathsf{W}_p[w, C]$) computed on the set of documents in the concept node C.

For each term w_i in w, the quadruple (w_i, F, μ, σ) is added to p's lexicon (Lx_p) with initial preference $\mathsf{Pref}^p(w_i, F) = \mathsf{Pref}^p(w, C) = \mu + \sigma$, where F is the set of features which uniquely characterizes C with respect to p's context repository, and $\mu = \mathsf{W}_p[w, C]$ and $\sigma = 0$ ("rate of success").

Step 1. (**Query Context choice**) A context ($\mathcal{C}$)—called **query context**, is selected by the user. The context is used by the user to classify the documents in the seeker's document repository. Only documents classified by the selected context are assumed to be currently in the field of attention of the user.

Step 2. (**Query Cluster and Focus identification**) One document (d, the **example**) in the context's domain is chosen by the user as the query— we call this action **querying by example**. The document determines the **query cluster** (K). The path in the query context between query cluster $C_n = K$ and the root of the query context—in symbols $\langle K, C_{n-1}, \ldots, C_1 \rangle$, is called the **focus of the query**.

Step 3. (**Query formation**) For every concept node C_i in the focus, the seeker computes the features that characterize C_i with respect to d (that is, the set $F_{s,C_i} = \{(w, v) \mid w \in \mathsf{Text}(d), d \in C_i, v = \mathsf{W}_p[w, d, \mathcal{C}]\}$), and retrieves the associated linguistic expressions ("concept labels") from the lexicon. The seeker orders each linguistic expression according to decreasing preference (i.e., the sum of weight and rate of success of the linguistic expression in the lexicon). For linguistic expressions with identical preference, the seeker takes first the linguistic expression that appears first in the lexicon. The resulting sequence of labels $\langle w_n, w_{n-1}, \ldots, w_1 \rangle$ is called **query expression**.

Step 4. (**Query submission**) The seeker sends to the target provider(s) the query expression. $\langle w_n, w_{n-1}, \ldots, w_1 \rangle$.

Step 5. (**Answer discovery - Language matching**) An attempt is made by each target provider to find possible features distinguishing the example (d) from the set of documents in a document repository local to the provider.

The provider's attempt is made by accessing to the provider's lexicon (Lx_p, essentially a kind of dynamic "local ontology" for somebody), according to linguistic expressions and their relative ordering in the query expression.

Step 6. (**Answer submission**) Suppose that w is a term in the *first* linguistic expressions of the query expression such that w appears in the provider's lexicon. Then, the provider sends to the seeker both w and the documents, or a suitable representation of them, possibly limited in the number by a user-driven parameter) which are characterized by the features (F) associated with w in the provider's lexicon with maximum preference.

Step 7.   (**Answer evaluation and back propagation**) The seeker evaluates each received document against the example (d), "vectorized" by a vector v_d composed by the weights ("inverse frequency") of the terms contained in the query expression. Evaluation is computed according to a local similarity metric and an user-driven parameter of acceptance (see [5,3] for technical details). The seeker sends back to the provider the result of the evaluation, say a message: `accepted` / `do not accepted`).

Step 8.   (**Re-classification—context evolution**) The documents that receive positive evaluation are accepted—these documents are similar to the example. The seeker shows them to the user, who may decide to download or to store each document. The seeker might provide a recommendation to the user about the cluster in the focus to use for storing. In this case, the documents are stored in the cluster corresponding to the successful linguistic expression in the query expression, Step 6. Alternatively, an independent classification procedure can be used; among others we refer to [2].

Step 9.   (**Lexicon updating—winning associations**) Suppose that the number of accepted documents is at least one. Then, the seeker and the provider increase the value of features (precisely, success rate σ) associated to w with maximum preference in their lexicon (cf. Steps 3, 6). The value of the updating is proportional to the number of accepted documents.

At the same time, the seeker decreases the value of features associated with any term in the lexicon that appears in the query expression except w ("competing associations"). Similarly, the provider decreases the value of any set of features associated with w in its lexicon that does not characterize the documents sent to the seeker.

Step 10. (**Lexicon updating—losing associations**) Suppose that the number of accepted documents is zero. Then, the seeker and the provider decrease the value of features (i.e., success rate σ) associated to w with maximum preference in their lexicon (cf. Steps 3, 6). The value of updating is proportional to the number of unaccepted documents.

On the basis of the foregoing steps, to be thought of as being performed at generic stage $t \in N$,[2] we define the **adaptive query interaction game** $\mathcal{G} = \langle u, s, p, Q, \mathcal{C} \rangle$, where $Q = \langle w_n, w_{n-1}, \ldots, w_1 \rangle$ is a query expression in the sense of Step 3. Observe: $\mathcal{G}$ is a repeated game in the sense of game theory (cf. [21]).

3   Community Formation, Reputation, and Trust

The formation of collaboration networks is an important latent effect in many computational systems of peers. Importantly, given the diverse skills, language, local knowledge and knowledge representation models that such collaborative

---

[2] Let N denote the set of natural numbers. For simplicity, in defining Steps 1-10 we have omitted time sup- and sub-scripts from notation.

peers involve, deciding which partners to cooperate with—what target providers an information seeker should have, see Step 4—is both critical and difficult. The formation of collaborative communities is crucial for efficient resource routing in unstructured peer-to-peer systems.

Two particularly important factors that influence cooperative behavior of peers are trust and reputation. In this section, we show how these factors contribute to community building through the analysis of query results and, as a main consequence, to the semantic routing of resources in P2P systems.

3.1   Query Propagation—Trust

We have seen how local knowledge, structured in a context, is used by a peer in the role of a seeker to make a query. After query formulation, the seeker checks what peers are connected ("active") and chooses, among those connected, the peer(s) to send the query to. A query session is then opened to manage the answers from each peer, or from the peers that are connected with the peer in charge to solve the query. Now, what "strategy" the seeker uses to select a provider and what referrals from the providers it uses to select the most relevant provider to solve the query is an important issue that we have not discussed so far. We discuss the issue below. An interesting and quite related paper about this topic is [33]; other references are listed therein.

Trust and reputation are complex, multifaceted issues and are related to other themes such as risk, competence, security, beliefs and perceptions, utility and benefit, and expertise [26]. In the selection of trustworthy peers, reputation becomes significant. You can think of reputation as the expectation about a peer's future behavior based on information about the peer's past behavior.

The *automatic generation* of a trust rating for peers—and therefore the identification of hubs—deserves thorough investigation, for which reason we now rely on the routing mechanism of Section 2. Formally, we introduce the following definition. (Recall that by N we denote the set $\{0, 1, 2, \ldots\}$ of natural numbers.)

Definition 2. Let peers s, p and query expression $Q = \langle w_n, w_{n-1}, \ldots, w_1 \rangle$ computed at time $t \in N$ by s in Step 3 of repeated game $\mathcal{G}$ be given. We say that s **trust p over Q at** t just in case

$$Tr(s, p, Q)_t \overset{\text{def}}{=} \sum_{i=1}^{n} \sigma_i > 0,$$

where $\sigma_i = \sigma$ in $(w_i, F, \mu, \sigma) \in Lx_s$ is calculated by restricting to p the interactions of s in the game $\mathcal{G} = \langle u, s, p, Q, \mathcal{C} \rangle$ up to stage t. We write $Tr(s, p, Q)$ to denote that s trust p over Q at some time.

Let peer s in the role of a seeker be given. The seeker faces the problem of selecting who among the peers is able to solve a query Q with highest probability, or who makes the most progress towards solving the query. To decide, the seeker constructs a list of peers to contact. After a finite number $t \in N$ of repeated playing of the adaptive query interaction game $\mathcal{G}$, the seeker manages a list $\langle p_1, p_2, \ldots, p_k \rangle$ of trusted peers to whom submit the query. The list is conventionally ordered according to decreasing trust:

$$Tr(s, p_1, Q)_t \geq Tr(s, p_2, Q)_t \geq \ldots \geq Tr(s, p_k, Q)_t.$$

The seeker' strategy of query resolution is then clear. The seeker first asks to p_1, second to p_2, finally to p_k, if it has not obtained relevant answers from previous peers in the list. It is important to note that the list of trusted peers evolves with the system. The game history suggests to each peer what peers are the "trusted-best" providers to solve specific queries. A further question arises: How a peer who receives a query for which it is not responsible *propagates* the query to relevant peers, at the least able to make some progress towards solving the query?[3] In the next subsection, we define "relevant" peers in terms of reputation.

3.2 Reputation Systems and Communities

Most existing reputation systems [25] require a central server to store and distribute the available information about trust and reputation of peers concerned; see for instance [32] for references. A challenge, see also [32], is to build a decentralized, scalable P2P trust management system that is efficient in both trust computation and trust data storage.

A *reputation system of peers* collects, distributes, and aggregates feedback about peers' past behavior. Following [25], a reputation system requires at least three properties to operate: a. peers are "long-lived," so that there is an expectation of future interaction; b. feedback about current interactions is captured, explicitly represented and distributed into the P2P network, so that it is available to all peers in all future transactions; c. feedback about current interactions becomes past feedback, which is paid attention to by the peers in making decisions. These requirements are at the basis of the following definition of "reputation."

Definition 3. Let peer p and query expression $Q = \langle w_n, w_{n-1}, \ldots, w_1 \rangle$ computed at time $t \in N$ by some peer s in Step 3 of repeated game $\mathcal{G}$ be given. We define the **reputation of** p **over** Q **at** t as follows.

$$Re(p, Q)_t \stackrel{\text{def}}{=} \sum_{s \in \Lambda \setminus \{p\}} Tr(s, p, Q)_t,$$

where Λ denotes the set of active peers in the system at time t. We define the **reputation of** p—in symbols $Re(p, \cdot)$, the maximum reputation $Re(p, Q)_t$ of p over every query expression Q computed at time t by some peer except p.

By a mechanism of query propagation, it is always possible that results for a given query come from peers that the seeker has *not directly* asked to solve.

---

[3] This question emphasizes the concept of *progressive* solution of a query, which is an important focus of the evolutive, self-adapting approach of this paper.

In order to define such mechanism, we have to define the "propagation space," namely, the set of active peers to whom the seeker should send the query. We now introduce the notion of community as our proposal for a **propagation space**. In particular, the next definition presents the concept of a "community of peers" in terms of the reputation that each active peer has gained in the system.

Definition 4. Let query expression Q computed at time $t \in N$ by some peer in Step 3 of repeated game $\mathcal{G}$ be given. We define a **community of peers for** Q **at time** t **in** $\mathcal{G}$—in symbols $\Omega(Q)_t$:

$$\Omega(Q)_t \stackrel{\text{def}}{=} \{p \in \Lambda \,|\, Re(p,Q)_t \text{ is defined and maximum}\},$$

where Λ denotes the set of active peers in the system at time t.

We return to query propagation and suppose that a peer s (the seeker) aims to solve a query Q at any stage $t \in N$ of game $\mathcal{G}$. We propose the following strategy to propagate Q over the network of peers, who interact pairwise by playing $\mathcal{G}$.

At time $t \in N$, the seeker s first looks at community $\Omega(Q)_t$ and chooses one peer in the community. The seeker's decision within the selected community is based on internal preferences, or simply "it takes it random." Let p be the chosen peer. Then, p either solves the query directly, if it is able to do so, or p submits Q to a third-party peer p' in the community $\Omega(Q)_t$, so that Q propagates from s to p' through p. Again, p's decision on what peer in the selected community to submit the query is open to personal preference and other factors, like for example user-interaction design and computational efficiency, which we do not investigate in this paper. Similarly, propagation of Q runs until either Q is solved or there are no new members to whom submit the query. In the former case, solution is back-propagated to s through all peers concerned ("propagation chain"); lexicon of the peers in the chain is updated to enforce winning associations (Step 9) in future interactions. In the latter case, a failure message is propagated backwards to s, together with feedback from each peer in the propagation chain according to Step 10 of the game.

As an important consequence of the foregoing procedure of query propagation, communities evolve with time, because reputation of each member of a community $\Omega(Q)_t$ modifies according to success or failure in solving the query. New members may entry $\Omega(Q)_t$, while some old members may leave $\Omega(Q)_t$ out.

4   Conclusion

The approach to semantic routing in P2P networks that we have presented in this paper is based on trust management and reputation. Starting from an adaptive mechanism of query-answering, a kind of repeated game, we have defined the reputation of each peer, in order to be able to logically cluster the P2P network by its contents, each forming a reputation-based community of peers with similar semantics. As a main consequence, the P2P network self-organizes, and the network clustering is not imposed, but rather emerges gradually by point-to-point interaction among the peers with the highest reputation. Communities of peers have been finally used to advance our proposal for semantic routing.

Our framework is useful to construct a variety of peer-to-peer applications where the "problem of naming" is relevant. Our approach has been inspired by language games [31] and by self-organizing distributed data structures [13], and some seminal ideas on naming games in artificial intelligence and robotics [27, 28] and advertising games [4] have been used.

Experimental work remains to be done to demonstrate the practical benefits of our model to peers' selection and effective resource routing. Initial experimental setting is in progress within a system of knowledge exchange [8,7,3].

References

1. K. Aberer and Z. Despotovic. Managing trust in a peer-to-peer information system. In H. Paques, L. Liu, and D. Grossman, editors, *Proceedings of CIKM-01*, pages 310–317, New York, NY, 2001. ACM Press.
2. G. Adami, P. Avesani, and D. Sona. Bootstrapping for hierarchical document classification. In *Proceedings of the Twelfth ACM International Conference on Informationand Knowledge Management(CIKM-03)*, pages 295–302, New York, USA, 2003. ACM Press.
3. A. Agostini. SDS games: Similar documents service by games. Technical report, ITC-IRST, Trento, Italy, May 2004.
4. A. Agostini and P. Avesani. Advertising games for web services. In R. Meersman, Z. Tari, and D. Schmit, editors, *Proceedings of the Eleventh International Conference on Cooperative Information Systems (CoopIS-03)*, pages 93–110, Berlin Heidelberg, 2003. Springer-Verlag LNCS 2888.
5. A. Agostini and P. Avesani. Adaptive querying to knowledge exchange. Technical report, ITC-IRST, Trento, Italy, January 2004.
6. A. Agostini and P. Avesani. On the discovery of the semantic context of queries by game-playing. In *Proceedings of the Sixth International Conference On Flexible Query Answering Systems (FQAS-04)*, pages 203–216, Berlin Heidelberg, 2004. Springer-Verlag LNAI 3055.
7. M. Bonifacio, P. Bouquet, G. Mameli, and M. Nori. KEx: A Peer-to-Peer solution for distributed knowledge management. In *Proceedings of the Fourth International Conference on Practical Aspects of Knowledge Management (PAKM-02)*, pages 490–500, Heidelberg, 2002. Springer-Verlag LNAI 2569.
8. M. Bonifacio, P. Bouquet, G. Mameli, and M. Nori. Peer - mediated distributed knowledge management. In *Proceedings of AAAI Spring Symposium on Agent Mediated Knowledge Management (AMKM-03)*, Stanford, CA, 2003. Stanford University.
9. A. Büchner, M. Ranta, J. Hughes, and M. Mäntylä. Semantic information mediation among multiple product ontologies. In *Proceedings of IDPT-99*, 1999.
10. P. Dell'Acqua, L. M. Pereira, and A. Vitória. User preference information in query answering. In T. Andreasen, A. Motro, H. Christiansen, and H. L. Larsen, editors, *Proceedings of FQAS-02*, pages 163–173, Berlin Heidelberg, 2002. Springer-Verlag LNAI 2522.
11. G. W. Flake, S. Lawrence, C. L. Giles, and F. M. Coetzee. Self-organization and identification of Web communities. *IEEE Computer*, 35(3):66–71, 2002.

12. G. Moro, A. M. Ouksel, C. Sartori. Agents and peer-to-peer computing: A promising combination of paradigms. In *Proceedings of AP2PC-02, Bologna, Italy, 2002.* pages 1–14. Springer-Verlag LNCS 2530.

13. A. M. Ouksel, G. Moro. G-Grid: A Class of Scalable and Self-Organizing Data Structures for Multi-dimensional Querying and Content Routing in P2P Networks. In *Proceedings of AP2PC-03, Melbourne, Australia, 2003.* pages 78–89. Springer-Verlag LNCS 2872.

14. T. Gaasterland, P. Godfrey, and J. Minker. An overview of cooperative answering. *Journal of Intelligent Information Systems*, 1(2):123–157, 1992.

15. H. Grice. Logic and Conversation. In P. Cole and J. Morgan, editors, *Syntax and Semantics*. Academic Press, New York, 1975.

16. Gene Kan. *Peer-to-Peer: Harnessing the Benefits of Disruptive Technologies*, chapter 8, pages 94–122. O'Reilly & Associates, 2001.

17. M. S. Khambatti, K. D. Ryu, and P. Dasgupta. Efficient discovery of implicitly formed peer-to-peer communities. *International Journal of Parallel and Distributed Systems and Networks*, 5(4):155–163, 2002.

18. J. Kubiatowicz, D. Bindel, Y. Chen, P. Eaton, D. Geels, R. Gummadi, S. Rhea, H. Weatherspoon, W. Weimer, C. Wells, and B. Zhao. Oceanstore: An architecture for global-scale persistent storage. In *Proceedings of ACM ASPLOS*, volume 35, pages 190–201. ACM, November 2000.

19. P. S. Marsh. *Formalising Trust as a Computational Concept*. PhD thesis, University of Stirling, 1994.

20. J. Minker. An overview of cooperative answering in databases (invited paper). In T. Andreasen, H. Christiansen, and H. L. Larsen, editors, *Proceedings of FQAS-98*, pages 282–285, Berlin Heidelberg, 1998. Springer-Verlag LNCS 1495.

21. M. J. Osborne and A. Rubinstein. *A Course in Game Theory*. The MIT Press, Cambridge, MA, 1994.

22. O. F. Rana and A. Hinze. Trust and reputation in dynamic scientific communities. *IEEE Distributed Systems Online*, 5(1), 2004.

23. Sylvia Ratnasamy, Paul Francis, Mark Handley, Richard Karp, and Scott Shenker. A scalable content addressable network. In *Proceedings of ACM SIGCOMM 2001*, pages 161–172, 2001.

24. Sylvia Ratnasamy, Scott Shenker, and Ion Stoica. Routing algorithms for DHTs: Some open questions. In *1st IPTPS*, 2002.

25. P. Resnick, R. Zeckhauser, E. Friedman, and K. Kuwabara. Reputation systems. *Communications of the ACM*, 43(12):45–48, 2000.

26. J. Sabater and C. Sierra. REGRET: A reputation in gregarious societies. In J. P. Müller, E. Andre, S. Sen, and C. Frasson, editors, *Proceedings of AGENTS-01*, pages 194–195, New York, NY, 2001. ACM Press. Also IIIA Technical Report, Artificial Intelligence Research Institute, Spain. Available online at www.iiia.csic.es/ sierra/articles/2001/reputation.pdf.

27. L. Steels. Self-organizing vocabularies. In C. Langton and T. Shimohara, editors, *Proceedings of the V Alife Conference*, Cambridge, MA, 1996. The MIT Press.

28. L. Steels and A. McIntyre. Spatially distributed naming games. *Advances in Complex Systems*, 1(4):301–324, 1998.

29. Ion Stoica, Robert Morris, David Karger, M. Francs Kaashoek, and Hari Balakrishnan. Chord: A scalable peer-to-peer lookup service for internet applications. In *SIGCOMM*, pages 149–160. ACM Press, 2001.

30. A. Trigoni. Interactive query formulation in semistructured databases. In T. Andreasen, A. Motro, H. Christiansen, and H. L. Larsen, editors, *Proceedings of the Fifth International Conference on Flexible Query Answering Systems (FQAS-02)*, pages 356–369, Berlin Heidelberg, 2002. Springer-Verlag LNAI 2522.
31. L. Wittgenstein. *Philosophical Investigations*. Blackwell, Oxford, UK, 1953.
32. L. Xiong and L. Liu. PeerTrust: Supporting reputation-based trust for peer-to-peer electronic communities. *IEEE Transactions on Knowledge and Data Engineering (TKDE), Special Issue on Peer-to-Peer Based Data Management*, 2004. To appear.
33. P. Yolum and M. P. Singh. Emergent properties of Referral Systems. In J. S. Rosenschein, T. Sandholm, M. Wooldridge, and M. Yokoo, editors, *Proceedings of the Second International Joint Conference on Autonomous Agents and Multiagent Systems (AAMAS-03)*, pages 592–599, New York, NY, 2003. ACM Press.
34. B. Yu and M. P. Singh. A social mechanism of reputation management in electronic communities. In M. Klush and L. Kerschberg, editors, *Proceedings of the Fourth International Workshop on Cooperative Information Agents (CIA-00)*, Berlin Heidelberg, 2000. Springer-Verlag LNAI 1860.

Integration of B2B Logistics Using Semantic Web Services

Javier Esplugas Cuadrado, Chris Preist, and Stuart Williams

HP Labs, Filton Rd, Stoke Gifford, Bristol BS32 8QZ, UK
javier.esplugas-cuadrado@hp.com
chris.preist@hp.com
skw@hp.com

Abstract. In this paper, we present a case study about the integration of a new partner into a freight logistics chain using semantic web services. We do this in the context of conceptual architecture of the EU Semantic Web-enabled Web Services project [5]. The case study is based on the process of substituting one of our freight forwarders (ocean shipping) with another logistic partner. The result of substitution must be the same functionally as existed before the substitution. We present the service description requirements which we encountered during its development. We discuss our experiences in using OWL-S to describe the services.

Keywords: Logistics, Semantic Web Services, Enterprise Integration, SCM

1 Introduction

In a world where global outsourcing and business-to-business integration are commonplace in product manufacturing, logistics interactions are becoming more and more significant. The prices of logistic transportation are between 4.1 % (Top performers) and 5.3 % (on average) of the cost of product development, excluding the costs of inventory[1]; When this is also included, logistics costs can reach as high as 13.7%. In a $100 Billion industry such an overhead is significant. Hence the selection of the right logistics provider in terms of price competitiveness and efficiency becomes critical for any enterprise. In a B2B context, logistics interactions between parties are supported by the use of electronic message exchanges. There are 3 main messaging standards used to do this; The UN-Standard EDIFact (Electronic Data Interchange for Administration Commerce & Transport) [2], the US-Standard ANSI X.12 [3] and more recently, RosettaNet PIPs (Partner Interchange Processes) [4].

One logistic shipment can use several freight forwarders (This is known as a multi-leg shipment). Management of such a shipment can be complex: Goods must transit smoothly from one logistic provider to another, and the messages sent and received by the different parties must be coordinated. We consider a scenario in which there is a three-leg shipment taking place between a supplier in the UK and a manufacturing plant in Russia. Unexpectedly, logistics provider two (responsible for a shipment between Southampton and St. Petersburg) is unable to provide the required service

C. Bussler and D. Fensel (Eds.): AIMSA 2004, LNAI 3192, pp. 96–105, 2004.
© Springer-Verlag Berlin Heidelberg 2004

and must be substituted. The logistics coordinator is responsible for locating a replacement and integrating it seamlessly into the logistics chain.

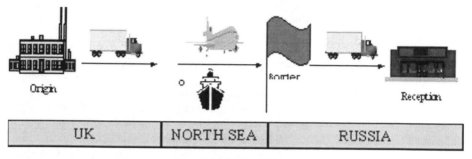

Fig. 1. Multi-leg Shipment

In this paper we present the service description requirements which we encountered during the development of this case study. We do this in the context of the SWWS conceptual architecture [5]. Figure 2 shows how our case study is organized within this architecture. In section 2, we discuss the knowledge representation requirements on the logistics service description at the business layer of the architecture. This is done in the context of a contract template, describing a set of possible logistics services. We also discuss how the discovery and pre-contractual conversations associated with the service are used to manipulate this contract template to come to an agreed definition of the service to be provided. In section 3, we discuss the requirements on the service description at the interaction layer of the architecture.

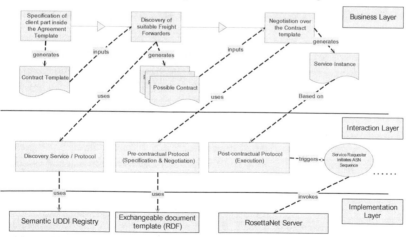

Fig. 2. Case study alignment with the EU SWWS Project Conceptual Architecture

2   Service Discovery and Contract Formation

2.1   The Contract and the Contract Template

From the perspective of the business layer of the architecture, a logistic service is characterized by a set of parameters. These parameters are: start location; destination location; start date/time; arrival date/time; number of packages; dimensions and weight of each package and the Incoterms to be provided. These parameters constitute the terms of the service. For example, a specific service may be the shipping of 12 pallets from Southampton to St. Petersburg, leaving at 10:00 AM on the 2nd of June to arrive by 10:00 PM on the 8th of June. In addition to its terms, a service will have payment information; the price of the service, the means of payment and the terms of payment. Thirdly, at the interaction layer of the architecture, a service will have interaction information defining the format and sequencing of messages (according to some message protocol or choreography) which will accompany its execution. When terms, payment and interaction information are agreed between a service provider and service consumer, this constitutes a *contract* specifying exactly what service will be provided.

   The role of the discovery and contract formation phases are for a service requestor to locate a service provider and agree a definition of the service to be provided. The key document used during these phases is the *contract template*. A contract template describes a contract as outlined above, but with all parameters left un-instantiated.

2.2   Discovery

During discovery, a service requestor interacts with a discovery service to determine if any service providers may be able to meet their needs. In the context of the conceptual architecture, the request and provider adverts consist of a contract template with constraints on some of the parameters. For example, a logistics service provider may advertise a contract template with the start location constrained to be a port in the UK and the destination to be a port in Russia, without specifying which, and leaving all other information (times, sizes, prices, etc) unconstrained. A requestor may state that they want a shipment of specific dimensions to leave Plymouth sometime after 10am on June 1st, to arrive in St Petersburg before midnight on June 9th. Discovery consists of determining whether the two partially constrained templates are compatible. The exact definition of compatibility is beyond the scope of this paper. See [8] [9] for existing proposals. If two templates are compatible, then the advertiser may be able to meet the requestor's needs, and the two parties enter into a pre-contractual conversation.

2.3   The Pre Contractual Phase

In the context of our case study, the pre-contractual phase consists of a set of conversations between the requestor and the possible service providers located through the discovery phase. The outcome, if successful, will be a specific contract agreed between the requestor and one service provider. Each conversation is a simple three-stage exchange;

1. The service requestor sends the provider a version of the contract template with parameters instantiated or constrained to define the class of service they require. This would be similar to the constrained template used for discovery, described in section 2.2. The requestor may also provide a time deadline by which responses are required.

2. The service provider replies with all possible contract instances which satisfy the constrained template. This will include a fixed price for the service. For example, a provider could offer the service instance described in section 2.1 for a price of £600.

3. The requestor selects one from the set of all responses, and sends an acceptance to the corresponding provider.

Note that such a protocol allows comparison but not negotiation of parameters such as price.

2.4   Using OWL-S Within Contract Templates and Contracts

The contract templates and contracts we developed as part of our case study contain OWL-S descriptions of services. This work has allowed us to identify areas where OWL-S requires augmenting to handle our case study.

In OWL-S, the service profile is the primary representation used for service discovery. It presents properties of the service such as: service name, service category, contact information, and service provider ratings. It also describes the required Inputs, Outputs, Preconditions and Effects of the service.

The OWL-S profile is primarily designed to categorise a service, rather than to give a complete and structured business-layer description of specifically what a service provider offers. For this reason we have augmented it with a structured description of a logistics service, using a simple logistics ontology allowing representation of appropriate geographical information (beyond 'service radius' of OWL-S), information about container dimensions and weight, and Incoterms.

Furthermore, the OWL-S profile assumes that profile parameters are fully instantiated within an advertisement, which means it cannot be straightforwardly used within a contract template and provides no means of constraining parameters. To overcome this, we have developed a set of 'constrained' classes (e.g 'UK port', 'Before June 10th', etc) which can be used within the description of a service advertisement or request. These are developed in OWL, which does not provide any mathematical reasoning, and hence the numerical range constraints (such as 'Before June 10th') are somewhat unnatural and are reasoned with by considering them as a set of instances.

The service profile currently (OWL v1.0) only provides a place-holder for preconditions of the service, without defining any structure for them. In the pre-contractual conversation we can expect a certain degree of flexibility in terms of the inputs used. For example, a service requester could either specify a pair of Date and time structures (start & arrival), or a start date and time plus a maximum permitted time for transportation. The different inputs will require different treatments by the service interactions (as defined in the OWL-S process model). However, there is no means to specify how the existence or the absence of some inputs affects the process model interpretation. This lack of expressivity of dependencies between inputs and the process model has also been observed [11] in a different application.

3   Description of the Service Execution

So far, we have focused our attention on the business-layer description of the logistics service. However, as we mentioned in section 2.1 a service also has an interaction layer description, describing the possible exchanges of messages between provider and requestor which can occur as the service is executed. Such a description may also be decided as part of the contract agreement process. Within our case study, our analysis determined that, at a certain level of abstraction, there is one single interaction protocol which is used by most logistics services. This interaction protocol provides for actioning and monitoring of the progress of the service provided by the freight forwarded. The way in which protocol interactions are related to the lifecycle of the freight forwarding service is shown in Figure 3.

- Awaiting action 1: An ASN (Advance Shipment Notice) message sequence will be initiated by the Service Requester when it is about to deliver the shipment to the collection site. Once the shipment is collected (no message sequence captures this event), the Service Requester can initiate an SSM (Shipment Status Message) message sequence at any time to receive status information from the service provider.
- Active phase 2: An ASN message sequence will be initiated by the Service Provider when it is about to deliver the shipment to its final destination.
- Active phase 3: Once the ASN sequence of the previous phase has completed, the service provider initiates both a POD (Proof of Delivery) and a FI (Freight Invoice) sequence. These sequences can occur in either order and indeed may overlap in time. The proof of delivery sequence informs the requestor that the delivery has been made successfully, and the freight invoice sequence requests payment for the service.
- Once the POD Sequence is finished, the service requester cannot initiate any more SSM sequences and the communication for this specific service is finished.

Each message exchange sequence (ASN, POD, FI and SSM) is a two way message exchange with no guarantee of security or delivery.
In addition to this conversational behavior, partners also need to have a shared understanding of the context in which the exchange occurs. Specifically, partners need to:

- Share a common vocabulary of concepts used within messages. Currently, logistics partners do this by an informal shared understanding. In our case study, we use an ontology to formalize this vocabulary.
- Share a common understanding of how actions in the physical world relate to the sending/receiving of messages. For the purpose of this case study, we assume this understanding is implicit. Figure 3 shows the model used.

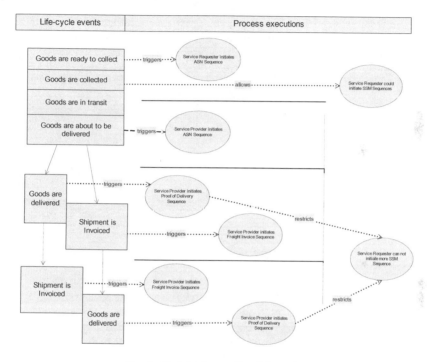

Fig. 3. Freight forwarding life-cycle

The abstract protocol can be implemented using any of the three standards (RosettaNet, EDIFact or X.12) and there may be differences between the way two logistics providers use the same standard. For this reason, two logistics partners may use quite different concrete realizations of the same abstract protocol. Hence, there is an important role for protocol mediation in this case study. However, discussion of this is beyond the scope of this paper and we present a single protocol based on the way these standards are typically used.

We now show how we create a description of the service execution protocol. Firstly we develop a complete specification of the protocol as a state machine from the perspective of each of the participants. This complete specification contains features which cannot currently be captured in the OWL-S process model. For that reason, we transform this state machine into a simpler process algebra representation, omitting such features. This can then be represented using the OWL-S process model.

In figure 4, we present the overall architecture of interaction. The service provider and consumer implement an abstract state machine embodying the behaviour required by the protocol. The required exchange of messages for ASN, SSM, POD and FI interactions are implemented using web service technology. The combination of all these web services results in the required abstract state machine.

The state machine giving a complete specification of the protocol from the perspective of the service provider is shown in figure 5. It shows how the sequences of business actions are translated into lower-level message request/indications. We can't make any assumptions on the reliability of the communications channel, therefore we must ensure that any state can receive/send re-transmits, can handle loss of confirmations, etc. To achieve the necessary degree of control we use timers and dynamically assigned variables (e.g. Max-Retransmissions = 5). In the interests of space, we have omitted the SSM message sequence from this state machine.

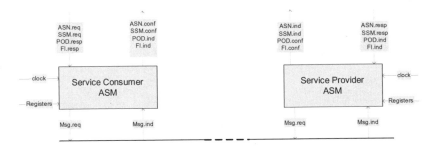

Fig. 4. Service-to-Service Abstract State machine conceptualization

OWL-S is neither able to represent timers nor exception handling. This need for exception handlers was already presented by Fensel and Bussler in [16]. For this reason, we present a simplified description of this protocol using process algebra (This time we include the SSM exchange) [10]. Again, this is from the perspective of the service provider. The description is in CCS [11] and has been implemented on the Edinburgh Concurrency Workbench [13]

With the exception of the omission of timeout information and exception handling, this is equivalent to the complete protocol presented in Figure 5. In Figure 6, we provide a UML process sequence diagram of the process algebra description.

```
agent P0 = receive_asn.ASN_1_RECEIVED \stopSSM;
agent ASN_1_RECEIVED = ('send_asn.ASN_2_SENT) |
                       (receive_ssm_request.SSM_RECEIVED
                        + stopSSM.0);
agent ASN_2_SENT = ('send_pod.POD_SENT) |
('send_fi.FI_SENT);
agent POD_SENT = 'stopSSM.0;
agent FI_SENT = 0;
agent SSM_RECEIVED = 'send_ssm_response.SSM_RESPONDER
                     + stopSSM.0;
agent SSM_RESPONDER = receive_ssm_request.SSM_RECEIVED
                      + stopSSM.0;
```

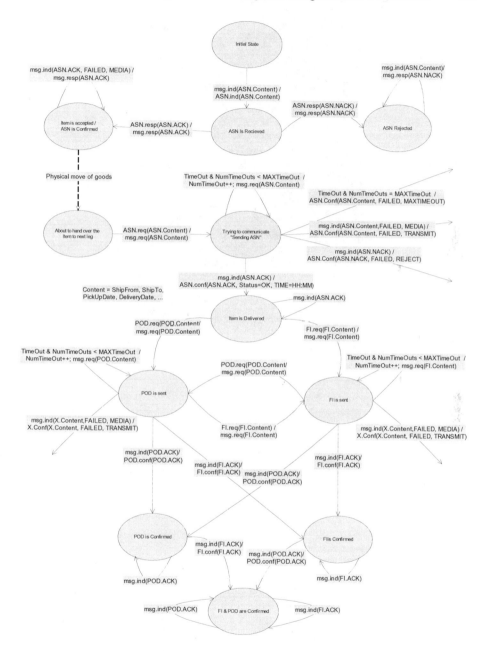

Fig. 5. The Service Provider State Machine

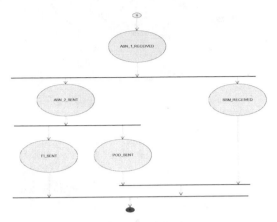

Fig. 6. UML Specification of the Process sequence

Implementing the Service Execution Model in OWL-S

We have implemented the process specified above using the OWL-S process model. The complete model is provided in [14], and mirrors closely the structure of Figure 6. For example, the split occurring at the second stage of the overall process is represented as follows;

```
<process:Split>
  <process:components rdf:parseType="Collection">
   <process:AtomicProcess rdf:about="#SSM_RECEIVED"/>
    <process:Sequence>
     <process:components rdf:parseType="Collection">
       <process:CompositeProcess rdf:ID="ASN_2_SENT"/>
       <process:CompositeProcess rdf:ID="State2">
     </process:components>
    </process:Sequence>
  </process:components>
</process:Split>
```

The requirements of our case study went beyond the capabilities of the OWL-S 1.0 process model in several ways. As we explained earlier, our protocol required the specification of timeouts (requiring timers in the process language) and exception handling. Furthermore, OWL-S 1.0 does not handle the synchronisation of parallel processes with the degree of control our application requires. Specifically, we want to synchronise any SSM_RECEIVED process to terminate when the POD_SENT process has been successfully completed, as SSM messages are no longer valid after this point. However, the 'join' operator of OWL-S only allows the joining of processes which previously were generated in the same split, so cannot synchronise two parallel processes which were initiated independently.

4   First Conclusions and Further Work

In this paper, we have presented a case study for semantic web services based on a multi-leg freight transportation scenario. We have also presented our experiences with applying existing semantic web services technology, in the form of OWL-S 1.0. Specifically, we identified the following requirements not currently met;

1. A more structured model of services at the 'business' layer of abstraction.
2. An ability to constrain service parameters in advertisements and requests.
3. Representation of timers in service process models.
4. Handling of exceptions in service process models.
5. Complex synchronization of parallel processes in service process models.

We are currently working in conjunction with others in the SWWS consortium on the design of a service description language able to meet requirements 1 and 2 and a conversation/choreography language able to meet requirements 3-5. We hope our experiences in this will feed into future versions of WSMO [15] and OWL-S [6]

References

[1]   McKinsey and Institute fur Supply Chain Management. Survey over 40 Multinationals and Consumer Goods in Europe. 2002-03

[2]   EDIFACT- United Nations Directories for Electronic Data Interchange for Administration, Commerce and Transport. Available at

[3]   X.12 - Accredited Standards Committee Reference Web-Site at   .

[4]   RosettaNet Consortium Reference Web-Site   .

[5]   Preist, C. A Conceptual Architecture for Semantic Web Services, submitted to International Semantic Web Conference (ISWC2004), Hiroshima, Japan

[6]   The OWL Services Coalition, OWL-S: Semantic Mark-up for Web Services v.1.0. Available at

[7]   The DAML/OWL Services Coalition, DAML-S: Semantic Markup for Web Services v.0.9. Available at

[8]   Paolucci, M., Kawamura, T., Payne, T.R. and Sycara, K: Semantic Matching of Web Service Capabilities. Proc. International Semantic Web Conference (2002) 333-347

[9]   Trastour, D., Bartolini, C. and Gonzalez-Castillo,J.: A Semantic Web Approach to Service Description for Matchmaking of Services. In Proceedings of the Semantic Web Working Symposium, Stanford, CA, USA, July 30 - August 1, 2001

[10] Object Management Group. OMG Unified Modelling Language Specification v1.5 formal 2003-03-1. Available at

[11] Richards D., Sabou M. Semantic Markup for Semantic Web Tools: A DAML-S description of an RDF-Store. In: Proceedings of the Second International Semantic Web Conference (ISWC2003), Florida, USA, 20-23 October 2003

[12] CSS Process Algebra - Milner, R., Communication and Concurrency. Prentice Hall, 1989

[13] Faron Moller, Perdita Stevens. The Edinburgh Concurrency Workbench. Reference Web Site

[14] Javier Esplugas, Chris Preist, Stuart Williams. 2003. SWWS - D8.2 Ontologies & Services

[15] Dumitru Roman, Holger Lausen, Uwe Keller. 2004. The Web Service Modelling Ontology WSMO. Available online via

[16] Fensel D. and Bussler C. 2002. The Web Service Modeling Framework WSMF. Electronic Commerce: Research and Applications, 1 (2002) 113-117.

Planning and Monitoring Web Service Composition*

M. Pistore[1], F. Barbon[2], P. Bertoli[2], D. Shaparau[2], and P. Traverso[2]

[1] University of Trento - ITALY
pistore@dit.unitn.it
[2] ITC-irst - Trento - ITALY
{barbon,bertoli,traverso,shaparau}@irst.itc.it

Abstract. The ability to automatically compose web services, and to monitor their execution, is an essential step to substantially decrease time and costs in the development, integration, and maintenance of complex services. In this paper, we exploit techniques based on the "Planning as Model Checking" approach to automatically compose web services and synthesize monitoring components. By relying on such a flexible technology, we are able to deal with the difficulties stemming from the unpredictability of external partner services, the opaqueness of their internal status, and the presence of complex behavioral requirements. We test our approach on a simple, yet realistic example; the results provide a witness to the potentiality of this approach.

1 Introduction

The emerging paradigm of web services provides the basis for the interaction and coordination of business processes that are distributed among different organizations, which can exchange services and can cooperate to provide better services, e.g., to third parties organizations or to individuals. One of the big challenges for the taking up of web services is the provision of computer automated support to the composition of service oriented distributed processes, in order to decrease efforts, time, and costs in their development, integration, and maintenance. The ability to automatically plan the composition of web services, and to monitor their execution is therefore an essential step toward the real usage of web services.

BPEL4WS (Business Process Execution Language for Web Services) [1] is an emerging standard for the specification and execution of service oriented business processes. BPEL4WS has been designed with two functions in mind. On the one hand, *executable* BPEL4WS programs allow the specification and execution of the processes internal to an organization (*internal processes* in the following). On the other hand, *abstract* BPEL4WS specifications can be used to specify and publish the protocol that external agents have to follow to interact with a web service (*external protocols* in the following). Therefore, BPEL4WS offers the natural starting point for web service composition.

In this paper, we devise a planning technique for the automated composition and automated monitoring of web services. Automated composition allows providing services

---

* The work is partially funded by the FIRB-MIUR project RBNE0195K5, "Knowledge Level Automated Software Engineering".

C. Bussler and D. Fensel (Eds.): AIMSA 2004, LNAI 3192, pp. 106–115, 2004.
© Springer-Verlag Berlin Heidelberg 2004

that combine other, possibly distributed, services, in order to achieve a given business goal. Starting from the description of the external protocols (e.g., expressed as an abstract BPEL4WS specification) and given a "business requirement" for the process (i.e. the goal it should satisfy, expressed in a proper goal language), the planner synthesizes automatically the code that implements the internal process and exploits the services of the partners to achieve the goal. This code can be expressed in a process execution language such as executable BPEL4WS.

Our planning techniques are also exploited to automatically generate a monitor of the process, i.e., a piece of code that is able to detect and signal whether the external partners do not behave consistently with the specified protocols. This is vital for the practical application of web services. Run-time misbehaviors may take place even for automatically composed (and possibly validated) services, e.g. due to failures of the underlying message-passing infrastructure, or due to errors or changes in the specification of external web services.

In order to achieve these results, our planner must address the following difficulties, which are typical of planning under uncertainty:

- **Nondeterminism**: The planner cannot foresee the actual interaction that will take place with external processes, e.g., it cannot predict a priori whether the answer to a request for availability will be positive or negative, whether a user will confirm or not acceptance of a service, etc.
- **Partial Observability**: The planner can only observe the communications with external processes; that is, it has no access to their internal status and variables. For instance, the planner cannot know a priori the list of items available for selling from a service.
- **Extended Goals**: Business requirements often involve complex conditions on the behavior of the process, and not only on its final state. For instance, we might require that the process never gets to the state where it buys an item costing more than the available budget. Moreover, requirements need to express conditional preferences on different goals to achieve. For instance, a process should try first to reserve and confirm both a flight and an hotel from two different service providers, and only if one of the two services is not available, it should fall back and cancel both reservations.

We address these problems by developing planning techniques based on the "Planning as model checking" approach, which has been devised to deal with nondeterministic domains, partial observability, and extended goals. A protocol specification for the available external services is seen as a nondeterministic and partially observable domain, which is represented by means of a finite state machine. Business requirements are expressed in the EaGLe goal language [8], and are used to drive the search in the domain, in order to synthesize a plan corresponding to the internal process defining the web-service composition. Plan generation takes advantage of symbolic model checking techniques, that compactly represent the search space deriving from nondeterministic and partially observable domains. These are also exploited to produce compact monitoring automata that are capable to trace the run-time evolution of external processes, and thus to detect incorrect interactions.

In this paper, we define the framework for the planning of composition and monitoring of distributed web services, describe it through an explanatory example, and implement the planning algorithm in the MBP planner. We provide an experimental evaluation which witnesses the potentialities of our approach.

2   A Web-Service Composition Domain

Our reference example consists in providing a furniture purchase & delivery service. We do so by combining two separate, independent existing services: a furniture producer, and a delivery service.

We now describe the protocols that define the interactions with the existing services. These protocols can be seen as very high level descriptions of the BPEL4WS external protocols that would define the services in a real application.

The protocol provided by the furniture producer is depicted in Fig. 1.3. The protocol becomes active upon a request for a given item; the item may be available or not — in the latter case, this is signaled to the request applicant, and the protocol terminates with failure. In case the item is available, the applicant is notified with informations about the product, and the protocol stops waiting for either a positive or negative acknowledgment, upon which it either continues, or stops failing. Should the applicant decide that the offer is acceptable, the service provides him with the cost and production time; once more, the protocol waits for a positive or negative acknowledgment, this time terminating in any case (with success or failure).

The protocol provided by the delivery service is depicted in Fig. 1.2. The protocol starts upon a request for transporting an object of a given size to a given location. This might not be possible, in which case the applicant is notified, and the protocol terminates failing. Otherwise, a cost and delivery time are computed and signaled to the applicant; the protocol suspends for either a positive or negative acknowledgment, terminating (with success or failure respectively) upon its reception.

The idea is that of combining these services so that the user may directly ask the combined service to purchase and deliver a given item at a given place. To do so, we exploit a description of the expected protocol the user will execute when interacting with the service. According to the protocol (see Fig. 1.1), the user sends a request to get a given item at a given location, and expects either a signal that this is not possible (in which case the protocol terminates, failing), or an offer indicating the price and cost of the service. At this time, the user may either accept or refuse the offer, terminating its interaction in both cases.

Thus a typical (nominal) interaction between the user, the combined purchase & delivery service P&S, the producer, and the shipper would go as follows:

1. the user asks P&S for a certain item I, that he wants to be transported at location L;
2. P&S asks the producer some data about the item, namely its size, the cost, and how much time does it take to produce it;
3. P&S asks the delivery service the price and cost of transporting an object of such a size to L;
4. P&S provides the user a proposal which takes into account the overall cost (plus an added cost for P&S) and time to achieve its goal;

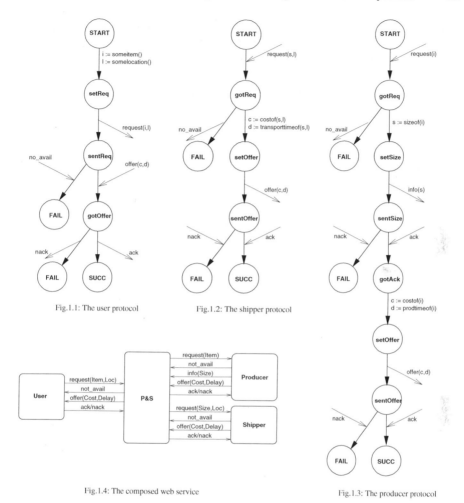

Fig.1.1: The user protocol

Fig.1.2: The shipper protocol

Fig.1.4: The composed web service

Fig.1.3: The producer protocol

Fig. 1. The protocols and their combination.

5. the user confirms its order, which is dispatched by P&S to the delivery and producer.

Of course this is only the nominal case, and other interactions should be considered, e.g., for the cases the producer and/or delivery services are not able to satisfy the request, or the user refuses the final offer.

3   Planning via Model Checking

The "Planning as Model Checking" framework [5] is a general framework for planning under uncertainty. It allows for *non-determinism* in the initial state and in the outcome of action execution. It allows modeling planning domains with different *degrees of run-time observability*, where e.g. the domain state is only partially visible via sensing, and for expressing *temporally extended planning goals*, i.e., goals that define conditions on sequences of states resulting from the execution of a plan, rather than just on final states.

In this framework, a domain is a model of a generic system with its own dynamics; formally, it is expressed as a (non-deterministic) finite state automaton. The domain is controlled by a plan which is also represented as a (deterministic) finite state automaton. During execution, the plan produces *actions*, which constitute the input of the domain, on the basis of the *sensing* coming from the domain and of its internal state. In turn, the domain evolves its state in response to the action, and produced a new output. That is, the execution can be seen as the evolution of the synchronous product of the automata (formal details are presented in [5]).

This generality involves a high complexity in the plan synthesis. In particular, partial observability involves the need for dealing with uncertainty about the current domain state: at every plan execution step, the executor must consider a set of equally plausible states, also called a *belief state* or simply *belief* [7,4]. When searching for a plan, also the planner must consider beliefs and the result of actions and sensing over them. Therefore, the search in a partially observable domain $\mathcal{D}$ can be described as search inside a correspondent fully observable "belief-level", or *knowledge-level*, domain $\mathcal{D}_K$ whose states are the beliefs of $\mathcal{D}$. Knowledge-level domain $\mathcal{D}_K$ can be produced by a power-set construction upon $\mathcal{D}$.

This leads to the important consequence that planning under partial observability can be performed by planning for full observability over the associated knowledge-level domain [3]:

Fact 1 *Let $\mathcal{D}$ be a ground-level domain and g be a knowledge-level goal for $\mathcal{D}$. Let also $\mathcal{D}_K$ be the knowledge level domain for $\mathcal{D}$. Then Π is a plan that achieves g on $\mathcal{D}$ if, and only if, Π achieves (the knowledge-level interpretation of) g on $\mathcal{D}_K$.*

Also notice that the knowledge-level domain describes all the valid observable behaviors of the domain. Therefore, we can use it as a monitor, to check at run time whether the domain really behaves as predicted in the domain model.

In the "Planning as Model Checking" framework, extended goals have been originally expressed as CTL [10] formulas, inheriting a standard semantics over the execution structure. Planning with CTL goals has been studied in [13,14] under the hypothesis of full observability and in [5,3] in the more general case of partial observability. However, CTL is often inadequate for planning, since it cannot express crucial aspects such as failure and recovery conditions, intentionality, and preferences amongst sub-goals. EaGLe [8] has been designed with the purpose to overcome these limitations of CTL and to provide a language for temporally extended planning goals in non-deterministic domains. EaGLe constructs permit to express goals of different strength (e.g. **DoReach** p requires achieving p, while **TryReach** p requires the controller to do its best to achieve p, but admits not reaching it); they handle failure, and sub-goal preferences (namely, in g_1 **Fail** g_2, goal g_1 is considered first, and only if its achievement or maintenance fails, then goal g_2 is used as a recovery or second-choice goal). The combination of these concepts is very powerful, and allows expressing goals such as e.g. **TryReach** c **Fail DoReach** d: here, the sub-goal **TryReach** c requires to find a plan that tries to reach condition c. During the execution of the plan, a state may be reached from which it is not possible to reach c.

When such a state is reached, goal **TryReach** c fails and the recovery goal **DoReach** d is considered. A formal semantics and a planning algorithm for EaGLe goals in fully observable domains appears in [8].

4   Planning for Web-Service Composition

In this section we describe how the techniques provided by the planning as model checking framework can be applied to solve the problem of planning and monitoring of web-service composition.

The first step to model the domain, and to put ourselves in a position to synthesize a combined web service, is to model each of the protocols of the external partners as a planning domain. The states of the domain are used to codify the states of the protocol, the current values of the variables, and the contents of the input and output channels.

The modeling of the state of the protocol and of its variables is straightforward. The modeling of channels is more complex; each channel features a channel state (empty or full), and in case it is full, auxiliary variables are used to store the values carried by the channel. For instance, in the case of the shipper, the input channel REQUEST conveys the item size and the location as data, and is hence modeled with variables REQUEST.STATUS, REQUEST.SIZE, and REQUEST.LOC.

The only actions in the model correspond to channel read/write operations, since these are the only operations available to an external agent for controlling the evolution of the protocol. A receive action can only be executed on an output channel of the protocol which is full; its execution empties the channel and updates the protocol state. A send action, on the other hand, is possible only on an empty input channel of the protocol; if the input channel carries values, the action also specifies the actual values transmitted on the channel; when this action is executed, the channel is marked as full, and the transmitted values are stored in the appropriate channel variables.

The transitions in the model capture different aspects of the evolution of the system. From one side, they describe the update of the channel variables due to send/receive actions executed by the agent interacting with the protocol. From the other side, they model the internal evolution of the protocol. This internal evolution may correspond to the receive/send operations complementary to the send/receive actions executed externally. Also, it may correspond to updates in the internal variables, when assignment steps of the protocols are executed. Finally, no-op transitions are introduced to model the possibility of protocols being idle.

The observations of the protocol are limited to the status of the input and output channels and to the values contained in a channel when it is read.

This construction defines the ground domain for each of the external partners. Given one of these ground domains, we can perform the power-set construction to obtain the associated knowledge level domain, which is used as a run-time monitor to check whether the behaviors of the external partners conform to the protocol, and trigger an appropriate handling of failures. (It is easy to extend it with a time-out mechanism to also trap the undesired condition where a portion of some protocol is stuck.)

The goal of the planning task is to synthesize the process that interacts with the three external processes in order to provide the purchase & delivery service to the users. The planning domain consists of the combination of the three ground-level domains for the external partners, i.e. of their synchronous product. The business goal of P&S can be described as follows:

1. The service should try to reach the ideal situation where the user has confirmed his order, and the service has confirmed the associated (sub-)orders to the producer and shipper services. In this situation, the data associated to the orders have to be mutually consistent, e.g. the time for building and delivering a furniture shall be the sum of the time for building it, and that for delivering it.
2. Upon failure of the above goal, e.g., because the user refuses the offer, the service must reach a fall-back situation where every (sub-)order has been canceled. That is, there must be no chance that the service has committed to some (sub-)order before the user cancels his order.

This goal can be expressed by the following EaGLe formula, where the **TryReach** and **DoReach** clauses represents the above portions 1 and 2 of the requirement.

$$\textbf{TryReach} \ (user.succ \land producer.succ \land shipper.succ \land$$
$$user.d = add\_delay(producer.d, shipper.d) \land$$
$$user.c = add\_cost(producer.c, shipper.c))$$
$$\textbf{Fail DoReach}(user.fail \land producer.fail \land shipper.fail)$$

The planning domain is only partially observable by the executor of the process that we want to synthesize. Thus, solving the problem implies using dedicated algorithms for planning under partial observability with EaGLe goals, or, alternatively, planning for the fully observable associated knowledge level domain. We pursue this latter approach, so that we can reuse existing EaGLe planning algorithms under full observability. We proceed as follows. We generate the knowledge level domain by combining the three monitors defined previously. Similarly to what happens for the ground level domains, this computation consists of a synchronous product. Inside the knowledge level domain, we mark as *success* the belief states which contain only states satisfying the ideal condition that the services *tries* to reach (i.e. $user.succ \land producer.succ \land shipper.succ \land user.d = add\_delay(producer.d, shipper.d) \land user.c = add\_cost(producer.c, shipper.c) \land empty\_channels$), and as *failure* the belief states which contain only states satisfying the condition that the service *has* to reach in case the preferred objective fails (i.e. $user.fail \land producer.fail \land shipper.fail \land empty\_channels$). Finally, we plan on this domain with respect to the aforementioned EaGLe goal. Fact 1 guarantees that the approach outlined above for planning under partial observability with EaGLe goals is correct and complete.

5   Experimental Results

In order to test the effectiveness and the performance of the approach described above, we have conducted some experiments using the MBP planner. Some extensions to the planner have been necessary to the purpose. First, we have implemented the procedure for translating protocols similar to the ones described in Fig. 1 into the ground-level planning domains represented in the input language of MBP. Second, we have implemented a routine that performs the power-set domain construction, building the monitors corresponding to the three external protocols. MBP already provides algorithms for planning with EaGLe goals, which we have exploited in the last step of the planning algorithm.

We have run MBP on four variants of the case study considered in this paper, of different degrees of complexity. In the easiest case, CASE 1, we considered a reduced domain with only the user and the shipper, and with only one possible value for each type of objects in the domain (item, location, delay, cost, size). In CASE 2 we have considered all three protocols, but again only one possible value for each type of object. In CASE 3 we have considered the three protocols, with two objects for each type, but removing the parts of the shipper and producer protocols concerning the size of the product. In CASE 4, finally, is the complete protocol. We remark that CASE 1 and CASE 2 are used to test our algorithms, even if they are admittedly unrealistic, since the process knows, already before the interaction starts, the item that the user will ask and the cost will be charged to the user. In CASE 3 and CASE 4, a real composition of services is necessary to satisfy the goal.

In all four cases we have experimented also with a variant of the shipper protocol, which does not allow for action $nack$.

The experiments have been executed on an Intel Pentium 4, 1.8 GHz, 512 MB memory, running Linux 2.4.18. The results, in Fig. 2, report the following information:

- Generate: the time necessary to generate the MBP description of knowledge domains from their description of the three external protocols.
- BuildMonitor: the time necessary to parse and build the three internal MBP models corresponding to the monitors of the three external protocols; after the models have been built, it is possible to monitor in real-time the evolution of the protocols.
- BuildDomain: the time necessary to parse and build the internal MBP model of the combination of the three knowledge level domains.
- Planning: the time required to find a plan (or to check that no plan exists) starting from the planning domain built in the previous step.
- Result: whether a plan is found or not.

The last two results are reported both in the original domains and in the domains without "$nack$" being handled by the shipper.

The experiments show that the planning algorithm correctly detects that it is not possible to satisfy the goal if we remove the $nack$ action handling in the shipper, since we cannot unroll the contract with the shipper and to satisfy the recovery goal **DoReach** $failure$ in case of failure of the main goal. Moreover, MBP has been able to complete all the planning and monitor construction tasks with a very good performance, even for the most complex protocol descriptions. Indeed, in the worse case, MBP takes around two minutes to complete the task; as a reference, we asked an experienced designer to develop the protocol combination, and this took him more than one hour.

		With shipper nack				Without shipper nack	
	Generate	BuildMonitor	BuildDomain	Planning	Result	Planning	Result
CASE 1	1 sec.	1 sec.	2 sec.	1 sec.	YES	0 sec.	NO
CASE 2	1 sec.	1 sec.	6 sec.	8 sec.	YES	6 sec.	NO
CASE 3	8 sec.	15 sec.	32 sec.	23 sec.	YES	14 sec.	NO
CASE 4	12 sec.	65 sec.	63 sec.	118 sec.	YES	23 sec.	NO

Fig. 2. Results of the experiments.

6 Related Work and Conclusions

In this paper, we define, implement and experiment with a framework for planning the composition and monitoring of BPEL4WS web services. As far as we know, there is no previous attempt to automatically plan for the composition and monitoring of service oriented processes that takes into account nondeterminism, partial observability, and extended goals.

The problem of simulation, verification, and automated composition of web services has been tackled in the semantic web framework, mainly based on the DAML-S ontology for describing the capabilities of web services [2]. In [12], the authors propose an approach to the simulation, verification, and automated composition of web services based a translation of DAML-S to situation calculus and Petri Nets, so that it is possible to reason about, analyze, prove properties of, and automatically compose web services. However, as far as we understand, in this framework, the automated composition is limited to sequential composition of atomic services for reachability goals, and do not consider the general case of possible interleavings among processes and of extended business goals. Moreover, Petri Nets are a rather expressive framework, but algorithms that analyze them have less chances to scale up to complex problems compared to symbolic model checking techniques.

Different planning approaches have been proposed for composing web services, from HTNs [16] to regression planning based on extensions of PDDL [9], but how to deal with nondeterminism, partial observability, and how to generate conditional and iterative behaviors (in the style of BPEL4WS) in these frameworks are still open issues.

Other planning techniques have been applied to related but somehow orthogonal problems in the field of web services. The interactive composition of information gathering services has been tackled in [15] by using CSP techniques. In [11] an interleaved approach of planning and execution is used; planning technique are exploited to provide viable plans for the execution of the composition, given a specific query of the user; if these plans turn out to violate some user constraints at run time, then a re planning task is started. Finally, works in the field of Data and Computational Grids is more and more moving toward the problem of composing complex workflows by means of planning and scheduling techniques [6].

While the results in this paper are extremely promising, there is a wide space for improving. In particular, the computationally complex power-set construction of the knowledge level domain can be avoided altogether by providing algorithms for natively planning with extended goals under partial observability. This is a is a main goal in our research line; a preliminary result appears in [3], focusing on the CTL goal language.

The extension of this work to the EaGLe language, and the exploitation of symbolic representation techniques for this problem, is far from trivial.

Finally, we intend to extend our experimentation on a set of realistic case studies expressed using the BPEL4WS language; this will require an extension of MBP to natively handle the language.

References

[1]   Andrews, T.; Curbera, F.; Dolakia, H.; Goland, J.; Klein, J.; Leymann, F.; Liu, K.; Roller, D.; Smith, D.; Thatte, S.; Trickovic, I.; and Weeravarana, S. 2003. Business Process Execution Language for Web Services, Version 1.1.

[2]   Ankolekar, A. 2002. DAML-S: Web Service Description for the Semantic Web. In *Proc. of the 1st International Semantic Web Conference (ISWC 02)*.

[3]   Bertoli, P., and Pistore, M. 2004. Planning with Extended Goals and Partial Observability. In *Proc. of ICAPS'04*.

[4]   Bertoli, P.; Cimatti, A.; Roveri, M.; and Traverso, P. 2001. Planning in Nondeterministic Domains under Partial Observability via Symbolic Model Checking. In Nebel, B., ed., *Proc. of IJCAI 2001*.

[5]   Bertoli, P.; Cimatti, A.; Pistore, M.; and Traverso, P. 2003. A Framework for Planning with Extended Goals under Partial Observability. In *Proc. ICAPS'03*.

[6]   Blythe, J.; Deelman, E.; and Gil, Y. 2003. Planning for Workflow Construction and Maintenance on the Grid. In *Proc. of ICAPS'03 Workshop on Planning for Web Services*.

[7]   Bonet, B., and Geffner, H. 2000. Planning with Incomplete Information as Heuristic Search in Belief Space. In *Proc. AIPS 2000*.

[8]   Dal Lago, U.; Pistore, M.; and Traverso, P. 2002. Planning with a Language for Extended Goals. In *Proc. AAAI'02*.

[9]   McDermott, D. 1998. The Planning Domain Definition Language Manual. Technical Report 1165, Yale Computer Science University. CVC Report 98-003.

[10] Emerson, E. A. 1990. Temporal and modal logic. In van Leeuwen, J., ed., *Handbook of Theoretical Computer Science, Volume B: Formal Models and Semantics*. Elsevier.

[11] Lazovik A.; Aiello M.; and Papazoglou M. 2003. Planning and Monitoring the Execution of Web Service Requests. In *Proc. of ICSOC'03*.

[12] Narayanan, S., and McIlraith, S. 2002. Simulation, Verification and Automated Composition of Web Services. In *Proc. of WWW-11*.

[13] Pistore, M., and Traverso, P. 2001. Planning as Model Checking for Extended Goals in Non-deterministic Domains. In *Proc. IJCAI'01*.

[14] Pistore, M.; Bettin, R.; and Traverso, P. 2001. Symbolic Techniques for Planning with Extended Goals in Non-Deterministic Domains. In *Proc. ECP'01*.

[15] Thakkar, S.; Knoblock, C.; and Ambite, J. L. 2003. A View Integration Approach to Dynamic Composition of Web Services. In *Proc. of ICAPS'03 Workshop on Planning for Web Services*.

[16] Wu, D.; Parsia, B.; Sirin, E.; Hendler, J.; and Nau, D. 2003. Automating DAML-S Web Services Composition using SHOP2. In *Proc. of ISWC2003*.

A Logic of Inequalities

Nikolai G. Nikolov

CLBME-Bulgarian Academy of Sciences
Bl. 105, Acad. G. Bontchev Str., Sofia 1113, Bulgaria
shte@clbme.bas.bg

Abstract. A logical system is presented that tolerates partial or total contradictions or incomplete information. Every set of formulas in such a system has a model. Other theoretical properties were also investigated concerning the generalization of the notion of contradiction from classical logic. Applications to knowledge representation were considered and a way was proposed to represent generic and explicit information while providing monotonic inference.

1 Introduction

This section presents the motivation behind the logical system we are going to develop as concerns implication, negation, and deduction.

1.1 Implication

First-order logic (FOL) has the choice of defining implication in a number of equivalent ways: (1) by a truth table; (2) by other connectives, as in $\neg a \vee b$; or (3) by stating that $I(a \rightarrow b) = 1$ iff $I(a) \leq I(b)$, where I is a valuation function mapping formulas to the set of truth values $\{0,1\}$. The third way seems most intuitively appropriate with respect to deduction by Modus Ponens.

Consider a lattice L of logical values, and a valuation function mapping into it. While formulas like $\neg a$, $a \wedge b$, $a \vee b$ can be interpreted with values from L - as long as their constituents can - the case with $a \rightarrow b$ is different. It expresses the fact that $I(a) \leq I(b)$, and this, no matter what L is chosen, is always a crisp statement - it can be either true or false.

We therefore generalize FOL to a L-valued logic where, instead of representing the 'derivative' definitions of '$\rightarrow$' (1), (2), we use the 'original definition (3). It should be noted that when $L = \{0,1\}$, the definitions coincide.

We will use '$\leq$' instead of '$\rightarrow$' in order to emphasize the intended reading of the implication.

C. Bussler and D. Fensel (Eds.): AIMSA 2004, LNAI 3192, pp. 116–125, 2004.

1.2   Negation

The idea of having a separate valuation function for the *falsity* of a proposition has appeared occasionally in the AI and logic literature (cf. [3], p. 178). This allows for simultaneous valuation of a proposition as true and false, and this way contradictions can be represented.

Other approaches do with a single valuation function, but make it map into a special truth-value lattice which include values for truth, falsity, lack of knowledge and contradiction [4,9] or other values in-between these [8].

While FOL and fuzzy logic (FL) do not provide room for incomplete information or contradiction, intuitionistic fuzzy logic (IFL) [1] is designed especially for modeling uncertainty (incompleteness). In it, a proposition p is valuated independently by $\mu(p)$, degree of truth of p, and $v(p)$, degree of falsity. Both are real numbers from [0,1], with the condition that for all p, $\mu(p)+v(p)\leq 1$.

In the present work, we adopt the view that a proposition is interpreted by a pair of degrees - a truth and a falsity degree. While this is no new idea, in our system this feature is going to have significant modeling power, as will be shown in the second part of the paper.

Another reading of the two degrees is that they represent the established degrees of proof and refutation, respectively. Thus, the interpetation of the negation of a proposition should be the same pair of values as the proposition's interpretation but in reverse order - the degree of refutation of a proposition is the degree of proof of its negation.

Yet another function of the two degrees will be to represent the distinction between specific (explicit) and generic (default) knowledge, so that deduction is made possible even in the presence of conflict between such items of knowledge.

1.3   Information Persistence

The degrees of truth and falsity of a formula are meant to represent the truth or falsity established on the basis of the given knowledge. Thanks to the separate representation of the two, we can claim monotonicity in both degrees - given a formula, if a truth degree can be established on the basis of a set of formulas S, then at least the same truth degree should be established from any $S' \supseteq S$. The same holds of the degree of falsity. However, since the degree of falsity of a formula is the degree of truth of its negation, with the accumulation of counter-evidence a formula can be refuted to a greater extent. Although the latter is a feature of non-monotonic logics, we will see how our system exhibits this by virtue of being monotonic in both degrees.

2   Basic Formal Model

In this paragraph we propose a formal model of the principles discussed so far. We begin with a propositional inequality logic (PInL). A PInL setting P = <A,L> consists of a set of propositional symbols A and a lattice L with an involution operation $^{-}$. We will use L as the range of our valuation function - for example, we can take $L = [0,1]$ and $x^- = 1-x$.

We assume the notation 1 for $\vee L$ and 0 for $\wedge L$.

Definition 1. We will call *formulas* of P the following:

- for all $p \in A$, p is a formula.
- if p is a formula, then $\neg p$ is a formula.
- if p and q are formulas, then $p \wedge q$ and $p \vee q$ are formulas.

Note that we do not include any versions of implication in the definition, nor do we plan to define it by other connectives. We choose to do so because no implication should be valuated with elements of L, but rather with $\{0,1\}$, as we discussed in the previous section.

Definition 2. *Valuation* is a function defined on the set of formulas of P ranging to L^2. For all formulas p, q, if $V(p)=<V^+_p,V^-_p>$ and $V(q)=<V^+_q,V^-_q>$, then

1. $V(\neg p) = < V^-_p,V^+_p >$
2. $V(p \wedge q) = < V^+_p \wedge V^+_q, V^-_p \vee V^-_p>$
3. $V(p \vee q) = < V^+_p \vee V^+_q, V^-_p \wedge V^-_p>$

Now we turn to the important issue of deduction. In first-order logic, semantic consequence is usually defined through the notion of deductive closure of a set of formulas. Starting with some initial axioms (the initial set of formulas), its deductive closure is the smallest set that contains all formulas true whenever the initial ones are true.

The formulas in the initial set can be regarded as statements each claiming the truth of the corresponding formula. The generalization of this to the many-valued case (and it is done so in fuzzy logic) would be to have a set of statements (or two-valued formulas) claiming that a given formula is true to some degree.

To this end, we define a notion which combines the properties of a truth-claiming statement and an implication formula.

Definition 3. By *inequality* we will mean an expression of either of these kinds: $d_\varphi \geq \lambda$ or $d_\varphi \geq d_\psi$, where $\lambda \in L$ and φ, ψ are formulas and for a formula p, d_p is either V^+_p or V^-_p. An inequality will be called *atomic* if the participating formulas are atomic. Inequalities of the first kind will be called *ground*.

The following definition relates a set of inequalities to valuations.

Definition 4. We will say that a valuation V *satisfies* a set of inequalities W $(V \models W)$ iff all of the inequalities in W hold for the component functions of V.

Proposition 1. For all sets W of atomic inequalities, there exists a valuation V that satisfies W.

Proof. Clearly the valuation that assigns to all p, $V^+_p=1$ and $V^-_p=1$, satisfies W, since ground inequalities are satisfied by 1's, and non-ground inequalities reduce to $1 \leq 1$.

Of course, the trivial valuation is far from useful for needs such as deduction. Therefore, we would need to formalize the intuitive notion of valuation that suits best a given set of inequalities.

The reason the trivial valuation is not useful is that it is, in a sense, maximal - it assigns the maximum possible value to each degree. We are interested in whether there is a minimal - and thus most useful - valuation for a given set of inequalities.

Definition 5. We will define a partial order between valuations as follows: $V_1 \leq V_2$ iff for all p, $V^+_{1(p)} \leq V^+_{2(p)}$ and $V^-_{1(p)} \leq V^-_{2(p)}$ where $V_{i(p)} = <V^+_{i(p)}, V^-_{i(p)}>$, $i=\{1,2\}$.

Definition 6. A valuation V will be called *minimal* for a set of inequalities W if $V \models W$ and there exists no other valuation $V' \models W$ such that $V' \geq V$.

Proposition 2. For every set of atomic inequalities W, there exists a unique minimal valuation V^*_W.

We postpone the proof of this proposition until we introduce several necessary notions.

Definition 7. A set of inequalities W will be called *transitively ≤-closed* if for all $d_1 \leq d_2$, $d_2 \leq d_3 \in W$, $d_1 \leq d_3 \in W$. For every set of inequalities W we construct its ≤ *closure* $W^\sim$ to be the intersection of all transitively ≤-closed sets that contain W; that intersection is also transitively ≤-closed.

Proof of Proposition 2. We will construct a valuation that is minimal for $W^\sim$, and then prove it to be what is needed. For all formulas φ, let

$$V^*(\varphi) = < \bigvee_{(V^+_\varphi \geq \lambda) \in W^\sim, \lambda \in L} \lambda, \quad \bigvee_{(V^+_\varphi \geq \lambda) \in W^\sim, \lambda \in L} \lambda >$$

Satisfaction. Clearly V^* satisfies all ground inequalities of $W^\sim$ and therefore of W. Consider an arbitrary non-ground inequality $d_1 \geq d_2 \subset W^\sim$. For all ground inequalities $(d_2 \geq \lambda) \in W^\sim$ there is a ground inequality $(d_1 \geq \lambda) \in W^\sim$ by the transitivity of $W^\sim$. Therefore,

$$\bigvee_{(d_2 \geq \lambda) \in W^\sim, \lambda \in L} \lambda \quad \leq \quad \bigvee_{(d_1 \geq \lambda) \in W^\sim, \lambda \in L} \lambda,$$

so $V^*(d_1) \geq V^*(d_2)$.

Minimality and uniqueness. Assume $V' < V^*$, $V' \models W$. Since every valuation satisfying W also satisfies $W^\sim$ by the transitivity of '≤' in L), and by definition V^* is the minimal valuation satisfying $W^\sim$, then $V^* \leq V'$.

An important property of InL is that, given a valuation V, we can introduce *measure of contradiction*, a number which will gradually vary from 0 (a given set of formulas is consistent in the classical sense) to 1 (the set of formulas is inconsistent in the classical sense), the in-between values showing the presence of partial evidence both for and against a formula. We can also have a *measure of uncertainty*, a number which will gradually vary from 0 (V is certain both about a formula and its negation) to 1 (there is no evidence neither about the formula nor about its negation), the in-between values showing again the presence of partial evidence. Moreover, it turns out that these two notions can be formalized by a single expression.

Assume (until the end of this section) that we have a norm $|.|$ on the elements of L: $L \rightarrow [0,1]$.

Definition 8. The *information content* $\iota_{V(p)}$ of a formula p according to a valuation V is the value $|V^+(p)| + |V^-(p)|$. The *minimal information content* of a set of formulas S according to a valuation V will be $\inf_{p \in S} \iota_{V(p)}$; the *maximal information content* will be $\sup_{p \in S} \iota_{V(p)}$, respectively.

It must be noted that $\iota_{V(p)}$ is a generalization of the notion of *degree of uncertainty* from intuitionistic fuzzy logic for the case $L=[0,1]$ and $V^+(p) + V^-(p) \leq 1$ (actually, its complement to 1).

Proposition 3. A set of formulas is contradictory (in the classical sense) iff its maximum information content according to the valuation V^* is greater than 1.

The notion of information content leads to another noteworthy property of propositional InL - a result we can call Locality theorem. Recall that the Compactness theorem for classical propositional logic states that a set of formulas S is consistent iff every finite subset of S is consistent. In propositional InL it is senseless to speak about consistent sets of formulas, as every set of formulas has a model. However, we can generalize the notion of consistency using the concept of information content. We have the notion of maximum information content of a set of formulas, which is just the meet of the information contents of all formulas in it. Now, whatever the maximum value, there must be a formula whose information content is arbitrarily close to it.

Proposition 4. (Locality theorem). For any set of formulas S and a real number r, if $\iota_{max}(S) > r$ then there exists a formula $\varphi \in S$ such that $\iota(\varphi) \geq r$.

It is easily seen that if we restrict L to $\{0,1\}$, the above result reduces to the Compactness theorem. In InL, we have the stronger claim that the property of being contradictory is a local one - namely, that there always is at least one formula that represents the level of contradiction or information incompleteness of the whole set.

For the rest of this section we will outline a version of predicate inequality logic (InPL). This simple version will be needed solely for presenting a knowledge representation approach (based on inequality logic) in the next section. We show how this approach motivates a specific extension of predicate inequality logic which will be developed in the subsequent section.

An InPL language $K = <P, C, V, r, L>$ consists of a set of predicate symbols P, constant symbols C, variable symbols V, arity function r: $P \rightarrow N$, and a lattice L with an involution operation $^-$. Again, we denote $\vee L$ by 1 and $\wedge L$ by 0.

Definition 9. By a *simple term* we will mean a constant symbol or a variable symbol.

Definition 10. We will call *formulas* of K the following:

- if $\lambda \in L$, λ is a formula.
- for all $p \in P$, $p(t_1,\ldots,t_{r(p)})$ is a formula, where $t_1,\ldots,t_{r(p)}$ are simple terms.
- if φ and ψ are formulas, then $\neg\varphi$, $\varphi\wedge\psi$ and $\varphi\vee\psi$ are formulas.

The set of formulas of K will be denoted by $\Phi(K)$.

The notion of statement is similar to that in the propositional case but with the additional option for quantifiers.

Definition 11. We will call a *quantifier block* any expression of the kind $Q_1 \ldots Q_n$, where Q_i is $\forall x$ or $\exists x$ for some variable symbol x.

Definition 12. Where φ and ψ are formulas of K and $\lambda \in L$, we will call *statements* of K the following: $\lambda \leq \varphi$, $\varphi \leq \lambda$, $\varphi \leq \psi$, $Q\lambda \leq \varphi$, $Q\varphi \leq \lambda$, $Q\varphi \leq \psi$ (in the last three statements Q is a quantifier block).

Definition 13. *Algebraic system* (cf. [11]) for K is a couple $<A,I>$ where A is a set and I is a function whose domain is $\Phi(K) \cup C \cup X$. If c is a constant or variable, then $I(c) \in A$; for a formula φ, $I(\varphi) = <I^+(\varphi), I^-(\varphi)>$ so that

- $I(\neg\varphi) = <\Gamma^-(\varphi), \Gamma^+(\varphi)>$
- $I(\varphi\wedge\psi) = <\Gamma^+(\varphi) \wedge \Gamma^+(\psi), \Gamma^-(\varphi) \vee \Gamma^-(\psi)>$
- $I(\varphi\vee\varphi) = <\Gamma^+(\varphi)\vee \Gamma^+(\psi), \Gamma^-(\varphi) \wedge \Gamma^-(\psi)>$

Definition 14. By *inequality* we will mean an expression of any of the following two kinds: $Qd_\varphi \geq \lambda$ or $Qd_\varphi \geq d_\psi$, where $\lambda \in L$ and φ, ψ are formulas, and Q is a quantifier block; also, for each p, d_p can be either V^+_p or V^-_p. We will call an inequality *atomic,* if only atomic formulas participate in it. Inequalities of the first kind will be called *ground*. We will call an inequality *closed* if all of its variables are quantified.

If not explicitly mentioned, below we will use closed inequalities.

The following definition relates sets of inequalities to algebraic systems.

Definition 15. We will say that an algebraic system M = <A,I> is a *model* of a set of inequalities W (M ⊨ W) iff all inequalities in W hold for the component functions of I, and the range of quantified variables is A.

Proposition 5. For all sets W of atomic inequalities there exists an algebraic system M that satisfies W.

Proof. The trivial interpretation assigning 1 to all formulas is a model of all sets of atomic inequalities (similarly to the case with PInL).

Definition 16. Let for two algebraic systems, M_1=<A_1,I_1> $\leq M_2$=<A_2,I_2> iff for any variable-free formula p, $\Gamma^+_1(p) \leq \Gamma^+_2(p)$ and $\Gamma^-_1(p) \leq \Gamma^-_2(p)$ where $I_i(p) - <\Gamma^+_i(p),$ $\Gamma^-_i(p)>$, i={1,2}.

Definition 17. We will call an algebraic system M *minimal* for a set of inequalities W, if M ⊨ W and for no other set of inequalities V' ⊨ W, V' ≤ V.

The problem of existence of a minimal algebraic system for a fixed object universe is easily solved and reduces to the corresponding propositional InL theorem.

Proposition 6. For every set of atomic inequalities W and object set A there exists a unique (up to renaming of the constants) minimal algebraic system $M^*_W = <A,I^*_W>$.

Proof outline. We construct a set of inequalities W_0 as follows:

- we replace every formula $\forall x \; \varphi$ with a set of formulas $\varphi/x=a_i$ (where x is replaced by an element of A)
- we replace every formula $\exists x \; \varphi$ with a formula $\varphi/x=c_i$ (where X is replaced by a new c_i).

The set W_0 can be treated as a set of propositional inequalities. By Theorem 2 there exists a unique minimal valuation V^*_W that satisfies it. We assign $I^*_W=V^*_W$ over the corresponding formulas.

3   Knowledge Representation by Inequality Logic

Let us consider an example:
   The age of a human being is between 0 and 130 years.
   C is a person.
   D's age is 135 years.
   We would expect the following answers from a system equipped with this knowledge:
   Problem 1. What is the age of C? Answer: 0..130 years
   Problem 2. Is D a human being? Answer: No.

Other problems with the representation of the above knowledge are:

Problem 3. Representation of unsharp boundaries (in the above example a person is allowed to be 130 but not 131 years old).

Problem 4. The rule stating the possible age to be 0..130 years should not prevent the system to use explicit information about a person who is 135 (i. e. default knowledge should be overridden if necessary).

First-order logic presents a solution only to the second of the above problems. Various aspects of the problems are treated by fuzzy, intuitionistic fuzzy, and default logics [12]. In the present section we will propose a systematic way to address these problems using inequality predicate logic.

We will first propose a way to represent explicit and generic knowledge in InL.

We interpret I^+ or I^- as degree of proof or refutation, respectively. Thus, the minimal interpretation of any formula for which no information is available is <0,0> - there are no evidence either for or against it. The degree of non-plausibility can be used to represent inherited (generic) knowledge - to state that a person's age is from 0 to 130 years (assuming this is the human lifespan), we may use the InPL inequality

$$man(x) \leq \neg age(x,(130,\infty))$$

(in this example, think of the set of truth values as just {'false','true'}). So, if x is a person, it is not plausible that his age be above 130 years. Conversely, we will use the degree of proof to represent specific, explicitly stated knowledge - if a person a is reported to be y years old, then $\mathrm{I}^+(age(a,y))$ is true. The two types of knowledge can co-exist without conflicts - inherited knowledge, represented throught the degree of non-plausibility of the reverse statement, serves as a default rule. Facts about a 135 years old person (or the biblical Methusaleh) will not block the work of a InPL-based system, but such a system will note the elevated non-plausibility of such a case.

Here is an example of how InPL inferences can be drawn using the degree of non-plausibility:

$$\mathrm{I}^+(man(x)) \leq \mathrm{I}^+(\neg age(x,(-\infty,0)))$$
$$\mathrm{I}^+(man(x)) \leq \mathrm{I}^-(age(x,(-\infty,0)))$$

If this rule is used to make deduction by Modus Ponens, the degree of non-plausibility of $age(x,(-\infty,0))$ and $age(x,(130,-\infty))$ increases to $\mathrm{I}^+(man(x))$.

Conversely, here is how to use the same rule to make deduction by Modus Tollens:

$$\mathrm{I}^-(\neg age(x,(-\infty,0))) \leq \mathrm{I}^-(man(x))$$
$$\mathrm{I}^+(age(x,(-\infty,0))) \leq \mathrm{I}^-(man(x))$$

and the degree of non-plausibility of man(x) increases to

$$\max \{ \mathrm{I}^+(age(x,(-\infty,0))), \mathrm{I}^+(age(x,(130,\infty))) \}.$$

Let us now consider, for the sake of explanation, a different way of representing the intervals - by adding a fact for each individual point value in each interval. Of course, these new facts will be uncountable, so such a representation is only of theoretical importance:

$$man(x) \leq \neg age(x,131)$$
$$man(x) \leq \neg age(x,132)$$

$$\dots$$

However this clarifies the inference mechanism better: during a Modus Tollens deduction, the exact rule is fired that corresponds to the explicitly stated knowledge of age of x.

We demonstrated how InPL can solve P2 (the two-way inference with InPL statements) and P4 (work with the degrees of proof and non-plausibility). We will now consider an approach to P3.

Since the set of truth values in InPL can be any lattice L, we can specify different degrees of non-plausibility of age(x,...) depending on the constant. Years in the middle of the 0..130 interval will increase the degree of non-plausibility less; the maximum increase, 1, will be reached outside of the interval, while in the ends the degree of non-plausibility will take intermediate values. Such rules are naturally represented by InPL inequalities:

$$I^+(man(x) \wedge \lambda_0) \le I^+(\neg age(x,0))$$
$$I^+(man(x) \wedge \lambda_{50}) \le I^+(\neg age(x,50))$$
$$I^+(man(x) \wedge \lambda_{100}) \le I^+(\neg age(x,100))$$
$$I^+(man(x) \wedge \lambda_{150}) \le I^+(\neg age(x,150))$$

where for example $\lambda_0 = 1$, $\lambda_{50} = 0.05$, $\lambda_{100} = 0.7$, $\lambda_{150} = 1$ (the degree of non-plausibility for a person to be at that age). The above rules look unusual by syntax, but they convey the following information: if x is a man then it is impossible for him to be i years old, and this statement has a degree of plausibility λ_i.

Rules for contraposition deduction by Modus Tollens can also be formulated.

Thus, representation of information of this kind now includes another possibility for a more flexible inference:

$1 \le age(d,135)$. (an InPL statement claiming age(d,135) with a degree of proof 1).
?- man(d).   Proof: 0; Non-plausibility: 1
$1 \le age(h,110)$.
?- man(h).   Proof: 0; Non-plausibility: 0.8

4 Inequality Logic Compared to Other Approaches

An interesting parallel between InL and **possibilistic logic** (PL). is that inequality valuation can be regarded as a necessity measure from PL. However, the essential properties of these two logics differ in the following:

- inequality logic does not rely on first-order interpretations. In contrast, PL uses necessity/possibility measure as a means for describing the possibility of first-order interpretations, which are then subject to preference.
- PL uses first-order inference (and resolution)
- PL does not distinguish explicitly between generic and factual knowledge. This is due to the representation of both types of knowledge through first-order formulas. In contrast, with CL generic/factual items of knowledge are naturally represented by the degrees of plausibility and non-plausibility.

InL is clearly a case of **multivalued logic**, and in particular, it can be a version of **fuzzy logic**. However, the systematic treatment of implication seems to solve issues of implication definition and Modus Ponens inference present in some of these logic [1].

InL does not have a dedicated mechanism for defaults as is present in **Default reasoning** [12]. However, an important feature of InL is that it is bi-monotonic (monotonic in both truth degrees) and therefore inference is always monotonic.

When this work was nearly finished, the author learned about a formalism called **evidence logic** (EL) [7][1]. Evidence logic deals with items of proof evidence and refutatory evidence of assertions, each to a certain (discrete) degree. While InL has a similar feature, it seems that it differs from EL in all other crucial aspects, namely the motivation for treating implication as order-relation even in the multi-valued case, and therefore introducing the notion of a statement to generalize both the concepts of an implication formula and the concept of a piece of evidence. Consequently, other important notions (sets of statements as generalizations of the sets of formulas from classical logic, satisfiability of a set of statements, measure of contradiction) are specific to inequality logic.

The same arguments hold when InL is compared to **intuitionistic fuzzy logic** [1] and other independently arised similar systems (**vague sets theory**, **neutrosophic logic** [13] - a difference of the latter from intuitionistic fuzzy logic is the lack of restriction on the sum truth + falsity + indeterminacy) that also estimate separately the truth and the falsity of a proposition. Moreover, it is often pointed out as a difficulty that models based on these logics should have a source of the actual degrees of truth and falsity for each fact. In InL, a solution to this would be the interpretation of the degree of non-plausibility as a means to represent generic knowledge, as discussed in the previous section - in this case, the necessary values would come from known possibilistic distributions of the corresponding variable (e.g. human lifespan in our example).

It is interesting to compare InL with **description logic with symbolic number restrictions** (DL-SNR, [2]) which, although quite different theoretically, addresses problems of numeric knowledge representation discussed here. DL-SNR augments the classic DL with means to add requirements on the numbers (ranges) of the described objects. For example, lifespan can be represented as a restriction on the possible values of the objects' age. Far from having studied thoroughly the specifics of our approach compared to DL-SNR (a much more developed theory), we envisage two possible directions where InL may have some advantage. First, InL is tolerant to partial or total contradictions, including contradictory numerical data: thus, it can represent knowledge about a 969-year old person while still maintaining the rule that human lifespan is between 0 and 130 years (at the expense of having only a local contradiction). Second, it can represent this gradually, not falling into total contradiction but distinguishing between the degrees of contradiction of reported facts about a 131- and a thousand-years-old human being.

5   Conclusion and Future Work

In this paper we have presented a logical system that generalizes the treatment of implication as order relation. The system is also featured by supporting independent

---

[1] The full text of [7] is not available to the author presently

estimations of the truth and the falsity of a proposition. Interesting theoretical properties were investigated concerning satisfiability of a set of formulas and the generalization of the notion of contradiction from classical logic. Applications to knowledge representation were considered and a way was proposed to represent generic and explicit information that can be in partial or total contradiction or under-specified. Monotonicity of inference is maintained in each degree (of proof and non-plausibility).

In a subsequent research, the author plans to focus on representation of distributed numerical data as InL terms, proof theory and complexity issues.

Acknowledgment. This work was supported by the National Scientific Fund of Bulgaria under contract I-1303/2003.

References

1. Atanassov, K., Intuitionistic Fuzzy Sets, Springer-Verlag, 1999.
2. Baader, F., Sattler, U., Description Logics with Symbolic Number Restrictions, Proceedings of the 12th European Conference on Artificial Intelligence, 1996, Budapest, Hungary.
3. Barwise, J., Moss, L. S., Vicious Circles: On the Mathematics of Non-Wellfounded Phenomena, CSLI Lecture Notes, CSLI Publications, Stanford University, 1996.
4. Belnap, N., A useful four-valued logic, in: Modern Uses of Multiple-Valued Logic, G. Epstein and J. M. Dunn, Eds., Reidel Publishing Company, 1977, pp. 7-37.
5. Cercone, N., The ECO Family, in: Semantic Networks, Fritz Lehmann, Ed., 1993.
6. Dubois, D., Lang, J., Prade, H., Possibilistic Logic, in D. M. Gabbay et al., Eds., Handbook of Logic in Artificial Intelligence and Logic Programming, Vol. 3, 439-513, Oxford University Press, 1994.
7. Faust, D., The Concept of Evidence, Int. Journal of Intelligent Systems, 15 (2000), 477-493.
8. Fortemps, P., Slowinski, R.,, A graded quadrivalent logic for ordinal preference modelling: Loyola-like approach, Fuzzy Optimization and Decision Making 1 (2002), 93-111.
9. Ginsberg, M., Bilattices and Modal Operators, Journal of Logic and Computation, 1(1):41-69, July 1990.
10. Iwanska, L., Shapiro, S., Eds., Language for Knowledge and Knowledge for language, AAAI Press/The MIT Press, 2000.
11. Rasiowa, H., Sikorski, R., The mathematics of metamathematics, Polish Academic Publisher, 1963.
12. Reiter, R. A logic for default reasoning, Artificial Intelligence, 13(1,2):81-132, 1980
13. Smarandache, F., Neutrosophy, American Research Press, 1998.
14. Zadeh, L., A new direction in AI: Towards a computational theory of perceptions, AI magazine, vol. 22, pp. 73-84, 2001.

Exploiting the Constrainedness in Constraint Satisfaction Problems

Miguel A. Salido[1] and Federico Barber[2]

[1] Dpto. Ciencias de la Computación e Inteligencia Artificial, Universidad de Alicante
Campus de San Vicente, Ap. de Correos: 99, E-03080, Alicante, Spain
msalido@dsic.upv.es
[2] Dpto. Sistemas Informáticos y Computación, Universidad Politécnica de Valencia
Camino de Vera s/n, 46071, Valencia, Spain
fbarber@dsic.upv.es

Abstract. Nowadays, many real problem in Artificial Intelligence can be modeled as constraint satisfaction problems (CSPs). A general rule in constraint satisfaction is to tackle the hardest part of a search problem first. In this paper, we introduce a parameter (τ) that measures the constrainedness of a search problem. This parameter represents the probability of the problem being feasible. A value of $\tau = 0$ corresponds to an over-constrained problem and no states are expected to be solutions. A value of $\tau = 1$ corresponds to an under-constrained problem which every state is a solution. This parameter can also be used in a heuristic to guide search. To achieve this parameter, a sample in finite population is carried out to compute the tightnesses of each constraint. We take advantage of this tightnesses to classify the constraints from the tightest constraint to the loosest constraint. This heuristic may accelerate the search due to inconsistencies can be found earlier and the number of constraint checks can significantly be reduced.

Keywords: Constraint Satisfaction Problems, complexity, heuristic search.

1 Introduction

Many real problems in Artificial Intelligence (AI) as well as in other areas of computer science and engineering can be efficiently modeled as Constraint Satisfaction Problems (CSPs) and solved using constraint programming techniques. Some examples of such problems include: spatial and temporal planning, qualitative and symbolic reasoning, diagnosis, decision support, scheduling, hardware design and verification, real-time systems and robot planning.

These problems may be soluble or insoluble, they may be hard or easy. How to solve these problems have been the subject of intensive study in recent years.

Some works are focused on the constrainedness of search. Heuristics of making a choice that minimises the constrainedness can reduce search [3].The constrainedness "knife-edge" that measures the constrainedness of a problem during search [10].

C. Bussler and D. Fensel (Eds.): AIMSA 2004, LNAI 3192, pp. 126–136, 2004.

Most of the work are focused on general methods for solving CSPs. They include backtracking-based search algorithms. While the worst-case complexity of backtrack search is exponential, several heuristics to reduce its average-case complexity have been proposed in the literature [2]. For instance, some algorithms incorporate features such as variable ordering which have a substantially better performance than a simpler algorithm without this feature [5].

Many works have investigated various ways of improving the backtracking-based search algorithms. To avoid *thrashing* [6] in backtracking, *consistency* techniques, such as *arc-consistency* and *k-consistency*, have been developed by many researchers. Other ways of increasing the efficiency of backtracking include the use of *search order* for variables and values. Thus, some heuristics based on *variable ordering* and *value ordering* [7] have been developed, due to the additivity of the variables and values. However, constraints are also considered to be *additive*, that is, the order of imposition of constraints does not matter; all that matters is that the conjunction of constraints be satisfied [1]. In spite of the additivity of constraints, only some works have be done on constraint ordering heuristic mainly for arc-consistency algorithms [9,4].

Here, we introduce a parameter that measures the "constrainedness" of the problem. This parameter called τ represents the probability of the problem being feasible and identify the tightnesses of constraints. This parameter can also be applied in a heuristic to guide search. To achieve this parameter, we compute the tightnesses of each constraint. Using this tightnesses, we have developed a heuristic to accelerate the search. This heuristic performs a constraint ordering and can easily be applied to any backtracking-based search algorithm. It classifies the constraints by means of the tightnesses, so that the tightest constraints are studied first. This is based on the principle that, in goods ordering, domain values are removed as quickly as possible. This idea was first stated by Waltz [11] *"The base heuristic for speeding up the program is to eliminate as many possibilities as early as possible"* (p. 60).

An appropriate ordering is straightforward if the constrainedness is known in advance. However in the general case, an good classification is suitable to tackle the hardest part of the search problem first.

In the following section, we formally define a CSP and summarize some ordering heuristics and an example of soluble and insoluble problem. In section 3, we define a well-known definition of constrainedness of search problems. A new parameter to measure the constrainedness of a problem is developed in section 4. In section 5, we present our constraint ordering heuristic. Section 6 summarizes the conclusions and future work.

2   Definitions and Algorithms

In this section, we review some basic definitions as well as basic heuristics for CSPs.

Briefly, a constraint satisfaction problem (CSP) consists of:

- a set of variables $V = \{v_1, v_2, ..., v_n\}$
- each variable $v_i \in V$ has a set D_{v_i} of possible values (its domain)
- a finite collection of constraints $C = \{c_1, c_2, ..., c_k\}$ restricting the values that the variables can simultaneously take.

A solution to a CSP is an assignment of values to all the variables so that all constraints are satisfied.

2.1   Constraint Ordering Algorithms

The experiments and analyses by several researchers have shown that the ordering in which variables and values are assigned during the search may have substantial impact on the complexity of the search space explored. In spite of the additivity of constraints, only some works have be done on constraint ordering. Heuristics of making a choice that minimises the constrainedness of the resulting subproblem can reduce search over standards heuristics [3].

Wallace and Freuder initiated a systematic study to identify factors that determine the efficiency of constraint propagation that achieve arc-consistency [9]. Gent et al. proposed a new constraint ordering heuristic in AC3, where the set of choices is composed by the arcs in the current set maintained by AC3 [4]. They considered the remaining subproblem to have the same set of variables as the original problem, but with only those arcs still remaining in the set. Walsh studied the constrainedness "knife-edge" in which he measured the constrainedness of a problem during search in several different domains [10]. He observed a constrainedness "knife-edge" in which critically constrained problems tend to remain critically constrained. This knife-edge is predicted by a theoretical lower-bound calculation.

Many of these algorithms focus their approximate theories on just two factors: the size of the problems and the expected number of solutions. However, this last factor is not easy to estimate.

2.2   Solubility and Insolubility

Will a problem be soluble or insoluble? Will it be hard or easy to solve? How can we develop heuristics for new problem domains? All these questions have been studied by researchers in the last decades in a large number of problems domains. Consider the example presented in [3] of colouring a graph with a fixed number of colours so that neighboring nodes have different colours. If the nodes in the graph are loosely connected, then problems tend to be soluble and it is usually easy to obtain one of the many solutions. If nodes are highly connected, then problems tend to be insoluble and it is not easy to find a solution. At intermediate levels of connectivity, problems can be hard to solve since they are neither obviously soluble nor insoluble.

Figure 1 shows colouring graphs with four nodes using three colours: red, blue and green. Nodes connected by an edge must have different colours. The connectivity of a node is the number of edges connected to the node. The connectivity of a graph is the average connectivity of its nodes. (A) is an under-constrained and soluble problem due to 18 states are solutions. (B) is a problem which is just soluble and 6 states are solutions but there is only an unique solution up to symmetry. (C) is an over-constrained and insoluble problem consisting of a clique of four nodes.

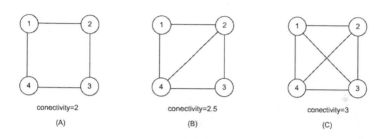

conectivity=2   conectivity=2.5   conectivity=3

(A)   (B)   (C)

Fig. 1. Colouring Graph with four nodes using three colours [3].

We can use connectivity to develop a simple but effective heuristic for graph colouring that colours the most constrained nodes first. Consider colouring the nodes in Figure 1B without such a heuristic, using instead their numerical order. We might colour node 1 red, then node 2 green, and node 3 blue. We would then be unable to colour node 4 without giving it the same colour as one of its neighbors. Instead, suppose we seek to colour the most constrained nodes first. Both informally, the constrainedness of the graph is directly related to its connectivity. This then suggest the heuristic of colouring the nodes in decreasing order of their connectivity. As node 2 and 4 have the highest connectivity, they are coloured first. If we colour node 2 red and node 4 green, then nodes 1 and 3 can be coloured blue. Ordering the nodes by their connectivity focuses on the hardest part of the problem, leaving the less constrained and easier parts till last.

This example shows that some parts of the problem are hardest than others and a variable ordering may accelerate the search. However many real problems maintains thousand of variables and constraints and remains difficult to identify which variables and constraints are tightest. So a sample in finite populations may be useful to identify the constrainedness of the problem and perform a constraint ordering to take advantage of the problem topology. It may be useful to carry out domain filtering over the tightest constraints and even analyse the loosest constraints because many of them may be redundant and therefore removed.

3   Constrainedness κ

Given a new search problem, it is appropriate to identify parameters to measure the constrainedness of the problem and to develop heuristics for finding a solution more efficiently.

In [3], Gent et al. present a parameter that measures the constrainedness of an ensemble of combinatorial problems. They assume that each problem in an ensemble has a state space S with $|S|$ elements and a number, Sol of these states are solutions. Any point in the state space can be represented by a N-bit binary vector where $N = log_2(|S|)$. Let $\langle Sol \rangle$ be the expected number of solutions averaged over the ensemble. They defined constrainedness, κ, of an ensemble by,

$$\kappa =_{def} 1 - \frac{log_2(\langle Sol \rangle)}{N} \tag{1}$$

Gent et al. proposed a straightforward way to compute $\langle Sol \rangle$ and therefore κ [3]. Consider constraint satisfaction problems, each variable $v \in V$, has a domain of values D_v of size d_v. Each constraint $c_i \in C$ of arity a restricts a tuple of variables $\langle v_1, ..., v_a \rangle$, and rules out some proportion $\acute{p}_{c_i}$ of possible values from the cartesian product $D_{v_1} \times ... \times D_{v_a}$. Without loss of generality we can define the tightnesses of a constraint as $\acute{p}_c$ or its complementary $1 - \acute{p}_c$. Problems may have variables with many different domain sizes, and constraints of different arities and tightnesses.

The state space has size $\prod_{v \in V} d_v$. Each constraint $c_i \in C$ rules out a proportion $\acute{p}_{c_i}$ of these states, so the number of solution is

$$\langle Sol \rangle = (\prod_{v \in V} d_v) \times (\prod_{c_i \in C} (1 - \acute{p}_{c_i})) \tag{2}$$

Substituting this into (1) gives

$$\kappa = \frac{- \sum_{c_i \in C} log_2(1 - \acute{p}_{c_i})}{\sum_{v \in V} log_2(d_v)} \tag{3}$$

κ lies in the range $[0, \infty)$. A value of $\kappa = 0$ corresponds to an under-constrained problem. A value of $\kappa = \infty$ corresponds to an over-constrained problem.

However, this parameter defines the constrainedness of constraint satisfaction problems in general, but not of an individual problem.

As we can observe, constrainedness in constraint satisfaction problem is closely related to probability. Unfortunately, it is difficult to compute this probability directly [3], mainly in a particular problem.

So, the main contribution of this papers focuses on computing this probability (or its complementary) for each constraint of the problem. These probabilities are computed by a sampling from finite populations. This sampling may be a simple random or systematic sampling, where there is a population, and a sample is chosen to represent this population. That is, the population is composed of the states lying within the convex hull of all initial states generated by means of the Cartesian product of variable domain bounds. The sample is composed by a set of random and well distributed states in order to represent the entire population. In case of continuous variables, they are discretized in base on an appropriate granularity. Each constraint is checked with the states of the sample and this gives us the probability p_{c_i} that constraint c_i satisfies the problem. Thus, we assume p_{c_i} the tightnesses of the constraint ($p_{c_i} \equiv 1 - \acute{p}_{c_i}$). In this way, we can obtain the parameter κ or the parameter τ developed in the following section.

4   Computing the Constrainedness τ

In this section, we introduce a parameter called τ that measures the constrainedness of the problem. This parameter represents the probability of the problem being feasible. This parameter lies in the range $[0, 1]$. A value of $\tau = 0$ corresponds to an over-constrained and no states are expected to be a solution ($\langle Sol \rangle = 0$). A value of $\tau = 1$ corresponds to an under-constrained and every state is expected to be a solution ($\langle Sol \rangle = \prod_{v \in V} d_v$). This parameter can also be used in a heuristic to guide search. To this end, we take advantage of the tightnesses of each constraint to classifying them from the tightest constraint to the loosest constraint. Thus, a search algorithm can tackle the hardest part of the problem first.

To compute τ a sample from a finite population is performed, where there is a population (states), and a sample is chosen to represent this population. The sample is composed by $s(n)$ random and well distributed states where s is a polynomial function.

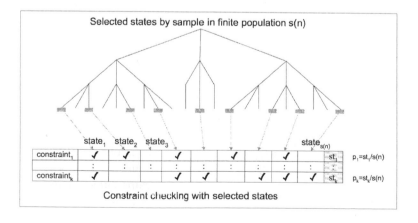

Fig. 2. From non-ordered constraint to ordered constraint

As in statistic, the user selects the size of the sample $s(n)$. We study how many states $st_i : st_i \leq s(n)$ satisfy each constraint c_i (see Figure 2). Thus, each constraint c_i is labeled with p_{c_i}: $c_i(p_{c_i})$, where $p_{c_i} = st_i/s(n)$ represents the proportion of possible states, that is, the tightnesses of the constraint.

In this way, given the set of probabilities $\{p_{c_1}, ..., p_{c_k}\}$, the number of solutions can be computed as:

$$\langle Sol \rangle := (\prod_{v \in V} d_v) \times (\prod_{c_i \in C} (p_{c_i})) \qquad (4)$$

This equation is equivalent to the obtained in [3]. However, our definition of constrainedness is given by the following equation:

$$\tau := \prod_{c_i \in C} (p_{c_i}) \qquad (5)$$

τ is a parameter that measures the probability that a randomly selected state is a solution, that is, the probability this state satisfies the first constraint (p_{c_1}), the second constraint (p_{c_2}) and so forth, the last constraint (p_{c_k}). In this way, we guarantee that a random state satisfies all constraints. This parameter lies in the range $[0, 1]$ that represent the constrainedness of the problem.

We present the pseudo-code of computing τ.

Computing the constrainedness τ

Inputs: A set of n variables, $v_1, ..., v_n$;
For each v_i, a set D_i of possible values (the domain)
A set of constraints, $c_1, ..., c_k$.
Outputs: The constrainedness τ.
1.- From the entire number of states generated by the Cartesian product of the variable domain bounds, a well distributed sample with $s(n)$ states is selected.
2.- With the selected sample of states $s(n)$, we compute how many states $st_i : st_i \leq s(n)$ satisfy each constraint $c_i, i = 1..k$. Thus, c_i is labelled with $p_{c_i} = st_i/s(n)$.
3.- $\tau := \prod_{c_i \in C}(p_{c_i})$

For example, let's see the random problem presented in Table 1. There are three variables, each variable lies in the range [1,10], and there are three constraints c_1, c_2, c_3. The first constraint satisfies 944 states, the second constraint satisfies 960 states and the third constraint satisfies 30 constraints. Thus the probability a random state satisfies the first constraint is $p_{c_1} = \frac{944}{1000} = 0.944$. Similarly, $p_{c_2} = 0.960$ and $p_{c_3} = 0.03$. So, the probability a random state satisfies all constraints is 0.027. However, only 29 states satisfy these three constraints, so the above probability that a random state satisfies all constraint is 0.029.

4.1   A Heuristic Using τ

To compute τ, it is necessary to obtain the tightnesses of each constraint, represented by the following set of probabilities $\{p_{c_1}, ..., p_{c_k}\}$. We take advantage of this information to classifying the constraint so that a search algorithm can

Table 1. random problem with 3 variables and 3 constraints

Z1,Z2,Z3: 1..10	Solutions	p_{c_i}	τ
$c1: -Z1 + Z2 + Z3 <= 13$	944	0.944	
$c2: -Z1 - 2*Z3 <= -6$	960	0.96	**0.027**
$c3: Z2 + 3*Z3 = 29$	30	0.03	
$c3\&c2\&c3$	29	**0.029**	dif=0.002

manage the hardest part of a problem first. Figure 3 shows the constraints in the natural order and classified by tightnesses. If the tightest constraints is very constrained ($\tau \approx 0$), the problem will be over-constrained. However, if this tightest constraints is under-constrained ($\tau \approx 1$) then, the problem will be under-constrained.

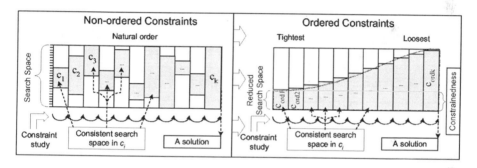

Fig. 3. From non-ordered constraints to ordered constraints: Constrainedness.

To achieve this objective, we classify the constraints in ascending order of the labels p_{c_i} so that the tightest constraints are classified first $p_{c_{ord1}}, p_{c_{ord2}}, ..., p_{c_{ordk}}$ (see Figure 3). Thus, a backtracking-based search algorithm can tackle the hardest part of a search problem first and inconsistencies can be found earlier and the number of constraint checks can significantly be reduced.

5   Evaluation of τ and the Resultant Heuristic

In this section, we evaluate our parameter τ and our heuristic. To estimate the constrainedness of random problems we compare τ with the actual constrainedness by obtaining all solutions of random problems. Furthermore, we study the performance of some well-known CSP solvers that incorporate our heuristic: Chronological Backtracking (BT), Generate&Test (GT), Forward Checking (FC) and Real Full Look Ahead (RFLA)[1], because they are the most appropriate

---

[1] Backtracking, Generate&Test, Forward Checking and Real Full Look Ahead were obtained from CON'FLEX. It can be found in: http://www-bia.inra.fr/T/conflex/Logiciels/adressesConflex.html.

techniques for observing the number of constraint checks. This evaluation will be carried out on the classical n-queen problem.

5.1   Evaluating τ

In our empirical evaluation, each random CSP was defined by the 3-tuple $< n, c, d >$, where n was the number of variables, c the number of constraints and d the domain size. The problems were randomly generated by modifying these parameters. We evaluated 100 test cases for each type of problem. We present the average actual constrainedness by obtaining all solutions, our estimator τ choosing a sample of $s(n) = 7n^2$ states, the number of possible states, the average number of possible solutions, the average number of estimate solutions using τ and the error percentage.

Table 2 shows some types of random problems. For example in problems with 5 variables, each with 5 possible values and 5 constraints $< 5, 5, 5 >$, the number of possible states is $d^n = 5^5 = 3125$, the average number of solutions is 125, so the actual constrainedness is 0.04. With a sample of $7n^2 = 175$ states, we obtain an average number of 6.64 solutions. Thus, our parameter $\tau = 0.038$ and the number of estimate solutions of the entire problem is 118.7. In this way, the error percentage is only 0.2%.

Table 2. Random instances $< n, c, d >$, n:variables, c:constraints and d:domain size

Problems	actual con-strainedness	Parameter τ	Number of States	Number of Solutions	Number of Estimated Sol.	% Error
$< 3, 5, 5 >$	0.09	0.07	125	11.2	8.7	2%
$< 3, 5, 10 >$	0.05	0.043	1000	50	43	0.7%
$< 3, 10, 5 >$	0.024	0.013	125	3	1.6	1.12%
$< 5, 5, 5 >$	0.04	0.038	3125	125	118.7	0.2%
$< 5, 10, 5 >$	0.008	0.01	3125	25	31.2	0.19%
$< 5, 10, 10 >$	0.0045	0.0034	100000	453	340	0.1%

5.2   Evaluating Our Heuristic

The n-queens problem is a classical search problem to analyse the behaviour of algorithms. Table 3 shows the amount of constraint check saving in the n-queens problem.

We incorporated our constraint ordering (CO) to well-known CSP solver: GT+CO, BT+CO, FC+CO and RFLA+CO. Here, the objective is to find all solutions. The results show that the amount of constraint check saving was significant in GT+CO and BT+CO and lower but significant in FC+CO and RFLA+CO. This is due to these techniques are more powerful than BT and GT.

Table 3. Constraint check saving using GT , BT, FC and RFLA in the n-queens problem.

queens	GT&GT+CO Constraint Check Saving	BT&BT+CO Constraint Check Saving	FC&FC+CO Constraint Check Saving	RFLA&RFLA+CO Constraint Check Saving
5	2.1×10^4	2.4×10^2	150	110
10	4.1×10^{11}	3.9×10^7	1.4×10^5	9.3×10^4
20	1.9×10^{26}	3.6×10^{18}	9.6×10^{14}	6.03×10^{11}
50	2.4×10^{70}	3.6×10^{52}	3.1×10^{44}	1.6×10^{32}
100	2.1×10^{143}	2.1×10^{106}	4.5×10^{93}	1.8×10^{66}
150	5.2×10^{219}	3.7×10^{161}	6.8×10^{142}	2.1×10^{100}
200	9.4×10^{295}	8.7×10^{219}	9.9×10^{198}	2.2×10^{134}

6   Conclusion and Future Work

In this paper, we introduce a parameter (τ) that measures the "constrainedness" of a search problem. τ represents the probability of the problem being feasible. A value of $\tau = 0$ corresponds to an over-constrained problem. $\tau = 1$ corresponds to an under-constrained problem. This parameter can also be used in a heuristic to guide search. To achieve this parameter, we compute the tightnesses of each constraint. We can take advantage of this tightnesses to classify the constraints from the tightest constraint to the loosest constraint. Using this ordering heuristic, the search can be accelerated due to inconsistencies can be found earlier and the number of constraint checks can significantly be reduced.

Furthermore, this heuristic technique is appropriate to solve problems as a distributed CSPs [8] in which agents are committed to solve their subproblems.

For future work, we are working on exploiting this constraint ordering to remove redundant constraints in large problems.

References

1. R. Bartak, 'Constraint programming: In pursuit of the holy grail', *in Proceedings of WDS99 (invited lecture), Prague, June*, (1999).
2. R. Dechter and J. Pearl, 'Network-based heuristics for constraint satisfaction problems', *Artificial Intelligence*, **34**, 1–38, (1988).
3. I.P. Gent, E. MacIntyre, P. Prosser, and T Walsh, 'The constrainedness of search', *In Proceedings of AAAI-96*, 246–252, (1996).
4. I.P. Gent, E. MacIntyre, P. Prosser, and T Walsh, 'The constrainedness of arc consistency', *Principles and Practice of Constraint Programming*, 327–340, (1997).
5. R. Haralick and Elliot G., 'Increasing tree efficiency for constraint satisfaction problems', *Artificial Intelligence*, **14**, 263–314, (1980).
6. V. Kumar, 'Algorithms for constraint satisfaction problems: a survey', *Artificial Intelligence Magazine*, **1**, 32–44, (1992).
7. N. Sadeh and M.S. Fox, 'Variable and value ordering heuristics for activity-based jobshop scheduling', *In proc. of Fourth International Conference on Expert Systems in Production and Operations Management*, 134–144, (1990).

8. M.A. Salido, A. Giret, and F. Barber, 'Distributing Constraints by Sampling in Non-Binary CSPs', *In IJCAI Workshop on Distributing Constraint Reasoning*, 79–87, (2003).
9. R. Wallace and E. Freuder, 'Ordering heuristics for arc consistency algorithms', *In Proc. of Ninth Canad. Conf. on A.I.*, 163–169, (1992).
10. T. Walsh, 'The constrainedness knife-edge', *In Proceedings of the 15th National Conference on AI (AAAI-98)*, 406–411, (1998).
11. D.L. Waltz, 'Understanding line drawings of scenes with shadows', *The Psychology of Computer Vision*, 19–91, (1975).

Orthogonal Operators for User-Defined Symbolic Periodicities

Lavinia Egidi and Paolo Terenziani

Dipartimento di Informatica - Università del Piemonte Orientale
Spalto Marengo, 33, 15100 Alessandria - Italy
{lavinia.egidi,paolo.terenziani}@mfn.unipmn.it

Abstract. We identify a set of orthogonal properties characterizing periodicities; based on these we define a lattice of classes (of periodicities). For each property, we introduce a language operator and, this way, we propose a family of symbolic languages, one for each *subset of operators*, one for each point in the lattice. So, the expressiveness and meaning of each operator, and thus of each language in the family, are clearly defined, and a user can select the language that *exactly* covers the properties of her domain. To the best of our knowledge, our language covering the top of the lattice (i.e., all of the properties) is more expressive than any other symbolic language in the AI and DB literature.

Keywords: user-defined periodicities, symbolic languages, orthogonal operators.

1 Introduction

Calendars and periodicity play a fundamental role in the human modeling of the world, and are extremely relevant in many applications, spanning from financial trading to scheduling, from manufacturing and process control to office automation and data broadcasting. In most practical applications, supporting a "standard" calendar (i.e., the Gregorian calendric system) does not suffice, since *user-defined* periodicities need to be used (see, e.g., [13]). Thus, many different AI and DB approaches have been devised to deal with periodicity and its related notions of *granularity* and *calendric systems* [2,13] (see, e.g., the survey in [15]). Besides *logical* approaches ([4] and approaches in classical temporal logics) and *mathematical* ones (e.g., Kabanza's *linear repeating points* [9]), *symbolic* approaches to user-defined periodicities are gaining an increasing relevance (consider, e.g., [11,12,3,14]). The latter provide a set of *operators* which can be combined in order to define complex periodicities in an *incremental* and *compositional* way.[1]

---

[1] For instance, in [11], "the first day of each month" can be modeled by first applying a basic operator in order to define "day" and "month", then applying a *dicing* operators, to split months into sets of days, and finally a *slicing* operator, to select the first day in each set.

C. Bussler and D. Fensel (Eds.): AIMSA 2004, LNAI 3192, pp. 137–147, 2004.

In this paper, we propose a *family* of new symbolic languages, that we designed according to the following intuitions:

1. the expressiveness of (symbolic) languages for periodicities can be charaterized on the basis of a set of *orthogonal properties*;
2. the less (symbolic) language operators are interdependent, the clearer is their underlying semantics: operators should correspond as much as possible to specific properties, without affecting each other;
3. there is no "best language" per se: the goodness of a language depends on the domain of application; the most suitable language is the one that meets more precisely the expressiveness requirements.

With this in mind,

- we identified (Sect. 2) five orthogonal properties that characterize user-defined periodicity. The definitional process was driven by considerations on the significance and usefulness of the structures that must be allowed, on homogeneity arguments and on orthogonality requirements (cf. Item 1 and 2 above);
- we defined, for any subset of these properties, a class of periodicities. The classes, ordered by set inclusion, form a lattice (Sect. 2). In [6] this lattice was used in order to classify different (symbolic) languages in the literature;
- we defined two basic (symbolic language) operators to express periodicities for which none of the five properties hold; and five additional operators, one for each property (Sect. 3). Any subset of the five operators, together with the basic ones, defines a language. Languages, ordered by set inclusion, define a lattice;
- we proved that the lattice of languages matches the lattice of periodicities, in that each node of the former has enough expressive power in order to define *exactly* the omologous node in the latter (Sect. 4).

Our symbolic approach makes easier the task of choosing a priori a language, since the choice only depends on the properties of interest in the given domain/application (see Issue 3 above). At a later stage, when the user needs to define a new periodicity, the choice of the operators required is easier because it depends on the properties of that periodicity.

To the best of our knowledge, our top language (i.e., the one that can deal with all of the properties) is more expressive than any other symbolic language in the AI and DB literature (see the comparison in [6]).

Moreover, the modularity of our approach can be exploited by language designers and implementers, since in order to operate on the whole family of languages, one can simply focus on the seven operators. For instance:

- the semantics of all the languages in the family can be provided on the basis of the semantics of the seven operators. In [7], a semantics in terms of Presburger Arithmetic is given;
- interpreters/compilers for each one of the languages can be built in a modular way.

In Sect. 5 we briefly compare our approach to others in the literature.

2   Properties

Intuitively, *periodicities* are events that repeat in a regular way in time. As in many approaches in the literature, we choose to focus only on the *temporal* aspects of periodic events, disregarding other properties (e.g., agent, location). We adopt *discrete, linearly ordered* and *unbounded* time; *time points* are the basic temporal primitives. The basic structures on time points are *time intervals* i.e., non empty sets of points. A *convex* time interval is the set of all points between two endpoints.

We take *calendars* as the basis of our construction, as in most symbolic approaches in the literature (e.g., [11,12,3,14]). Calendars ("minutes", "days", "months") model the discrete time axis, partitioning it into a regularly repeating pattern of adjacent intervals [11]. In particular, a *chronon calendar* defines the tick of the given (temporal) system. We call *Cal* the set of all calendars.

Approaches in the literature witness that the need for more complex structures has been felt. An analysis of the various proposals led us to identify five crucial properties. We propose here definitions filtered through our intuition and our demand for orthogonality.

Operators to *select* some portions of the time line, dropping others, have been provided in, e.g., [11,12,3,14]. The resulting periodicities have the non-adjacency property. We give a preliminary definition of the property, that captures the above:

NA - (prelim). *A periodicity P has the* non-adjacency *property, if it has an interval I, that is not P's rightmost interval, such that for no $J \in P$, $Meet(I, J)$, where $Meet([s_1, e_1], [s_2, e_2]) \leftrightarrow s_2 = e_1 + 1$ (see [1]).*

For instance, "Mondays" has the non-adjacency property, as well as (ex.1) "Mondays from 8 to 18".

In some cases, one may want to capture the fact that a periodic event occurs over time intervals with gaps (i.e., holes) in them (see, e.g. [3]). For instance, (ex.2) "Working hours on Mondays, from 8 to 12 and from 14 to 18", may be represented using a gap interval for each Monday.

G - *A periodicity P has* Gaps *if it contains gap intervals.*

Notice that the property of having gaps is orthogonal with respect to non-adjacency, since the former is about inner holes in intervals, and the latter about outer gaps between intervals. For instance, (ex.2) has both the NA and the G property, while (ex.1) has only NA, and "each day, with the lunch-break gap (from 12 to 14)" has only G.

Intervals may overlap [5] (exact overlaps, i.e., multiple occurrences of the same interval, are special cases). For instance, (ex.3) "Tom's and Mary's working hours on Mondays" may be a case of (exact) overlap—consider e.g., the same periodicity (ex.2) for both Tom and Mary.

In order to disambiguate the relationship between gaps and overlaps, we introduce the notion of extent. We define the *extent* of an interval (or sets thereof) as the interval whose endpoints are the minimum and maximum points belonging to the interval (or sets thereof).

O - *A periodicity P has* Overlaps *if the extents of some of the intervals have non-empty intersection.*

So, O is a property of interval extents, and therefore totally independent from G.

In order to preserve our intuition of non-adjacency, and to keep O and NA orthogonal, we settle on a more articulate version of NA-(prelim):

NA - *A periodicity has the* non-adjacency *property if it can't be split in a finite number of periodicities that don't satisfy NA-(prelim),*
(i.e., if it can't be split in a finite number of periodicities that have adjacent intervals).

Other approaches pointed out the importance of dealing with *bounded* periodicities (consider, e.g., [2]) or with periodicities consisting of a finite aperiodic set of intervals plus a periodic part [10]. We introduce the property of being *eventually periodic* (terminology taken from [8]) to model both (notice that a bounded periodicity can be seen as a degenerate eventually periodic one with an empty periodic part).

EP - *A periodicity P is* Eventually Periodic *if it can't be expressed giving a repeating pattern and a positive period.*

Consider, e.g., (ex.4) "Tuesday January 13, 2004 plus Tom's and Mary's working hours on Mondays (defined as in ex.3), starting from January 14, 2004".

EP does not interact with G and NA, since EP is a property of the sequence of intervals as a whole, whereas the other two are local properties. Also, EP and O are orthogonal, since the periodic and/or aperiodic parts may have overlaps or not.

Finally, Leban et al. [11] pointed out the importance of grouping intervals into structured collections. For instance, the periodicity in (ex.4) may be structured by grouping intervals into collections, one for each month (ex.5). Nested groupings (e.g., into months and years) are also allowed.

To cope with structure, *order−n* collections are introduced by Leban et al. We extend the definition to deal with multiple occurrences, by defining order-n collections as multisets:

Definition 1 (Collections). *For each $n > 0$, an* order-n collection *is a multiset of order-$(n − 1)$ collections. A time interval is an* order-0 collection.

It is customary to use the set notation (with braces) for order-n collections with $n > 0$.

S - *A periodicity has* Structure *if it is an* order-n collection, *with $n > 1$.*

So, non-structured periodicities are *order*-1 *collections*, while *order-n collections* with $n > 1$ are needed for structured periodicities. S is orthogonal to NA, G, O and EP, since it operates at a different level.

So far, we defined five orthogonal properties. Even though the definitions are tailored in order to meet user needs, and obtain only meaningful structures, we must place further constraints on the combinations of the five properties that we wish to allow, based on homogeneity observations.

Remark 1 (Homogeneity). In order-n collections, braces are not annotated, i.e. no semantics can be attached to them. Therefore, to preserve a clean semantics, we only admit *homogeneous* structures, i.e. structures *in which all data has been grouped according to the same calendars.*

A consequence of this choice is that *overlaps between order-n collections (n > 0) are not possible.*

Based on the properties above, we build richer classes from *Cal*:

Definition 2 (Classes of periodicity). *Let Cal denote the class of calendars, together with the null event.* $Cal^{\pi_1,\dots,\pi_k}$ *is the class of calendars together with all periodicities that may satisfy only properties in* $\{\pi_1,\dots,\pi_k\}$.

3 Orthogonal Operators

We define two basic operators, that can be applied only initially and never after the other operators.

- **Chronon_Cal:**
  No input;
  Output: an order-1 collection right and left infinite, containing adjacent one-element no-gap intervals.
- **Cal_Def:**
  Input: a calendar C in *Cal*, an 'anchor' time point p which is the start point of an interval in C, and a list of positive natural numbers $n_1, \dots n_k$;
  Output: a calendar, built by grouping cyclically $n_1, \dots n_k$ intervals of C starting from p (both directions), i.e. the set of all intervals $I_{h,j}$, $h \in \mathbb{N}$, $j = 1, \dots, k$ defined as follows: considering C as a set of intervals ordered according to the natural ordering, let $l(h) = ap + h \cdot \sum_{i=1}^{k} n_i$ and ap be the index of the interval $J_{ap} \in C$ starting at the anchoring point, then
  - the starting point of $I_{h,j}$ is the starting point of the interval of position $1 + l(h) + \sum_{i=1}^{j-1} n_i$ in calendar C;
  - the ending point of $I_{h,j}$ is the ending point of the interval of position $l(h) + \sum_{i=1}^{j} n_i$ in calendar C.

In the following we need two relational operators on intervals:

Definition 3 (NSDur, SDur). *Let* $E(J)$, $E(J')$ *be the extents of intervals* J, J'. J *is* non strictly during J' *(J* **NSDur** *J') if* $E(J')$ *contains* $E(J)$; J *is* strictly during J' *(J* **SDur** *J') if* $E(J')$ *contains* $E(J)$ *and the endpoints of* $E(J)$ *are both different from the endpoints of* $E(J')$.

Then we can introduce the five operators, paired with the five orthogonal properties. We place constraints on the inputs that they can take, based on the following remarks: (a) in the cases of *Select* and *Drop*, the structure of the second argument is explicitly disregarded, therefore we prescribe an unstructured input; (b) for homogeneity reasons (see Remark 1) unions make sense only over order-1 collections, which reflects on the definitions of *Union* and *Replace*; (c) operators must either modify intervals or treat them as black boxes, for orthogonality (this reflects on the definitions of *Replace* and *Group_by*); (d) intuition suggests that a user first collects raw data and then organizes it logically, therefore *Group_by* can only be applied last (all other operators have unstructured inputs); notice that this is consistent also with (a) and (b) above.

- **Select (for non adjacency)**
  Input: $N = \{n_1, ..., n_k\}$, $n_i \in I\!N$, order-1 collections C_1 and C_2;
  Output: An order-1 collection (or the empty set) containing for all $J_h \in C_2$ and $i = 1, \ldots, k$, intervals $I_{h,i}$ defined as follows:

$$I_{h,i} = n^{th}(\{I \in C_1 | I \text{ NSDur } J_h\}, n_i)$$

  where $n^{th}(C, m)$ selects the m-th interval in the collection C. if it exists, it is the empty set otherwise.
  • See Remarks (a) and (b), above.
- **Drop (for gaps)**
  Input: $N = \{n_1, ..., n_k\}$, $n_i \in I\!N$, order-1 collections C_1 and C_2;
  Output: An order-1 collection containing for each $I_h \in C_1$ the interval I'_h obtained dropping from I_h, for $i = 1, \ldots, k$, the points belonging to the interval $n^{th}(\{J \in C_2 | J \text{ SDur } I_h\}, n_i)$.
  • See Remarks (a) and (b) above.
- **Union (for overlaps)**
  Input: two order-1 collections C_1 and C_2;
  Output: the order-1 collection containing all intervals of C_1 and C_2 (notice that this is a *multiset union*, i.e. multiple occurrences are allowed).
  • For the constraints on the arguments, see Remark (b) above.
- **Replace (for eventual periodicity)**
  Input: Left and right infinite order-1 collections C_1, C_2 and C_3 (where C_1 and C_3 can be the empty set, but not C_2) and time points p_1, p_2 such that $p_1 < p_2$ and if p_1 belongs to some intervals of C_1 or C_2, it is their right endpoint, and similarly for p_2 relative to C_2 and C_3;
  Output: An order-1 collection containing all intervals of C_1 up to and including point p_1, all intervals of C_2 from $p_1 + 1$ to p_2 (included), and all intervals of C_3 from point $p_2 + 1$.
  • This operator corresponds to the intuition that a complex periodicity consists of bounded portions of basic periodicities. It is defined on order-1 collections—see Remark (b). For the constraints on p_i, see Remark (c).
- **Group_By (for structure)**
  Input: An order-n collection C and a calendar C', such that for each interval $i \in C$ there is an interval $j \in C'$ such that i NSDur$j$;
  Output: An order-$(n + 1)$ collection $C_{new} = \{T_h\}$ containing for each interval $I_h \in C'$ the order-n collection $T_h = \{S'_{i,h}\}$ that, for each order-$(n - 1)$ subcollection S_i of C whose extent has nonempty intersection with I_h (i.e. $E(S_i) \cap I_h \neq 0$), contains the order-$(n - 1)$ subcollection $S'_{i,h}$ obtained dropping from S_i the intervals that are not contained in I_h.

- The constraint on the second input stems from orthogonality—See remark (c) above. See also Remark (d).

We define the periodicities in the examples from Sec. 2 (we choose *hours* as the chronon calendar, and the first hour of Jan 1st, 2004, as the origin; we don't detail the obvious definitions of *days*, *months* and *weeks*):

- (ex.1) $Mon8\text{-}18 = Select(2, Days8\text{-}18, weeks)$ where
  $Days8\text{-}18 = Select(2, C, days)$ and $C = Cal\_Def(hours, 0, \langle 8, 10, 6 \rangle)$
- (ex.2) $WH = Drop\,(\langle 4, 5 \rangle, Mon8\text{-}18, hours)$
- (ex.3) $M\text{+}T = Union(WH, WH)$
- (ex.4) $P = Replace(\emptyset, 288, days, 312, M\text{+}T)$,
- (ex.5) $Group\_by(P, months)$.

We prove that each operator affects a single property:

Theorem 1 (Orthogonality). {Select, Drop, Union, Group_By, Replace} *is an orthogonal set of operators.*

Proof (Sketch). We defined an operator introducing each property. We now show, for each property, that no other operator can introduce it.
NA. The definition of NA itself is tailored so that Union can't introduce it. The use of SDur ensures that *Drop* doesn't introduce it. The same holds for Replace, because of the constraints on p_i. The constraints on the definition of Group_By guarantee that the latter doesn't affect the underlying sequence of intervals.
G. The only operators that affect intervals are *Cal_Def* and *Drop*. Only *Drop* can introduce gaps, since *Cal_Def* compounds adjacent intervals.
O. Select and Drop can't introduce overlaps by their nature. Replace can't because disjoint portions of periodicities are used to obtain the new one. Group_By doesn't affect the underlying sequence of intervals.
EP. Select, Drop and Group_By work periodically, and the period of their output is the least common multiple (*lcm*) of the periods of the inputs, if those were unbounded and with no aperiodic part. Similarly, Union doesn't add EP, since if periodicities C_1 and C_2 are not bounded and have no aperiodic part, $C = \text{Union}(C_1, C_2)$ is a pure unbounded periodicity with period $p = lcm(p_1, p_2)$ and repeating pattern the multiset union of $lcm(p_1, p_2)/p_2$ adjacent occurrences of $RP(C_2)$ and $lcm(p_1, p_2)/p_1$ repetitions of $RP(C_1)$ over the same extent—where p_i (resp. $RP(C_i)$) is the period (resp. repeating pattern) of C_i.
S. By definition, Select, Drop, Union and Replace output order-1 collections. Therefore, only Group_By can add structure. □

4   Expressiveness

The operators we defined can be combined to obtain a family of languages. Let $\mathcal{L}$ be the basic language {$Chronon\_Cal, Cal\_Def$}. We prove that it defines exactly the class Cal. Adding any combination of the other operators to it, we define a lattice of languages, ordered by set inclusion. We prove that the lattice of languages matches exactly the lattice of classes of periodicities, in the sense that language $\mathcal{L} \cup \{O_{\pi_1}, \ldots, O_{\pi_k}\}$ defines all and only the periodicities in $Cal^{\pi_1 \cdots \pi_k}$ (where O_{π_i} is the operator that introduces property π_i).

The first part of this result is proven by Thm. 1. The converse (that the languages are expressive enough to define the corresponding classes) is proven by induction. In order to simplify the proof, it is convenient to fix an order in which operators are applied. This is not restrictive for our goals: in the lattice, all classes corresponing to all the combinations of properties are present, and therefore it is not relevant in which order the properties are added or removed. Lemma 1 proves the induction steps:

Lemma 1. *1. $\mathcal{L} = \{Chronon\_Cal, Cal\_Def\}$ defines at least* Cal.
 2. The language $\mathcal{L} \cup \{Select\}$ defines at least Cal^{NA}.
 3. If $\mathcal{L} \cup \{O_1, \ldots, O_k\}$ defines at least Cal (resp. Cal^{NA}), then $\mathcal{L} \cup \{O_1, \ldots, O_k, Drop\}$ defines at least Cal^G (resp. $Cal^{NA,G}$).
 4. If $\mathcal{L} \cup \{O_1, \ldots, O_k\}$ defines at least $Cal^{\pi_1, \ldots \pi_k}$, with $\{\pi_1, \ldots \pi_k\} \subseteq \{NA, G\}$, then $\mathcal{L} \cup \{O_1, \ldots, O_k, Union\}$ defines at least $Cal^{\pi_1, \ldots, \pi_k, O}$.
 5. If the language $\mathcal{L} \cup \{O_1, \ldots, O_k\}$ defines at least $Cal^{\pi_1, \ldots \pi_k}$, with $\{\pi_1, \ldots \pi_k\} \subseteq \{NA, G, O\}$, then $\mathcal{L} \cup \{O_1, \ldots, O_k, Replace\}$ defines at least $Cal^{\pi_1, \ldots, \pi_k, EP}$.
 6. If the language $\mathcal{L} \cup \{O_1, \ldots, O_k\}$ defines at least $Cal^{\pi_1, \ldots \pi_k}$, with $\{\pi_1, \ldots \pi_k\} \subseteq \{NA, G, O, EP\}$, then $\mathcal{L} \cup \{O_1, \ldots, O_k, Group\_By\}$ defines at least $Cal^{\pi_1, \ldots, \pi_k, S}$.

Proof. Let $RP(C)$ be the repeating pattern of C and $p(C)$ its period.

1. Let C be a generic calendar, whose repeating pattern consists of intervals of widths $w_1, \ldots, w_n$. Let ap be the starting point of one occurrence of the repeating pattern. Then

$$C = Cal\_Def(ap, Chronon\_Cal(), \langle w_1, \ldots, w_h \rangle).$$

2. Let $C \in Cal^{NA}$. If $C \in Cal$, then the thesis follows from Item 1.
 Otherwise, define C_1 so that $RP(C_1)$ is obtained adding to $RP(C)$ all convex intervals necessary to have adjacent intervals, and adjacent occurrences of the repeating pattern; $C_1 \in Cal$. Let C_2 be a periodicity with $RP(C_2)$ the extent of $RP(C_1)$, and $p(C_2) = p(C_1)$; $C_2 \in Cal$. Both C_1 and C_2 belong to Cal and are definable in $\mathcal{L}$.
 Let $N = \{n_1 \ldots, n_k\}$ be the positions of the intervals of C in $RP(C_1)$. Then, $C = Select(N, C_1, C_2)$, as required.
3. Let $C \in Cal^G$ (resp. $Cal^{NA,G}$). If it doesn't have property G, then the thesis follows from Item 1 (resp. Item 2).
 So, let us assume that it has gap intervals. Then let C_1 be the interval closure of C, i.e. the periodicity consisting of the extents of all intervals in C. Of course, the interval closure has the same properties as the original periodicity, except for gaps. Thus $C_1 \in Cal$ (resp. Cal^{NA}) and can be defined in $\mathcal{L} \cup \{O_1, \ldots, O_k\}$, by hypothesis.

We add gaps appropriately one interval at a time in the repeating pattern of C_1, using suitable periodicities C_2. C_2 is identical to C_1 except for the interval I that we need to modify. That one is replaced in C_2 by the subintervals that must be removed, and all the other, adjacent ones, to make sure that if C has adjacent intervals, so has C_2. N is set to $\{n_1, n_2 \ldots, n_k\}$ to identify the intervals in C_2 that must be removed from I. Then $\mathrm{Drop}(N, C_1, C_2)$ yields a new periodicity with the same gaps as C in all occurrences of I. The other intervals are unchanged.

With a finite number of applications of Drop as above, C is obtained. (After the first application, C_1 will have, legitimately, gaps.)

4. Let C be any periodicity in $Cal^{\pi_1,\ldots,\pi_k,O}$. If it has no overlaps, it can be defined in $\mathcal{L} \cup \{O_1, \ldots, O_k\}$ by hypothesis.

   Otherwise, it can be split in a finite number of periodicities with no overlaps. This introduces no gaps and no structure. It doesn't need introduce EP since if C is purely periodic, then overlaps must repeat periodically. It doesn't need to introduce NA either, by the definition of NA. Therefore we obtain a finite number of periodicities belonging to $Cal^{\pi_1,\ldots,\pi_k}$, by hypothesis definable in $\mathcal{L} \cup \{O_1, \ldots, O_k\}$. By a finite number of applications of Union we obtain C as required.

5. Let $C \in Cal^{\pi_1,\ldots,\pi_k,EP}$. If it doesn't have the property EP, it can be defined in $\mathcal{L} \cup \{O_1, \ldots, O_k\}$ by hypothesis.

   Otherwise, in the most general case, split it in two infinite periodicities and a finite one. Define C_1 by removing the right bound to the left infinite periodicity obtained (call that bound p_1), and C_3 similarly (defining p_2 as the left bound that has been removed); define C_2 by extending the aperiodic part A to a periodicity with $RP(C_2) = A$ and $p(C_2)$ the width of the extent of $RP(C_2)$. (If the periodicity C is finite to the left (resp. right), then C_1 (resp. C_3) is empty. Notice that it is always possible to choose p_1 or p_2 so that C_2 is not empty.) These extensions don't introduce G, nor NA, nor O, but simply reproduce them periodically if they appear in C.

   Therefore $C_i \in Cal^{\pi_1,\ldots,\pi_k}$, and by hypothesis are definable in $\mathcal{L} \cup \{O_1, \ldots, O_k\}$. And $C = \mathrm{Replace}(C_1, p_1, C_2, p_2, C_3)$.

6. Let $C \in Cal^{\pi_1,\ldots,\pi_k,S}$. If it has no structure, it can be defined in $\mathcal{L} \cup \{O_1, \ldots, O_k\}$ by hypothesis.

   So, let C have structure. First assume that it is an order-2 collection. Remove its order-1 braces (i.e. the inner braces), transforming it to an order-1 collection C_1. Define C_2 as a periodicity whose intervals are the extents of the order-1 subcollections of C. Notice that C_2 has no EP, by the definition of S. It has no gaps, no overlaps, and no structure by definition, and has NA only if C has NA. Therefore $C_1, C_2 \in Cal^{\pi_1,\ldots,\pi_k}$ and can be defined in $\mathcal{L} \cup \{O_1, \ldots, O_k\}$. Moreover, $C = \mathrm{Group\_By}(C_1, C_2)$.

   If C is an order-n collection, the same construction can be applied $n-1$ times, adding braces from the inside out, to the order-1 collection obtained removing all structure from C. $\qquad\square$

Let O_{π_k} be the operator introducing property π_k (thus $O_{NA}=Select$, $O_G=Drop$, etc.). We prove that $Cal^{\pi_1 \cdots \pi_k}$ is the minimal closure of Cal, with respect to $\{O_{\pi_1}, \ldots, O_{\pi_k}\}$, using Theorem 1 and Lemma 1:

Theorem 2. $\mathcal{L} \cup \{O_{\pi_1}, \ldots, O_{\pi_k}\}$ *defines exactly* $Cal^{\pi_1 \cdots \pi_k}$.

Proof. By Theorem 1, $\mathcal{L} \cup \{O_{\pi_1}, \ldots, O_{\pi_k}\}$ defines at most $Cal^{\pi_1 \cdots \pi_k}$.

The converse is proven by induction on k. For $k = 0$, the basis of the induction is Lemma 1, Item 1. For positive k, the inductive step is proven using Lemma 1 as follows: if $S \in \{\pi_1 \ldots \pi_k\}$, by Item 6; otherwise, if $EP \in \{\pi_1 \ldots \pi_k\}$ (but not S), by Item 5; otherwise, if S and EP are not in $\{\pi_1 \ldots \pi_k\}$, but O is, by Item 4; otherwise, if $G \in \{\pi_1 \ldots \pi_k\}$, by Item 3; if only NA holds, by Item 2. $\square$

5   Conclusions

We presented a family of symbolic languages for user-defined periodicity, that has significant features and solves some drawbacks of languages in the literature.

The modularity of our approach allows for a clear management of properties characterizing periodicities. We explicitly avoid side-effects, that impair the clarity of semantics elsewhere. Consider, for instance, in the language of [11], the definition of "the first Monday of each month": group Mondays into months, using *Dice*, then select the first Monday in each group, with the *Slice* operator "[1]\". Counterintuitively, this defines a collection of collections each containing a Monday.

Moreover, modularity allows to obtain the desired expressiveness for an application without the burden of unnecessary features. This is not obvious. For intance, consider [3], in which it is explicitly stated that all the structure carried over from [11] is of no use, but is there as an unavoidable heritage. The effort to get rid of the structure was then done in [14], and results in rather complex operators.

Our top language is more expressive than any other symbolic language in the literature, to the best of our knowledge, since it allows to deal with all the five properties we defined, including the special case of exact overlaps, not treated by any other symbolic approach.

But the expressiveness is enhanced not only in a quantitative way, but also qualitatively. Indeed, our design of the languages is based on an analysis of the structures that it makes sense to define, in view of usage, homogeneity constraints and our aim at modularity. Overlaps are a notable example—for instance, in [11] order-n collections ($n > 0$) can overlap, resulting in structures of no clear meaning (cf. Remark 1).

References

1. J.F. Allen, Maintaining Knowledge about Temporal Intervals, *Communications of the ACM* 26(11):832-843, 1983.

2. C. Bettini, C. Dyreson, W. Evans, R. Snodgrass, X. Wang, A Glossary of Time Granularity Concepts, in *Temporal Databases: Research and Practice*, Springer Verlag, 1998.
3. C. Bettini, R. De Sibi, Symbolic Representation of User-defined Time Granularities, *Proc. TIME'99*, IEEE Computer Society, 17-28, 1999.
4. J. Chomicki, and T. Imielinsky, Finite Representation of Infinite Query Answers, *ACM ToDS* 18(2), 181-223, 1993.
5. D. Cukierman, and J. Delgrande, Expressing Time Intervals and Repetition within a Formalization of Calendars, *Computational Intelligence* 14(4), 563-597, 1998.
6. L. Egidi and P. Terenziani, A lattice of classes of user-defined symbolic periodicities, *TIME'04*, 2004.
7. L. Egidi and P. Terenziani, A mathematical framework for the semantics of symbolic languages representing periodic time, *TIME'04*.
8. Enderton, *A Mathematical Introduction to Logic*, Academic Press, New York, 1972.
9. F. Kabanza, J.-M. Stevenne, and P. Wolper, Handling Infinite Temporal Data, *Journal of Computer and System Sciences* 51, 3-17, 1995.
10. A. Kurt, M. Ozsoyoglu, Modelling and Querying Periodic Temporal Databases, *Procs. DEXA'95*, 124-133, 1995.
11. B. Leban, D.D. McDonald, and D.R. Forster, A representation for collections of temporal intervals, *AAAI'86*, 367-371, 1986.
12. M. Niezette, and J.-M. Stevenne, An Efficient Symbolic Representation of Periodic Time, *Proc. CIKM*, 1992.
13. M. Soo, and R. Snodgrass, Multiple Calendar Support for Conventional Database Management Systems, *Proc. ITD*, 1993.
14. P. Terenziani, Symbolic User-defined Periodicity in Temporal Relational Databases, *IEEE TKDE* 15(2), 489-509, 2003.
15. A. Tuzhilin and J. Clifford, On Periodicity in Temporal Databases, *Information Systems* 20(8), 619-639, 1995.

Solving Constraints Between Lines in Euclidean Geometry

Philippe Balbiani and Khalil Challita

Irit-CNRS, Université Paul Sabatier
118 route de Narbonne, 31062 Toulouse Cedex 4, France
{balbiani,challita}@irit.fr

Abstract. We consider constraints satisfaction problems between lines in Euclidean geometry. Our language of constraints is based on the binary relation of parallelism. Our main results state that (1) solving constraints between lines in dimension 2 can be done in polynomial time whereas (2) solving constraints between lines in dimension 3 is NP-hard.

Keywords: Spatial reasoning - Constraint satisfaction problems - Euclidean geometry.

1 Introduction

The growing field of qualitative spatial reasoning finds its application in a variety of areas, such as Geographic Information Systems [8,9], Databases [17], Multimedia [21], Computer Vision and Artificial Intelligence. Most researchers have dealt with three main classes of spatial information. *Topological* relations describe how the interiors, the exteriors and the boundaries of two regions relate [5,8,19,20]. *Directional* relations describe the relative position of two regions to one another [10,13,22]. For instance, Ligozat [13] studies the algebra of cardinal relations between points in dimension 2. *Distance* relations describe the relative distance of two regions [9,24]. In artificial intelligence, variables usually denote points [4] or regions [6,19]. The latter alternative is more often preferred because a region takes into account the space that might be occupied by an object, and thus enables us to study a wider class of common problems. Affine geometry, one of the most prominent mathematical models of space, arises from the study of points, lines and planes by means of properties stated in terms of incidence. In coordinate geometry, lines are sets of points satisfying linear equations. Completely determined by two of their points, they can also be considered as abstract entities. They have certain mutual relations like, for instance, parallelism. Lines are to be found in many axiomatizations of affine geometry. However, we had great difficulty finding any examples of qualitative forms of spatial reasoning based solely on them. To confirm this claim, we have not been able to find any explicit reference to a qualitative spatial reasoning framework devoted to the study of lines in Euclidean geometry.

In this paper, we consider constraints satisfaction problems between lines in Euclidean geometry. Our language of constraints is based on the binary relation of parallelism. Our main results state that solving constraints between lines in dimension 2 can be

C. Bussler and D. Fensel (Eds.): AIMSA 2004, LNAI 3192, pp. 148–157, 2004.

done in polynomial time whereas solving constraints between lines in dimension 3 is NP-hard. The article is organized as follows. In section 2, we introduce relevant notions concerning constraint networks in general, and state some results about the consistency problem of constraints between lines in the Euclidean plane. Sections 3 and 4 generalize these results to a language enabling us to express ordering constraints or quantitative constraints between lines in dimension 2. In section 5, we establish that the complexity problem of networks of constraints between lines in dimension 3 is NP-hard, even for atomic ones.

2   Lines in Dimension 2

From now on, by PO, EQ, DC we respectively mean: "having one point in common", "equal", "parallel and distinct". Two lines in the plane, denoted by d and d', are exactly in one of the following relations: $d\{PO\}d'$, $d\{EQ\}d'$, $d\{DC\}d'$. Let $E = \{PO, EQ, DC\}$ be the set of the jointly exhaustive and pairwise disjoint relations that compare the position of any couple of lines in a plane.

The definitions needed for describing a constraint satisfaction problem (CSP), are defined by Montanari [16]. A network of linear constraints $\mathcal{R}$ is a couple (I, C), where $I \subseteq I\!N$ is a finite set of variables, and C is a mapping from I^2 to the set of the subsets of E (i.e. 2^E). The network $\mathcal{R}$ is atomic if for all $i, j \in I$, if $Card(C(i,j)) > 1$ then $C(i,j) = E$. We say that $\mathcal{R}$ is path-consistent if for all $i, j, k \in I$, $C(i,j) \subseteq C(i,k) \circ C(k,j)$. The composition table of the relations considered is given in figure 1, where the symbols $<$ and $>$ account for the relation $\{DC\}$. A scenario (or an assignment) is a function V that maps I to a set of lines, in the Euclidean plane. A scenario is consistent if for all $i, j \in I$, the relation that holds between the lines $d_i = V(i)$ and $d_j = V(j)$ is in $C(i,j)$. A relation $r \in C(i,j)$ is feasible if there exists a consistent scenario such that the lines d_i and d_j are in the relation r. A network of constraints is minimal if every relation in it is feasible. The notion of $k - consistency$, adapted from Freuder [11], leads naturally to strong k-consistency, as defined by Vilain and Kautz [23]. We say that $\mathcal{R}$ is k-consistent if, given any consistent assignment of $k - 1$ of its variables to lines in the Euclidean plane, there exists a consistent assignment of any k^{th} variable of the network. It is strongly k-consistent if it is j-consistent for all $j \leq k$. A network is said to be globally consistent if it is strongly n-consistent, for $n = Card(I)$. Given a network of constraints, the question that arises is whether or not there is a consistent scenario for it. The algorithm of path consistency is explored and analyzed in [14,15]. The constraints propagation algorithm due to Allen [1], that replaces each constraint $C(i,j)$ by $C(i,j) \cap (C(i,k) \circ C(k,j))$, transforms in polynomial time each network $\mathcal{R}$ into a path-consistent one, whose set of consistent scenarios is the same as for $\mathcal{R}$.

Example 1. Path-consistent but not globally consistent network of linear constraints: $I = \{1, 2, 3, 4, 5\}$ and $C(1,2) = C(1,5) = C(3,4) = C(3,5) = \{PO, EQ\}$, $C(1,3) = C(1,4) = C(2,3) = C(2,4) = \{PO, DC\}$, $C(2,5) = \{PO, DC, EQ\}$, $C(4,5) = \{DC, EQ\}$. Indeed, if we consider its subnetwork where $C(1,2) = C(3,4) = \{EQ\}$ and $C(1,3) = C(1,4) = C(2,3) = C(2,4) = \{DC\}$, we find it impossible to consistently assign the fifth variable. We can easily check that the above network is minimal.

The following result is an immediate corollary of proposition 2 (see below).

Proposition 1. *The consistency problem of networks of linear constraints is decidable in polynomial time, by means of a deterministic algorithm.*

Consider a network (I, C) of constraints between lines in the Euclidean plane. If this network is consistent then, obviously, we can find a consistent scenario V such that for all i in I, $V(i)$ is a nonvertical line. Indeed, as the constraint networks we consider are finite, we take care during the construction of a scenario V not to assign to a variable i a line parallel to the the vertical axis, in order to avoid having equations of the form $x = c$, where $c \in \mathbb{R}$.

3   Oriented Parallelism

From now on in this section, we only consider nonvertical lines in the Euclidean plane. It is a well-known fact that such lines are defined by a linear equation of the form $y = ax+b$ where a and b are real numbers. Given two parallel lines in the Euclidean plane, we give an orientation to their respective positions. Informally, for a line d_i, we wish to be able to distinguish the parallel lines that lie to its left from those that are to its right.

$\circ$	EQ	$<$	$>$	PO
EQ	EQ	$<$	$>$	PO
$<$	$<$	$<$	$<, >, EQ$	PO
$>$	$>$	$<, >, EQ$	$>$	PO
PO	PO	PO	PO	$<, >, EQ,PO$

Fig. 1. Composition table of oriented 2D relations.

Definition 1. *For any two lines d_i and d_j of the Euclidean plane with equations $y = a_i x + b_i$ and $y = a_j x + b_j$:*

- $d_i\{<\}d_j$ iff $(a_i = a_j) \wedge (b_i < b_j)$.
- $d_i\{>\}d_j$ iff $(a_i = a_j) \wedge (b_i > b_j)$.
- $d_i\{PO\}d_j$ iff $(a_i \neq a_j)$.
- $d_i\{EQ\}d_j$ iff $(a_i = a_j) \wedge (b_i = b_j)$.

An oriented 2D network is a linear constraint network of lines in a Euclidean plane, where the relations are taken from the set $E = \{PO, EQ, <, >\}$.

The binary relations $<$ and $>$ are the inverse of each other (i.e. $d_i\{<\}d_j$ iff $d_j\{>\}d_i$). We have the equivalence $d_i\{DC\}d_j \Leftrightarrow ((d_i\{<\}d_j) \vee (d_i\{>\}d_j))$. The composition table of these relations is given in figure 1. We used the consistency-based composition of relations [3] to compute it: if $\alpha, \beta \in E$, then $\alpha \circ \beta$ contains all the relations $\gamma \in E$ such that there exists lines d_i, d_j, d_k of the plane satisfying $d_i\{\alpha\}d_j$, $d_j\{\beta\}d_k$ and $d_i\{\gamma\}d_k$.

Example 2. Oriented 2D network which is not minimal: $I = \{1, 2, 3, 4\}$ and $C(2, 1) = C(3, 1) = C(4, 1) = C(4, 2) = C(4, 3) = \{>, EQ\}$, $C(2, 3) = \{<, >\}$. Indeed, the relation between the first and the fourth variables cannot be reduced to $\{EQ\}$.

The most important question about networks of constraints concerns the tractability of the consistency problem. The following proposition states that solving networks of constraints with oriented 2D relations can be done in deterministic polynomial time.

Proposition 2. *The consistency problem of oriented 2D networks is decidable in polynomial time, by means of a deterministic algorithm.*

Proof. In his work [13], and in order to compare the different positions of points with cartesian coordiantes (a_i, b_i), and (a_j, b_j) in the Euclidean plane, Ligozat defined the following nine relations: $(<, <), (<, =), (<, >), (=, <), (=, =), (=, >), (>, <), (>, =), (>, >)$. To each set Γ of oriented 2D relations we can associate a set Γ^C of cardinal relations such that an oriented 2D relation satisfied by the lines d_i (with equation $y = a_i x + b_i$) and d_j (with equation $y = a_j x + b_j$) is in Γ iff the cardinal relation satisfied by the points (a_i, b_i) and (a_j, b_j) is in Γ^C:

$\emptyset^C = \emptyset$.

$\{PO\}^C = \{(<, <), (<, =), (<, >), (>, <), (>, =), (>, >)\}$.

$\{EQ\}^C = \{(=, =)\}$.

$\{<\}^C = \{(=, <)\}$.

$\{>\}^C = \{(=, >)\}$.

$\{EQ, <\}^C = \{(=, =), (=, <)\}$.

$\{EQ, >\}^C = \{(=, =), (=, >)\}$.

$\{<, >\}^C = \{(=, <), (=, >)\}$.

$\{PO, EQ\}^C = \{(<, <), (<, =), (<, >), (>, <), (>, =), (>, >), (=, =)\}$.

$\{PO, <\}^C = \{(<, <), (<, =), (<, >), (>, <), (>, =), (>, >), (=, <)\}$.

$\{PO, >\}^C = \{(<, <), (<, =), (<, >), (>, <), (>, =), (>, >), (=, >)\}$.

$\{PO, EQ, <\}^C = \{(<, <), (<, =), (<, >), (>, <), (>, =), (>, >), (=, =), (=, <)\}$.

$\{PO, EQ, >\}^C = \{(<, <), (<, =), (<, >), (>, <), (>, =), (>, >), (=, =), (=, >)\}$.

$\{PO, <, >\}^C = \{(<, <), (<, =), (<, >), (>, <), (>, =), (>, >), (=, <), (=, >)\}$.

$\{EQ, <, >\}^C = \{(=, =), (=, <), (=, >)\}$.

$\{PO, EQ, <, >\}^C = \{(<, <), (<, =), (<, >), (>, <), (>, =), (>, >), (=, -), (-, <), (=, >)\}$.

By construction, the consistency problem of an oriented 2D network is polynomially reducible to the consistency problem of a network of cardinal constraints. Moreover, we easily check that the sets of cardinal relations defined above are preconvex. We conclude our proof by recalling that the consistency problem of networks of preconvex cardinal constraints is decidable in polynomial time [13].

4   Metric Constraints in Dimension 2

Our aim in this section is to define quantitative relations that allow us to compare the distance that separates two parallel lines of the Euclidean plane. We will first consider relations that enable us to tell if, for two parallel lines d_i and d_j, the distance between them (denoted later on by $d(d_i, d_j)$), is less or equal to a certain value. The latter relation will then be augmented by another one, allowing us to tell whether or not the distance from d_j to d_i is superior to a real number.

Definition 2. *Let $h \geq 0$. For any couple (d_i, d_j) of lines in the Euclidean plane:*

- *$d_i\{P_h^+\}d_j \Leftrightarrow d_i$ is parallel to d_j and $d(d_i, d_j) \leq h$.*
- *$d_i\{P_h^-\}d_j \Leftrightarrow d_i$ is parallel to d_j and $d(d_i, d_j) \geq h$.*

A metric 2D network is a linear constraint network of lines in a Euclidean plane, where the relations are of the form $\{PO\}$, $\{P_h^+\}$ and $\{P_h^-\}$.

Remarks. For $h > 0$, consider two parallel lines in the Euclidean plane (d_i, d_j), distant of h, which equations are $y = a_i x + b_i$ and $y = a_j x + b_j$. These lines are identical iff $d_i\{P_0^+\}d_j$. Moreover, $d_i\{P_h^+\}d_j \Leftrightarrow ((a_i = a_j) \wedge |b_i - b_j| \leq D_a)$, where the real D_a satisfies the equation $h = \frac{D_a}{\sqrt{1+a_i^2}}$. Symmetrically, $d_i\{P_h^-\}d_j \Leftrightarrow ((a_i = a_j) \wedge |b_i - b_j| \geq D_a)$. Hence, the constraints $\{P_h^+\}$ and $\{P_h^-\}$ are strictly equivalent to the constraints $\{[-D_a, D_a]\}$ and $\{[-\infty, -D_a] \cup [D_a + \infty]\}$. Thus we can invariably switch between $d_i\{P_h^+\}d_j$ and $(b_i - b_j) \in [-D_a, D_a]$ (the same reasoning applies to $d_i\{P_h^-\}d_j$). For the composition of relations of the form $\{P_h^+\}$ and $\{P_h^-\}$ (showed in figure 2), we use the definition of its counterpart, given in [7]: for any two intervals T and S, the composition $T \circ S$ admits only values r for which there exist $t \in T$ and $s \in S$, such that $r = t + s$. Recall a result concerning TCSP networks, established by Dechter *et al.* [7]: the path-consistency algorithm terminates when applied to an *integral* TCSP, where the extreme points of all its intervals are rational numbers. Later on, when looking for a consistent scenario of a metric 2D network, we can take the distances between all of its lines to be integers. Thus, the path-consistency of such a network can be established using Montanari's proof [16].

$\circ$	P_h^+	P_h^-	PO
P_r^+	P_{r+h}^+	P_{h-r}^-	PO
P_r^-	P_{r-h}^-	P_R	PO
PO	PO	PO	PO, P_R

Fig. 2. Composition of metric 2D networks' relations.

Let $h \leq 0$. For any line of the Euclidean plane d_i, the set of lines d such that $d\{P_h^-\}d_i$ represents by convention all the parallel lines that are equal or parallel to d_i. In that case, the relation $\{P_h^-\}$ will be denoted by $\{P_R\}$. Let us consider the inner difficulty of proving the consistency of a given metric 2D network of constraints.

Proposition 3. *The consistency problem of metric 2D networks is NP-complete.*

Proof. Given a metric 2D network $\mathcal{R} = (I, C)$, for all $i, j \in I$, let $P^- = \{P_{t_1}^-, \ldots, P_{t_p}^-\}$ and $P^+ = \{P_{l_1}^+, \ldots, P_{l_q}^+\}$ be the sets of all corresponding parallel constraints appearing in $C(i,j)$. It is clear that the disjunction of constraints P^- (resp. P^+) can equivalently be reduced to $\{P_{h_{ij}^-}\}$ (resp. $\{P_{h_{ij}^+}\}$), where $h_{ij}^- = min\{t_k : 1 \leq k \leq p\}$ (resp. $h_{ij}^+ = max\{l_k : 1 \leq k \leq q\}$). Let $\mathcal{R}' = (I, C')$ be the constraint network obtained in the following way: replace $\{P_h^-\}$ by $\{P_{h_{ij}^-}\}$ and $\{P_h^+\}$ by $\{P_{h_{ij}^+}\}$. Then, by replacing in $\mathcal{R}'$ $\{P_h^-\}$ by $\{DC\}$, $\{P_h^+\}$ by $\{DC, EQ\}$ and $\{P_R\}$ by $\{DC, EQ\}$, we can polynomially check if the resulting network of linear constraints is consistent or not (due to proposition 1). If it is consistent, let $\mathcal{R}'' = (I, C'')$ be a ! solution, which is an atomic linear constraint network. We then switch back to a subnetwork $\mathcal{R}'_\alpha = (I, C_\alpha)$ of $\mathcal{R}'$, where every relation $\{DC\} = C''(i,j)$ is replaced by the original parallel one (i.e. $\{P_{h_{ij}^+}\}$ or/and $\{P_{h_{ij}^-}\}$). Thus, for all $i, j \in I$, either $C_\alpha(i,j) = \{PO\}$ or $C_\alpha(i,j) \subseteq \{P_{h_{ij}^+}, P_{h_{ij}^-}\}$. Checking the consistency of $\mathcal{R}'_\alpha$ leads us to find a consistent scenario for the variables $i, j \in I$, where $C_\alpha(i,j) \subseteq \{P_{h_{ij}^+}, P_{h_{ij}^-}\}$. Knowing that the consistency problem of a $TCSP$ is NP-complete [7], our proposition is proven.

Corollary 1. *The consistency problem of metric 2D networks, where the only allowed parallel constraints are of the form $\{P_h^+\}$, is in P.*

This result stems directly from the fact that the consistency problem of an STP (which is by definition an atomic $TCSP$) is in P [7].

5   Lines in Dimension 3

To compare the different positions of lines in the space, we add a fourth relation representing the non-coplanarity (NC) between two lines. The set $E = \{PO, EQ, DC, NC\}$ contains relations that are jointly exhaustive and pairwise disjoint, where each one is equal to its inverse. We already know from the decidability of elementary geometry [12] that the consistency problem of networks of linear constraints in the Euclidean space is decidable. We next show that this problem is NP-hard, by polynomially reducing the problem "Not-all-equal SAT" to the problem of lines in the space. The decision problem "Not-all-equal SAT" comes from classical propositional logic. Given a conjunction of clauses containing exactly 3 literals, the issue at stake is to determine whether there exists a valuation satisfying it and such that in no clause are all 3 literals equal in truth value. See [18] for details.

Definition 3. *A spatial network is a linear constraint network of lines in a Euclidean space.*

As in section 3, we use the consistency-based composition of relations to compute the table in figure 3: if $\alpha, \beta \in E$, then $\alpha \circ \beta$ contains all the relations $\gamma \in E$ such that there exist lines d_i, d_j, d_k in the space satisfying $d_i\{\alpha\}d_j$, $d_j\{\beta\}d_k$ and $d_i\{\gamma\}d_k$.

$\circ$	EQ	DC	PO	NC
EQ	EQ	DC	PO	NC
DC	DC	DC, EQ	PO, NC	PO, NC
PO	PO	PO, NC	PO, NC, DC,EQ	PO, NC, DC
NC	NC	PO, NC	PO, NC, DC	PO, NC, DC,EQ

Fig. 3. Composition table of spatial relations.

Example 3. Here are some examples of spatial networks, containing four elements.

1. Non-consistent and path-consistent atomic spatial network: $C(1,2) = \{DC\}$, $C(1,3) = C(1,4) = C(2,3) = C(2,4) = \{PO\}$, $C(3,4) = \{NC\}$. Indeed, we cannot consistently assign the fourth variable. This shows that the polynomial method of path consistency (Allen's triangulation) doesn't provide a complete decision procedure for the consistency problem of spatial networks.
2. Non-globally consistent and path-consistent spatial network: $C(1,2) = C(1,3) = C(2,3) = \{DC\}$, $C(1,4) = C(2,4) = \{PO\}$, $C(3,4) = \{NC\}$. If we assign to the third variable a line d_3 included in the plane defined by the parallel lines d_1 and d_2, we find it impossible to consistently assign the fourth one.

Proposition 4. *The consistency problem of spatial networks is NP-hard.*

Proof. Let $\phi = (C_1 \wedge \ldots \wedge C_n)$ be a conjunction of n clauses having exactly 3 literals. We next associate to ϕ a spatial network $\mathcal{R}_\phi$. For our purpose, $VAR = \{p, q, r, \ldots\}$ will designate the set of atoms appearing in ϕ, and $\{d_p, d_q, d_r, \ldots\}$ their associated lines in $\mathcal{R}_\phi$. In the network $\mathcal{R}_\phi$, the lines $\{d_0, d_1, d_0', d_1', d, d'\}$ that constitute our basic structure must satisfy the conditions: $d_0\{PO\}d_1$, $d_0'\{PO\}d_1'$, $d_0\{DC\}d_0'$, $d_1\{DC\}d_1'$, $d_0\{NC\}d_1'$, $d_1\{NC\}d_0'$, $d\{PO\}d_0$, $d\{PO\}d_1$, $d\{PO\}d_0'$, $d\{PO\}d_1'$, $d'\{PO\}d_0'$, $d'\{PO\}d_1'$, $d'\{NC\}d$. For all $1 \le i \le n$, and for all atoms p appearing in the clause $C_i = l_{i_1} \vee l_{i_2} \vee l_{i_3}$, we associate the lines d_p and $d_{\neg p}$. These lines must satisfy the conditions: $d_p\{PO\}d_0$, $d_p\{PO\}d_1$, $d_p\{DC, PO\}d'$, $d_{\neg p}\{PO\}d_0$, $d_{\neg p}\{PO\}d_1$, $d_{\neg p}\{DC, PO\}d'$, et $d_p\{NC\}d_{\neg p}$.
The intuitive interpretation of the literals in ϕ is: for each literal l, l is true if the line d_l is included in the plane (P), defined by the lines (d_0, d_1), otherwise l is false.
Notice that all lines d_l are either parallel to d' and are included in (P), or they intersect d', d_0 and d_1. We easily check that for each atom appearing in a clause C_i, the construction of the lines d_p and $d_{\neg p}$ is mutually exclusive, in the sense that one of them is included in (P), whereas the other passes through it.

To successfully complete our reduction, for each clause $C_i = l_{i_1} \vee l_{i_2} \vee l_{i_3}$, at least one line $d_{l_{ij}}$ must be included in (P), and another one $d_{l_{ik}}$ must pass through it, where $(j, k \in \{1, 2, 3\})$. To achieve our aim, for all $1 \leq j \leq 3$, the lines $d_{l_{ij}}$ and d must satisfy the following condition: $d_{l_{ij}}\{PO, NC\}d$. For each clause C_i, we represent the lines $d_{l_{ij}}$ in such a way that for every distinct $j, k, t \in \{1, 2, 3\}$, there exists d'' satisfying $d_{l_{ij}}\{PO\}d''$, $d_{l_{ik}}\{PO\}d''$ and $d_{l_{it}}\{NC\}d''$. This condition ensures that at most two lines are either parallel to d' or intersect it.

This proves that a formula ϕ is satisfiable iff $\mathcal{R}_\phi$ is consistent. As the reduction made above is done in polynomial time in the length of the formula ϕ, the proposition is established. Hence, determining consistency of networks of constraints between lines in the Euclidean space is untractable. The following proposition implies that it is still untractable if one considers networks of atomic constraints.

Proposition 5. *Any spatial network is polynomially reducible to an atomic one.*

Proof. Let (I, C) be a spatial network. In order to prove this result, we need to check that for each $i, j \in I$ such that $C(i, j)$ is a disjunction of constraints of the set $E = \{PO, EQ, DC, NC\}$, the variables i, j and the constraint $C(i, j)$ can be equivalently replaced by an atomic spatial network. For all cases stated below, we replace $C(i, j)$ by $\{PO, EQ, DC, NC\}$ and then add some relevant variables.

1. $d_i\{EQ, DC\}d_j$: we add the variables d_u, d_v together with the following constraints $((d_u\{PO\}d_v) \wedge (d_i\{PO\}d_u) \wedge (d_i\{DC\}d_v) \wedge (d_j\{PO\}d_u) \wedge (d_j\{DC\}d_v))$.
2. $d_i\{EQ, PO\}d_j$: we add the variables d_u, d_v, d_w together with the following constraints $((d_u\{PO\}d_v) \wedge (d_u\{DC\}d_w) \wedge (d_v\{NC\}d_w) \wedge (d_i\{PO\}d_u) \wedge (d_i\{PO\}d_v) \wedge (d_i\{PO\}d_w) \wedge (d_j\{PO\}d_u) \wedge (d_j\{PO\}d_v) \wedge (d_j\{PO\}d_w))$.
3. $d_i\{EQ, NC\}d_j$: we add the variables d_u, d_v, d_w together with the following constraints $((d_u\{NC\}d_v) \wedge (d_u\{NC\}d_w) \wedge (d_v\{NC\}d_w) \wedge (d_i\{PO\}d_u) \wedge (d_i\{PO\}d_v) \wedge (d_i\{PO\}d_w) \wedge (d_j\{PO\}d_u) \wedge (d_j\{PO\}d_v) \wedge (d_j\{PO\}d_w))$.
4. $d_i\{PO, NC\}d_j$: we add the variables d_u, d_v, d_w together with the following constraints $((d_i\{PO\}d_w) \wedge (d_j\{PO\}d_w) \wedge (d_w\{NC\}d_u) \wedge (d_i\{PO\}d_u) \wedge (d_j\{PO\}d_u) \wedge (d_i\{DC\}d_v) \wedge (d_j\{PO\}d_v))$.
5. $d_i\{DC, NC\}d_j$: we add the variables d_u, d_v, d_t, d_w, d_z that respectively satisfy the same constraints as those satisfied by d_0, d_1, d_0', d_1', d, defined during the proof of proposition 4. Moreover, we impose the following conditions $((d_i\{PO\}d_u) \wedge (d_i\{PO\}d_v) \wedge (d_i\{NC\}d_z) \wedge (d_j\{PO\}d_t) \wedge (d_j\{PO\}d_w) \wedge (d_j\{NC\}d_z))$.
6. $d_i\{DC, PO\}d_j$: we add the variables d_u, d_v, d_w together with the following constraints $((d_u\{DC\}d_w) \wedge (d_i\{PO\}d_w) \wedge (d_i\{PO\}d_u) \wedge (d_j\{PO\}d_w) \wedge (d_j\{PO\}d_u) \wedge (d_v\{NC\}d_i) \wedge (d_v\{PO\}d_j))$.
7. $d_i\{EQ, DC, PO\}d_j$: we add the variables d_u, d_v together with the following constraints $((d_i\{PO\}d_u) \wedge (d_i\{PO\}d_v) \wedge (d_j\{PO\}d_u) \wedge (d_j\{PO\}d_v) \wedge (d_u\{DC\}d_v))$.
8. $d_i\{EQ, NC, PO\}d_j$: we add the variables d_u, d_v together with the following constraints $((d_i\{PO\}d_u) \wedge (d_i\{PO\}d_v) \wedge (d_j\{PO\}d_u) \wedge (d_j\{PO\}d_v) \wedge (d_u\{NC\}d_v))$.

9. $d_i\{DC, PO, NC\}d_j$: we add the variables d_t, d_u, d_v, d_w together with the following constraints $((d_u\{PO\}d_v) \wedge (d_v\{DC\}d_w) \wedge (d_u\{NC\}d_w) \wedge (d_t\{PO\}d_u) \wedge (d_t\{PO\}d_v) \wedge (d_t\{PO\}d_w) \wedge (d_i\{PO\}d_u) \wedge (d_i\{PO\}d_v) \wedge (d_i\{NC\}d_t) \wedge (d_j\{PO\}d_t) \wedge (d_j\{PO\}d_w))$.

10. $d_i\{DC, EQ, NC\}d_j$: we add the variables d_u, d_v, d_w together with the following constraints $((d_v\{DC\}d_u) \wedge (d_u\{PO\}d_w) \wedge (d_w\{PO\}d_v) \wedge (d_i\{DC\}d_u) \wedge (d_i\{NC\}d_w) \wedge (d_j\{DC, PO\}d_u) \wedge (d_j\{DC, PO\}d_v))$.

The path consistency property enables us to check that the resulting network has the same set of consistent scenarios as (I, C). Also note that for a spatial network of n elements, there are at most n^2 constraints. We conclude that our reduction is polynomial in the size of the network (I, C), and is done in time $O(n^2)$.

Corollary 2. *The consistency problem of atomic spatial networks is NP-hard.*

In the proof of proposition 4, it suffices to transform the relations $\{PO, NC\}$ and $\{PO, DC\}$ into atomic ones.

6 Conclusion and Perspectives

In this paper we studied several path-consistent constraint networks of lines in the Euclidean plane and space. Our main goal was to determine the complexity of the consistency problem of a network of linear lines. We have already shown that for a network of linear lines, this problem is in P. Considering some special relations between two parallel lines in a plane, we established that the complexity problem of an oriented 2D linear network (i.e. when the orientation of parallel lines is taken into account) is still in P, whereas the one concerning a metric 2D network (i.e. when the distance separating two parallel lines is considered) is NP-complete. We then showed that the consistency problem of atomic networks of lines in the Euclidean space is NP-hard, by polynomially reducing the problem "Not-all-equal SAT" to the problem of lines in the space.

Our next step is to determine the complexity of oriented and metric networks in the Euclidean space. But first, an important question that arises is whether the consistency problem of spatial networks is in NP. Given such a network $\mathcal{R}$, we need to exhibit a non deterministic program running in polynomial time in the length of the spatial network's variables, that computes a consistent scenario for $\mathcal{R}$.

Acknowledgements. Khalil Challita benefits from grants, allowed by the Lebanese National Council for Scientific Research and by the Paul Sabatier University.

References

1. Allen, J., *Maintaining knowledge about temporal intervals*, Communications of the Association for Computing Machinery, **26**, pp. 832–843, 1983.
2. Balbiani, P., *Raisonner à propos des droites et des cercles: réseaux de contraintes et systèmes déductifs*, Reconnaissance des Formes et Intelligence Artificielle (RFIA), 2004.

3. Bennett, B., Isli, A., Cohn, A.G. *When does a composition table provide a complete and tractable proof procedure for a relational constraint language?*, in: Proceedings of International Joint Conference on Artificial Intelligence (IJCAI), 1997.
4. Clarke, B. *Individuals and points*, Notre Dame Journal of Formal Logic, **26**, pp. 61–75, 1985.
5. Cui, Z., Cohn, A., Randell, D. *Qualitative and topological relationships in spatial databases* in: Proceedings of SSD-93, pp. 296–315, 1993.
6. Jean-François Condotta *Problèmes de satisfaction de contraintes spatiales : algorithmes et complexité*, Thèse de l'université Paul Sabatier, 2000.
7. Dechter, R., Meiri, I., Pearl, J. *Temporal constraint networks*, Artificial Intelligence, pp. 61–95, 1991.
8. Egenhofer, M.J. *Reasoning about binary topological relationships*, in: proceedings of SSD-91, pp. 143–160, 1991.
9. Frank, A.U. *Qualitative spatial reasoning about distances and directions in geographic space*, Languages and Computing, pp. 343–371, 1992.
10. Freska, C. *Using orientation information for qualitative spatial reasoning*, in: Proceedings of COSIT-92, Lecture Notes in Computer Science, Springer, pp. 162–178, 1992.
11. Freuder, E. *A Sufficient condition for backtrack-free search*, Journal of the ACM, pp. 24–32, 1982.
12. Henkin, L., Suppes, P., Tarski, A. *The axiomatic method*, North Holland, 1959.
13. Ligozat, G. *Reasoning about cardinal directions*, Journal of Visual Languages and Computing, **9**, pp. 23–44, 1998.
14. Mackworth, A. *Consistency in networks of relations*, Artificial Intelligence, pp. 99–118, 1977.
15. Mackworth, A., Freuder, E. *The complexity of some polynomial network consistency algorithms for constraint satisfaction problems*, Artificial Intelligence, pp. 65–74, 1985.
16. Montanari, U. *Networks of constraints: Fundamental properties and application to picture processing*, Information Sciences, pp. 95–132, 1974.
17. Papadias, D., Theodoridis, T., Sellis, T., Egenhofer, M.J. *Topological relations in the world of minimum bounding rectangles: a study with R-trees*, in: Proceedings in ACM SIGMOD-95, pp. 92–103, 1995.
18. Papadimitriou, C. *Computational complexity*, Addison Wesley, USA, 1994.
19. Randell, D., Cui, Z., Cohn, A. *A spatial logic based on regions and connection*, in Nebel, B., Rich, C., Swartout, W. (editors): Proceedings of the Third International Conference on Principles of Knowledge Representation and Reasoning. Morgan Kaufman, pp. 165–176, 1992.
20. Renz, J., Nebel, B. *On the complexity of qualitative spatial reasoning: a maximal tractable fragment of the region connection calculus*, Proceedings IJCAI-97, Nagoya, Japan, pp. 522–527, 1997.
21. Sistla, A.P., Yu, C., Haddad, R. *Reasoning about Spatial Relations in Picture Retrieval Systems*, in: Proceedings in VLDB-94, pp. 570–581, 1994.
22. Skiadopoulos, S., Koubarakis, M. *Composing cardinal directions relations*, in: Proceedings of the Seventh International Symposium on Spatial and Temporal Databases (SSTD'01), Lecture Notes in Computer Science, Springer, pp. 299–317, 2001.
23. Vilain, M., Kautz, H. *Constraint propagation algorithms for temporal reasoning*, Proceedings of the Fifth National Conference on Artificial Intelligence. American Association for Artificial Intelligence, pp. 377–382, 1986.
24. Zimmermann, K. *Enhancing qualitative spatial reasoning- Combining orientation and distance*, in: Proceedings of COSIT-93, Lecture Notes in Computer Science, Springer, pp. 69–76, 1993.

An Oracle Based Meta-learner for Function Decomposition

R. Shyam Sundar Yadav and Deepak Khemani

Dept. of Computer Science and Engineering,
Indian Institute of Technology Madras,
Chennai 600036, India.
shyam@cs.iitm.ernet.in, khemani@iitm.ac.in

Abstract. Function decomposition is a machine learning algorithm that induces the target concept in the form of a hierarchy of intermediate concepts and their definitions. Though it is effective in discovering the concept structure hidden in the training data, it suffers much from under sampling. In this paper, we propose an oracle based meta learning method that generates new examples with the help of a bagged ensemble to induce accurate classifiers when the training data sets are small. Here the values of new examples to be generated and the number of such examples required are automatically determined by the algorithm. Previous work in this area deals with the generation of fixed number of random examples irrespective of the size of the training set's attribute space. Experimental analysis on different sized data sets shows that our algorithm significantly improves accuracy of function decomposition and is superior to existing meta-learning method.

Keywords: Machine learning, Function decomposition, Bagging, Meta-learning.

1   Introduction

Function decomposition is a machine learning and data mining algorithm proposed by Zupan et. al. [12] that discovers hierarchical structure of the target concept hidden in the training data. As opposed to other symbolic learning algorithms which represent the classifier in terms of rules or decision trees, function decomposition induces the classifier in the form of a set of intermediate function (or concept) definitions and associations among them. Given a set of training examples described by a set of input attributes and a class label, function decomposition first divides this data set into two by partitioning the input attribute set. These two are then recursively divided resulting in a hierarchy of concepts. Generalization also occurs in this discovery of hierarchical structure.

It is empirically shown that function decomposition is effective in finding the correct concept structure underlying the training data and accurate in predicting the class values of unseen examples. However, it is more sensitive to training data and suffers much from under sampling [12]. When training set is small, it does

C. Bussler and D. Fensel (Eds.): AIMSA 2004, LNAI 3192, pp. 158–167, 2004.

not guarantee the discovery of correct intermediate concepts and thus tends to be less accurate. Thus it becomes inapplicable to find accurate classifiers from a sparse training data.

In this paper, we present an oracle based meta-learning method called *oracle* HINT that generates additional examples with the help of a bagged ensemble, adds them to the training data and then induces a classifier from this new training data. This method is inspired from combined multiple models (CMM) approach to induce accurate classifiers [3]. The main idea behind this approach can be summarized as follows. In general, when the training data is sparse, the learning algorithm's heuristics may not allow it to find the accurate classifier. So, the learning algorithm's heuristics may benefit if the algorithm is given some additional examples. The class values of additional examples can be found from an ensemble constructed from the same training data, as ensemble is shown to be more accurate than a single classifier [2].

However, the proposed method differs from CMM in two important ways: (1) the new examples that have to be generated are automatically determined by the method (2) the number of new examples generated changes from one data set to another and is found by the method, where as in CMM the values for the new examples are generated randomly following the distribution inherent in the classifier produced by bagged ensemble and the number of new examples is set to 1000 irrespective of the size of the training data set. These two modifications are necessary in order to properly guide the heuristics of learning algorithm by providing the right examples and to vary the number of new examples according to training set's domain size, as generating too many examples may mislead the meta-learning algorithm in the case of small attribute spaces. The proposed method is experimentally evaluated to verify its accuracy gains as well as its superiority to CMM approach.

The rest of the paper is organized as follows. Section 2 reviews the related work. Section 3 first describes the function decomposition algorithm and then presents our method, *oracle*HINT. Empirical evaluation of our method is presented in Section 4. Finally Section 5 concludes by specifying directions to future work.

2   Related Work

Asenhurst [1] first proposed decomposition method for the design of switching circuits. His decomposition method was used to decompose a truth table of a specific boolean function to be then realized with standard binary gates. Recently, his method was improved to allow incompletely specified switching functions [7]. Luba [4] presented a method for the decomposition of multi-valued switching functions in which each multi-valued variable is encoded by a set of Boolean variables. The authors also identified the usefulness of function decomposition for machine learning.

Within the machine learning framework, there are approaches that are based on problem decomposition but where the problem is decomposed by an expert and not automatically discovered by machine. A well-known example is structured induction applied by Shapiro [9]. This approach is based on a manual decomposition of the problem and an expert assisted selection of examples to construct rules for the concepts in the hierarchy.

Recently Zupan et. al. [11] proposed a new method for function decomposition in the context of machine learning. The main objectives of this method are to automatically derive the hierarchical structure hidden in the training set and to induce classifiers that generalize from training data. The current paper tries to improve the accuracy of this function decomposition method in the case of small training sets with the help of an ensemble. One such approach where an ensemble is used to improve the quality of classifier can be found in [3]. The main idea of this method is to generate 1000 new examples following the distribution present in the classifier produced by an ensemble, find the class values of these new examples using that ensemble and then induce a classifier from the original training examples *and* these new examples.

3   An Oracle Based Function Decomposition

In this section, we first briefly describe the function decomposition method, then analyze the reasons for its inaccuracy when the training data is sparse, and finally present our method.

3.1   Function Decomposition

Given a set of training examples E_F that partially describes the function $y = F(\underline{X})$ and a partition $A|B$ of input attributes such that $A \cap B = \phi$ and $A \cup B = X$, the goal of the core part of the algorithm is to find two new intermediate concepts $c_i = G(A, c_j)$ and $c_j = H(B)$ by constructing two new example sets E_G and E_H respectively. This process is called *single step decomposition* or *basic decomposition step*.

The two examples sets are discovered in the following way. Given an example set E_F and a disjoint partition of X to $A|B$, single step decomposition step first constructs a partition matrix, $P_{A|B}$ which is a tabular representation of example set E_F with all combinations of values of attributes in A as row labels and of B as column labels. Each example $e_i \in E_F$ has its corresponding entry in $P_{A|B}$ with a row index $A(e_i)$ and a column index $B(e_i)$. Those entries which do not have corresponding examples in E_F are unspecified. An example data set and a partition matrix are shown in the Figure 1 for illustrative purpose.

Each column in the partition matrix denotes the behaviour of F when the attributes in B are constant. The columns which have the same entries for all rows are said to be compatible to one another. All columns of partition matrix are given numeric values that describe the intermediate function c_j such that compatible columns get the same value. This numbering of columns is found by coloring the *column incompatibility graph*, a graph whose vertices are columns of partition matrix and whose edges connect two vertices if the columns they

$x1$	$x2$	$x3$	y
lo	lo	lo	lo
lo	lo	hi	lo
lo	hi	hi	hi
med	med	lo	med
med	hi	lo	med
med	hi	hi	hi
hi	lo	lo	hi
hi	med	lo	med
hi	med	hi	med
hi	hi	lo	hi

x_2	lo	lo	med	med	hi	hi
$x_1\ x_3$	lo	hi	lo	hi	lo	hi
lo	lo	lo	-	-	-	hi
med	-	-	med	-	med	hi
hi	hi	-	med	med	hi	-
c	1	1	2	2	1	3

Fig. 1. An example data set that partially specifies $y = F(x1, x2, x3)$ and a Partition matrix for the partition $\{x1\}|\{x2, x3\}$.

represent are incompatible. The intermediate concept values are shown in the last line of the partition matrix of Figure 1.

Now, the column labels along with these numeric values constitute the example set E_H for the concept $c_j = H(B)$. The second example set E_G is also derived from partition matrix in the following way. For any value of c_j and combination of values of attributes in A, $c_i = G(A, c_j)$ is determined by looking for an example e_i in row $A(e_i)$ and in any column labeled with the value of c_j. If such example exists, an example with the attribute set $A \cup \{c_j\}$ and class $c_i = F(e_i)$ is added to E_G. Decomposition generalizes every unspecified entry of $P_{A|B}$ in a row a and a column b, if a corresponding example e_i with $a = A(e_i)$ and column $B(e_i)$ with the same label as b is found.

This basic decomposition step is recursively applied to the two intermediate functions until the overall complexity of decomposed function is less than the complexity of original function or the original function contains fewer than than two attributes.

Note that the basic decomposition step requires the partition of input attribute set along with the example set that has to be decomposed. This correct partition of input attributes is also found with the help of basic decomposition step. Every possible partition of input attribute set is evaluated by basic decomposition step and the one that requires minimum number of values to encode the intermediate function is chosen as the best partition of input attributes. The size of second partition (B) is limited by an upper bound, b (=3), similar to [11].

3.2   Problems Due to Sparseness of Data

When the training data set is small, most of the entries of partition matrix are unspecified. In such a scenario, the basic decomposition step may not have enough support (number of entries that match) to make two columns compatible. Moreover, there is a chance of making two columns compatible even though the two columns may not have same entries, because of unspecified entries which match with any value. This affects the discovery of both the number of labels required to encode intermediate function and value of intermediate concept for each column. Thus, the function decomposition algorithm may not have enough information to find the correct definitions of intermediate concepts.

3.3   The *Oracle*HINT Meta-learning Algorithm

In this sub section, we present our oracle based function decomposition method, called oracleHINT. The method mainly consists of three modules: Partition selector, Training set expander and Oracle. Training set expander finds the input values of new examples whereas the class values of these additional examples are determined with the help of a bagged ensemble (called Oracle) constructed using function decomposition as the base algorithm. The main purpose of partition selector is to evaluate all the partitions and choose the best partition. The algorithm is shown in the Figure 2. The details of three modules are given in the following.

Oracle. At every level of decomposition, the example set E_{F_i} that needs to be decomposed into E_G and E_H is passed to oracle which then constructs a bagged ensemble from it. The next role of oracle is to find the class values of new examples. The new examples presented to oracle are complete in the sense that values are specified for all input attributes.

Training set expander. The main role of training set expander is to populate the partition matrix such that basic decomposition step possesses sufficient information to find the correct intermediate concept definition. Given a partition matrix and intermediate concept labels for all columns, training set expander first groups the columns according to their labels. Then for each group, it finds the input attribute values of the unspecified entries. Note that these can be obtained by looking at the row and column indices of unspecified entries. These unspecified entries constitute the new example set. The main idea here is to re-evaluate the correctness of concept labels of partition matrix columns (and hence the intermediate concept definition) by providing additional information for each group. This procedure is illustrated in the Figure 3 for the partition matrix of Figure 1.

Note that all the unspecified entries are added to additional example set here. However, it is not the case in general, as there is an upper bound on the number of examples added to each partition matrix. The reason behind this upper bound is this: since bagged ensemble is only slightly accurate than the base algorithm, generation of too many examples may mislead the meta learning algorithm. In general, for every group the algorithm adds at most k ($= 10$) unspecified entries of each row. Moreover, there is an upper bound, N ($= 1500$), on the total number of examples added to the best partition at all levels.

For efficient implementation, we followed similar approach of [11]. The algorithm first sorts the examples E_F based on the values of attributes in A and

---

oracleHINT(Example Set E_{F_0})
  Mark the initial example set E_{F_0} decomposable
  $j \leftarrow 1$
  $newExamples \leftarrow 0$
  while there exists a decomposable set E_{F_i} that partially specifies
       $c_i = F_i(x_1, ..., x_m)$ with $m > 2$ **do**
    construct bagged ensemble (oracle) from E_{F_i}
    evaluate all possible partitions $A|B$ of $X = (x_1, ..., x_m)$ such that
      $A \cup B = X, A \cap B = \phi$, and $\|B\| \leq b$
    if $newExamples < N$ **do**
      select all partitions that result in intermediate concepts with
        the same minimum cardinality
      for each such partition p **do**
        group the partition matrix according to the column labels
        for each row r and each group g of the partition matrix **do**
          add $n_p = min(k$, number of unspecified entries present in row r
          and group g) examples in each group
        end for
      end for
    end if
    re-evaluate the selected partitions
    select the best partition $A|B$, call it p_{best}
    $newExamples \leftarrow newExamples + n_{best}$
    if E_{F_i} is decomposable using $A|B$ **then**
      decompose E_{Fi} to E_G and E_H, such that $c_i = G(A, c_j)$ and
      mark E_G and E_H decomposable
      $j \leftarrow j + 1$
    else mark E_{F_i} non-decomposable
  end while

Fig. 2. The *oracle*HINT meta-learning algorithm

vales of c_i. The examples with the same $A(e_i)$ constitute groups that correspond to rows in partition matrix $P_{A|B}$. Within each group, examples with the same value of c_i constitute subgroups. We further sort each subgroup according to their class label to obtain sub-subgroup. Note that it does not imply that two columns that are in the same subgroup have the same class label. The input values of new examples can easily be obtained in the following way. First arrange the columns of partition matrix according to their class label in a temporary list called *gpColumnsByColor*. Then for each sub-subgroup, find the class value of first column and then use gpColumnsByColor to find the remaining columns that are absent in that particular sub-subgroup and have the same class value. These form the B part of new examples. The A part is obtained by the values of the group (or row) in which this sub-subgroup exists.

x_2	lo	lo	hi	med	med	hi
$x_1\ x_3$	lo	hi	lo	lo	hi	hi
lo	lo	lo	-	-	-	hi
med	-	-	med	med	-	hi
hi	hi	-	hi	med	med	-
c	1	1	1	2	2	3

$x1$	$x2$	$x3$
lo	med	lo
lo	med	hi
lo	hi	lo
med	lo	lo
med	lo	hi
med	med	hi
hi	lo	hi
hi	hi	hi

Fig. 3. Rearranged partition matrix and input values of Additional examples

Partition selector. Given a training set E_{F_i}, partition selector chooses all partitions which result in intermediate concepts that have the same minimum size with the help of basic decomposition step. Our experiments with function decomposition revealed that many partitions result in the same sized intermediate concepts because of sparseness of data. It then passes these partition matrices along with the concept labels to training set expander which adds new examples. The next role of partition selector is to re-evaluate these partition matrices (after addition of examples) and choose the best partition.

4   Empirical Evaluation

This section presents the empirical evaluation of the proposed method. Apart from verifying *oracle*HINT meta-learning method, we also evaluate combined multiple model approach to HINT in order to asses that guided generation of additional examples and varying the number of additional examples according to the size of the domain will indeed result in more accurate classifiers. Thus the issues that are addressed in the empirical study include (1) the accuracy gains provided by *oracle*HINT to HINT (2) superiority of *oracle*HINT over CMMHINT in improving accuracy.

The function decomposition method, HINT, we implemented was the one proposed in [11]. This does not deal with the noise data and continuous classes. We also implemented CMMHINT, CMM with function decomposition as the base learner. The number of additional examples (N) generated in this case is experimentally calculated by varying the number from 1000 to 2000 in steps of 500. $N = 1500$ yielded better results and hence this number is chosen for CMMHINT as well as the upper bound for *oracle*HINT. The number of models generated for bagged ensemble and CMMHINT is set to 10.

The experiments are carried out on 8 data sets taken from UCI Machine learning repository [10]. The characteristics of these datasets are shown in the Table 1. There are basically two kinds of datasets: full training sets taken from large domains and a small portion of available training data taken from small domains. The datasets Wisconsin breast cancer, Vote, Breast cancer and Lym-

Table 1. Characteristics of the Data sets used in the experimental study

Dataset	♯examples	♯attrs	♯classes	♯val/attrs
Wisconsin breast cancer	683	9	2	10
Vote	435	16	2	3
Breast cancer	277	9	4	5.67
Lymphography	148	8	4	3.28
Monk1 (5%)	24	6	2	2.8
Monk2 (20%)	84	6	2	2.8
Car (10%)	172	6	4	3.5
Balance (30%)	187	4	3	5

phography fall in the first category while Monk1, Monk2, Car and Balance come under second category. [1] The proportion of training data taken for second category is also included in the Table 1 and shown next to the data set name. These two kinds of data sets are taken in order to analyze the effects of input domain's size on the number of additional examples generated.

Classification accuracies are measured using 10-fold stratified cross valida tion. The average and the standard deviation of the accuracies for all the methods are shown in the Table 2. From the table, it is evident that *oracle*HINT improves the accuracy of HINT on all the datasets. Moreover, it outperforms CMMHINT in all but two data sets where the accuracy is slightly lower (0.36% and 0.67%). The average gain of accuracy provided by *oracle*HINT and CMMHINT are 8.59% and 2.55% respectively. *Oracle*HINT is more accurate than HINT and CMMHINT with a confidence of 99% and 98% respectively, according to a paired t-test. The number additional of examples generated by *oracle*HINT for each of the data set is shown in the Table 3. From the table it is clear that *oracle*HINT generates new examples according to the size of the training set's domain. Note that at every level, additional examples are added for several candidate parttitions. The number indicated here is the sum of the number of examples added for the best selected partition found after re-evaluation at all levels.

For the Wisconsin breast cancer data set, *oracle*HINT and CMMHINT improved the accuracy of HINT by 3.14% and 0.44% respectively. Note that the number of new examples generated by *oracle*HINT in this case is only 1375 as compared to 1500 generated by CMMHINT. This means that with a fewer number of appropriate new examples, *oracle*HINT is able to produce a clas- sifer that is 2.7% more accurate than CMMHINT. In the case of Vote data set, *oracle*HINT generated 1528 new examples and is able to produce a classifier that is 6.59% and 1.55% more accurate than HINT and CMMHINT respectively. That is with only 28 additional examples, when comparaed to CMMHINT, *oracle*HINT produced a more accurate classifier which is a clear evidence of our

---

[1] Lymphography and Breast Cancer data sets were obtained from the University Med- ical Centre, Institute of Oncology, Ljubljana, Yugoslavia. Thanks go to M. Zwitter and M. Soklic for providing the data.

Table 2. Classification accuracies (%) of HINT, *oracle*HINT and CMMHINT

Data set	HINT	*oracle*HINT	CMMHINT
Wisconsin breast cancer	92.68 ± 2.18	95.82 ± 1.8	93.12 ± 3
Vote	88.18 ± 7.03	94.77 ± 4.32	89.63 ± 17.64
Breast cancer	67.14 ± 14	70 ± 7.35	70.36 ± 9.31
Lymphography	54 ± 12.8	56 ± 13.1	56.67 ± 15.28
Monk1	83.33 ± 22	93.33 ± 13.3	86 ± 22
Monk2	85.5 ± 16.6	95 ± 15	93.33 ± 7.37
Car	86.67 ± 7.93	92.69 ± 5.56	88.46 ± 6.44
Balance	78.42 ± 8.95	91.05 ± 10.27	82.63 ± 9.43

Table 3. Number of new Examples Generated by *oracle*HINT

Dataset	No.of new Examples
Wisconsin breast cancer	1375
Vote	1528
Breast cancer	1059
Lymphography	1512
Monk1	172
Monk2	217
Car	170
Balance	193

claim that producing suitable new examples in stead of random examples would greatly benifit the meta-learning algorithm to induce accurate classifiers.

However, in the two data sets, the accuracy of *oracle*HINT falls just below that of CMMHINT. For the Breast cancer domain, the accuracy gain provided by CMMHINT is 3.22% where as *oracle*HINT gained 2.86%. However, the *oracle*HINT algorithm generated only 1059 new examples as contrast to 1500 generated by CMMHINT. Thus *oracle*HINT used a fewer number of new examples to produce a classifier that is closely equivalent (in terms of accuracy) to that of CMMHINT which means that all new examples would have been helpful to the heuristics of the meta-learner.

In the case of small domains, both meta-learning algorithms, as expected, perform uniformly better than HINT and *oracle*HINT outperforms CMMHINT on all data sets. The accuracy gains provided by *oracle*HINT are very high averaging over 9.54% while that of CMMHINT average over 4.12%. Note that the number of additional exmaples generated *oracle*HINT for these data sets is approximately 200. However, they are able to produce classifiers that are 5% more accurate than that of CMMHINT on the average. Since no domain's total size is more than 1500, we can imply that many examples generated in the case of CMMHINT caused it to induce less accurate classifiers.

5 Conclusions

In this paper we presented a novel meta-learning approach for function decomposition to induce accurate classifiers. The existing work [3] in this area deals with the generation of some fixed number of random examples. The main contribution of the proposed method is the generation of suitable examples and the automatic discovery of the number of examples required. The advantages of these two modifications to the existing work are experimentally verified.

In the case of large domains, many partitions result in the same sized intermediate concepts thus making all of them candidates to be further investigated. In such case generating examples for each partition may increase the time complexity of the meta-learner drastically. So, possible future direction includes finding a new measure that can distinguish and rank the candidate partitions. We are currently working on one such measure related to compatibility ratio which measures the confidence with which a particular partition defines the intermediate function.

References

1. Asenhurst, L.: The decomposition of switching functions. *Technical Report*, Bell laboratories. pages 541-602, 1952.
2. Breiman, L.: Bagging predictors. *Machine Learning*, pages 123-140, 1996.
3. Domingos, P.: Knowledge acquisition from examples via multiple models. *Proc. of the Fourteenth International Conference on Machine Learning*, pages 148-156, 1997.
4. Luba T.: Decomposition of multiple-valued functions. *25th Intl. Symposium on Multiple-Valued Logic*, pages 255-261, 1995.
5. Michie, D.: Problem decomposition and the learning of skill. *Machine Learning: ECML-95*, Notes in Artificial Intelligence, pages 17-31, 1995.
6. Michalski, R.S.: Understanding the nature of learning: issues and research directions. *Machine Learning: An Artificial Intelligence Approach*, pages 3-25, 1986. Morgan Kaufmann.
7. Perkowski, M.A. et. al.: Unified approach to functional decomposition of switching functions. *Technical report*, Warsaw University of Technology and Eindhoven University of Technology. 1995.
8. Pfahringer,B.: Controlling constructive induction in CiPF. Machine Learning: ECML-94, pages 242-256, 1994. Springer-Verlag.
9. Shapiro, A.D.: *Structured induction in expert systems*. Turing Institute Press in association with Addison-Wesley Publishing Company. 1987.
10. Merz, C.J., Murphy. P.M. and Aha, D.W.: UCI repository of machine learning databases. Department of Information and Computer Science, University of California at Irvine, Irvine, CA. 1997.
11. Zupan, B., Bohanec, M., Demsar, J. and Bratko, I.: Machine Learning by function decomposition. *Proc. of the Fourteenth International Conference on Machine Learning*, pages 421-429, 1997.
12. Zupan, B., Bohanec, M., Demsar, J. and Bratko, I.: Learning by discovering concept hierarchies. *Artificial Intelligence*, 109:211-242, 1999.

Bagged Voting Ensembles

S.B. Kotsiantis and P.E. Pintelas

Educational Software Development Laboratory
Department of Mathematics
University of Patras, Hellas

Abstract. Bayesian and decision tree classifiers are among the most popular classifiers used in the data mining community and recently numerous researchers have examined their sufficiency in ensembles. Although, many methods of ensemble creation have been proposed, there is as yet no clear picture of which method is best. In this work, we propose Bagged Voting using different subsets of the same training dataset with the concurrent usage of a voting methodology that combines a Bayesian and a decision tree algorithm. In our algorithm, voters express the degree of their preference using as confidence score the probabilities of classifiers' prediction. Next all confidence values are added for each candidate and the candidate with the highest sum wins the election. We performed a comparison of the presented ensemble with other ensembles that use either the Bayesian or the decision tree classifier as base learner and we took better accuracy in most cases.

1 Introduction

In contrast to statistics where prior knowledge is expressed in the form of probability distributions over the observations and over the assumed dependencies data mining techniques make their prior knowledge explicit by restricting the space of assumed dependencies without making any distributional assumptions. Recently, the concept of combining data mining algorithms is proposed as a new direction for the improvement of the performance of individual algorithms. An ensemble of classifiers is a set of classifiers whose individual decisions are combined in some way to classify new instances. In [5] is provided an accessible and informal reasoning, from statistical, computational and representational viewpoints, of why ensembles can improve results. The main reason may be that the training data can not provide sufficient information for selecting a single best classifier from the set of hypotheses, because the amount of training data available is too small compared to the size of the hypothesis space.

Several methods have been recommended for the design of ensemble of classifiers [5]. Mechanisms that are used to make ensemble of classifiers include: i) Using different subset of training data with a single data mining method, ii) Using different training parameters with a single training method, iii) Using different data mining methods. Even though, many methods of ensemble design have been proposed, there is as yet no clear picture of which method is best. This is in part because only a limited number of comparisons have been attempted and several of those have aggregated on com

C. Bussler and D. Fensel (Eds.): AIMSA 2004, LNAI 3192, pp. 168–177, 2004.

paring boosting to bagging [1, 4, 25]. Both boosting and bagging are generic techniques that can be employed with any base data mining technique. They operate by selectively re-sampling from the training data to generate derived training sets to which the base learner is applied.

This paper explores an alternative method for constructing good ensembles that does not rely on a single data mining algorithm. The idea is very simple: use different subsets of the same training dataset with the concurrently usage of a voting methodology that combines a Bayesian and a decision tree algorithm. Using voting methodology, we expect to obtain better results based on the belief that the majority of experts are more likely to be correct in their decision when they agree in their opinion. In fact, the comparison with other ensembles that use either the Bayesian or decision tree algorithm on 30 standard benchmark datasets showed that the proposed ensemble had better accuracy on the average.

Section 2 presents the most well- known methods for building ensembles, while section 3 discusses the proposed ensemble method. Experiment results and comparisons of the presented combining method in a number of datasets with other ensembles that also use as base learner either the decision tree or the Bayesian classifier are presented in section 4. We conclude in Section 5 with summary and further research topics.

2 Ensembles of Classifiers

As we have already mentioned the concept of combining classifiers is proposed as a new direction for the improvement of the performance of individual classifiers. The goal of classification result integration algorithms is to generate more certain, precise and accurate system results. This section provides a brief survey of methods for constructing ensembles.

Bagging [4] is a ``bootstrap" ensemble method that creates individuals for its ensemble by training each classifier on a random redistribution of the training set. Each classifier's training set is generated by randomly drawing, with replacement, N examples - where N is the size of the original training set; many of the original examples may be repeated in the resulting training set while others may be left out. After the construction of several classifiers, taking a vote of the predictions of each classifier performs the final prediction.

In [4], it was made the important observation that instability (responsiveness to changes in the training data) is a prerequisite for bagging to be effective. A committee of classifiers that all agree in all circumstances will give identical performance to any of its members in isolation. Bagging decision trees has been proved to be very successful for many data mining problems [1, 4, 25].

Another method that uses different subset of training data with a single data mining method is the boosting approach [7]. Boosting is similar in overall structure to bagging, except that keeps track of the performance of the data mining algorithm and concentrates on instances that have not been correctly learned. Instead of choosing the t training instances randomly using a uniform distribution, it chooses the training instances in such a manner as to favor the instances that have not been accurately learned. After several cycles, the prediction is performed by taking a weighted vote of the predictions of each classifier, with the weights being proportional to each classifier's accuracy on its training set.

AdaBoost is a practical version of the boosting approach [7]. There are two ways that Adaboost can use these weights to construct a new training set to give to the base data mining algorithm. In boosting by sampling, examples are drawn with replacement with probability proportional to their weights. The second method, boosting by weighting, can be used with base data mining algorithms that can accept a weighted training set directly. With such algorithms, the entire training set (with associated weights) is given to the base data mining algorithm. Adaboost requires less instability than bagging, because Adaboost can make much larger changes in the training set.

MultiBoosting [21] is another method of the same category that can be considered as wagging committees formed by AdaBoost. Wagging is a variant of bagging; bagging uses re-sampling to get the datasets for training and producing a weak hypothesis, whereas wagging uses re-weighting for each training example, pursuing the effect of bagging in a different way. A number of experiments showed that MultiBoost achieves greater mean error reductions than any of AdaBoost or bagging decision trees at both committee sizes that were investigated (10 and 100) [21].

Another approach for building ensembles of classifiers is to use a variety of data mining algorithms on all of the training data and combine their predictions. When multiple classifiers are combined using voting methodology, we expect to obtain good results based on the belief that the majority of experts are more likely to be correct in their decision when they agree in their opinion [9].

Another method for combining classifiers - called Grading- trains a meta-level classifier for each base-level classifier [19]. The meta-level classifier predicts whether the base-level classifier is to be trusted (i.e., whether its prediction will be correct). The base-level attributes are used also as meta-level attributes, while the meta-level class values are + (correct) and − (incorrect). Only the base-level classifiers that are predicted to be correct are taken and their predictions combined by summing up the predicted probability distributions. Stacked generalization [20], or Stacking, is another sophisticated approach for combining predictions of different data mining algorithms. Stacking combines multiple classifiers to induce a higher-level classifier with improved performance. In detail, the original data set constitutes the level zero data and all the base classifiers run at this level. The level one data are the outputs of the base classifiers. A data mining algorithm is then used to determine how the outputs of the base classifiers should be combined, using as input the level one data. It has been shown that successful stacked generalization requires the use of output class distributions rather than class predictions [20].

3   Presented Methodology

The combination of two methods that agree everywhere cannot lead to any accuracy improvement no matter how ingenious a combination method is employed. Naïve

Bayes (NB) [6] and C4.5 [15] differ a lot in their predictions since it was proved after a number of comparisons, that the methodology of selecting the best classifier of NB and C4.5 according to 3-cross validation gives better accuracy in most cases than bagging or boosting or multiboost NB and C4.5 [10].

Bagging uses a voting technique which is unable to take into account the heterogeneity of the instance space. When majority of the base classifiers give a wrong prediction for a new instance then the majority vote will result in a wrong prediction. The problem may consist in discarding base classifiers (by assigning small weights) that are highly accurate in a restricted region of the instance space because this accuracy is swamped by their inaccuracy outside the restricted area. It may also consist in the use of classifiers that are accurate in most of the space but still unnecessarily confuse the whole classification committee in some restricted areas of the space. To overcome this problem we have suggested the bagged sum rule voting using two data mining algorithms. When the sum rule is used each voter has to give a confidence value for each candidate. In our algorithm, voters express the degree of their preference using as confidence score the probabilities of classifiers prediction [20]. Next all confidence values are added for each candidate and the candidate with the highest sum wins the election. The algorithm is briefly described in Figure 1.

MODEL GENERATION
Let n be the number of instances in the training data.
For each of t iterations (t=10 in our experiments):
• Sample n instances with replacement from training data.
• Built two classifiers (NB, DT) from the sample
• Apply sum voting of the data mining algorithms
• Store the resulting model.

CLASSIFICATION
For each of the t models:
  Predict class of instance using model.
Return class that has been predicted most often.

Fig. 1. The proposed ensemble

The time complexity increases to twice that of bagging. This time increase is, however, compensated for by the empirical fact that the Bagged Voting provides better generalization performance with much smaller ensemble size than bagging,

In [12] is showed that the generalization error, E, of the ensemble can be expressed as $E = \bar{e} - \bar{d}$; where $\bar{e}$ and $\bar{d}$ are the mean error and diversity of the ensemble respectively. This result implics that increasing ensemble diversity while maintaining the average error of ensemble members, should lead to a decrease in ensemble error. Bagged voting leads to larger diversity among member classifiers even though individual classifiers may not achieve an optimal generalization performance. For example, if the increase in diversity ($\bar{d}$) is larger than the increase in average error ($\bar{e}$) of individual classifier, we have a decrease in the generalization error of an ensemble. For this reason, the Bagged Voting scheme is useful in terms of ensemble diversity.

It has been observed that for bagging, an increase in committee size (sub-classifiers) usually leads to a decrease in prediction error, but the relative impact of each successive addition to a committee is ever diminishing. Most of the effect of each technique is obtained by the first few committee members [1, 4, 9, 23]. For this reason, we used 10 sub-classifiers for the proposed algorithm.

It must be also mentioned that the proposed ensemble can be easily parallelized. The computations required to obtain the classifiers in each bootstrap sample are independent of each other. Therefore we can assign tasks to each processor in a balanced manner. By the end each processor has obtained a part of the Bagged Voting ensemble. In the case we use the master-slave parallel programming technique, the method starts with the master splitting the work to be done in small tasks and assigning them to each slave (C4.5 and NB classifiers). Then the master performs an iteration in which if a slave returns a result (this means it finished its work) then the master assigns it another task if there are still tasks to be executed. Once all the tasks have been carried out the master process obtains the results and orders the slaves to finish since there are not more tasks to be carried out. This parallel execution of the presented ensemble can achieve almost linear speedup.

4   Comparisons and Results

For the comparisons of our study, we used 30 well-known datasets mainly from domains from the UCI repository [2]. We have also used data from language morphological analysis (dimin) [3], agricultural domains (eucalyptus, white-colar) [13] and prediction of student dropout (student) [11].

In order to calculate the classifiers' accuracy, the whole training set was divided into ten mutually exclusive and equal-sized subsets and for each subset the classifier was trained on the union of all of the other subsets. Then, cross validation was run 10 times for each algorithm and the median value of the 10-cross validations was calculated (10x10 cross-validation). It must be mentioned that we used the free available source code for algorithms by [22].

In the following tables, we represent with "vv" that the proposed ensemble (Bagged Voting) looses from the specific ensemble. That is, the specific algorithm performed statistically better than the proposed according to t-test with $p<0.001$. In addition, in Tables, we represent with "v" that the proposed ensemble looses from the specific ensemble according to t-test with $p<0.05$. Furthermore, in Tables, "**" indicates that Bagged Voting performed statistically better than the specific ensemble according to t-test with $p<0.001$ while "*" according to $p<0.05$. In all the other cases, there is no significant statistical difference between the results (Draws). It must be mentioned that the conclusions are mainly based on the resulting differences for $p<0.001$ because a p-value of 0.05 is not strict enough, if many classifiers are compared in numerous datasets [17]. However, as one can easily observe the conclusions remain the same with $p<0.05$. In the last rows in all Tables one can see the aggregated results in the form (a/b/c). In this notation "a" means that the proposed ensemble is significantly more accurate than the compared algorithm in a out of 30 datasets, "c" means that the proposed ensemble is significantly less accurate than the compared algorithm in c out of 30 datasets, while in the remaining cases (b), there is no significant statistical difference between the results. In the following Tables, we also present the average error rate of all tested dataset for each ensemble.

The decision on limiting the number of sub-classifiers is important for practical applications. For both Bagging and Boosting, much of the reduction in error appears to have occurred after ten to fifteen classifiers. But Adaboost continues to measurably improve their test-set error until around 25 classifiers for decision trees [14]. For this reason, we used 25 sub-classifiers for our experiments. Firstly, we compare the presented methodology with bagging, boosting and MultiBoost version of NB (using 25 sub-classifiers). Secondly, we compare the presented methodology with bagging, boosting and MultiBoost version of C4.5 (using 25 sub-classifiers). In the last rows of the Table 1 one can see the aggregated results. The presented ensemble is significantly more accurate than bagging NB in seven out of the 30 datasets, while it has significantly higher error rate in none dataset. At this point, it must be also mentioned that the proposed ensemble and the bagging version of NB with 25 sub-classifiers need similar training times. In addition, the presented ensemble is significantly more accurate than boosting NB in 3 out of the 30 datasets, whilst it has significantly higher error rate in one dataset. The presented ensemble has also significantly lower error rates in four out of the 30 datasets than Multiboost NB, whereas it is significantly less accurate in one dataset. What is more, the presented ensemble needed much less time for training than boosting and multi-boosting version of NB algorithm.

The presented ensemble is significantly more accurate than bagging C4.5 in three out of the 30 datasets, while it has significantly higher error rates in none dataset. In addition, the presented ensemble is significantly more accurate than boosting C4.5 in three out of the 30 datasets whilst it has significantly higher error rates in one dataset. Furthermore, the presented ensemble has significantly lower error rates in two out of the 30 datasets than Multiboost C4.5, whereas it is significantly less accurate in one dataset. It must be also mentioned that the resulting statistical differences for $p < 0.05$ are even better for the presented ensemble.

To sum up, on the average the performance of the presented ensemble is more accurate than the other well-known ensembles that use only the NB algorithm from 5.5% to 13.5%. Moreover, on the average the performance of the presented ensemble is more accurate than the other well-known ensembles that use only the C4.5 algorithm from 4% to 7%. What is more, the presented ensemble needed much less time for training than bagging, boosting and multi-boosting version of C4.5 algorithm.

Subsequently, we compare the presented methodology with other well-known ensembles that use either C4.5 or NB as base classifiers. We compare the proposed methodology with:

- Stacking methodology that constructs the meta-data set by the entire predicted class probability distributions [20]. We used NB, C4.5 as base classifiers and MLR [20] as meta-level classifier.
- Voting methodology using NB, C4.5 as base classifiers [5]
- Grading methodology using the instance based classifier IBk with ten nearest neighbors as the meta level classifier [19] and NB, C4.5 as base classifiers.

Table 1. Comparing Bagged Voting ensemble with bagging, boosting and MultiBoost version of NB and C4.5

	Bagged Voting	Bagging NB	Boosting NB	Multi-boost NB	Bagging C4.5	Boosting C4.5	Multi-boost C4.5
anneal	97.93	87.27**	95.2 *	94.13 **	98.83	99.61 v	99.59 v
badge	100	99.69	99.66	99.66	100	100	100
balance	86.68	90.29 v	92.11 vv	92.29 vv	82.33**	76.91**	79.26 **
breast-cancer	72.08	72.73	68.57	69.01	73.37	66.50**	68.27
breast-w	96.15	96.07	95.55	95.58	96.31	96.51	96.51
colic	83.24	78.94 *	77.46 *	79.28	85.23	82.01	83.13
credit-g	75.63	75.13	75.09	74.71	74.17	72.79	74.35
diabetes	76.17	75.57	75.88	76.2	75.67	72.81 *	74.21
dimin	97.56	92.77**	92.93 **	93.95 **	97.07**	96.03 **	96.17 **
eucalyptus	63.51	54.87**	59.06 *	59.24 *	65.02	64.89	64.73
haberman	75.2	74.86	73.94	73.94	72.06	71.12 *	71.12 *
heart-c	83.04	83.24	83.14	83.56	79.54	79.6	79.87
heart-h	84.03	84.16	84.67	84.8	79.91 *	78.28 *	80.11 *
heart-statlog	84.37	83.41	82.3	82.7	81.11	80.15	81.37
hepatitis	83.61	84.39	84.23	84.67	81.63	82.74	83.59
ionosphere	90.66	81.94**	91.12	91.66	92.23	93.62 v	93.54
iris	95.4	95.53	95.07	95.07	94.8	94.47	94.47
kr-vs-kp	99.31	87.80**	95.10**	95.22 **	99.45	99.62 v	99.62 v
labor	90.87	93.4	88.93	90.07	83.83**	89.1	88.1
lymphotherapy	82.06	83.5	80.67	82.64	79.14	83.09	83.24
monk1	81.03	73.35 *	72.37 *	72.42 *	82.32	96.54 vv	94.36 vv
mushroom	100	95.73**	100	100	100	100	100
primary-tumor	47.34	49.47	49.71	49.71	44.4	41.65 *	41.65 *
soybean	93.57	92.83	92.02	93.15	92.78	93.19	93.21
student	86.81	85.59	85.12	85.47	86.49	81.44 *	81.68 *
titanic	78.22	77.86 *	77.86 *	77.88 *	77.93	78.89	78.71
waveform	82.1	80.00**	80.01 **	80.29 **	82.81	83.32	83.73 v
white-clover	66.81	62.79	70.74	71.14	68.69	72.71	71.55
wine	97.18	97.52	96.57	96.57	95.5	96.62	96.84
zoo	96.23	95.07	97.23	97.23	93.29	95.38	95.77
Aver. Error	15.11	17.14	16.26	15.93	16.14	16.01	15.71
W/D/L (p<0.001)		0/23/7	1/26/3	1/25/4	0/27/3	1/26/3	1/27/2
W/D/L (p<0.05)		1/19/10	1/21/8	1/22/7	0/26/4	4/18/8	4/20/6

In the last rows of the Table 2 one can see the aggregated results. The presented ensemble is significantly more accurate than voting in two out of the 30 datasets, whilst it has significantly higher error rate in none dataset. The resulting statistical differences for p<0.05 are even better for the presented ensemble. It must be also mentioned that on the average the performance of the presented ensemble is more accurate than voting about 9.5%.

Table 2. Comparing Bagged Voting ensemble with Stacking, Voting and Grading ensembles

	Bagged Voting	Stacking	Voting	Grading
anneal	97.93	98.51	98.7	98.86
badge	100	100	100	100
balance	86.68	90.23 v	78.41**	90.3 v
breast-cancer	72.08	71.35	71.66	72.04
breast-w	96.15	96.01	95.74	96.08
colic	83.24	85.02	83.07	84.07
credit-g	75.63	74.81	72.58*	74.06
diabetes	76.17	76.39	75.9	75.63
dimin	97.56	97.2*	97.26 *	97.25 *
eucalyptus	63.51	63.6	61.63	61.29
haberman	75.2	73.88	74.34	72.78
heart-c	83.04	83.11	80.1	81.46
heart-h	84.03	83.58	83.95	82.76
heart-statlog	84.37	84.04	80.89	81.63
hepatitis	83.61	84.00	81.98	82.51
ionosphere	90.66	89.97	88.04	92.51
iris	95.4	95.33	95.53	94.87
kr-vs-kp	99.31	99.44	99.38	99.3
labor	90.87	93.57	86.87	90.33
Lymphotherapy	82.06	81.58	78.66	82.39
monk1	81.03	81.02	81.28	79.22
mushroom	100	100	100	100
primary-tumor	47.34	45.93	45.64	47.5
soybean	93.57	93.06	93.47	93.31
student	86.81	86.9	86.73	85.99
titanic	78.22	77.76	77.94	77.9
waveform	82.1	81.84	77.32**	79.55 **
white-clover	66.81	56.43**	65.31	65.93
wine	97.18	97.01	95.84	96.51
zoo	96.23	95.95	95.18	96.15
Aver. Error	*15.11*	*15.42*	*16.55*	*15.59*
W/D/L(p<0.001)		*0/29/1*	*0/28/2*	*0/29/1*
W/D/L(p<0.05)		*1/27/2*	*0/26/4*	*1/27/2*

Similarly, the proposed ensemble is significantly more accurate than Stacking in two out of the 30 datasets, while it is significantly less accurate in one dataset. The average relative accuracy improvement of the proposed ensemble is about 2% better in relation to Stacking. Furthermore, the presented ensemble has significantly lower error rates in one out of the 30 datasets than Grading, whereas it is significantly less accurate in none dataset. Besides, the presented ensemble needed much less time for training than Grading while the average relative accuracy improvement is about 3%.

To sum up, the presented methodology of combining NB and C4.5 algorithms could be an off-the self method-of- choice for a data mining task where there is no a priori knowledge available about the domain and the primary goal of data mining is to develop a classifier with lowest possible classification error.

5   Conclusions

It is known that if we are only concerned for the best possible classification accuracy, it might be difficult or impossible to find a single classifier that performs as well as a good ensemble of classifiers. In this study, we built an ensemble of classifiers using two different data mining methods: the Naive Bayes and the C4.5 algorithm.

Our approach answers to some extend such questions as generating uncorrelated classifiers and control the number of classifiers needed to improve accuracy in the ensemble of classifiers. While ensembles provide very accurate classifiers, too many classifiers in an ensemble may limit their practical application. To be feasible and competitive, it is important that the data mining algorithms run in reasonable time. In our method, we limit the number of sub-classifiers to 10. It was proved after a number of comparisons with other ensembles, which use either C4.5 or NB as base classifiers, that the Bagged Voting methodology gives better accuracy in most cases. It must be also mentioned that the proposed ensemble can be easily parallelized achieving almost linear speedup.

In spite of these results, no general method will work always. In a future work, it would be interesting to study the impact of the number of base classifiers on the necessary data partitions required to keep a certain level of performance of the proposed ensemble

Instability of the base data mining algorithms is a major factor in the ability to generate diversity in the form of anti-correlations between the various base-classifiers in the pool, which is the key for variance reduction. Therefore, one can expect that the relative advantage of our technique will be increased more if we added another one unstable base-classifier such as neural networks. We plan to investigate this direction. Moreover, there is no reason to restrict this approach to combining classifiers. Combining different regressions is another important problem which could be handled by this approach replacing voting with averaging.

Finally, there are some other open problems in ensemble of classifiers, such as how to understand and interpret the decision made by an ensemble of classifiers because an ensemble provides little insight into how it makes its decision. For data mining applications, comprehensibility is crucial, voting methods normally result in incomprehensible classifier that cannot be easily understood by end-users. These are the research topics we are currently working on and hope to report our findings in the near future.

References

1.   Bauer, E. & Kohavi, R., "An empirical comparison of voting classification algorithms: Bagging, boosting, and variants". Machine Learning, 36 (1999), 105–139.
2.   Blake, C.L. & Merz, C.J., UCI Repository of machine learning databases. Irvine, CA: University of California, Department of Information and Computer Science (1998). [http://www.ics.uci.edu/~mlearn/MLRepository.html]
3.   Van den Bosch, A. and W. Daelemans., Memory-based morphological analysis. Proc. of the 37th Annual Meeting of the ACL (1999), University of Maryland, pp. 285-292 (http://ilk.kub.nl/~antalb/ltuia/week10.html).

4. Breiman L., "Bagging Predictors". Machine Learning, 24(3), (1996) 123-140. Kluwer Academic Publishers.
5. Dietterich, T.G., Ensemble methods in machine learning. In Kittler, J., Roli, F., eds.: Multiple Classifier Systems. LNCS Vol. 1857, Springer (2001) 1–15
6. Domingos P. & Pazzani M., "On the optimality of the simple Bayesian classifier under zero-one loss". Machine Learning, 29, (1997) 103-130.
7. Freund Y. and Schapire R. E., Experiments with a New Boosting Algorithm, Proceedings: ICML'96, p. 148-156.
8. Hall L.O., Bowyer K.W., Kegelmeyer W.P., Moore T.E. and Chao C., Distributed learning on very large datasets. In ACM SIGKDD Workshop on Distributed and Parallel Knowledge Discovery (2000).
9. Chuanyi J. & Sheng M., "Combinations of weak classifiers". IEEE Trans. Neural Networks, 8(1):32–42, 1997.
10. Kotsiantis S., Pintelas P., On combining classifiers, Proceedings of HERCMA 2003 on computer mathematics and its applications, Athens, Sept. 25-27, 2003.
11. Kotsiantis S., Pierrakeas C. and Pintelas P., Preventing student dropout in distance learning systems using machine learning techniques, Proceedings of 7th International Conference on Knowledge-Based Intelligent Information and Engineering Systems (KES), Oxford, Sept. 3-5, 2003, Lecture notes series, Springer-Verlag Vol 2774, pp 267-274.
12. Krogh, A., & Vedelsby, J., "Neural network ensembles, cross validation and active learning". In Advances in Neural Information Processing Systems (1995) 7.
13. McQueen, R.J., Garner, S.R., Nevill-Manning, C.G., and Witten, I.H., "Applying machine learning to agricultural data". Journal of Computing and Electronics in Agriculture (1994).
14. Opitz D. & Maclin R., "Popular Ensemble Methods: An Empirical Study", Artificial Intelligence Research, 11 (1999): 169-198, Morgan Kaufmann.
15. Quinlan J.R., C4.5: Programs for machine learning. Morgan Kaufmann, San Francisco, 1993.
16. Quinlan, J. R., Bagging, boosting, and C4.5. In Proceedings of the Thirteenth National Conference on Artificial Intelligence (1996), pp. 725–730, AAAI/MIT Press.
17. Salzberg, S., "On Comparing Classifiers: Pitfalls to Avoid and a Recommended Approach", Data Mining and Knowledge Discovery, Vol. 1, (1997) pp. 317–328.
18. Schapire, R. E., Freund, Y., Bartlett, P., & Lee, W. S., "Boosting the margin: A new explanation for the effectiveness of voting methods". The Annals of Statistics, 26, (1998) 1651–1686.
19. Seewald, A. K., Furnkranz, J., An evaluation of grading classifiers. In Advances in Intelligent Data Analysis: Proceedings of the Fourth International Symposium IDA (2001), pages 221–232, Berlin, Springer.
20. Ting K. and Witten I., "Issues in Stacked Generalization", Artificial Intelligence Research 10, (1999) 271-289.
21. Webb G. I., "MultiBoosting: A Technique for Combining Boosting and Wagging", Machine Learning, 40, (2000) 159–196, Kluwer Academic Publishers.
22. Witten I. & Frank E., Data Mining: Practical Machine Learning Tools and Techniques with Java Implementations, Morgan Kaufmann, San Mateo, 2000.

Cluster Validation for High-Dimensional Datasets

Minho Kim, Hyunjin Yoo, and R.S. Ramakrishna

Department of Information and Communications, GIST
1 Oryong-dong, Buk-gu, Gwangju, 500-712, Republic of Korea
{mhkim, hjyoo, rsr}@gist.ac.kr

Abstract. Cluster validation is the process of evaluating performance of clustering algorithms under varying input conditions. This paper presents a new solution to the problem of cluster validation in high-dimensional applications. We examine the applicability of conventional cluster validity indices in evaluating the results of high-dimensional clustering and propose new indices that can be applied to high-dimensional datasets. We also propose an algorithm for automatically determining cluster dimension. By utilizing the proposed indices and the algorithm, we can discard the input parameters that PROCLUS needs. Experimental studies show that the proposed cluster validity indices yield better cluster validation performance than is possible with conventional indices.

Keywords: high-dimensional clustering, cluster validity index, unsupervised learning

1 Introduction

Clustering operation attempts to partition a set of objects into several subsets. The idea is that the objects in each subset are indistinguishable under some criterion of similarity. It is one of the most important tasks in data analysis. It finds application in bioinformatics, web data analysis, information retrieval, CRM (Customer Relationship Managements), text mining, and scientific data exploration, to name only a few major areas [11], [13].

Clustering refers to unsupervised learning as opposed to classification. That is, it does not make use of class information about each data object during learning. However, most clustering algorithms require that input parameters be appropriately tuned for optimal results. For example, algorithms such as K-means require k, the number of clusters, as input. As is well known, the quality of their clustering results depends rather significantly on the parameter. In order to suitably adjust (tune) the input parameters, clustering algorithms have to utilize class information. But this contradicts the very spirit of pure clustering. In recent times *cluster validity indices* (CVIs) have attracted attention as a means to resolve this dilemma [6], [7], [9], [10], [14], [15], [16], [17]. CVIs can signal perfect tuning of input parameters by assuming the minimum (or maximum) value for optimal clustering result. The latter can be defined through the number of clusters and *purity*. That is, the clustering result is optimal if the number of clusters is the same as that which best fits a dataset while at the same

C. Bussler and D. Fensel (Eds.): AIMSA 2004, LNAI 3192, pp. 178–187, 2004.
© Springer-Verlag Berlin Heidelberg 2004

time, purity is as high as possible. Here, purity is the sum of data objects in the majority class in each cluster.

Most of the existing CVIs address clustering results in low-dimensional datasets. These CVIs are based on distances between data objects. The distance utilizes the feature (attribute) vector of data objects for its definition.

In [5], however, it has been shown that when the feature vector of each data object belongs to a high-dimensional space, distances between pairs of data objects in a dataset are almost the same for a wide spectrum of data distributions and distance functions. This is tantamount to a loss in the ability of distance functions to measure the dissimilarity (or similarity) between data objects, especially in high-dimensional datasets. This is the *curse of high-dimensionality*. It follows that acceptable clustering results are beyond the reach of conventional clustering algorithms.

The research community is understandably seized of the matter [1], [2], [3], [12]. However, the clustering algorithms for high-dimensional applications require 'optimized' input parameters. To address this issue, one can naively utilize conventional CVIs. The CVIs, as noted above are based on distance functions which are ineffective in high-dimensional datasets; and hence, it is clear that conventional CVIs may fail to identify optimal clustering.

This paper makes use of *PROCLUS* [2], a well-known high-dimensional clustering algorithm, as the clustering algorithm for high-dimensional datasets. PROCLUS also requires input parameters just like other clustering algorithms. It requires two parameters: the number of clusters and the average number of cluster dimensions of each cluster. Here, a dimension is defined as *a cluster dimension* if data objects in a cluster are more highly correlated in that dimension than in any other dimension. With a view to compute the average number of cluster dimensions, we propose an algorithm for automatically determining the cluster dimensions. As for the other parameter, the number of clusters, we propose new CVIs. The new CVIs will be used for evaluating the performance of PROCLUS obtained by varying the number of clusters and choosing the best from among them. Finally, we also experimentally evaluate the performance of the proposed algorithm in automatic cluster dimension determination. The proposed CVIs will also come under experimental scrutiny.

The rest of the paper is organized as follows. Section 2 discusses clustering high-dimensional datasets and briefly reviews PROCLUS. The proposed algorithm for automatically determining cluster dimensions is provided in section 3. In section 4, designing of new cluster validity indices are described. Experimental results and conclusions are given in sections 5 and 6, respectively.

2   Clustering in High-Dimensional Datasets and PROCLUS

As for high-dimensional datasets, it is unlikely that all the dimensions are strongly correlated with a cluster. The dimensions along which there is only a weak correlation or, more often than not, no correlation at all, interfere with the clustering process. Actually, this inference follows from the fact that under specific conditions and distribution of high-dimensional datasets, distances between pairs of data objects are almost identical [5].

The feature (dimension) selection step is invariably the first step in many of the known clustering algorithms. This step excludes all the "extraneous" dimensions, thereby removing the noise emanating from them. However, since this step precedes clustering, there is a risk of losing vital information. Practical high-dimensional datasets are usually endowed with the property that a group of data objects are closely clustered in a dimension set while a different group of data objects are closely clustered in a different dimension set. Also, the sizes of these dimension sets for a particular cluster may be different. Therefore, it is almost impossible to determine a single dimension set that is acceptable for all the clusters [2].

These two problems can be addressed by exploiting the fact that different groups of data objects are correlated along different sets of dimensions in high-dimensional datasets. This was first observed and subsequently discussed in detail by Agrawal et. al. [1] and Aggarwal et. al. [2], [3], respectively. This is described below. Let C_e be a set of data objects in a d-dimensional space. A subset C (of C_e) is said to be a *projected cluster* along D ($|D| \leq d$) if the objects in C are closely related with respect to dimensions in D. The PROjected CLUStering algorithm is based upon this notion [2]. PROCLUS requires the number of clusters nc and the average number of cluster dimensions l as two input parameters.

Here is a brief on the notations and definitions which will be used in the sequel. C_i is a set of data objects, i.e., $C_i = \{x_1, \cdots, x_{N_i}\}$ and it represents a cluster. The *centroid* x_{c_i} of C_i is defined by $x_{c_i} = \sum_{j=1}^{N_i} x_j / N_i$. The *medoid* m_i is a real data object that represents a cluster C_i. It is usually close to x_{c_i}. The radius of a cluster C_i centered at a medoid m_i is defined by: $r_{m_i} = \sum_{j=1}^{N_i} d(x_i, m_i) / N_i$. In PROCLUS, *Manhattan segmental distance function*, a variant of the Manhattan distance function, is defined in order to evaluate the distance in a projected cluster. Let D be a subset of a d-dimensional set ($|D| \leq d$). Then, the Manhattan segmental distance function with respect to the dimension set D for two d-dimensional data objects x_1 and x_2 is defined by: $d_D(x_1, x_2) = \sum_{m \in D} |x_{1,m} - x_{2,m}| / |D|$.

Now, we can pose the problem of projected clustering as follows:

$$\Theta = \arg_{\{C_i\},\{D_i\}} \min \left\{ \sum_{i=1}^{k} \frac{|C_i| \cdot r_{m_i,D_i}}{N} \right\}, \tag{1}$$

where $\sum_{i=1}^{k} \frac{|C_i| \cdot r_{m_i,D_i}}{N}$ is the average projected cluster radius, N is the total number of data objects, and $r_{m_i,D_i} = \sum_{j=1}^{N_i} d_{D_i}(x_i, m_i) / N_i$. This means that the problem of projected clustering is equivalent to finding a set of clusters $\{C_i\}$ along with a set of their corresponding dimension sets $\{D_i\}$ that minimizes the average projected cluster radius.

3 Automatic Determination of Cluster Dimensions

The scheme for finding cluster dimensions in PROCLUS requires l, the average number of cluster dimensions, as an input parameter. The clustering result is strongly dependent on the value of l. If an inappropriate value of l, (for instance, larger value than the optimal one) were used, dimensions unrelated with data objects in a local area would be included in the corresponding cluster dimension set. This leads to incorrect assignment of data objects and finally results in unacceptable clustering. However, this problem can be solved through reasonable assumptions complying with projected clustering and intuitive heuristics.

Let $X_{i,j}$ be the average distance between data objects in the local area L_i along the jth dimension, where L_i is the area within the distance δ_i from a medoid m_i of a cluster C_i and $\delta_i = \min_{j \neq i} d(m_i, m_j)$. Since data objects in a cluster are highly correlated in cluster dimensions while they are uncorrelated in the other dimensions, there is a valley in the graph of sorted $X_{i,j}$ values. Here, the valley refers to the location at which X_{ij} (in the sorted graph) changes rapidly. From this analysis, one is naturally led to the following definition of *cluster dimension*: if some X_{ij} value in the sorted X_{ij} graph is below the valley, then its corresponding dimension is the *cluster dimension*. This intuitive definition relies on the reasonable assumption that the X_{ij} sorted graph does indeed have a valley.

This is similar to the approach adopted for finding the neighborhood radius ε in DBSCAN [8]. Our algorithm for effectively locating the valley in the X_{ij} sorted graph is given in Fig. 1.

```
for each medoid mᵢ
do
    (1)  {Xᵢⱼ′}ₛₒᵣₜₑᵈ = Sort( {Xᵢⱼ} )
    (2)  Hᵢⱼ′ = HighPassFiltering({Xᵢⱼ′}ₛₒᵣₜₑᵈ )
    (3)  Locₘᵢₙ = Find the location of minimum Hᵢⱼ′
    (4)  Dᵢ = {j | j′ < Locₘᵢₙ, where j = original order of
         j′}
end
```

Fig. 1. Algorithm of automatic cluster dimension selection

A few words on the algorithm are in order. First, we generate $\{X_{ij}'\}_{sorted}$ by sorting $\{X_{ij}\}$ in line (1) of Fig. 1. j' is a new index used while sorting $\{X_{ij}\}$. Thus, the "original order of j'" in line (4) refers to its corresponding original index j in $\{X_{ij}\}$. In order to effectively find the valley, we perform high-pass filtering. We can use any filter that can find the minimum value in the valley. In the experiments, we utilize a variant of a simple, well-known 2-dimensional high-pass filter, with (-1, 2, -1) as its kernel. In line (3), we find the location of the minimum value of $H_{ij'}$, which corresponds to a valley. Finally, all the dimensions whose associated values are below or equal to the valley are taken to be cluster dimensions. The performance of the proposed algorithm is evaluated in section 5.

4 New CVIs for Validating High-Dimensional Clustering

The performance of many clustering algorithms is critically dependent on the characteristics of the dataset and input parameters. Improper input parameters for a specific dataset may lead to clusters which deviate from those in the dataset. In order to determine the input parameters that lead to clusters that best fit a given dataset, we need techniques for evaluating the clusters themselves. Popular techniques employ cluster validity indices (CVI).

A very important factor in defining CVIs is the distance function. All the functions in conventional CVIs make use of all the dimensions. However, in the context of high-dimensional datasets, most distance functions are not very useful due to the curse of dimensionality. Since the function $\|\cdot\|$ used in some conventional CVIs, such as SD and S_Dbw, is also a kind of distance function, the same problem lurks in the background. This leads to the reasonable inference that CVIs based on these distance functions cannot properly evaluate results of the clustering algorithms for high-dimensional datasets. Experimental results tend to support this observation (please see section 5).

Therefore, we have to define new CVIs which can measure how well a clustering result fits a given dataset in high-dimensional applications. For this purpose, new CVIs for high-dimensional clustering have to be capable of expressing the meaning of compactness of a cluster and separability among clusters with respect to high-dimensional datasets as in [4]. As compactness and separability are also based on distance functions, we should start by redesigning distance functions in order to develop new CVIs for validating high-dimensional clustering.

A hint on how to proceed may be gleaned from $d_{D_i}(\cdot,\cdot)$ of PROCLUS (section 2). According to [4], data objects in a good cluster should be close to one another. This function comes in handy because any new compactness measure has to, in essence, incorporate this feature in high-dimensional clustering applications. The reason is that a dimension set D_i is composed of dimensions in which data objects in a cluster D_i are correlated and $d_{D_i}(\cdot,\cdot)$ is a distance function reflecting only these dimensions. $d_{D_i}(\cdot,\cdot)$ is also effective for a new definition of separability. This is explained below:

- First, if there exist two clusters whose data objects are very close to each other, $d_{D_i}(c_1,c_2)$ has relatively small value since they have the same or very similar dimension sets. And this can indicate that the two clusters need to be merged. Here, c_i and c_j are centroids of clusters C_i and C_j, respectively.
- Second, if two clusters are well separated, $d_{D_i}(c_i,c_j)$ has relatively high value since two clusters have different cluster dimensions. Even though the two clusters share the same cluster dimension set, $d_{D_i}(c_i,c_j)$ also has relatively high value because they should be well separated in the space defined by the common cluster dimension set.

SD and S_Dbw among CVIs make use of $\|\sigma\|$. This also can be redefined as $\|\sigma\|_{D_i}=\sqrt{\sum_{m\in D_i}\sigma_m^2/|D_i|}$. Since we have prepared new distance functions $d_{D_i}(\cdot,\cdot)$ and

$\|\sigma\|_{D_i}$, we can now define various new CVIs by replacing $d(\cdot,\cdot)$ and $\|\sigma\|$ with these new functions. Newly designed CVIs are given in eqn. (2) ~ (6) (Since some of existing CVIs, viz., Dunn and S_Dbw, are computationally very expensive and thus impractical, we do not define their corresponding CVIs for high-dimensional clustering.)

$$DB_{HD}(nc) = \frac{1}{nc}\sum_{i=1}^{nc}\left(\max_{j=1\cdots nc, j\neq i}\frac{S_{D_i}+S_{D_j}}{d_{D_i,j}}\right)$$

$$S_{D_i} = \frac{1}{n_i}\sum_{x\in C_i}d_{D_i}(x,c_i), \quad d_{D_i,j} = d_{D_i}(c_i,c_j) \tag{2}$$

$$XB_{HD}(nc) = \frac{\sum_{k=1}^{nc}\sum_{j=1}^{N}u_{kj}^2 d_{D_k}(x_j,c_k)^2}{N\cdot\min_{i=1\ldots nc}\left\{\min_{\substack{j=1\ldots nc\\i\neq j}}d_{D_i}(c_i,c_j)^2\right\}} \tag{3}$$

$$I_{HD}(nc) = \left(\frac{1}{nc}\times\frac{E_{HD,1}}{E_{HD,nc}}\times D_{HD,nc}\right)^p, (p=2)$$

$$E_{HD,nc} = \sum_{k=1}^{nc}\sum_{j=1}^{N}u_{kj}d_{D_k}(x_j,c_k) \tag{4}$$

$$D_{HD,nc} = \max_{i=1\ldots nc}\left\{\max_{\substack{j=1\ldots nc\\i\neq j}}d_{D_i}(c_i,c_j)\right\}$$

$$v_{sv,HD}(nc) = v_{uN,HD}(nc) + v_{oN,HD}(nc)$$

$$v_{u,HD}(nc) = \frac{1}{nc}\sum_{i=1}^{nc}\left(\frac{1}{n_i}\sum_{x\in C_i}d_{D_i}(x,c_i)\right) \tag{5}$$

$$v_{o,HD}(nc) = \frac{nc}{d_{\min}}, \quad d_{\min} = \min_{i=1\ldots nc}\left\{\min_{\substack{j=1\ldots nc\\i\neq j}}d_{D_i}(c_i,c_j)\right\}$$

$$SD_{HD}(nc) = a\cdot Scat_{HD}(nc) + Dis_{HD}(nc), \quad a = Dis_{HD}(nc_{\max})$$

$$Scat_{HD}(nc) = \frac{1}{nc}\sum_{i=1}^{nc}\frac{\|\sigma(c_i)\|_{D_i}}{\|\sigma(X)\|_D}$$

$$Dis_{HD}(nc) = \frac{D_{\max,HD}}{D_{\min,HD}}\sum_{i=1}^{nc}\left(\sum_{j=1}^{nc}d_{D_i}(c_i,c_j)\right)^{-1} \tag{6}$$

$$D_{\max,HD} = \max_{i=1\ldots nc}\left\{\max_{\substack{j=1\ldots nc\\i\neq j}}d_{D_i}(c_i,c_j)\right\}, \quad D_{\min,HD} = \min_{i=1\ldots nc}\left\{\min_{\substack{j=1\ldots nc\\i\neq j}}d_{D_i}(c_i,c_j)\right\}$$

5   Experimental Results

In this section, we first evaluate the performance of the algorithm for automatically determining the cluster dimension proposed in section 3 and then, we evaluate the performance of conventional and newly proposed CVIs for high-dimensional datasets. The quality of a clustering result is generally evaluated under the following criteria:

- The number of clusters (nc) found by the clustering algorithm
- Cluster purity: This is computed by summing the number of data objects of a majority class in each cluster.

That is, a clustering result is said to be of "good quality" if it has the same number of clusters as does a given dataset and at the same time has as high a cluster purity as possible. The number of clusters is related to cluster purity. This can be inferred from the frequently observed phenomenon that cluster purity deteriorates noticeably if the estimated number of clusters is different from that of a given dataset. In this paper, we will not evaluate cluster purity because that has already been done in [2] and our results are almost the same as those in [2]. PROCLUS shows very high cluster purity provided that we make use of the exact number of clusters nc as well the average number of cluster dimensions l. Because our modified PROCLUS utilizes the algorithm for automatic cluster dimension determination, the input parameter l is not required. Therefore, in this section, we experiment with the modified PROCLUS by varying the input parameter nc (the number of resulting clusters). We also evaluate the performance of CVIs by comparing the estimated number of clusters with that of a given dataset.

Datasets used in the experiments were generated through the method given in [2]. They represent various situations and are divided into two categories. One category consists of those datasets whose cluster dimension sets for different clusters are disjoint, i.e., $\forall i, j \ (i \neq j) \ D_i \cap D_j = \varnothing$. Datasets in this category are t1, t3, t5, and t7. The other category includes the clusters that may share cluster dimensions among them, i.e., $D_i \cap D_j \neq \varnothing \ (i \neq j)$. Datasets t2, t4, t6, and t8 belong to this category. The latter category is more common in real world applications. In order to create truly representative datasets, we allow more than two clusters to be contained in the same subspace. All the datasets except t1 and t2 are of this kind. t5 and t6 are generated by increasing the number of clusters sharing the same subspace. Finally, t7 and t8 are generated by decreasing distances among clusters using the same subspace from datasets t3 and t4, respectively.

Table 2 summarizes lists of cluster dimensions estimated through the proposed algorithm for automatically determining cluster dimensions for various datasets. In the table, each line for each dataset lists cluster dimensions of the respective cluster. Cluster dimensions are sorted in ascending order with respect to their X_{ij} values. It can be seen that the sizes of the cluster dimension set (of each dataset) turn out to be the same as those of the given datasets and they are listed in the "size" column of the table. Also, the cluster dimensions are the same as those of the given datasets. The proposed algorithm is seen to be quite effective in automatically determining cluster dimensions under various circumstances.

Table 1. Estimated cluster dimensions for various datasets

Dataset	Cluster dimensions	size	Dataset	Cluster dimensions	size
t1	2, 1, 3, 0	4	t2	0, 26, 3, 16, 4, 22, 9	7
	28, 31, 30, 29	4		13, 20, 27, 26	4
	24, 21, 23, 22	4		4, 16, 24, 20, 22, 29, 9	7
	15, 16, 14, 17	4		14, 10, 1, 9, 26, 16, 22	7
	8, 7, 9, 10	4		0, 22, 27, 8, 26, 20, 3	7
t3	0, 1, 2	3	t4	22, 3, 11, 0, 9, 17, 19	7
	6, 7, 8	3		22, 3, 4, 16, 29, 25	6
	24, 25, 26	3		27, 3, 11, 22, 16, 0, 21, 9	8
	14, 13, 12	3		29, 11, 26, 4, 0	5
	1, 0, 2	3		1, 17, 11, 22, 12, 19, 3	7
	19, 20, 18	3		1, 17, 12, 19, 11, 22, 3	7

Now, performance of CVIs is evaluated. The first experiment makes use of the simplest datasets t1 and t2. All the conventional CVIs, viz., v_{sv}, I, XB, and DB (except SD for t1 and v_{sv} for t2) indicate different number of clusters from that of given datasets. In other words, they fail to estimate the actual number of clusters. It can also be seen that SD and v_{sv} succeed to some extent. But, they fail to find the exact number of clusters for almost all other test datasets (we have omitted other results due to the limitation of space). This means that finding exact number of clusters in t1 and t2 by SD and v_{sv} is just a coincidence and that it does not indicate their true performance. In the long run, conventional CVIs fail to find the number of clusters in high-dimensional datasets. Undoubtedly, the reason is the curse of dimensionality as already discussed. Since conventional CVIs fail on the simplest datasets in this experiment and, moreover, we will use more complex datasets in subsequent experiments, we no longer persist with them.

Table 2. Suggested number of clusters by new cluster validity indices and their correctness for various datasets. Correctness is marked by O or X in the parenthesis

	t1	t2	t3	t4	t5	t6	t7	t8	# correct
$v_{sv,HD}$	5 (O)	5 (O)	6 (O)	6 (O)	8 (O)	8 (O)	5 (X)	6 (O)	7
I_{HD}	5 (O)	5 (O)	6 (O)	6 (O)	8 (O)	8 (O)	6 (O)	6 (O)	8
SD_{HD}	5 (O)	5 (O)	4 (X)	5 (X)	7 (X)	7 (X)	5 (X)	5 (X)	2
XB_{HD}	5 (O)	5 (O)	7 (X)	5 (X)	4 (X)	2 (X)	5 (X)	5 (X)	2
DB_{HD}	5 (O)	5 (O)	6 (O)	6 (O)	7 (X)	7 (X)	5 (X)	5 (X)	4

Results for new CVIs proposed in section 4 are summarized in table 2. In this experiment, we also use t1 and t2. All the new CVIs have their optimal values at the correct number of clusters. This implies that d_{D_i} and $\|\sigma\|_{D_i}$ incorporated into the new CVIs are very effective for measuring the distance between data objects in high-dimensional spaces.

In the second experiment, we use more complex datasets than in the first experiment. The objective of this experiment is to evaluate the performance of the proposed CVIs under various situations. Table 2 shows the results for dataset t3 and t4 in which two clusters are in the same subspace. As for this dataset, SD_{HD} and XB_{HD} return incorrect results. As for dataset t6 generated by having more clusters than t4 sharing the same subspace(s), SD_{HD}, XB_{HD}, and DB_{HD} yield wrong results as shown in table 2. Finally, clusters sharing a subspace in dataset t7 are located more closely than those in the previous datasets. All the proposed CVIs except I_{HD} fail to estimate the correct number of clusters.

Here, we observe that SD_{HD} and XB_{HD} fail on all the (somewhat) complex datasets t3 ~ t7. The reason why the two CVIs fail is because their intra-cluster distances are not properly defined. In SD_{HD}, $Scat_{HD}(nc) = \frac{1}{nc} \cdot \sum_{i=1}^{nc} \|\sigma(c_i)\|_{D_i} / \|\sigma(X)\|_D$ can be seen as the intra-cluster distance. Here, $\|\cdot\|$ is defined in the same way as is the Euclidean distance function. However, [2] states that there is no appropriate normalized variant of the Euclidean distance function for high-dimensional applications. But, we simply defined this variant by: $\| x_1 - x_2 \|_{D_i} = \sqrt{\sum_{m \in D_i} (x_{1,m} - x_{2,m})^2 / |D_i|}$. This amounts to empirically verifying the claim made in [2]. As for XB_{HD}, its intra-cluster distance can be defined as $\sum_{k=1}^{nc} \sum_{j=1}^{N} u_{kj}^2 d_{D_i}(x_j, c_k)^2 / N$. Here the sum of distances of data objects from respective centroids is divided by the total number of data objects, N. This averaging may smooth out steep deviations caused by data objects in some clusters generated by unnecessary merging. That is, in case the number of data objects in a needlessly merged cluster is relatively small, the deviations caused by this cluster may be masked by averaging.

As summarized in table 2, I_{HD} shows the best performance among various CVIs proposed in this paper. The performance of $v_{sv,HD}$ is the second best and those of SD_{HD} and XB_{HD} are the worst.

6 Conclusions

In this paper, we have discussed the problem of cluster validation for high-dimensional datasets and presented a solution. The key to the solution lies in chalking out a path to counter the curse of dimensionality. We reviewed the PROCLUS algorithm with a view to shed light on this problem. The influence of this curse on conventional CVIs was also discussed. We followed this up with five new CVIs for cluster validation in high-dimensional applications. Experimental studies revealed that conventional CVIs fail to test validity of results returned by PROCLUS even for datasets whose clusters are well separated. More specifically, they could not estimate the exact number of clusters in given datasets, thereby failing a vital performance test. The new CVIs proposed in this paper succeeded in finding the exact number of clusters. We also carried out experiments on complex datasets representing multifarious situations. SD_{HD} and XB_{HD} turned out to be the worst and I_{HD} the best in performance. We have also proposed a new algorithm for automatically determining cluster dimensions. This dispenses with an important input parameter which PROCLUS needs (i.e., the average size of the set of cluster dimensions). The proposed CVIs are expected to be useful in evaluating results of various high-dimensional clustering algorithms besides PROCLUS.

References

[1] Agrawal, R., Gehrke, J., Gunopulos, D., Raghavan, P.: Automatic Subspace Clustering of High Dimensional Data for Data Mining Applications. Proc. ACM-SIGMOD Int'l Conf. Management of Data (1998) 94-105
[2] Aggarwal, C.C., Procopiuc, C., Wolf, J.L., Yu, P.S., Park, J.S.: Fast Algorithms for Projected Clustering. Proc. ACM SIGMOD Int'l Conf. Management of Data (1999) 61-72
[3] Aggarwal, C.C., Yu, P.S.: Redefining Clustering for High-Dimensional Applications. IEEE Trans. Knowledge and Data Engineering 14(2) (2002) 210-225
[4] Berry, M.J.A., Linoff, G.: Data Mining Techniques: For Marketing, Sales, and Customer Support. John Wiley & Sons (1997)
[5] Beyer, K.S., Goldstein, J., Ramakrishnan, R., Shaft, U.: When Is `Nearest Neighbor' Meaningful?. Proc. Int'l Conf. Database Theory (ICDT), (1999) 217-235
[6] Davies, D.L. Bouldin, D.W.: A Cluster Separation Measure. IEEE Trans. Pattern Analysis and Machine Intelligence (PAMI) 1(2) (1979) 224-227
[7] Dunn, J.C.: A Fuzzy Relative of the ISODATA Process and its Use in Detecting Compact Well-Separated Clusters. J. Cybernetics 3 (1973) 32-57
[8] Ester, M., Kriegel, H.-P., Sander, J., Xu, X.: A Density-based Algorithm for Discovering Clusters in Large Spatial Databases. Proc. Int'l Conf. Knowledge Discovery and Data Mining (KDD) (1996) 226-231
[9] Halkidi, M., Vazirgiannis, M.: Quality Scheme Assessment in the Clustering Process. Proc. Principles and Practice of Knowledge Discovery in Databases (PKDD). Lecture Notes in Artificial Intelligence Vol. 1910 (2000) 265-276
[10] Halkidi, M., Vazirgiannis, M.: Clustering Validity Assessment: Finding the Optimal Partitioning of a Dataset. Proc. Int'l Conf. Data Mining (ICDM) (2001) 187-194
[11] Han, J., Kamber, M.: Data Mining: Concepts and Techniques. Morgan Kaufmann (2001)
[12] Hinneburg, A., Keim, D. A.: An Optimal Grid-Clustering: Towards Breaking the Curse of Dimensionality in High-Dimensional Clustering. Proc. Int'l Conf. Very Large DataBases (VLDB) (1999) 506-517
[13] Jain, A.K., Murty, M.N., Flynn, P.J.: Data Clustering: A Review. ACM Computing Surveys 31(3) (1999) 264-323
[14] Kim, D.-J., Park, Y.-W., Park, D.-J.: A Novel Validity Index for Determination of the Optimal Number of Clusters. IEICE Trans. Inf. & Syst., E84-D(2) (2001) 281-285
[15] Maulik, U., Bandyopadhyay, S.: Performance Evaluation of Some Clustering Algorithms and Validity Indices. IEEE Trans. Pattern Analysis and Machine Intelligence (PAMI) 24(12) (2002) 1650-1654
[16] Schwarz, G.: Estimating the Dimension of a Model. Annals of Statistics 6(2) (1978) 461-464
[17] Xie, X.L., Beni, G.A.: A Validity Measure for Fuzzy Clustering. IEEE Trans. Pattern Analysis and Machine Intelligence (PAMI) 3(8) (1991) 841-846

Emergent Behaviours Based on Episodic Encoding and Familiarity Driven Retrieval

Emilia I. Barakova

RIKEN BSI, 2-1, Hirosawa, Wako-shi, Saitama, 351-0198 Japan.
emilia@brain.riken.jp

Abstract. In analogy to animal research, where behavioural and internal neural dynamics are simultaneously analysed, this paper suggests a method for emergent behaviours arising in interaction with the underlying neural mechanism. This way an attempt to go beyond the indeterministic nature of the emergent behaviours of robots is made. The neural dynamics is represented as an interaction of memories of experienced episodes, the current environmental input and the feedback of previous motor actions. The emergent properties can be observed in a two staged process: exploratory (latent) learning and goal oriented learning. Correspondingly, the learning is dominated to a different extent by two factors: novelty and reward. While the reward learning is used to show the relevance of the method, the novelty/familiarity is a basis for forming the emergent properties. The method is strongly inspired by the state of the art understanding of the hippocampal functioning and especially its role in novelty detection and episodic memory formation in relation to spatial context.

1 Introduction

Emergence of behaviour in biological organisms can be understood by simultaneous study of at least two different scales of organization: neural and behavioural. The term emergence may suggest that the intelligent behaviour is merely a consequence of unknown and uncontrolled internal dynamics of a system of connected simple elements. In this paper the emergence of behaviour is understood as a consequence of assumed neural dynamics that closely models the functionality of the hippocampal formation. The functionality is assigned to the neural structures as much as supported by behavioural experiments. Yet, this paper aims at a computational model oriented towards a robot implementation.

The choice of the hippocampal formation as the brain structure where the dynamics causing an emergent behaviour takes place is made due to several reasons. Among them, the involvement of the hippocampus in episodic memory formation [1][2][3] and its role in familiarity discrimination, are considered, and illustrated through emergent behaviours within a navigation task.

Many biologically inspired robotic systems are built by simulating insect-like behaviours, for a review see [4]. Such a setting supposes a reactive nature of behaviour - it is determined mainly by sensing. The simulations following the functionality of the mammalian brain that include memory or motivational features are seldom implemented into a robot without a severe simplifications. The theoretical models of the hippocampus and basal ganglia, however, suggest neural solutions that incorporate those features, and

C. Bussler and D. Fensel (Eds.): AIMSA 2004, LNAI 3192, pp. 188–197, 2004.
© Springer-Verlag Berlin Heidelberg 2004

produce results on a behavioural scale, often not in the range of the computational expense, affordable for a realistic robotics task [5][6][7].

This paper puts forward memory driven behaviour. In particular, memories of experienced episodes are considered as carriers of contextual information, and therefore as a substratum for emergence of complex behaviours: the animat continuously gathers information about the surrounding world through experiencing sequences of events. Higher organisms can encode such subjectively experienced episodes, so their further actions are determined to a big extent of these remembered episodes. Episodic memory formation is generally associated with the encoding in the hippocampus.

While the emergent phenomena are modelled through the hippocampal system, the behaviour manifests itself through a motor system. To rightfully describe the organism-environmental interaction the third, sensory system needs to be modelled. The overall model has to satisfy requirements coming from the behavioural setup as well as requirements that concern memory formation and reuse. The specificity of the model is that it attempts navigation, determined mainly by the experienced memories of connected events (episodes). In doing that we expect to observe manifestation of novel behaviour that has emerged on the basis of encoding different memories about similar situations.

Therefore, every individual event has to be seen in context. For a realistic task this is possible only if memorizing is flexible in both encoding and retrieval. Flexibility, as opposed to exact storage puts forward the need to selectively store the incoming perceptual information, judging which is new, or very similar to the experienced one. The criteria of familiarity facilitates the ability to infer appropriate behaviour in a novel environment or for performing a novel task. The efficient encoding trough the familiarity judgement is a basis for life-long learning.

The paper is organized as follows: In Section 2 suggests a hypothesis and the corresponding working model for novelty gated hippocampal encoding; In Section 3 the framework and the scheme from the last two chapters is bridged to the computations, derived by theoretical findings to lay a computational ground for further modelling. The connection between the two levels of the emergency scheme is shown in short in Section 4. The results that show the efficacy of the novelty encoding are not shown in this study. Instead, some results from the functionality of the overall scheme are shown in Section 5. Section 6 offers a discussion of the state and the perspectives of this research.

2   The Model

Approaching the novelty and familiarity discrimination problem from the perspective of an embodied agent has the following meaning: first, novelty has to be considered in relation to behaviour; and second, the information that has to be judged for novel or familiar is derived by the experienced episodes of events. The episode paradigm will be elaborated on first.

Episodic and autobiographical memories have intrinsic relation to sensory and perceptual events (Conway [8]). The term "episodic memory" is used differently by the researchers. In definition, given in [8], which extends the widely accepted definition of Tulving [9], the episodic memory has event specific, sensory-perceptual details of recent experiences that lasted for comparatively short periods of time (minutes to hours).

To make these definitions more transparent for the purposes of our model, let us clarify that perception includes sensing, as well as memory, anticipation behavioural goals, etc. [10][11]. Further in this text sensing and perception will be distinguished, so that sensing implies the external (sensory-bound) patterns, while the perception is the combined representation, formed by the sensory, memory and eventually top-down behavioural or attentional influence.

The encoding of episodes takes place in CA3 area, while the representation that guides the goal-oriented behaviour is formed in CA1 area. The overall processing, naturally includes the contextual temporal information and accounts for novelty, and efficient encoding.

The computation in proposed model accentuates on the representation of CA1 area, as a physical component with comparative function. The relation between the incoming in and outgoing from CA1 area signals is as follows. The information from the learned episode from CA3 and the sensory-bound information coming directly from EC forms the pattern in CA1 that controls the up coming behaviour and signals for novelty.

This functionality has been confirmed by experimental studies to a large extent. Our aim is a model that closely resembles the actual computations in the hippocampus and is applicable for a robotic implementation. Therefore we hypothesize the exact mechanism of novelty detection and context transfer between the two representations. We assume that the two representations - in CA1 and in CA3 area act together for the novelty detection and future action choice. The CA1 representation determines the action choice and signals for novelty, while CA3 supplies it with contextual information.

The computational scheme that illustrates the hypothesized functionality is as follows. Two simultaneously active neural networks, corresponding to CA3 and CA1 area perform the major computations. The neurons in CA3 area account for temporal aspect and the formation of episodes, the representation in CA1 area is prone to detect novelty.

The third structure, EC provides the input patterns to both areas. The same patterns, as formed in EC area are projected simultaneously to CA1 area trough the direct pathway, and to CA3 area (trough DG, which is not modelled here) to further reach CA1 area. The projection to CA3 area is mainly topological. In the itinerary of the indirect pathway, in the CA3 area the broad lateral connectivity promotes formation of episodes, where the temporal characteristics of the formed episodes are taken into consideration.

The representation, projected to CA1 area is not assumed topological, i.e. the connectivity between EC and CA1 is full. The pattern that reaches CA1 area via the direct pathway is organized on pattern similarity. Since the same projected pattern from EC area reaches within a small time interval the areas in CA1 and CA3, the connection between the currently most active neurons in this two areas is also strenghtened.

Let the representation that is formed in CA1 area is denoted by E. It evolves under the action of the following competing influences: sensory S, memory M and behavioural B. For a robotic framework it is feasible to consider discrete processing. Therefore formally an episode E is a set of n discrete events e, defined by a considerable difference in the event representations. A single event e that is expressed by a specific firing pattern in CA1 area is defined by s, m and b,

$$e = \{s, m, b\} \tag{1}$$

where the sensory component s introduces the current influence from the external world and constitutes by feedforward connections; memory component m represents the temporal impact of the sensory patterns, and is constituted by the lateral connections; the behavioural component b represents the influence that the previous action has brought on the current even. All three components are multidimensional vectors. The change from one to another event requires a change in at least one component that is bigger than an internal threshold, indicating the detection of a novel event.

The memory component consists of encoded episodes of events (memory with a temporal reference) M as formed in CA3 area. M is a set of n discrete events occurring in a temporal order m_t, $t \in [1,...,n]$) defined by a considerable difference in the event representations.

$$M = \{m_t\}, t \in [1,...n] \tag{2}$$

Learning of an episode means that associations can rapidly be formed among items presented in temporal proximity. This is especially valid for events, or routes, where the temporal order is of importance. Therefore by episode learning the order or the temporal association has appeared important rather than or along with another common feature, and this has influenced the encoding. So, the events that have been learned as an episode will tend to be recalled together and after each other, even if presentation order is changed. To summarize, the proposed model, as shown in , is as follows. Three structures, resembling EC, CA1 and CA3 areas form the representation that is further used for navigation. The computations are performed in the superficial CA1 and CA3 areas. The representation, which is denoted by E describes the activation pattern in CA1 area. It contains set of elements, which are not necessarily in the order of their temporal appearance. In contrast, M is a set of temporally related patterns. It refers to the activation pattern of CA3 area. The two representations are physically and computational connected.

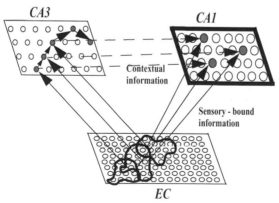

Fig. 1. Schematic representation of the proposed model. The CA3 and CA1 areas respond differently to the same patterns. The CA3 area provides temporal context to the CA1 representation.

3   Biological Learning

This section outlines the biologically plausible representational and learning mechanisms within and between the different neural structures. Some of the formulas are adopted from the related work (like place cells definition, the specific Hebbian and Temporal Hebbian learning schemes). These are the preliminary elements that will support the choice of the model and justify the simplifications that are made for the robotics implementation.It is widely known that the cells in the rat hippocampus fire when the rat is at particular location of the environment [12]. Because of that property, these cells are called also place cells. If the rat moves through the environment, at every particular position a number of place cells fire. Cells that code for places in nearest vicinity fire most strongly, while the cells that code for more distant locations fire less. The activity of the place cell firing can be modelled by a Gaussian for the open environments, where place cells show non-directional firing. Therefore, the movement of a simulated rat at every position of the environment is characterized by a particular pattern of firing, containing of the active place cells in its vicinity. The activity of each cell can be represented in the following way:

$$s_{i,\,t}(r) = -\left(\frac{\|r - c_i\|}{\exp(2\sigma^2)}\right) \qquad (3)$$

where c_i is the location in the space of the centre of the cell i's place field, r is the position of the simulated rat, and σ represents the width of the place field. s corresponds to the sensory representation within a single event.

The sensory as well as behavioural signals are encoded into constellations of the active place cells. The unique pattern of activity corresponds to a certain position r in the environment. The level of activity of every place cell depends on the distance between the rat position and the place fields centres. Fig. 2.a) shows two single activation patterns from the rat route, which represent the pattern of activation of the simulated EC area. These patterns are dependant on the external-world and are further transmitted through the direct pathway.

The learning mechanism of the feed-fortward connections from a EC area, to both CA1 and CA3 area is the modified Hebbian rule as shown in Eq. (4).

$$\Delta w_{ij}^{CA-EC} = \alpha_1 g\left(EC_i CA_j - w_{ij}^{CA-EC} CA_j^2\right) \qquad (4)$$

where α_1 is learning rate, notation $CA\text{-}EC$ shows the starting and destination layer of the connection (coming from EC, reaching CA layer) the indices i and j denote neurons on the input and output layer, correspondingly. The CA layer is not denoted as CA1 or CA3, because the learning rule is used for EC-CA1 as well as EC-CA3 learning. The term $w_{ij}^{CA-EC} CA_j^2$ of Eq. (4) is needed due to internal instability of the Hebbian rule. The difference in the feedforward learning in EC-CA1 and EC-CA3 stems from the different connectivity. In EC-CA3 area the predominant are the topological connections - the simulation is done as the neurons from the first (EC) layer project to a topologically correspondent area, in a way that every input neuron is connected to 20% of the output neurons. Differently, the learning between EC and CA1 area is done on the self-organizing principle, since the connectivity between those two layers is full. The lateral inhibition connections, denoted as LI have a sharpening effect on the transmitted to the CA areas activations.

$$\Delta w_j^{LI-CA} = \alpha_2 g\left(Li \cdot CA_j - \alpha_3 w_j^{LI-CA} CA_j^2\right) \qquad (5)$$

where α_2, α_3 are learning rates, and g is a gating factor.

The biological and computational plausibility of the learning process as described in Eq. (4),(5) have been shown previously in [13] where the learning parameters choices is explained in detail.

By far, the representation made within the layer denoted as CA3 does not have the intrinsic capacity for temporal association. This quality is obtained by applying a Hebbian rule with asymmetric time window over the lateral connections only. The asymmetric time window has been simulated to correspond to the experimental measurements as found by [14], see also [15]. The lateral learning rule is adapted from the one suggested in [16], so that it overcomes the computational constrains of the asymmetric time window function. Due to the so introduced temporal aspect, the learning in CA3 results in episode learning. A plot of a sample learned episode performed by the set of equations (4-5) and the adapted learning rule by [16] is shown in Fig. 3.

4   Connection Between the Neural and Behavioural Representations

The actor-critic model [18] most closely resembles the behavioural part of the organism-environmental interaction, in the following sense: At any moment t, the embodied animat is able to choose an action on the environment, as well as environment provides it with a feedback. In the case considered here the simulated animat can choose from 8 possible actions - or more exactly from 8 directions of movement.

By a physical robot they are to be restricted to 3. The critic is the feedback influence that reaches CA1 area in this model. The actor-critic mechanism regards the actions of the animat that are directed in finding a particular goal. The familiarity gating is entirely performed in the feed-forward track. The goal oriented behaviour will be used only for illustration of the animat behaviour, and not to optimize its performance. The mechanism of actor-critic optimization, based on place cells representation is suggested in [17].

However, the two studies have completely different objective - in [17] the reinforcement algorithm causes improved behaviour, while in our case the learned episodes are a substratum of the emergent behaviour, i.e. the first paper models dopamine like effects, while we work on episodic memory based behaviour.

The actor-critic mechanism used for the simulations is modified from the original [18][17] in a way that it accounts for a more realistic movement of both rat and robot. To be consistent with the text above and with the previous notation, the critic is denoted with b. The value of b when the animat is at a position r as represented in CA1 area, has the following form:

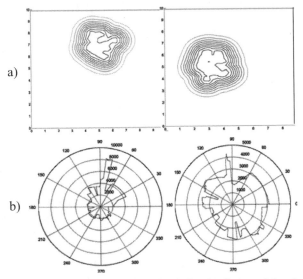

Fig. 2. Samples of sensory patterns provided by a) the simulation of the place cells formation process, and b) the omnidirectional range sensor of a robot.

$$b(r^{CA1}) = \sum_i w_i f_i(r^{CA1}) \qquad (6)$$

where w_i is the weight between the output cell and the i-th place cell as formed in CA1 area. At the made experiments, the actor makes use of 8 action cells $a_j, j = 1...8$. At position r, the activity of the each action cell is:

$$a_j(r) = \sum_i v_{ji} f_i(r^{CA1}) \qquad (7)$$

where a_j stays for the j-th action cell, and v is the adaptive weight between the action cell and the i-th place cell. The first step for the movement direction is taken randomly with a probability P_j. However, the next movement direction is chosen in a random way, but the possibilities are restricted according to the choices made in the previous movements $P_j(t-1), P_j(t-2)$, so there is not a random walk like trajectory, but smoother orbits with eventual sudden turns.

The actor weights are adapted according to:

$$\Delta v_{ij} \propto \delta f_i(r_t) g_j(t) \qquad (8)$$

where $g_j(t) = 1$ if action j was chosen at the moment t, $g_j(t) = 0$ otherwise.

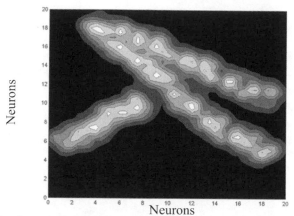

Fig. 3. Episodes, formed after Hebbian learning with lateral inhibition and novelty gating. Every input pattern activates multiple neurons. The actual path corresponds to the neurons, activated at highest.

5   Emergent Behaviours and Robotic Implications

Emergent properties arise at a particular level of system description by interaction of relatively simple lower level components - between themselves and with the environment. In this paper as the lower level of organization is considered the functional simulation of the hippocampal formation, and as the higher level the resulting behaviour.

At the lower level, the sensory bound representation of the direct pathway, and the episodic representation of the indirect pathway, come together in CA1 area, where the comparison (novelty/familiarity judgements) takes place. Note that at the same time, the CA1 area gets input from the current pattern of EC area and a pattern from CA3 area that does not have incorporated the pattern that EC area currently projects.

In Fig. 2.b) are shown the omnidirectional views taken by range sensors, when a robot is at a specific position of the environment. The similarity between the nature and the shapes of both types of signals, the one obtained by distance dependant superposition of place cell firing with respect to the rat positioning (Fig. 2.a, the inner contour) and the range sensor readings of a robot with respect to the robots current position, Fig. 2.b), justifies the use of patterns as illustrated in Fig. 2.b) for a robot simulation. For the novelty detection, the network build on the basis of the proposed computational scheme is simplified. The Hebbian learning followed by a lateral inhibition is replaced by a modification of the competitive Hebbian learning algorithm [19][20], which makes a single neuron to represent an input pattern. It is necessary to organize the map which has fine representation for frequently visited places but coarse representation for others. This problem is elegantly solved by the proposed algorithm.The connections between events within an episode are formed as an internal property of the learning process that is a principle difference from existing models with temporal history encoding [21]. An online comparison of the incoming sensory-bound patterns with those encoded into episodes is made. Once a recognition of the similarity between an experienced episode and the current sequence of events is encountered, the behaviour is entirely guided by the encoded memories. When memory of a similar situation is not available, the behaviour is random goal-searching. In Fig. 4. are illustrated two groups of behaviours: merely random, when no related memory episode have been encountered, and two memory based behaviours that are initiated when the similarity between the upcoming environmental sequence appears familiar with already experienced episodes of memories.

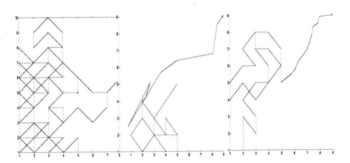

Fig. 4. Behaviour of the simulated rat. a) random goal-searching behaviour; b) and c) familiarity driven behaviours, emerging after a period of exploration.

6   Discussion

This paper features episodic memory encoding as a substratum for emergence of behaviours and goal oriented navigation, performed solely on the recollected episodes. The episode formation and behavioural choices are based on novelty/familiarity discrimination. The impact of novelty is two-fold: it allows an efficient encoding (exploration phase) and it is a basis for flexible reuse of memories in the recall (exploitation phase). The same computational paradigm is used in both cases, which makes an on-line implementation feasible.

Mimicking an animal by a robot simulation has its roots in the many parallels that can be found between them. The most obvious parallels stem from the embodied nature of an animal and a robot: both have a physical body, gather external information and behave accordingly. Going beyond this coarse comparison, we search for a simulation that aims exactness at the level of internal representation, the hippocampal representation in particular.

The functional efficiency of the hippocampal encoding, while performing both tasks - episodic encoding and novelty detection, suggests an optimal computational scheme, which may be beneficial for a robotics task. A detailed hippocampal simulation on its turn is a substratum for realistic emergent behaviours and can benefit the experimental sciences.

A new concept for hippocampal model underlying behaviour simulation that has been presented incorporates the novelty/familiarity gated learning and builds a functional connection between novelty detection and episode formation. A different approach has been taken to the sensory input. The functional and structural resemblance between sensory patterns of a robotic range sensors and place cells representation was observed, so the robotics simulation is based on so derived patterns.

References

[1]   Bunsey, M. , Eichenbaum, H. B.: Conservation of hippocampal memory function in rats and humans. Nature (London), 379, (1996), 255-257.

[2]   Eichenbaum, H., Dudchenko, P., Wood, E., Shapiro, M., Tanila, H.: The Hippocampus, Memory, and Place Cells: Is It Spatial Memory or a Memory Space? Neuron. Cell Press, Vol. 23, (1999) 209-226.

[3]   Stark, C.E., Squire, L.R.: Simple and associative recognition memory in the hippocampal region. Learn. Mem. **8,** (1998) 190-197.

[4]   Franz, M.O., Mallot, H.A.: Biomimetic robot navigation. Robotics and Autonomous Systems **30**, (2000) 133-153.

[5]   Arleo, A., Gerstner, W.: Spatial cognition and neuro-mimetic navigation: A model of hippocampal place cell activity. Biological Cybernetics, 83,(2000) 287-299.

[6]   Burgess, N., Recce, M., O'Keefe, J.: A model of hippocampal function. Neural Networks, 7, (1994) 1065-1081.

[7]   Touretzky, D. S., Redish, A. D.: Theory of rodent navigation based on interacting representations of space. Hippocampus, 6, (1996) 247-270

[8]   Conway, M. A.: Sensory-perceptual episodic memory and its context: autobiographical memory. Phil. Trans. R. Soc. Lond. B **356**, (2001) 1375-1384.

[9]   Tulving, E., Donaldson, W.: Organization of memory. New York: Acad. Press, (1972).

[10]   Barakova, E., Lourens, T.: Prediction of rapidly changing environmental dynamics for real time behaviour adaptation. Dynamic Perception, IOS press, (2002) 147-152.

[11]   Pfeifer, R., Scheier, C.: Understanding Intelligence, The MIT Press, (1999).

[12]   O'Keefe, J., Nadel, L.: The Hippocampus as a Cognitive Map, Oxford Press, (1971).

[13]   Schweighofer N., Doya K. and Lay F.: Unsupervised learning of granule cell sparse codes enhances cerebellar adaptive control, Neuro science 103, (2002) 35-50.

[14]   Zhang, L., Tao, H., Holt, C., Harris, W., Poo, M.: A critical window for cooperation and competition among developing retinotectal synapses. Nature, 395, (1998).

[15]   Markram, H., Lubke, H., Frotscher, M., Sakmann, B.: Regulation of synaptic efficacy by coincidence of postsynaptic aps and epsps. Science, 275, (1997) 213-215.

[16]   Dayan, P., Abbott, L.F.: Theoretical Neuroscience: Computational and Mathematical Modeling of Neural Systems, MIT Press, Cambridge MA (2001).

[17]   Foster, D.J., Morris, R.G.M., Dayan P.: A model of hippocampally dependent navigation, using the temporal difference learning rule. Hippocampus 10, (2000) 1-16.

[18]   Sutton, R.S. and Barto, A.G.: Reinforcement Learning: An Introduction MIT Press, Cambridge, MA, (1998).

[19]   Fritzke B.: Growing cell structures- a self organizing network for unsupervised and supervised learning, Neural Networks, vol.7 (1995). 1441-1460.

[20]   Martinetz T., Schulten, K.: Topology representing networks, Neural Networks, v.7 n.3, (1994) 507-522.

[21]   Barakova, E., Zimmer, U.: Dynamic Situation and Trajectory Discrimination by Means of Clustering and Summation of Raw Range Data, AISTA, Australia, (2000).

Increasing the Classification Accuracy of Simple Bayesian Classifier

S.B. Kotsiantis and P.E. Pintelas

Educational Software Development Laboratory
Department of Mathematics
University of Patras, Hellas

Abstract. Simple Bayes algorithm captures the assumption that every feature is independent from the rest of the features, given the state of the class feature. The fact that the assumption of independence is clearly almost always wrong has led to a general rejection of the crude independence model in favor of more complicated alternatives, at least by researchers knowledgeable about theoretical issues. In this study, we attempted to increase the prediction accuracy of the simple Bayes model. Because the concept of combining classifiers is proposed as a new direction for the improvement of the performance of individual classifiers, we made use of Adaboost, with the difference that in each iteration of Adaboost, we used a discretization method and we removed redundant features using a filter feature selection method. Finally, we performed a large-scale comparison with other attempts that have tried to improve the accuracy of the simple Bayes algorithm as well as other state-of-the-art algorithms and ensembles on 26 standard benchmark datasets and we took better accuracy in most cases using less time for training, too.

1 Introduction

Probabilistic classifiers and, in particular, the simple Bayes classifier, are among the most popular classifiers used in the machine learning community and increasingly in many applications. The study of probabilistic classification is the study of approximating a joint distribution with a product distribution. Probabilistic classifiers operate on data sets where each example x consists of feature values $<a_1, a_2 \ldots a_i>$ and the target function y can take on any value from a pre-defined finite set $V=(v_1, v_2 \ldots v_j)$. Classifying unseen examples involves calculating the most probable target value v_{max} and is defined as: $v_{max} = \max_{v_j \in V} P(v_j \mid a_1, a_2, \ldots, a_i)$. Using Bayes theorem v_{max} can be rewritten as: $v_{max} = \max_{v_j \in V} P(a_1, a_2, \ldots, a_i \mid v_j) P(v_j)$.

Bayes rule is used to estimate the conditional probability of a class label y, and then assumptions are made on the model, to decompose this probability into a product of conditional probabilities. Under the assumption that features values are conditionally independent given the target value, the formula used by the simple Bayes classifier is:

C. Bussler and D. Fensel (Eds.): AIMSA 2004, LNAI 3192, pp. 198–207, 2004.

$$v_{\max} = \max_{v_j \in V} P(v_j) \prod_i P(a_i \mid v_j),$$ where V is the target output of the classifier and

$P(a_i|v_j)$ and $P(v_i)$ can be calculated based on their frequency in the training data.

The application of previous formula is straightforward for the categorical features. For numerical features, one can model the component marginal distributions in a wide variety of ways. The simplest would be to adopt some parametric form e.g. marginal Gaussian estimators [5]. Another problem with this formula is the zero counts. Zero counts are obtained when a given class and feature value never occur together in the training set, and is problematic because the resulting zero probabilities will wipe out the information in all the other probabilities when they are multiplied. A solution to this problem is to incorporate a small-sample correction into all probabilities, such as the Laplace correction [5]. If a feature value does not occur given some class, its probability is set to 1/N, where N is the number of examples in the training set.

The assumption of independence is clearly almost always wrong. However, a large-scale comparison of simple Bayesian classifier with state-of-the-art algorithms for decision tree induction and instance-based learning on standard benchmark datasets found that simple Bayesian classifier sometimes is superior to each of the other learning schemes even on datasets with substantial feature dependencies [5]. An explanation why simple Bayes method remains competitive, even though it provides very poor estimates of the true underlying probabilities can be found in [9].

However, there are comparisons where the accuracy of the simple Bayes algorithm is near the bottom as for instance in the experiment of [14]. Nevertheless, in that case too, this algorithm had the best accuracy per needed training time. It predicts the class feature in a very short time. Another advantage of simple Bayesian classifier is that during classification can use as inputs, data with missing values, whereas in decision tree and neural network cannot.

In this study, we increase the training time of the simple Bayes algorithm so as to take better results. We use the simple Bayes along with the usage of discretization, feature selection and boosting. We performed a large-scale comparison with other attempts that have tried to improve the accuracy of the simple Bayes algorithm as well as other state-of-the-art algorithms and ensembles on 26 standard benchmark datasets and we actually took better accuracy in most cases using less time for training, too.

Description of some of the attempts that have been tried to improve the performance of simple Bayesian classifier is given in section 2. Section 3 discusses the proposed algorithm for improving the performance of simple Bayesian classifier. Experiment results in a number of data sets are presented in section 4, while brief summary with further research topics are given in Section 5.

2 Previous Attempts for Improving the Performance of Simple Bayes Classifier

The most well known attempt for improving the performance of the simple Bayes algorithm is the discretization of the continuous features into intervals, instead of using the default option to utilize the normal distribution to calculate probabilities. Numerous discretization methods have been examined such as the partition of the range of the features into k equal sized intervals and the partition of the range into intervals containing the same number of instances. A brief survey of these attempts and an empirical study comparing the performance of the most well-known discretization methods is given in [6], concluding that all the tested discretization methods can outperform the version of the simple Bayesian classifier that assumes normal distributions for continuous features. The same authors also concluded that the entropy-based method [7] performed somewhat better than the others. Entropy-based discretization is a supervised incremental top down method which recursively selects the cut-points minimizing entropy until a stopping criterion based on the MDL criterion ends the recursion.

The performance of the simple Bayesian Classifier on domains with redundant features can be also improved by removing redundant features [13]. The 'selective Bayesian classifier', has been explored by numerous researchers such as [13], [16]. A well-known filter that computes the empirical mutual information between features and the class, and discards low-valued features was used by [23]. Other researchers have explored the possibility of using a decision tree algorithm as a pre-processor to discover useful feature subsets for simple Bayes classifier. A simple method that uses C4.5 decision trees [18] to select features has been described by [20].

On the other hand, a wrapping forward search strategy to select features for use with simple Bayes was used in [13]. In [16], the author uses constructive induction and feature deletion (BSEJ algorithm) to alleviate the feature inter-dependence problem of the simple Bayesian classifier. BSEJ uses the wrapper model to join and delete features. A greedy search, at each step, either deletes one feature or creates a new one through joining (generating the Cartesian product of) two features. BSEJ starts from the set of all the original features, and stops when neither joining nor deleting can improve upon the accuracy of the simple Bayesian classifier. In [12] the researchers used the best first backward selection method as search method for applying the wrapper approach. They showed that this combination has very good results with simple Bayes algorithm.

More elaborate attempts to overcome the assumption of independence between features are based on including extra terms describing the relationship between the features [10]. Of course, this means that the simple form of the simple Bayes model is sacrificed. In fact, these particular authors approached things from the opposite direction, identifying weaknesses of the approach based on constructing an overall model of the joint distribution, and restricting themselves to models which included all the two way marginals of which had the class label as one component.

Recently, an iterative approach of simple Bayes is presented in [11]. The iterative Bayes begins with the distribution tables built by the simple Bayes and then the algorithm iteratively cycles through all the training examples using a hill-climbing technique. Experimental evaluation of iterative Bayes showed minor but consistent gain in accuracy in relation to simple Bayes [11]. However, the contingency tables are incrementally updated each time a training example is seen, which implies that the order of the examples could influence the final decision.

Another attempt for improving the simple Bayes model was the Bayesian trees [27]. A Bayesian tree-learning algorithm builds a decision tree, and generates a local simple Bayesian classifier at each leaf. The tests, leading to a leaf, can alleviate feature inter-dependencies for the local simple Bayesian classifier. In [27], the authors also proposed the application of lazy learning techniques to Bayesian tree induction and presented the resulting lazy Bayesian rule-learning algorithm, called LBR. For each test example, it builds a most appropriate rule with a local simple Bayesian classifier as its consequent.

Lately in the area of ML the concept of combining classifiers is proposed as a new direction for the improvement of the performance of individual classifiers. In [2], the researchers built an ensemble of simple Bayes classifiers using bagging [4] and boosting procedures [8]. Another way that has been examined for generation of ensemble of simple Bayesian classifiers is by using different feature subsets randomly and taking a vote of the predictions of each classifier that uses different feature subset [25].

3 Presented Algorithm

As we have already mentioned, comparing the performance of the most well known discretization methods, in [6], the authors concluded that the entropy-based method [7] performed slightly better. For this reason, we use the entropy-based method as discretization method in our algorithm. Full description of the discretization method is beyond the scope of this paper since it can be found in [7].

Feature wrappers selection techniques often achieve better results than filters due to the fact that they are tuned to the specific interaction between the induction algorithm and its training data [6]. However, they tend to be much slower than feature filters because they must repeatedly call the induction algorithm. In the authors' opinion, the advantage of filter approach outweighs its disadvantage. In general, filters execute many times faster than wrappers, and therefore stand a much better chance of scaling to databases with a large number of features than wrappers do. Thus, we have selected to use the filter approach embedded to our algorithm. The well-known filter that computes the empirical mutual information between features and the class [23], and discards low-valued features was modified for our algorithm. The mutual information gain criterion has a strong bias in favor of features with many different values, thus we rectify this bias by a kind of normalization – gain ratio that sometimes is used from decision tree algorithms [18] was used by the proposed algorithm. Features are selected by keeping those for which gain ratio exceeds a fixed threshold e. In order to have a robust selection, we set e to 0.02 of the gain ratio filter, in an attempt to discard only features with negligible impact on predictions. However, such a low threshold can discard many features.

The ensembles of simple Bayesian classifiers have traditionally not been a focus of research. The reason is that simple Bayes is an extremely stable learning algorithm, and bagging is mainly variance reduction technique, thus not being able to benefit from its integration. However, simple Bayes can be effectively used in ensemble techniques, which perform also bias reduction, such as boosting [2]. The authors of [2] also report that there is a problem with boosting which is the robustness to noise. This is expected because noisy examples tend to be misclassified, and the weight will be increased for these examples. For this reason, we have chosen to use Adaboost with only 10 classifiers. Thus, the proposed algorithm (BoostFSNB) is summarized in (Figure 1). It makes use of Adaboost, with the difference that in each iteration of Adaboost, it uses the entropy discretization method and it removes redundant features using the gain ratio filter feature selection method.

```
    Assign weight=1  to each training example
    for i=1 to 10
        {  for i=1 to number of features
            {
            S= Sorted values of i feature;  Splitting(S)
            if Entropy-MDLP-Criterion=SATISFIED then break
            else {
                T = GetBestSpitPoint(S); S₁ = GetLeftPart(S,T);  S₂ = GetRightPart(S,T); Split-
ting(S₁)
                Splitting(S₂)  }
            }
            for i=1 to number of features
            { G= Gain Ratio of i feature
            if (G<0.02) then remove i feature from data set
            }
    Apply Simple Bayes to weighted data set and store the resulting model
    Compute error e of model and store error;  if (e=0) or (e>0.5) then break
        for k=1 to number of training examples
            {
            if (Classification(k)=correct) then multiply weight of example by e/(1-e)
            Normalize weight of all examples
            }
    Output the final classifier:
    For each model add –log(e/(1-e)) to weight of class predicted and return class with highest
sum
```

Fig. 1. The proposed algorithm

Because the proposed algorithm is a combination of models, the produced classifier is less easily interpretable than the simple Bayes model. However, BoostFSNB as a weighted sum of simple Bayes models, remains much more easily interpretable than Neural Networks and Support Vector Classifiers [21]. In [24], the authors showed that boosting improves the accuracy of the simple Bayesian classifier in 9 out of the tested 14 data sets. However, they concluded that the mean relative error reduction of boosting over the simple Bayesian classifier in the 14 data sets was only 1%, indicating very marginal improvement due to boosting. On the contrary, the proposed algorithm has mean relative error reduction about 20% over the simple Bayesian classifier in the tested data sets. The main reason is that the embedding feature selection technique makes the simple Bayes slightly unstable and as a result more suitable for Adaboost.

In the following section, we present the experiments. It must be mentioned that the comparisons of the proposed algorithm are separated in three phases: a) with the other attempts that have tried to improve the accuracy of the simple Bayes algorithm, b) with other state-of-the-art algorithms and c) with other well-known ensembles.

4 Comparisons and Results

For the purpose of our study, we used 26 well-known datasets from many domains from the UCI repository [3]. These data sets were hand selected so as to come from real-world problems and to vary in characteristics. In order to calculate the classifiers' accuracy, the whole training set was divided into ten mutually exclusive and equal-sized subsets and for each subset the classifier was trained on the union of all of the other subsets. Then, cross validation was run 10 times for each algorithm and the median value of the 10-cross validations was calculated. In Table 1, one can see the comparisons of the proposed algorithm with the other attempts that have tried to improve the classification accuracy of the simple Bayes algorithm. Four well-known algorithms were used for the comparison: discretize simple Bayes [6], selective simple Bayes with forward selection [13], Tree Augmented Naïve Bayes [10] and lazy Bayesian rule-learning algorithm [27]. It must be mentioned that we also present the accuracy of the simple Bayes algorithm as borderline. In addition, a representative algorithm for each of the other sophisticated machine learning techniques was tested. The most well known learning algorithm to estimate the values of the weights of a neural network - the Back Propagation (BP) algorithm [15] - was the representative of the ANNs. SMO algorithm was the representative of the Support Vector Machines [17]. We also used the 3-NN algorithm as a representative of kNN[1].

In Table 1, we represent with *"vv"* that the proposed BoostFSNB algorithm *looses* from the specific algorithm. That is, the specific algorithm performed statistically better than BoostFSNB according to t-test with $p<0.001$. In addition, in Table 1, we represent with *"v"* that the proposed BoostFSNB algorithm *looses* from the specific algorithm according to t-test with $p<0.05$. Furthermore, in Table 1, "**" indicates that BoostFSNB performed statistically better than the specific classifier according to t-test with $p<0.001$ while "*" according to $p<0.05$. In all the other cases, there is no significant statistical difference between the results (*Draws*). It must be mentioned that the conclusions are mainly based on the resulting differences for $p<0.001$ because a p-value of 0.05 is not strict enough, if many classifiers are compared in numerous data sets [22]. However, as one can easily observe the conclusions remain the same with $p<0.05$. In the last rows of the Table 1 one can see the aggregated results in the form (*a/b/c*). In this notation "*a*" means that the proposed algorithm is significantly more accurate than the compared algorithm in *a* out of 26 data sets, "*c*" means that the proposed algorithm is significantly less accurate than the compared algorithm in *c* out of 26 data sets, while in the remaining cases (*b*), there is no significant statistical difference between the results. Thus, the proposed algorithm is significantly more accurate than simple Bayes (NB) in 12 out of the 26 data sets, while it has significantly higher error rates than simple Bayes in three data sets. The average error rate of our algorithm is also about 20% less than that of simple Bayes algorithm.

In addition, the proposed algorithm has significantly lower error rates in 11 out of the 26 data sets than the simple discretize version of simple Bayes (DiscNB), while it is significantly less accurate in three data sets. Furthermore, the proposed algorithm is significantly more accurate than the wrapping feature selection version of simple Bayes (WrapperNB) in 11 out of the 26 data sets using less time for training, too. In only one data set, the proposed algorithm has significantly higher error rate. Moreover, the proposed algorithm is significantly more accurate than LBR algorithm in 6 out of the 26 data sets and even though, the proposed algorithm has significantly higher error rates in other six data sets it uses much less time for training and classification. Additionally, the average error rate of the proposed algorithm is 2.5% less than LBR. Finally, the proposed algorithm is significantly more accurate than Tree Augmented Naïve Bayes (TAN) algorithm in 4 out of the 26 data sets, while it is significantly less accurate in two data sets.

Table 1. Comparing the proposed algorithm with other attempts to improve the simple Bayes

	Boost FSNB	NB	DiscNB	Wrap-perNB	TAN	LBR	BP	SMO	3NN
anneal	99.31	86.59**	95.9 **	89.57 **	98.11*	98.01 **	94.97 **	96.89 **	97.29 **
autos	75.6	57.41 **	65.17 **	63.61 **	74.78	73.8	48.84 **	56.55 **	67.23 **
balance	81.9	90.53 vv	71.56 **	90.53 vv	70.8**	72.17 **	85.67 vv	87.62 vv	86.74 vv
breast-cancer	72.17	72.7	72.7	71.64	69.28**	72.35	72.95	69.92	73.13
breast-w	95.98	96.07	97.2 vv	95.5 *	97 v	97.21 vv	96.35	96.81 v	96.61 v
colic	82.63	78.7 **	79.54**	83.91 v	82.8	82.33	83.07	82.69	80.95 *
credit-a	85.9	77.86 **	86.22	85.3	86.07	86.1	85.94	84.91	84.96 *
credit-g	72.83	75.16 vv	75.04 vv	73.79 v	74.3 vv	74.9 v	74.86 vv	75.11 vv	72.21
diabetes	75.38	75.75	75.26	76.06	75.36	75.38	77.04 vv	77.07 v	73.86 **
heart-c	82.42	83.34	83.47 v	78.75 **	82.97	83.54 v	82.98	84.03	81.82
heart-h	83.51	83.95	84.2	82.63	84.84 v	84.54 v	84.16	83.26	82.33 *
heart-statlog	82.19	83.59 v	82.56	82.78	82.63	82.59	83.3 v	83.81	79.11 **
hepatitis	84.14	83.81	84.28	82.55	84.83	84.91	84.29	85.03	80.85 **
hypothyroid	98.72	95.3 **	98.19 *	95.19 **	99.16 v	99.12 v	93.44 **	93.49 **	93.21 **
ionosphere	92.14	82.17 **	89.29 **	90.14 **	91.03 *	90 **	87.07 **	87.93 **	86.02 **
iris	94.2	95.53 v	93.33	94.27	92.93 *	93.2 *	84.8 **	84.87 **	95.2 v
kr-vs-kp	94.58	87.79 **	87.79 **	94.34	92.28 **	96.79 vv	98.92 vv	95.78 vv	96.56 vv
labor	91.33	93.57	88.57 *	85 **	92.1	87.5 **	88.93	94	87.83 *
Lymph/rapy	83.69	83.13	85.1	81.22 *	86.3 v	85.45	82.26	85.94	81.74
mushroom	100	95.76 **	95.76 **	99.62 **	99.96 **	99.96 **	99.97 *	100	100
prim.-tumor	46.49	49.71 vv	49.71 vv	43.45 **	47.76 v	48.85 vv	24.9 **	29.2 **	44.98 *
segment	93.08	80.16 **	91.16 **	89.17 **	95.16 vv	93.94 vv	91.35 **	89.72 **	96.12 vv
sonar	78.19	67.71 **	76.23	71.25 **	76.41 *	76.04*	78.67	77.88	83.76 vv
vote	95.08	90.02 **	90.02 **	95.63	94.62	94.11*	96.32 vv	96.23 v	93.08 **
waveform	81.61	80.01 **	79.97 **	81.94 v	80.1 *	83.42 vv	86.56 vv	86.94 vv	77.67 **
zoo	95.64	94.97	93.21 **	92.67 **	95.45	93.21 **	60.43 **	93.16 *	92.61 **
Average error	*14.66*	*17.62*	*16.32*	*16.52*	*16.11*	*15.02*	*18.15*	*16.2*	*15.73*
W-D-L (p<0.001)		*12/11/3*	*11/12/3*	*11/14/1*	*4/20/2*	*6/14/6*	*8/12/6*	*7/15/4*	*10/12/4*
W-D-L (p<0.05)		*12/9/5*	*13/9/4*	*13/9/4*	*9/10/7*	*9/8/9*	*9/10/7*	*8/11/7*	*15/5/6*

The proposed algorithm is also significantly more precise than BP algorithm with one hidden layer in 8 out of the 26 data sets, whilst it has significantly higher error rates in six data sets. In addition, the proposed algorithm is significantly more accurate than SMO algorithm in 7 out of the 26 data sets, whereas it has significantly higher error rates in four data sets. The proposed algorithm is significantly more precise than 3NN algorithm in 10 out of the 26 data sets, while it has significantly higher error rates in four data sets. In brief, we managed to improve the performance of the simple Bayes Classifier obtaining better accuracy than other well known methods that have tried to improve the performance of the simple Bayes algorithm. The proposed algorithm also gave better accuracy than other sophisticated state-of-the-art algorithms on most of the 26 standard benchmark datasets. Moreover, BoostFSNB needed 31 times less time for training (on the average) in the tested data-sets than BP and 2.5 times than SMO.

Subsequently, we compare the performance of BoostFSNB with bagging decision trees and boosting decision trees that have been proved to be very successful for many machine-learning problems [19]. Similarly with the proposed algorithm, Quinlan (1996) used 10 classifiers for bagging and boosting C4.5 algorithm. In Table 2, we present the accuracy of the simple Bayes algorithm after applying the bagging and boosting procedures (with 25 classifiers) as [2] used in their experiments. In the last rows of the Table 2 one can see the aggregated results.

Table 2. Comparing the proposed algorithm with well known ensembles

	BoostFSNB	AdaboostC4.5	BaggingC4.5	BaggingNB	AdaboostNB
anneal	99.31	99.59 v	98.82 **	87.27 **	95.2 **
autos	75.6	85.46 vv	81.48 vv	57.71 **	57.12 **
balance	81.9	78.35 **	82.68	90.29 vv	92.11 vv
breast-cancer	72.17	66.89 **	73.1	72.73	68.57 **
breast-w	95.98	96.08	96.18	96.07	95.55 *
colic	82.63	81.63	84.99 vv	78.94 **	77.46 **
credit-a	85.9	84.01 **	86.38	77.81 **	81.16 **
credit-g	72.83	70.75 **	73.38	75.13 vv	75.09 vv
diabetes	75.38	71.69 **	75.23	75.57	75.88
heart-c	82.42	78.79 **	79.86 **	83.24	83.14
heart-h	83.51	78.68 **	80.24 **	84.16	84.67 v
heart-statlog	82.19	78.59 **	80.93	83.41 v	82.3
hepatitis	84.14	82.38 *	82.05 *	84.39	84.23
hypothyroid	98.72	99.65 vv	99.57 vv	95.53 **	95.27 **
ionosphere	92.14	93.05 v	91.63	81.94 **	91.12
iris	94.2	94.33	94.73	95.53 v	95.07 v
kr-vs-kp	94.58	99.59 vv	99.43 vv	87.8 **	95.1 vv
labor	91.33	87.17 *	83.67 **	93.4	88.93
lymphotherapy	83.69	80.87 *	78.44 **	83.5	80.67 *
mushroom	100	100	100	95.73 **	100
primary-tumor	46.49	41.65 **	42.81 **	49.47 vv	49.71 vv
segment	93.08	98.12 vv	97.25 vv	80.41 **	80.16 **
sonar	78.19	79.13	77.25	67.96 **	81.21 v
vote	95.08	95.51	96.25 vv	90.09 **	95.19
waveform	81.61	81.4	81.63	80 **	80.01 **
zoo	95.64	95.18	93.7 *	95.07	97.23 v
Average error	14.66	15.44	14.94	17.57	16.07
W-D-L (p<0.001)		(9/13/4)	(6/14/6)	(12/11/3)	(8/14/4)
W-D-L (p<0.05)		(12/8/6)	(8/14/6)	(12/9/5)	(10/8/8)

The proposed algorithm is significantly more accurate than boosting C4.5 algorithm with 10 classifiers in 9 out of the 26 data sets. In only four data sets, the proposed algorithm has significantly higher error rates. In addition, the proposed algorithm is significantly more accurate than bagging C4.5 algorithm with 10 classifiers in 6 out of the 26 data sets, while on other six data sets, the proposed algorithm has significantly higher error rates using in any case less than half time for training. Additionally, the average error rate of the proposed algorithm is 2% less than bagging C4.5 algorithm. In brief, we took better accuracy than boosting and bagging decision trees on the most of the 26 standard benchmark datasets, using less time for training, too. In addition, the proposed algorithm is significantly more accurate than single boosting simple Bayes (AdaBoostNB) algorithm (using 25 classifiers) in 8 out of the 26 data sets, while in four data sets, the proposed algorithm has significantly higher error rates. Moreover, the proposed algorithm is significantly more accurate than single bagging simple Bayes algorithm (using 25 ensembles) in 12 out of the 26 data sets, whereas it has significantly higher error rates in only four data sets.

5 Conclusions

Ideally, we would like to be able to identify or design the single best learning algorithm to be used in all situations. However, both experimental results [14] and theoretical work [15] indicate that this is not possible. The simple Bayes classifier has much broader applicability than previously thought. Besides its high classification accuracy, it also has advantages in terms of simplicity, learning speed, classification speed and storage space.

To sum up, we managed to improve the performance of the simple Bayesian Classifier combining the usage of discretization, feature selection and boosting procedures. We performed a large-scale comparison with other attempts that have tried to improve the accuracy of the simple Bayes algorithm as well as other state-of-the-art algorithms and ensembles on 26 standard benchmark datasets and we took better accuracy in most cases using less time for training, too. Using less time for training the proposed algorithm stands a much better chance of scaling to data mining applications.

In future research it would be interesting to examine the performance of the presented algorithm in extremely imbalanced data sets. We believe that the embedded boosting process of the presented algorithm enables it to operate comparatively well in such difficult data sets, too.

References

1. D. Aha, Lazy Learning, Dordrecht: Kluwer Academic Publishers, 1997.
2. E. Bauer, and R. Kohavi. An empirical comparison of voting classification algorithms: Bagging, boosting, and variants, Machine Learning, 36 (1999): 105–139.
3. C.L. Blake and C.J. Merz, UCI Repository of machine learning databases [http://www.ics.uci.edu/~mlearn/MLRepository.html]. Irvine, CA: University of California, Department of Information and Computer Science (1998).
4. L. Breiman, Bagging Predictors. Machine Learning, 24 (1996): 123-140.
5. P. Domingos and M. Pazzani, On the optimality of the simple Bayesian classifier under zero-one loss, Machine Learning, 29(1997): 103-130.
6. J. Dougherty, R. Kohavi and M. Shami. Supervised and unsupervised discretization of continuous features. In Proceedings of the twelfth International Conference of Machine Learning. Morgan kaufmann (1995).
7. U. Fayyad and K. Irani, Multi-interval discretization of continuous-valued attributes for classification learning. In Proceedings of the Thirteenth International Joint Conference on Artificial Intelligence, Morgan Kaufmann (1993): 1022-1027.

8. Y. Freund and R. E. Schapire, Experiments with a New Boosting Algorithm, In Proceedings of ICML'96, 148-156.
9. J. H. Friedman, On bias, variance, 0/1-loss and curse-of-dimensionality. Data Mining and Knowledge Discovery, 1(1997): 55-77.
10. N. Friedman, D. Geiger and M. Goldszmidt, Bayesian network classifiers. Machine Learning, 29(1997): 131-163.
11. J. Gama, Iterative Bayes. Intelligent Data Analysis, 6(2000): 463 – 473.
12. R. Kohavi and G. John, Wrappers for feature subset selection, Artificial Intelligence, 2(1997): 273-324.
13. P. Langley and S. Sage, Induction of selective Bayesian classifiers. In Proc. of the 10th Conference on Uncertainty in Artificial Intelligence, Seattle, (1994): 399-406.
14. D. Michie, D. Spiegelhalter and C. Taylor, Machine Learning, Neural and Statistical Classification, Ellis Horwood, 1994.
15. T. Mitchell, Machine Learning, McGraw Hill, 1997.
16. M. Pazzani, Searching for dependencies in Bayesian classifiers. Artificial Intelligence and Statistics IV, Lecture Notes in Statistics, Springer-Verlag: New York, 1997.
17. J. Platt, Using sparseness and analytic QP to speed training of support vector machines. In M. S. Kearns, S. A. Solla, and D. A. Cohn (Eds.), Advances in neural information processing systems 11, MA: MIT Press, 1999.
18. J.Quinlan, C4.5: Programs for machine learning. Morgan Kaufmann, San Francisco, 1993.
19. J. R. Quinlan, Bagging, boosting, and C4.5. In Proceedings of the Thirteenth National Conference on Artificial Intelligence (1996), 725–730.
20. C. Ratanamahatana and D. Gunopulos, Feature Selection for the Naive Bayesian Classifier using Decision Trees, Applied Artificial Intelligence, 17 (2003): 475–487.
21. G. Ridgeway, D. Madigan and T. Richardson,. Interpretable boosted Naive Bayes classification. In Proceedings of the Fourth International Conference on Knowledge Discovery and Data Mining, Menlo Park (1998): 101-104.
22. S. Salzberg, On Comparing Classifiers: Pitfalls to Avoid and a Recommended Approach, Data Mining and Knowledge Discovery, 1(1997): 317–328.
23. M. Singh, and G. Provan, Efficient learning of selective Bayesian network classifiers. In Proc of the 13th International Conference on Machine Learning (1996): 453-461, Bari.
24. K. Ting and Z. Zheng,. Improving the Performance of Boosting for Naive Bayesian Classification, N. Zhong and L. Zhou (Eds.): PAKDD'99, LNAI 1574, pp. 296-305, 1999.
25. Tsymbal, S. Puuronen and D. Patterson, Feature Selection for Ensembles of Simple Bayesian Classifiers, In Proceedings of ISMIS (2002): 592-600, Lyon, June 27-29.
26. Witten and E. Frank, Data Mining: Practical Machine Learning Tools and Techniques with Java Implementations. Morgan Kaufmann, San Mateo, 2000.
27. Z. Zheng, and G.I. Webb, Lazy learning of Bayesian rules. Machine Learning, 41 (2000): 53-84

Outlier Detecting in Fuzzy Switching Regression Models

Hong-bin Shen [1], Jie Yang [1], and Shi-tong Wang [2]

[1] Institute of Image Processing & Pattern Recognition, Shanghai Jiaotong University,
Shanghai, China, 200030
zjshenhongbin@yahoo.com.cn   (H-b. Shen)
jieyang@sjtu.edu.cn   (J. Yang)
[2] Dept. of Information, Southern Yangtse University, Jiangsu, China, 214036

Abstract. Fuzzy switching regression models have been extensively used in economics and data mining research. We present a new algorithm named FCWRM (Fuzzy C Weighted Regression Model) to detect the outliers in fuzzy switching regression models while preserving the merits of FCRM algorithm proposed by Hathaway. The theoretic analysis shows that FCWRM can converge to a local minimum of the object function. Several numeric examples demonstrate the effectiveness of algorithm FCWRM.

Keywords: fuzzy switch regression, outlier, fuzzy clustering

1   Introduction

Switching regression models have been extensively used in economics [1 ~ 3] and data mining research fields. Many scholars discussed switching regression models in various details [4 ~ 6]. In [4], the authors proposed FCRM algorithm to solve the switching regression problems based on the famous FCM clustering algorithm. In FCRM, the distance between the data vectors and cluster centers is represented by the difference between the output of different models and the expected output. When FCRM finally converges, it will produce estimates of the parameters of different models and at the same time assign a fuzzy label to each datum in the dataset.

Outliers are data values that lie away from the general regression models and identifying outlying observation is an important aspect of the regression model-building process. For outliers often imply some important features or rules, how to locate outliers have attracted more and more attention and several different methods have been proposed to attain this goal[6]. Some of the methods can only work well for the regression model containing only one single outlier point, such as Cook's Distance, and others can find multi-outliers in the *linear* regression models. The purpose of this paper is to present a new approach for identifying the outliers in both linear and nonlinear regression models or the mixture of them while keeping the advantages of Hathaway's approach FCRM [4], that is, the approach proposed in this paper will also produce estimates of the parameters accurately and at the same time

C. Bussler and D. Fensel (Eds.): AIMSA 2004, LNAI 3192, pp. 208–215, 2004.

assign a fuzzy label to each datum in the regression dataset. For this purpose, we will assign a weight factor to each data vector in the dataset and this weight factor can be interpreted as the importance of the datum. According to the information theory, the information with lower frequency is more important than those happened frequently, that is to say, the outliers will have much larger weight factors than those normal data points in the models, which will be demonstrated by algorithm FCWRM. With the weight obtained, we can detect the outliers in the switch regression models easily and quickly.

2   Fuzzy Switching Regression Models with Outliers

2.1   Outlier in the Switching Regression Models

Data points that lie away from other observations are called outliers. Each outlier needs to be examined *carefully* to determine if it represents a possible value from the population being studied, in which case it should be retained, or if it is an error in which case it can be excluded. It may be that an outlier is the most important feature of a dataset. Fig.1 illustrates such a switching regression model including 2 outlier points in the dataset.

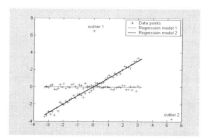

Fig. 1. A sample of fuzzy C regression model with outliers

In this paper, we assign a weight factor to each datum in the dataset and then we can construct a new algorithm of FCWRM (Fuzzy C Weighted Regression Model). By iterative function of the weight factor derived from the new objective function, every datum vector will obtain a weight factor when the algorithm finally converges, which can be used as a new criteria for finding the outlier information in the dataset. Furthermore, it can also produce estimates of $\{\bar{\beta}_1, \bar{\beta}_2, ..., \bar{\beta}_c\}$ and at the same time assign a fuzzy label to each datum in the regression dataset.

2.2   FCWRM Algorithm

By assigning a weight factor to each datum of the dataset, we can obtain a new objective function of FCWRM as follows:

$$J_{FCWRM} = \sum_{i=1}^{C}\sum_{k=1}^{N} \mu_{ik}{}^{m} \frac{1}{w_k{}^{q}} d_{ik}(\vec{\beta}_i) \tag{1}$$

Where N is the number of the datum in the dataset and $\sum_{k=1}^{N} w_k = w$, and w is total weight of the points in the dataset. The aim of FCWRM is to add a small weighting value w_k (large value for $\frac{1}{w_k{}^{q}}$) to the datum that belongs to at least one of the switching regression models. Generally speaking, outliers are far away from all the models, in this case, we will assign a large value w_k to each outlier (small value for $\frac{1}{w_k{}^{q}}$). The parameter q plays an important role in the clustering process. When q is large enough, then the weight value of each datum is almost equal to $\frac{w}{N}$, in other words, the weight plays the same influence on all the data samples; and if $q \to 0$, then the influence of the weight will reach the maximum.

Considering this constraint of $\sum_{k=1}^{N} w_k = w$, we have the following Lagrange function without constraints:

$$J_{FCWRM}{}' = \sum_{i=1}^{C}\sum_{k=1}^{N} \mu_{ik}{}^{m} \frac{1}{w_k{}^{q}} d_{ik}(\vec{\beta}_i) + \lambda(\sum_{k=1}^{N} w_k - w) \tag{2}$$

Where λ is the Lagrange coefficient. Differentiating (2) with respect to w_k, we obtain the following partial differentiation equation:

$$\frac{\partial J_{FCWRM}{}'}{\partial w_k} = -q \cdot \frac{1}{w_k{}^{q+1}} \cdot \sum_{i=1}^{C} \mu_{ik}{}^{m} \cdot d_{ik}(\vec{\beta}_i) + \lambda \tag{3}$$

with $\dfrac{\partial J_{FCWRM}{}'}{\partial w_k} = 0$, we will obtain:

$$\lambda = q \cdot \frac{1}{w_k{}^{q+1}} \cdot \sum_{i=1}^{C} \mu_{ik}{}^{m} \cdot d_{ik}(\vec{\beta}_i) \tag{4}$$

Resolving (4) for w_k

$$w_k = \left(\frac{q \cdot \sum_{i=1}^{C} \mu_{ik}{}^{m} \cdot d_{ik}(\vec{\beta}_i)}{\lambda}\right)^{\frac{1}{q+1}} \tag{5}$$

with $\sum_{k=1}^{N} w_k = w$:

$$w = \sum_{k=1}^{N} (\frac{q \cdot \sum_{i=1}^{C} \mu_{ik}^{m} \cdot d_{ik}(\vec{\beta}_i)}{\lambda})^{\frac{1}{q+1}} \tag{6}$$

so

$$\lambda^{\frac{1}{q+1}} = \sum_{k=1}^{N} (q \cdot \sum_{i=1}^{C} \mu_{ik}^{m} \cdot d_{ik}(\vec{\beta}_i))^{\frac{1}{q+1}} \cdot \frac{1}{w} \tag{7}$$

$$\lambda = (\sum_{k=1}^{N} (q \cdot \sum_{i=1}^{C} \mu_{ik}^{m} \cdot d_{ik}(\vec{\beta}_i))^{\frac{1}{q+1}} \cdot \frac{1}{w})^{q+1} \tag{8}$$

According to (4), (8):

$$w_k = \frac{(q \cdot \sum_{i=1}^{C} \mu_{ik}^{m} \cdot d_{ik}(\vec{\beta}_i))^{\frac{1}{q+1}}}{\sum_{k=1}^{N} (q \cdot \sum_{i=1}^{C} \mu_{ik}^{m} \cdot d_{ik}(\vec{\beta}_i))^{\frac{1}{q+1}}} \cdot w = \frac{(\sum_{i=1}^{C} \mu_{ik}^{m} \cdot d_{ik}(\vec{\beta}_i))^{\frac{1}{q+1}}}{\sum_{k=1}^{N} (\sum_{i=1}^{C} \mu_{ik}^{m} \cdot d_{ik}(\vec{\beta}_i))^{\frac{1}{q+1}}} \cdot w \tag{9}$$

(9) is the iterative function of the weight factor.

Now we present the following *FCWRM* algorithm:

Algorithm *FCWRM:* Fuzzy C Weighted Regression Model

---

1. Let $S = \{(\vec{x}_1, y_1), (\vec{x}_2, y_2), ..., (\vec{x}_N, y_N)\}$ denotes the dataset.

2. Initialize $C(2 \le C \le N), m(m > 1), q(q \ge 1), t = 0, error$, where *error* is a small constant.

3. Initialize $U^{(t)}, W^{(t)} = [w_k]$ which satisfy $\sum_{k=1}^{N} w_k = w$

4. In accordance with $U = [\mu_{ik}], W = [w_k]$, compute the weighted membership degree matrix $U^{(W)} = [\tilde{\mu}_{ik}]$ where $\tilde{\mu}_{ik}^{m} = \frac{\mu_{ik}^{m}}{w_k^{q}}$

5. Based on $U^{(W)}$, we obtain the new objective function $\tilde{J}_{FCWRM} = \sum_{k=1}^{N} \sum_{i=1}^{C} \tilde{\mu}_{ik}^{m} \frac{1}{w_k^{q}} d_{ik}(\vec{\beta}_i)$

6. According to $\frac{\partial \tilde{J}_{FCWRM}}{\partial \vec{\beta}_i} = 0$, compute $\vec{\beta}^{(t)}$

7. With $\vec{\beta}^{(t)}$ obtained in step 6, compute the error matrix $E = [d_{ik}(\vec{\beta}_i)]$.

8. According to $E = [d_{ik}(\vec{\beta_i})]$, update $U^{(t)} \rightarrow U^{(t+1)}$ satisfying the following rules:

$$
\mu_{ik} = \begin{cases}
\dfrac{1}{\displaystyle\sum_{j=1}^{C}\left(\dfrac{d_{ik}(\vec{\beta_i})}{d_{jk}(\vec{\beta_i})}\right)^{\frac{1}{m-1}}} & if \quad I_k = \Phi \\[2em]
\displaystyle\sum_{i\in I_k}\mu_{ik} = 1 & if \quad I_k \neq \Phi, i \in I_k \\[1em]
0 & if \quad I_k \neq \Phi, i \notin I_k
\end{cases}
\tag{10}
$$

Where $I_k = \{i \mid 1 \leq i \leq C, d_{ik} = 0\}$

9. With $U^{(t+1)}, E = [d_{ik}(\vec{\beta_i})]$, update $W^{(t)}$ to $W^{(t+1)}$ based on formula (9)

10 . If $\|U^{(t+1)} - U^{(t)}\| < error$ stop algorithm

11 . Otherwise $t \leftarrow t+1$, go to step 4

2.3 Convergence of FCWRM

Now, let us investigate the convergence properties of this new FCWRM algorithm:

Theorem 1: Let $\phi(U) = J_{FCWRM}$, where $U = [\mu_{ik}]_{C \times N}$, $w_k (k = 1,2,..., N)$ is fixed, and $d_{ik}(\vec{\beta_i}) \neq 0$, for all $1 \leq i \leq C, 1 \leq k \leq N$, then U is a local minimum of $\phi(U)$ if and only if μ_{ik} is computed via (10).

Proof: The only-if part has been proved according to the derivation of μ_{ik}. To show the sufficiency, we examine $H(\phi)$, the $CN \times CN$ Hessian of the Lagrangian of $\phi(U)$ evaluated at the U given by (10). Using Lagrange multiplier method, we find that the problem is equivalent to minimizing

$$
L(W, \lambda) = J_{FCWRM} - \sum_{k=1}^{N}\lambda_k(\sum_{t=1}^{C}\mu_{ik} - 1)
\tag{11}
$$

From (11), we have

$$
h_{st,ik}(U) = \frac{\partial}{\partial\mu_{st}}\left[\frac{\partial\phi(U)}{\partial\mu_{ik}}\right] = \begin{cases} m(m-1)\mu_{ik}^{m-2}\dfrac{1}{w_k^q}d_{ik}(\vec{\beta_i}) > 0 & if \quad s = i, \\[1em] 0 & otherwise \end{cases}
\tag{12}
$$

Where μ_{st} is computed from (10). Thus, $H(U) = [h_{st,ik}(U)]$ is a diagonal matrix. Since $m > 1$, and $d_{ik}(\vec{\beta}_i) > 0, w_k > 0$ for all $1 \le i \le C, 1 \le k \le N$, we know from the above formula that Hessian $H(U)$ is positive definite and consequently, (10) is also a sufficient condition for minimizing $\phi(U)$.   □

Theorem 2: Let $\phi(W) = J_{FCWRM}$, where $U = [\mu_{ik}]_{C \times N}$ is fixed, and $d_{ik}(\vec{\beta}_i) \ne 0$, for all $1 \le i \le C, 1 \le k \le N$, $m > 1$. Then $w_k(k = 1,2,...,N)$ is a local minimum of $\phi(W)$ if and only if $w_k(k = 1,2,...,N)$ is computed via (9).

Proof: The necessity was proved based on the derivation of $w_k(k = 1,2,...,N)$. To show the sufficiency, we have from (2) that

$$\frac{\partial}{\partial w_j}\left[\frac{\partial \phi(w)}{\partial w_k}\right] = \begin{cases} q(q+1)\sum_{i=1}^{C}\mu_{ik}^{m}\dfrac{1}{w_k^{q+2}}d_{ik}(\vec{\beta}_i) & > 0 & \text{if} \quad j = k \\ 0 & & \text{otherwise} \end{cases} \tag{13}$$

i.e. the Hessian is positive definite and consequently (9) is a sufficient condition for minimizing $\phi(w)$.   □

With Theorem 1 and 2, similar to Bezdek's proof in [4], we can prove that

$$J_{FCWRM}(U^{t+1}, W^{t+1}) \le J_{FCWRM}(U^t, W^t) \tag{14}$$

In other words, J_{FCWRM} is a decreasing function with t. So, the FCWRM algorithm will finally converge.

3 Simulations

In this section, we use the numerical simulation results to illustrate the effectiveness of algorithm FCWRM. Set $m = 2, w = 250, q = 1$.

Example 1— In this example, we test FCWRM on the nonlinear system with $C = 2$ which is also used by Hathaway in [4] as the benchmark sample. The dataset is generated with the following nonlinear system with the same parameter of [4]:

$$\begin{cases} RE1: y_k = \beta_{10} + \beta_{11}x_k + \beta_{12}x_k^2 \\ RE2: y_k = \beta_{20} + \beta_{21}x_k + \beta_{22}x_k^2 \end{cases} \tag{15}$$

Fig. 2 shows the datasets of 4 cases used in this example named A, B, C, D.

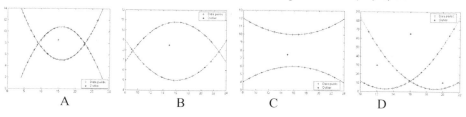

A   B   C   D

Fig. 2. The nonlinear system with outliers of 4 cases used in this example

We test FCWRM on these 4 cases 10 times and Table 1 illustrates the mean weight factors of normal datum vectors and that of the outliers in the datasets.

Table 1. Results of FCWRM on A, B, C, D datasets

Algorithm	Dataset	$\overline{W}_1$	$\overline{W}_2$
FCWRM	A	0.66	198.91
	B	2.24	87.57
	C	1.08	211.77
	D	1.21	34.88

Where $\overline{W}_1$ and $\overline{W}_2$ denote the mean weight factor of normal datum and outlier points respectively. From Table 1, we can detect the outlier information of the 4 datasets easily with the weight factor obtained.

Example 2—In this example, we deal with mining mixture structure involving curve and line in the same model while trying to find the outliers in the dataset which is shown in Fig. 3. The dataset is generated from the following mixture system with parameters.

$$\begin{cases} RE1: y_k = -8 + x_k + \varepsilon_1 \\ RE2: y_k = 21 - 2x_k + 0.625x_k^2 + \varepsilon_2 \end{cases} \tag{16}$$

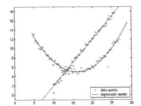

Fig. 3. A mixture of curve and line dataset   **Fig. 4.** Mining results with outliers

Fig. 4 shows the first two data vectors when we sort all the observations according to their weight factors in descent order, which are considered as the outliers in this paper and the result is somehow satisfactory. Obviously, if we want to select *n* observations from the dataset as the outlier candidate, the first *n* observations of the sorted datums in accordance with their weights in descent order are the answer. We can demonstrate again that FCWRM algorithm is an effective algorithm that can also mine the outliers from the mixture structure.

4   Conclusions

This paper proposed a new algorithm FCWRM to find the outlier information in the regression models. The best advantage of FCWRM is that we can detect the outliers in the dataset easily by the weight obtained while producing the accurate estimate of the parameters of the regression models. Our theoretic analysis shows that FCWRM can converge to a local minimum of the objective function. Simulations are done to show the validity and effectiveness of FCWRM.

References

1. D. S .Hamermesh, "Wage bargains, threshold effects, and the Phillips curve," Quart. J. Econ. 84 (1970) 501—517
2. R. E. Quandt, "A new approach to estimating switching regressions," J. Amer. Statist. Assoc. 67 (1972) 306—310
3. R. E. Quandt and J. B. Ramsey, "Estimating mixtures of normal distributions and switching regressions," J. Amer. Statist. Assoc. 73 (1978) 730—752.
4. R. Hathaway and J. Bezdek, "Switching regression models and fuzzy clustering," IEEE Trans. Fuzzy Syst. 1,3 (1993) 195—204.
5. S. B. Caudill and R. N. Acharyal, "Maximum-likelihood estimation of a mixture of normal regressions: starting values and singularities," Commun. Stat.-Simul. 27, 3 (1998) 667—674.
6. David.M.Sebert, Douglas C. Montgomery, Dwayne A. Rollier, "A Clustering Algorithm for identifying multiple outliers in linear regression", Computational Statistics and Data Analysis, 27(1998) 461—484.

PubMiner: Machine Learning-Based Text Mining System for Biomedical Information Mining

Jae-Hong Eom and Byoung-Tak Zhang

Biointelligence Lab., School of Computer Science and Engineering,
Seoul National University,
Seoul 151-744, South Korea
{jheom, btzhang}@bi.snu.ac.kr

Abstract. PubMiner, an intelligent machine learning based text mining system for mining biological information from the literature is introduced. PubMiner utilize natural language processing and machine learning based data mining techniques for mining useful biological information such as protein-protein interaction from the massive literature data. The system recognizes biological terms such as gene, protein, and enzymes and extracts their interactions described in the document through natural language analysis. The extracted interactions are further analyzed with a set of features of each entity which were constructed from the related public databases to infer more interactions from the original interactions. An inferred interaction from the interaction analysis and native interaction are provided to the user with the link of literature sources. The evaluation of system performance proceeded with the protein interaction data of *S.cerevisiae* (bakers yeast) from MIPS and SGD.

Keywords: Natural Language Processing, Data Mining, Machine Learning, Bioinformatics, and Software Application

1 Introduction

New scientific discoveries are founded on the existing knowledge which has to be easy to get to and thus usable by the scientific community. Electronic storage allows the customized extraction of information from the literature and its combination with other data resources such as heterogeneous databases. The scientific community is growing so that even for a rather specialized field it becomes impossible to stay up-to-date just through personal contacts in that particular community. The growing amount of knowledge also increases the chance for new ideas based on combining solutions from different fields. And there is a necessity of accessing and integrating all scientific information to be able to judge the own progress and to get inspired by new questions and answers [1].

Since the human genome sequences have been decoded, especially in biology and bioinformatics, there are more and more people devoted to this research domain and hundreds of on-line databases characterizing biological information such as sequences, structures, molecular interactions, and expression patterns [2]. Even though

C. Bussler and D. Fensel (Eds.): AIMSA 2004, LNAI 3192, pp. 216–225, 2004.
© Springer-Verlag Berlin Heidelberg 2004

the widespread topics of research, the end result of all biological experiments is a publication in the form of text. Information in text form such as MEDLINE[1], however, is a greatly underutilized source of biological information to the biological researchers. It takes lots of time to obtain the important and precise information from huge databases with daily increase. Thus knowledge discovery from a large collection of scientific papers is very important for efficient biological and biomedical research. Until now, a number of tools and approaches have been developed to resolve such needs. There are many systems analyzing abstracts in MEDLINE to offer bio-related information services. For example, Suiseki [3] and BioBiblioMetrics [4] focus on the protein-protein interaction extraction and visualization. MedMiner [5] utilizes external data sources such as GeneCard [6] and MEDLINE for offering structured information about specific keywords provided by the user. AbXtract [7] labels the protein function in the input text and XplorMed [8] presents the user specified information through the interaction with user. GENIES [9] discovers more complicated information such as pathways from journal abstracts. Recently, MedScan [10] employed full-sentence parsing technique for the extraction of human protein interactions from MEDLINE. And there a number of approaches related to text mining for biology and other fields [11].

Generally, these conventional systems rely on basic natural language processing (NLP) techniques when analyzing literature data. And the efficacy of such systems greatly depends on the rules for processing unrefined information. Such rules have to be refined by human experts, entailing the possibility of lack of clarity and coverage. In order to overcome this problem, we used machine learning techniques in combination with conventional NLP techniques. Our method also incorporated several data mining techniques for the extensive discovery, i.e., detection of the interactions which are not explicitly described in the text.

We have developed PubMiner (Publication Text Mining system) which performs efficient mining of gene and protein interactions. For the evaluation, the budding yeast (*S. cerevisiae*) was used as a model organism. The goal of our text mining system is to design and develop an information system that can efficiently retrieve the biological entity-related information from the MEDLINE, where the biological entity-related information includes biological function of entities (e.g., gene, protein, and enzymes), related gene or protein, and relation of gene or proteins. Especially we focus on interactions between entities.

The paper is organized as follows. In Section 2, the overall architecture of Pub-Miner is described. In Section 3, we describe the methodology of the relation inference module of PubMiner. In Section 4, performance evaluation of each component is given. Finally, concluding remarks and future works are given in Section 5.

2 System Description

The system, PubMiner, consists of three key components: natural language processing, machine learning-based inference, and visualization module.

---

[1] http://www.pubmed.gov

2.1 Interaction Extraction

The interaction extraction module is based on the NLP techniques adapted to take into account the properties of biomedical literature. It includes a part-of-speech (POS) tagger, a named-entity tagger, a syntactic analyzer, and an event extractor. The POS tagger based on hidden Markov models (HMMs) was adopted for tagging biological words as well as general ones. The named-entity tagger, based on support vector machines (SVMs), recognizes the region of an entity and assigns a proper class to it. The syntactic analyzer recognizes base phrases and detects the dependency represented in them. Finally, the event extractor finds the binary relation using the syntactic information of a given sentence, co-occurrence statistics between two named entities, and pattern information of an event verb. General medical term was trained with UMLS meta-thesaurus [12] and the biological entity and its interaction was trained with GENIA [13] corpus. The underlying NLP approaches for named entity recognition are based on the system of Hwang *et al.* [14] and Lee *et al.* [15] with collaborations. More detailed descriptions of language processing are elucidated in [16]. Figure 1 shows the schematic architecture of the interaction extraction module.

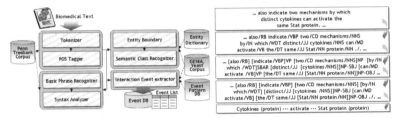

Fig. 1. The schematic architecture of the interaction extraction module (left) and the example of sentence parsing (right). The resulting event DB contains interactions between entities. Event pattern database was constructed from the GENIA corpus and tuned to yeast domain with manually tagged documents.

2.2 Inference

The relation inference module, which finds common features and group relations, is based on data mining and machine learning techniques. A set of features of each component of the interaction are collected from public databases such as *Saccharomyces* Genome Database (SGD) [17] and database of Munich Information Center for Protein Sequences (MIPS) [18] and represented as a binary feature vector. An association rule discovery algorithm, Apriori [19] was used to extract the appropriate common feature set of interacting biological entities. In addition, a distribution-based clustering algorithm [20] was adopted to analyze group relations. This clustering method collects group relation from the collection of document which contains various biological entities. And the clustering procedure discovers common characteristics among members of the same cluster. It also finds the features describing inter-cluster (between clusters) relations. PubMiner also provides graphical user interface to select various options for the clustering and mining. Finally, the hypothetical interactions are generated for the construction of interaction network. The hypotheses correspond to the inferred generalized association rules and the procedure of association discovery is described in Section 3. The inferred relations as well as the original relations are stored in the local database in a systematic way for efficient management of information. Figure 2 describes the schematic architecture of relation inference module.

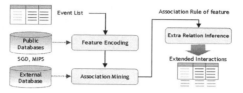

Fig. 2. The schematic architecture of relation inference module. For feature encoding, feature definition of public database such as SGD and MIPS are used. The event list represents the set of interactions which was constructed from previous interaction extraction module. The extended interactions include inferred interaction through the feature association mining.

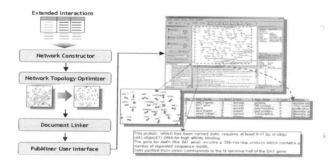

Fig. 3. The workflow diagram of the visualization module (left) and its interface (right). The dashed lines in the resulting interaction graph represent the inferred interactions.

2.3 Visualization

The visualization module shows interactions among the biological entities as a network format. It also shows the documents from which the relations were extracted and inferred. In addition, diverse additional information, such as the weight of association between biological entities could be represented. Thus the user can easily examine the reliability of relations inferred by the system. Moreover, this module shows interaction networks with minimized complexity for comprehensibility and can be utilized as an independent interaction network viewer with predefined input format. Figure 3 shows the overall architecture of visualization module and its interface.

3   Methods

In this section we describe the methodology of the relation inference module of Pub-Miner. Basically, the relation inference is based on the machine learning theory to find the optimal feature sets. Additionally, association rule discovery method which is widely used in data mining field is used to find general association among the selected optimal features.

3.1 Feature Selection

In our application, each interaction event is represented by their feature association. Thus the selection of optimal feature subset is important to achieve the efficiency of system and to eliminate non-informative association information. Therefore, Pub-Miner uses feature dimension reduction filter which was earlier introduced by Yu *et al.* [21], named fast correlation-based filter (FCBF), to achieve these objectives. Here, we call this FCBC procedure as feature dimension reduction filter (FDRF) for our application.

Each feature of data can be considered as a random variable and the *entropy* is used as a measure of the uncertainty of the random variable. The entropy of a variable X is defined as:

$$H(X) = -\sum_i P(x_i)\log_2(P(x_i)),\tag{1}$$

And the entropy of X after observing values of another variable Y is defined as:

$$H(X\,|\,Y) = -\sum_j P(y_j)\sum_i P(x_i\,|\,y_j)\log_2(P(x_i\,|\,y_j)),\tag{2}$$

where $P(y_j)$ is the prior probability of the value y_j of Y, and $P(x_i\,|\,y_j)$ is the posterior probability of X being x_i given the values of Y. The amount by which the entropy of X decreases reflects additional information about X provided by Y and is called *information gain* [22], given by

$$IG(X\,|\,Y) = H(X) - H(X\,|\,Y)\tag{3}$$

According to this measure, a feature Y is considered to be more correlated to feature X than feature Z, if $IG\,(X\,|\,Y) > IG\,(Z\,|\,Y)$. Symmetry is a desired property for a measure of correlation between features and information gain. However, information gain is biased in favor of features with more values and the values have to be normalized to ensure they are comparable and have the same affect. Therefore, here we use the *symmetrical uncertainty* as a measure of feature correlation [23], defined as:

$$SU(X,Y) = 2\left[\frac{IG(X\,|\,Y)}{H(X)+H(Y)}\right],\ 0 \le SU(X,Y) \le 1\tag{4}$$

With symmetrical uncertainty (SU) as feature association measure, we use the feature selection procedure of Yu *et al.* [21] to reduce the computational complexity of association mining. To decide whether a feature is relevant to the protein interaction (interaction class) or not, we use two measures, c–correlation and f–correlation which use the threshold SU value δ decided by user. The class C in Figure 4 is divided into two classes, conditional protein class (C_C) and result protein class (C_R) of interaction.

Definition 1. (c–correlation $SU_{i,c}$, f–correlation $SU_{j,i}$). Assume that dataset S contains N ($f_1,\dots, f_N$) features and a class C (C_C or C_R). Let $SU_{i,c}$ denote the SU value that measures the correlation between a feature f_i and the class C (called c–correlation), then a subset S' of relevant features can be decided by a threshold SU value δ, such that $\forall f_i \in S'$, $1 \le i \le N$, $SU_{i,c} \ge \delta$. And the pair-wise correlation between all features (called f–correlation) can be defined in same manner of c–correlation with a threshold value δ. The value of f–correlation is used to decide whether relevant feature is redundant or not when considering it with other relevant features.

Given training dataset $S = (f_1, \ldots, f_N, C)$, where $C = C_C \cup C_R$ and
User-decided threshold δ, do following procedure for each class C_C and C_R.

1. **Repeat** Step 1.1 to 1.2, for all i, $i = 1$ to N.
   1.1 **Calculate** $SU_{i,c}$ for f_i.
   1.2. **Append** f_i to S'_{list} when $SU_{i,c} \geq \delta$.
2. **Sort** S'_{list} in descending order with $SU_{i,c}$ value.
3. **Set** f_p with the first element of S'_{list}.
4. **Repeat** Step 4.1 to 4.3, for all $f_p \neq NULL$.
   4.1 **Set** f_q with the next element of f_p in S'_{list}.
   4.2 **Repeat** Step 4.2.1 to 4.2.3, for all $f_q \neq NULL$.
      4.2.1 **Set** $f'_q = f_q$.
      4.2.2 if $SU_{p,q} \geq SU_{q,c}$,
            Remove f_q from S'_{list} and **Set** f_q with the next element of f'_q in S'_{list}.
            else **Set** f_q with the next element of f_q in S'_{list}.
      4.2.3 **Set** f_q with the next element of f_q in S'_{list}
   4.3 **Set** f_p with next the element of f_p in S'_{list}.
5. **Set** $S_{best} = S'_{list}$

Output the most informative optimal feature subset: S_{best}

Fig. 4. The procedures of feature dimension reduction filter (FDRF).

3.2 Mining Feature Association

Association Mining

To predict protein–protein interaction with feature association, we adopt the association rule discovery data mining algorithm (so-called Apriori algorithm) proposed by Agrawal *et al.* [19]. Generally, an association rule $R\ (A \Rightarrow B)$ has two values, *support* and *confidence*, representing the characteristics of the association rule. Support (*SP*) represents the frequency of co-occurrence of all the items appearing in the rule. And confidence (*CF*) is the accuracy of the rule, which is calculated by dividing the *SP* value by the frequency of the item in conditional part of the rule.

$$SP(A \Rightarrow B) = P(A \cup B), \ CF(A \Rightarrow B) = P(B \mid A) \qquad (5)$$

where $A \Rightarrow B$ represents association rule for two items (set of features) A and B in that order. Association rule can be discovered by detecting all the possible rules whose supports and confidences are larger than the user-defined threshold value called minimal support (SP_{min}) and minimal confidence (CF_{min}) respectively. Rules that satisfy both minimum support and minimum confidence threshold are taken as to be *strong*. Here we consider these strong association rules as interesting ones.

In this work, we use the same association rule mining and the scoring approach of Oyama *et al.* [24] for performance comparison with respect to the execution time.

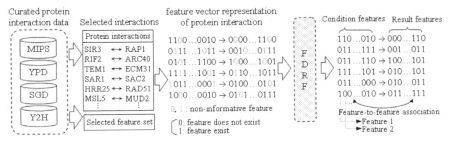

Fig. 5. Representation of protein interaction by feature vectors. Each interaction is represented with binary feature vector (whether the feature exists or not) and their associations. The FDRF sets those features as "don't care" (D/K) which have *SU* value less than given *SU* threshold δ. This is intended to consider in association mining only those features that have greater *SU* value than a given threshold. The features marked D/K are regarded as D/K also in association rule mining (i.e., these features are not counted in the calculation of support and confidence). These features are not shown in the vector representation of right side of Figure 5.

Entity Interaction with Feature Association

An interaction is represented as a pair of two proteins that directly bind to each other. To analyze protein–protein interactions with feature association, we consider each interacting protein pair as a transaction of data mining. These transactions with binary vector representation are described in Figure 5. Using association rule mining, then, we extract association of features which generalize the interactions.

4   Experimental Results

Performance of Entity Extraction

In order to test our entity recognition and interaction extraction module, we built a corpus from 1,000 randomly selected scientific abstracts from PubMed identified to contain biological entity names and interactions through manual searches. The corpus was manually analyzed for biological entities such as protein, gene, and small mole-cule names in addition to any interaction relationships present in each abstract within the corpus by biologist within our laboratory. Analysis of the corpus revealed 5,928 distinct references to biological entities and a total of 3,182 distinct references to interaction relationships. Performance evaluation was conducted over the same set of 1,000 articles, by capturing the set of entities and interactions recognized by the sys-tem and comparing this output against the manually analyzed results previously de-scribed. Table 1 shows the statistics of abstract document collection for extraction performance evaluation.

Table 1. The statistics for the document collection.

# of abstracts in collection	# of biological entities	# of interactions
1,000	5,928	3,182

We measured the recall and the precision for both the ability to recognize entity names in text in addition to the ability of the system to extract interactions based on the following calculations:

$$\text{Recall} = TP / (TP + FN), \quad \text{Precision} = TP / (TP + FP)$$

where, TP (true positive) is the number of biological entities or interactions that were correctly identified by the system and were found in the corpus. FN (false negative) is the number of biological entities or interactions that the system failed to recognize in the corpus and FP (false positive) is the number of biological entities or interactions that were recognized by the system but were not found in the corpus. Performance test results of the extraction module in the PubMiner are described in Table 2.

Table 2. The precision and recall performance of the entities and interaction extraction.

Rcognition Categories	Recall	Precision
Biological entities	83.5	93.1
Interactions of entities	73.9	80.2

Performance of Feature Selection and Association Mining

To test the performance of inference of PubMiner through feature selection (reductions), we used protein–protein interaction as a metric of entity recognition and interaction extraction. The major protein pairs of the interactions are obtained from the same data source of Oyama et al. [24]. It includes MIPS, YPD and Y2H by Ito et al. and Uetz et al., respectively [18]. Additionally, we use SGD [17] to collect more abundant feature set. Table 3 shows the statistics of interaction data for each data source and filtering with FDRF of Figure 4.

Table 3. The statistics for the protein–protein interaction dataset.

Data Source	# of interactions	# of initial features	# of filtered features
MIPS	10,641		
YPD	2,952		
SGD	1,482	6,232 (total)	1,293 (total)
Y2H (Ito et al.)	957		
Y2H (Uetz et al.)	5,086		

We performed feature filtering procedure of Figure 4 as a first step of our inference method ($\delta=0.73$) after the feature encoding with the way of Figure 5. Next, we performed association rule mining under the condition of minimal support 9 and minimal confidence 75% on the protein interaction data which have reduced features. And with the mined feature association, we predicted new protein–protein interaction which have not used in association training setp. The accuracy of prediction is measured whether the predicted interaction exists in the collected dataset or not. The results are measured with 10 cross-validation.

Table 4. Accuracy of the proposed method and the effect (in elapsed time) of filtering optimal informative features with FDRF. Total interactions for prediction is selected from Table 3.

Prediction method (Association ming)	# of interactions			Accuracy	Elapsed Time
	Total	Excluded	Predicted		
Without FDRF	4,628	463	423	91.4 %	212.34 sec
With FDRF	4,628	463	439	94.8 %	143.27 sec

Table 4 gives the advantage of obtained by filtering non-informative (redundant) features and the inference performance of PubMiner. The accuracy of interaction prediction increased about 3.4% with FDRF. And the elapsed time of FDRF based association mining, 143.27 sec, include the FDRF processing time which was 19.89 sec. The elapsed time decrease obtained by using FDRF is 32.5%. Thus, it is of great importance to reduce number of feature of interaction data for the improvement of both accuracy and execution time. Thus, we can guess that the information theory based feature filtering reduced a set of misleding or redundnt features of interaction data and this feature reduction eliminated wrong associations and boosted the over all pocessing time. And the feature association shows the promising results for inferencing implicit interaction of biological entities.

5   Conclusions

In this paper, we presented a biomedical text mining system, PubMiner, which screens the interaction data from literature abstracts through natural language analysis, performs inferences based on machine learning and data mining techniques, and visualizes interaction networks with appropriate links to the evidence article. To reveal more comprehensive interaction information, we employed both the data mining approach with optimal feature selection method in addition to the conventional natural language processing techniques. The proposed method achieved the improvement of both accuracy and processing time. From the result of Table 4, it is also suggested that with smaller granularity of interaction (i.e., not protein, but a set of features of proteins) we could achieve further detailed investigation of the protein–protein interaction. Thus we can say that the proposed method is suitable for an efficient analysis of interactive entity pair which has many features and this approach is also suitable as a back-end module of general literature mining.

But, current public interaction data produced by high-throughput methods (e.g., Y2H) have many false positives. And several interactions of these false positives are corrected by recent researches through reinvestigation with new experimental approaches. Thus, study on the new method for resolving these problems related to false positive screening with respect to literature mining further remain as future works.

Acknowledgements. This research was supported by the Korean Ministry of Science and Technology under the NRL Program and the Systems Biology Program.

References

1. Andrade, M.,A., and Borka, P.: automated extraction of information in molecular biology. *FEBS Letters* **476** (2000) 12–17
2. Chiang, J.,H., *et al.*:: GIS: a biomedical text–mining system for gene information discovery. *Bioinformatics* **20**(1) (2004) 120–121
3. Blaschke, C., *et al.*: Automatic extraction of biological information from scientific text: protein–protein interactions. In *Proc. of ISMB–1999*, Heidelberg, Germany (1999) 60–67
4. BioBiblioMetrics. http://www.bmm.icnet.uk/~stapleyb/biobib/
5. Tanabe, L., *et al.*: MedMiner: an internet text-mining tool for biomedical information, with application to gene expression profiling. *BioTechniques* **27** (1999) 1210–1217
6. Safran, M., *et al.*: Human gene-centric databases at the Weizmann institute of science: GeneCards, UDB, CroW 21 and HORDE. *Nucleic Acids Res.* **31**(1) (2003) 142–146
7. Andrade, M.,A., Valencia, A.,: Automatic extraction of keywords from scientific text: application to the knowledge domain of protein families. *Bioinformatics* **14**(7) (1998) 600–607
8. Perez-Iratxeta, C., *et al.*: XplorMed: a tool for exploring MEDLINE abstracts. *Trends Biochem. Sci.* **26** (2001) 573–575
9. Friedman, C., *et al.*: GENIS: a natural-language processing system for the extraction of molecular pathways from journal articles. *Bioinformatics* **17**(Suppl.1) (2001) S74–S82
10. Daraselia, N., *et al.*: Extracting human protein interactions from MEDLINE using a full-sentence parser. *Bioinformatics* **20**(5) (2004) 604–611
11. Nédellec C., *et al.*: Machine learning for information extraction in genomics – state of the art and perspectives. In: Sirmakessis, S. (ed.) : Text Mining and its Applications. *Studies in Fuzzi. and Soft Comp.* **138**. Springer–Verlag, Berlin Heidelberg New York (2004) 99–118
12. Humphreys, B. L., et al.: The Unified Medical Language System: an informatics research collaboration. *J. Am. Med. Inform. Assoc.* **5** (1998) 1–11
13. Kim J.D., *et al.*: GENIA corpus - semantically annotated corpus for bio-textmining. *Bioinformatics* 19(Suppl 1) (2003) i180–182
14. Hwang, Y.S., *et al.*: Weighted probabilistic sum model based on decision tree decomposition for text chunking. *Int. J. Comp. Proc. Orient. Lang.* **16**(1) (2003) 1–20
15. Lee, K.J., *et al.*: Two-phase biomedical NE recognition based on SVMs. In *Proc. of ACL 2003 Workshop on Natural Language Processing in Biomedicine* (2003) 33–40
16. Eom, J.H., *et al.*: PubMiner – a machine learning-based biomedical text mining system. *Technical Report (BI–TR0401)*, Biointelligence Lab., Seoul National University (2004)
17. Christie, K.R., *et al.*: Saccharomyces Genome Database (SGD) provides tools to identify and analyze sequences from Saccharomyces cerevisiae and related sequences from other organisms. *Nucleic Acids Res.* **32**(1) (2004) D311–D314
18. Mewes, H.W., *et al.*: MIPS: analysis and annotation of proteins from whole genomes. *Nucleic Acids Res.* **32**(1) (2004) D41–D44
19. Agrawal, R., *et al.*: Mining association rules between sets of items in large databases. In *Proc. of ACM SIGMOD–1993*, Washington D.C., USA (1993) 207–216
20. Slonim, N., and Tishby, N.: Document clustering using word clusters via the information bottleneck method. In *Proc. of SIGIR–2000*, Athens, Greece (2000) 208–215
21. Yu, L. and Liu, H.: Feature selection for high dimensional data: a fast correlation-based filter solution. In *Proc. of ICML–2003*, Washington D.C., USA (2003) 856–863
22. Quinlan, J.: C4.5: Programs for machine learning. Morgan Kaufmann. (1993)
23. Press, W.H., *et al.*: Numerical recipes in C. Cambridge University Press. (1988)
24. Oyama, T., *et al.*: Extraction of knowledge on protein–protein interaction by association rule discovery. *Bioinformatics* **18** (2002) 705–714

Advances in Profile Assisted Voicemail Management

Konstantinos Koumpis

Vienna Telecommunications Research Center - ftw.
Tech Gate Vienna, 1 Donau City St.
1220 Vienna, Austria
koumpis@ftw.at

Abstract. Spoken audio is an important source of information available to knowledge extraction and management systems. Organization of spoken messages by priority and content can facilitate knowledge capture and decision making based on profiles of recipients as these can be determined by physical and social conditions. This paper revisits the above task and addresses a related data sparseness problem. We propose a methodology according to which the coverage of language models used to categorize message types is augmented with previously unobserved lexical information derived from other corpora. Such lexical information is the result of combining word classes constructed by an agglomerative clustering algorithm which follows a criterion of minimum loss in average mutual information. We subsequently generate more robust category estimators by interpolating class-based and voicemail word-based models.

Keywords: automatic categorization, speech recognition, stochastic language models, class-based clustering, voicemail.

1 Introduction

The enormous growth of available spoken audio recordings has led to a comparable growth in the need for methods to assist users in managing the knowledge contained therein [1]. Standard knowledge management approaches typically organize content in portals, use text search and analysis tools, and rely heavily on text as the medium for transferring knowledge. The ongoing migration of computing for information access from the desktop and telephone to mobile devices such as personal digital assistants (PDAs) and smart phones introduces new challenges as these devices offer limited audio playback and display capabilities. Voicemail represents a growing volume of real-world speech data that involves a conversational interaction between a human and a machine with no feedback from the machine, and for which manual organization is a time consuming task, particularly for high-volume users. There are situations in which users would prefer to receive messages of certain content types and leave the remaining ones to be reviewed later at a more convenient location or time. For example, imagine a user attending a business meeting abroad requiring constant information flow

C. Bussler and D. Fensel (Eds.): AIMSA 2004, LNAI 3192, pp. 226–235, 2004.

from his head office but not messages from his local recreation club. On the contrary, the same person being on holiday would most likely be interested only in messages related to friends and family rather than those concerning work.

As text categorization utilities are becoming central into advanced email tools, users are likely to wish their migration into voicemail too. Voicemail recipients today rely almost exclusively on caller line identity, the presentation of the caller's telephone number or name, to filter incoming messages. A few alternative solutions have been proposed for efficient voicemail retrieval which include browsing and searching of message transcriptions via a graphical user interface [2], generation and delivery of text summaries on mobile phone displays using wireless protocols [3], extraction of the identity and phone number of the caller from voicemail messages [4], and re-ordering voicemail messages based on criteria of urgency and business relevance [5]. A profile assisted voicemail management system can instead sift through a stream of arriving messages to find those relevant to predefined categories. Each message can be in exactly one, multiple or no category at all. Unlike search queries, user profiles are persistent, yet adaptive, and tend to reflect long term information needs.

Many standard machine learning techniques have been applied to automated text categorization problems, such as decision trees, naive Bayes, neural networks, k-nearest neighbour classifiers and support vector machines [6,7,8]. Stochastic language models are of particular interest as input features because they can incorporate local dependencies and thus preserve semantics, as a result of modelling word sequences within the framework of standard Markov based approximations. Character level language models have been found to be effective in text classification [9] and author attribution [10] tasks. This paper deals with a corpus containing transcriptions of spoken messages. Spoken language is different from written language as it is often ungrammatical, lacks punctuation and capitalization, and its textual representation almost always contains substitution, deletion and insertion errors. Training stochastic language models using a small corpus, such as voicemail, carries the risk of assigning zero probabilities to a large number of likely events. Because some words are similar to other words in their meaning and syntactic function one can expect getting better estimates with fewer parameters by grouping words into classes.

The rest of the paper is divided into five sections. Section 2 describes the voicemail data and the categorization protocol used, respectively. Section 3 discusses the methodology employed to perform message categorization, and experimental results are given in section 4. Finally, we summarize our conclusions and discuss future work in section 5.

2   Voicemail Data

We have used the LDC Voicemail Corpus-Part I [11]. This corpus contains 1801 messages (14.6 hours, averaging about 90 words per message). As a training set for the categorization tasks we used 1789 out of 1801 available messages (151K words) of the corpus. The reason for which 12 messages had to be excluded from the training set was that they did not contain enough information to determine their category. For evaluation purposes we used the test set of the corpus comprising 42 messages (2K words) as well as the test set of the Voice-mail Corpus-Part II comprising 50 messages (4K words). Apart from the human transcriptions (denoted SR-HT), which contained some noise in the form of rep-etitions and broken words, we also used transcriptions with a word error rate (WER) of 42.5% produced by a hybrid multi-layer perceptron / hidden Markov model speech recognizer (denoted SR-SPRACH) [12]. Additionally, we obtained another set of transcriptions with a WER of 31% (denoted SR-HTK) produced by the more complex HTK Switchboard system adapted to voicemail [13].

Table 1. Taxonomy for the message priority- and content-based categorization tasks. Further details and examples can be found in [14].

Priority-based categorization

Category	Description
high	an immediate action by the recipient is required, expected or implied (often following a request)
medium	some attention by the recipient will be required
low	rather trivial content, no need for immediate attention

Content-based categorization

Category	Description
technical	specific technical issues related to projects
office	daily issues (excl. technical)
business	complementary professional tasks not covered by the above
family	related to family members (spouse, children, parents etc.) or concern family issues
friends	related to friends (incl. colleagues but not concerning work)
private	miscellaneous content concerning the recipients not covered by any of the above

2.1   Voicemail Categorization Protocol

Voicemail messages are typically short, conveying the reason for the call, the information that the caller requires from the voicemail recipient and a return telephone number. Herein we consider two tasks, categorization by *content* and by *priority*. The categories in both tasks are mutually exclusive and exhaustive, that is, every message belongs to one, and only one, of the categories. The data labelling is a result of subjective analysis of the message transcriptions. The at-tributes that the message recipient will perceive along with the categorization criteria, are determined by individual needs. These needs change over time and with the physical and social environment. As the data is not organized per voice-mail subscriber, we assumed a general voicemail recipient profile, which might not be fully compatible with the criteria of each individual voicemail recipient. Finally, during the labelling process for the categorization tasks no attempt was made to associate the message priority or content with the identity of speakers and thus the task does not share similarities with speaker recognition [15].

Table 1 outlines the taxonomy related to the priority- and content-based categorization tasks. Given the relatively small size and the nature of the corpus, we decided to use 3 and 6 categories, respectively because in a dense category space there would be only few example messages in each category. The distribution of messages in the training and test sets for the priority- and content-based tasks are given subsequently in Table 2.

Table 2. Category distributions across the training and test sets for priority and content, respectively.

Priority-based categorization

Category	Training set	Test set
high	37.4%	29.3%
medium	51.4%	54.3%
low	11.1%	16.3%

Content-based categorization

Category	Training set	Test set
technical	13.1%	5.3%
office	16.9%	23.4%
business	38.7%	35.1%
family	5.9%	12.8%
friends	16.4%	12.8%
private	9.0%	10.6%

3   Categorization Using Stochastic Language Models

We approach voicemail categorization in a Bayesian learning framework. We assume that the message transcription was generated by a parametric model (in our current implementation this is limited to a language model), and use training data to calculate Bayes optimal estimates of the model parameters. Then, using these estimates we classify new test messages using Bayes rule to turn the generative model around and calculate the probability that a category would have generated the test message in question. Categorization then becomes the task of selecting the most probable category. Details of the above approach are given bellow.

A language model is essentially an information source which emits a sequence of symbols w_i from a finite alphabet, i.e., the vocabulary. The probability of any word sequence $w_1, w_2, ..., w_i$ is given by:

$$p(w_1, w_2, ..., w_N) = \prod_{i=1,...,N} p(w_i|w_1, ..., w_{i-1}) \qquad (1)$$

A simple yet effective approach to approximate the above is the n-gram model [16] according to which the occurrence probability of any test word sequence is conditioned upon the prior occurrence of $n-1$ other words:

$$p(w_i|w_1, ..., w_{i-1}) \approx p(w_i|w_{i-n+1}, ..., w_{i-1}) \qquad (2)$$

n-gram language models have the advantage of being able to cover a much larger variation than would normally be derived directly from a corpus in the form of explicit linguistic rules, such as a formal grammar. Open vocabularies can also be easily supported by n-gram language models and are used in all experiments reported in this paper.

The task of classifying a message transcription $\mathcal{M}$ into a category $c \in C = \{c_1, c_2, ..., c_C\}$ can be expressed as the selection of the category which has the largest posterior probability given the message transcription:

$$c^+ = \arg\max_{c \in C}\{p(c|\mathcal{M})\} \qquad (3)$$

$$= \arg\max_{c \in C}\{p(\mathcal{M}|c)p(c)\} \qquad (4)$$

In the above expression the language model is used to estimate the likelihood $p(\mathcal{M}|c)$ whilst the prior $p(c)$ is assumed to be the same with that of the training set. For computational reasons, products of probabilities in Equation 4 are replaced by sums of negative log probabilities. Categorizing a message involves calculating a sum of negative logs for each category, where the length of the sum equals to the number of n-grams contained in the test message. Each term in the sum is proportional to the frequency with which the corresponding n-gram sequence has occurred in the training data. Note that if one assumes equal priors the above criterion becomes equivalent to perplexity [17], a measure expressing the average number of possible branches after a word in a sequence. Comparing the above measure across different categories for each test message allows the highest ranked category along with a rank value to be returned. The number of returned categories can be specified by the user so that the categorization results may be given in the form of an n-best list for further processing. Such 'soft' decisions allow a message to appear in more than one relevant category giving greater flexibility during retrieval. Finally, adding new messages to a trained n-gram model only requires the recording of word occurrence statistics for those messages.

3.1   Class-Based n-Gram Models

Training n-grams for categorization using a small corpus carries the risk of assigning zero probabilities to a large number of likely events not present in the available data. The perplexity of test word sequences containing such unseen events will increase significantly. Based on the hypothesis that some words are similar to other words in their meaning and syntactic function, we can derive likely, yet unobserved, word sequences to reduce the effects of data sparseness. Further, this approach can update the probabilities of rarely observed word sequences. For example, if the word "speech" is completely missing from the

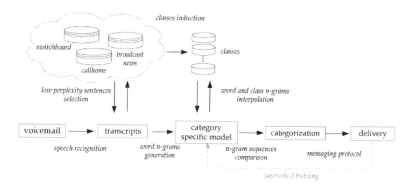

Fig. 1. Overview of the methodology to augment language models with word classes for categorizing spoken messages.

training data while the words "voice" and "spoken" are included, there is still a good chance to be able to model it using a class which contains semantically similar words to the above. An overview of the methodology followed is depicted on Figure 1. Word clustering can provide useful semantically related groups, similar to an automatically generated thesaurus. Suppose that we partition a vocabulary of V words into G classes using a function f_g, which maps a word, w_i, into its class g_i. The resulting model

$$p(w_i|w_{i-2}, w_{i-1}) = p(g_i|g_{i-2}, g_{i-1})p(w_i|g_i) \tag{5}$$

produces text by first generating a string of classes $g_1,g_2,...,g_n$ and then converting it into words w_i with probability $p(w_i|g_i)$, for $i = 1, 2,...,n$. Word classes can be defined either manually or automatically. Manual definition makes use of part-of-speech tags and stem information while automatic definition clusters words as part of an optimization method. For the purposes of this study we adopted an agglomerative clustering algorithm [18]. This algorithm performs a bottom-up clustering, starting with a separate cluster for each of the G most frequent words and at each step merge that pair for which the loss in average mutual information is minimum. Different words in the same class are only distinguished according to their relative frequencies in the training set as a whole and therefore large and relevant sets should be used to generate accurate word classes.

In order to reduce the amount of computation along with the risk of generating irrelevant classes, we selected subsets of various American English transcriptions from the publically available Broadcast News, Switchboard and CallHome corpora. The criterion employed was low sentence perplexity (in practice, <200) over a trigram language model trained on each of the priority and content voicemail categories described in section 2.1. We also required that sentences used to induce word classes contained at least ten words. The corresponding vocabularies for the sentences selected were divided into 1000 classes. Prior to the interpolation with the word-based voicemail language models we retained in the classes those words that occurred at least ten times in the selected data and we included no more than the ten most frequent words of any class.

4   Experimental Results

Categorization performance in all subsequent experiments is measured in terms of *overall accuracy*, which is defined as:

$$Acc = \frac{\#correctly\ categorized\ messages}{\#messages\ considered} \tag{6}$$

We examined the effects of the following factors in relation to the above best-category only performance measure:

WER quantifies the mismatches between the reference category language models and those of the test messages due to transcription errors.

n-**gram order** introduces a trade-off between capturing enough context and having poor model estimates due to data sparsity.

smoothing replaces the original counts with modified counts so as to redistribute the probability mass from the more commonly observed events to the less frequent and unseen events. Various smoothing techniques were compared, namely linear, absolute, Good Turing and Witten Bell [19].

The results for the priority- and content-based tasks are given in Figures 2 and 3, respectively. The training set is the same, whether we test on manually transcribed or automatically recognized data. We expect that the performance when testing with automatically transcribed data can be improved by using training data that is automatically generated too. We used neither a stop-list nor stemming as in our previous experiments [14] they were found to hurt accuracy. The larger training data set employed (approx. 80% more messages) offered consistent but relatively small improvements over the baseline word-based language models we had previously reported. This suggests that the stochastic language models employed for the categorization tasks are not too sensitive to training set size variations, as far as statistics for a sufficient number of *n*-grams have been calculated.

The accuracy in priority-based categorization task was significantly higher than the content-based one due to the smaller degree of confusability (3 vs. 6 target categories). The interpolated word- and class-based *n*-gram models (right column figures) offered improved accuracy than the word-based *n*-gram models (left column figures). Class-based clustering from multiple corpora allowed the models to hypothesize out-of-vocabulary words, which often hold the most significance when testing with unseen data. The average absolute improvement due to class-based clustering in categorization accuracy was 2-5%. Despite that the clustering algorithm employed generates pairs of words, roughly equal gains were observed between the bigram and trigram models since all models back-off to lower order *n*-grams. As it had been observed in previous experiments, transcription errors had a significant impact on categorization accuracy. Moving from human transcriptions to automatic transcriptions with WERs of either 31.0% or 42.5% reduces the accuracy by about 20% absolute.

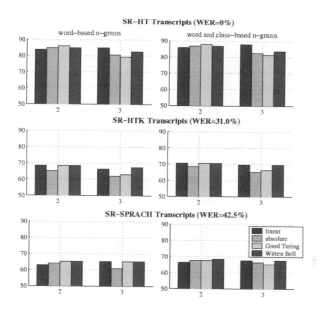

Fig. 2. Accuracy (%) in the priority-based categorization task using different smoothing techniques. The rows of subfigures correspond to transcripts of different WERs, while the n-gram order is shown on the horizontal axis.

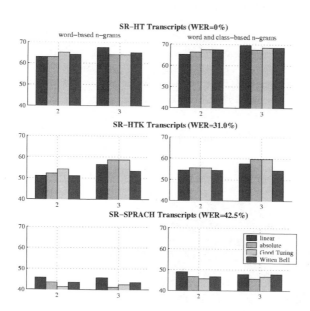

Fig. 3. Accuracy (%) in the content-based categorization task. The subfigure layout follows that of Fig. 2.

The differences across the four smoothing techniques were small. Among them, linear and Witten Bell performed slightly better on average, followed by Good Turing. It is though possible to combine different language models to improve accuracy. Methods as simple as majority voting can be employed to help reduce errors that individual smoothing techniques introduce.

The slight differences across the results made apparent the limitations in system evaluation introduced by a small test set. Although the combined test sets of Voicemail Corpora I and II demonstrated the effects of transcription errors, they were not adequate to demonstrate clear patterns related to other factors. Another issue to be investigated is how to treat messages for which the level of agreement among annotators is low. The use of Kappa statistic [20] could help indicate in a definitive way the correct category, if any, that a message belongs to. In future experiments we also plan to use the training set of Voicemail Corpus II as a validation and as a test set. Finally, the parametric model we employed for voicemail categorization was based only on textual information. It remains to be investigated if any prosodic features can be effectively associated with particular categories.

5 Conclusion

Voicemail data introduces several challenges to information management systems, including ambiguities related to short messages, uncertainties associated with speech recognizers and the need for scalability and portability in new domains and users. We have approached voicemail management in a Bayesian learning framework using stochastic language models to represent individual messages and groups of messages reflecting user profiles. Although still limited by the challenging speech recognition environment and the lack of any deep semantic analysis, we have reported improvements by training on a larger data set and by augmenting the language models with class-based models derived automatically from other corpora.

Acknowledgments. This work is supported by a Marie Curie fellowship.

References

1. Moreno, P., Thong, J.M.V., Logan, B., Jones, G.J.F.: From multimedia retrieval to knowledge management. IEEE Computer **35** (2002) 58–66
2. Hirschberg, J., Bacchiani, M., Hindle, D., Isenhour, P., Rosenberg, A., Stark, L., Stead, L., Whittaker, S., Zamchick, G.: SCANMail: Browsing and searching speech data by content. In: Proc. Eurospeech, Aalborg, Denmark (2001)
3. Koumpis, K., Ladas, C., Renals, S.: An advanced integrated architecture for wireless voicemail retrieval. In: Proc. 15th IEEE Intl. Conf. on Information Networking, Beppu, Japan (2001) 403–410
4. Huang, J., Zweig, G., Padmanabhan, M.: Information extraction from voicemail. In: 39th Annual Meeting of Assoc. for Computational Linguistics, Toulouse, France. (2001)

5. Ringel, M., Hirschberg, J.: Automated message prioritization: Making voicemail retrieval more efficient. In: Proc. Conf. on Human Factors in Computing Systems (Ext. Abstracts), Minneapolis, MN, USA (2002) 592–593
6. Yang, Y.: An evaluation of statistical approaches to text categorization. Journal of Information Retrieval **1** (1999) 67–88
7. Lewis, D.D., Schapire, R.E., Callan, J.P., Papka, R.: Algorithms for linear text classifiers. In: Proc. 19th annual Intl. ACM SIGIR Conf. on Research and Development in Information Retrieval. (1996) 298–306
8. Sebastiani, F.: Machine learning in automated text categorization. ACM Computing Surveys **34** (2002) 1–47
9. Teahan, W.J., Harper, D.J.: Using compression based language models for text categorization. In: Proc. Workshop on Language Modeling and Information Retrieval, Carnegie Mellon University, USA (2001) 83–88
10. Peng, F., Schuurmans, D., Kaselj, V., Wang, S.: Automated authorship attribution with character level language models. In: Proc. 10th Conf. of European Chapter of Assoc. for Computational Linguistics, Budapest, Hungary (2003) 19–24
11. Padmanabhan, M., Eide, E., Ramabhardan, G., Ramaswany, G., Bahl, L.: Speech recognition performance on a voicemail transcription task. In: Proc. IEEE ICASSP, Seattle, WA, USA (1998) 913–916
12. Koumpis, K., Renals, S.: The role of prosody in a voicemail summarization system. In: Proc. ISCA Workshop on Prosody in Speech Recognition and Understanding, Red Bank, NJ, USA (2001) 87–92
13. Cordoba, R., Woodland, P.C., Gales, M.J.F.: Improving cross task performance using MMI training. In: Proc. IEEE ICASSP. Volume 1., Orlando, FL, USA (2002) 85–88
14. Koumpis, K.: Automatic categorization of voicemail transcripts using stochastic language models. In: Proc. 7th Int. Conf. on Text, Speech and Dialogue, Brno, Czech Republic (2004)
15. Charlet, D.: Speaker indexing for retrieval of voicemail messages. In: Proc. IEEE ICASSP. Volume 1., Orlando, FL, USA (2002) 121–124
16. Gotoh, Y., Renals, S.: Statistical language modelling. In Renals, S., Grefenstette, G., eds.: Text and Speech Triggered Information Access. Springer-Verlag (2003) 78–105
17. Jelinek, F., Mercer, R.L., Bahl, L.R., Baker, J.K.: Perplexity - a measure of difficulty of speech recognition tasks. In: Proc. 94th Meeting Acoustical Society of America, Miami Beach, Florida, USA (1977)
18. Brown, P.F., Pietra, V.J.D., deSouza, P.V., Lai, J.C., Mercer, R.L.: Class-based n-gram models of natural language. Computational Linguistics **18** (1992) 467–479
19. Chen, S., Goodman, J.: An empirical study of smoothing techniques for language modeling. Computer Speech and Language **13** (1999) 359–394
20. Carletta, J.: Assessing agreement on classification tasks: The kappa statistic. Computational Linguistics **22** (1996) 249–254

Computing Speech Acts*

Gemma Bel Enguix[1,2] and M. Dolores Jimenez Lopez[2]

[1] Department of Computer Science, University of Milan-Bicocca
Via Bicocca degli Arcimboldi, 8, 20126 Milan, Italy
gbe@astor.urv.es
[2] Research Group on Mathematical Linguistics, Universitat Rovira i Virgili
Pl. Imperial Tarraco, 1, 43005 Tarragona, Spain
mdjl@astor.urv.es

Abstract. Human-computer interfaces require models of dialogue structure that capture the variability and unpredictability within dialogue. In this paper we propose to use a computing paradigm –membrane systems– in order to define such a dialogue model. We introduce *Primary Dialogue Membrane Systems* (shortly, PDMS) as a biological computing model that computes pragmatic minimal units –speech acts– for constructing dialogues. We claim that PDMS provide a simple model where the passage from the real dialogue to the membrane system model can be achieved in a highly formalized way.

Keywords: Membrane Systems, Dialogue Modelling, Speech Acts.

1 Introduction

Membrane systems –introduced in [12]– are models of computation inspired by some basic features of biological membranes. They can be viewed as a new paradigm in the field of natural computing based on the functioning of membranes inside the cell. Briefly, in a membrane system multisets of objects are placed in the compartments defined by the membrane structure –a hierarchical arrangement of membranes, all of them placed in a main membrane called the *skin membrane*– that delimits the system from its environment. Each membrane identifies a *region*, the space between it and all the directly inner membranes, if any exists. Objects evolve by means of reaction rules also associated with the compartments, and applied in a maximally parallel, nondeterministic manner. Objects can pass through membranes, membranes can change their permeability, dissolve and divide. Membrane systems can be used as generative, computing or decidability devices. This new computing model seems to have several intrinsically interesting features such as, for example, the use of multisets and the inherent parallelism in its evolution. For a formal definition of membrane systems we refer to [13].

---

* This research has been supported by a Marie Curie Fellowship of the European Community programme *Human Potential (IHP)* under contract number HPMF-CT-2002-01582 and by a Marie Curie European Reintegration Grant (ERG).

C. Bussler and D. Fensel (Eds.): AIMSA 2004, LNAI 3192, pp. 236–245, 2004.

Membrane systems provide a powerful framework for formalizing any kind of *interaction*, both among agents and among agents and the environment. An important idea of membrane systems is that generation is made by evolution, when the configuration of membranes undergoes some modifications, given by certain rules. Therefore, most of evolving systems can be formalized by means of membrane systems. Indeed, they have been already applied to linguistics in [3] and other suggestions for specific applications have been given in [13]. In linguistics and natural language processing, membrane systems are specially suitable for dealing with fields where contexts, and mainly evolving contexts, are a central part of the theory. A topic where context and interaction among agents is essential is the field of dialogue modelling and its applications to the design of effective and user-friendly computer dialogue systems. This paper is a attempt to compute speech acts by means of membrane systems, this is, to generate by means of a natural-formal device the final product of interaction in human communication: dialogue. Theory of speech acts was introduced by Austin [2] and Searle [15], and it is now a central theory of pragmatics and human communication.

In what follows, after giving a brief summary of approaches to dialogue modelling in section 2, we introduce some linguistic concepts related to pragmatics and dialogue in section 3. Then, in section 4, some new concepts in membrane systems for computing with speech acts are defined and Primary Dialogue Membrane Systems are introduced. Section 5 gives an example of an artificial non-formal dialogue extracted from a Shakespeare's comedy. We close the paper with some final remarks and references.

2   Some Approaches to Dialogue Modelling

In the last fifty years or so, analysis of conversation has formed an increasingly important part of language study. Philosophy, psychology, sociology, linguistics, cognitive science, artificial intelligence, human-computer interaction and software engineering have examined conversation from a variety of perspectives. Researchers of dialogue often adopt two related –and sometimes conflicting– research goals:

1. to develop a theory of dialogue that includes a theory of cooperative task-oriented dialogue in which the participants are communicating for the accomplishment of some goal-directed task;
2. and to develop algorithms and procedures to support a computer's participation in a cooperative dialogue.

Different approaches to modelling dialogue have been proposed both from theoretical and practical perspectives. In general, we can distinguish –according to [10]– two different approaches in dialogue management studies:

1. *Structural approach*, characterized by using dialogue grammars to capture regularities of dialogue in terms of exchanges and moves and with the aim of trying to identify adjacency-pairs. (cf. [9], [14]).

2. *Intention-plan-based approach* that classifies speaker's beliefs and intentions into speech acts and uses planning operators to describe them. (cf. [1]).

Both approaches regard natural language as purposeful behaviour, but they differ in how this behaviour is to be described. The former sees dialogues as products and disposes participants' beliefs and intentions into a predefined dialogue structure. The latter, instead, focuses on participants' goals, and stresses relations between acts that contain appropriately sets of beliefs and intentions as their preconditions and effects.

The approach presented in [9] for describing processing of utterances in a discourse can be placed within the structural approach. The framework proposed stresses the role of purpose and processing in conversation. This model distinguishes basically three interrelated and interacting components in the structure of a discourse: 1) a *linguistic structure*; 2) an *intentional structure*; 3) and an *attentional structure*. Those three components of discourse structure supply all the information needed by the speaker in order to determine how an utterance fits with the rest of the discourse.

Within the same structural approach can be placed Frohlich and Luff's work. In [7], various aspects of 'technology of conversation' –as have been described in conversational analysis literature– are applied to human-computer interaction in order to generate orderly sequences of talk.

An example of the *intention-plan-based approach* to conversation is the model presented in [1]. It is argued that much of linguistic behaviour can be explained by assuming a plan based model of language. Language is viewed as an instance of goal-oriented behaviour. Utterances are produced by speech acts that are executed in order to have some effect on the hearer, effects that typically involve modifying the hearer's beliefs or goals.

However, *structural* and *intention-plan-based* approaches are not the only perspectives from which conversation has been tackled within the fields of artificial intelligence and computational linguistics. A very interesting research line is the one that applies the theory of *multi-agent systems* to the study of conversational interchanges. In [11] conversation is defined as the result of coordinated interactions among agents to reach a common goal: the conversational goal. In [8] we find another example of application of distributed artificial architectures to dialogue modelling. In that paper, CARAMEL is presented as a general architecture that intends to be applied to several different matters, among them dialogue management.

Another interesting model for conversation in the area of computational linguistics, hard to be placed in any of the above items of classification, is Bunt's *Dynamic Interpretation Theory* (DIT) [4]. DIT emerges from the study of spoken human-human information dialogue and aims at 'uncovering fundamental principles in dialogue both for the purpose of understanding natural dialogue phenomena and for designing effective, efficients and pleasant computer dialogue systems.'. In DIT, conversations are viewed in an *action perspective*. Language is considered a tool to perform context-changing actions.

What we have said in this section evidences the importance of conversation in language study and shows somehow the susceptibility of conversation to be tackled from very different points of view. In this paper, we propose a new way of facing the modelling of conversation: a *membrane computing model*. In our model, the membranes are considered to be agents with specific personal background – represented by the notion of domain – which exchange and compute "speech acts".

3   Dialogue and Speech Acts

The most classical distinction in computational dialogues is the one established between *task-oriented* (TO) and *non task-oriented* (NTO), based on the cooperation of participants in the consecution of conversational goals. In task-oriented dialogues (TO): a) agents collaborate, b)there exist conversational goals, and c) opening and termination can be solved with external measure elements. In non task-oriented dialogues (NTO): a) agents coact, but they do not necessarily collaborate, b) There are not conversational goals or at least, if they exist, they are private, and c) opening and termination are not defined.

Besides the above classification, [6] provides an interesting gathering which includes, among others, the following items: a) *Personal Settings*: Conversations characterized by the free exchange of turns among the two or more participants. b) *Institutional Settings*: The participants engage in speech exchanges that resemble ordinary conversation, but are limited by institutional rules.

Taking the main features of both classifications, we think it is possible to distinguish three types of dialogues, which are shown in table 1.

1. *primary*: personal non-task oriented dialogues with free turn-taking,
2. *oriented*: personal task oriented dialogues with free turn-takikng; and
3. *formal*: institutional task oriented dialogues with non-free tarn-taking.

Table 1. Structural types of dialogues

TYPE	SETTINGS	TASKS	TURN-TAKING
PRIMARY	Personal	NTO	free
ORIENTED	Personal	TO	free
FORMAL	Institutional	TO	non-free

We have established three types of dialogue that, obviously, need different formalizations. In this paper we concentrate on *primary dialogues*. We present a formal definition of a a computing device for computation of acts in this type of dialogues.

Now, before going on with the introduction of the computing device, we have to introduce the main units in the system we want to define. Basic elements we deal with in here are *speech acts*. An speech act can be defined as a communicative event whose final meaning is not only related to syntax but also to the illocutionary strength of the speaker. Speech acts has been traditionally a central topic in pragmatics, now they have an increasing importance in the so-called dialogue games [5], an attempt to start a formal study of pragmatic situations. Combining both theories, and adapting their main concepts to a *computational description*, we propose to distinguish the following types of acts in human communication: 1) *Query-yn* (yes, no), 2) *Query-w* (what), 3) *Answer-y* (yes), 4) *Answer-n* (no), 5) *Answer-w* (what), 6) *Agree*, 7) *Reject*, 8) *Prescription*, 9) *Explain*, 10) *Clarify*, 11) *Exclamation*. This list includes the most usual acts and may be modified any moment depending on the convenience and accuracy of the theory.

Acts are usually gathered in topics during a conversation. For starting, closing, or changing a topic, some special expressions are usually used. They are *structural acts*, and should be added to the the above list of sequences, obtaining: 12) *Open*, 13) *Close*, 14) *Changetopic*. Structural acts have some special features which make them different. *Open* is the first act, or at least the first instruction, in every dialogue or human interaction. However, *close* is not always present, in the same way that, many times, topics are not closed in conversations, and new ones arise without and ending for the previous. On the other hand, *changetopic* is a sequence of transition which cannot be followed by every agent. Nevertheless, these concepts have to be adapted to the diversity of realistic situations, which may be quite unexpected. In a dialogue, not every agent has every type of speech act. Depending on the *competence* of each agent, some speech acts can be blocked. For instance, only an agent with certain power can use the act *prescription*. The distribution of speech acts among the agents will be very important in the development of the dialogue.

4   Defining PDMS

Membrane systems were formaly described in [12], whereas an adaptation to linguistics was introduced in [3] giving rise to *Linguistic membrane systems* (in short, LMS). These theoretical formalizations are the basis for *Primary Dialogue Membrane System* (PDMS), which are defined as follows:

Definition 1
$$\Pi = \{\mu, \mathcal{V}, \mathcal{M}, \mathcal{T}, \mathcal{R}\},$$

where

- μ *is the membrane system;*
- $\mathcal{V}$ *is the set of alphabets associated to types of speech acts;*
- $\mathcal{M} = (\{u..w\}, D, \tau)$ *is the initial configuration of each membrane, being:*
  - $\{u...w\}$ *the set of acts over* $\mathcal{V}^\star$;
  - D, *the domain of the membrane;*
  - T *is any element of* $\mathcal{T}$.
- $\mathcal{T}$ *is the turn-taking set;*
- $\mathcal{R} = \{R_1, .., R_n\}$ *is the set of rules of every membrane of the system, where the order in which rules are given is also a preference for using them.*

In order to understand the working of the system, we have to explain the way some parts of the system work, especially the following aspects: a) configuration of alphabets, b) domains, c) shape of the rules, d) the turn-taking protocol $\mathcal{T}$, e) halting criteria, and f) the configuration of output.

Configuration of Alphabets. Basic elements of PDMS are speech acts. These speech acts are gathered in several types, following the classification given above. Every one of these types is an ordered set of elements which can be used just one time, according to the precedence.

We define a maximal set of alphabets $\mathcal{V} = \{\omega, \#, \kappa', \kappa, \alpha^y, \alpha^n, \alpha, \gamma, \varphi, \tau, \varepsilon, \lambda, \xi\}$, where every element is a set of speech acts, as follows:

- $\omega = \{o_1, o_2, ..o_n\}$, speech acts of type *open*.
- $\# = \{\#_1, \#_2, ..\#_n\}$, speech acts of type *close*.
- $\kappa' = \{q'_1, q'_2, ..q'_n\}$, speech acts of type *query-yn*.
- $\kappa = \{q_1, q_2, ..q_n\}$, speech acts of type *query-w*.
- $\alpha^y = \{a_1^y, a_2^y, ..a_n^y\}$, speech acts of type *answer-y*.
- $\alpha^n = \{a_1^n, a_2^n, ..a_n^n\}$, speech acts of type *answer-n*.
- $\alpha = \{a_1, a_2, ..a_n\}$, speech acts of type *answer-w*.
- $\gamma = \{g_1, g_2, ..g_n\}$, speech acts of type *agree*.
- $\varphi = \{f_1, f_2, ..f_n\}$, speech acts of type *reject*.
- $\pi = \{p_1, p_2, ..p_n\}$, speech acts of type *prescription*.
- $\varepsilon = \{e_1, e_2, ..e_n\}$, speech acts of type *explain*.
- $\lambda = \{l_1, l_2, ..l_n\}$, speech acts of type *clarify*.
- $\xi = \{x_1, x_2, ..x_n\}$, speech acts of type *exclamation*.

Shape of the rules. Rules are understood as the way the membranes-agents exchange elements and interact each other. Every rule in the system has in the left side the indication of the turn-taking. At the right side it has, a) the generation in reply to the explicit invitation to talk, which can include the order δ, introduced in [12] for dissolving membranes, and b) the agent whom the speech act is addressed to, if it exists. The turn-taking allows applying just one rule.

Domains. In PDMS, *domain* of a membrane is related to the competence of an agent in a dialogue, this is, what the agent knows and can say. It is defined as the set of speech acts that every membrane is able to utter. It can include entire sets of acts defined for the system or just single acts coming from some set. Of course, just speech acts defined in $\mathcal{V}$, this is, existing in the possible world described by μ, can be used. $DM_n = \{u, .., w \in \mathcal{V}\}$.

Turn-Taking Protocol. For primary dialogues, turn-taking must be free, this is, it is not given as a sequence, but as a set of active elements, at the beginning of the computation. Every turn is distributed by the agent that is talking. When somebody asks, explains, or clarifies something, in a dialogue, he/she does it to somebody among the others. Then, we establish that the addresser in each turn can choose next speaker. It does it by means of the *turn-taking rule* included at the end of each rule of the system. This is denoted by means of a

letter depending of the speech act uttered in such rule. We establish, then, the
following turn-taking symbols related to every speech act: O (open), # (close,)
Q' (Query-yn), Q (Query-w), A^y (Answer-y), A^n (Answer-n), A (Answer-w), G
(Agree), F (Reject), P (Prescription), E (Explain), L (Clarify), X (Exclamation),
H (Changetopic). We include H for *changetopic* among these symbols, which is
not related to any set of speech acts, because any type (except answer) can be
a good reply to it. If no indication of turn is given in a rule, the turn goes to
every membrane able to reply, this is, every membrane containing a rule with
the required symbol in the left. If there are several membranes able to act, then
the turn is indicated by the number of the membrane, which also establishes an
order of precedence in the computation, this is $M_1 < M_2 < M_3 < .. < M_n$.

Halting Criteria. We establish that the system stops if one of the following
conditions is fulfilled: i)No rule can be applied in any membrane, b) just one
membrane remains in the system, c) no more acts are available.

Configuration of the Output. For PDMS there are not output membranes. For
the *configuration of the output*, we define the Generation Register (GR). The
generation register gives account of the changes in the configuration of the system
in every step. To look at the GR is the way to know what the final result of the
system is.

5   Example

We offer in this section a very simple example of the functioning of PDMS. This
is taken from the Shakespeare's play *The comedy of errors* act 3 scene 2. The
number of agents in the dialogue are three, Luciana, related to M_1, Antipholus,
which is represented in M_2, and finally Dromio, M_3. One of them, Luciana,
disappears after talking, generating a new membrane. Then, the others start a
dialogue between them.

$$\Pi = \{\mu, \mathcal{V}, \mathcal{M}, \mathcal{T}, \mathcal{R}\},$$

where:
$\mu = [_0 [_1]_1 [_2]_2]_0$,
$\mathcal{V} = \{\kappa, \alpha, \varepsilon, \varphi\}$, where:

$\kappa = \{q_1 : $ `Why, how now, Dromio! where runn'st thou so fast?`,
$q_2 : $ `Do you know me, sir? am I Dromio? am I your man?`,
$q_3 : $ `What woman's man? and how besides thyself? besides`
`thyself?`,
$q_4 : $ `What claim lays she to thee?`$\}$
$\alpha = \{a_1 : $ `Thou art Dromio, thou art my man, thou art thyself`,
$a_2 : $ `Marry, sir, besides myself, I am due to a woman; one`
`that claims me, one that haunts me, one that will have`
`me.`,
$a_3 : $ `Marry sir.`$\}$
$\varepsilon = \{e_1 : $ `I'll fetch my sister, to get her good will.`$\}$

$\varphi = \{f_1 : \texttt{I am an ass, I am a woman's man and besides myself.}\}$
$\mathcal{T} = \{O, Q, A, E, F\}.$
$\mathcal{M} = M_1 \cup M_2 \cup M_3,$ where:
    $M_1 = \{\emptyset, \varepsilon, O\},\; M_2 = \{\emptyset, \kappa \cup \alpha, \emptyset\},\; M_3 = \{\emptyset, \alpha \cup \pi \cup \{q_2\}, \emptyset\}$
$\mathcal{R} = R_1 \cup R_2 \cup R_3,$ where:
    $R_1 = \{r_1 : O \to e\delta, [[\ ]_3]_0; E_2\},$
    $R_2 = \{r_1 : E \to q; Q_3,\; r_2 : Q \to a; A_3,\; r_3 : F \to q; Q_3,\; r_4 : A \to q; Q_3\},$
    $R_3 = \{r_1 : Q \to q; Q_2,\; r_2 : Q \to a; A_2,\; r_3 : A \to f; F_2\}.$

For simplifying the rule of generation of membrane M_3 we give its domain in the initial configuration. Therefore, the system starts in the first configuration with two membranes, and after the first step one of the is deleted and another one is created, as we show in figure 1.

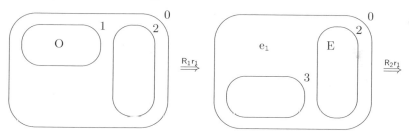

Fig. 1. Initial configuration and first step.

After the deletion creation of membranes, the dialogue becomes an exchange between just two agents. Finally, the system stops because the rule to be applied is $R_2 r_4$ and there is not any q in the set κ to be introduced in the system. Figure 2 shows the two last configurations of the system.

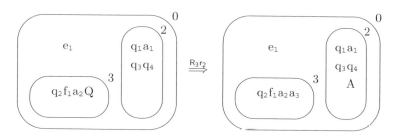

Fig. 2. Transition in the last step of the system

The output of the computation must be found in the Generation Register, whose configuration is the one showed in table 2.

Table 2. Generation register

$$
\begin{aligned}
&C_0 : [O]_1 \\
&C_1 : [e]_1 \ \delta, \ [E]_2, \\
&C_2 : \qquad [q_1]_2, \ [Q]_3 \\
&C_3 : \qquad [Q]_2, \ [q_2]_3 \\
&C_4 : \qquad [a_1]_2, \ [A]_3 \\
&C_5 : \qquad [F]_2 \ [f_1]_3 \\
&C_6 : \qquad [q_3]_2 \ [Q]_3 \\
&C_7 : \qquad [A]_2, \ [a_2]_3 \\
&C_8 : \qquad [q_4]_2, \ [Q]_3 \\
&C_9 : \qquad [A]_2 \ [a_3]_3
\end{aligned}
$$

Looking at table 3 and knowing that everything generated in M_1 belongs to Luciana, what is generated in M_2 is the speech of Antipholus and M_3 refers to Dromio, we have the following outcome:

Luciana I'll fetch my sister, to get her good will.
Exit
Enter DROMIO of Syracuse
Antipholus Why, how now, Dromio! where runn'st thou so fast?
Dromio Do you know me, sir? am I Dromio? am I your man? am I myself?
Antipholus Thou art Dromio, thou art my man, thou art thyself.
Dromio I am an ass, I am a woman's man and besides myself.
Antipholus What woman's man? and how besides thyself? besides thyself?
Dromio Marry, sir, besides myself, I am due to a woman; one that claims me, one that haunts me, one that will have me.
Antipholus What claim lays she to thee?
Dromio Marry sir.

where δ represents the *exit* of a character and the creation of a membrane means the rule *enter*.

6   Final Remarks

In this paper we have introduced some elements for a formal modeling of human communication in the framework of pragmatics using membrane systems. Basic issues related to a membrane system approach to conversation have been developed in order to test the suitability of the model. Nevertheless, since this is just an initial approximation to the possibility of describing conversation by means of membrane systems, many important aspects remain to be approached. Anyway we think that to apply membrane systems to linguistic topics has several advantages, among which we stress the flexibility of the model. In this sense, we point out that, depending on the consideration of the membranes and domains (agents, societies, languages), several branches of linguistics can be broached.

Considering membranes as agents, and domains as a personal background and linguistic competence, the application to dialogue is almost natural, and simple from the formal point of view. Many variations can be introduced to the basic model presented in this paper in order to account for different features of conversation, and this can be a good research area for the future. Perhaps membrane systems can help to formalize different types of dialogue, introducing small variants in the configuration of rules, alphabets, domains or relationship between membranes.

Finally, although the model is defined for formally describing human communication, we think that it can be applied to the generation of conversations in the framework of human-computer or computer-computer interface.

References

1. Allen, J.F., Perrault, C.R.: Analyzing Intention in Utterances. *Artificial Intelligence* **15** (1980) 143-178.
2. Austin, J.L.: *How to Do Things With Words*. Oxford University Press, New York (1962).
3. Bel Enguix, G.: Preliminaries about Some Possible Applications of P Systems in Linguistics. In: Păun, Gh., Rozenberg, G., Salomaa, A., Zandron, C. (eds.): *Membrane Computing*. LNCS 2597. Springer, Berlin (2003).
4. Bunt, H.C.: *DIT-Dynamic Interpretation in Text and Dialogue*. ITK Research Report, no. 15. Tilburg University, The Netherlands (1990).
5. Carlson, L.: *Dialogue games*. Reidel, Dordretch (1983).
6. Clark, H.H.: *Using Language*. Cambridge University Press, Cambridge (1996).
7. Frohlich, D., Luff, P.: Applying the Technology of Conversation to the Technology for Conversation. In: Luff, P., Gilbert, N., Frohlich, D. (eds.): *Computers and Conversation*. Academic Press, London (1990) 187-220.
8. Grau, B., Sabah, G.,Vilnat, A.: Control in Man-Machine Dialogue. *Think* **3** (1994) 32-55.
9. Grosz, B. J., Sidner, C.L.: Attention, Intentions and the Structure of Discourse. In: Nagao, M.: *Language and Artificial Intelligence*. Elsevier Science Publishers B.V., North-Holland (1987) 3-32.
10. Jokinen, K.: Goal Formulation Based on Communicative Principles. In: *COLING'96. Proceedings of the 16th International Conference on Computational Linguistics*. Vol 2. Copenhagen (1996) 598-603.
11. Moulin, B., Rousseau, D., Lapalme, G.: A Multi-Agent Approach for Modelling Conversations. In: *AI'94. Natural Language Processing. Proceedings of the Fourtheenth International Avignon Conference*. Vol. 3. Paris (1994) 35-50.
12. Păun, Gh.: Computing with Membranes. *Journal of Computer and System Sciences* **61** (2000) 108-143.
13. Păun, Gh.: *Membrane Computing. An Introduction*. Springer, Berlin (2002).
14. Reichman, R.: *Getting Computers to Talk Like You and Me. Discourse Context, Focus, and Semantics (An ATN Model)*. MIT Press, Cambridge (1985).
15. Searle, J.: *Speech Acts: An Essay in the Philosophy of Language*. Cambridge University Press, Cambridge (1969).

High Performance Part-of-Speech Tagging of Bulgarian

Veselka Doychinova and Stoyan Mihov

Institute for Parallel Processing
Bulgarian Academy of Sciences
stoyan@lml.bas.bg

Abstract. This paper presents an accurate and highly efficient rule-based part-of-speech tagger for Bulgarian. All four stages – tokenization, dictionary application, unknown words guessing and contextual part-of-speech disambiguation – are implemented as a pipeline of a couple deterministic finite state bimachines and transducers. We present a description of the Bulgarian ambiguity classes and a detailed evaluation and error analysis of our tagger. The overall precision of the tagger is over 98.4% for full disambiguation and the processing speed is over 34K words/sec on a personal computer. The same methodology has been applied for English as well. The presented realization conforms to the specific demands of the semantic web.[1]

1   Introduction

Part-of-speech tagging has important applications to many areas of computational linguistics including syntax analysis, corpus linguistics, grammar checking, text-to-speech generation etc. The part-of-speech tagger is an essential resource for many semantic web applications like information extraction and knowledge acquisition. Recent efforts for providing a semantic-based multilingual infrastructure of the world wide web require new formal models and methods for language engineering. For the specific needs of the semantic web, in addition to the preciseness, a part-of-speech tagger has to provide the following features:

– High performance – crucial in respect to the vast amount of information presented on the web;
– XML and Unicode compliance;
– Technology applicable to other languages.

Our solution addresses all of the above mentioned problems.

For English and some other languages there are various accurate part-of-speech taggers based on different methodologies [3–5, 15]. Steven Abney gives a survey on the main methods in [1]. Most of the known approaches do not provide high performance.

---

[1] This work was funded by a grant from VolkswagenStiftung.

C. Bussler and D. Fensel (Eds.): AIMSA 2004, LNAI 3192, pp. 246–255, 2004.
© Springer-Verlag Berlin Heidelberg 2004

Emmanuel Roche and Yves Schabes introduce in [11] a deterministic tagger which has significantly better performance than the other systems [2, 4, 5]. The authors compose the contextual rules from the Brill tagger into a sequential transducer. Tokenizer, dictionary and guesser are implemented using other techniques. We extend this approach by:

- providing an uniform technique for the representation and utilization of the tokenizer, dictionary, guesser and the contextual rules;
- application of bimachines for supporting rewriting rules with no restrictions on the length of the left and right context;
- support of lexical and morphological constraints in the contextual rules;
- processing the text without modifying it – by inserting XML tags in the original.

Reports for Bulgarian part-of-speech taggers are given by Hristo Tanev and Ruslan Mitkov in [14] and by Kiril Simov and Petya Osenova in [13]. The development of the first tagger was performed without relying on a large tagged corpus. The reported resulting precision of it is 95% for 95% recall. For the development of the second tagger a corpus consisting of 2500 sentences was used. The achieved precision is 95.17%.

Our part-of-speech tagger is developed using a large manually tagged corpus kindly provided by Svetla Koeva from the Institute for Bulgarian Language. The corpus consists of 197K tokens (over 150K words) randomly extracted from an 1M words Bulgarian corpus, structured along the standards of the Brown University corpus. This is a running text of edited Bulgarian prose divided into 500 samples of over 2000 words each, representing a wide range of styles and varieties of prose.

In our research initially we tried to train the Brill tagger [2] for Bulgarian. We used a 160K tokens tagged corpus for training. The results were disappointing – although the tagger performed very well on the training corpus – 98,7%, on a unseen 40K tokens corpus it performed poorly – 95,5%. We suppose that the reason for the low accuracy on Bulgarian texts is a consequence of the inflectional nature of the Bulgarian morphology leading to a large amount of wordforms and the free word order in the Bulgarian sentence.

We present a rule-based approach [3, 15] leading to 98.4% precision implemented by finite state devices [8, 11, 12]. The first step to solving the ambiguity is tokenizing the text. For the second step we use a 75K base forms grammatical dictionary [9], which assigns to each known word its most-probable tag and the set of all possible tags (its ambiguity class). If a word is not in the dictionary, a guesser is consulted in the third step. Finally, 148 manually constructed contextual rules are applied on the text to handle the ambiguities.

We present the ambiguity classes and the tagset in the next section. Afterwards we proceed with the tokenizer, lexicon and guesser description. Section 4 describes the contextual rules. The evaluation results are presented in Section 5. Implementation details are given in Section 6. Finally the conclusion presents some general comments and directions for further work.

2   Restricted Tagset and Ambiguity Classes

The problem of correct part-of-speech tagging is a consequence of the implicit ambiguity of the words in respect of their morphology, syntactic function and meaning. For example, in the sentence: *Напразно тичат инкасаторите в бели престилки - навсякъде всичко е наред.*, the word *бели* could be tagged as five different forms: a plural adjective, a plural noun, a present singular verb, a past singular verb and an imperative verb. And whereas in this case the solution is quite straightforward, for the correct tagging of the verbs *завърши* and *стане* in the sentence *Нямаше търпение да завърши висше образование, да стане козметичен хирург.* a more complex analysis is required.

It is hard to use all 946 different morphological tags from the dictionary in our rule-based method. Moreover, some distinctions in the given text cannot be determined reliably without full syntactic and semantic analysis. For example the dative and accusative cases of pronouns in short form are hardly distinguishable. Hence, the tagset should be quite restricted but it should still provide the deserved functionality. In our tagset only morphological characteristics, which are considered essential for part-of-speech tagging are taken into account. For example, past singular verbs have the same tag, although only second and third person forms are ambiguous. All forms, which differ in number are divided. Verbs are also classified according to whether they are in present or past tense. Pronouns are grouped according to gender and short forms. The final tagset has 40 tags given in Table 1.

Table 1. Bulgarian part-of-speech tagset.

Nmfs	feminine and masculine singular nouns, singular neutral nouns w. definite article	PLs	singular personal pronoun
Nns0	singular neutral nouns without definite article	PLp	plural personal pronouns
		PL	personal reflexive pronoun
Np	plural nouns	PLz	short forms of personal reflexive pronoun
Nv	vocative nouns	PLsz	short forms of singular personal pronouns
Nc	countable masculine nouns	PLpz	short forms of plural personal pronouns
Amfs	singular feminine and masculine adjectives, singular neutral adjectives with definite article	PPmfs	singular feminine and masculine possessive pronoun
		PPns	singular neutral possessive pronouns
Ans0	singular neutral adjectives without definite article	PPp	plural possessive pronouns
		PPz	short forms of possessive pronouns
Ap	plural adjectives	POmfs	demonstrative, relative, indefinite, collective, negative and interrogative singular masculine and feminine pronouns
VRs	singular present tense verbs		
VRp	plural present tense verbs	POns	demonstrative, relative, indefinite, collective, negative and interrogative singular neutral pronouns
VPs	singular past tense verbs		
VPp	plural past tense verbs		
VXs	singular present tense active voice participle	POp	demonstrative, relative, indefinite, collective, negative, interrogative plural pronouns
VXp	plural present tense active voice participle		
		ADV	adverbs
VYs	singular past tense active voice participle	NUMO	ordinal numerals
VYp	plural past tense active voice participle	NUMC	cardinal numerals
VQs	singular past tense passive voice participle	CONJ	conjunctions
		PREP	prepositions
VQp	plural past tense passive voice participle	PUNCT	punctuation
VZ	adverbial participle	MISC	particles, interjection, other miscellaneous tokens
VI	imperative verbs		

In respect of the tagset the words in our dictionary are divided into 259 ambiguity classes. 47 of them consist of more than 100 words. As shown on Table 2 the largest class consists of present and past verbs, followed by the one of masculine and countable nouns. The first column presents the number of entries in the class and the second one shows the occurrence frequency on 1000 words derived from a 20M words untagged corpus. Statistics on the right shows how many times words from the class have appeared with a corresponding tag in our manually tagged representative corpus.

Table 2. Main Bulgarian ambiguity classes.

Entries	Freq.	Class	Examples	Realization
12967	32.30	VPs/VRs	абдикира|абонира|абортира|абсолютизира	689/4162
5376	17.10	Nc/Nmfs	абажура|абзаца|аблатива|абонамента	274/1754
4575	4.69	Amfs/VQs	адаптираната|адаптирана|адаптираният|адаптирания	571/148
3192	2.79	Amfs/Ap	абисински|абитуриентски|аборигенски|абсолвентски	222/228
3165	10.05	VI/VPs/VRs	агни|бави|безбожничи|безделничи	15/430/636
2182	18.38	ADV/Ans0	абсолютно|абстрактно|абсурдно|авантюристично	2122/1011
2141	1.37	Np/VQs	абортирания|авансирания|анонсирания|аранжирания	260/16
1881	0.53	VI/VRp	ахнете|барнете|бафнете|белнете	17/45
1521	2.97	Ap/VQp	адаптираните|адаптирани|активираните|активирани	343/87
594	0.69	Ans0/VQs	адаптирано|активирано|арестувано|асфалтирано	57/50
554	0.56	VQs/VRp	барнат|близнат|блъвнат|блъснат	20/61
408	1.11	Amfs/VYs	аглутиниращата|аглутинираща|аглутиниращият	142/1
394	0.46	VI/VRs	бди|бележи|блести|бръмчи	1/100
387	0.69	Amfs/VXs	буренясалата|буренясала|буренясалият|буренясалия	46/31
350	2.52	Amfs/Nmfs	абаджийска|абхазката|абхазка|авантюристката	115/292
273	1.71	Np/VRp	багрите|барабаните|бедите|благословите	196/24
260	6.42	Np/VI/VPs/VRs	багри|барабани|беди|благослови	475/4/117/276
219	0.41	Ap/Np	абхазките|авантюристките|адвентистките	26/44
168	0.60	ADV/Ans0/VQs	вдъхновено|вп编рено|втренчено|вцепенено	50/43/8
136	0.43	Ap/VYp	аглутиниращите|аглутиниращи|благоденстващите	69/0
129	0.68	Np/VXs	белилата|белила|бесилата|бесила	35/47
126	0.50	Ap/VXp	буренясалите|буренясали|велите|вели	30/10
111	1.24	Nmfs/VXs	белилото|бесилото|билото|бил	43/72
106	0.51	Amfs/Np/VQs	активирания|вдъхновения|възвишения|въздържания	4/88/0

3 Tokenizer, Dictionary, and Guesser

3.1 Tokenizer

We built a sophisticated tokenizer, which marks and categorizes tokens as numeral expressions, dates, hours, abbreviations, URLs, items, punctuation, words, abbreviations etc. Words in Latin and Cyrillic are differently marked when capitalized or upper case. Punctuation is classified according to the type and the function of the sign. Sentence boundaries are recognized as well.

The tokenizer is implemented as a composition of 53 contextual rewriting rules. Some of the rules require that the length of the right context is unlimited. All tokenization rules are composed into 4 bimachines.

3.2 Dictionary

The dictionary assigns to each dictionary word in the text its ambiguity class and its initial tag. Usually the initial tag is the most probable tag for the ambiguity class. For example, the class which consist of adverbs and neutral adjectives gets adverb as a most probable tag, because in the corpus these words are adverbs 2122 times and adjectives 1011 times. There are exceptions from this principle in some cases. For example in the class singular present tense verb / singular past tense verb, the perfective verbs are initially tagged as past verbs and the imperfective and dual aspect verbs are tagged as present verbs, because usually the perfective verbs are used in present tense with *да* or *ще* and in this way there is a more reliable context information to transform the past verb tag to present. In the sentences:

Тръгна пеша и стигна до стадиона за около час. – *тръгна* and *стигна* are past verbs.
Кога да тръгна, за да стигна навреме? – *тръгна* and *стигна* are present verbs.

Table 3. Result of dictionary application.

	tokens	share
All tokens:	101207	
Dictionary coverage	97760	96.59%
Correct initial tag from dictionary	91128	90.04%
Wrong initial tag from dictionary	6632	6.55%

The dictionary contains about 1M wordforms. Since each wordform can occur in lower case, upper case or capitalized, the dictionary contains 3M strings. It is implemented as one (big) rewriting rule and represented by a sequential transducer using the construction method presented in [10].

The overall dictionary performance is given in Table 3.

3.3 Guesser

The words that are not in the dictionary are handled by the guesser. The constructed rules are analysing the suffix for guessing the word's morphology and for assigning the initial part-of-speech tag and the ambiguity class. For example, the word *суопнахме*, which was found in a computer text is an english word with a Bulgarian suffix for plural third person verb. Hence, it will be correctly tagged by the guesser. Words with the suffix *ирания*, receive a tag for ambiguity class, which allows them to be tagged as a masculine singular adjective, a plural noun or a singular passive participle. For some words there is only one option. Such are the words with suffix *аемо*, *тел* and others.

The capitalized words in the middle of the sentence, which in most cases are unknown proper names are tagged as singular nouns. The same applies to Latin text.

After the guesser is applied to the text the precision reaches 93.28%. The total number of the words in our 100K tokens corpus that have not been found in the dictionary is 3447. For all of them the guesser has suggested its initial tag, which is wrong in only 4.72% of the cases treated by the guesser. Table 4 presents the exact numbers.

Table 4. Guesser performance.

	tokens	share
All tokens:	101207	
Not in Dictionary	3447	3.41%
Correct initial tag from dictionary	91128	90.04%
Correct initial tag from Dictionary and Guesser	94412	93.29%
Wrong initial tag from guesser	163	0.16%

The guesser is implemented as a composition of 73 rewrite rules all compiled into a single bimachine.

4   Contextual Disambiguation Rules

The part-of-speech ambiguity ratio for our corpus is 1.51 tags/word, which means that in average every second word is ambiguous. For solving the ambiguities we apply 148 contextual rules, which can utilize part-of-speech, lexical or dictionary information on the context. Below some exemplary rules are given:

```
change ADV to Amfs if next word is Nmfs
change Np to VRs if previous 1 or 2 word is "ще/MISC"
change Nmfs to VPs if word is perfective verb and previous word is
"ce/MISC"
```

A rule is applied if and only if the context is fulfilled and the ambiguity class of the targeted word allows the new tag.

Experiments have shown that the rule order significantly influences the results. Because of that the rules are applied in a certain order to handle specific ambiguities. For example the rules that change a noun into past verb precede the rules that change a past verb into present verb.

All 148 contextual rules are composed into 2 bimachines which we apply in a pipeline.

5   Evaluation Results and Error Analysis

5.1   Preciseness Results

After all the rules are applied to the training corpus the overall accuracy reached 98.44%. Totally 5610 tags were changed by the context rules. For the unseen test corpus the result is slightly worse - the accuracy is 98.29% and the context rules changed 5297 tags. Table 5 presents the details.

Table 5. Tagger results on training and test corpus.

	Training corpus		Test corpus	
	tokens	share	tokens	share
All tokens:	101207		96146	
Correct initial tags from dictionary & guesser	94412	93.29%	89599	93.19%
Correct tags by Tagger	99630	98.44%	94505	98.29%
Tags changed by context rules	5610	5.54%	5297	5.51%

At that point a few new rules were developed to handle specific cases that were found mainly in the test corpus. We have got a slight increase of the preciseness after applying the additional rules:

	Additional rules	Overall result
Training corpus	+0.15%	98.59%
Test corpus	+0.16%	98.46%

5.2   Error Analysis

After the application of the tagger on both corpora 2900 words received a wrong tag. 2117 of them were not changed by the contextual rules and 783 cases handled by the context rules were not tagged correctly. From the 783 cases 452 times the tagger changed a correct initial tag given by the dictionary or guesser and 331 times both – initial and context rules tags were wrong.

The largest group of wrong tags is adverb / neutral adjective. Most of those errors were made because in many cases the syntactic context of both adverbs and adjectives is similar. For example when the following word is a neutral noun we have no reliable context for distinguishing the two cases.

*Закъснението на самолета причинява * само/Ans0 известно забавяне на програмата.*

*Като статистическа величина БВП отчита стойността на крайните стоки и услуги за определен период, * обикновено/Ans0 тримесечие или година.*

The same applies to dual aspect verbs. Our statistics showed that in most cases the dual aspect verbs are in present so the dictionary initially gives them the relevant tag. Certainly, some cases were incorrectly tagged using this statistic approach.

*Така лидерът на СДС Екатерина Михайлова * коментира/VRs изявлението на Първанов по повод вота на недоверие на правителството.*

The ambiguity, which remains in the singular adjective / singular noun class is difficult in the case of proper nouns. Our context rules cannot completely solve this ambiguity at that point. For solving it a thorough semantic analysis is necessary.

Пристигнахме късно от Света/Amfs Гора.

* Дарън/Amfs Ралфс от Щатите поднесе сензацията на Световното първенство по ски алпийски дисциплини.

Short forms of pronouns are known to be very movable in the Bulgarian sentence. Generally, they are likely to be personal pronouns in contiguity with a verb and possessive pronouns in contiguity with a noun. But there are many difficult cases where the short form is between a noun and a verb.

Изображението се е запазило в душата ми/PPz.

*Мама * ми/PPz е обещала да отидем в ботаническата градина.*

Most errors were made in cases where semantic analysis is required for disambiguation.

*Целта беше да * й/PLsz грабне вниманието.*

*Следователно с Волкерс и с романа му "Нещо сладко" осъществяваме едно закъсняло запознанство с една практически неизвестна * ни/PLpz литература.*

The main ambiguity classes, which are wrongly tagged are given in Table 6.

Table 6. Main errors by the tagger.

325 words Ans0/ADV (бързо, обикновено)
199 words PLz/MISC (се, си)
156 words VRs/VPs (води, каза)
143 words Amfs/Nmfs (бос, свят, лек, имена)
134 words PPz/PLsz (му,ми,й,ти)
130 words Np/Nmfs (листа, крака, господа)
101 words PPz/MISC (си)
 80 words PPz/PLpz (им, ни)
 69 words Np/VRs (работи, води, мисли)
 50 words Np/VPs (обяви, отговори, уреди)

The 10 classes in Table 6 represent 43.10% of all errors. The rest of the wrongly tagged words are distributed into 110 ambiguity classes.

6   Implementation Details

As already mentioned the whole tagger is implemented as a composition of 275 rewriting rules. For the construction of the rules we used the methods presented in [8, 7, 6]. The rules are then composed and represented by bimachines by the techniques presented in [12]. For the construction of the sequential transducer for the rewriting dictionary rule we developed a new method presented in [10]. In this way the tagger consists of 7 bimachines and 1 sequential transducer applied in a pipeline.

The text is transduced by each of the finite state devices deterministically. After each step the text is enriched with additional information which is used by the following steps. At the end only part-of-speech tags are left. The tagger is capable of processing of Unicode and the markup is down by inserting XML tags without modifying the input text.

The size of the tagger is 82002KB including all data and the executable. We measured the processing speed on a Pentium III 1GHz computer running Linux. The performance is measured for the whole process of tagging, including the disk operations needed for reading in and writing out the text file. The performance is **34723 words/sec**.

The processing speed is proportional to the number of devices in the pipeline. Theoretically we could compose all the rules into one single bimachine. In that case we would have about 8 times faster processing. The problem is that the size of this device would be unacceptable for the current technology. Nevertheless we could trade off speed for size if needed. For example by representing our tagger by 208 bimachines the size is 21123KB by a processing speed of 1550 words/sec.

The same technique was tested by realizing an English tagger. We constructed the bimachine pipeline by composing the rules from the Brill system [2] trained on the Penn Treebank Tagged Wall Street Journal Corpus. In addition to the technique presented in [11] we implemented the extended version of Brill's system, which is supplemented by a guesser and the contextual rules are able to make use of lexical relationships. All 148 guesser rules were composed into 3 bimachines. The 70K words dictionary was implemented as a sequential transducer. The 288 contextual rules were composed into 13 bimachines. The size of our implementation is 56340KB. As expected our system delivered identical result compared to the result of Brill's system and performed with a processing speed of 16223 words/sec.

7   Conclusion

We presented a Bulgarian part-of-speech tagger with 98.4% precision. The analysis of the ambiguity classes showed that the problem of part-of-speech disambiguation for Bulgarian is as complex as the one for English, but the ambiguities are consequences of other language phenomena. We showed that the cases where the tagger assigns a wrong tag require a more complex syntactic or semantic analysis. Hence, further improvement of the tagger preciseness would require much more efforts.

The methodology presented in the paper provides a very efficient, language independent implementation of all stages of the process. We successfully applied the same technique with the rules of the Brill tagger for English.

Further we plan to exploit the presented methodology for other languages and other applications like information extraction, grammar checking and prosody and phonetic description generation.

Acknowledgments: We are grateful to Svetla Koeva for the valuable discussions during the beginning of our research.

References

1. Steven P. Abney, Part-of-Speech Tagging and Partial Parsing, In Ken Church and Steve Young and Gerrit Bloothooft, editor, Corpus-Based Methods in Language and Speech Kluwer Academic Publishers, Dordrecht, 1996.
2. Eric Brill, Some advances in rule-based part of speech tagging, Proceedings of the Twelfth National Conference on Artificial Intelligence (AAAI-94), Seattle, Wa., 1994.
3. Jean-Pierre Chanod, Pasi Tapanainen, Tagging French - comparing a statistical and a constraint-based method, Proceedings of Seventh Conference of the European Chapter of the Association for Computational Linguistics, 1995.
4. Kenneth Church, A stochastic parts program and noun phrase parser for unrestricted texts, Proceedings of the Second Conference on Applied Natural Language Processing, Austin, Texas, 1988.
5. Doug Cutting, Julian Kupiec, Jan Pedersen, and Penelope Sibun, A practical part-of-speech tagger, Proceedings of Third Conference on Applied Natural Language Processing (ANLP-92), pages 133–140, 1992.
6. Hristo Ganchev, Stoyan Mihov and Klaus U. Schulz, One-Letter Automata: How to Reduce k Tapes to One. CIS-Bericht, Centrum für Informations- und Sprachverarbeitung, Universität Munchen, 2003.
7. Dale Gerdemann and Gertjan van Noord, Transducers from Rewrite Rules with Backreferences, Proceedings of EACL 99, Bergen Norway, 1999.
8. Ronald Kaplan and Martin Kay, Regular Models of Phonological Rule Systems, Computational Linguistics 20(3), 331-378, 1994
9. Svetla Koeva, Grammar Dictionary of the Bulgarian Language Description of the principles of organization of the linguistic data, Bulgarian language magazine, book 6, 1998.
10. Stoyan Mihov and Klaus U. Schulz, Efficient Dictionary-Based Text Rewriting using Sequential Transducers, CIS-Bericht, Centrum für Informations- und Sprachverarbeitung, Universität Munchen, 2004. To appear.
11. Emmanuel Roche, Yves Schabes, Deterministic Part-of-Speech Tagging with Finite-State Transducers, Computational Linguistics, Volume 21, Number 2, June 1995.
12. Emmanuel Roche and Yves Schabes, Introduction, Finite-State language processing, E Roche, Y Schabes (Eds), MIT Press, 1997.
13. Kiril Simov, Petya Osenova, A Hybrid System for MorphoSyntactic Disambiguation in Bulgarian, Proceedings of the RANLP 2001 Conference, Tzigov Chark, Bulgaria, 5-7 September 2001.
14. Hristo Tanev; Ruslan Mitkov, Shallow Language Processing Architecture for Bulgarian, Proceedings of COLING 2002: The 17th International Conference on Computational Linguistics, 2002.
15. Atro Voutilainen, A syntax-based part-of-speech analyser , Proceedings of Seventh Conference of the European Chapter of the Association for Computational Linguistics, 1995.

The Definite Article of Bulgarian Adjectives and Numerals in DATR

Velislava Stoykova

Institute of the Bulgarian Language, Bulgarian Academy of Sciences,
52, Shipchensky proh. str., bl. 17, 1113 Sofia, Bulgaria
vili1@bas.bg

Abstract. The paper describes the inflectional feature of definiteness in Bulgarian language. It takes into account the specific morphosyntactic properties of the adjectives and the numerals, and argues for a related computational approach of interpretation. The DATR language for lexical knowledge presentation is accepted as a framework for constructing a model of Bulgarian adjectives and numerals inflectional morphology. The particular type hierarchies are defined, and the basic architecture of the model is explained in terms of its linguistic motivation.

1 Introduction

The most interesting grammar feature of standard Bulgarian language in which it differs with all Slavic languages is the feature of definiteness. Taken together with the fact that Bulgarian language does not use cases to express syntactic structures, it requires a specific sequence of tasks to be resolved for natural language processing applications.

It is important to note that the definite article in Bulgarian is an ending morpheme [7]. This fact gives a priority to morphological interpretations instead of syntactic ones. At the level of syntax, the definite article shows the subject (when it is not a proper name) since Bulgarian language uses a relatively free word order.

So, giving a detailed formal morphological interpretation of the definite article is an essential preliminary condition for part-of-speech parsing of Bulgarian.

2 The Semantics of Definiteness in Bulgarian

According to the traditional academic descriptive grammar works [7], the semantics of definiteness in standard Bulgarian language is expressed in three ways: lexical, morphological, and syntactic.

The lexical way of expressing definiteness is closely connected with the lexical semantics of a particular lexeme, so that, it would not be of semantic value for our formal interpretation. It is because of the fact that most of the formal grammar interpretations are supposed to deal with one-sense lexeme, which is the simplest possible type of lexeme.

C. Bussler and D. Fensel (Eds.): AIMSA 2004, LNAI 3192, pp. 256–266, 2004.

At the syntactic level, the definiteness in Bulgarian could express various types of semantic relationships like a case (to show subject), part-of-whole, deixis etc. Some authors tend to analyse this feature as a way to compensate for the lack of case declensions.

It is important to note that instead of the very many existing descriptive grammar works devoted to the problem, the semantics of definiteness in Bulgarian seems still not a sufficiently well studied phenomenon.

2.1   The Formal Morphological Markers of the Definite Article

As it has been pointed, the syntactic function of definiteness in Bulgarian is expressed by a formal morphological marker which is an ending morpheme [7]. It is different for the genders, however, for the masculine gender two types of definite morphemes exist – to determine a defined in a different way entities, which have two phonetic variants, respectively.

For the feminine and for the neuter gender only one definite morpheme exists, respectively. For the plural two definite morphemes are used depending on the ending vocal of the main plural form.

The following part-of-speech in Bulgarian take a definite article: nouns, adjectives, numerals (both cardinals and ordinals), possessive pronouns, and reflexive-possessive pronoun.

The definite morphemes are the same for all part-of-speech, however, in the further description we are going to analyze the inflectional morphology simply for the adjectives and the numerals.

3   Some Preliminaries for Possible Formal Interpretation

As it has been pointed, the very complicated semantics of the feature of definiteness in Bulgarian requires a related specific formal approach of interpretation. In fact, it should consists of two embedded in one system stages.

The first one is a formal interpretation of the inflectional morphology, and the second should give a syntactic interpretation of the first. The first stage requires to apply standard computational morphology approaches like a rule-based concatenation of morphemes and construction of relevant rules for their combinations, whereas the second requires an effective syntactic processing of various generated inflecting forms.

Obviously, such a semantically complicated model could hardly be found among the existing formal models like HPSG, for example, especially designed mostly for syntactic processing and normally producing only one type of inflecting forms.

We considered the DATR language for lexical knowledge presentation as a suitable formal framework for modeling the inflectional morphology of Bulgarian definite article.

4   The DATR Language

The DATR language is a non-monotonic language for defining the inheritance networks through path/value equations [6]. It has both an explicit declarative semantics and an explicit theory of inference allowing efficient implementation, and at the same time, it has the necessary expressive power to encode the lexical entries presupposed by the work in the unification grammar tradition [3,4,5].

In DATR information is organized as a network of nodes, where a node is a collection of related information. Each node has associated with it a set of equations that define partial functions from paths to values where paths and values are both sequences of atoms. Atoms in paths are sometimes referred to as attributes.

DATR is functional, it defines a mapping which assigns unique values to node attribute-path pair, and the recovery of this values is deterministic. It can account for such language phenomena like regularity, irregularity, and subregularity, and allows the use of deterministic parsing.

The DATR language has a lot of implementations, however, our application was made by using QDATR 2.0 (consult URL http://www.cogs.susx.ac.uk/lab/nlp/datr/datrnode49.html for a related file bul_det.dtr). This PRO-LOG encoding uses Sussex DATR notation [10].

DATR allows construction of various types of language models (language theories), however, our model is presented as a rule-based formal grammar and a lexical database. The particular query to be evaluated is a related inflecting word form, and the implementation allows to process words in Cyrillic alphabet.

5   The Principles of DATR Encoding of Bulgarian Adjectives Inflectional Morphology

We are not intended to follow any particular morphological theory, however, our DATR analysis is linguistically motivated.

In particular, we define morphemes to be of semantic value and consider them as a realisation of a specific morphosyntactic phenomenon (as the definite morphemes are a morphosyntactic realization of the feature of definiteness).

We are encoding words following the traditional notion of the lexeme, and we accept the different phonetic alternations to be of semantic value.

The approach we use is related and indebted to those of Cahill and Gazdar [1,2] used to account for German adjectives inflectional morphology, however, we do not apply their account of morphotactics.

Our model represents an inheritance network consisting of various nodes which allows us to account for all related inflecting forms within the framework of one grammar theory.

5.1   The Inheritance Hierarchy of the Adjectives

Bulgarian adjectives have four grammar feature: gender, number, definiteness, and comparison of degree (only for those of quality) [8]. According to their semantics, Bulgarian adjectives are divided into two types: relative and of quality.

All grammar features of adjectives are inflectional and they depend upon agreement on the noun the adjective modifies. So, all of them should be accounted for in our morphological interpretation.

It is interesting to note that the above inflectional features of the adjectives express an internal dependency. Thus, adjectives have three different inflectional forms to account for the feature of gender which, at the same time, are equally marked for the number as singular.

That means if we generate all gender inflecting forms, we will automatically generate singular form. Which shows the priority of the feature of gender over the feature of number, and suggests that the feature of gender has a wider semantic scope than that of the number.

Another interesting fact is that the rule for forming different gender word forms and the rule for forming plural form are similar. Normally, all these forms are generated by attachment of a particular inflecting morpheme to the base form of the adjective.

Such similarity in structure suggests that the rules generating gender inflecting forms and the rule generating plural form would be organaised in one common node of the semantic network.

Also, an interesting relationship of dependency could be viewed between the morphemes expressing the feature of comparison of degree (which are prefix morphemes) and the morphemes for the feature of gender and number. That relationship shows a priority of the feature of gender.

So, in our interpretation we accept the feature of gender as a specific trigger to change the values of number, comparison of degree, and definiteness word forms.

Following these preliminary assumptions, we generate first the gender inflectional forms, than the plural form, the defined inflectional form, and the compared inflectional form.

We are going to use the notation accepted in Stoykova [9] for the encodings of the discussed above grammar features. Particularly for the feature of the definite article, we accept the identical node DET defined also in Stoykova [9]. The Bulgarian adjectives type hierarchy is given in Figure 1.

Our DATR analysis of adjectives starts with the node DET which defines inflecting morphemes for the definite article as follows:[1]

```
DET:
      <sing undef>          ==
      <sing def_2 masc>     == _ja
      <sing def_2 masc_1>   == _a
      <sing def_1 masc>     == _jat
      <sing def_1 masc_1>   == _ut
      <sing def_1 femn>     == _ta
      <sing def_1 neut>     == _to
```

[1] Here and elsewhere in the description we use Latin alphabet to present morphemes instead of Cyrillic used normally. Because of the mismatching between both some of the typically Bulgarian phonological alternations are assigned by two letters, whereas in Cyrillic alphabet they are marked by one.

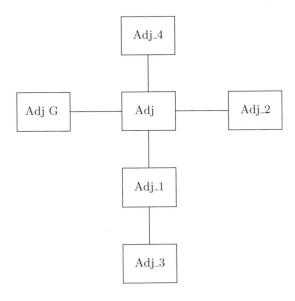

Fig. 1. The adjectives type hierarchy.

```
<plur undef>          ==
<plur def_1>          == _te.
```

Node AdjG is a basic node in our DATR account of the adjectives. It defines grammar rules for generating all inflectional word forms for the feature of gender, number, and definiteness. It is constructed according to the discussed above preliminaries.

```
AdjG:
      <sing undef masc> == "<root>"
      <sing undef femn> == "<root gend>" _a
      <sing undef neut> == "<root gend>" _o
      <sing def_2 masc> == "<plur undef masc>" DET
      <sing def_1 masc> == "<plur undef masc>" DET
      <sing def_1>      == "<sing undef>" DET
      <plur undef>      == "<root gend>" _i
      <plur def_1>      == "<plur undef>" DET.
```

Node Adj inherits all grammar rules of node AdjG but it employs also the grammar rules for generating the word forms for the feature of comparison of degree. It is constructed according to the analysed above assumptions about the sequence of the process of the generation of inflecting forms, and defines the adjectives of quality.

```
Adj:
    <> == AdjG
    <compar> == po_  "<>"
    <superl> == naj_ "<>".
```

Node Adj_1 inherits the grammar rules of node Adj but changes the rules for generating singular forms for feminine and for neuter gender to use the palatal gender morphemes.

```
Adj_1:
    <> == Adj
    <sing undef femn> == "<root gend>" _ja
    <sing undef neut> == "<root gend>" _jo.
```

Node Adj_2 defines the inflectional morphology of those adjectives which realise two types of phonetic alternation during the process of inflection. At this node an additional word inflectional base form <root plur> is used to account for the specific phonetic alternations of the base form in forming plural.

```
Adj_2:
    <> == Adj
    <plur undef> == "<root plur>" _i.
```

Node Adj_3 defines the inflection of a type of adjectives which are of common gender. They take only a feminine gender value, which in fact is optional, and are considered as a gender-neutral but have all other grammar features of the adjectives.

```
Adj_3:
    <> == Adj_1
    <sing undef masc> == "<sing undef femn>"
    <sing undef neut> == "<sing undef femn>"
    <sing def_2 masc> == "<sing def_1 femn>"
    <sing def_1 masc> == "<sing def_1 femn>"
    <sing def_1 neut> == "<sing def_1 femn>".
```

Node Adj_4 inherits all grammar rules of node Adj. The new employed grammar rule changes the inflectional morpheme for neuter gender into -e.

```
Adj_4:
    <> == Adj
    <sing undef neut> == "<root gend>" _e.
```

6   The Principles of DATR Encoding of Bulgarian Numerals Inflectional Morphology

For our interpretation of definiteness of the numerals we are going to follow linguistic motivation. The underlying semantic principles of the encodings are similar to those described for the adjectives. An additional principle we are going to follow is the use of word-formation morphemes as a condition to define the numerals type hierarchy.

6.1   The Inheritance Hierarchy of the Numerals

All grammar features that the numerals in Bulgarian express are connected with their specific semantics, which share both the features of the nouns and those of the adjectives.

The semantics of the numerals express either a quantity or a sequence. Concerning their grammar features, the numerals are similar to the adjectives because they use the agreement. At the same time, if they are used independently, they are similar in their grammar feature to the nouns.

With respect to their semantics, the numerals are divided into two types: cardinals and ordinals. With respect to their word formation they are divided into simple and compound.

This duality in the semantics of the numerals is going to be the important point in our encoding. The Bulgarian numerals type hierarchy is given in Figure 2.

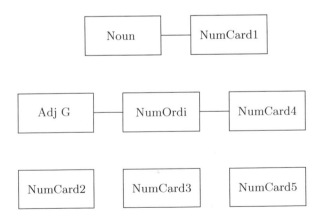

Fig. 2. The numerals type hierarchy.

We start our encoding of the numerals with assigning the definite morphemes, and we employ the node DET as it is defined for the adjectives.

```
DET:
    <sing undef>            ==
    <sing def_2 masc>       == _ja
    <sing def_2 masc_1>     == _a
    <sing def_1 masc>       == _jat
    <sing def_1 masc_1>     == _ut
    <sing def_1 femn>       == _ta
    <sing def_1 neut>       == _to
    <plur undef>            ==
    <plur def_1>            == _te.
```

The definition of the node NumCard1 is given to be exactly the same as those employed for the interpretation of the nouns in Stoykova [9]. NumCard1 describes the cardinal numerals which use the inflectional rules of the nouns.

```
NumCard1:
          <> == Noun.
```

Node NumCard2 describes the cardinal numerals, which end in -a, -ta, and use word formation suffixes -ma, -mina, -ina, -tina, -ka.

```
NumCard2:
          <sing undef> == "<root>"
          <sing def_1> == "<root>" DET: <sing def_1 femn>.
```

Node NumCard3 defines the cardinal numerals, which end in -e, -i, -o, and use word formation suffixes -nki, -ki.

```
NumCard3:
          <sing undef> == "<root>"
          <sing def_1> == "<root>" DET: <plur def_1>.
```

Node NumCard4 describes the inflectional morphology of 'one', and is defined as follows:

```
NumCard4:
          <> == NumOrdi
          <sing def_1 masc> == "<root>" _i DET
          <sing def_2 masc> == "<root>" _i DET.
```

Node NumCard5 describes the inflectional morphology of 'two'.

```
NumCard5:
  <sing undef masc> == "<root>"
  <sing undef femn> == "<root gend>" _e
  <sing undef neut> == "<sing undef femn>"
  <sing def_1 masc> ==  <sing undef masc> DET: <sing def_1 femn>
  <sing def_1 femn> ==  <sing undef femn> DET: <plur def_1>
  <sing def_1 neut> == "<sing def_1 femn>".
```

Node NumOrdi defines the ordinal numerals to inherit all grammar features of the adjectives.

```
NumOrdi:
        <> == AdjG.
```

7   Evaluating Different Inflecting Forms

The proposed encoding gives a detailed morphological account of the feature of definiteness of all possible inflectional types of Bulgarian adjectives and numerals. According to the defined grammar rules, it is possible to generate all the inflecting forms.

The lexemes, themselves, are defined as different nodes, and are attached to related word inflectional ones inheriting in this way the particular inflectional grammar rules. The lexical information is given by the paths <root>, <root gend>, and <root plur> so, to account for the different types of roots phonetic alternations. The above distribution of the lexical knowledge is given because our model does not account for the morphotactics. Such account of morphotactics is rather difficult to be done for Bulgarian because of the fact that the syllable is not identical to the morpheme.

The example lexemes for the Bulgarian words for 'smooth' (gladuk) and 'seven' (sedem) are evaluated for their inflecting forms in the Appendix.

8   Conclusions

The proposed DATR-theories of the inflectional morphology of Bulgarian adjectives and numerals use traditional linguistic notions for encoding the feature of definiteness. Further, it would be possible to extend the application to account for the syntactic interpretations of definiteness.

References

1. Cahill L. and Gazdar G. 1997. The inflectional phonology of German adjectives, determiners and pronouns. *Linguistics*, 35(2):211–245.
2. Cahill L. and Gazdar G. 1999. The Polylex architecture: multilingual lexicons for related languages. *Traitement automatique des langues*, 40.

3. Evans R. and Gazdar G. 1989a. Inference in DATR. *Fourth Conference of the European Chapter of the Association for Computational Linguistics*, 66–71.
4. Evans R. and Gazdar G. 1989b. The semantics of DATR. In Anthony G. Cohn, ed. *Proceedings of the Seventh Conference of the Society for the Study of Artificial Intelligence and Simulation of Behaviour*, London: Pitman/Morgan Kaufmann, 79–87.
5. Evans R. and Gazdar G. 1990. The DATR papers. *CSRP 139, Research Report, vol. 1*, University of Sussex, Brighton.
6. Evans R. and Gazdar G. 1996. DATR: A language for lexical knowledge representation. *Computational Linguistics*, 22(2):167–216.
7. Gramatika na suvremennia bulgarski knizoven ezik. 1983. *Morphologia*, tom. 2.
8. Stojanov S. 1963. Emploi et signification de l'article defini dans la langue Bulgare litteraire moderne. II partie - Les adjectifs, les numeraux, les pronoms et les participes. *Annuaire de l'Universite de Sofia, Faculte philologique*, LVII(1):625–712.
9. Stoykova V. 2002. Bulgarian noun – definite article in DATR. In Donia Scott, ed. *Artificial Intelligence: Methodology, Systems, and Applications. Lecture Notes in Artificial Intelligence 2443*, Springer-Verlag, 152–161.
10. The DATR Web Pages at Sussex. 1997. *http://www.cogs.susx.ac.uk/lab/nlp/datr/*

Appendix

```
Gladuk: <> == Adj
        <root> == gladuk
        <root plur> == gladk.

Gladuk: <sing undef masc> == gladuk.
Gladuk: <sing undef femn> == gladka.
Gladuk: <sing undef neut> == gladko.
Gladuk: <plur undef> == gladki.
Gladuk: <compar sing undef masc> == po-gladuk.
Gladuk: <compar sing undef femn> == po-gladka.
Gladuk: <compar sing undef neut> == po-gladko.
Gladuk: <compar plur undef> == po-gladki.
Gladuk: <superl sing undef masc> == naj-gladuk.
Gladuk: <superl sing undef femn> == naj-gladka.
Gladuk: <superl sing undef neut> == naj-gladko.
Gladuk: <superl plur undef> == naj-gladki.
Gladuk: <sing def_1 masc> == gladkijat.
Gladuk: <sing def_2 masc> == gladkija.
Gladuk: <sing def_1 femn> == gladkata.
Gladuk: <sing def_1 neut> == gladkoto.
Gladuk: <plur def_1> == gladkite.
Gladuk: <compar sing def_1 masc> == po-gladkijat.
Gladuk: <compar sing def_2 masc> == po-gladkija.
Gladuk: <compar sing def_1 femn> == po-gladkata.
Gladuk: <compar sing def_1 neut> == po-gladkoto.
Gladuk: <compar plur def_1> == po-gladkite.
```

```
Gladuk: <superl sing def_1 masc> == naj-gladkijat.
Gladuk: <superl sing def_2 masc> == naj-gladkija.
Gladuk: <superl sing def_1 femn> == naj-gladkata.
Gladuk: <superl sing def_1 neut> == naj-gladkoto.
Gladuk: <superl plur def_1> == naj-gladkite.

Sedem: <> == NumCard3
        <root> == sedem.

Sedem: <sing undef> == sedem.
Sedem: <sing def_1> == sedemte.
```

Towards a Better Understanding of the Language Content in the Semantic Web

Pavlin Dobrev[1], Albena Strupchanska[2], and Galia Angelova[2]

[1] ProSyst Bulgaria Ltd., 48 Vladaiska Str., Sofia, Bulgaria, `pavlin@prosyst.com`
[2] Bulgarian Academy of Sciences, Institute for Parallel Information Processing,
25A Acad. G. Bonchev Str., 1113 Sofia, Bulgaria, {`albena`, `galia`}`@lml.bas.bg`

Abstract. Internet content today is about 80% text-based. No matter static or dynamic, the information is encoded and presented as multilingual, unstructured natural language text pages. As the Semantic Web aims at turning Internet into a machine-understandable resource, it becomes important to consider the natural language content and to assess the feasibility and the innovation of the semantic-based approaches related to unstructured texts. This paper reports about work in progress, an experiment in semantic based annotation and explores scenarios for application of Semantic Web techniques to the textual pages in Internet.

1   Introduction and State of the Art

The ultimate aim of the Semantic Web is to make the web resources more meaningful to computers by augmenting the presentation markup with semantic markup, i.e. meta-data annotations that describe the content. It is widely expected that the innovation will be provided by agents and applications dealing with ontology acquisition, merging and alignment, annotation of www-pages towards the underlying ontologies as well as intelligent, semantic-based text search and intuitive visualisation. However, the current progress in all these directions is not very encouraging despite the number of running activities. Isolated results and tools are available for e.g. automatic and semi-automatic annotation of web pages, for knowledge-based information retrieval, for ontology learning and so on but it is still difficult to grasp a coherent picture of how the Semantic Web will drastically change the information age by offering quite new kinds of services. Another discouraging obstacle is that the ontologies in the Semantic Web are not clearly seen at the horizon. Due to these reasons, it makes sense to develop and evaluate experimental settings which might provide on-hand experience with semantic based systems and show the desired benefits as well as the potential gaps in the current research efforts.

A summary of the relevant state of the art should sketch the status in several core Semantic Web directions. One of them is **ontology availability, development and evolution** which is considered as the first challenge for the Semantic Web [1]. Isolated ontologies are available in a number of fields and initiatives like the

C. Bussler and D. Fensel (Eds.): AIMSA 2004, LNAI 3192, pp. 267–276, 2004.

„standard upper ontology" aim at the design and building of certain acceptable domain-independent ontologies intended to be reused and extended for particular domain. There is a number of public taxonomies (even very large, in the medical domain for instance) but the most elaborated semantically-based resources like CyC or LinkBase® are not publicly accessible. In fact, the availability of underlying ontologies is an issue at the core of the Semantic Web enterprise. Many tools for building ontologies and reusing existing ones have been developed. Environments like Protégé [2] or Chimaera [3] offer sophisticated support for ontology engineering and merging. Protégé is an integrated software tool used by system developers and domain experts to develop knowledge-based systems. It offers an editing environment with several third party plug-ins. Protégé allows to export the created ontology in a number of formats and has also a flexible plug-in structure that provides modular extension of the functionalities. OntoEdit [4] is another sophisticated ontology editor that supports methodology-based ontology construction and that takes comprehensive advantage of Ontobroker inference capabilities.

Because of the numerous isolated conceptual resources, **ontology mapping** is also a hot area of research. Today matching between ontologies and schema is still largely done manually in a labor-intensive and error-prone process. As a consequence, semantic integration issues have now become a serious bottleneck in a wide variety of applications. The high costs of overcoming this bottleneck have triggered numerous research activities on how to describe mappings, manipulate them, and generate them semi-automatically but unfortunately there has been little cross-fertilization between the results. There are, most generally, two approaches to ontology mappings: based on heuristics that identify structural and naming similarities between models [5] and using machine learning techniques in order to learn mappings between models/ontologies [6]. In both cases, the systems require feedback from the users to refine the proposed mappings. US activities in **ontology alignment and merging** [7] face the fact that different domain-dependent ontologies are organized along different principles for acquisition of concepts and their natural language labels; choosing 42 sample terms from EIA Glossary of Energy terms, it turned out that only 22 of them matched one or more SIMS domain model terms fully or partially, and no single algorithm for automatic label alignment was found [8].

Another important issue is the **(automatic or semi-automatic) annotation of pages** in the Semantic Web. Annotation is considered as one of the most effort-consuming tasks that has to be performed by especially developed tools. Recent annotation tools support manual and non ambiguous pages annotation according to predefined typology of events, locations, names, and non ambiguous domain terms (see for instance [9]). Selecting manually text fragments as concept labels is not very efficient, moreover different annotators may tend to build the semantic indices in their own way and will need precisely formulated standardization rules how to anchor pieces of terms to the ontological concepts. Please note that many technical terms are made up of multiple words (e.g. *delta doped resonant tunneling diodes*) and the only way to accurately distinguish them is the analysis of qualified noun phrases rather than individual words, which is problematic for automatic recognition and processing by language technologies and even for human beings. So at present it remains unclear how the different annotation practices could be standardized to produce pages annotated in a similar manner.

Another open question is **how many semantic anchors are appropriate per page**: should all possible semantic indices be inserted (even against different ontologies) or only the domain-specific concepts should be anchored to one chosen ontology? . The realistic scenarios are well-defined domain-specific tasks in compact areas - e.g SPIRIT [10] uses a multilingual ontology for mapping geographical concepts and target only annotation of named entities and geographic objects.

At last, the present **language technologies** still did not prove their feasibility for automatic collection of the necessary Semantic Web data; as a result, the majority of running projects in the field still rely on manually-acquired demonstration ontologies in narrow domains. There is still no evidence that **knowledge-intensive information retrieval** provides much better results [11]. To conclude, in our view the development of the Semantic Web is at certain initial phase of data collection, elaboration of design scenarios, development of prototypical applications that may become success stories, and their evaluation and market assessment.

Concerning the **visualisation** in Semantic Web, Kimani et al. [12] classifies existing approaches, where our approach would be sorted as generated rendering with direct manipulation interaction style. Our experimental tool provides visualisation and navigation support. Magpie [13] shows an approach for semantic-based assistance in user's web page navigation. It is a framework supporting the interpretation of web pages that is integrated in the standard web browser. The user chooses particular domain ontology from which ontology-based lexicon is automatically extracted. Then the ontology dependent entities in the web pages are annotated automatically using the *ontology-based lexicon* approach. The user chooses the classes of entities to be highlighted in the web page s/he browses. By right-clicking on a highlighted entity a context dependent menu is shown. The choices in the menu depend on the class of the selected entity within the selected ontology. Magpie services act as an auxiliary knowledge resource, which is at the disposal of users.

In this paper we report about on-going research work addressing the text of the www-pages in the future Semantic Web. We discuss in Section 2 existing semantic structures and annotation according to them, which is called *indexing* in the information science. In fact, while indexing, the present terminological collections - domain nomenclatures, classifications, and ontologies - are applied as semantic backbones in (multilingual) text archives. To know more about automatic annotation is of crucial importance for the appearance of the next generation technologies, since their proper semantic resources are not available yet with the necessary volume, content and format and it still remains an open question when and how they will arise. In Section 3 we present an experiment in manual semantic annotation of real www-pages against a financial ontology in English that is considered as a semantic backbone when building the semantic index. The experiment allowed us to get an idea about the potential difficulties in the annotation process, which include on-the-fly resolution of several kinds of ambiguities like manual choice of the anchored phrases from the natural language pages, choice of ontology node and so on. These ambiguities are embedded elements of the Semantic Web due to the fact that the complexity of the whole enterprise implies multiple choices in many tasks and there will be no (most probably there cannot be) standard solutions for all users. We present as well an experimental visualisation tool, which we develop at present to assist the semantic-based search of annotated web pages. The tool is implemented at concept demonstration level and allows for browsing of semantically-related pages from the perspective of a single underlying ontology. Section 4 discusses applications that may benefit from the availability of semantic-based search and its visualisation. Section 5 contains the conclusion.

2   Annotation of Pages and Conceptual Resources

As we said, the task of linking a free text fragment (a word or a phrase) to a term from certain terminological collection is well known in the computational linguistics and the information science. This is the so-called *indexing*. The most successful indexing applications deal with the medical domain where indexing according to medical classifications is systematically performed in practical settings by software tools and thousands of health professionals who at least have to edit the indexed text. The annotation traditions and standards for specialised texts (patient records) are established since decades, moreover some very large terminological collections are especially designed to spin the indexing process – for instance SNOMED, which among others helps calculating the price of the medical treatments. The more advanced the system is, the more automatic the indexing procedures are, providing high precision of terms recognition. The world leader in indexing software is the company Language and Computing (Belgium) which develops the medical ontology LinkBase® and indexing software against different medical classifications [14]. Annotation with 100% precision is impossible [15]; however, the benefit is that the same document becomes accessible via the synonyms of the annotated terms [14]. So we believe that the annotation task as defined in the Semantic Web could use the indexing experience gathered in medical informatics. There should be domain-dependent conventions how to recognise the ontology terms in the free text to be indexed; please note that the concept and relation labels can be verbalised in a free text in a variety of ways. Another lesson learnt from the medical indexing, which we apply in our current experiment, is to annotate in the text all occurrences of all ontology labels, which we are able to recognise (or the software we develop is able to recognise). However, annotation is not elementary from semantic point of view, even against medical terms that are relatively well-defined collections. Let us illustrate some key semantic problems, which are not frequently discussed.

Consider Figure 1 and the free text uploaded in the leftmost scrolling window. It contains the two subsequent words *investment portfolio*. In the ontology uploaded in the second scrolling window, there are two separate concepts with labels INVESTMENT and PORTFOLIO (they are not visible in Figure 1). Only domain expert who reads and interprets correctly the text will be able to decide how to define the semantic indices from the phrase *investment portfolio* to the concepts investment and portfolio. As natural language is rather vague and the individual reader interprets the meaning, another domain expert could link the phrase and the two concepts differently. In other words, even the manual annotation is a task to be performed with certain (small) percentage of disagreement by highly specialised automatic annotation. Due to this reason, running projects in this field target automatic annotation of some kind of entities only, e.g. named entities.

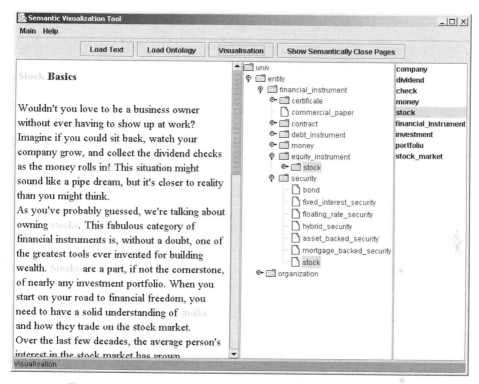

Fig. 1. Visualisation of semantically annotated text and its semantic indices

Regarding automation of annotation in the Semantic Web, a lot of (even commercial) annotation tools have been developed to support manual annotation in the relevant context. Annotea [16] allows annotations in RDF and provides mechanism for publishing annotations on the web. It uses XPointer for locating the annotations in the annotated document and a bookmark schema, which describes the bookmark and topic metadata. Other annotation tools include an ontology browser for the exploration of the ontology and instances and a HTML browser that will display the annotated parts of the text. OntoMat-Annotizer [17] allows the annotator to highlight relevant parts of the web page and create new instances via drag'n'drop interactions. It supports the user with the task of creating and maintaining ontology-based DAML+OIL markups. OntoMat is based on the S-CREAM framework [18], which comprises inference services, crawler, document management system, ontology guidance and document viewers. OntMat supports semi-automatic annotation of web pages based on the information extraction component Amilcare [19]. It provides a plug-in interface for extensions. Another annotation tool that integrates Amilcare is MnM [20]. It can handle multiple ontologies at the same time. MnM makes it possible to access ontology servers through APIs, such as OKBC, and also to access ontologies specified in a markup format, such as RDF and DAML+OIL. The extraction of knowledge structures from web pages is through the use of simple user-defined knowledge extraction patterns.

Regarding the available conceptual resources, the overview of existing public constructions displays primarily the multiple perspectives to classification of reality objects, relations and their attributes and features. The reader may consider as an example three taxonomies in computer science: *(i)* the ACM taxonomy of keywords, designed by the IEEE Computer Society [21], *(ii)* a taxonomy in Computer Graphics Interfaces, developed within a NSF-funded project as a searchable database index for a large part of the ASEC Digital Library [22] and *(iii)* the SeSDL Taxonomy of Educational Technology, which gives links to the British Educational Thesaurus BET [23]. These three hierarchies are built for different purposes and a careful study of their concepts shows that less of 5% of the nodes are common. As a rule, even for these „intersecting" concepts the classification into subconcepts is different. Similar variety exists concerning the emerging ontologies.

We considered in depth the public financial "branch" of the MILO ontology [24] which contains all concepts mentioned at least three times in the Brown corpus and additionally, is relatively easy for people to understand and practical for computational use. MILO is integrated under SUMO [25] and its financial part covers 246 basic entities (terms). In Teknowledge's ontologies, terms belong to one of five basic types: class, relation, function, attribute, or individual. Terms are the vocabulary of the ontology and MILO adopted some naming conventions to differentiate types of terms at sight, which were useful in the annotation process. We mapped MILO to a financial ontology we developed earlier for educational purposes in the LARFLAST project [26]. Three quarters of the terms coincide, however the design decisions are different. For instance, in MILO *dividend* is a relation while for us it is a concept. It looks difficult even for knowledge engineers to formulate precise rules how to align the meaning of *concepts* to *relations*. Mapping of such ontologies will require complex semantic resources, which define better the meanings, and in-depth inference. Most probably, as it happens today with the indexing software, it will be impossible to achieve 100% correctness of mappings and alignment.

3   The Experiment

We annotated manually the text of 132 real www-pages using the LARFLAST ontology that has 280 concepts and relations. While selecting the pages we noticed the following. There are millions of Web pages with financial information in Internet but the majority of them refer to few ontology terms only. This is due to the well-known fact that in general, text meaning *IS NOT* verbalisation of domain knowledge. The pages we found (via Google and searching for keywords) discuss for instance banking and stock exchange information, deals, company descriptions; thousands (newspaper) articles concern financial matters in general and therefore, words like *stock* and *bond* appear here and there in the texts. On the other hand, the ontology is a compact formal encoding of domain knowledge. Only textbooks, manuals, surveys contain very frequently the ontology terms as - by default- these kinds of texts are descriptions of domain knowledge. In other words, the annotation of the static web content at present would face the serious problem that the stories presented in web pages refer to many domain ontologies by addressing only few concepts from several ontologies. For instance, a document discussing *stocks and bonds for investments in computer and aircraft industry* could concern three domain ontologies. In this way the decision of how to annotate (against which ontology) is rather difficult and we restricted our experiment to strictly specialised texts that belong to the financial domain although these kinds of texts are relatively rare in Internet.

We implemented the ViSem tool supporting the visualisation of semantic indices and providing some kinds of semantic-based text search. ViSem works over an archive of html-pages annotated according to an ontology encoded in DAML+OIL/OWL-format. Figure 1 shows the tool interface in "Visualisation" mode. Texts are loaded by the button "Load text" and appear in the leftmost text window. The ontology is open by the "Load ontology" button, in the second scrolling window. After loading a www-page and its ontology, ViSem analyses the semantic index and displays the list in the rightmost side of its main window: in the order of appearance, the text phrases from the leftmost window which are semantically anchored to terms from the chosen ontology (please note the list can be empty). In "Visualisation" mode, after selecting an item from the list in column 3, ViSem shows (colours) in the leftmost text all words and phrases linked to the highlighted term. The same colour is used for colouring the ontology label too. Originally our idea was to link the text and ontology term by a line, as we believe the visualisation by straight line will be the best intuitive illustration. However, supporting a second presentation layer over the text layer would require too much implementation efforts worth to be invested in a bigger project only. Please note that the visualisation of links by colouring is the most often approach at present and almost all annotation tools work in this way.

ViSem is implemented in Java using Swing graphical library. In ViSem we reuse ideas and code from our tool CGWorld which supports the graphical acquisition of conceptual graphs in Internet [27]. Ontology processing is built on top of Jena's API. Jena is a Java framework for building Semantic Web applications. It provides a programmatic environment for RDF, RDFS and OWL [28].

4   Application Scenarios

If the Semantic Web makes the web resources more meaningful to computers, then what is the benefit for human users, given the fact that humans develop ontologies and annotate (millions of) web-pages? In the context of our small experiment we try to answer this questions by exploring different application scenarios where the semantically indexed archive and its ontology improve the information services.

The first useful application is the semantic-based text search. It is illustrated in Figure 2. The user selects a concept from the ontology and clicks the button **Show semantically close pages**. Then the most relevant page, which is semantically linked to the highlighted concept, is loaded in the leftmost window. Belonging to the same domain and annotated against the same ontology, this page obligatory contains many terms from the ontology. Please note that in this case, the present information retrieval techniques will not distinguish between the pages shown in Figure 1 and Figure 2. They are 100% similar, as they practically contain the same words, and ranking them in a list would depend on the algorithms of the searching engine. So the only way of finer ranking is to have semantic-based indices as they are suggested today in the Semantc Web.

The second application scenario we envisage is support of comprehension while reading www-pages which could be useful for domain novices or for foreigners who read a page in unknown language and do not grasp the meaning of all specific terms. ViSem supports at the moment the following services: *(i)* after highlighting a phrase in the left-most window, via the right button menu, the user can view **properties and attributes**, **relations**, and **multiple inheritance**. This may help understanding the meaning of the semantically-anchored phrase (in a earlier project, which investigated knowledge-based machine-aided translation, we integrated for similar purposes a module for natural language generation to provide more readable explanations for non-professionals [29]).

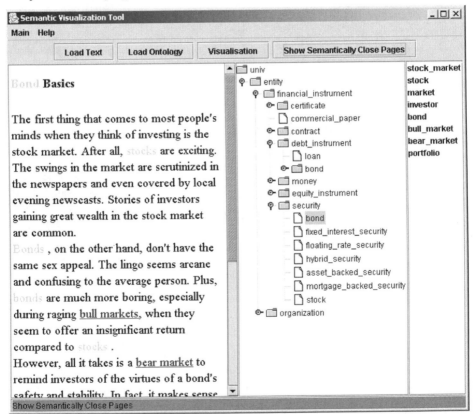

Fig. 2. The most relevant corpus page, which is semantically linked to *bond*

Another useful application of semantically-indexed archives of www-pages is the emerging "educational Semantic Web". Current eLearning systems need increased abilities in quality, quantity, and interaction and the Semantic Web agents (i.e. content, that is aware of itself) will play crucial role in the next generation learning management systems which take content from various sources and aggregate it. In our previous project [26] we implemented personalised information retrieval as the system was offering to the learner dynamically retrieved readings, which are "most relevant" to the concept he/she does not know well or know wrongly. Unfortunately, information retrieval by keywords does not work well for educational purposes as it does not recognise the text genre and the majority of the "relevant" pages contain much technical data (e.g. banking information) which is not a good teaching source. Semantic indexing, however, works via the ontology thus proposing content to students who need it. In this way the Semantic Web can be used as a technology for realising sophisticated eLearning scenarios for all actors involved in the learning process, including teachers in collaborative courseware generating system.

5   Conclusion

In this paper we report about on-going experiment designed after a careful study of the recent developments in the Semantic Web. As our focus is on the text of the Internet pages, we explore scenarios for annotation and semantic-based search with compact ontologies. It seems the annotation as such will be problematic, as the indexing is problematic even in the well-defined domains. It also looks likely that in the foreseeable future, we will have numerous non-coherent ontologies, as they exist today in the domain of medicine, developed by different organisations and in different natural languages, with manual alignment defined by explicit correspondences. On the other hand we believe that the semantic-based text processing is feasible at least in narrower, well-defined domains. So we plan to continue our experiment by annotating financial pages against MILO as well and exploring the semantic search with several ontologies.

References

[1]   Benjamins R., and Jesús Contreras, The six challenges for the Semantic Web. White paper 2002, http://www.isoco.com/isococom/whitepapers/files/SemanticWeb-whitepaper-137.pdf
[2]   PROTEGE, http://protege.stanford.edu/
[3]   McGuinness D., Fikes R., Rice J., and S. Wilder. An environment for merging and testing large ontologies. In *Proceedings of KR 2000*, pp. 483–493. Morgan Kaufmann, 2000.
[4]   Sure Y., Angele J.and S. Staab OntoEdit: Guiding Ontology Development by Methodology and Inferencing. In Proc. of the International Conference on Ontologies, Databases and Applications of SEmantics ODBASE 2002
[5]   Noy N, and Musen M. PROMPT:Algorithm and Tool for Automated Ont. Merging and Alignment. In Proc. Of the 17th National Conference on Artificial Intelligence (AAAI-2000),Austin, TX, 450-455.
[6]   Doan A, Madhavan J. Domingos P., and Halevy A. Learing to Map between Ontologies on the Semantic Web. In Proc. 11th Int. World Wide Web Conf. (WWW2002)
[7]   The Energy Data Collection (EDC) project: deep focus on hydra-headed metadata. www.digitalgovernment.org/news/stories/2002/images/metadatafinal.pdf
[8]   Hovy E., and J. Clavans. Comparison of Manual and Automatic Inter-Ontology Alignment, 2002, http://altamira.isi.edu/alignment

[9] Vargas-Vera M., Motta E., Domingue J., Shum S. B. and M. Lanzoni. Knowledge Extraction by using an Ontology-based Annotation Tool. Proc. 1st Int. Conf. on Knowledge Capture, (K-CAP'01), Workshop on Knowledge Markup & Semantic Annotation, Victoria, B.C., Canada, 2001

[10] SPIRIT, Spatially-Aware Information Retrieval on the Internet, IST FP5 project in Semantic Web, http://www.geo-spirit.org/

[11] Sparck-Jones, Karen, "What is the Role of NLP in Text Retrieval?," in Tomek Strzalkowski (ed.), Natural Language Information Retrieval, Kluwer, 1999, pp. 1-24.

[12] Kimani St., Catarci T., and I. Cruz. Web Rendering Systems: Techniques, Classification Criteria and Challenges. In Vizualizing the Semantic Web Geroimenko, V.Chen Ch. (Eds.), Berlin: Springer 2002, pp. 63 – 89.

[13] John Domingue, Martin Dzbor, Enrico Motta: Semantic Layering with Magpie. Handbook on Ontologies 2004, pp.533-554

[14] TeSSI®: Get more out of your unstructured medical documents. Language & Computing, White paper April 2004, see www.landc.be

[15] Natural Language Processing in Medical Coding. Language & Computing, White Paper April 2004, www.landc.be

[16] http://www.w3.org/2001/Annotea/

[17] http://sourceforge.net/projects/ontomat

[18] Handschuh, S., Staab, S. and F. Ciravegna, „S-CREAM - Semi-Automatic Creation of Metadata," Semantic Authoring, Annotation and Markup Workshop, 15th European Conference on Artificial Intelligence, (ECAI'02), Lyon, France, 2002, pp. 27-33.

[19] Ciravegna F., Dingli A., Petrelli D. and Yorick Wilks: "Document Annotation via Adaptive Information Extraction" Poster at the 25th Annual International ACM SIGIR Conference on Research and Development in Information Retrieval August 11-15, 2002, in Tampere, Finland

[20] Vargas-Vera M., Motta E., Domingue J., Lanzoni M., Stutt A. and Fabio Ciravegna. MnM: Ontology Driven Semi-Automatic and Automatic Support for Semantic Markup", In Proc. of the 13th International Conference on Knowledge Engineering and Management (EKAW 2002), ed Gomez-Perez, A., Springer Verlag, 2002.

[21] ACM Computing Classification System, www.computer.org/mc/keywords/keywords.htm

[22] CGI Taxonomy, http://www.siggraph.org/education/curriculum/projects/Taxonomy2001.htm

[23] SeSDL Taxonomy, www.sesdl.scotcit.ac.uk/taxonomy/ed_tech.html

[24] Nichols D. and A. Terry. User's Guide to Teknowledge Ontologies. Teknowledge Corp., December 2003, ontology.teknowledge.com/Ontology_User_Guide.doc

[25] Pease A., Niles I., and J. Li, 2002. The Suggested Upper Merged Ontology: A Large Ontology for the Semantic Web and its Applications. In Working Notes of the AAAI-2002 Workshop on Ontologies and the Semantic Web, Edmonton, Canada, July 28-August 1, 2002. http://projects.teknowledge.com/AAAI-2002/Pease.ps

[26] Angelova G., Boytcheva S., Kalaydjiev O., Trausan-Matu S., Nakov P. and Albena Strupchanska. Adaptivity in Web-Based CALL, In Proc. ECAI-2002, July 2002, Lyon, France, pp. 445-449. (see the LARFLAST ontology at http://www.larflast.bas.bg)

[27] Dobrev P. and K. Toutanova, CGWorld - Architecture and Features, In Proc. of the 10th International Conference on Conceptual Structures: Integration and Interfaces, pp. 261 – 270; http://www.larflast.bas.bg:8080/CGWorld

[28] JENA, http://jena.sourceforge.net

[29] Projects DB-MAT and DBR-MAT, 1992-1998 : knowledge-based machine aided translation, see http://nats-www.informatik.uni-hamburg.de/~dbrmat and http://www.lml.bas.bg/projects/dbr-mat.

A Study on Neural Networks and Fuzzy Inference Systems for Transient Data

Fevzullah Temurtas

Sakarya University, Department of Computer Engineering, Adapazari, Turkey

Abstract. In this study, a Neural Network (NN) structure with tapped time delays and Mamdani's fuzzy inference system (FIS) are used for the concentration estimation of the Acetone and Chloroform gases inside the sensor response time by using the transient sensor response. The Coated Quartz Crystal Microbalance (QCM) type sensor is used as gas sensors. The estimation results of Mamdani's FIS are very closer to estimation results of ANN for the transient sensor response. Acceptable good performances are obtained for both systems and the appropriateness of the NN and FIS for the gas concentration determination inside the sensor response time is observed.

1 Introduction

The volatile organic vapours in ambient air are known to be reactive photo-chemically, and can have harmful effects upon long-term exposure at moderate levels. These type organic compounds are widely used as a solvent in a large number of the chemical industry and in the printing plants [1,2].

Two of the applied concentration estimation methods are using of neural networks (NNs) and fuzzy inference systems (FISs) [2-7]. Usually, the steady state responses of the sensors are used for concentration estimations of the gases in the estimation using NNs and FISs [2-7]. Steady state response means no signals varying in time. But, for realizing the determination of the concentrations before the response times and decreasing the estimation time, the transient responses of the sensors must be used. Transient response means varying signals in time. The response values change very fast at the beginning of the measurement in the transient responses of the sensors. That is, slope is bigger at the beginning and decrease with time. So, a NN structure with tapped time delays [2,4] and Mamdan's [8] FIS using the response and slope of response is used for realizing the estimation of Acetone and Chloroform gas concentrations before the response times and decreasing the estimation time. The QCM type sensor, which shows good performance regardless of the ambient temperature- humidity variations as well as the concentration changes was used as gas sensors. The performance and the suitability of the proposed method are discussed based on the experimental results.

C. Bussler and D. Fensel (Eds.): AIMSA 2004, LNAI 3192, pp. 277–284, 2004.
© Springer-Verlag Berlin Heidelberg 2004

2   Sensors and Measurement System

The Quartz Crystal Microbalances (QCM) is useful acoustic sensor devices. The principle of the QCM sensors is based on changes Δf in the fundamental oscillation frequency to upon ad/absorption of molecules from the gas phase. The detailed explanation of the measurement and gas control systems and sensor are addressed in [2]

In this study, the frequency shifts (Hz) versus concentrations (ppm) characteristics were measured by using QCM sensor for Acetone and Chloroform gases. At the beginning of each measurement gas sensor is cleaned by pure synthetic air. Each measurement is composed of five periods. Each period consists of 10 minutes cleaning phase and 10 minutes measuring phase. During the periods of the measurements, at the first period 500 ppm, and at the following periods 1000, 3000, 5000, and 8000 ppm gases are given.

For the preparation of measurement data sets, firstly, cleaning phase data removed from the measured responses. Then, the cleaning phase base frequency shifts (5-15 Hz.) subtracted from sensor responses. Approximately 1800 instantaneous sensor responses were obtained for given six PPM values in both the training and test set. Instantaneous here means values at one point in time. Figure 1 shows the frequency shift and slope of frequency shift graphs for Chloroform.

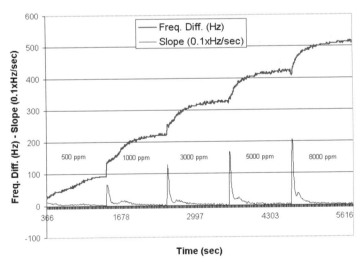

Fig. 1. Frequency shift and slope of frequency shift graphs for Chloroform.

3   Decreased Estimation Time by Using Artificial Neural Network

At the first study, a multi-layer feed-forward NN with tapped time delays [2,4] is used for determination of the concentrations of Acetone and Chloroform gases inside the sensor response time. The network structure is shown in Figure 2. The input, Δf is the sensor frequency shift value, t_s is data sampling time equal to 2 sec and the output, *PPM* is the estimated concentration. The inputs to the networks are the frequency shift and the past values of the frequency shift. The networks have a single hidden layer and a single output node. The activation functions for the hidden layer nodes and the output node are sigmoid transfer function.

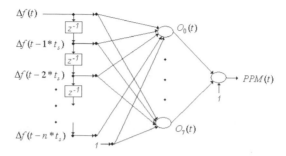

Fig. 2. Multi-layer feed-forward neural network model with a time delayed structure

The information about the trend of the transient sensor responses can be increased by increasing the numbers of data. This requires additional neural network inputs. For illustrating the effect of the numbers of inputs, four different numbers of inputs to the networks are used. These are,

- the frequency shift and the two past values of the frequency shift $(n = 3)$,
- the frequency shift and the four past values of the frequency shift $(n = 5)$,
- the frequency shift and the seven past values of the frequency shift $(n = 8)$,
- the frequency shift and the nine past values of the frequency shift $(n = 10)$.

The back propagation (BP) method is widely used as a teaching method for an ANN. [11].The BP algorithm with momentum gives the change $\Delta w_{ji}(k)$ in the weight of the connection between neurons i and j at iteration k as

$$\Delta w_{ji}(k) = -\alpha \frac{\partial E}{\partial w_{ji}(k)} + \mu \Delta w_{ji}(k-1) \tag{1}$$

where α is called the learning coefficient, μ the momentum coefficient, E the sum of squared differences error function, and $\Delta w_{ji}(k-1)$ the weight change in the immediately preceding iteration.

The performance of the BP algorithm is improved if the learning rate is allowed to change during the training process in response to the complexity of the local surface error. Training time can also be decreased by the use of an adaptive learning rate, which attempts to keep the learning rate step size as large as possible while keeping learning stable. This algorithm is commonly known as the gradient descent with momentum and adaptive learning rate (GDX) [9]. GDX is one of the high performance BP training algorithms which used in this paper.

Other high performance BP training algorithm which used in this study is Resilient BP (RP) [9-11]. RP was developed by Riedmiller and Braun [11]. In contrast to other gradient algorithms, this algorithm does not use the magnitude of the gradient. It is a direct adaptation of the weight step based local gradient sign. The RP algorithm generally provides faster convergence than most other algorithms [10,11]. Local information for each weight's individual update value, $A_{ji}(k)$, on the error function E is obtained according to [9-11].

When the update value for each weight is adapted, the delta weights are changed as follows:

$$\Delta w_{ji}(k) = \begin{cases} -A_{ji}(k), if \ \dfrac{\partial E}{\partial w_{ji}(k-1)} \dfrac{\partial E}{\partial w_{ji}(k)} > 0 \\[2mm] A_{ji}(k), if \ \dfrac{\partial E}{\partial w_{ji}(k-1)} \dfrac{\partial E}{\partial w_{ji}(k)} < 0 \\[2mm] 0, else \end{cases} \tag{2}$$

More details about RP algorithm can be found in [10-12].

Table 1. A replicate data set of Chloroform presented to NN structures for the training (n = 4)

Normalized Five ANN inputs (n + 1 = 5)					Normalized Desired Output PPM$_{true}$
$\Delta f(t)$	$\Delta f(t-t_s)$	$\Delta f(t-2*t_s)$	$\Delta f(t-3*t_s)$	$\Delta f(t-4*t_s)$	
0.021	0.018	0.012	0.006	0.000	0.05
0.027	0.021	0.018	0.012	0.006	0.05
0.030	0.027	0.021	0.018	0.012	0.05
...	...	...	...	...	...
0.096	0.096	0.096	0.096	0.096	0.05
...	...	...	...	...	...
0.122	0.083	0.042	0.020	0.000	1
0.155	0.122	0.083	0.042	0.020	1
0.187	0.155	0.122	0.083	0.042	1
...	...	...	...	...	...
0.515	0.515	0.514	0.513	0.514	1

The measured transient sensors responses were used for the training and test processes. Two measurements were made using same QCM sensor for this purpose. One measurement was used as training set and other measurement was used as test set. The measured data is normalized between 0 and 1. Table 1 shows a replicate data set of Chloroform presented to ANN structures for the training process.

4 Decreased Estimation Time by Using Fuzzy Inference System

At the second study, a fuzzy logic based algorithm which includes Mamdani's fuzzy inference method [7,8] was proposed for realizing the estimation of Acetone and Chloroform gas concentrations before the response times. In this system, two inputs, frequency change of the sensor Δf, and slope of Δf ($S\Delta f$) (Figure 1) and one output, concentration of the introduced gas PPM are used.

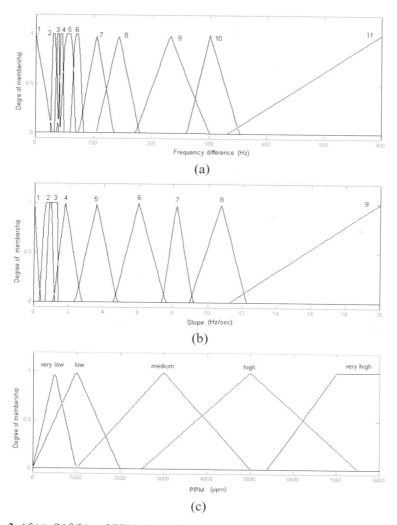

Fig. 3. Δf (a), $S\Delta f$ (b) and PPM (c) membership functions for chloroform gas with $n = 8$.

From the relations of the inputs and output, extracted fuzzy rules and corresponding defuzzification equation are as follows:

Rule l: IF Δf is A_i and $S\Delta f$ is B_j THEN PPM is C_k $(l = 1,2,\ldots,40)$

$$\tag{4}$$

$$\mu_{\Delta fi} = A_i(\Delta f), \qquad \mu_{S\Delta fi} = B_i(S\Delta f), \qquad \mu_{PPMk} = C_i(PPM) \tag{5}$$

$$PPM = \frac{\displaystyle\sum_{k=1}^{5} \mu_{PPMk} * PPMk}{\displaystyle\sum_{k=1}^{5} \mu_{PPMk}} \tag{6}$$

where, $i = 1,2,\ldots,11$, $j = 1,2,\ldots,9$ and $k = 1,2,\ldots,5$.

Equations which used for the calculation of $S\Delta f$ is given in (5).

$$S\Delta f(t) = \frac{\Delta f(t) - \Delta f(t - n * t_s)}{n * t_s} \tag{7}$$

where, $\Delta f(t)$ is the frequency change of the sensor at time t, $\Delta f(t-n*t_s)$ is n^{th} past value of the $\Delta f(t)$ and t_s is data sampling time equal to 2 sec. In this study, four different n values 3, 5, 8, 10 were used.

Figure 3 shows the sample Δf, $S\Delta f$ and PPM membership functions for Chloroform gas with n = 8 and Figure 4 illustrates an example of Mamdani's fuzzy inference, aggregation and defuzzification for the concentration estimation.

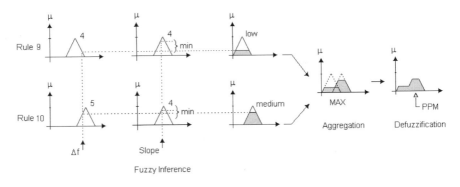

Fig. 4. An example of Mamdani's fuzzy inference, aggregation and defuzzification.

5   Performance Evaluation

For the performance evaluation, we have used the mean relative absolute error, $E(RAE)$ [2]:

$$E(RAE) = \frac{1}{n_{test}} \sum_{tetset} \left(\frac{\left| (PPM_{predicted} - PPM_{true}) \right|}{PPM_{true}} \right) \quad \forall PPM_{true} \neq 0 \tag{8}$$

where, $PPM_{predicted}$ is estimated concentration, PPM_{true} is real concentration and n_{test} is number of test set data.

6 Results and Discussions

The ability of the fuzzy logic and neural network structures to estimation of the Acetone and Chloroform gas concentrations related to the n values is given in table 2. Acceptable good [2-7] estimation values are obtained from the both FIS and NN structures and the results of the FIS structure are very closer to the results of the NN structure using GDX algorithm for both Acetone and Chloroform gases. As seen in this table, estimation times are generally at the level of seconds while sensor response times are at the level of minutes for both systems. This means that the determination of the concentrations of the Acetone and Chloroform gases inside the sensor response time is achieved by using the both FIS and NN structures. This table shows also that RP training algorithm provides faster convergence than GDX algorithms in the concentration estimation of Acetone and Chloroform gases for this study.

Table 2. Concentration estimations results (Sensor response time is ~250 sec)

Gas	n values	Estimation time (sec)	E(RAE) (%) for FIS	E(RAE) (%) for NN(GDX)	E(RAE) (%) for NN(RP)
Chloroform	3	6	5.75	5.94	2.34
	5	10	4.91	4.47	0.99
	8	16	3.56	3.22	0.57
	10	20	3.14	2.94	0.46
Acetone	3	6	5.07	4.24	2.13
	5	10	3.78	3.18	0.82
	8	16	2.92	2.58	0.47
	10	20	2.64	2.36	0.39

From the same table, it can be seen easily that, accuracy of the estimation can be improved by increasing the n values. This means that the optimum estimation results can be adjusted and achieved by using suitable number of data sampling range.

In this study, it is seen that acceptable good estimation results can be achieved for the estimation of the Acetone and Chloroform gas concentrations before the steady state response of the QCM sensor using both FIS and NN systems and FIS structure is simple applicable to the transient sensor data.

The NN structure with tapped time delays is useful for realizing the determination of the concentrations inside the response times and optimum estimation results can be achieved by using enough number of NN inputs and suitable training algorithm.

Unlike the NN structure whose adaptation to the handle systems including cheap microcontrollers is not easy [13], the fuzzy logic can be easily adapted to the handle systems for detection of gas concentration inside the sensor response time because of the simplicity of the fuzzy structure. The results of the fuzzy logic are comparable good and closer to those of the NN structure for estimation of the Acetone and Chloroform gas concentrations. And the optimum estimation time can be selected according to the desired acceptable error by using suitable number of data sampling range.

F. Temurtas

References

1. Ho, M.H., Gullbault, G.G., Rietz, B.: Continuos Detection of Toluene in Ambient Air with a Coated Piezoelectric Crystal, Anal. Chem., 52(9), (1980)
2. Temurtas, F., Tasaltin, C., Temurta , H., Yumusak, N., Ozturk, Z.Z.: Fuzzy Logic and Neural Network Applications on the Gas Sensor Data : Concentration Estimation, ISCIS03, Lecture Notes in Computer Science, Vol. 2869, (2003), 178-185
3. Temurtas, F., Gulbag, A., Yumusak, N.: A Study on Neural Networks using Taylor Series Expansion of Sigmoid Activation Function, ICCSA'04, Lecture Notes in Computer Science, Vol. 3046, (2004), 386-394
4. Temurtas, F., Tasaltin, C., Temurta , H., Yumusak, N., Ozturk, Z.Z.: A Study on Neural Networks with Tapped Time Delays: Gas Concentration Estimation, ICCSA04, Lecture Notes in Computer Science, Vol. 3046, (2004), 395-402
5. Yea, B., Osaki, T., Sugahara, K., Konishi, R.: The concentration estimation of inflammable gases with a semiconductor gas sensor utilizing neural networks and fuzzy inference, Sensors and Actuators-B, 41 (1997) 121-129
6. Pardo, M., Faglia, G., Sberveglieri, G., Corte, M., Masulli, F., Riani, M.: A time delay neural network for estimation of gas concentrations in a mixture, Sensors and Actuators B, 65 (2000) 267–269
7. Caliskan, E., Temurtas, F., Yumusak, N.: Gas Concentration Estimation using Fuzzy Inference Systems, SAU FBE Dergisi, Vol. 8 (1) (2004)
8. Mamdani, E.H., and Assilian, S.: An experiment in linguistic synthesis with a fuzzy logic controller, International Journal of Man-Machine Studies, 7 (1), (1975) 1-13
9. Hagan, M. T., Demuth, H. B., Beale, M. H.: Neural Network Design, Boston, MA: PWS Publishing, (1996)
10. Riedmiller, M.: Advanced supervised learning in multilayer perceptrons from backpropagation to adaptive learning algorithms, Int. J. of Computer Standards and Interfaces, Special Issue on Neural Networks, 5 (1994)
11. Riedmiller, M, and Braun, H.: A Direct Adaptive Method for Faster backpropagation learning: The RPROP Algorithm, Proceedings of the IEEE Int. Conf. On Neural Networks, San Francisco, CA, March 28, 1993.
12. Sagiroglu, S., Besdok, E., Erler, M.: Control Chart Pattern Recognition Using Artificial Neural Networks, Turk J Elec Engin, 8(2) (2000).
13. Avci, M., Yildirim, T.: Generation of Tangent Hyperbolic Sigmoid Function For Microcontroller Based Digital Implementations Of Neural Networks, TAINN 2003, Canakkale, Turkey (2003)

Automatic Design of Hierarchical TS-FS Model Using Ant Programming and PSO Algorithm

Yuehui Chen, Jiwen Dong, and Bo Yang

School of Information Science and Engineering, Jinan University,
Jinan 250022,P.R.China
{yhchen,csmaster , yangbo}@ujn.edu.cn

Abstract. This paper presents an approach for designing of hierarchical Takagi-Sugeno fuzzy system (TS-FS) automatically. The hierarchical structure is evolved using Ant Programming (AP) with specific instructions. The fine tuning of the rule's parameters encoded in the structure is accomplished using Particle Swarm Optimization (PSO) algorithm. The proposed method interleaves both optimizations. Starting with random structures and rules' parameters, it first tries to improve the hierarchical structure and then as soon as an improved structure is found, it fine tunes its rules' parameters. It then goes back to improving the structure again and, provided it finds a better structure, it again fine tunes the rules' parameters. This loop continues until a satisfactory solution (hierarchical Takagi-Sugeno fuzzy model) is found or a time limit is reached. The performance and effectiveness of the proposed method are evaluated using time series prediction problem and compared with the related methods.

1   Introduction

Fuzzy logic system [1] has been successfully applied to a number of scientific and engineering problems in recent years. The problems in designing of fuzzy logic system include: (1) how to automatically partition the input-output space for each input-output variable; (2) how many fuzzy rules are really needed for properly approximating an unknown nonlinear systems; (3) how to determine the fuzzy rule base automatically. As it is well known the curse-of-dimensionality is an unsolved problem in the fields of fuzzy and neurofuzzy systems.

   The problems mentioned above can be partially solved by the recent developments of hierarchical fuzzy systems. As a way to overcome the curse-of dimensionality, it was suggested in [2] that to arrange several low-dimensional rule base in a hierarchical structure, i.e. a tree, causing the number of possible rules to grow in a linear way with a number of inputs. But no method was given on how the rules base could be determined automatically. In [3] the author described a new algorithm which derives the rules for hierarchical fuzzy associative memories that were structured as a binary tree. In [4-6], a specific hierarchical fuzzy system is proposed and its universal approximation property was proved. But the main problems in fact lies that this is a specific hierarchical fuzzy systems which lack of flexibility in the structure adaptation,

C. Bussler and D. Fensel (Eds.): AIMSA 2004, LNAI 3192, pp. 285–294, 2004.
© Springer-Verlag Berlin Heidelberg 2004

and it is difficult to arrange the input variables for each sub-model. In [7] a genetic algorithm-based approach was proposed to optimize the hierarchical structure and the parameters of 5-inputs hierarchical fuzzy controller for the low-speed control problem. Based on the analysis of importance of each input variable and the coupling between any two input variables, the problem of how to distribute the input variables to different (levels of) relational modules for incremental and aggregated hierarchical fuzzy relational systems was addressed [8].

This paper presents an approach to design hierarchical TS-FS model. The hierarchical structure is evolved using AP [9] with specific instructions. The fine tuning of the rule's parameters encoded in the structure is accomplished using PSO algorithm. The proposed method interleaves both optimizations. Starting with random structures and rules' parameters, it first tries to improve the hierarchical structure and then as soon as an improved structure is found, it fine tunes its rules' parameters. It then goes back to improving the structure again and, provided it finds a better structure, it again fine tunes the rules' parameters. This loop continues until a satisfactory solution (hierarchical TS-FS model) is found or a time limit is reached.

The paper is organized as follows: Section 2 introduces a simple TS-FS model. The new encoding method and evaluation of the hierarchical TS-FS are presented in Section 3. A hybrid learning algorithm for evolving the hierarchical TS-FS model is given in Section 4. Section 5 presents some simulation results for the time series forecasting problem. Finally in section 6 and 7 we present some concluding remarks.

2   Takagi-Sugeno Fuzzy Systems (TS-FS)

Fuzzy inference systems are composed of a set of if-then rules. A Sugeno-Takagi fuzzy model has the following form of fuzzy rules [1]:

$$R_j : If \ x_1 \ is \ A_{1j} \ and \ x_2 \ is \ A_{2j} \ and \cdots and \ x_n \ is \ A_{nj}$$

$$Then \ y = g_j(x_1, x_2, \cdots, x_n), \ (j = 1, 2, \cdots, N)$$

$$g_j(x_1, x_2, \cdots, x_n) = \omega_0 + \omega_1 x_1 + +\omega_2 x_2 + \cdots + +\omega_n x_n$$

where $g_j(.)$ is a crisp function of x_i. The overall output of the fuzzy model can be obtained by:

$$y = \frac{\sum_{j=1}^{N} g_j(\cdot) T_{i=1}^{m_j} \mu_{ij}(x_i)}{\sum_{j=1}^{N} T_{i=1}^{m_j} \mu_{ij}(x_i)} \tag{1}$$

where $1 \leq m_j \leq n$ the number of input variables that appear in the rule premise, N is the number of fuzzy rules, n is the number of inputs, $\mu_{ij}(x_i)$ is the membership function for fuzzy set A_{ij} and T is a t-norm for fuzzy conjunction.

A number of researches have been devoted to identify the TS-FS model. The parameters to be determined are the division of input space, the shapes of membership functions in the antecedent parts and the linear weights in the consequent parts.

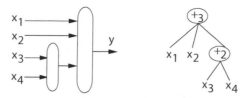

Fig. 1. Left: an example of possible hierarchical TS-FS model with 4 inputs and 3 hierarchical layers, Right: the tree structural representation of the corresponding hierarchical TS-FS model, where the used instruction set is $I = \{+_2, +_3,\ x_1, x_2, x_3, x_4\}$.

3 Hierarchical TS-FS: Encoding and Evaluation

A hierarchical fuzzy logic system not only provide a more complex and flexible architecture for modeling nonlinear systems, but can also reduce the size of rule base to some extend. But there is no systematic method for designing of the hierarchical TS-FS model yet. The problems in designing of hierarchical fuzzy logic system include:

- Selecting a proper hierarchical structure;
- Selecting the inputs for each TS fuzzy sub-model;
- Determining the rule base for each TS fuzzy sub-model;
- Optimizing the parameters in the antecedent parts and the linear weights in the consequent parts of the TS fuzzy sub-model.

In this sense, finding a proper hierarchical TS-FS model can be posed as a search problem in the structure and parameter space. Fig.1 (left) shows an example of possible hierarchical TS-FS models with 4 input variables and 3 hierarchical layers.

3.1 Encoding

A tree-structural based encoding method with specific instruction set is selected for representing a hierarchical TS-FS in this research. The reasons for choosing this representation are that (1)the trees have a natural and typical hierarchical layer; (2)with pre-defined instruction sets, the tree can be created and evolved using the existing tree-structure-based approaches, i.e., AP, Genetic Programming (GP) and PIPE algorithms [13].

Assume that the used instruction set is $I=\{+_2, +_3,\ x_1, x_2, x_3, x_4\}$, where $+_2$ and $+_3$ denote non-leaf nodes' instructions and taking 2 and 3 arguments, respectively. x_1, x_2, x_3, x_4 are leaf nodes' instructions and taking zero argument each. In addition, the output of each non-leaf node is calculated as a single T-S fuzzy sub-model (Section 2). For this reason the non-leaf node $+_2$ is also called a 2-inputs T-S fuzzy instruction/operator. Fig.1 (right) shows tree structural representation of the hierarchical TS-FS model shown in Fig.1 (left).

It should be noted that in order to calculate the output of each TS-FS sub-model (non-leaf node), parameters in the antecedent parts and consequent parts of the TS-FS sub-model should be encoded into the tree.

3.2 Calculation of the Hierarchical TS-FS Tree

The output of a hierarchical TS-FS tree can be calculated in a recursive way. For simplicity, the calculation process of the tree (Fig.1 (right)) is given for displaying the
method.

Assume that each input variable is divided into two fuzzy sets and the used fuzzy
membership function is

$$\mu(a,b;x) = \exp(-\frac{x-a}{b})^2 \tag{2}$$

Firstly we calculate the output of the T-S fuzzy sub-model (node $+_2$). Assume that
the used fuzzy sets for variables x_3, x_4 are A_{11}, A_{12}, A_{21}, and A_{22}, respectively. Therefore, the corresponding fuzzy rules of node $+_2$ can be formed as follows [12]:

$$R1: if\ x_3\ is\ A_{11}\ \ and\ \ x_4\ is\ A_{21}\ then\ y_1 = k_1(a_0 + a_1x_3 + a_2x_4)$$
$$R2: if\ x_3\ is\ A_{11}\ \ and\ \ x_4\ is\ A_{22}\ then\ y_2 = k_2(a_0 + a_1x_3 + a_2x_4)$$
$$R3: if\ x_3\ is\ A_{12}\ \ and\ \ x_4\ is\ A_{21}\ then\ y_3 = k_3(a_0 + a_1x_3 + a_2x_4)$$
$$R4: if\ x_3\ is\ A_{12}\ \ and\ \ x_4\ is\ A_{22}\ then\ y_4 = k_4(a_0 + a_1x_3 + a_2x_4)$$

The output of node $+_2$ can be calculated based on the T-S fuzzy model:

$$y = \frac{\sum_{i=1}^4 \sigma_i y_i}{\sum_{i=1}^4 \sigma_i} \tag{3}$$

where

$$\sigma_1 = \mu_{A_{11}}(x_3)\mu_{A_{21}}(x_4), \quad \sigma_2 = \mu_{A_{11}}(x_3)\mu_{A_{22}}(x_4),$$
$$\sigma_3 = \mu_{A_{12}}(x_3)\mu_{A_{21}}(x_4), \quad \sigma_4 = \mu_{A_{12}}(x_3)\mu_{A_{22}}(x_4).$$

Secondly, we calculate the overall output of the hierarchical T-S fuzzy model. It has
three inputs, x_1, x_2 and y, the output of the T-S fuzzy sub-model (node $+_2$). Assume
that, the used fuzzy sets for variables x_1, x_2 and y are: B_{11}, B_{12}, B_{21}, B_{22}, B_{31} and B_{32},
respectively. The overall output of tree in Fig.1 (right) can be calculated based on the
following fuzzy rules:

$$R1: if\ x_1\ is\ B_{11}, x_2\ is\ B_{21}, y\ is\ B_{31}\ then\ z_1 = c_1(d_0 + d_1x_1 + d_2x_2 + d_3y)$$
$$R2: if\ x_1\ is\ B_{11}, x_2\ is\ B_{21}, y\ is\ B_{32}\ then\ z_2 = c_2(d_0 + d_1x_1 + d_2x_2 + d_3y)$$
$$R3: if\ x_1\ is\ B_{11}, x_2\ is\ B_{22}, y\ is\ B_{31}\ then\ z_3 = c_3(d_0 + d_1x_1 + d_2x_2 + d_3y)$$
$$R4: if\ x_1\ is\ B_{11}, x_2\ is\ B_{21}, y\ is\ B_{32}\ then\ z_4 = c_4(d_0 + d_1x_1 + d_2x_2 + d_3y)$$
$$R5: if\ x_1\ is\ B_{12}, x_2\ is\ B_{21}, y\ is\ B_{31}\ then\ z_5 = c_5(d_0 + d_1x_1 + d_2x_2 + d_3y)$$
$$R6: if\ x_1\ is\ B_{12}, x_2\ is\ B_{21}, y\ is\ B_{32}\ then\ z_6 = c_6(d_0 + d_1x_1 + d_2x_2 + d_3y)$$
$$R7: if\ x_1\ is\ B_{12}, x_2\ is\ B_{22}, y\ is\ B_{31}\ then\ z_7 = c_7(d_0 + d_1x_1 + d_2x_2 + d_3y)$$
$$R8: if\ x_1\ is\ B_{12}, x_2\ is\ B_{22}, y\ is\ B_{32}\ then\ z_8 = c_8(d_0 + d_1x_1 + d_2x_2 + d_3y)$$

The overall output of the tree is

$$z = \frac{\sum_{j=1}^{8} \mu_j z_j}{\sum_{j=1}^{8} \mu_j}$$
(4)

where

$$\mu_1 = \mu_{B_{11}}(x_1)\mu_{B_{21}}(x_2)\mu_{B_{31}}(y), \; \mu_2 = \mu_{B_{11}}(x_1)\mu_{B_{21}}(x_2)\mu_{B_{32}}(y)$$
$$\mu_3 = \mu_{B_{11}}(x_1)\mu_{B_{22}}(x_2)\mu_{B_{31}}(y), \; \mu_4 = \mu_{B_{11}}(x_1)\mu_{B_{22}}(x_2)\mu_{B_{32}}(y)$$
$$\mu_5 = \mu_{B_{12}}(x_1)\mu_{B_{21}}(x_2)\mu_{B_{31}}(y), \; \mu_6 = \mu_{B_{12}}(x_1)\mu_{B_{21}}(x_2)\mu_{B_{32}}(y)$$
$$\mu_7 = \mu_{B_{12}}(x_1)\mu_{B_{22}}(x_2)\mu_{B_{31}}(y), \; \mu_8 = \mu_{B_{12}}(x_1)\mu_{B_{22}}(x_2)\mu_{B_{32}}(y)$$

Where all the parameters k_i (i=1, 2, 3, 4), a_0, a_1, a_2, and the shape parameters used in fuzzy sets A_{11}, A_{12}, A_{21}, and A_{22}, are encoded in the node $+_2$. The parameter c_j (j=1, 2, ..., 8) , d_0, d_1, d_2, d_3 and the shape parameters used in fuzzy sets B_{11}, B_{12}, B_{21}, B_{22}, B_{31} and B_{32} are attached to the node $+_3$ of the tree. All these parameters are randomly generated alone with the creation of the tree at initial step, and will be optimized by the PSO algorithm.

3.3 Objective Function

In this work, the fitness function used for AP and PSO is given by Root Mean Square Error (RMSE):

$$Fit(i) = \sqrt{\frac{1}{P}\sum_{j=1}^{P}(y_1^j - y_2^j)^2}$$
(5)

where P is the total number of training samples, y_1^j and y_2^j are the actual and model outputs of j-th sample. $Fit(i)$ denotes the fitness value of i-th individual.

4   An Approach for Evolving the Hierarchical TS-FS

4.1 Ant Programming for Evolving the Architecture of the Hierarchical TS-FS

Ant programming is a new method which applies the principle of the ant systems to automated program synthesis [9]. In the AP algorithm, each ant will build and modify the trees according to the quantity of pheromone at each node. The pheromone table appears as a tree. Each node owns a table in which it memorizes the rate of pheromone to various possible instructions (Fig.2).

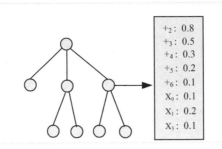

$+_2$:	0.8
$+_3$:	0.5
$+_4$:	0.3
$+_5$:	0.2
$+_6$:	0.1
X_0:	0.1
X_1:	0.2
X_3:	0.1

Fig. 2. Pheromone tree, in each node a pheromone table holds the quantity of pheromone associated with all possible instructions.

First, a population of programs is generated randomly. The table of pheromone at each node is initialized at 0.5. This means that the probability of choosing each terminal and function is equal initially. The higher the rate of pheromone is, the higher the probability to be chosen. Each program (individual) is then evaluated using a predefined objective function. The table of pheromone is update by two mechanisms:

(1) Evaporation decreases the rate of pheromone table for every instruction on every node according to following formula:

$$P_g = (1-\alpha)P_{g-1} \tag{6}$$

where P_g denotes the pheromone value at the generation g, α is a constant ($\alpha = 0.15$).

(2) For each tree, the components of the tree will be reinforced according to the fitness of the tree. The formula is:

$$P_{i,s_i} = P_{i,s_i} + \frac{\alpha}{Fit(s)} \tag{7}$$

where s is a solution (tree), $Fit(s)$ its fitness, s_i the function or the terminal set at node i in this individual, α is a constant $\alpha = 0.1$, P_{i,s_i} is the value of the pheromone for the instruction s_i in the node i.

A brief description of AP algorithm for structure optimization of the hierarchical TS-FS is as follows:

1) Set the elitist tree as NULL and its fitness value as a biggest positive real number of the computer at hand. Every component of the pheromone tree is set to an average value;

2) Random generation of ants (trees) based on the pheromone tree and corresponding parameters encoded in the hierarchical TS-FS;

3) Evaluation of ants using Eqn. (5);

4) Update of the pheromone table according to Eqn. (6) and Eqn. (7);

5) Go to step 1) unless a better tree is found. The criterion concerning with the better tree found is distinguished as follows: if the fitness value of the best tree is smaller than the fitness value of the elitist tree, or the fitness values of two trees are equal but the nodes of the former is lower than the later, then we say that the better tree is found. The best and elitist trees are the best tree of the current generation and the one found so far, respectively.

4.2 Parameter Optimization with PSO

For the parameters optimization of the hierarchical TS-FS, a number of global and local search algorithms, i.e., GA, EP, gradient based learning method can be employed. The basic PSO algorithm is selected for parameter optimization due to its fast convergence and ease to implementation.

The PSO [10] conducts searches using a population of particles which correspond to individuals in evolutionary algorithm (EA). A population of particles is randomly generated initially. Each particle represents a potential solution and has a position represented by a position vector x_i. A swarm of particles moves through the problem space, with the moving velocity of each particle represented by a velocity vector v_i. At each time step, a function $Fit(i)$ (Eqn. (5) in this study) representing a quality measure is calculated by using x_i as input. Each particle keeps track of its own best position, which is associated with the best fitness it has achieved so far in a vector P_i. Furthermore, the best position among all the particles obtained so far in the population is kept track of as P_g. In addition to this global version, another version of PSO keeps track of the best position among all the topological neighbors of a particle.

At each time step t, by using the individual best position, $P_i(t)$, and the global best position, $P_g(t)$, a new velocity for particle i is updated by

$$v_i(t+1) = v_i(t) + c_1\varphi_1(P_i(t) - x_i(t)) + c_2\varphi_2(P_g(t) - x_i(t)) \tag{8}$$

where c_1 and c_2 are positive constant and φ_1 and φ_2 are uniformly distributed random number in [0,1]. The term v_i is limited to the range of $\pm v_{max}$. If the velocity violates this limit, it is set to its proper limit. Changing velocity this way enables the particle i to search around its individual best position, P_i, and global best position, P_g. Based on the updated velocities, each particle changes its position according to the following equation:

$$x_i(t+1) = x_i(t) + v_i(t+1). \tag{9}$$

4.3 The Proposed Learning Algorithm

The general learning procedure for the optimal design of the hierarchical TS-FS model can be described as follows.

1) Create the initial population randomly (hierarchical TS-FS and their corresponding parameters);
2) Structure optimization by AP algorithm.
3) If the better structure is found, then go to step 4), otherwise go to step 2);
4) Parameter optimization by PSO algorithm. In this stage, the tree structure is fixed, and it is the best tree taken from the end of run of the structure search. All of the parameters encoded in the best tree formulated a parameter vector to be optimized by PSO;
5) If the maximum number of PSO search is reached, or no better parameter vector is found for a significantly long time (say 100 steps for maximum 2000 steps) then go to step 6); otherwise go to step 4);
6) If satisfied solution is found, then stop; otherwise go to step 2).

5   Experiments

The proposed approach has been evaluated in the Mackey-Glass chaotic time-series prediction problem. The chaotic Mackey-Glass differential delay equation is recognized as a benchmark problem that has been used and reported by a number of researchers for comparing the learning and generalization ability of different models. The Mackey-Glass chaotic time series is generated from the following equation:

$$\frac{dx(t)}{dt} = \frac{ax(t-\tau)}{1+x^{10}(t-\tau)} - bx(t) \tag{10}$$

where $a=0.2$ and $b=0.1$, $\tau > 17$ the equation shows chaotic behavior. In our simulations, $\tau = 30$ has been adopted. To make the comparison with earlier work fair [8], we predict the $x(t+6)$ using the input variables $x(t-30)$, $x(t-24)$, $x(t-18)$, $x(t-12)$, $x(t-6)$ and $x(t)$, where $t=130$ to $t=1329$. It corresponds to a 6-inputs, 1-output mapping.

Table 1. The importance degree of each input variables for Mackey-Glass time-series

x_i	x_0	x_1	x_2	x_3	x_4	x_5
$Impo(x_i)$	0.247	0.332	0.072	0.113	0.056	0.180

1000 sample points used in our study. The first 500 data pairs of the series were used as training data, while the remaining 500 were used to validate the model identified. The used instruction set is $I = \{+_2, +_3, \ldots, +_6, x_0, x_1, x_2, x_3, x_4, x_5\}$, where x_0, x_1, x_2, x_3, x_4, x_5 denote $x(t-30)$, $x(t-24)$, $x(t-18)$, $x(t-12)$, $x(t-6)$ and $x(t)$, respectively.

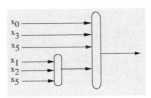

Fig. 3. The structure of the evolved hierarchical TS-FS model for predicting of Mackey-Glass time-series with RMSE 0.0167

The results are obtained from training of hierarchical TS-FS with 20 different experiments. The average *RMSE* value for training and test data sets are 0.0179 and 0.0167, respectively. The structure of the evolved hierarchical TS-FS model was shown in Fig.3. Based on [8], the importance degree of each input variables is evaluated and listed in Table 1. It can be seen that the most important variables are arranged into the first layer of the hierarchical TS-FS models by AP algorithm automatically.

A comparison has been made to show the actual time-series, the hierarchical TS-FS model output and the prediction error (Fig.4). A comparison result of different methods for forecasting Mackey-Glass data is shown in Table 2.

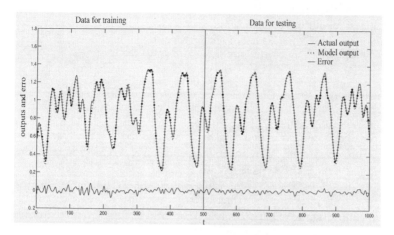

Fig. 4. Actual time-series, model output and prediction error for training and test data sets.

Table 2. Comparison of the incremental type multilevel FRS (IFRS) [8], the aggregated type multilevel FRS (AFRS) [8], and the hierarchical TS-FS in Mackey-Glass time-series prediction

Model	Hierar. layer	No. of rules	No. of para.	RMSE(train)	RMSE(test)
IFRS	4	25	58	0.0240	0.0253
AFRS	5	36	78	0.0267	0.0256
H-TS-FS	3	24	33	0.0179	0.0167

6 Discussion

One major advantage of using a hierarchical TS-FS or a multilevel fuzzy system other than a single-level one is that the number of fuzzy rules and fuzzy operations involved in modeling process can be reduced significantly as compared with those required by the single-level counterparts. Due to the limitations to solve the hierarchical TS-FS analytically, we choose to identify the hierarchical TS-FS via an evolutionary optimization approach.

Firstly, the hierarchical structure and the rules' parameters can be flexibly encoded into a TS-FS tree. And then, the AP and the PSO algorithms are employed to evolve the hierarchical structure and parameters alternatively. In the methods of IFRS and AFRS [8], the hierarchical structure and input selection are assigned based on: (1) analysis of the importance of each input variables; (2) analysis of the coupling between input variables. In contrast to the IFRS and AFRS, the hierarchical structure and input selection in this research are accomplished using an evolutionary procedure automatically.

The effectiveness of the proposed methods has been demonstrated in time-series prediction problem. Compared to the IFRS and AFRS the generated hierarchical TS-FS model has some advantages in terms of the approximation accuracy, the number of rules and the number of free parameters.

This paper provides a method, alternatively searches between the tree structure space and parameter space by using the AP and PSO algorithms. But other tree-structure based evolutionary algorithms, i.e., Genetic Programming, Probabilistic Incremental Program Evolution and parameter learning algorithms, i.e., Genetic Algorithm, Evolutionary Strategy, can also be used to solve the problem.

7 Conclusions

Based on a novel representation and calculation of the hierarchical TS-FS models, an approach for evolving the hierarchical TS-FS is proposed in this paper. The hierarchical architecture and inputs selection of the hierarchical TS-FS were accomplished using AP algorithm, and the rules' parameters embedded in the hierarchical TS-FS model are optimized using a PSO algorithm. Simulation result shown that the evolved hierarchical TS-FS models were effective for predicting of chaotic time-series. The simulation is constructed under the assumption of that the hierarchical layer is three and each input variable is divided into two fuzzy sets. It is direct to generalize the proposed method to the complex cases. The preliminary results are encouraging. Our future works will concentrate on improving the convergence speed of the proposed method and apply it to the complex control problems.

References

1. Takagi, T. and Sugeno, M.: Fuzzy identification of systems and its application to modeling and control. IEEE Trans. Syst. Man, Cybern., 15, (1985) 116-132
2. Brown, M., Bossley K.M., Mills D.J. and Harris C.J.: High dimensional neurofuzzy systems: overcoming the curse of dimensionality. Proc. 4th Int. Conf. on Fuzzy Systems. (1995) 2139-2146
3. Rainer, H.: Rule generation for hierarchical fuzzy systems. Proc. of the annual conf. of the North America Fuzzy Information Processing. (1997) 444-449
4. Wang, L.-X.: Analysis and design of hierarchical fuzzy systems. IEEE Trans. Fuzzy Systems, 7, (1999) 617-624
5. Wang, L.-X. : Universal approximation by hierarchical fuzzy systems. Fuzzy Sets and Systems, 93, (1998) 223-230
6. Wei, C. and Wang, L.-X. : A note on universal approximation by hierarchical fuzzy systems. Information Science, 123, (2000) 241-248
7. Lin, L. C. and Lee, G.-Y. : Hierarchical fuzzy control for C-axis of CNC tuning centers using genetic algorithms. Journal of Intelligent and Robotic Systems, 25, (1999) 255-275
8. Duan, J.-C. and Chung, F.-L. : Multilevel fuzzy relational systems: structure and identification. Soft Computing 6 (2002) 71-86
9. Birattari, M., Di Caro, G., and Dorigo M.: Toward the formal foundation of Ant Programming. In Third International workshop, ANTS2002. LNCS 2463, 2002 188-201
10. Kennedy, J. et al.,: Particle Swarm Optimization. Proc. of IEEE International Conference on Neural Networks. IV (1995) 1942-1948
11. Kasabov, K. et al.,: FuNN/2 - A fuzzy neural network architecture for adaptive learning and knowledge acquisition. Information Science 101 (1997) 155-175
12. Ying, H.: Theory and application of a novel fuzzy PID controller using a simplified Takagi-Sugeno rule scheme. Information Science, 123 (2000) 281-293
13. Chen, Y. et al.,: Nonlinear System Modeling via Optimal Design of Neural Trees, International Journal of Neural Systems, 14 (2004) 125-137

Forecasting Stock Price by SVMs Regression

Yukun Bao[1], Yansheng Lu[2], and Jinlong Zhang[3]

[1]Department of Management Scince & information System, School of Management,
Huazhong University of Science and Technology, Wuhan 430074, China

[2] College of Computer Science, Huazhong University of Science and Technology, Wuhan
430074, China

[3]Department of Management Scince & information System, School of Management,
Huazhong University of Science and Technology, Wuhan 430074, China

Abstract. Forecasting stock price is one of the fascinating issues of stock
market research. Accurately forecasting stock price, which forms the basis
for the decision making of financial investment, is probably the biggest
challenge for capital investment industry, which leads it a widely
researched area. Time series forecasting and neural network are once
commonly used for prediction on stock price. This paper deals with the
application of a novel neural network technique, support vector machines
(SVMs) regression, in forecasting stock price. The objective of this paper is to
examine the feasibility of SVMs regression in forecasting stock price. A data
set from shanghai stock market in China is used for the experiment to test the
validity of SVMs regression. The experiment shows SVMs regression a
valuable method in forecasting the stock price.

Keywords: Stock price forecasts; SVMs regression; Machine learning

1 Introduction

Stock price forecasts are valuable for investors, which tell out the investment
opportunities. Toward the fascinating goal, research efforts have been made to find
superior forecasting methods. Financial time series forecasting is regarded as one of
the most challenging applications of modern time series forecasting. But numerous
studies have found that univariate time series, such as Box-Jenkins ARIMA models
are as accurate as more expensive linear regression or vector autoregressive models
[1,2,3]. The success of linear models, however, is conditional upon the underlying
data generating process being linear and not being random. One view in financial
economics is that market prices are random and that past prices cannot be used as a
guide for the price behavior in the future. Chaos theory, however, suggests that a
seemingly random process may in fact have been generated by a deterministic
function that is not random [4,5]. In such a case, ARIMA methods are no longer a

C. Bussler and D. Fensel (Eds.): AIMSA 2004, LNAI 3192, pp. 295–303, 2004.
© Springer-Verlag Berlin Heidelberg 2004

useful tool for estimation and forecasting. Research efforts turn to new methods. One of them is the study of neural networks.

Neural networks have been successfully used for modeling financial time series [6,7]. Especially, several researchers report modest, positive results with the prediction of market prices using neural networks [8,9,10], but not by using price and volume histories alone, and no one uses technical analysis pattern heuristics. Neural networks are universal function approximations that can map any non-linear function without a priori assumptions about the properties of the data [11]. Unlike traditional statistical models, neural networks are data-driven, non-parametric weak models, and they let "the data speak for themselves".Consequently, neural networks are less susceptible to the problem of model misspecification as compared to most of the parametric models. Neural networks are also more noise tolerant, having the ability to learn complex systems with incomplete and corrupted data. In addition, they are more flexible, having the capability to learn dynamic systems through a retraining process using new data patterns. So neural networks are more powerful in describing the dynamics of financial time series in comparison to traditional statistical models [12,13,14,15].

Recently, a novel neural network algorithm, called support vector machines (SVMs), was developed by Vapnik and his co-workers [16]. Unlike most of the traditional neural network models that implement the empirical risk minimization principle, SVMs implement the structural risk minimization principle which seeks to minimize an upper bound of the generalization error rather than minimize the training error. This induction principle is based on the fact that the generalization error is bounded by the sum of the training error and a confidence interval term that depends on the Vapnik–Chervonenkis (VC) dimension. Based on this principle, SVMs achieve an optimum network structure by striking a right balance between the empirical error and the VC-confidence interval. This eventually results in better generalization performance than other neural network models. Another merit of SVMs is that the training of SVMs is equivalent to solving a linearly constrained quadratic programming. This means that the solution of SVMs is unique, optimal and absent from local minima, unlike other networks' training which requires non-linear optimization thus running the danger of getting stuck in a local minima. Originally, SVMs have been developed for pattern recognition problems [17]. However, with the introduction of Vapnik's ε-insensitive loss function, SVMs have been extended to solve non-linear regression estimation problems and they have been shown to exhibit excellent performance [18,19].

This paper consists of five sections. Section 2 presents the principles of SVMs regression and the general procedures of applying it. By raising an example from stock market in China, the detailed procedures involving data set selection, data preprocessing and scaling, kernel function selection and so on are presented in Section 3. Section 4 discusses the experimental results followed by the conclusions drawn from this study and further research hints in the last section.

2 SVMs Regression Theory

Given a set of data points $G = \{(x_i, d_i)\}_i^n$ (x_i is the input vector, d_i is the desired value and n is the total number of data patterns), SVMs approximate the function using the following:

$$y = f(x) = w\phi(x) + b \tag{1}$$

where $\phi(x)$ is the high dimensional feature space which is non-linearly mapped from the input space x. The coefficients w and b are estimated by minimizing

$$R_{SVMs}(C) = C\frac{1}{n}\sum_{i=1}^{n} L_\varepsilon(d_i, y_i) + \frac{1}{2}\|w\|^2, \tag{2}$$

$$L_\varepsilon(d, y) = \begin{cases} |d - y| - \varepsilon & |d - y| \geq \varepsilon \\ 0 & \text{otherwise} \end{cases} \tag{3}$$

In the regularized risk function given by Eq. (2), the first term $C(\frac{1}{n})\sum_{i=1}^{n} L_\varepsilon(d_i, y_i)$ is the empirical error (risk). They are measured by the ε-insensitive loss function given by Eq. (3). This loss function provides the advantage of enabling one to use sparse data points to represent the decision function given by Eq. (1). The second term $\frac{1}{2}\|w\|^2$, on the other hand, is the regularization term. C is referred to as the regularized constant and it determines the trade-off between the empirical risk and the regularization term. Increasing the value of C will result in the relative importance of the empirical risk with respect to the regularization term to grow. ε is called the tube size and it is equivalent to the approximation accuracy placed on the training data points. Both C and ε are user-prescribed parameters.

To obtain the estimations of w and b, Eq. (2) is transformed to the primal function given by Eq. (4) by introducing the positive slack variables ξ_i and ξ_i^* as follows:

Minimize $R_{SVMs}(w, \xi^{(*)}) = C\sum_{i=1}^{n}(\xi_i + \xi_i^*) + \frac{1}{2}\|w\|^2$

Subjected to $\begin{array}{l} d_i - w\phi(x_i) - b_i \leq \varepsilon + \xi_i, \\ w\phi(x_i) + b_i - d_i \leq \varepsilon + \xi_i^*, \xi^{(*)} \geq 0 \end{array}$ (4)

Finally, by introducing Lagrange multipliers and exploiting the optimality constraints, the decision function given by Eq. (1) has the following explicit form [18]:

$$f(x, a_i, a_i^*) = \sum_{i=1}^{n}(a_i - a_i^*)K(x, x_i) + b \tag{5}$$

In Eq. (5), a_i and a_i^* are the so-called Lagrange multipliers. They satisfy the equalities $a_i * a_i^* = 0$, $a_i \geq 0$ and $a_i^* \geq 0$ where $i = 1, 2, ..., n$ and are obtained by maximizing the dual function of Eq. (4) which has the following form:

$$R(a_i,a_i^*) = \sum_{i=1}^{n} d_i(a_i - a_i^*) - \varepsilon \sum_{i=1}^{n}(a_i + a_i^*)$$

$$-\frac{1}{2}\sum_{i=1}^{n}\sum_{j=1}^{n}(a_i - a_i^*)(a_j - a_j^*)K(x_i,x_j)$$

(6)

with the constraints

$$\sum_{i=1}^{n}(a_i - a_i^*),$$

$$0 \leq a_i \leq C, \qquad i = 1,2...,n,$$

$$0 \leq a_i^* \leq C, \qquad i = 1,2...,n.$$

Based on the Karush–Kuhn–Tucker (KKT) conditions of quadratic programming, only a certain number of coefficients $(a_i - a_i^*)$ in Eq. (5) will assume non-zero values. The data points associated with them have approximation errors equal to or larger than ε and are referred to as support vectors. These are the data points lying on or outside the ε-bound of the decision function. According to Eq. (5), it is evident that support vectors are the only elements of the data points that are used in determining the decision function as the coefficients $(a_i - a_i^*)$ of other data points are all equal to zero. Generally, the larger the ε, the fewer the number of support vectors and thus the sparser the representation of the solution. However, a larger ε can also depreciate the approximation accuracy placed on the training points. In this sense, ε is a trade-off between the sparseness of the representation and closeness to the data.

$K(x_i,x_j)$ is defined as the kernel function. The value of the kernel is equal to the inner product of two vectors X_i and X_j in the feature space $\phi(x_i)$ and $\phi(x_j)$, that is, $K(x_i,x_j) = \phi(x_i) * \phi(x_j)$. The elegance of using the kernel function is that one can deal with feature spaces of arbitrary dimensionality without having to compute the map $\phi(x)$ explicitly. Any function satisfying Mercer's condition [16] can be used as the kernel function. The typical examples of kernel function are as follows:

Linear: $K(x_i,x_j) = x_i^T x_j$.

Polynomial: $K(x_i,x_j) = (\gamma x_i^T x_j + r)^d, \gamma > 0.$

Radial basis function (RBF):

$K(x_i,x_j) = \exp(-\gamma \|x_i - x_j\|^2), \gamma > 0.$

Sigmoid: $K(x_i,x_j) = \tanh(\gamma x_i^T x_j + r)$.

Here, γ, r and d are kernel parameters. The kernel parameter should be carefully chosen as it implicitly defines the structure of the high dimensional feature space $\phi(x)$ and thus controls the complexity of the final solution.

From the implementation point of view, training SVMs is equivalent to solving a linearly constrained quadratic programming (QP) with the number of variables twice as that of the training data points.

Generally speaking, SVMs regression for forecasting follows the procedures:
1.Transform data to the format of an SVM and conduct simple scaling on the data;
2.Choose the kernel functions;
3.Use cross-validation to find the best parameter C and γ;
4. Use the best parameter C and γ to train the whole training set;
5.Test.

3 Forecasting Stock Price

3.1 Data Sets

We select daily closing prices of Haier (a famous corporation in China) of shanghai stock exchange between April.15, 2003 and Nov. 25, 2003. Haier is a famous electrical appliance manufacturer in China and electrical appliance market in China is in stable situation. This is to say, there is no great fluctuation in market volume, market competition is fair and market profit rate is at a reasonable level. During that time, the stock market in China is calm and no special political events affected the stock except the SARS. But it didn't affect the electrical appliance market. So we choose it as the sample of our experiment. There are totally 140 data points from   . We used 100 data points in front of the data series as training data sets and the rest 40 data points as testing data.

3.2 Data Preprocessing and Scaling

In order to enhance the forecasting ability of model, we transform the original closing prices into relative difference in percentage of price (RDP)[20]. As mentioned by Thomason [20], there are four advantages in applying this transformation. The most prominent advantage is that the distribution of the transformed data will become more symmetrical and will follow more closely a normal distribution. This modification to the data distribution will improve the predictive power of the neural network.
The input variables are determined from four lagged RDP values based on 5-day periods (RDP-5, RDP-10, RDP-15 and RDP-20) and one transformed closing price (EMA15) which is obtained by subtracting a 15-day exponential moving average from the closing price. The optimal length of the moving day is not critical but it should be longer than the forecasting horizon of 5 days [20]. EMA15 is used to maintain as much information as contained in the original closing price as possible, since the application of the RDP transform to the original closing price may remove some useful information. The output variable RDP+5 is obtained by first smoothing the closing price with a 3-day exponential moving average because the application of a smoothing transform to the dependent variable generally enhances the prediction performance of the SVMs. The calculations for all the indicators are showed in table 1.

Table 1. Input and output variables

Indicator	Calculation
Input variables	
EMA15	$P(i) - \overline{EMA_{15}(i)}$
RDP-5	$(p(i) - p(i-5))/p(i-5)*100$
RDP-10	$(p(i) - p(i-10))/p(i-10)*100$
RDP-15	$(p(i) - p(i-15))/p(i-15)*100$
RDP-20	$(p(i) - p(i-20))/p(i-20)*100$
Output variable	
RDP+5	$(\overline{p(i+5)} - \overline{p(i)})/\overline{p(i)}*100$
	$(\overline{p(i)} = \overline{EMA_3(i)}$

3.3 Performance Criteria

The prediction performance is evaluated using the following statistical metrics, namely, the normalized mean squared error (NMSE), mean absolute error (MAE), directional symmetry (DS) and weighted directional symmetry (WDS). NMSE and MAE are the measures of the deviation between the actual and predicted values. The smaller the values of NMSE and MAE, the closer are the predicted time series values to the actual values. DS provides an indication of the correctness of the predicted direction of RDP+5 given in the form of percentages (a large value suggests a better predictor). The weighted directional symmetry measures both the magnitude of the prediction error and the direction. It penalizes the errors related to incorrectly predicted direction and rewards those associated with correctly predicted direction. The smaller the value of WDS, the better is the forecasting performance in terms of both the magnitude and direction.

3.4 Kernel Function Selection

We use general RBF as the kernel function. The RBF kernel nonlinearly maps samples into a higher dimensional space, so it, unlike the linear kernel, can handle the case when the relation between class labels and attributes is nonlinear. Furthermore, the linear kernel is a special case of RBF as (Ref. [13]) shows that the linear kernel with a penalty parameter $\tilde{C}$ has the same performance as the RBF kernel with some parameters (C, γ). In addition, the sigmoid kernel behaves like RBF for certain parameters [14].
The second reason is the number of hyper-parameters which influences the complexity of model selection. The polynomial kernel has more hyper-parameters than the RBF kernel.

Finally, the RBF kernel has less numerical difficulties. One key point is $0 < K_{ij} \leq 1$ in contrast to polynomial kernels of which kernel values may go to infinity $(\gamma x_i^T x_j + r > 1)$ or zero $(\gamma x_i^T x_j + r < 1)$ while the degree is large.

3.5 Cross-Validation and Grid-Search

There are two parameters while using RBF kernels: C and γ. It is not known beforehand which C and γ are the best for one problem; consequently some kind of model selection (parameter search) must be done. The goal is to identify good (C, γ) so that the classifier can accurately predict unknown data (i.e., testing data). Note that it may not be useful to achieve high training accuracy (i.e., classifiers accurately predict training data whose class labels are indeed known). Therefore, a common way is to separate training data to two parts of which one is considered unknown in training the classifier. Then the prediction accuracy on this set can more precisely reflect the performance on classifying unknown data. An improved version of this procedure is cross-validation.

We use a grid-search on C and γ using cross-validation. Basically pairs of (C, γ) are tried and the one with the best cross-validation accuracy is picked. We found that trying exponentially growing sequences of C and γ is a practical method to identify good parameters (for example, $C = 2^{-5}$, 2^{-3},..., 2^{15}, $\gamma = 2^{-15}$, 2^{-13},..., 2^3).

4 Results and Discuss

In Fig. 1 the horizontal axis is the trading days of the test set and the vertical axis is stock price. It could be found that actual stock price run down from above the predicted one to below it at the 2nd trading day; in the following four trading days the actual stock price goes down further; it tells that it is a timing for selling at 2nd day. Actual stock price run up from below the predicted stock price to above it at the 6th trading day; in the following two trading days actual stock price stays above the closing price of the 6th trading day; it tells that it is timing for buying at 6th day. On the following days, it could be done like this. The timing area for buying and selling derived from Fig. 1 tells the investment values.

5 Conclusion

The use of SVMs in forecasting stock price is studied in this paper. The study concluded that SVMs provide a promising alternative to the financial time series forecasting. And the strengths of SVMs regression are coming from following points: 1) usage of SRM; 2) few controlling parameters; 3) global unique solution derived from a quadratic programming.

But further research toward an extremely changing stock market should be done, which means the data fluctuation may affect the performance of this method. Another further research hint is the knowledge priority used in training the sample and determining the function parameters.

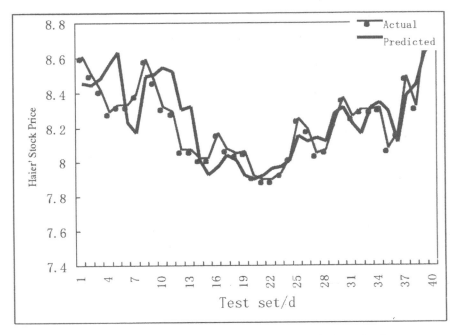

Fig. 1. Comparison between actual and predicted Haier's stock price

References

[1] D.A. Bessler and J.A. Brandt. Forecasting livestock prices with individual and composite methods. Applied Economics, 13, 513-522, 1981.
[2] K.S. harris and R.M. Leuthold. A comparison of alternative forecasting techniques for live stock prices: A case study. North Central J. Agricultural Economics, 7, 40-50, 1985.
[3] J.H. Dorfman and C.S. Mcintosh. Results of a price forecasting competition. American J. Agricultural Economics, 72, 804-808, 1990.
[4] S.C. Blank. Chaos in future markets? A nonlinear dynamic analysis. J. Futures Markets, 11, 711-728, 1991.
[5] J. Chavas and M.T. Holt. Market instability and nonlinear dynamics. American J. Agricultural Economics, 75, 113-120, 1993.
[6] Hall JW. Adaptive selection of U.S. stocks with neural nets. In: GJ Deboeck (Ed.), Trading on the edge: neural, genetic, and fuzzy systems for chaotic financial markets. New York:Wiley, 1994.
[7] Yaser SAM, Atiya AF. Introduction to financial forecasting. Applied Intelligence, 6, 205-213, 1996.

[8]   G. Grudnitski, L. Osburn, Forecasting S&P and gold futures prices: an application of neural networks, The Journal of Futures Markets, 13 (6) 631–643, 1993.

[9]   S. Kim, S. Chun, Graded forecasting using an array of bipolar predictions: application of probabilistic neural networks to a stock market index, International Journal of Forecasting 14 (3), 323–337, 1998.

[10] E. Saad, D. Prokhorov, D. Wunsch, Comparative study of stock trend prediction using time delay, recurrent and probabilistic neural networks, IEEE Transactions on Neural Networks, 9 (6), 1456-1470, 1998.

[11] Cheng W, Wanger L, Lin CH. Forecasting the 30-year US treasury bond witha system of neural networks. Journal of Computational Intelligence in Finance 1996;4:10–6.

[12] Sharda R, Patil RB. A connectionist approach to time series prediction: an empirical test. In: Trippi, RR, Turban, E, (Eds.), Neural Networks in Finance and Investing, Chicago: Probus Publishing Co., 1994, 451–64.

[13] Haykin S. Neural networks: a comprehensive foundation. Englewood CliKs, NJ: Prentice Hall, 1999.

[14] Zhang GQ, Michael YH. Neural network forecasting of the British Pound=US Dollar exchange rate. Omega 1998;26(4):495–506.

[15] Kaastra I, Milton SB. Forecasting futures trading volume using neural networks. The Journal of Futures Markets 1995;15(8):853–970.

[16] Vapnik VN. The nature of statistical learning theory. New York: Springer, 1995.

[17] Schmidt M. Identifying speaker with support vector networks. Interface '96 Proceedings, Sydney, 1996.

[18] Muller KR, Smola A, Scholkopf B. Prediction time series with support vector machines. Proceedings of International Conference on Artificial Neural Networks, Lausanne, Switzerland, 1997, p 999

[19] Vapnik VN, GolowichSE, Smola AJ. Support vector method for function approximation, regression estimation, and signal processing. Advances in Neural Information Processing Systems 1996;9:281-287.

[20] Thomason M. The practitioner methods and tool. Journal of Computational Intelligence in Finance 1999;7(3):36–45.

[21] Keerthi, S. S. and C-.J. Lin. Asymptotic behaviors of support vector machines with Gaussian kernel. Neural Computation 15 (7), 1667–1689.

[22] Lin, H.-T. and C.-J. Lin. A study on sigmoid kernels for SVM and the training of non-PSD kernels by SMO-type methods. Technical report, Department of Computer Science and Information Engineering, National Taiwan University. Available at http://www.csie.ntu.edu.tw/~cjlin/papers

Harmonic Detection Using Neural Networks with Conjugate Gradient Algorithm

Nejat Yumusak[1], Fevzullah Temurtas[1], and Rustu Gunturkun[2]

[1] Sakarya University, Department of Computer Engineering, Adapazari, Turkey
[2] Dumlupinar University, Technical Education Faculty, Kutahya, Turkey

Abstract. In this study, the Elman's recurrent neural networks using conjugate gradient algorithm is used for harmonic detection. The feed forward neural networks are also used for comparison. The conjugate gradient algorithm is compared with back propagation (BP) and resilient BP (RP) for training of the neural networks. The distorted wave including 5th, 7th, 11th, 13th harmonics were simulated and used for training of the neural networks. The distorted wave including up to 25th harmonics were prepared for testing of the neural networks. The Elman's recurrent and feed forward neural networks were used to recognize each harmonic. The results of the Elman's recurrent neural networks are better than those of the feed forward neural networks. The conjugate gradient algorithm provides faster convergence than BP and RP algorithms in the harmonics detection.

1   Introduction

AC power systems have a substantial number of large harmonic generating devices, e.g. adjustable speed drives for motor control and switch-mode power supplies used in a variety of electronic devices such as computers, copiers, fax machines, etc. These devices draw non-sinusoidal load currents consisting primarily of lower-order 5th, 7th, 11th, and 13th harmonics that distort the system power quality. [1]. Harmonic standards (e.g. IEEE 519 and IEC 555) have been developed to address limits in allowable harmonics [2,3].

An effective way for harmonic elimination is the harmonic compensation by using active power filter. Active power filter detect harmonic current from distorted wave in power line, then generates negative phase current as same as detected harmonic to cancel out the harmonic in power system. Using of the artificial neural networks is one of the methods for harmonic detection. [4-8].

The back propagation (BP) algorithm is widely recognized as a powerful tool for training neural networks (NNs). But since it applies the steepest descent method to update the weights, it suffers from a slow convergence rate and often yields suboptimal solutions. A variety of related algorithms have been introduced to address that problem. A number of researchers have carried out comparative studies of training algorithms [9-12]. The resilient BP (RP) and Fletcher-Reeves conjugate gradient (CGF) algorithms [9-12] used in this study is one of these type algorithms.

C. Bussler and D. Fensel (Eds.): AIMSA 2004, LNAI 3192, pp. 304–311, 2004.
© Springer-Verlag Berlin Heidelberg 2004

In this study, the method to apply the Elman's recurrent neural networks [6,7] for harmonic detection process in active filter is described. The feed forward neural networks were also used for comparison. The distorted wave including 5th, 7th, 11th, and 13th harmonics are used to be input signals for these neural networks at the training state. The output layer of network is consisted of 4 units in according to each order of harmonic. By effect of learning representative data, each component of harmonic is detected to each according unit. That means neural network structures can decompose each order of harmonic and detect only harmonic without fundamental wave in the same time.

2   Elman's Recurrent Neural Network for Harmonic Detection

Because of non-sinusoidal load currents consisting primarily of lower-order 5th, 7th, 11th, and 13th harmonics that distort the system power quality, we consider about 5th, 7th, 11th, and 13th harmonics detection. At the first step we used the feed forward neural network [6,7]. This network was a multilayer network (input layer, hidden layer, and output layer). The hidden layer neurons and the output layer neurons use nonlinear sigmoid activation functions.

At the second step, because of the time series nature of the distorted wave, we used Elman's recurrent neural network (RNN) [6,7] for harmonic detection as seen in Figure 1. This network is also a multilayer network (input layer, recurrent hidden layer, and output layer). The hidden layer neurons and the output layer neurons use nonlinear sigmoid activation functions.

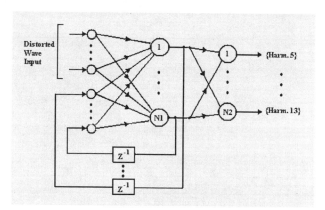

Fig. 1. Elman's recurrent neural network structures for harmonics detection

In this study, 20 hidden layer neurons and 4 output layer neurons were used for both FNN and Elman's RNN and the number of the inputs were 4 for both network structures.

3   Training of the Networks

The back propagation (BP) method is widely used as a teaching method for an ANN [12]. The BP algorithm with momentum gives the change $\Delta w_{ji}(k)$ in the weight of the connection between neurons i and j at iteration k as

$$\Delta w_{ji}(k) = -\alpha \frac{\partial E}{\partial w_{ji}(k)} + \mu \Delta w_{ji}(k-1) \tag{1}$$

where α is called the learning coefficient, μ the momentum coefficient, E is the sum of squared differences error function, and $\Delta w_{ji}(k)$ the weight change in the immediately preceding iteration. The performance of the BP algorithm is improved if the learning rate is allowed to change during the training process in response to the complexity of the local surface error.

The high performance BP training algorithm used in this study is Fletcher-Reeves conjugate gradient algorithm (CGF). The BP algorithm with momentum and Resilient BP (RP) [10] are also used [8] for comparison.

In contrast to other gradient algorithms, the RP algorithm does not use the magnitude of the gradient. It is a direct adaptation of the weight step based local gradient sign [9,10,12]. Local information for each weight's individual update value, $A_{ji}(k)$, on the error function E is obtained according to [10,12].

When the update value for each weight is adapted, the delta weights are changed as follows:

$$\Delta w_{ji}(k) = \begin{cases} -A_{ji}(k), if \ \dfrac{\partial E}{\partial w_{ji}(k-1)} \dfrac{\partial E}{\partial w_{ji}(k)} > 0 \\[3ex] A_{ji}(k), if \ \dfrac{\partial E}{\partial w_{ji}(k-1)} \dfrac{\partial E}{\partial w_{ji}(k)} < 0 \\[3ex] 0, else \end{cases} \tag{2}$$

More details about RP algorithm can be found in [9,10,12].

In conjugate gradient algorithm a search is carried out along conjugate directions. The first iteration of all the conjugate gradient algorithms starts out by searching in the steepest descent direction, i.e., the negative of the gradient.

$$p_{ji}(0) = -\frac{\partial E}{\partial w_{ji}(0)} \tag{3}$$

A line search is performed to determine the optimal distance to move along the current search direction:

$$w_{ji}(k+1) = w_{ji}(k) + \alpha p_{ji}(k) \tag{4}$$

Then the next search is performed so that it is conjugate to the previous directions. The new search is determined by combining the new steepest descent direction with the previous search direction:

$$p_{ji}(k) = -\frac{\partial E}{\partial w_{ji}(k)} + \beta_{ji}(k)p_{ji}(k-1) \tag{5}$$

CGF implements the Fletcher-Reeves update of the conjugate gradient algorithm where the constant $\beta_{ji}(k)$ is computed as

$$\beta_{ji}(k) = \frac{\dfrac{\partial E}{\partial w_{ji}(k)} \dfrac{\partial E}{\partial w_{ji}(k)}}{\dfrac{\partial E}{\partial w_{ji}(k-1)} \dfrac{\partial E}{\partial w_{ji}(k-1)}} \tag{6}$$

which is the ratio of the norm squared of the current gradient to the norm squared of the previous gradient. More details about CGF algorithm can be found in [12,13].

In order to make neural network enable to detect harmonics from distorted wave, it is necessary to use some representative distorted waves for learning. These distorted waves are made by mixing the component of the 5th, 7th, 11th, and 13th harmonics in fundamental wave. For this purpose, 5th harmonic up to 70%, 7th harmonic up to 40%, 11th harmonic up to 10% and 13th harmonic up to 5% were used and approximately 2500 representative distorted waves were generated for training process.

During the training process, the distorted waves were used for recognition. As the result of recognition, output signal from each output unit gives the coefficient of each harmonic included in the input distorted wave and these harmonics are eliminated from the distorted wave (see Figure 2). Equations [6-8] used in the elimination process are shown in (6), and (7).

$$I_f(t) = I_d(t) - \sum_h I_h(t) \tag{7}$$

$$I_h(t) = A_h Sin(2\pi ft + \theta) \tag{8}$$

where, If(t) is the active filtered wave, $I_d(t)$ is the distorted wave, $h = 5,7,11,13$, A_h are coefficients of lower-order 5th, 7th, 11th, and 13th harmonics, $f = 50$ Hz, θ is phase angle and equal to zero in this study.

4 The Quality of Power System Waves

The common index used to determine the quality of power system currents and voltages are total harmonic distortion (THD) [6-8], which is defined as

$$THD = \sqrt{\frac{\sum_{2}^{\infty} I_h^2}{I_1^2}} \qquad (9)$$

where I_h represents the individual harmonics and I_1 is the fundamental component of the load wave.

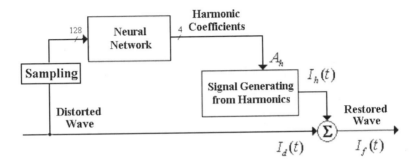

Fig. 2. Process for restoring wave

5   Results and Conclusions

The non sinusoidal load currents consist also that the higher order harmonics such as 17th, 19th, etc., but they do not carry any significant current [14]. So, for the performance evaluation of the neural network structures, 5th harmonic up to 70%, 7th harmonic up to 40%, 11th harmonic up to 10% and 13th harmonic up to 5%, 17th harmonic up to 5%, 19th harmonic up to 2.5%, 23rd harmonic up to 2.5%, 25th harmonic up to 2% were used [15] and approximately 250 representative distorted waves were generated as a test set.

For the training and test processes, input signals of the neural networks are the amplitudes of one period of distorted wave. The amplitudes are taken 128 point at regular interval of time axis. The amplitudes are used to be input signals of the neural networks without any pre processing. At the training phase, the higher order harmonics such as 17th, 19th, etc., are ignored for THD calculations.

Figure 3 shows the training results of the feed forward neural networks. As seen in this figure, the results of the RP training algorithm are better then that of the standard back propagation algorithm. From the same figure, it can be seen easily that CGF training algorithm provides faster convergence than other algorithms in the harmonics detection.

Figure 4 shows the training results of Elman's recurrent neural networks. As seen in this figure, the results of the RP training algorithm is better then that of the standard back propagation algorithm and the CGF training algorithm provides faster convergence than others.

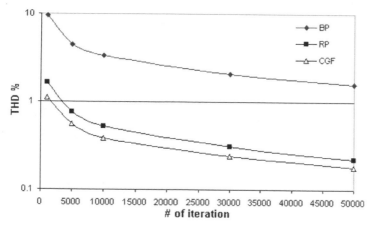

Fig. 3. Training results of feed forward neural network

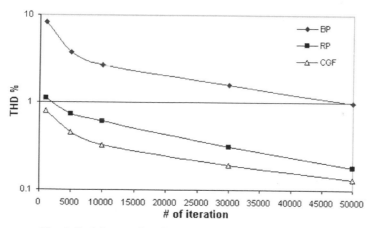

Fig. 4. Training results of Elman's recurrent neural networks

After the training process is completed, the general distorted waves (test set) were used for recognition. As the result of recognition, output signal from each output unit means the coefficient of each harmonic which is including in the input distorted wave and these harmonics are eliminated from the distorted wave.

Table 1 shows the average THD values of restored waves obtained by using the feed forward and Elman's recurrent neural networks for training and the test set. The sample source wave and the restored waves are shown in Figure 5.

The recommendation IEEE 519 allows a total harmonic distortion (THD) of 5% in low-voltage grids [16]. As seen in the table, average THD value is 46.36% before compensation and obtained average THD values are less then 5% after compensation for all networks. These THD values are suitable to the recommendation IEEE 519.

Because the higher order harmonics are ignored for THD calculations at the training phase, training THD values are smaller than test THD values as seen in the table. The 3.65% of training THD values come from the higher order harmonics such as 17th, 19th, etc which are not used in the training. This means that there is an improvement potential. The THD values obtained by using Elman's recurrent neural networks are better than the THD values obtained by using the feed forward neural networks. This can be because of that the feedback structures of the Elman's RNN are more appropriate for the time series nature of the waves.

Table 1. Average THD values

Neural Network	Training Algorithm	Training Average *THD* (%){5^{th}, ..., 13th harmonics}	Test Average *THD* (%){5^{th}, ..., 25th harmonics}
Before compensation		46.22	46.36
Feed forward NN	BP	1.96	4.14
	RP	0.22	3.65
	CGF	0.18	3.65
Elman's RNN	BP	0.97	3.77
	RP	0.18	3.65
	CGF	0.13	3.65

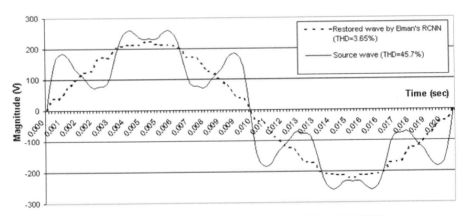

Fig. 5. Sample source and restored waves (by Elman's RCNN)

As the result, the possibility of the feed forward and Elman's recurrent neural networks to detect harmonics is confirmed by compensating the distorted waves and it can be said that the feed forward and Elman's recurrent neural networks are effective to use for active filter. And it is also confirmed that the CGF training algorithm provides faster convergence than the BP and RP training algorithms in the harmonics detection.

References

1. Unsal, A., Von Jouanne, A.R., Stonic, V.L.: A DSP controlled resonant active filter for power conditioning in three phase industrial power system, Signal Processing, Vol. 82 (2001) 1743-1752
2. IEEE Standarts 519-1992, IEEE Recommended Practice and Requirements for Harmonics Control in Electric Power Systems, Piscataway, NJ, (1992)
3. IEEE Recommended Practices for Power System Analysis, IEEE Inc., New York, NY (1992)
4. Pecharanin, N., Sone, M., Mitsui, H.: An application of neural network for harmonic detection in active filter, ICNN (1994) 3756-3760
5. Rukonuzzaman, M., Nakaoka, M.: Adaptive neural network based harmonic detection for active power filter, IEICE Transactions On Communications, E86B (5) (2003) 1721-1725
6. Temurtas, F., Gunturkun, R., Yumusak, N., Temurtas, H., Unsal, A.: An application of Elman's Recurrent Neural Networks to Harmonic Detection, IEA-AIE 04, Lecture Notes in Artificial Intelligence, 3029 (2004) 1043-1052
7. Temurtas, F., Gunturkun, R., Yumusak, N., Temurtas, H.: Harmonic Detection using Feed Forward and Recurrent Neural Networks for Active Filters, Electric Power Systems Research, in press (2004)
8. Temurtas, F., Gunturkun, R., Yumusak, N., Temurtas, H., Cerezci, O.: Elman's Recurrent Neural Networks using Resilient Back Propagation for Harmonic Detection, PRICA 04, Lecture Notes in Artificial Intelligence, in press (2004)
9. Sagiroglu, S., Besdok, E., Erler, M.: Control Chart Pattern Recognition Using Artificial Neural Networks, Turk J Elec Engin, 8(2) (2000).
10. Riedmiller, M, and Braun, H.: A Direct Adaptive Method for Faster backpropagation learning: The RPROP Algorithm, Proceedings of the IEEE Int. Conf. On Neural Networks, San Francisco, CA, March 28, 1993.
11. Brent, R.P.: Fast Training Algorithms for Multi-layer Neural Nets, IEEE Transactions on Neural Networks 2 (1991) 346–354
12. Hagan, M. T., Demuth, H. B., Beale, M. H.: Neural Network Design, Boston, MA: PWS Publishing, (1996)
13. Fletcher, R., Reeves, C.M.: Function minimization by conjugate gradients, Computer Journal 7, (1964) 149-154
14. Ryckaert, W.R.A., Ghijselen, J.A.L., Melkebeek, J.A.A.: Harmonic mitigation potential of shunt harmonic impedances, Electric Power Systems Research, Vol. 65 (2003) 63-69
15. Reid, W.E.: Power quality issues – standards and guidelines, IEEE Trans. on Ind. App., Vol. 32(3) (1996) 625- 632
16. Nunez-Zuniga, T.E., Pomilio, J.A.: Shunt active power filter synthesizing resistive loads, Vol. 17(2) (2002) 273-278

Neural Model of Osmotic Dehydration Kinetics of Fruits Cubes

Ieroham Baruch[1], Próspero Genina-Soto[2], Boyka Nenkova[3],
and Josefina Barrera-Cortés[2]

[1] CINVESTAV-IPN, Department of Automatic Control, av. IPN no 2508, A.P. 14-740,
07360 Mexico D.F., Mexico

[2] CINVESTAV-IPN, Department of Biotechnology and Bioengineering,
av. IPN no 2508, A.P. 14-740,
07360 Mexico D.F., Mexico

[3] IIT-BAS, Geo Milev, BAS bl. 2,
1113 Sofia, Bulgaria

Abstract. The paper proposed to use a Recurrent Neural Network model (RNN) for process prediction of the osmotic dehydration kinetics of nature product cubes (apple, sweet potatoes and potatoes) at different operational conditions of temperature and concentration of the osmotic solution. The proposed RNN model has five inputs, three outputs and eight neurons in the hidden layer, with global and local feedbacks. The learning algorithm is a modified version of the dynamic backpropagation one. The learning and generalization mean squared errors are below 2%. The learning was performed in 701 epochs, 40 iterations each one. The statistical analysis confirms the good quality of the proposed RNN model.

1   Introduction

The Osmotic Dehydration (OD) is a mass transfer operation of increasing interest in food preservation technologies. It is done by immersion of a natural product into a hypertonic solution for achieving a flow of water outwards the solid, as well as a countercurrent flow of solution into the product. For developing food treatment technology based on the OD process, it is necessary to know the OD kinetics for fixing the desired dehydration and impregnation levels involved in such process, [1].

For modeling the mass transfer phenomena during the OD process, analytical and empirical models have been reported. Some empirical models are those, developed by Lenart and Flink, [2] and Azuara, et al., [3]. Analytical models have been developed by Beristain et al., [4], who proposed a phenomenological model based on the Fick's second law. Raoult-Wack et al., [5], have developed a compartment model and Toupin et al. (1989), [6], stated a complex mathematical model based on transport

C. Bussler and D. Fensel (Eds.): AIMSA 2004, LNAI 3192, pp. 312–320, 2004.

phenomena. An inconvenient of most of these models is that they involved some empirical constants that ought to be known previously, in order to be used.

Artificial Neural Networks (ANN) models seemed suitable for modeling the osmotic dehydration process, [7]. They have been applied in various fields since 1985 and are beneficial for modeling complicated and atypical experimental conditions without having to put forward hypotheses on the underlying physical and/or chemical mechanisms, [8]. These models also take nonlinearities and interactions between input variables of the model into account with very few parameters, [9].

This study was designed to test and validate the efficiency of the Recurrent Neural Network (RNN) model for predicting profiles kinetics of water loss in fruits such as sweet potato roots, potatoes and apples. The profile kinetics is determined at two temperatures (26°C and 50°C) and three concentrations of the osmotic solution (30:100, 50:100 and 70:100), [10].

2   Description of the Osmotic Dehydration Process Experiment

The nature products (sweet potato roots, potatoes and apple) were obtained from a local market. The osmotic solutions were prepared using distilled water and commercial refined sucrose as osmotic agent.

The Osmotic dehydration (OD) process experiment requires following a sequence of operation. The nature product cubes of 3.5 cm are put in a container of 4L containing osmotic solutions at fixed concentration and temperature. The homogenization of the osmotic solution is obtained by a mild agitation of 100 rpm, [10]. The osmotic dehydration process is treated with osmotic solutions of different sucrose concentrations (30:100, 50:100 and 70:100 w/w) and temperature (26°C and 50°C). The osmotic dehydration process is carried out during an exposition time of 168 hours. During this time, the nature cubes are tested at 8, 24, 72 and 168 hours.

The global OD kinetics is obtained by the weight evolution of the cubes. The cubes are withdrawn from the solution. Immediately, they are blotted with a tissue paper and weighted on tarred receptacles prior to returning them to the reactor.

The water lost is determined by weight difference of dried and osmosis cubes.

3   Input-Output Pattern of Learning

The input-output pattern of learning is shown on the Fig. 1. The variables determining the OD process are the temperature (T) and the osmotic solution concentration (OSC). The RNN model included these variables in the input pattern of learning as well as the dimensional lost of water (C/Co) for the three fruits studied: sweet potato roots (SPR), potatoes (P) and apples (A).

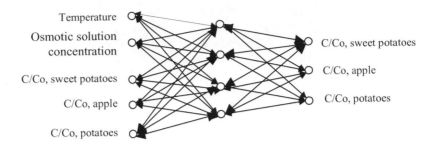

Temperature

Osmotic solution concentration

C/Co, sweet potatoes

C/Co, apple

C/Co, potatoes

C/Co, sweet potatoes

C/Co, apple

C/Co, potatoes

Fig. 1. Input-Output Pattern of Learning.

The output pattern of learning is conformed only by the dimensional lost of water (C/Co) of the three fruits mentioned below and corresponding at a next time of the OD process.

4   Recurrent Neural Network Topology and Learning

In the present paper, a two layer completely parallel RNN model it is proposed to be used as a neural predictive model of the OD process. The RNN two-layer architecture contains one hidden and one output layer, both recurrent – with local and global feedbacks. The proposed RNN model is inspired from the RNN model given in [11], but here it is extended by a global feedback and by a local feedback in the output layer, so it takes the form:

$$X(k+1) = S[A_1X(k) + BU(k) + DY(k)] \qquad (1)$$
$$Y(k+1) = S[CX(k)+A_2(k)Y(k)] \qquad (2)$$
$$A_1= \text{block-diag } (A_{1,ij}); \, |\, A_{1,ij}\, | < 1; \, A_1= \text{block-diag } (A_{2,ij}); \, |A_{2,ij}\, |<1 \qquad (3)$$

Where, Y, X and U are output, state and input vectors, respectively, with dimensions l, n, m, respectively; A_1, A_2 are (nxn) and (lxl)- local feedback block-diagonal weight matrices respectively; $A_{1,ij}$, $A_{2,ij}$ are diagonal blocks of A_1, A_2 with (1x1) or (2x2) dimensions; B and C are (nxm) and (lxn)- weight matrices; D is a (nxl)- global output closed loop matrix; S[.] is a vector-valued sigmoid activation function. The equation (3) represents the local stability conditions, imposed on all diagonal blocks of the feedback matrices A_1, A_2. The saturation function could be used as approximation of the sigmoid function so to improve the RNN architecture, facilitating its realization, [11]. The stability of the RNN model is assured by the activation functions S and by the local stability conditions (3). The global feedback has been introduced so to reduce the measurement data noise during the RNN learning. For training the RNN it is used a modified dynamic backpropagation algorithm, which has the form:

$$W_{ij}(k+1) = W_{ij}(k) + \eta \, \Delta W_{ij}(k) + \alpha \, \Delta W_{ij}(k-1) \qquad (4)$$

Where: W_{ij} is a general weight, denoting the ij-th weight element of each weight matrix (C, D, A_1, A_2, B) in the RTNN model to be updated; ΔW_{ij} (ΔC_{ij}, ΔD_{ij}, $\Delta A_{1,ij}$, $\Delta A_{2,ij}$

and ΔB_{ij}) is the weight correction of W_{ij}; finally, η and α are the learning rate parameters. The stability of this learning algorithm has been proved in [11]. In the discrete-time RNN model, the weight corrections of the updated matrices described by equations (1), (2), are given as follows:

■ For the output layer:

$$R_1 = [T_j(k) - Y_j(k)]\, Y_j(k)\, [1 - Y_j(k)] \tag{5}$$
$$\Delta C_{ij}(k) = R_1\, X_i(k) \tag{6}$$
$$\Delta A_{2,ij}(k) = R_1\, Y_i(k) \tag{7}$$

Where: ΔC_{ij}, $\Delta A_{2,ij}$ are weight corrections of the ij-th elements of the (lxn) learned matrix C and (lxl) learning matrix A_2; T_j is a j-th element of the target vector; Y_j is a j-th element of the output vector; X_i is an i-th element of the output vector of the hidden layer, R_1 is an auxiliary variable.

■ For the hidden layer:

$$R_2 = C_i(k)\, [T(k)-Y(k)]\, X_j(k)\, [1 - X_j(k)] \tag{8}$$
$$\Delta B_{ij}(k) = R_2\, U_i(k) \tag{9}$$
$$\Delta D_{ij}(k) = R_2\, Y_i(k) \tag{10}$$
$$\Delta A_{1,ij}(k) = R_2\, X_i(k-1) \tag{11}$$

Where: ΔB_{ij}, ΔD_{ij}, are weight corrections of the ij-th elements of the (nxm) learned matrix B and the (nxl) learned matrix D; C_i is a row vector of dimension (1xl), taken from the transposed matrix C'; [T-Y] is a (lx1) output error vector, through which the error is back-propagated to the hidden layer; U_i is an i-th element of the input vector U; X_i is an i-th element of the vector X; $\Delta A_{1,ij}$ is the weight correction of the ij-th elements of the (nxn) block-diagonal matrix A_1; R_2 is an auxiliary variable.

5 Experimental Results

The graphical results for the last epoch of RNN learning with experimental data, are given on Fig. 2. The RNN used for modeling and identification of the OD process has five inputs, eight neurons in the hidden layer and three outputs (5, 8, 3). The number of neurons in the hidden layer is determined in an experimental way, according to the Mean Square Error (MSE%) of learning. The learning algorithm is a version of the dynamic backpropagation one, specially designed for this RNN topology. The described above learning algorithm is applied simultaneously to 5 degradation kinetic data sets (patterns), containing 40 points each one. The 5 data sets are considered as an epoch of learning. After each epoch of learning, the 5 pattern sets are interchanged in an arbitrary manner from one epoch to another. An unknown kinetic data set, repeated 5 times, is used as a generalization data set. The learning is stopped when the MSE of learning becomes below of a prescribed error limit (MSE%<2%). So it is done for the generalization, where MSE%<2%. An additional measure of weight convergence was also applied, which is the relationship $|\Delta W_{ij}(k)|/|W_{ij}(k)|*100\% < 2\%$ for all updated parameters. This error was obtained after 701 epochs of learning.

The graphical results, shown on Fig. 2, compare the experimental data for the 5 OD kinetics studied. The variables compared are the relative residual water content of each fruit tested and the mean square error for the 701 epochs of learning. The generalization of the RNN was carried out reproducing the OD kinetics, which is not included in the training process. This OD process was carried out at 20°C and an osmotic solution concentration of 30:100. The graphical generalization results obtained are shown on Fig. 3. The graphics compare the experimental data with the output data, generated by the RNN during the last epoch of generalization. The MSE% of generalization, given on the end of the last graphic is below 2%.

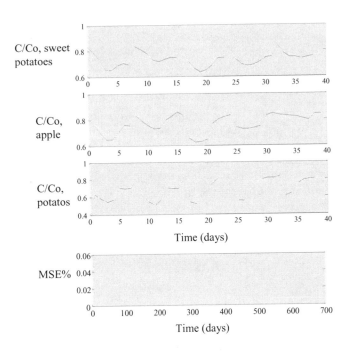

Fig. 2. Graphical results of learning. Experimental data (continuous line) vs. RNN outputs (dashed line) are plotted subsequently for the last epoch of learning, corresponding to the 5 OD kinetics used in the learning process of the RNN model. The variables shown are relative residual water content of the natural fruits: sweet potatos roots, potatoes and apple, as well as the mean square error of learning during 701 epochs of learning. The learning rate is of 1.2 and the momentum rate is of 0.2.

The MSE% corresponding to 20 runs of the program at the end of the 701-th epoch of learning/generalization is given on Table 1. The operational conditions of this OD process are in the range of operational conditions studied.

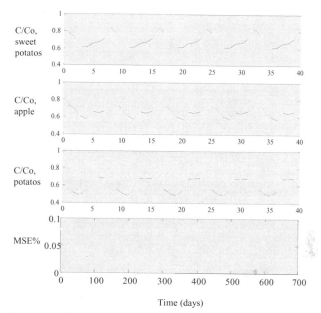

Fig. 3. Graphical results of generalization. Experimental data (continuous line) vs. RNN outputs (dashed line), repeated seven times for the last epoch of learning, are plotted for five OD kinetics. The variables shown are relative residual water content of the natural fruits: sweet potatos roots, potatoes and apple, as well as the mean square error of generalization during 701 epochs of generalization.

Table 1. Means squared error (%) in the end of the 701-th epoch of learning/generalization for 20 runs of the program.

No.	1	2	3	4	5
Learning	0.68	0.63	0.73	0.76	0.75
Generalization	0.69	0.67	0.72	0.92	0.88
No.	6	7	8	9	10
Learning	0.68	0.71	0.72	0.65	0.68
Generalization	0.69	0.65	0.79	0.67	0.69
No.	11	12	13	14	15
Learning	0.73	0.75	0.63	0.76	0.63
Generalization	0.72	0.88	0.67	0.92	0.67
No.	16	17	18	19	20
Learning	0.76	0.68	0.73	0.75	0.71
Generalization	0.92	0.69	0.72	0.88	0.65

According to the results obtained, the capacity of the RNN model to reproduce similar degradation process, entering with an incomplete or noisy input data set is confirmed.

The cost function ξ minimized during the learning is the average of the instantaneous error e_i of the output layer, i is the number of outputs defined on Fig.3, and it is given by the following equation:

$$\xi = \frac{1}{2}\sum_i e_i^2 \tag{12}$$

Where: the number of outputs is three. The average cost ξ_{av} for one epoch of learning is:

$$\xi_{av} = \frac{1}{N}\sum_{j=1}^{N}\xi_j \tag{13}$$

Where j is the number iterations for one epoch, and N is equal to 40. The average cost for all epochs $\xi_{av,ep}$ of learning is:

$$\xi_{av,ep} = \frac{1}{Nep}\sum_{j=1}^{Nep}\xi_{av_j} \tag{14}$$

Where j is the epoch number and Nep is equal to 701. The mean average cost ε for all runs of learning is:

$$\varepsilon = \frac{1}{n}\sum_{k=1}^{n}\xi_{av_k} \tag{15}$$

Where k is the run number and n is equal to 20. The standard deviation σ with respect to the mean value is:

$$\sigma = \frac{1}{n}\sum_{i=1}^{n}\Delta_i^2 \tag{16}$$

Where the deviation Δ is:

$$= \xi_{av} - \varepsilon \tag{17}$$

The graphical results of the given in Table 1 statistical data are depicted on Fig. 4 - for the RNN learning and on Fig. 5 - for the RNN generalization. The mean and the standard deviation values are respectively:

- For learning:

$\varepsilon = 0.706\%$; $\sigma = 0.045\%$.

- For generalization:

$\varepsilon = 0.754\%$; $\sigma = 0.103\%$.

In Fig. 4 and Fig. 5, it is seen that about two or three run data are outside the standard deviation which is due to the different initial weights values, chosen in arbitrary manner as equiprobable numbers over small range.

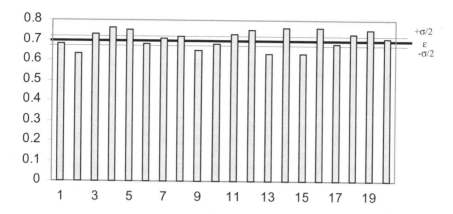

Fig. 4. Graphical representation of the Mean squared error (%) in the end of the 701-th epoch of learning for 20 runs of the program, together with the mean value and the standard deviation.

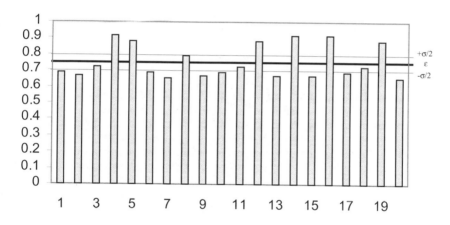

Fig. 5. Graphical representation of the Mean squared error (%) in the end of the 701-th epoch of generalization for 20 runs of the program, together with the mean value and the standard deviation.

It is important to say that the experimental data in the OD process have an average standard deviation of ± 2-10%. According the mean square error of approximation obtained during RNN model learning, it could be said that the RNN model could be used successively to predict the OD process.

6 Conclusions

The paper proposed to use a Recurrent Neural Network model to predict the OD process. The multi-input multi-output RNN proposed, have five inputs, three outputs and eight neurons in the hidden layer, as well as global and local feedbacks. The weight update learning algorithm is a version of the well-known dynamic backpropagation algorithm, directed to the RNN learning. The obtained approximation and generalization error at the end of the 701-th epoch is below 2%. The learning process is applied simultaneously for five OD kinetics data of different temperature, osmotic solution concentration and different relative residual water content of the natural fruits: sweet potatos roots, potatoes and apples, where good convergent results, including statistics, have been obtained. After training and generalization, the RNN model is capable to evolve the relative residual water content of the natural fruits: sweet potatos roots, potatoes and apple, entering with an incomplete or noisy input data set. The last statistical results confirm the good work of the learning and generalization program, which gives similar results in various runs.

References

1. Raoult-Wack, A.L.: Recent advances in the osmotic dehydration of foods. Trends in Food Science and Technology 5 (1994) 255-260.
2. Lenart, A., Flink, J.M.: Osmotic Concentration of Potatoes. II. Spatial Distribution of the Osmotic Effect. Journal of Food Technology 19 (1984) 65-89.
3. Azuara, E., Beristain, C.I., Gutiérrez, G.F.: A Method for Continuous Kinetic Evaluation of Osmotic Dehydration. Lebensmittel-Wissenschast & Technologie 31 (1998) 317-321.
4. Beristain, C.I., Azuara, E., García, H.S.: Development of A Mathematical Model to Predict Kinetics of Osmotic Dehydration. Journal of Food Science and Technology 29, no 4 (1992) 239-242.
5. Raoult-Wack, A.L., Petitdemange, F., Giroux, F., Guilbert, S, Ríos, G., Lebert, A.: Simultaneous Water and Solute Transport in Shrinking Media. Part 2. A Compartmental Model for Dewatering and Impregnation Soaking Process, Drying Technology 9, no 3 (1991) 613-630.
6. Toupin, C.J., Marcotte, M., Le Maguer, M.: Osmotically-Induced Mass Transfer in Plant Storage Tissues, A Mathematical Model. Part I. Journal of Food Engineering, no 10 (1989) 13-38.
7. Bichop, C: Neural Networks and Their Applications. Review of Scientific Instruments 65, no 5 (1994) 1803-1832.
8. Baughman, D.R., Liu, Y.A.: Neural Networks in Bioprocessing and Chemical Engineering. Ed. Academic Press, New York (1995) 1-17.
9. Valdez-Castro, L., Baruch, I., Barrera-Cortés, J.: Neural Networks Applied to the Prediction of Fed-Batch Fermentation Kinetics of Bacillus Thuringiensis. Bioprocess and Biosystems Engineering 25 (2003) 229-233.
10. Genina-Soto, P., Barrera-Cortés, J., Gutiérrez-López, G., Nieto, E. A.: Temperature and Concentration Effects of Osmotic Media on OD Profiles of Sweet Potato Cubes. I. J. Drying Technology 19, no. 3 (2001) 547-558.
11. Baruch, I., Flores, J. M., Nava, F., Ramirez, I. R., Nenkova, B.: An Advanced Neural Network Topology and Learning, Applied for Identification and Control of a D.C. Motor. Proc. of the First International IEEE Symposium on Intelligent Systems, IS'02, Varna, Bulgaria, Vol. I (2002) 289-295.

Robust and Adaptive Load Frequency Control of Multi-area Power Networks with System Parametric Uncertainties Using Temporal Difference Based MLP Neural Networks

Farzan Rashidi and Mehran Rashidi

Control Research Department, Engineering Research Institute, Tehran
P.O.Box: 13445-754, Iran
and

Abstract. In this paper a robust and adaptive Temporal Difference learning based MLP (TDMLP) neural network for power system Load Frequency Control (LFC) is presented. Power systems, such as other industrial processes, are nonlinear and have parametric uncertainties that for controller design had to take the uncertainties into account. For this reason, in the design of LFC controller the idea of TDMLP neural network is being used. Some simulations with two interconnections are given to illustrate proposed method. Results on interconnected power system show that the proposed method not only is robust to increasing of load perturbations and operating point variations, but also it gives good dynamic response compared with traditional controllers. It guarantees the stability of the overall system even in the presence of generation rate constraint (GRC). To evaluate the usefulness of proposed method we compare the response of this method with RBF neural network and PID controller. Simulation results show the TDMLP has the better control performance than RBF neural network and PID controller.

1   Introduction

In power systems, one of the most important issues is the load frequency control (LFC), which deals with the problem of how to deliver the demanded power of the desired frequency with minimum transient oscillations [1]. Whenever any suddenly small load perturbations resulted from the demands of customers occur in any areas of the power system, the changes of tie-line power exchanges and the frequency deviations will occur. Thus, to improve the stability and performance of the power system, generator frequency should be setup under different loading conditions. For this reason, many control approaches have been developed for the load frequency control. Among them, PID controllers [2], optimal [3], nonlinear [4] and robust [5] control strategies, and neural and/or fuzzy [6-7] approaches are to be mentioned. An industrial plant, such as a power system, always contains parametric uncertainties. As the operating point of a power system and its parameter changes continuously, a fixed controller may no longer be suitable in all operating conditions. In this paper, because

C. Bussler and D. Fensel (Eds.): AIMSA 2004, LNAI 3192, pp. 321–330, 2004.
© Springer-Verlag Berlin Heidelberg 2004

of the inherent nonlinearity of power system a new artificial neural network based intelligent controller, which has the advance adaptive control configuration, is designed. The proposed controller uses the capability of the MLP neural network based on Temporal Difference (TD) learning for the design of LFC controller. In this work, for the design of MLP neural network the idea of TD learning and applying it to nonlinear power system is being used. The motivation of using the TD learning for training of the MLP neural network is to take the large parametric uncertainties into account so that both stability of the overall system and good performance have been achieved for all admissible uncertainties. Moreover, the proposed controller also makes use of a piece of information which is not used in conventional controllers (an estimate of the electric load perturbation, i.e. an estimate of the change in electric load when such a change occurs on the bus). The load perturbation estimate could be obtained either by a linear estimator, or by a nonlinear neural network estimator in certain situations. It could also be measured directly from the bus. We will show by simulation that when a load estimator is available, the neural network controller can achieve extremely dynamic response. In this study, the TDMLP neural network is considered for control interconnected power system with two areas with power tie-lines to supply different consumers. The simulation results obtained are shown that the proposed controller not only has good performance in the presence of the generation rate constraint (GRC), but also gives good dynamic response compare to RBF neural network and PID controller. This paper is organized as follows: Section 2 describes the power system and its mathematical model. In section 3, the whole structure of the proposed TDMLP neural network is shown. Section 4 describes the application of TDMLP in LFC. Section 5 shows the simulation results that have been compared with RBF neural network and PID controller. Some conclusion remarks are discussed in section 6.

2   Mathematical Model of Power System

The power networks are usually large-scale systems with complex nonlinear dynamics. However, for the design of LFC, the linearized model around operating point is sufficient to represent the power system dynamics [1]. Fig.1 shows the block diagram of ith area power system. Each area including steam turbines contains governor and reheater stage of the steam turbine. According to Fig.1, time-constants of the T_{ri}, T_{ti} and T_{gi} are considered for the reheater, turbine and governor of the thermal unit, respectively. Wherever the actual model consists of the generation rate constraints (GRC) and it would influence the performance of power systems significantly, the GRC is taken into account by adding a limiter to the turbine and also to the integral control part all of areas to prevent excessive control action.

The GRC of the thermal unit is considered to be 0.3 p.u. per minute ($\delta = 0.005$). All areas have governors with dead-band effects which are important for speed control under small disturbances. The governor dead-band is also assumed to be 0.06%. Based on the suitable state variable chosen in Fig. 1, the state space model of this system can be obtained as follows:

$$\dot{x}(t) = Ax(t) + Bu(t)$$
$$y(t) = Cx(t)$$

(1)

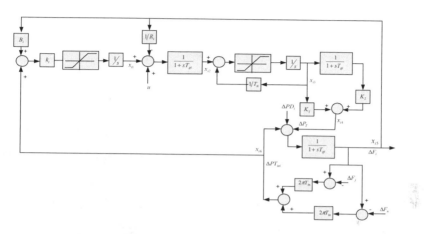

Fig. 1. Block-Diagram of the ith area power system [8]

Where x is a 12 by 1 state vector and $u = [U_1 \quad U_2 \quad \Delta P_{D1} \quad \Delta P_{D2}]^T$. The outputs are defined to be the frequency deviations (ΔF_i) and the deviation of transmission power line (ΔP_{tie}). The values of A, B and C matrices has been described in [8].

Table 1. System uncertainties

Uncer.	$\underline{a_i}$	a_{i0}	$\overline{a_i}$	Δa_i
$1/T_{gi}$	8.33	10.42	12.5	**2.07**
$1/T_{gi}R$	2.983	4.7	6.51	**1.81**
$1/T_{ti}$	2.78	3.473	4.167	**0.6935**
$1/T_{ri}$	0.0833	0.1042	0.125	**0.0208**
K_p/T_p	4	8	12	**4**
$1/T_{pi}$	0.033	0.0665	0.1	**0.0335**
T_{12}	**0.049**	**0.0707**	**0.093**	**0.0223**

As the important characteristics of power systems such as: changing of the generation, loading conditions and system configuration are. Therefore, parameters of the linear model described previously, depend on the operating points. In this paper the range of the parameter variations are obtained by change of simultaneously T_n, T_{12} by 50% and all other parameters by 20% of their typical values. Denoting the ith parameter by a_i, the parameter uncertainty is formulated as:

$$a_i = a_{i0} + \delta_i a_i, \ |\delta_i| \leq 1, \ i = 1,2,..., \ a_{i0} = \frac{a_i + \overline{a_i}}{2}, \ \Delta a_i = \overline{a_i} - a_{i0} \tag{2}$$

Where $\overline{a_i}$ and a_i stand for the maximum and minimum value, respectively. Table 1 shows the system uncertainties with their nominal, maximum and minimum values.

3   Temporal Difference Learning Based MLP Neural Networks

3.1   Temporal Difference Learning

Most of new learning algorithms like reinforcement learning, Q-learning and the method of temporal differences are characterized by their fast computation and in some cases lower error in comparison with the classical learning methods. Fast training is a notable consideration in some control applications. In reinforcement learning, there is no teacher available to give the correct output for each training example, which is called unsupervised Learning. The output produced by the learning agent is fed to the environment and a scalar reinforcement value (reward) is returned. The learning agent tries to adjust itself to maximize the reward [9-10]. Often the actions taken by the learning agent to produce an output will affect not only the immediate reward but also the subsequent ones. In this case, the immediate reward only reflects partial information about the action. This is called delayed-reward [11]. Temporal difference (TD) learning is a type of reinforcement learning for solving delayed-reward prediction problems. Unlike supervised learning, which measures error between each prediction and target, TD uses the difference of two successive predictions to learn that is Multi Step Prediction. The advantage of TD learning is that it can update weights incrementally and converge to a solution faster [12-13]. In a delay-reward prediction problem, the observation-outcome sequence has the form $x_1, x_2, x_3,..., x_m, z$ where each x_t is an observation vector available at time $t, 1 \leq t \leq m$ and z is the outcome of the sequence. For each observation, the learning agent makes a prediction of z, forming a sequence: $P_1, P_2, P_3,..., P_m$. Assuming the learning agent is an artificial neural network, update for a weight w of the network with the classical gradient descent update rule for supervised learning is:

$$\Delta w = -\alpha \nabla_w E \tag{3}$$

Where α is the learning rate, E is a cost function and $\nabla_w E$ is the gradient vector. A simple form of E can be

$$E = \frac{1}{2}\sum_{t=1}^{m}(P_t - z)^2 \qquad (4)$$

Where P_t and z have been described at above. From equations (2) and (3), Δw will be calculated as follows:

$$\Delta w = -\alpha\sum_{t=1}^{m}(P_t - z)\nabla_w P \qquad (5)$$

In [14] Sutton derived the incremental updating rule for equation (4) as:

$$\Delta w_t = \alpha(P_{t+1} - P_t)\sum_{k=1}^{t}\nabla_w P_k \;,\; t = 1,2,...,m \text{ and } P_{m+1} \overset{def}{=} z \qquad (6)$$

To emphasize more recent predictions, an exponential factor λ is multiplied to the gradient term:

$$\Delta w_t = \alpha(P_{t+1} - P_t)\sum_{k=1}^{t}\lambda^{t-k}\nabla_w P_k \qquad (7)$$

Where $0 \le \lambda \le 1$. This results in a family of learning rules, $TD(\lambda)$, with constant values of λ. But there are two special cases:
First, when $\lambda = 1$, equation (6) falls back to equation (5), which produces the same training result as the supervised learning in Equation (4).
Second, when $\lambda = 0$, equation (6) becomes

$$\Delta w_t = \alpha(P_{t+1} - P_t)\nabla_w P_k \qquad (8)$$

Which has a similar form as equation (4). So the same training algorithm for supervised learning can be used for $TD(0)$.

3.2   TDMLP Neural Network

Multilayer perseptrons are an important class of neural networks that have been applied successfully to solve some difficult and diverse problems by training them in a supervised manner with some learning algorithms such as error correction learning rule, delta rule and etc. The classical generalized delta rule for multi-layer feedforward network is [15]:

$$\Delta w_l = \alpha y_{l-1}^T \delta_l \qquad (9)$$

Where w_l is a $m \times n$ weight matrix connecting layer $l-1$ and l, m is the size of layer $l-1$ and n is the size of layer l, α is the learning rate (a scalar), y_{l-1}^T is transpose of the column vector y_{l-1} which is the output in layer $l-1$, δ_l is a column vector of error propagated from layer l to $l-1$, $l = 0$ for the input layer. For output layer and for hidden layer the vector of backpropagated error, δ_l, is deferent and defined as:

$$\delta_l = \begin{cases} (T-Z)* f_l'(net_l) & if \; l \; is \; an \; output \; layer \\ f_l'(net_l)* w_{l+1}\delta_{l+1} & if \; l \; is \; a \; hidden \; layer \end{cases} \tag{10}$$

Where $f_l'(.)$ is the derivative of transfer function, f_l, in layer l, net_l is the weighted sum in layer l, δ_{l+1} is the delta value backpropagated from the upper layer of layer l, * denotes the element-wise vector multiplication, T is the target vector, Z is the output vector. To applying TD learning to the multi-layer feedforward network, we extract the term $(T-Z)$ from the original δ_l and obtain the δ_l^* as a new delta rule. So we define δ_{k+1}^* as:

$$\delta_{k+1}^* = diag[f'_{k+1}(net_{k+l})] \tag{11}$$

Where $diag$ is the diagonal matrix and 1 is the output layer. If l is a hidden layer, equation (11) can be written as:

$$\delta_l^* = f_l'(net_l)* w_{l+1}.\delta_{l+1}^* \tag{12}$$

With the new delta, equation for change of each weight is rewritten as:

$$[\Delta w_l]_{ij} = \alpha[y_{l-1}]_i[\delta_l]_j = \alpha(T-Z)^T.([y_{l-1}]_i[\delta_l^*]_j) \tag{13}$$

Where $[\delta_l^*]_j$ is the jth element in vector δ_l^* and $[y_{l-1}]_i$ is the ith element in vector y_{l-1}. Unlike the original delta which is a vector backpropagated from an upper to a lower layer, now the new delta, δ_l^* is a $m \times n$ matrix where m is the size of output layer and n is the size of layer l. The error term $(T-Z)$ is needed for calculation of every weight increment. Comparing gradient decent in supervised learning in equation (5) and the backpropagation with new delta in equation (11) $\nabla_w P(t)$, the gradient term at time t for weight w' is:

$$\nabla_{w'} P_t = ([y_{l-1}]_i[\delta_l^*]_j)^T \tag{14}$$

Where $w' = [w_l(l)]_{ij}$ is the ijth element in the weight matrix w_l at the time t. By substituting this result to the formula of $TD(\lambda)$ learning in equation (7), we have:

$$[\Delta w_{lt}(t)]_{ij} = \alpha(P(t+1)-P(t))^T \sum_{k=1}^{t} \lambda^{t-k} ([y_{l-1}(k)]_i[\delta_l^*(k)]_j)^T \tag{15}$$

Where $\Delta w_{lt}(t)$ is the matrix of increment of weight connecting layer l and $l-1$ for prediction P_t. The term inside summation is called the history vector, denoted by $[h(t)]_{ij}$. We now obtain updating rules of TD learning by backpropagation. The weight update is performed by equation (15) with the new delta.

3.3   Training Procedure

Compared to the original backpropagation algorithm, the new procedures for $TD(\lambda)$ learning requires some more storage for keeping the following values:

A. The previous output vector, P_{t-1}, at time t, which is used in computing every weight change.

B. The history vector, $h_l(t,i,j) = \sum \lambda^{t-k} [\delta_l^*(k)]_j [y_{l-1}(k)]_i$ for each weight-connecting ith node in layer $l-1$ to jth node in layer l. It has the same size as the output vector. Each weight shall have its own history vector. The training procedure involves 3 stages (at time t):

   1. Feedforward: calculation of new prediction P_t.

   2. Weight update: calculation of weight increments by equation (15) using the history terms at time $t-1$.

   3. Backprop: calculation of the new deltas at time $t+1$;, for each layer l, starting from the output layer. The history term is updated by:

$$h_l(t,i,j) = [\delta_l^*(t+1)]_j [y_{l-1}(t+1)]_i + \lambda h_l(t-1,i,j)_i \qquad (16)$$

4   Design of TDMLP Neural Network for Power System LFC

The objective of the controller design in interconnected power system is damping of the frequency and tie-line power deviations oscillations, stability of the overall system for all admissible uncertainties and load disturbances. Fig.2 shows the block diagram of the closed-loop system, consists of TDMLP controller. The simulation results on a single machine power system show that the performance of MLP neural network is much better than conventional PID controllers. Therefore, for the design of the nonlinear LFC controller in two areas power systems the MLP neural network is being used. Since the objective of LFC controller design in interconnected power system are damping the frequency and tie-line power deviations with minimizing transient oscillation under the different load conditions. Thus, frequency deviations, tie-line power deviations and the load perturbation are chosen as MLP neural network inputs. Moreover, in order to evaluate the control signal (u), the MLP neural network controller makes use of a piece of information which is not used in the conventional and modern controller (an estimate of the load perturbation $\Delta\hat{P}D_i$).

In general, the load perturbation of the large system is not directly measurable. Therefore, it must be estimated by a linear estimator or by a nonlinear neural network estimator, if the nonlinearities in the system justify it. Such an estimator takes as inputs a series of k samples of the frequency fluctuations at the output of the generator $[\Delta F(n) \quad \Delta F(n-1) \quad ... \quad \Delta F(n-k+1)]^T$, and estimates the instantaneous value of the load perturbation based on this input vector. The implementation of such an estimator is beyond the scope of this paper. Here, we assume that the load estimate $\Delta \hat{P} D_i$ is available, i.e. $\Delta \hat{P} D(n) = \Delta PD(n)$. Thus, frequency deviations, tie-line power deviations and the load perturbation are chosen as the MLP neural network inputs. The outputs of the neural network are the control signals, which are applied to the governors. The data required for the MLP neural network training is obtained from the TDL design in different operating conditions and under various load disturbances.

5   Simulation Results

For small sampling time, it can be shown that the discrete-time model is almost the same as the continuous-time model. Hence, the simulations have been carried out in MATLAB software using continuous-time domain functions. In this study, the application of TDMLP neural controller for LFC in two areas power system is investigated. The performance of this method is compared with the RBF neural controller and PID controller, which has been widely used in power system.

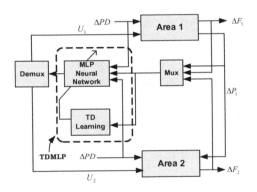

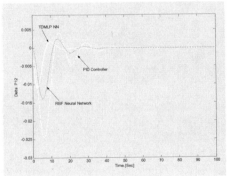

Fig. 2. Block-Diagram of the TDMLP neural network applied to LFC

Fig. 3. The performance of controllers with nominal parameters

Fig. 3 to 5 depicts performances of the TDMLP, RBF and PID controllers when different load step disturbances in two areas are applied to the system. Fig.3 shows the tie-line power deviations when a 2% and 0.5% load step disturbances are applied in areas 1 and 2, respectively. Fig.4 shows the performances of controllers with applying a 0.5% and 1.5% load step disturbances to 1 and 2 areas, respectively, whereas the parameters are decreased from their nominal values to the minimum values. Fig.5 shows the responses of the controllers when the parameters are increased from their nominal values to their maximum values and a 2% and 0.8% load step disturbance are applied to 1 and 2 areas, respectively.

To show the performance of the proposed controller, we run several tests, not shown here. The obtained simulation results show that the proposed TDMLP neural network is very effective and not only has good performance, even in the presence of the GRC, but also ensures the stability of the overall system, especially when the parameters and the operating conditions of the system are changed.

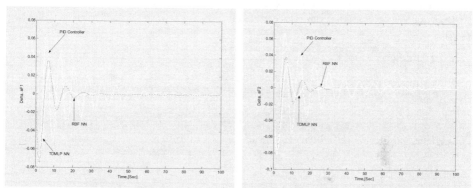

Fig. 4. The performance of the controllers for frequency deviations with minimum parameters

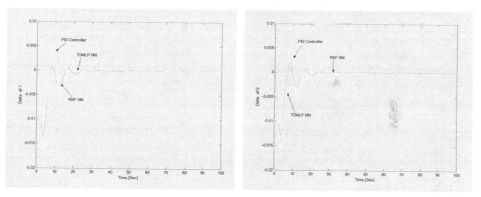

Fig. 5. The performance of the controllers for frequency deviations with maximum parameters

From these figures, it is seen that the proposed method is superior compared to other controllers against to increasing of the step load disturbances in the areas of power systems, especially when the system parameters are changing.

6   Conclusion

This paper showed an application of the neural network to automatic generation control in the power system. In this paper, a TDMLP neural network load frequency control was proposed to improve the performance and stability of the power system. This control strategy was chosen because the power systems involve many parametric uncertainties with varying operating conditions. In this work, transient behavior of the frequency of each area and tie-line power deviations in the power system with two areas is considered under any load perturbations in any area. The simulation results showed that proposed controller is effective and can ensure that the overall system will be stable for all admissible uncertainties and load disturbances, also The TDMLP controller can achieve good performance even in the presence of GRC, especially when the system parameters are changing. And the performance of the proposed controller is better than RBF neural network and PID controller to the load disturbances at any area in the interconnected power system.

References

[1]   Tetsuo Sasaki; Toshihisa Kadoya; Kazuhiro Enomoto, "Study on Load Frequency Control Using Redox Flow Batteries", IEEE Trans. on Power Systems, pp.1-8, 2003
[2]   Young-Hyun Moon; Heon-Su Ryu; Jong-Gi Lee; Seogjoo Kim;" Power system load frequency control using noise-tolerable PID feedback", IEEE International Symposium on Industrial Electronics, Volume: 3, pp. 1714-1718, 2001
[3]   el-din Azzam, M.;" An optimal approach to robust controller design for load-frequency control", Transmission and Distribution Conference and Exhibition, Vol. 1, pp. 180-183, 2002
[4]   Jafari-Harandi M. and S. M. T. Bathee, "Decentralized variable-structure and fuzzy logic load frequency control of multi-area power systems", Fuzzy Logic Symposium, Malaysia, 1997.
[5]   Wang, Y.; Zhou, R.; Wen, C.;" Robust controller design for power system load frequency control", First IEEE Conference on Control Application, Vol. 2, pp. 642-646, 1992
[6]   Talaq, J.; Al-Basri, F.;" Adaptive fuzzy gain scheduling for load frequency control", IEEE Transactions on Power Systems, Vol. 14, Issu 1, pp. 145-150, 1999
[7]   Beaufays F. et al, "Application of neural networks to load frequency control in power system", Neural Networks, Vol. 7, No.1, PP. 183-194, 1994.
[8]   Shayeghi, H. A. Shayanfar, "Application of ANN Technique for Interconnected Power System Load Frequency Control", Internationa Power System Conference, PSC04, Tehran, pp. 33-40, 2003
[9]   P. Dayan, "Temporal Differences: $TD(\lambda)$ for General λ", Machine Learning, in press, 1991
[10] R. P. Lippmann, "An Introduction to Computing with Neural Nets", IEEE ASSP Magazine, 4-22, 1987
[11] R. S. Sutton, "Temporal Credit Assignment in Reinforcement Learning", Doctoral Dissertation, Department of Computer and Information Science, University of Massachusetts, Amherst, 1984
[12] R. S. Sutton and A. G. Barto, "A Temporal Difference Model of Classical Conditioning", Proceedings of the Ninth Annual Conference of the Cognitive Science Society, 355-378, Seattle, WA: Lawrence Erlbaum, 1987
[13] Perlovsky L.I., "Emotions, Learning and control," proc. of IEEE Int. symp. On Intelligent control/Intelligent systems and semiotics, Cambridge MA, pp. 132-137, 1999
[14] R.S.Sutton, "Learning to Predict by the Methods of Temporal Differences," Machine Learning, 3: 9-44, 1988
[15] D.E.Rumelhart, G.E.Hinton, and R.J.Williams, "Learning Internal Representations by Error Propagation," Parallel Distributed Processing (PDP): Exploration in Microstructure of Recognition (Vol. 1), Chapter 8, MIT Press, Cambridge, Massachusetts, 1986

Rule Based Neural Networks Construction for Handwritten Arabic City-Names Recognition

Labiba Souici, Nadir Farah, Toufik Sari, and Mokhtar Sellami

Departement d'informatique, Laboratoire LRI
University Badji Mokhtar BP 12 Annaba
ALGERIA
souici@lri-annaba.net

Abstract. A recent innovation in artificial intelligence research has been the integration of multiple techniques into hybrid systems. These systems seek to overcome the deficiencies of traditional artificial techniques by combining techniques with complementary capabilities. At the crossroads of symbolic and neural processing, researchers have been actively investigating the synergies that might be obtained from combining the strengths of these two paradigms. In this article, we deal with a knowledge based artificial neural network for handwritten Arabic city-names recognition. We start with words perceptual features analysis in order to construct a hierarchical knowledge base reflecting words description. A translation algorithm then converts the symbolic representation into a neural network, which is empirically trained to overcome the handwriting variability.

1 Introduction

Nowadays, artificial neural networks (ANNs) are widely used in different fields especially to find a response to the challenge of automatic pattern recognition [4] but even today's most powerful computers are unable to reach human performance.
Neural networks have been heavily researched and many architectures and training techniques have been proposed. ANNs can be basically categorized into two types:

- Those where each neuron corresponds to a specific concept, working mode is fully explainable and with no learning phase. They thus fall into the category of transparent systems or networks with local representation [5].
- Those where a concept is distributed over several neurons, working mode is opaque and learning is done by adaptively updating weights of their connections. They are thus called black box systems with distributed representation [5].

Most of the networks used for pattern recognition are distributed ones [4]. They show advantages for gradual analog plausibility, learning, robust fault-tolerant processing and generalization. However, there is not yet a problem independent way to choose a good network topology. Learning phase is intensive, time consuming and needs a

C. Bussler and D. Fensel (Eds.): AIMSA 2004, LNAI 3192, pp. 331–340, 2004.

large database. Moreover, it is difficult to explain the networks behavior and to analyze the origin of their errors.

On the other side of *modeling a mind* by ANNs, *making a mind* can be achieved by symbolic approaches. Their representations have advantages of easy interpretation, explicit control, fast initial coding, dynamic variable binding and knowledge abstraction. This approach is not adapted to the approximate or incomplete information processing so the theoretical knowledge must be at a time correct and complete and its processing is sequential.

Both symbolic and neural paradigms have their own advantages and deficiencies. Most importantly, the virtues of one approach could compensate the deficiencies of the other.

In recent years, the research area of symbolic and neural hybridization has seen a remarkably active development. Furthermore, there has been an enormous increase in the successful use of hybrid intelligent systems in many diverse areas [7, 20].

Our research addresses Arabic handwriting recognition, in previous works we have used neural nets with distributed representation for character recognition [13] and local representation for word recognition [15].

In this paper, we deal with the combination of both approaches (symbolic and connectionist) in building a knowledge based artificial neural network (KBANN) system for Arabic handwriting city-names recognition.

The following sections introduce a general state of the art on mail sorting then an overview on the proposed system architecture is presented. A focus is done on feature extraction and recognition steps in sections 4 and 5. At the end of the paper, experimental results are discussed and future directions are highlighted.

2   State of the Art of Mail Sorting

The postal address reading is considered as the most successful applications of pattern recognition [12, 17]. They are writer independent, off-line systems processing large vocabularies (several thousands of words). However, the redundancy existing between the city name and the zip code can be exploited to improve their performance. A great amount of mail is processed every day by the postal services in the world. As an example, in 1997 the US Postal Service processed about 630 millions of letters per day [16]. With this large quantity of mail the use of automatic systems for postal addresses sorting is therefore primordial. The text to extract can involve: zip code, city name, street number and name, postal box, etc. These data can be in printed, isolated handwritten or cursive forms. Components of mail sorting system are: image acquisition, address field localization, text reading and finally the determination of the mail destination. The localization of the address field includes, [2, 3, 6, 16], a pre-processing step : thresholding and binarization, segmentation in lines and in bounding boxes [9] and a segmentation-detection step of the way number and name, apartment number, postal box, city and country names, etc. The address determination, i.e. final customer or local delivery point, consist in recognizing localized units such as characters, words, punctuations, etc. and to interpret the recognized symbols according to the data base of valid addresses. For character and word recognition, all known techniques of pattern recognition can be applied. Nevertheless, the more investigated seems to be statistical methods such as K nearest neighbours (KNN), Hidden markov models (HMM), artificial neural nets (ANN) etc. Srihari in [16], implemented several classifiers: a structural, a hierarchical, a neuronal and a template matching based recognizers individually and in combination for character recognition, then he developed an HMM module for word recognition. In [3], HMM letters are combined in HMM words for the recognition of way names in French postal addresses.

All the above techniques and many others are operational in commercialized systems all around the world but they are generally dedicated to roman or Asian script processing. Nevertheless, no such system exists for Arabic script, in spite of the fact that more than 20 countries use it.

3 General Architecture of Our System

In this paper, we propose a KBANN based system for handwritten city-names recognition in Algerian postal addresses (fig. 1).

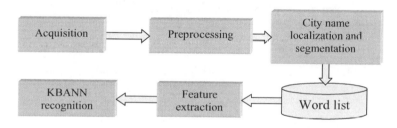

Fig. 1. General architecture of the system.

3.1 Acquisition and Preprocessing

Addresses are acquired in gray levels at 200DPI (dots per inch) resolution. We apply on each image a median filter with 3x3 window as structuring element in order to eliminate the background and reduce the noise. A mean local thresholding operation transforms the image to a binary matrix (1 for the text and 0 for the background) [2, 6, 10].

3.2 City Name Localization and Extraction

We extract the writing of the line which containing the city name and the zip code (it is generally the line before the last one). To localize the city name, we use a technique based on word gap statistics [6]. We compute gaps between connected components extracted by vertical projections of the whole address. The gap mean value is used as segmentation threshold. Gaps greater than the threshold represent word-gaps. The more closely connected component to the left corresponds to the zip code while the right ones correspond to the city name, heart of our concern. Arabic text is written and read from right to left and a city name can be composed of several words. This module generates a lit of words corresponding to the city name for the feature extraction module.

4 Feature Extraction

Among the 28 basic arabic letters, 6 are not connectable with the succeeding letter, thus, an Arabic word may be decomposed into sub-words, High or low secondary components exist for 15 letters which have one to three dots. Some of these characters have the same primary component and differ only by the position and/or the number of dots. We can also find loops, ascenders and descenders in arabic writing [1] (see figure 2).

Evidence from psychological studies of reading indicates that humans use perceptual features such as ascenders, descenders loops and word length in fluent reading [8]. Algorithms based on word shape features are often said to be *holistic* approach, as opposed to *analytical* ones that determines the identity of the word from its characters.

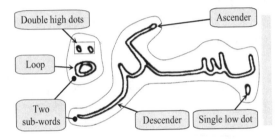

Fig. 2. Features in the word بسكرة

Our previous experiments with holistic arabic literal amounts recognition [14, 15] proved the usefulness of perceptual features and diacritical dots.

In this work, the same set of features is retained and extracted by contour tracing and Freeman chain coding [11]. The features used to describe the 55 words of Algerian city names lexicon are shown in table 1, with their number of possible occurrences.

Table 1. Chosen features in the city-name lexicon

Code	Meaning
xSW	Sub-words number (x=1..5)
xA	Ascenders number (x=0..5)
xL	Loops number (x=0..3)
xD	Descenders number (x=0..3)
xSHD	« Single High Dot » number (x=0..3)
xSLD	« Single Low Dot » number (x=0..2)
xDHD	« Double High Dots » number (x=0..2)
xDLD	« Double Low Dots » number (x=0..2)
xTHD	« Triple High Dots » number (x=0..1)

Ideally, the considered lexicon is described by a set of features (see table 2) ordered as in table 1.

Table 2. Words description in city-names lexicon

N°	Description	Word	N°	Description	Word
1	1-000-10010	عين	28	2-210-11010	البيض
2	1-010-01200	تبسة	29	2-230-00200	قالمة
3	1-011-01000	بو	30	2-310-10001	الشلف
4	1-100-02010	جيجل	31	2-320-11100	الجلفة
5	1-110-00210	تسمسيلت	32	3-002-01020	عريريج
6	1-110-20101	خنشلة	33	3-021-20100	تندوف
7	1-120-00110	مسيلة	34	3-023-10000	وزو
8	1-120-00110	ميلة	35	3-101-00210	تيارت
9	1-120-10010	سطيف	36	3-111-10200	تمنراست
10	1-121-00000	معسكر	37	3-111-11210	تيبازة
11	1-130-20210	قسنطينة	38	3-132-00200	ورقلة
12	2-000-00020	سيدي	39	3-201-10020	إليزي
13	2-001-02000	برج	40	3-201-30010	غليزان
14	2-001-10120	تيزي	41	3-220-00110	المدية
15	2-020-00110	سعيدة	42	3-310-01110	البليدة
16	2-021-00100	سوق	43	3-320-10100	الدفلة
17	2-021-10201	تموشنت	44	3-330-10100	النعامة
18	2-101-01001	بشار	45	4-111-00000	مرداس
19	2-110-02110	بجاية	46	4-111-10110	غرداية
20	2-110-11100	عنابة	47	4-122-10000	وهران
21	2-110-11200	باتنة	48	4-211-00000	أهراس
22	2-111-00000	أم	49	4-222-01110	البويرة
23	2-111-01100	بسكرة	50	4-302-11000	الجزائر
24	2-131-20100	مستغانم	51	4-321-01110	البواقي
25	2-210-00110	سكيكدة	52	4-421-10000	الطارف
26	2-210-02000	بلعباس	53	5-202-00000	أدرار
27	2-210-10100	تلمسان	54	5-311-00010	الوادي
			55	5-521-10000	الأغواط

For example, the description of the word عنابة (Table 2, word N :20) is 2-110-11100, this means that this words has: 2SW-1A, 1L, 0D, 1SHD, 0SLD, 1DHD, 0DLD, 0TPH (see table 1 for the used abbreviations).

5   Design of KBANN Classifier

The designed classifier is inspired by the KBANN approach (Knowledge Based Artificial Neural Network) developed by Towell in 1991 and tested in the fields of molecular biology, DNA sequence analysis and process control. Towell presented theoretical and experimental validations of his approach. KBANN results were better than eight other empirical and hybrid approaches [18, 19].

Theoretical knowledge expressed by rules is used to determine the initial topology of the neural network. The network is then refined using standard neural learning algorithm and a set of training examples.

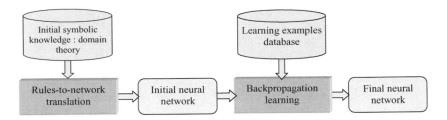

Fig. 3. Knowledge base and neural network integration

In our approach, we have used the KBAN integration depicted in fig 3. It is therefore necessary to:
1. Construct a knowledge base describing the words with their features. The rule sets must be hierarchically structured.
2. Translate the rules into a neural network with a translation algorithm.
3. Refine the neural network with an empirical learning process (back-propagation algorithm).

5.1   Knowledge Base Construction

Study of the extracted features (section 4) is used to create a hierarchical classification for words in the considered lexicon and to deduce (from table 2) a set of rules having the following form:

IF Characteristic THEN Assignment.

To illustrate each rules level, we only give an example concerning the word shown in fig 2. (see table 1 for the used abbreviations).

Level 1 rules : contains 5 rules defining word classes Ci according to their sub-words number (the sub-words separation is generally done by writers).

if 2SW then C2

Level 2 rules: contains 41 rules defining word sub-classes according to their ascenders, loops and descenders numbers.

if C2 and 1A and 1L and 1D then C2_111

Level 3 rules : contains 55 rules defining word *sub-sub*-classes according to their diacritical dots numbers.

if C2_111 and 0SHD and 1SLD and 1DHD and 0DLD and 0THD then بسكرة

5.2   Rules to Network Translation

A translation algorithm transfer's theoretical knowledge (symbolic rules) towards an ANN. Fig 4 shows relations between a set of rules and an ANN. This way of defining networks avoids some of the problems inherent to ANNs and empirical learning. The initial architecture of the network is obtained in an automatic way and we don't have any more worries to determine the number of layers, neurons and interconnections. Besides this, rules give to the network an initial knowledge and represent dependency relations between the input attributes and the desired answers.

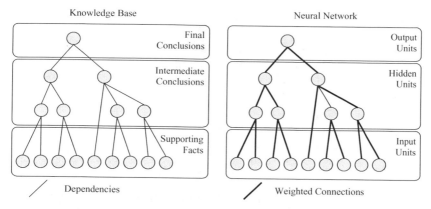

Fig. 4. Correspondences between knowledge base and neural network [19]

Table 3 briefly describes the four steps of the used translation algorithm.

Table 3. Rules-to-network translation algorithm [19]

Step 1 : Rule rewriting
This step ransforms the set of rules into a format that clarifies its hierarchical structure and makes it possible to directly translate the rules into a neural network. Rules rewriting doesn't change knowledge but only the written rules representation.
Step 2 : Network mapping and numbering
This step establishes a mapping between a set of rules and a neural network. Using this mapping (Fig 3), the algorithm creates networks that have one to one correspondence with elements of the rule set. Weights on all links specified by the rule set, and units activation are initialized so that the network responds in exactly the same manner as the rules upon which it is based.
The knowledge based networks code weights and thresholds according to the rule type:
- Weights of connections for a positive premise are initialized to: Weight = +W;
- Weights of connections for a negative premise are initialized to: Weight = -W;
- Thresholds of conjunction resulting units are initialized to: Threshold = (-P + 0.5) * W;
- Thresholds of disjunction resulting units are initialized to: Threshold = - 0.5 * W;
The W value is a constant value specified by the user. Bigger is W, bigger will be the gap between a positive conclusion and a negative one. The P value indicates the number of positive premises (without negation) in the antecedents list for a conclusion unit.
The translation algorithm also numbers units in the obtained neural network. This number is not useful by itself, but it is a necessary precursor to the following steps.
Step 3 : Units and connections adding
This step adds hidden units to the initial neural network, there by giving it the ability to learn derived features not specified in the initial rule set but suggested by the expert. This may be optional because initial rules are often sufficient to obviate the need for adding hidden units. It is also possible to add input units for providing the initial network with input features not referred to by the rule set but which a domain expert believes are relevant.
Step 4 :. Weights perturbing
The final step in the rules-to-network translation is to perturb all the weights in the network by adding a very small random value to each weight. This perturbation is too small to have an effect on the network computations prior to training. However, it is sufficient to avoid problems caused by symmetry.

The obtained initial architecture of the network is probably more close to the final one than any random configuration of weights. Thus, the random initialization of weights and its negative consequences on the training phase can be controlled and minimized. Towell showed in his research [18, 19] that this type of approach reduces the training time and the number of examples to really learn.

---

338   L. Souici et al.

5.3 Neural Network Architecture and Training

The obtained network has the following architecture:
- An input layer with 34 neurons representing the set of chosen features with their possible occurrences (see Table 1).
- Two hidden layers: the first contains 5 neurons and the second 41 neurons (see section 5.1).
- An output layer with 54 neurons corresponding to the 55 words of the city-name lexicon. Note that there is a feature discrimination problem between words n°:7 and 8 (in table 2). We assume that they correspond to the same output neuron. This ambiguity can be solved later by zip code confrontation.

The network obtained from symbolic rules can be trained on classified examples to refine the knowledge previously introduced in the network, using back-propagation algorithm.

6 Results and Discussion

In addition to the application of KBANN approach for the considered problem, we have also implemented a standard multilayer perceptron (MLP). The latter has the same inputs and outputs as the former but it has only one hidden layer which size is heuristically determined and experimentally adjusted. KBANN and MLP classifiers properties and results are summarized in table 4.

Table 4. Comparison between KBANN and MLP for city-names recognition.

		MLP classifier	KBANN classifier
Architecture	Input neurons	34	34
	Hidden layer	1	2
	Hidden neurons	48	5+41
	Output neurons	54	54
Training phase	Database size *	55x30 writers =1650 words **	55x10 writers =550 words**
	Time	≈ 3 Hours	≈ 20 minutes
	Recognition rate	≈ 94 %	≈ 96 %
Testing phase	Database size *	55x 10 writers	55 x 10 writers
	Recognition rate	≈ 80 %	≈ 92 %

* Training and testing databases are distinct (different writers).
** The KBANN training database is a part of the MLP one.

Table 4 highlights the strengths of the KBANN compared to classical MLP for handwritten Arabic city-names recognition. It shows that KBANN training is accelerated and needs fewer examples. During testing phase, KBANN generalizes better than MLP on the same test set.

7   Conclusion and Future Work

In this article, we proposed a hybrid neuro-symbolic (KBANN) system for the recognition of handwritten city-names in Algerian postal addresses. The perceptual features analysis led to the construction of a hierarchical knowledge base reflecting words description. A translation algorithm converted the symbolic representation into a neural network then, an empirical learning phase was necessary to overcome the variability of writing and ill-detected features.

Neuro-symbolic integration supports the thesis that a system which learns from both theory and data can outperform a system that learns from theory or data alone. The obtained results for our application verify this hypothesis.
The knowledge insertion (rules) into the network solves the problems related to architecture specification and weights initialization in neural networks. It accelerates significantly the training process by setting initial connection weights on the basis of the domain theory rather than at random, thus the convergence is guaranteed in due time. We experimentally verified this assumption and we noticed that training takes about 10 times less than randomly initialized multilayer neural network.

The network structure given by the rule-to-network translation has a direct correspondence with the original set of rules. The intermediate concepts are preserved.
The network training can be achieved on a smaller set of examples since the initial network can code theoretical knowledge. In addition, the rules are clearly presented in the network and they explain its behavior versus the MLP black box.
Some future directions are suggested below to further improve our work:
- The insertion of fuzzy concepts within the rules may be interesting due to the handwriting fuzzy nature.
- The combination of KBANN with other kinds of simple and hybrid classifiers for the same application in order to improve recognition accuracy.
- The implementation of a complete multilingual (Arabic, Latin) addresses interpretation system including the script identification and the processing of all address components.

References

1.   Amin A: Off-line arabic character recognition: The state of the art. Pattern Recognition, Vol 31, N°5 (1998) 517-530

2.   Bennasri A., Zahour A., Taconet B.: Arabic script preprocessing and application to postal addresses. ACIDCA'2000, Vision & Pattern Recognition, Monastir, Tunisia (2000) 74-79
3.   Bertille J.M., Gilloux M., El Yacoubi A. : Localisation et reconnaissance conjointes de noms de voies dans les lignes distribution des adresses postales. SRTP/RD/Traitement automatique ligne distribution, Transition n°7 (1994) 16-25
4.   Bishop C. M.: Neural networks for pattern recognition. Clarendon Press, Oxford (1995)
5.   Côté M., Lecolinet E., Suen C.Y.: Automatic reading of cursive scripts using a reading model and perceptual concepts: The percepto system. IJDAR: International Journal on Document Analysis and Recognition, Vol 1 (1998) 3-17
6.   Dowton A.C., Leedham C.G.: Preprocessing and presorting of envelope images for automatic sorting using OCR. Pattern Recognition, Vol. 23, n°. 3/4 (1990) 347-362
7.   Hilario M.: An overview of strategies for neurosymbolic integration. In: Sun R. & Alexandre F. (Eds.). Connectionist-Symbolic Integration: From Unified to Hybrid Approaches, Chapter 2., Lawrence Erlbaum Associates (1997)
8.   Madhvanath S., Govindaraju V.: The role of holistic paradigms in handwritten word recognition. IEEE Transactions on Pattern Analysis and Machine Intelligence, Vol 23, N°:2, February (2001)
9.   Mahadevan U., Srihari S.N.: Parsing and recognition of city, state and ZIPcodes in handwritten addresses. ICDAR'99 (1999) 325-328.
10. Otsu N.: A threshold selection method from gray-level histogram. IEEE Transaction on image processing (1979) 62-66
11. Pavlidis T.: Algorithms for Graphic and Image Processing", Rockville, MD : Computer science press (1982)
12. Plamondon R. and Srihari S.N.: On-line and off-line handwritten recognition: a comprehensive survey. IEEE Trans. on PAMI, Vol. 22, n°. 22 (2000) 63-84.
13. Sari T., Souici L., Sellami M.: Off-line Handwritten Arabic Character Segmentation and Recognition System: ACSA-RECAM. IWFHR'2002, 8th International Workshop on Frontiers in Handwriting Recognition, Niagara-on-the-Lake, Ontario, Canada, August (2002)
14. Souici L., Aoun A., Sellami M.: Global recognition system for Arabic literal amounts. International Conference on Computer Technologies and Applications, ICCTA'99, Alexandria, Egypt, August (1999)
15. Souici-Meslati L., Rahim H., Zemehri M. C Sellami M. Système Connexionniste à Représentation Locale pour la Reconnaissance de Montants Littéraux Arabes. CIFED'2002, Conférence Internationale Francophone sur l'Ecrit et le Document, Hammamet, Tunisie, Octobre (2002)
16. Srihari S. N.: Recognition of handwritten and machine printed text for postal address interpretation. Pattern Recognition Letters: Special issue on postal processing and character recognition, Vol 14, N°: 4, April (1993) 291-302
17. Srihari S.: Handwritten address interpretation: a task of many pattern recognition problems. Int. Journal of Pattern Recognition and Artificial Intelligence, 14 (2000) 663–674
18. Towell G. G., Shavlic J. W.: Knowledge-based artificial neural networks. Artificial Intelligence, Vol 70 (1994) 119-165
19. Towell G. G.: Symbolic knowledge and neural networks : insertion, refinement and extraction. PhD thesis, University of Wisconsin, Madison, WI (1991)
20. Wermter S., Sun R.: Hybrid neural systems. Springer (2000)

A Generic E-learning Engineering Framework Embracing the Semantic Web

Johannes Lischka and Dimitris Karagiannis

University of Vienna, Inst. for Computer Science and Business Informatics, Dept. of
Knowledge Engineering
A-1210 Vienna, Bruenner Strasse 72, Austria
johannes.lischka@univie.ac.at, dk@dke.univie.ac.at

Abstract. E-Learning has become a serious discipline in IT supported management with the aim of enabling life-long learning. Unfortunately, E-Learning is a bottom-up based technical approach and the vision of life-long learning is not yet reached, because it demands the existence of resource pools as a basis enabling cross referencing of topics, skills and all other resources within an organizational memory. Fortunately, new technologies coming from the Semantic Web and Web-Services communities will be able to overcome some of the hindering technical obstacles providing interoperability between different platforms and programming paradigms so that resources can be personalized and presented on arbitrary clients. This paper embraces these technologies and presents a generic E-Learning Engineering approach that fits them into a top-down IT-supported management framework so that business goals may be transformed into a technical environment. Furthermore, this approach also sets grounds for closing the gap to E-Business (e.g. Performance Management like the Balanced Scorecard).

1 Introduction and Motivation – The "Technical" Dilemma

E-Learning is one of the many E-technologies that emerged on the verge of the 21st century promising life-long learning for everyone with perfect integration into an organizational or global memory. "Learn wherever and whenever you want" seems to be the slogan.

But like many other Information Technology (IT) related disciplines, E-Learning applications lack the ability to bridge the gap between organizational and technical requirements which one may call a "technical" Dilemma. Hence, strategic demands for integrated methodologies with support for organizational and technical management methods are neglected. Unfortunately, isolated and non-standards equipped applications are created that bear the tendency to get monolithic legacy applications.

This paper gives a comprehensive overview of the existing E-Learning landscape trying to assemble an engineering stack (layered approach) for E-Business integrated E-Learning with Semantic Web technologies. The approach is three-fold and results in a holistic E-Learning Engineering Framework. First, existing E-Learning standards

C. Bussler and D. Fensel (Eds.): AIMSA 2004, LNAI 3192, pp. 341–350, 2004.

and specifications are surveyed and are fitted into a broader Engineering stack including Business Orchestration and Web-Services execution. Second, this technical E-Learning Engineering Framework needs to be linked into a Business Methodology. These two issues will be scrutinized in Chapter 2. Third, Chapter 3 takes the theory into action and presents a conceptual E-Learning Engineering Framework based on the ADVISOR Modeling Framework. Finally, Chapter 4 looks into the future of E-Learning and especially points out the requirements posed by the European Commission on federal governments within the E-Learning Action Plan.

The aim of this paper therefore is to reverse the "technical" Dilemma in E-Learning by introducing an organizational-driven top-down discipline that is supported by IT with the help of an engineering approach [1]. The so called E-Learning Engineering Framework takes most of its wit from existing Business Engineering [2] ideas transferring it into the domain of E-Learning. With the help of E-Learning Engineering it should be possible to fit learning management into an organizational framework. Like many disciplines in the usual business – procurement, supply-chain management, accounting, etc. – E-Learning also needs to fit into a global strategy in order to measure and increase general efficiency [3].

2   Proposed Solution to the "Technical" Dilemma

As already pointed out, the solution to solving the dilemma in E-Learning is the introduction of a top-down engineering approach called E-Learning Engineering. E-Learning Engineering can be defined as applying Software Engineering to instructional design [4] or as *methods and techniques that deal with the creation of E-Learning applications*"[5].

It also is responsible for managing and engineering the organizational Resource Pool that is the foundation for E-Learning Engineering.

2.1   Description of the E-learning Environment: E-learning Modeling Methods

Modeling Methods on a technical level in terms of reuse and interoperability may be represented in two different ways syntactically: in XML [6] or in the syntax of the Resource Description Framework (RDF) [7].

The motivation to use (Semantic Web) ontologies based on RDF syntax (and related ontology languages like OWL [8]) is simple: RDF is a network-based representation formalism based on Subject-Predicate-Object triples (statements) that embraces the ideas of object-orientation and resource sharing and therefore is much more powerful than hierarchic XML. Furthermore, RDF identifies resources with Uniform Resource Identifiers (URI) and is not restricted to documents like XML [9]. The most highly developed Modeling Method in E-Learning is the RDF-binding of the Learning Objects Metadata (LOM) information model [10].

Another striking argument to choose RDF as underlying syntactical model is the level of acceptance within the Semantic Web community and the fact that also semantic standards seem to emerge bringing LOM and the Dublin Core Metadata Element Set (RDF-binding) [11] closer [12].

2.1.1 Existing E-learning Ontologies

So far, E-Learning ontologies have also been developed with a bottom-up approach deciding first about technical aspects of how to map information models to a technical binding. Concrete examples are complex and rare [12, 13]. Modeling Methods for describing other resources taking part in E-Learning are only poorly developed at this point of time. The Dublin Core Metadata Element Set or the vCard RDF-binding [14] are possibilities to express other relationships. But specific RDF-bindings for Learner Profiles (e.g. Reusable Competency Definitions [15]) do not exist[1].

2.1.2 Querying Ontologies and the Connection to Web-Services

With the use of RDF a Semantic Web for E-Learning is in the near grasp and also embraces the concept for a Service-oriented Architecture (SOA) and currently evolving Web-Services. This new architecture moves away from classical monolithic and proprietary Client-Server applications to interoperable Peer-to-Peer services using globally distributed Resource Pools.

The only drawback to realizing such a scenario is the immaturity of the development of RDF query interfaces. In order to answer simple questions like "Which is the best Learning Object for a set of arbitrary restrictions?" or "Which Learning Objects fit a Learner's Profile?" or more complex questions like "What are my tasks to fulfill the curriculum this term?" or "Is the University doing well according to the strategy" powerful Application Programming Interfaces (API) need to be provided in order to exchange knowledge coming from different ontologies.

2.1.3 Overview of Existing E-learning Modeling Methods

Despite of XML related drawbacks – efforts already exist to implement RDF-bindings [16, 17] – the information models of existing standards and specifications should be sufficient to create a framework of layers that shows the different levels of abstraction in E-Learning.

The so-called E-Learning Framework is depicted in Figure 1 and is input to the more global E-Learning Engineering Framework characterized in Chapter 3 (the Learning Resources Sequencing Layer is part of the proposed E-Learning Engineering Framework, see Figure 3).

2.2 Integration of E-learning into the Business Strategy and Methodology

Chapter 1 already pointed out the tight coupling of a layered framework approach with a methodology, i.e. *"a systematic approach that yields into a predefined target"* [18].

Methodologies for the procedures in E-Learning already exist, e.g. the Plato-Cookbook [19], E-Learning Strategy by Rosenberg [20], Six Steps [21], ADVISOR [22] and Courseware Engineering [23].

---

[1] The question remains, whether other Modeling Methods (e.g. Competency Definitions) need to be taken from specific E-Learning standards, especially in the context of the Semantic Web that per se enables interoperability among existing ontologies through RDF (or de-facto standards like LDAP).

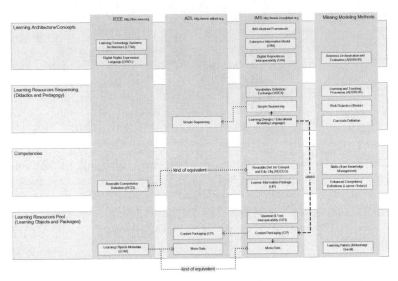

Fig. 1. E-Learning Framework.

But especially in a complex context, an adequate methodology has yet to be defined. Furthermore it is of vital importance to align E-Learning according to global business targets and Knowledge Management methodologies [24].

One of the main tasks in the future of the proposed E-Learning Engineering Framework will cover exactly this alignment of several domain-specific methodologies.

3 Service-Oriented E-learning Engineering Framework

The proposed E-Learning Engineering Framework has the aim of resolving the shortcomings described in Chapter 2.2. This is done primarily by introducing a top-down approach accompanied by a corresponding methodology. The use of ontologies and Web-Services to process the modeled resources is only a technical aspect of the problem[2] – the execution of domain requirements into a technical implementation. As the Semantic Web and RDF seem to stand on solid grounds it was the obvious choice.

The encapsulation of different representations residing in different layers[3] has got several advantages: on the one hand the visualizations (models) created by Modeling Methods contain a great deal of information in a simple way so that both organizational and IT-expert have common grounds to talk about. On the other hand, domain experts are able to design their learning landscape independent of other domains. This concept of abstraction and encapsulation of domain-specific

---

[2] The power of the generic E-Learning Engineering Framework lies in the openness towards customizable Modeling Methods that are able to cover any level of detail of an E-Learning scenario. Depending on a specific implementation, the output can be transformed into any Unicode text-format.

[3] E.g. a Learning Process comprises higher level information than a simple learning resource.

information was greatly successful in the Model-View-Controller concept in Software Engineering. The E-Learning Engineering Framework takes these findings into account, treating the rendering of information supposed for different platforms (View), the ontological resource description (Model) and the execution via Web-Services (Controller). With this conceptual approach, openness, interoperability, extensibility and the possibility to measure details residing in any layer are guaranteed.

In order to depict a holistic view for E-Leaning, the E-Learning Modeling Methods described in Chapter 2.1.3 have to be augmented with Modeling Methods (ontologies) that describe business flows and interrelations as well as technical workflows via Web-Services[4].

The following Chapter 3.1 discusses the need for Process-orientation as conceptual basis for describing information- and data-flows before Chapter 3.2 is dedicated to the actual E-Learning Engineering Framework.

3.1 Process-Orientation and Service-Orientation: Motivation

Process-orientation and Service-orientation are two mutual concepts. Coming from Business Process Management, process flows were the organizational answer to depicting ad-hoc or standard processes over several departments of an organization. This set the foundation for automation of technical IT-services activities via Workflow Management Systems and created highly flexible organizational structures that are able to react quickly to new requirements.

The concept of messaging between peers of IT-systems that provide tiny bits of implementations called services is mirrored in the SOA paradigm (in contrast to Client-Server Architecture). The goal is to describe information- or data-flows according to the organizational requirements that are executed with Web-Services, today's SOA leveraging internet protocols.

A process-oriented representation Modeling Method therefore is the perfect match to depict a chain of activities over heterogeneous resources executed with interoperable services along a value chain. Hence, it also allows the mapping of activity costs for activity-based costing and evaluation (i.e. process cycle times, process costs, etc.).

The same ideas of Process-orientation can be adopted for E-Learning[5]. Conceptually speaking, Learning or Teaching Processes implement the organizational flows of Business Processes and therefore depict the information- and data-flow for learners and teachers as a top-level concept. Heterogeneous skills (Learner Profiles) and document resources (Learning Objects) can be distributed around the world connected by internet technologies (XML, RDF, URI, etc.) that have to be put into the correct context by these Learning and Teaching Processes[6]. An example of a Learning Process in ADVISOR Modeling Method (see Chapter 3.2) is depicted in Figure 2.

---

[4] The implementation of Web-Services workflows is still work in progress. A modeled example of future implementations is depicted in Figure 2.

[5] For other approaches consider [31, 32].

[6] Both Learner Profiles and Learning Objects can be modeled as RDF resources in the ADVISOR modeling tool [27].

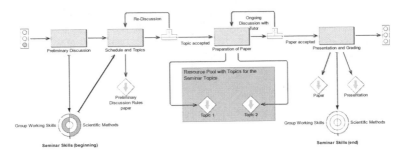

Fig. 2. Process-oriented E-Learning Modeling Method.

Similar to Business Processes, Learning and Teaching Processes can be evaluated in terms of times and costs. These quantitative measures define the interface for further evaluation in E-Business scenarios [28] (e.g. Performance Management with the Balanced Scorecard).

3.2   The Service-Oriented E-learning Engineering Framework in Detail

In order to fit the E-Learning Framework into a SOA, additional layers have to be considered. According to [25] the following layers exist: Discovery, Contracts, Business Process/Workflow, Transactions, Choreography, Conversations, Non-functional description, XML-based messaging and Network.

The Competency and Learning Resource Pool layers from the E-Learning Framework (Figure 1) both describe static relationships and therefore reside outside a SOA. The Learning Resources Sequencing layer can be incorporated into the SOA on the Business Process/Workflow layer. The Learning Architecture is not necessarily of any use anymore, because architectural issues are treated by SOA itself.

Figure 3 therefore depicts the resulting E-Learning Engineering Framework.

3.3   ADVISOR's Modeling Methods According to the E-learning Engineering Framework

As a conclusion to the E-Learning Engineering Framework being the conceptual input, the ADVISOR platform [22, 26] as Ontology Engineering Tool has been customized to visualize all of the required information via generic Modeling Methods. All relevant information ranging from Business Processes, Web-Services Workflows, Organizational Responsibilities, Learning and Teaching Processes and Learning Resources can be modeled (Figure 2 is an example of a Learning Process).

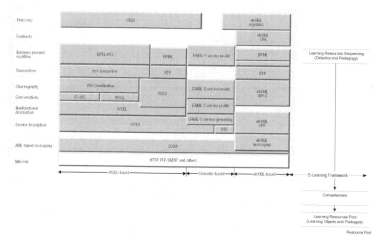

Fig. 3. The E-Learning Engineering Framework (extension of [25]).

As a test-bed to show the technical feasibility of the approach to execute the ADVISOR models with Web-Services, Figure 4 [27] shows the Service-oriented approach for handling RDF resources with arbitrary SOAP-speaking clients.

The Service Provider is the heart of the execution environment. Two entities are embedded within the provider, a Web-Services container and the learning Resources Pool which in this case is represented by the learning resources that were modeled with ADVISOR's RDF Modeling Methods. The Service Requestor is able to communicate with the Service Provider and its linked learning resources by means of SOAP messages.

The approach has to be extended to handle all ADVISOR models. Currently, Web-Services include simple computation of suitable Learning Objects for a given Learner Profile.

The modular E-Learning Engineering Framework presents an open interface for exchanging measures for Performance Management techniques like the Balanced Scorecard. Evaluation measures can be created for the whole model pool (e.g. Class Statistics, Usage of Learning Objects and Conformance to Business Targets).

4   Conclusion and Future Perspectives in E-learning

E-Learning gradually matures from a monolithic technical solution to enhance learning with IT to be a technology integrated into E-Business value chains. To reach this goal, an open and interoperable architecture has to be introduced. Especially in the context of complex scenarios (see Chapter 4.1) this implies the usage of Semantic Web technologies like RDF to meta-tag Learning Resources and to provide Process-oriented models of information- and data-flow.

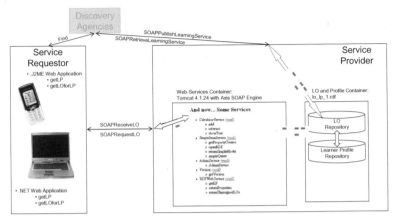

Fig. 4. Test-bed for the E-Learning Engineering Framework.

This paper suggests a so-called E-Learning Engineering Framework that satisfies all these requirements by providing a modular and layered approach. The tool ADVISOR implements the E-Learning Engineering Framework by providing relevant Modeling Methods for treating RDF Learning Resources.

Finally, a test-bed showed the feasibility of this approach.

4.1 E-europe

Modular structures and Learning Resource Pools are a major demand for E-Learning as a strategic governmental issue. The European Commission forces federal European governments and solution providers into implementing the guidelines of the E-Learning Action Plan.

One clear implication is the need for an open and interoperable framework to treat these requirements especially when thinking of the European Masters Programs [29]. With the help of the E-Learning Engineering Framework, a partial solution has been provided already and can be seen as a platform for open discussion to fit the needs of such a complex scenario.

4.2 E-business-Integrated Semantic E-learning

Technologically speaking, the main efforts for the future will be the development of interfaces between ADVISOR and Run-Time Environments. ADVISOR has to satisfy the interfaces existing Learning Management Systems (LMS) – at the moment the IMS Content Package format is supported – and future environments based on open Learning Resource Pools and Web-Services Workflow Engines and Intelligent Agents for fully automated model-driven E-Learning. The test-bed showing the results of RDF Web-Services on different client platforms is only one dimension of ongoing developments.

Another critical issue is the integration of E-Learning into E-Business and Performance Management. The integration of E-Learning into Enterprise Resource Planning (ERP) systems like SAP R/3 has to be dealt with. ADVISOR enables a Process-oriented view on E-Learning and could manage measures for any kind of its models.

4.3 Concluding Statement

The paper proposed the convergence of E-Learning, the Semantic Web and E-Business by introducing a generic Engineering approach with RDF tagged Learning Objects for a Semantic E-Learning and sets the foundation for closing the gap to E-Business and performance management by using a process-oriented paradigm.

Future work in the area of E-Learning embracing Semantic Web technologies and its use will boil down life-long learning without any borders of time or place. That is realizing person-centered communication scenarios where researchers and students can work together according to their Profiles and their corresponding interests identified by referenced (Learning) Resources and calendar information based on Semantic Web ontologies [30].

References

1. Donovan, J. J.: Business Re-Engineering with Information Technology, Prentice Hall, Englewood Cliffs, New Jersey, 1994
2. Giaglis, G. M.: Integrated Design and Evaluation of Business Processes and Information Systems, In: Communications of AIS Volume 2, Article 5, 1999
3. Affeld, D.: Mit Best Practice im Supply Chain Management (SCM) zur Optimierung der Wertschöpfungskette, In: Voegele, A. R., Zeuch, M. P. (Eds.), Supply Network Management, Gabler Verlag, 2002
4. Engineering E-Learning: Engineering E-Learning, http://www.elearning-engineering.com/learning/e-learning/engineering-elearning.htm, access Nov/14th/2003
5. Universität Oldenburg: E-Learning Engineering, http://www-is.informatik.uni-oldenburg.de/forschung/forschung_elearning_inhalt.htm, access Nov/14th/2003
6. W3C: Extensible Markup Language (XML), http://www.w3.org/XML/, access Dec/20th/2003
7. W3C: Resource Description Framework (RDF), http://www.w3.org/RDF/, access Dec/20th/2003
8. W3C: Web-Ontology (WebOnt) Working Group, http://www.w3.org/2001/sw/WebOnt/, access Dec/20th/2003
8. Nilsson, Mikael, Palmer, Matthias, Brase, Jan: The LOM RDF binding - principles and implementation, http://rubens.cs.kuleuven.ac.be:8989/ariadne/CONF2003/papers/MIK2003.pdf, access Dec/20th/2003
10. IEEE: IEEE LTSC | WG12 | PAR 1484.12.4, http://ltsc.ieee.org/wg12/par1484-12-4.html, access Dec/20th/2003
11. DCMI: Expressing Simple Dublin Core in RDF/XML, http://www.dublincore.org/documents/2002/07/31/dcmes-xml/, access Dec/20th/2003

12. Brase, Jan, Nejdl, Wolfgang: Ontologies and Metadata for eLearning, In Staab, S., Studer, R. (Eds.): Handbook on Ontologies, Springer-Verlag, 2003
13. KMR: RDF binding of LOM metadata, http://kmr.nada.kth.se/el/ims/metadata.html, access Dec/20th/2003
14. W3C: Representing vCard Objects in RDF/XML, http://www.w3.org/TR/2001/NOTE-vcard-rdf-20010222/, access Dec/20th/2003
15. IEEE: WG20: Reusable Competency Definitions, http://ltsc.ieee.org/wg20/index.html, access Dec/20th/2003
16. IMS: IMS Resource Description Framework(RDF) Bindings, http://www.imsglobal.org/rdf/index.cfm, access Jul/28th/2003
17. IMS: IMS Content Packaging Specification, http://www.imsglobal.org/content/packaging/index.cfm, access Jul/28th/2003
18. Zschocke, D.: Modellbildung in der Ökonomie, Verlag Franz Vahlen, München, 1995
19. Seufert, Sabine, Back Andreas, Häusler, Martin: E-Learning: Weiterbildung im Internet - Das Plato-Cookbook für internetbasiertes Lernen, SmartBooks Publishing, 2001
20. Rosenberg, Marc J.: E-Learning: Strategies for delivering Knowledge in the Digital Age, McGraw-Hill, 2001
21. Hall, Brandon: Six Steps to Developing a Successful E-Learning Initiative: Excerpts from the E-Learning Guidebook, McGraw-Hill, 2002
22. Lischka, H., Bajnai, J., Karagiannis, D., Chalaris, G.: The Virtual Global University - The Realization of a fully Virtual University - Concept and Experiences, In Auer, M. E., Auer, U. (Eds.): Proceedings of the workshop ICL, 2002
23. Klein, Müge, Stucky, Wolffried: Ein Vorgehensmodell zur Erstellung virtueller Bildungsinhalte, vieweg, Wiesbaden, 2001
24. Karagiannis, D; Stefanidis, G., Woitsch, R.: The PROMOTE approach - Modelling Knowledge Management Processes to describe organisational knowledge systems, In proceedings of OKLC 2002 Athens, 2002
25. Turner, Mark, Budgen, David, Brereton, Pearl: Turning Software into a Service, In Computer.org, IEEE Computer Society, October 2003
26. BOC: ADVISOR, http://www.boc-eu.com/advisor/start.html, access Dec/20th/2003
27. Lischka, J., Karagiannis, D.: Modeling and Execution of E-Learning Resources, in Conference Proceedings of the ACM SAC 2004
28. Bajnai, J., Lischka, J.: Planning and Simulation in an E-Learning Engineering Framework, in Proceedings of the AACE EDMEDIA 2004
29. EU Commission: The ERASMUS University Charter, http://www3.socleoyouth.be/static/en/overview/overview_erasmus_ic_reform/erasmus_university_charter_info.htm, access Jun/20th/2004
30. Lischka J. et al.: Roadmap for Reaching Semantic E-Learning – Test Cases; to appear in Proceedings of ICL 2004
31. Kraemer, W., Zimmermann, V.: Learning Life Cycle Management - Integration von Lernen in die Geschäftsprozesse, http://www.im-c.de/homepage/pdf/m_wolfgang_kraemer_volker_zimmermann.pdf, access Jun/20th/2004
32. IMS: IMS Learning Design Information Model, http://www.imsglobal.org/learningdesign/ldv1p0/imsld_infov1p0.html, access Jun/20th/2004

An Integrated Environment for Building Distributed Multi-agent Educational Applications

Tasos Triantis and Panayiotis Pintelas

Educational Software Development Laboratory,
Department Mathematics, University of Patras, Greece
{triantis, pintelas
http://www.math.upatras.gr/esdlab/

Abstract. In this paper, we present an integrated graphical environment, called X-Genitor, which supports the design and the development of educational applications for distance learning based on the multi-agent technology. The agents that participate in the educational system interact with each other in order to accomplish the common goal of educating the trainees to a particular educational subject. The X-Genitor allows the author to describe, specify and design the behavior of the produced educational application as well as to design and develop the appropriate learning units that will be presented to the trainee during an educational process. An innovation of the X-Genitor architecture is that the produced educational applications support the individualized and distance learning through the attachment of a mobile user interface agent to each trainee.

1 Introduction

In our days distance learning tends to become one of the basic means of human education for all the ages and without upper limit on the number of students. Internet, due to its nature, provides the base for the evolution of the distance learning if the suitable software exists. So far, the traditional learning management systems (LMS) do not provide an efficient way for the distinction of the different levels of student's intelligence as well as they do not emerge adaptive abilities to the students. Being general tools they only pay attention to the presentation technologies and not to the educational method, they present static information, which is unable to be renewed and they are based on a non-adaptable and extensible instructional strategy.

In contrast with such traditional LMS, a wide variety of academic and commercial agent construction tools (environments) have been developed such as Zeus [12] and JADE [11]. A large number of such environments can also be found in portals such as [9] and in network of excellence such as [10]. After a careful research and study of the existing agent construction environments, we decided to implement another integrated MAS (Multi Agent System) construction tool based on the following perspectives.

Firstly, from author's point of view, most of the existing construction environments are developing MAS for general purposes and none for educational applications.

C. Bussler and D. Fensel (Eds.): AIMSA 2004, LNAI 3192, pp. 351–360, 2004.

Secondly, these environments provide a variety of tools in order to easy the agent construction for users that have already some or more knowledge of agent technology. Our goal is to provide authors with an easy to use authoring tool that supports the lifecycle of an educational application (such as managing instructional strategy, managing educational content, publishing educational application), and requires no knowledge of agent technology which is achieved via a graphical formal model that encapsulate well known agent theory such as BDI [1].

Thirdly, from the software engineering point of view, in contrast with the existing environments, X-GENITOR's goals and features is the support of all main phases of software development (such as design, validation, documentation and application production), which is achieved via an Intermediate Design Representation (IDR) that is produced during the design and it is used along to the implementation of the educational application.

Thus, X-GENITOR, which is an evolution of GENITOR [3] an authoring system for constructing Intelligent Tutoring Systems (ITSs), gives the capability to the author to design, specify, describe and produce a distributed educational application based on multi-agent system (MAS) technology.

X-GENITOR involves both the technologies of intelligent agents and the distributed networked applications. Multi-agent approach is suitable for educational applications due to its ability of managing a very complex, dynamic, continually growing and distributed amount of information as well as due to its confrontation of education as a set of distributed expertise's.

The implementation of the X-GENITOR involves the production of a graphical formal method for specifying the intelligent agents and describing their behavior, which is the mechanism that allows the agent to attend, understand the events of its environment and reason about how to act. In addition, X-GENITOR uses an organizational framework, which defines the interaction, the roles and authority redactions among agents. Finally, X-GENITOR provides the production of the intelligent agents through the translation of their specifications, an inter-agent communication language and a communication protocol.

X-GENITOR's architecture is presented in section 2 while its functional view is given in section 3. Section 4 presents a use case of designing an application. In section 5 an application developed with X-GENITOR are shortly presented and finally, conclusions and future work are discussed in section 6.

2   X-Genitor Architecture

X-GENITOR is a software system, which allows the production of distributed educational multi-agent applications (EMAS) using a formal specification model. X-GENITOR's main goal is to allow a author having no knowledge of the agent technology to design the educational multi-agent application as well as to, produce the appropriate Learning Units. A Learning Unit (LU) is considered to be the smallest educational material, which will be displayed by the educational software to the trainee. The design phase of the application involves the specification of (a) the instructional strategy that the educational system should adopt during teaching procedure; (b) the roles and capabilities of each agent that populate the multi-agent system; (c) the inter-relations among the agents. Based on author's design, the authoring system produces and deploys automatically the educational multi-agent system to the student.

The formal specifications model that the author uses is called AOMFG (Agent Oriented Multi Flow Graphs) [8], which in general is a graphical model for the formal specification of multi agent systems, which combines strict formalism (such as intentional logics, modal logic etc.) and practical use by reflecting several modalities and mental notions in its structure. The model functions as a bridge between agent theory and real agent systems. It is based on the widely used Belief-Desire-Intention (BDI) formalism. The BDI architecture constitutes the theoretical background of the model and according to this, an agent in a multi agent system is viewed as having the three mental attitudes of belief, desire and intention.

In addition, it employs the most commonly used principles of state-based machines, programming languages, Cognitive Engineering and interaction specification models. The graphical nature of the model, which is based on the well-known High Level Petri Nets, provides a friendly way for multi agent systems specification by hiding from users the underlying use of mathematical formalism, which may be hard to use by non-specialists.

X-GENITOR provides the ability to the author to design his/her EMAS graphically based on the syntax and semantics of the AOMFG. An EMAS design consists of a set of graphs ordered in a **forest of tree structures**. This forest of trees composes the intermediate representation of the application design (IDR – Intermediate Design Representation), which is used by X-GENITOR system during the overall process of EMAS production.

X-GENITOR's architecture consists of the following modules as shown in Figure 1.

The **Graphical Agent Plans Editor** takes as input the AOMFG structure and is responsible for:

1. Providing the author with the appropriate graphical tools according to the selected model structure,
2. Depicting the graphical design,
3. Checking the design's syntax,
4. And interpreting the set of graphs of the design into the IDR.

The **Validation module** takes as input the IDR and provides the author with the ability of the graphical validation of his/her design. Given an initial mark as well as rules that either are defined by the author or the AOMFG semantics, validation module depicts the control flow of the agent behavior over the graphs. During validation, author participation is needed by simulating either agent's internal or environment's events that may be occurring during EMAS's execution. Application's environment consists of other applications and system resources as well as the end-user that uses it. Validation procedure may be applied to each agent separately.

The **Documentation module** takes as input the IDR and produces the documentation of the design. The documentation consists of the graphs and the added by the author descriptions for each graph.

The **Translator module** takes as input the IDR and translates the intermediate design representation into a specific programming language. The production of the translation is programming code, which is compiled into a self-executable file. Translator module's architecture consists of following sub-modules:

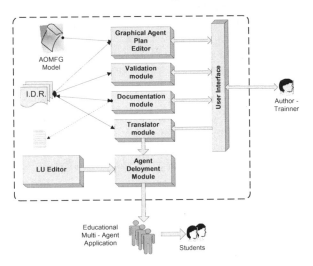

Fig. 1. X-Genitor Architecture

☐ **Programming Language translator**: takes as input the IDR and produce as output each agent's plans translated into a programming language. In X-GENITOR, the language that was adopted is Prolog.

☐ **Programming Language Compiler**: takes as input the agent's plans in the form of programming code and compiles them.

The **Agent Deployment module** is responsible for the deployment of each agent to its physical distributed location, over the network as well as for the start up of the whole MAS application Starting-up a distributed MAS application requires the initialization of each agent separately despite of the its physical location.

The **LU Editor** allows the author to design and produce the appropriate LUs based on HTML technology. A LU is a hypermedia construct of multimedia material. In addition, each LU is described by attributes that represent both static information used to identify the unit (i.e. title, type, location, size, etc.) and dynamic information that describes the behaviour of the unit (i.e. pedagogical prerequisites and objectives, display constraints etc.).

2.1   Agent Architecture

The translation module produces an executable agent whose architecture consists of the following sub-modules:

User Interface (UI): is the *listener* of end user's events on agent. Depending on the interaction between the agent and the end user (the Agent-User Interaction has been defined by the author) the UI can either be simple or complex. In any case, during the design time, the author selects the appropriate, for the agent, UI from precompiled UI Library.

Integration Module: is responsible for transferring environment's events (either user events or communication events) to the Compiled Agent Design module for further processing. The integration module is the Amzi Prolog's Logic Server [14].

Communication Mechanism: is responsible for sending and receiving agents' messages. The adopted technology for the implementation of this module is CORBA [13].

Compiled Agent Design: comprises the knowledge base and the reason-about mechanisms of each agent. Its structure is based on the well-known BDI logical framework where each agent is viewed as having the three mental attitudes of belief, desire and intention (BDI). In addition the three mental attitudes of BDI architecture, every agent contains a plan library. Its agent's plans were designed by the author.

Having the first three modules pre-implemented as a separate executable application, it is possible, due to the integration module, to add different compiled (in prolog) Compiled Agent Designs and produce different ready-to-run agent applications

3   The Multi Agent Tutoring Architecture

Currently, most of the multi-agent educational systems (e.g. [4], [5]) implement (some or all) the modules of a traditional ITS as separate autonomous agents and the whole tutoring system is delivered to the learner through either a web-based user interface or a mobile agent. X-GENITOR's developed applications comprise a tutoring architecture [6] on the basis of distributing both domain knowledge and expertise into several agents, which allows the efficient management of distributed information resources and the dynamic synthesis of the information that is presented to the learner.

In X-GENITOR each educational application may consist of one *instructional agent* and many *domain expert* agents, the configuration of which dynamically changes during the teaching process

The instructional agent undertakes the responsibility to control the information that is presented to the trainee based on a specific instructional strategy, which is embodied to instructional agent's knowledge base. This instructional strategy is implemented as a set of teaching plans; each plan is a sequence of teaching steps, each of which can be carried out by a team of expert agents. Note that the instructional agent is only aware of the specialty of the domain expert agents required per plan step; it then dynamically configures agent teams, based on the set of agents that are active within the system at a particular instance of time.

A domain expert agent is responsible for providing information and educational material to the trainee about its particular domain of knowledge. A domain expert contains a set of plans for recalling and presenting information modules (Learning Units) to the instructional agent. To this end, it is aware of the information resources, which are associated with a specific domain of the educational subject that the tutoring system deals with. In general, each domain expert agent can contribute a part of knowledge or an approach in different parts or cases of the subject; then a team of agents can collectively teach a subject that is beyond the individual capabilities and knowledge of each of the domain expert agents. The synthesis and the management of the distributed expert knowledge are the responsibility of the instructional agent.

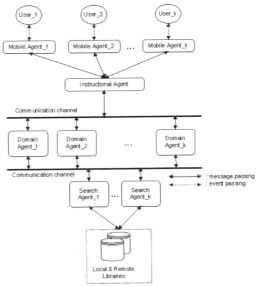

Fig. 2. The Multi Agent Tutoring Architecture

A pool of search agents undertakes the responsibility of searching for educational material through local or remote information resources on behalf of each domain expert agent, who filters the results of the search according to its domain knowledge.

During each step of the teaching process, based on the instructional strategy, the instructional agent forms a team of domain expert agents (based on the specialty and availability of each). Vertical communication between the instructional agent and the expert agents includes:

☐ The request from the instructional agent to each expert agent to execute one of its plans,

☐ The acceptance or rejection of the request by the expert agent

☐ The response of the expert agent to the instructional agent with the information modules that, according to the expert agent, provide a better match to the request of the instructional agent

Moreover, the members of each team communicate horizontally by exchanging messages in order to best meet the tutoring objectives. Such communication may involve:

☐ One expert agent requesting another expert agent to execute one of its plans

☐ One expert agent requesting another expert agent to act as its replacement for the execution of a plan

☐ The acceptance or rejection of the request by the expert agent

☐ The response of an expert agent to the request of another expert agent with the information modules that, according to the called expert agent, provide a better match to the request of the calling expert agent

Then, each domain expert agent serves as a source of information (possibly synthesizing and) providing the appropriate educational material. In order to implement this teaching practice, two fundamental issues have to be resolved:

☐ Subject experts are available. They are capable of working independently, of sensing the educational context and of co-operating with the teacher and provide the knowledge bits he/she asks from each of them

☐ The teaching material is structured in a way that it can be efficiently communicated. Moreover, it includes a description of its content that can be used by the teacher to synthesize a broader course

In order to achieve modular, open and dynamically changing behavior of the system, the communication channel of the above architecture is an agent called Facilitator [2]. Facilitator is not involved in the teaching procedure. This is the reason why Facilitator is not shown in the architecture of the educational system. The role of Facilitator is to provide "yellow pages" services to other agents. In other words, Facilitator is responsible for maintaining an accurate, complete and timely list of the services that a registered agent can provide. When each agent is started, his first responsibility is to register himself and his services to Facilitator.

Each trainee accesses the application remotely through a mobile agent. The mobile agent technology was adopted in the described architecture in order to meet the following features:

1. Distance learning: Each Mobile User Interface Agent moves through the network to trainee's place and interacts with him/her.
2. Individualized education: Each Mobile User Interface Agent is personalized to each trainee in order to track his/her actions and informs the instructional agent.
3. Reduction of network traffic. The information transmitted over the network is minimized, which has strong cost implications for devices connected by public wireless networks.
4. Support for disconnected operation. The mobile agent is still operational even though the client that it is situated on is disconnected from the network. The learning procedure is partially available to the trainee through mobile agent's caching mechanism.
5. Security: the mobile-agent adequately protects the tutoring system itself and LUs' copyrights through the use of encryption algorithm.

4 Designing an Application – A Use Case

The production procedure of an educational application via X-Genitor is as follows. During the design process, the author should define the number of the agents that populate the applications as well as the role of each one. According to the architecture described in section 3, X-Genitor supports two types of roles: the instructional role and the domain expert role. An instructional agent is aware of the overall educational subject as well as of the appropriate instructional strategy that will be adopted during teaching procedure. A domain expert agent provides knowledge, information, and educational material about its particular domain of knowledge.

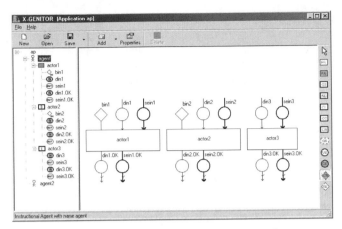

Fig. 3. X-GENITOR's Graphical Agent Plans Editor

Considering that each agent is constructed according to BDI architecture, via the specification editor and the graphical formal model, the author should design each agent's knowledge base (beliefs, desires, Intentions) and capabilities (plans). The instructional strategy should be embodied into instructional agent's plan library.

During design, author has also the ability to (1) re-use parts of plans of agents that have already been designed previously (these plans are already been saved into X-Genitor's plan library); (2) validate the design of each agent separately. Validation procedure depicts the control flow of the agent behavior over the graphs. During validation, author's participation is necessary by simulating either agent's internal or environment's events that may be occurring during application's execution. Application's environment consists of other applications and system resources as well as the student that uses it.

As soon as, the author is convinced that the specification he/she gave meet to application's scope, he/she may produce the executable multi-agent application through the translator.

So far, the author has specified the plans of the agents and the next step is to insert the agents' knowledge. With a specific editor one is able to write in a simple way the LU, which will be in an "html" form and may include apart from text, pictures and sound, video etc. In order to make the recall of information from the domain expert agents possible, the author must give apart from the LUs a meta-information in which key-words about what the LUs include will be mentioned.

Given that the application's construction procedure ended, through the delivery module, the author may deploy either the application on a selected server machine or the constructed LUs over local or remote LUs libraries.

From trainee's point of view, each trainee accesses the application remotely through a mobile agent. As long as the trainee register himself once, through a web interface, a mobile user interface agent will follow him/her wherever he/she wants to start/continue the educational process. The mobile agent's responsibilities are to display the LUs to the student as well as to track student's actions and to inform instructional agent about them.

5 Constructed Applications

X-GENITOR has been used to develop three tutoring applications in the medical education field, Dermatology Tutor, CT-Scan Tutor and Orthopaedics Tutor [7]. Traditional Medical Education adopts a system-oriented approach: each system of the human body is examined from several perspectives of medical interest. On the other hand, any computer based medical education (CBME) software would deal not only with distributed, and dynamically changing knowledge, but also with the challenge of deploying educational services over the infrastructure of the organization. Here we shortly describe the first one.

Dermatology Tutor [7] is an educational multi agent system that teach psoriasis. Each medical discipline of the subject (e.g. physiology, anatomy, immunology, microbiology etc.) is taught by a specialized domain expert agent. In particular, the tutoring society for teaching psoriasis consists of the following agents: Dermatology Agent, Histology, Physiology, Biology, Biochemistry, Microbiology, Radiology and Immunology agent. Each of them specializes on the corresponding medical domain and can provide knowledge and information about the domain matters. In addition, Dermatology Agent is the instructor agent of the tutoring system and is responsible for composing this information by designing and applying an overall tutoring strategy which is contained in its plans.

6 Conclusions

The construction of previous discussed applications was made by people who had no knowledge of agent technology and were experts in the medical subjects that the applications deal with. During the evaluation of the X-Genitor and its applications the following conclusions were emerged.

1. The AOMFG graphical formal model is the key for allowing an author (non familiar with agent technology) to design an educational application, which will present to the trainee educational material based on a specific instructional strategy. The desired strategy is embodied into the capabilities and the roles of each agent.
2. The IDR allows the same author to validate and produce the desired application by just pressing the appropriate button.

After designing and implementing educational systems for medical education, we are now in the process of applying the described architecture to alternative educational subjects. Currently, the research team is designing an application for teaching aspects of educational software evaluation. Evaluating educational multimedia software is a difficult subject matter, since it ought to cover an extensive range of topics. It should be based on a predefined set of specifications and predictable results arising from the use of the evaluated product. This application deals with the process of evaluating educational multimedia software and in particular it considers the subjects of the evaluation factors and the guidelines needed for selecting and evaluating educational software.

Finally, there are two improvements/extensions that used be made to the X-GENITOR in the near future. The first one is the embodiment of a visual simulation tool, which will allow the author to evaluate his/her application before publishing it. The second one is based on the issue that AOMFG is a formal model for designing general purposes agent application. Thus the main point that X-GENITOR should be adjusted/improved is allowing the author not only to choose but also to create his/her own roles for its agent in the application

References

1. M. Georgeff, B. Pell, M. Pollack, M. Tambe, and M. Wooldridge. The Belief-Desire-Intention Model of Agency. In J. P. Muller, M. Singh, and A. Rao, editors Intelligent Agents V Springer-Verlag Lecture Notes in AI Volume 1365, March 1999
2. Genesereth M. R. and Ketcpel S. P. (1994). Software Agents. Communications of ACM, 37(7): 48-53.
3. A. Kameas and P. Pintelas, "The functional architecture and interacion model of a GENerator of Intelligent TutORing applications", Journal of Systems and Software (JSS), 36(3), 1997, pp 233-245.
4. L Y. Deng, T. K. Shih, T. Huang, Y. Liao, Y. Wang and H. Hsu, "A Distributed Mobile Agent Framework for Maintaining Persistent Distance Education", Journal Of Information Science And Engineering Vol.18 No.4, July 2002, pp489-506
5. R. Silveira and R. Vicari, "Developing Distributed Intelligent Learning Environment with JADE – Java Agents for Distance Education Framework", Proceedings of 6th International Conference, Intelligent Tutoring Systems, Springer-Verlag Heidelberg, LNCS 2363, June 2002, pp. 105–118.
6. A. Triantis and P. Pintelas. "A Mobile Multi Agent Architecture for Web Based Learning", In proceedings of International Conference in Advanced Learning Technologies 2004, 30 August – 1 September 2004, Finland (To be appeared)
7. A. Triantis, A. D. Kameas, I. D. Zacharakis, G. Kagadis, G. Sakellaropoulos, G. Nikifiridis and P. Pintelas, "Towards a Generic Multi-agent Architecture of Computer Based Medical Education Applications", proceedings 2d Panhellenic Conference "Information and Communication Technologies in Education", Patra, October 2000, pp. 255-264
8. Zaharakis I. (1999). About Intelligent Agents' Formal Specifications. Ph.D. Thesis. Department of Mathematics, Univ. Of Patras.
9. UMBC AgentWeb: A Portal Related to Agents. Edited by Tim Finin & Yannis Labrou of UMBC Cogito (   )
10. AgentLink is the European Commission's IST-funded Coordination Action for Agent-Based Computing and is coordinated by the University of Liverpool and University of Southampton (http://www.agentlink.org/)
11. F. Bellifemine, A. Poggi, G. Rimassa. Developing multiagent systems with a FIPA-compliant agent framework. In Software - Practice & Experience, John Wiley & Sons, Ltd. vol no. 31, 2001, pp. 103-128
12. ZEUS: A Tool-Kit for Building Distributed Multi-Agent Systems Hyacinth Nwana, Divine Ndumu, Lyndon Lee and Jaron Collis In Applied Artifical Intelligence Journal, Vol 13 (1), 1999, p129-186.
13. OMG, Object Management Group, Agent Technology Green Paper Agent Working Group, OMG Document (2000) ,Version 0.91.
14. Steiner, T. Prolog Goes Middleware: Java-based Embedding of Logic Servers, PC AI Journal, 2001, Vol. 15 (4), pp 25-29.

A Tutoring System Supporting Experimentation with Virtual Macroeconomic Environments*

Manuel Núñez, Ismael Rodríguez, and Fernando Rubio

Dept. Sistemas Informáticos y Programación.
Universidad Complutense de Madrid, E-28040 Madrid. Spain.
{mn,isrodrig,fernando}@sip.ucm.es

Abstract. In this paper we present the capabilities and behavior of the tutoring system MAS, a system to experiment with (simulations of) complex macroeconomic environments. The users of the system may assume either the role of the State or the role of a company belonging to a specific productive sector. In fact, our system allows students to interact and modify the behavior, both in the short and long-term, of a real scale economy.

1 Introduction

One of the main disadvantages that students of Social Sciences confront is the disability to *practice* with systems close enough to what they will find during their professional lives. For the purpose of this paper let us consider the case of Economics. More specifically, let us take the topic of economic theory. A student will be usually confronted with exercises and assignments where he has to show his command on the theoretical models that he has learnt. A typical advanced exercise in microeconomics consists in calculating a general equilibrium for an economy with one producer, one consumer, and two goods. If we consider the macroeconomic side, students may expect to compute the GDP (Gross Domestic Product) according to some given data, or to discuss whether a given differential equation (with at most half a dozen parameters) adequately reflects reality. Obviously, the gap between these assignments and the *real world* is huge. In fact, students often miss to have something close to a *hands on* experience. Even though there exist tools to support some of the topics (most notably to analyze econometric data) they are usually very biased to numerical calculations.

Actually, the empirical study of new political, demographic, and social systems has been confronted with the difficulty of managing, with enough precision, environments containing a huge amount of relevant variables. Thus, the definition of new models has been sometimes lessened because it was difficult to verify their validity. The main problem consisted, on the one hand, in the impossibility of

---

* Research partially supported by the Spanish MCYT project TIC2003-07848-C02-01 and the Junta de Castilla-La Mancha project PAC-03-001.

C. Bussler and D. Fensel (Eds.): AIMSA 2004, LNAI 3192, pp. 361–370, 2004.

manipulating the real environment and, on the other hand, in the disability to generate realistic artificial environments. Hence, these fields have been favored with the combination of powerful computers and complex simulators. This is specially important in the case of simulating the behavior of systems that cannot be manipulated, as the economic behavior of a society. Thus, the validity of a new theory can be contrasted by simulating the environment and by comparing the obtained and expected results. Afterwards, by using different test values, one can estimate the behavior of the real system in conditions that could never be applied to the real environment. Examples of such systems can be found in [16, 4]. In fact, together with verbal argumentation and mathematics, computer simulation is becoming the third *symbol system* available to social scientists [12].

The development of simulators is turning Social Sciences in general, and Economics in particular, into more *inductive sciences* [5]. Let us remark that this current trend is useful not only for research but also for didactic purposes. In fact, students may profit from the ability to manipulate environments that without these programs could not been studied. Besides, they can observe the relation among *low level* factors (that is, the value of the corresponding variables) and high level factors (that is, the global behavior of the system). Thus, by using these simulators, students can have an overall vision of the considered system. In addition, they can even define new models and contrast their utility. A good candidate to be *simulated* is the economic behavior of a society. In fact, there are already some experimental simulators and algorithms taking into account partial views of the economy (e.g. [3] at the microeconomic level).

In this paper we present a new tutoring system that we call MAS (acronym for MAcroeconomic Simulator). MAS is built on top of CEES [14], which represents the core of the tutoring system. CEES was a *toy simulator* in the sense that users could interact with an economy but were not *guided* out of their mistakes. However, the complex computations and algorithms underlying the implementation of CEES have been reused in the creation of MAS, which presents, in particular, new tutoring capabilities. The main technical characteristic of MAS is that the underlying economic model (i.e. the algorithm computing how the economy evolves, and that is based on classical text books like [15]) generates a simulation that adequately reflects the majority of relevant macroeconomic aspects. In our tutoring system high level behavior (at the macroeconomic level) appears as a consequence of the interrelation between the different economic agents (providers of goods and providers of work) when they try to increase their own profit (microeconomic level). Actually, traditional economic theory was always separating macroeconomics from microeconomics. However, it is nowadays recognized that macroeconomic phenomena cannot be correctly explained without taking into account the microeconomic side (see e.g. [15]). Let us remark that the economic models that we consider are much more complex than most macroeconomics models in use. So, our system is able to explain how the economy of a society works in a more adequate way than models found in the literature usually focussing on one particular characteristic. As a measure of the complexity of the underlying economic models, MAS controls more than one thousand *heterogenous* variables in order to compute the current state of the economy, while most theoretical economic models control, in the most involved cases, a couple of tens.

It is worth to point out that the current version of MAS is more than a mere passive simulator where a user observes the behavior of the economy without interacting with it. On the contrary, it is an *interactive* system that allows a user to play the role of the most important economic institutions (i.e. the State or a private company), so that the effect of different decisions on the global economy can be checked. Thus, adequate interfaces are provided where the relevant parameters can be modified. For instance, if the user plays the role of an entrepreneur then he can regulate both the demanded amount of work and of raw materials, the price of his products, the salaries of the workers, etc. Besides, as State, the player regulates parameters as the progressiveness of income taxes, the indirect taxes rate, and unemployment benefits. Actually, MAS allows various users to play the role of different institutions in the same simulation (e.g. one user is the State, and several users represent private companies), so that the decisions of each player affect the others. Finally, MAS provides several *views* of the economic behavior, by means of graphical representations, according to the different parameters to be considered (e.g. prices, employment levels, stocks, etc).

The rest of the paper is structured as follows. In Section 2, we describe the main features of the tutoring system MAS. We will also briefly introduce the idea of *business cycle*. This notion is essential to our system. For example, a student playing the role of the state might be assigned to ease the length of the waves, while another playing the role of an entrepreneur might try to take advantage of the peak of the cycle. Next, in Section 3, we comment on the algorithm underlying the behavior of MAS. In Section 4 we give some examples of typical assignments and how they are developed in MAS. In Section 5 we give some details concerning the implementation of the system. Finally, in Section 6 we present our conclusions and some lines for future work.

2 Main Features of MAS

In this section we explain the main functionalities of our system. The main aim of MAS consists in providing students with an *easy-to-use* tool where they can practice the knowledge previously gained in the classroom. So, students will be able to check whether they have fully assimilated the concepts they were supposed to. We have designed MAS to help undergraduate students having another (main) source of learning (i.e. a teacher, or even a good book). However, the current system contains features to provide students with some independence. Actually, taking as starting point the help subsystem developed for our tutoring system WHAT [6, 7], the concepts covered by an intermediate course on macroeconomics can be documented by means of a friendly navigation interface. Topics can be accessed in three different ways: by using an index of topics, by incremental searches, or by an alphabetic list of keywords.

In order to ensure a personalized treatment, students login into the system by giving their ID-number and password. This allows the system to recover the data from previous sessions. This mechanism tries to avoid *attacks* to previous sessions of students. For example, an attacker could ask the system for either previous or partially solved assignments and provide wrong answers. Then, when the *real* student logs in, he will find out that his economies are in a different (for worst) point.

Exercises and assignments are temporally and thematically classified according to the underlying curriculum model. MAS offers three different categories of exercises.[1] In the first category we consider exercises where students are confronted with a given situation and they have to deduce properties such as how the situation was produced, or how it can be *repaired*. Since most (families of) exercises do not have a unique correct answer, these exercises are solved by filling successive multiple-choice forms. Depending on the previous answers (e.g. there is big demand of raw materials) the next form will be generated. In the second category we find exercises where the student gets a running economy and is asked to modify some of the parameters under his control (e.g. if he plays the role of the state then he can modify the tax rate) to change, in a given way, the behavior of the economy. Finally, in the last category students are asked not only to modify the values of the parameters but to change the proposed economic model to vary the behavior of an economy. For example, a student may be required to change the way in which aggregate demand is formed.

2.1 An Introduction to Business Cycles

Next we briefly present the struggling forces which provoke *business cycles* in real economies. Business cycles are patterns of growth/decrease of the economy which repeat themselves cyclicly. These theories are nowadays well-established in the economic theory literature. In order to avoid technical details we give a naïve, but intuitive, view of this concept, by considering only supply and demand. Actually, current theories of business cycles fit into this explanation (including the so-called *real business-cycle* and *new Keynesian* approaches) because they explain cycles by shocks in the supply and/or the demand sides (see for example [9, 1, 2] for additional explanations on these models).

Let us consider an economy where the demand of goods surpasses the supply. In this situation prices rise, so profit expectations increase. In order to boost production, entrepreneurs hire new employees. Thus, unemployment decreases, so entrepreneurs are forced to rise salaries to attract new man-power. Salaries, in general, are higher and unemployed workers who found a job have a new additional purchasing power. This situation induces an increase of the aggregate demand which surpasses again the recently boosted supply. The unsatisfied demand makes prices to grow up. So, once again, predictions suggest an increment of profit. Entrepreneurs boost again production and the whole process repeats. The chain reaction is based on this vicious circle which makes the wealth of an economy to grow constantly. We have an *expansion* stage.

---

[1] In Section 4 we present some concrete examples of typical assignments in MAS.

But this process does not last forever. Economic growth lies in the fact that aggregate demand and production costs rise *coupled*, so that profit margins stay more or less stable. Thus, an unbalance in this tradeoff can break the chain reaction. If production costs increase with respect to the demand then the profit of the entrepreneur is reduced. This unbalance will eventually happen in the long term mainly due to two reasons. First, good sources of natural resources will be all under exploitation. So, in order to boost production, companies will be forced to look for some other cultivation lands or deposits which actually are not so productive. Second, the decrease of unemployment will induce an increment of salaries. These two reasons will force entrepreneurs either to give up their business or to attempt to balance income and costs by rising prices. In the former case, fired employees lose their purchasing power. In the latter case, employees would reject to buy expensive goods. In both cases we have that the aggregate demand retracts. Thus, the accumulated stock will not be sold and employees will be fired. The rise of unemployment will induce a decrease of salaries. Besides, unemployed people have no more money to spend. So, the aggregate demand deteriorates even more. This situation forces entrepreneurs to reduce again the production and to fire more people. This process is repeated in a new chain reaction. The decreasing stage finishes when the retraction of aggregate demand and the reduction of production costs get unbalanced. If production costs decrease more than demand then investment will generate profit again. This unbalance will be induced by reasons opposed to those explained above. So, the economy starts to grow and the expanding part of the cycle starts again.

3   The Algorithm Controlling the Behavior of MAS

In this section we give some hints about the algorithm governing the economic behavior of our simulator. As we have previously said, this algorithm was originally introduced in the CEES system. Thus, the interested reader is referred to [14] for a detailed explanation. Given the current state of the economy, the algorithm computes the state of the economy in the next instant. So, time is split into steps (e.g. weeks, months, years). An iterated execution of the algorithm gives us the state of the economy in any arbitrary future time. We slightly depart from the usual conception that economy consists of three sectors. In order to have a more precise description, we split the primary sector into two sectors: *Alimentation* and *raw materials*. In this case, the latter must be understood in a broad system as it contains those industries needed to assure the productive cycle of companies. That is, in addition to proper raw materials we consider sectors as energy, industrial machinery, industrial construction, etc. Let us remark that some of these industries are usually included in the secondary sector. Thus, we will consider four productive sectors: *Alimentation, industry of goods, services*, and *raw materials*. We denote the first three productive sectors by *sectors of goods*. The latter sector must be understood, in a broad sense, as those materials that are needed by companies to perform the productive process. For instance, it includes industries as energy, mining, heavy industry, construction, etc.

The algorithm includes 9 phases split into 20 steps. In Figure 1 we depict them. All the steps are influenced by previous ones, as all of them modify the whole state of the economy. In that diagram, only non-obvious relations are depicted (i.e., those needing the creation of specific relationship data).

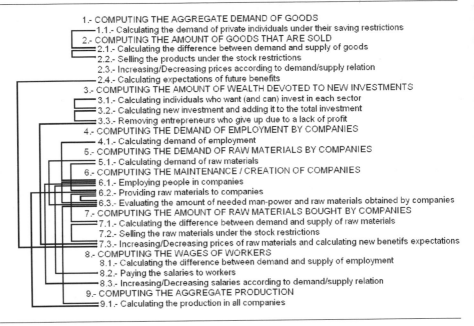

Fig. 1. Structure of the algorithm of MAS.

As an example of the mathematical basis underlying MAS we present the default definition of the rate of expenditure by an individual in each of the available products. From the total amount that an individual decides to spend, $ProductDemand_i$ indicates the percentage to be spent in the product i. Each product i is associated with a *consumption* sector (alimentation, industry, and services, respectively) by means of a function $s:N \longrightarrow \{1,2,3\}$. In addition, $\pi:\{1,2,3\} \longrightarrow R$ computes the *priority* that the individual assigns to consumption in each of the sectors. Finally, b and c are constant and different for each individual. They indicate the minimal quality threshold for the product and the additional influence of price in demand, respectively.

$$aux_i = \frac{PurchasingPower^{\pi(s(i))} \cdot \left(b - \frac{1}{Quality_i}\right)}{Price_i^{\frac{1}{PurchasingPower}} + c} \qquad ProductDemand_i = \frac{aux_i}{\sum_j aux_j}$$

The terms aux_i compute the *rough* percentage of money to be spent in each product. These terms are afterwards *normalized* so that $ProductDemand_i$ gives the real percentage. Let us remark that the demand increases with quality and diminishes with price. Besides, the influence of price in demand is bigger if the purchasing power is low.

4 Examples of Exercises in MAS

Even though the previous sections have described the general behavior and characteristics of MAS, it may not be yet clear the kind of exercises that students have to confront. In this section we will show a couple of examples presenting *typical* assignments to be solved in MAS.

The simplest assignments consists, as explained in Section 2, in trying to understand what is going on in a partial view of an economy. For example, let us consider Figure 2 (left) where, in order to reduce the required space, we have *deleted* the rest of the MAS graphical interface. The student has to determine which two sectors can generate such a joint behavior. First, he has to deduce that the given initial conditions were not natural enough, according to the model, so that there is a first stage of stabilization where the Economy tries to fit properly into the model (students know that they have to discard the *beginning* of the analyzed data). Afterwards, the stable cyclic behavior begins. In order to solve the *mistery*, it is enough to realize that the sector depicted in the down part of the graphic almost follows the derivative of the other one. Thus, it easily follows (at least, we expect so!) that the first evolution represents the sector of raw materials while the second one represents the industry sector.

One of the main requirements for a *good* government is to soften the cyclic behavior of the economy. Even though it will be almost impossible to avoid cycles (even undesirable) big *waves* produce a lot of instability and uncertainty in the economic agents. In fact, a very reduced form of state can help in this task. In Figure 2 (center) we show a simulation of a completely free market, while in the right hand side we present the behavior of an economy where a simple state (with no public companies) collects some taxes that are used to pay low unemployment benefits. Thus, one of the assignments is to change the relevant parameters in the state (tax collection, public expenditure, etc) so that the economy is converted from the first to the second graphic.

We will also ask students to deal with the influence of different company tactics in an economy. In this sense, it is worth to point out that a *huge* firm can strongly influence the evolution of cycles. In fact, it is even possible to stop a expansion or a depression as a result of the investments of our company. Another typical assignment regarding firm policies is to analyze the effects of *price dumping*. This technique consists in selling products under the production costs until the competence disappears. Once the market is controlled, the company can monopolistically act (with the consequent increase of prices). We will give initial conditions for the firm of the student and we will ask him to apply this policy. He should be able to realize that these initial conditions are very relevant in the success of dumping. Actually, it works only after a minimal threshold of portion of the market was initially owned and a great stored capital was available by the company (in order to confront the initial loses).

The last exercise that we are going to comment was created as a consequence of our experimentation with CEES [14], the subsystem used by MAS where the algorithm to compute the state of the economy is located. While testing the reliability of CEES we did not consider, by default, that *strange* behaviors were due to conceptual errors. Actually, it is a fact that in any society almost *anything* can happen if the specific conditions appear simultaneously. Hence, we tried to take advantage of these behaviors instead of discarding them. For example, during the development of the simulator we found out the existence of a very rare situation where a depression was accompanied by an inflationary spiral. This phenomenon is called *stagflation* and we were not previously aware of it. We found out that one of its possible causes is that, due to some factors, companies are forced to increase salaries though their profit is negative. Afterwards, we compared this situation with standard behaviors, where salaries use to decrease in depressions. We identified the main factors provoking this rare behavior in our model (e.g., excessive influence of the *still* low unemployment in the beginning of the depression), and we corrected them. Thus, one of the assignments (at the end of the course) consists in showing an economy presenting stagflation and asking the student to take the economy out of it.

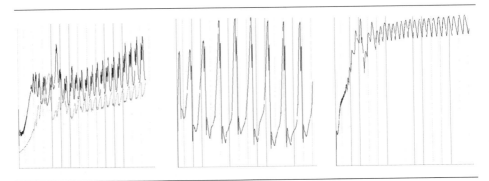

Fig. 2. Industry and Raw Materials sectors (left), completely unrestricted economy (center), and lowly restricted economy (right).

5   Implementation Details

In this section we give some details about the implementation of our tutoring system MAS. We will also review the main characteristics of the implementation of CEES since this subsystem is vital for the correct behavior of MAS. We would like to emphasize that the methodology that we followed to design the integrated system MAS/CEES can be described as a *symbiosis* between the implementation of the simulator and the learning of advanced macroeconomic concepts. Initially, we identified the set of basic operators (at the human level) producing the economic process (e.g. purchasing, selling, work, demand of goods, etc). Next, we identified the main results giving raise to the correct interrelation among these concepts (e.g. business cycles and their control, state regulations by means of taxes and unemployment benefits, monopolies and oligopolies, etc). Afterwards, we looked for economic explanations to the basic forces producing the high level behavior of the system (e.g. if there is an excess of supply then the entrepreneur will decrease the prices).

The architecture of MAS is split into different components. First, the client-side component provides a Web interface for users. This component consists of HTML pages with embedded Javascript code that are dynamically generated by the server in response to queries of users. Through this environment users are confronted with the proposed assignments. The server-side component selects the questions to send to each user, composes the HTML pages before sending them to the client, records the answers, provides simple statistics of the system use, and computes the results of questions concerning complex economic behaviors by forwarding the suitable initial conditions to CEES and executing the algorithm it provides. This feature allows MAS to dynamically create new questions by performing random small modifications to the initial conditions of other already known questions. In this case, MAS obtains the correct answer to the new question in advance by executing the algorithm provided by CEES and considering the values returned by it. Finally, the last component of MAS is the economic engine that provides such analysis, that is, CEES. MAS runs on top of CEES, since the latter implements the algorithm governing the economic predictions performed by MAS. The structure of the economy model guided the decomposition of the design in classes (State of the Economy, Productive sector, Labor sector, Entrepreneur, Worker, etc.), the needed operations (buy, sell, consume, invest, look for a job, migrate of sector, etc.), and the needed attributes (salary, savings, amount of people, etc.).

6 Conclusions and Future Work

We have presented MAS, a tutoring system to deal with macroeconomic environments. We think that MAS is indeed a very useful tool to help students in the task of learning the main characteristic of a complex economic system. It is worth to remark that MAS is built on top of CEES, a powerful subsystem that implements the algorithm governing the behavior of an economy.

As future work we would like to migrate the architecture of MAS/CEES to a more standardized technology of economic simulation (e.g. Swarm [10]). This change would allow us to easily compare simulation results and to share components in order to study design alternatives. A second line of future work consists in including some of the main economic factors which have not been included in the current version. This is the case of the loan system, a stock exchange, and international commerce. Finally, we plan to apply some of the economical mechanisms underlying MAS to the systems presented in [11, 8, 13]. In these works, simple microeconomic concepts are applied to concurrent and e-commerce systems, respectively. We are confident that relevant *high level* emerging properties can be indeed found in the distributions of resources.

Acknowledgments. The authors would like to thank the anonymous referees for valuable comments on a previous version of the paper.

References

[1]   G.A. Akerlof and J.L. Yellen. A near-rational model of the bussiness cycle, with wage and price inertia. *Quarterly Journal of Economics*, 100:823–838, 1985.

[2]   R. Barro, editor. *Modern Business Cycle Theory*. Harvard University Press, 1989.

[3]   J.Q. Cheng and M.P. Wellman. The WALRAS algorithm: A convergent distributed implementation of general equilibrium outcomes. *Computational Economics*, 12:1–24, 1998.

[4]   J. Frolova and V. Korobitsin. Simulation of gender artificial society: Multi-agent models of subject-object interactions. In *ICCS 2002, LNCS 2329*, pages 226–235. Springer, 2002.

[5]   F. Hahn. The next hundred years. *Economic Journal*, 101:47–50, 1991.

[6]   N. López, M. Núñez, I. Rodríguez, and F. Rubio. Including malicious agents into a collaborative learning environment. In *8th Int. Conf. on Intelligent Tutoring Systems, LNCS 2363*, pages 51–60. Springer, 2002.

[7]   N. López, M. Núñez, I. Rodríguez, and F. Rubio. WHAT: Web-based Haskell Adaptive Tutor. In *10th Artificial Intelligence: Methodologies, Systems, and Applications, LNAI 2443*, pages 71–80. Springer, 2002.

[8]   N. López, M. Núñez, I. Rodríguez, and F. Rubio. A multi-agent system for e-barter including transaction and shipping costs. In *18th ACM Symposium on Applied Computing, SAC'03*, pages 587–594. ACM Press, 2003.

[9]   R.E. Lucas. An equilibrium model of the bussiness cycle. *Journal of Political Economy*, 83:1113–1144, 1975.

[10]   F. Luna and B. Stefansson. *Economic Simulations in Swarm: Agent-Based Modelling and Object Oriented Programming*. Kluwer Academic Publishers, 2000.

[11]   M. Núñez and I. Rodríguez. PAMR: A process algebra for the management of resources in concurrent systems. In *FORTE 2001*, pages 169–185. Kluwer Academic Publishers, 2001.

[12]   T. Ostrom. Computer simulation: the third symbol system. *Journal of Experimental Social Psychology*, 24:381–392, 1998.

[13]   I. Rodríguez. Formal specification of autonomous commerce agents. In *19th ACM Symposium on Applied Computing, SAC'04*, pages 774–778. ACM Press, 2004.

[14]   I. Rodríguez and M. Núñez. CEES: Complex Economic Environments Simulator. In *ICCS 2003, LNCS 2658*, pages 658–667. Springer, 2003.

[15]   J.E. Stiglitz. *Principles of Macroeconomics*. W.W. Norton & Company, Inc, 1993.

[16]   R. Suppi, P. Munt, and E. Luque. Using PDES to simulate individual-oriented models in ecology: A case study. In *ICCS 2002, LNCS 2329*, pages 107–116. Springer, 2002.

An Agent Based Approach for Migrating Web Services to Semantic Web Services[*]

László Zsolt Varga, Ákos Hajnal, and Zsolt Werner

Computer and Automation Research Institute, Kende u. 13-17, 1111 Budapest, Hungary
{laszlo.varga, ahajnal, werner}@sztaki.hu
http://www.sztaki.hu/

Abstract. Semantic web services are considered as the concept bringing the web to its full potential by combining the best features of web services, agent technology, grid and the semantic web. In this paper we present an agent based architecture for migrating existing web services to the semantic web service environment. We developed the WSDL2Agent tool to support the migration. The tool automatically generates a Protégé project. With human interaction semantic information not present in the WSDL description can be added in Protégé and the project can be exported in OWL format. From the enhanced OWL description we can directly derive the skeletons of the elements of the Web Services Modeling Framework. The tool automates the most tedious tasks of the migration process and the users can focus on the semantic aspects.

Keywords: multi-agent systems, web services, semantic web services

1 Introduction

Nowadays computers are networked into the Internet and if an organization is not connected, then it has serious competitive drawback. In this environment individual software products must change from isolated applications into interoperating components in a world wide network of information and business transactions. These requirements do not allow the application of individual solutions and the focus turns to standardized data, information and knowledge exchange. Providing solutions to these needs are among the goals of several technologies including the web services technology [1], the semantic web technology [2], the grid [3] and agent based computing [4]. The grid is going to provide access to information and computing resources as pervasive as access to electricity is today. Currently the grid turns towards web services as underlying technology. Web services increase the web's potential by providing a way of automated discovery and invocation of software services using web protocols and data representation. Although web service protocols and data are machine readable, they do not provide the necessary level of "understanding" of the web content. Semantic web provides description techniques for describing content on the necessary

---

[*] This work was partly supported by the "Multiagent systems and applications" joint research project between the Hungarian and the Bulgarian Academy of Sciences.

C. Bussler and D. Fensel (Eds.): AIMSA 2004, LNAI 3192, pp. 371–380, 2004.

semantic level. Semantic web services extend web services with semantic web capabilities [5, 6]. Semantic description techniques are part of agent based computing, therefore it seems reasonable to investigate how agent technology could help migrate web services and the web service technology to the semantic web services environment. Agent technology also offers autonomous and proactive behaviors which may be necessary for semantic web services to adapt to unforeseen changes and requirements in dynamic service discovery and composition.

The research contribution of this paper is the description of an agent based architecture and a method for the migration of web services to the semantic web service environment. The technology contribution of this work is the implementation of the WSDL2Agent tool and the application of the tool to the Google web service.

In section 2 first we summarize the main concepts of web services and semantic web services. In section 3 we introduce a novel agent based architecture for migrating web services to the semantic web service environment. Section 4 presents the WSDL2Agent tool which automates mechanic steps of the migration process. The tool and its usage are demonstrated through the Google web service in section 5. In the end we compare our results with similar work and outline possible continuations.

2   Web Services and Semantic Web Services

The purpose of web services is to provide document- or procedure-oriented functionality over the network enhancing static web information towards interacting services. The web service is an abstract notion of certain functionality, the concrete piece of software implementing the web service is called provider agent [1], while other systems that wish to make use of the web services are called requester agents. Requester agents can interact with the provider agent via message exchange using SOAP (Simple Object Access Protocol) messages typically conveyed over HTTP.

The interface of the web service is described in machine-readable format by a WSDL (Web Services Description Language [7]) document. It defines the service as a set of abstract network end-points called ports and a set of operations representing abstract actions available at these ports. For each operation the possible input and output messages are defined and decomposed into parts. The data types of parts are described using the XSD (XML Schema Definition [8]) type system, which may be either built-in XML data types or custom, even nested structures e.g. complex types or arrays. The abstract definitions of ports, operations, and messages are then bound to their concrete network deployment via extensibility elements: internet location, transport protocol, and transport serialization formats. At present, WSDL is applicable to describe the syntactic level of web service access, but it does not provide semantic information about web services.

The semantic web services group of the DAML program has developed a DAML+OIL as well as an OWL based web service ontology [9]. The upper ontology for web services contains the service profile, the service model and the service grounding. The service profile provides a high-level description of a service and its provider in a way which would typically be presented to users when browsing a service registry. The service model details both the control structure and the data flow structure of the service. The grounding of a service specifies the details of how to access the service which is a mapping from an abstract to a concrete specification.

Semantic enabled web services [10] are an extension of the web service concept with semantic descriptions of data and services. Semantic web services will allow the intelligent and automatic web service discovery, selection, mediation and composition into complex services. The Web Services Modeling Framework (WSMF) [11] provides the model for developing, describing and composing semantic web services. The model consists of four main elements: ontologies, goal repositories, web service descriptions and mediators. The ontologies provide the terminology used by the other elements. The goal repositories contain specifications of objectives that should be solved by web services. The web services descriptions define the web services from various aspects including the services offered, input/output data, failures, service binding, quality and price information, provenance data, reliability information, etc. Mediators bypass interoperability problems of different vocabulary and interaction styles.

The Semantic Web Services Initiative Architecture committee (SWSA) of the DAML program is developing a reference architecture to support Semantic Web Service technologies. Our work is based on WSMF, because the SWSA architecture is not yet available, but it is known that the SWSA will take the current WSMF as a starting point.

3 Agent Based Semantic Web Service Architecture

Agents as autonomous and proactive software components can provide the glue for tightening software components together in the semantic web. The Agentcities initiative [12] has already created a world wide testbed with an infrastructure for experimenting with agent services based on agent technology standards [13]. The testbed infrastructure contains many elements needed for semantic web services: message transport; communication languages; ontologies; platform, agent and service directory services; monitoring tools; website based system for managing namespace and URL references to defined ontologies and other semantic definitions; several test applications; composite services. Based on the experiences in the Agentcities testbed we define an agent based semantic web service layer above existing web services as shown in Fig. 1.

Existing web services described by WSDL files constitute the web service layer. Each web service is represented in the semantic web service layer by a proxy agent capable of invoking the web service as well as playing the role of the mediator. A plain proxy agent without mediator capabilities can be automatically generated with the WSDL2Jade tool and the methods described in [14]. The proxy agent generated with WSDL2Jade is capable to invoke the web service. This only allows the deployment of agents based on existing web services and was useful to deploy agents in the Agentcities testbed. Now we are going to discuss how the proxy agent can be extended to play the role of the mediator in WSMF.

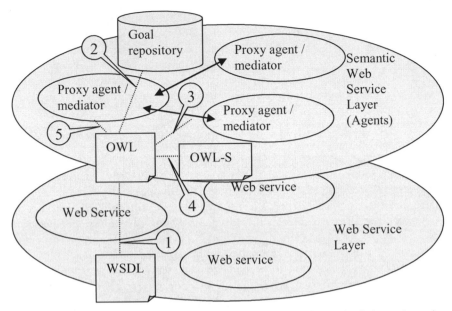

Fig. 1. Agents provide a semantic web service layer above the layer of existing web services

The WSDL description of the web service is represented with an OWL file in the semantic web service layer (link 1 in Fig. 1). The OWL file is generated with the tools and methods described in the next section. The OWL file is a description of the capabilities of the proxy agent in a semantic description language which makes easier the additions of extensions towards semantic web services. The OWL file is the basis of several components in the semantic web service layer. The goal descriptions of the proxy agent are extracted from this file and put into the goal repository (link 2 in Fig. 1). The OWL file contains the description of the input and output data of the web service and is used in the ontology of the content language of the communication between the proxy agents (link 3 in Fig. 1). The ontology of the content language can also be exported to the OWL-S file describing the semantic web services provided by the proxy agent (link 4 in Fig. 1). Finally the skeleton of the proxy agent is generated from the OWL file (link 5 in Fig. 1). If the OWL description is extended with mediator capabilities, then the proxy agent created through link 5 provides mediator services as well.

4   Creating the Components of the Architecture

In order to be able to create the WSMF components of the agent based semantic web services architecture described in the previous section, we have created the WSDL2Agent tool which is applicable to convert any WSDL file to a Protégé project file. The Protégé knowledge engineering tool [15] allows us to visualize and edit the web service description and convert it into various formats, such as RDF, OIL, DAML+OIL, and OWL. First we are going to discuss how the Protégé representation of the WSDL file can be created, then we will discuss how this Protégé representation can be used to create the WSMF components.

For input and output messages of a web service operation the conversion assigns Protégé classes (also known as frames) with fields (called slots in Protégé) corresponding to message parts. In accordance with conventions used in agent technology, classes representing operation input messages are called AgentActions, and classes representing output messages are called Predicates. Furthermore, class names are prefixed with a string which is the concatenation of port name and operation name in WSDL to make them unique as it is required by Protégé. To indicate web service invocation faults we generate a special predicate called ErrorPredicate. Since slot names must be globally unique as well in the knowledge domain (regardless of container classes), slot names are prefixed with the unique string of the class name they belong to. Similarly to input and output messages complex types defined in WSDL are also represented by Protégé classes with slots corresponding to the elements included in the complex type. These latter classes do not need to be prefixed with port name, operation name strings, since complex type names are unique in the WSDL.

In order to be able to generate the proxy agent skeleton form the OWL file (link 5 in Fig. 1) using the Ontology Bean Generator for Jade [16] the generated classes are organized in the structure defined by the Ontology Bean Generator. Classes representing complex types are child classes of a special class called Concept, agent action classes are successors of class AgentAction (which is also subclass of Concept), and predicate classes must inherit from class Predicate. In addition, a so called AID class instance must be present for successful agent code generation.

Another important aspect of WSDL to Protégé model generation is the question of type conversion, i.e. how the XML Schema type parts and complex type fields can be translated into Protégé slot types. Protégé supports four primitive value types: boolean, float, integer, and string. In addition, a value type called 'symbol' can represent enumerations of string values, and 'any' value type means that the slot can take any value of the above types. Since XML Schema has a much wider range of built-in data types than Protégé, the data type mapping may be imprecise for certain XML types. XML - Protégé type conversion rules are omitted here because of lack of space, but they are available on the web page of WSDL2Agent [17].

The mapping of complex types needs recursion. If there is a message part or a complex type field with type referring to another complex type 'B', then WSDL2Agent creates a class for the referred type 'B' and associates the referring type with a slot having type 'class' with a single allowed parent class 'B'.

One-dimensional array type fields in WSDL, such as int[], are represented by slots with multiple cardinality and with type corresponding to the scalar case (e.g. integer). In the case of multi-dimensional arrays, intermediate wrapper classes are created. Each intermediate class contains a slot referring to a lower number dimension class with multiple cardinality.

Using the above techniques the WSDL file is transformed into a Protégé project file in which XML data types are converted to Concept classes, web service operations are converted to AgentAction classes, and web service operation results are converted into Predicate classes. Concept classes are edited to add more semantics to them. AgentAction classes are edited to add mediator functionality to the proxy agents. These extensions need human intervention and cannot be done automatically. Once the extensions are added, the components of the WSMF model can be derived.

The Predicate classes contain the goals that can be achieved by invoking the web services, therefore the Predicate classes are exported to the goal repository of the WSMF model. The Concept classes describe the information exchanged between the proxy agents, therefore they are exported to the ontology describing the content language of the communication between the proxy agents. Concept and Predicate classes are also part of the OWL-S file describing the semantic web services of the proxy agent. Using the Ontology Bean Generator, the skeleton of the proxy agent is generated from the created Protégé project.

5   Example: The Google Web Service

In this section the above described agent based approach for creating semantic web services from existing web services is demonstrated on the Google web service [18].

Google Web APIs service consists of three parts which are accessible via three operations called *doGoogleSearch*, *doGetCachedPage*, and *doSpellingSuggestion*. The doGoogleSearch service is applicable to search in Google's index of web pages by submitting the query string (and search parameters) for which Google web service sends the set of search results back. The doGetCachedPage operation returns the cached contents of a specified URL when Google's crawlers last visited the page. Finally, doSpellingSuggestion service can be used to obtain a suggested spell correction for the submitted expression.

These operations and message formats are defined in the WSDL file downloadable from the Google web site along with the documentation describing the semantics of the messages. For simplicity we present only the search operation and how we can obtain its semantic web service representation. The WSDL file contains the following XML description of the input and output messages of the doGoogleSearch operation:

```
<message name="doGoogleSearch">
  <part name="key" type="s:string" />
  <part name="q" type="s:string" />
    . . .
</message>

<message name="doGoogleSearchResponse">
  <part name="return" type="s0:GoogleSearchResult" />
</message>
```

In the input message the 'key' parameter corresponds to the registration code (needs to be requested at the web page of Google), parameter 'q' is the search string. Other parameters are omitted here. The 's' namespace prefix in part types refers to the standard XML Schema namespace "http://www.w3.org/2001/XMLSchema" (declared in WSDL's <definitions> element), therefore each part has an XML's built-in data type.

The output message has a single part called 'return' with type referring to a local complex type (namespace prefix s0 refers to the target namespace) called Google-SearchResult which is defined in the <types> section in the WSDL file:

```
<s:complexType name="GoogleSearchResult">
 <s:all>
  <s:element name="documentFiltering" type="s:boolean" />
  <s:element name="searchComments" type="s:string" />
  <s:element name="estimatedTotalResultsCount" type="s:int" />
  <s:element name="estimateIsExact" type="s:boolean" />
  <s:element name="resultElements" type="s0:ResultElementArray" />
  . . .
 </s:all>
</s:complexType>
```

The GoogleSearchResult structure contains built-in XML type fields containing details about the search itself and further complex types, e.g. ResultElementArray (containing the actual list of search results) which is an array of ResultElement complex type representing a single search hit:

```
<s:complexType name="ResultElement">
  <s:all>
    <s:element name="summary" type="s:string" />
    <s:element name="URL" type="s:string" />
    <s:element name="snippet" type="s:string" />
    <s:element name="title" type="s:string" />
    . . .
  </s:all>
</s:complexType>
```

It contains a textual summary of the web page found, the URL, the snippet, the title, and other information like cached size and directory category. These fields have built-in XML type, except one complex type field which is not detailed here to save space.

A view of the model generated by WSDL2Agent is shown in Fig 2. The ontology of the web service is exported to an OWL file using the OWL Plugin. By building a new project from the exported OWL file the web service data model can be visualized, edited as an OWL ontology: OWL specific metadata can be introduced, logical class descriptions can be added, logic reasoners can be accessed.

The *GoogleSearchPortDoGoogleSearch*Predicate is exported to the goal repository as the goal of the *GoogleSearchPortDoGoogleSearch*AgentAction. Its OWL representation as generated by WSDL2Agent and exported from Protégé is the following:

```
<owl:Class rdf:ID="GoogleSearchPortDoGoogleSearchPredicate">
  <rdfs:subClassOf rdf:resource="#Predicate"/>
</owl:Class>
<owl:ObjectProperty
    rdf:ID="googleSearchPortDoGoogleSearchPredicate_return_value">
  <rdf:type

rdf:resource="http://www.w3.org/2002/07/owl#FunctionalProperty"/>
  <rdfs:domain
    rdf:resource="#GoogleSearchPortDoGoogleSearchPredicate"/>
  <rdfs:range rdf:resource="http://www.w3.org/2002/07/owl#Class"/>
  <protege:allowedParent rdf:resource="#GoogleSearchResult"/>
</owl:ObjectProperty>
```

This is a raw representation from the WSDL file, but with human intelligence more semantics can be added from the textual description of the web service using Protégé.

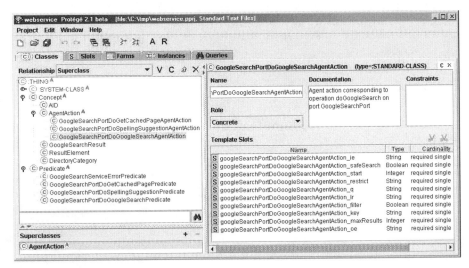

Fig. 2. The model generated from Google's WSDL file in Protégé's visual development environment

The *GoogleSearchPortDoGoogleSearch*AgentAction is exported to the ontology for the content language between proxy agents as well as to the OWL-S description of the semantic web services of the proxy agent. The OWL representation of the agent action together with the key property is the following:

```
<owl:Class rdf:ID="GoogleSearchPortDoGoogleSearchAgentAction">
  <rdfs:subClassOf>
    <owl:Class rdf:about="#AgentAction"/>
  </rdfs:subClassOf>
</owl:Class>

<owl:FunctionalProperty
rdf:ID="googleSearchPortDoGoogleSearchAgentAction_key">
  <rdfs:range
    rdf:resource="http://www.w3.org/2001/XMLSchema#string"/>
  <rdf:type
    rdf:resource="http://www.w3.org/2002/07/owl#DatatypeProperty"/>
  <rdfs:domain
    rdf:resource="#GoogleSearchPortDoGoogleSearchAgentAction"/>
</owl:FunctionalProperty>
```

In the case of both Protégé projects and OWL projects the Ontology Bean Generator plugin can be used to produce agent code from the model. The generated agent code can then be completed and run in Jade agent platform [19] resulting in an agent which understands and communicates with the terms specified by the ontology.

6   Analysis and Related Work

Using the tool and the approach presented in this paper, we can generate the basis of the WSMF elements for semantic web services. This helps to migrate web services to the WSMF model, because the translation of the information in the WSDL file may be tedious for even a single complex web service. An automatic tool cannot add semantics to a WSDL description, therefore the semantic markup of the web service must be done with human interaction. The tool translates the WSDL description to a Protégé project file where the semantic markup can be done easier. Once the semantic description is complete, the goal repository, the ontology of the content language for the communication between proxy agents and mediators, as well as the skeleton of the proxy agent code and the core of the OWL-S description can be derived directly.

As it is observed in [20] in the case of Amazon Web service to DAML-S conversion the human syntactic translation of the grounding takes about a week, while only a few hours needed to complete the process models and profiles. The usage of automated tools thus drastically reduces the effort required, and developers can focus on the semantic information when migrating existing web services to the semantic web.

The WSDL2DAMLS tool described in [20] can directly generate a DAML-S description form a WSDL file. The WSDL2DAMLS tool also needs human intervention, because the WSDL file does not contain the needed semantic information. Although the WSDL2DAMLS tool produces a DAML-S file, it does not produce other elements of the WSMF model. The DAML-S file contains the ontology of the content language which can be used between mediators, but does not contain the mediators themselves. Therefore our WSDL2Agent tool is complimentary to WSDL2DAMLS, because it also contains the mediator concept.

7   Conclusion and Outlook

In this paper we have presented an agent based architecture for migrating existing web services to the semantic web service environment. We have developed a tool [17] to support the migration. The tool automatically generates an OWL description of the agent providing the semantic web service. Human interaction is needed to add semantic information not present in the WSDL description. From the enhanced OWL description we can directly derive the skeletons of the elements of the WSMF. The most tedious tasks of the migration process are automated and the users can focus on the semantic aspects. The WSDL2Agent tool gives a novel solution and complements the WSDL2DAMLS tool.

The work presented in this paper can be continued in the direction of providing tools to automatically extract and derive the goal repository, the ontology and the OWL-S description from the OWL file generated by WSDL2Agent. Another interesting possibility is to investigate how WSDL2DAMLS and WSDL2Agent can be combined in order to provide smoother transition from web services to semantic web services. At the time of writing this paper WSDL2Agent supports WSDL1.1. Support for the recently published WSDL 2.0 specification is being implemented.

References

1. Web Services Architecture, W3C Working Group Note 11 February 2004, http://www.w3.org/TR/ws-arch/
2. Berners-Lee, T., Hendler, J., & Lassila, O. (2001). The Semantic Web. Scientific American 284(5), 34-43.
3. Foster, I., & Kesselman, C., eds. (1999). The Grid: Blueprint for a New Computing Infrastructure. San Francisco: Morgan Kaufmann.
4. Wooldridge, M. (2002). An Introduction to Multiagent Systems. Chichester: John Wiley & Sons
5. McIlraith, S. , Son, T. C. , and Zeng, H.: Semantic Web services. IEEE Intelligent Systems, 16(2), pp. 46–53, 2001.
6. Hendler, J.: Agents and the Semantic Web, IEEE Intelligent Systems, vol. 16, no. 2, Mar./Apr. 2001, pp. 30–37.
7. Web Services Description Language (WSDL) 1.1, W3C Note 15 March 2001, http://www.w3.org/TR/wsdl
8. XML Schema Part 0: Primer, W3C Recommendation, 2 May 2001, http://www.w3.org/TR/xmlschema-0/
9. The DAML Services Coalition (alphabetically Ankolenkar, A., Burstein, M., Hobbs, J.R., Lassila, O., Martin, D.L., McDermott, D., McIlraith, S.A., Narayanan, S., Paolucci, M., Payne, T.R., Sycara, K.): DAML-S: Web Service Description for the Semantic Web. The First International Semantic Web Conference (ISWC), Sardinia (Italy), June, 2002.
10. Bussler, C., Maedche, A., Fensel, D.: A Conceptual Architecture for Semantic Web Enabled Web Services. ACM Special Interest Group on Management of Data: Volume 31, Number 4, Dec 2002.
11. Fensel, D., Bussler, C., Ding, Y., Omelayenko, B.: The Web Service Modeling Framework WSMF. Electronic Commerce Research and Applications, 1(2), 2002.
12. Willmott, S.N., Dale, J., Burg, B., Charlton, P., O'brien, P.: "Agentcities: A Worldwide Open Agent Network", Agentlink News 8 (Nov. 2001) 13-15, http://www.AgentLink.org/newsletter/8/AL-8.pdf
13. Dale, J., Mamdani, E.: Open Standards for Interoperating Agent-Based Systems. In: Software Focus, 1(2), Wiley, 2001.
14. Varga, L.Z., Hajnal, A.: Engineering Web Service Invocations from Agent Systems, Lecture Notes in Computer Science Vol. 2691, Marik, V., Müller, J., Pechoucek, M. (Eds.), Multi-Agent Systems and Applications III, CEEMAS 2003, Prague, Czech Republic, June 16-18, 2003, Proceedings, p. 626., ISBN-3-540-40450-3
15. Gennari, J., Musen, M., Fergerson, R., Grosso, W., Crubézy, M., Eriksson, H., Noy, N., Tu. S.: The evolution of Protégé-2000: An environment for knowledge-based systems development. International Journal of Human-Computer Studies, 58(1):89-123, 2003.
16. van Aart, C.J., Pels, R.F., Giovanni C. and Bergenti F. Creating and Using Ontologies in Agent Communication. Workshop on Ontologies in Agent Systems 1st International Joint Conference on Autonomous Agents and Multi-Agent Systems, 2002.
17. WSDL2Agent available online at http://sas.ilab.sztaki.hu:8080/wsdl2agent/
18. Google Web API, http://www.google.com/apis/
19. Bellifemine, F., Poggi, A., Rimassa, G.: "JADE - A FIPA-compliant agent framework", In Proc. of the Fourth International Conference and Exhibition on the Practical Application of Intelligent Agents and Multi-Agents (PAAM'99), London, UK, (1999) pp. 97-108.
20. Paolucci, M., Srinivasan, N., Sycara, K., Nishimura, T.: Toward a Semantic Choreography of Web Services: From WSDL to DAML-S, In Proceedings of the First International Conference on Web Services (ICWS'03), Las Vegas, Nevada, USA, June 2003, pp 22-26.

Constructing a BDI Agent to Deploy in an Interactive Computer Game Environment

In-Cheol Kim

Department of Computer Science, Kyonggi University
San 94-6 Yiui-dong, Paldal-gu, Suwon-si, Kyonggi-do, 442-760, Korea
kic@msu.edu

Abstract. In this paper, we introduce the architecture and the path-planning behavior of KGBot. KGBot is an intelligent character agent deploying in an interactive computer game environment. It has been implemented as a bot client in the Gamebots system. KGBot adopts a general BDI engine, UM-PRS, as its central decision-making part. Considering its limited range of view, KGBot uses an extended real-time search algorithm, RTA-RG, for planning paths. Through some experiments, we investigate the efficiency of the UM-PRS engine and that of the real-time search algorithm for controlling KGBot in this complex virtual environment.

1 Introduction

As computer games become more complex, the need for intelligent non-player characters(NPC) is growing. Computer game worlds are usually dynamic and real-time environments. They also include complex 3D spaces and multiple interacting characters. Any agent in such an environment should have a lot of intelligent capabilities such as learning a map of their 3D environment, planning paths, coordinating with its teammates, and so on. There are a number of projects for designing and implementing such intelligent character agents deploying within a simulated virtual environment such as interactive computer game world. The examples are the Soarbot project [5] and the Gamebots project [10]. In this paper, we introduce the architecture and the path-planning behavior of a game agent, of which the name is KGBot. KGBot has been implemented as a bot client in the Gamebots system. KGBot adopts UM-PRS [4] as its decision-making part. UM-PRS is a general-purpose reasoning system, integrating traditional goal-directed reasoning and reactive behavior. We will explain the benefits from embedding the UM-PRS engine. In order to deploy well in this game environment, KGBot needs a fast on-line search algorithm which interleaves planning for a plausible next move and executing the move. However, most of existing real-time search algorithms such as RTA* and LRTA* do not consider the limitation of agent's view. Considering its limited range of view, KGBot uses an extended real-time search algorithm, RTA-RG, for planning paths. We will conduct some experiments to evaluate the efficiency of the UM-PRS engine and that of the real-time search algorithm for controlling KGBot in this complex virtual environment.

C. Bussler and D. Fensel (Eds.): AIMSA 2004, LNAI 3192, pp. 381–388, 2004.
© Springer-Verlag Berlin Heidelberg 2004

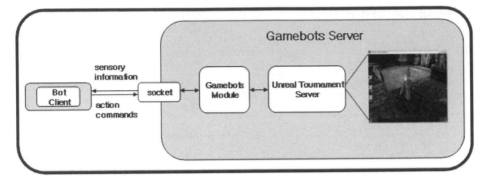

Fig. 1. Gamebots System

Fig. 2. Distributed Waypoints and an Agent's View

2   Computer Game Environment

Our agent, KGBot, is supposed to deploy within a simulated virtual environment which is made by Epic's Unreal Tournament(UT) game [3] and ISI's Gamebots system [10]. UT falls into a category of online video games known as first-person shooters, where all real time players exist in a 3D virtual world with simulated physics. As implied by 'first person' in the genre's name, every player's senses are limited by their location, bearings, and occlusion within the virtual world. Gamebots is a domain for research in multi-agent systems. It utilizes UT, which is one of the fast-paced multi-agent interactive computer games. Gamebots contains an additional module for UT that allows characters in the game to be controlled via network sockets connected to bot clients. Fig. 1 represents the overall architecture of Gamebots system. The Gamebots server feeds sensory information for the characters over the network connections. Based on this information, the bot client can decide what actions the character should take and issues commands back over the network to the game to have the character move, shoot, or talk.

Sensory information sent to the remote bot client is a complete list of everything within the agent's view at that moment, as well as the agent's own state such as health and location. It also contains some dynamic and game critical items such as other players and flying projectiles. However, due to the underlying bot implementation in UT, all vision messages simplify a world object down to a set of location and rotation coordinates called a waypoint. All bots do not have a direct sense of the map architecture, such as walls and floors. Instead, the map architecture is conveyed implicitly through the set of waypoints. Fig. 2 depicts the waypoints distributed over a complex 3D map and the current view of the character. Only the waypoints within the current view of the character can be recognized by the corresponding bot client. In this virtual environment, the bot clients, or the character agents must display intelligent behaviors to play successfully, such as planning paths, learning a map of their 3D environment, using resources available to them, coordinating with their teammates, and engaging in strategic planning which takes their adversaries into account.

3   Agent Architecture

Our KGBot is an intelligent bot client of Gambots system, which can control its remote character to roam through a complex 3D world space and play a domination game against some opponent characters. As mentioned above, KGBot must meet some requirements: showing real-time decision-makings and responses, building a complete map of the 3D environment, searching the hidden domination points, planning the shortest path, cooperating with teammates such as other bot players or human players, modeling opponent's behaviors, and so on. A general Belief-Desire-Intention(BDI) engine called UM-PRS is embedded in KGBot. It plays a role of the decision maker to determine the best action to meet the current situation. UM-PRS [4] is a general-purpose reasoning system, integrating traditional goal-directed reasoning and reactive behavior. In contrast to most traditional deliberative planning systems, UM-PRS continuously tests its decisions against its changing knowledge about the world, and can redirect the choices of actions dynamically while remaining purposeful to the extent allowed by the unexpected changes to the environment. UM-PRS consists of *World Model, Goals, Knowledge Areas(KAs), Intention Structure,* and *Interpreter.* The world model is a database of facts which are represented as relations. A goal can be either a top-level goal or a subgoal activated by the execution of a KA body. A KA is a declarative procedure specification of how to satisfy a system goal or query. A KA consists of name, documentation, purpose, context, body, effect, and failure section. KA purpose specifies the goal that successful execution of the KA body will satisfy. KA context specifies the situations in which the KA may be applied. The context is checked throughout the execution of a KA, to make sure that the KA is still applicable to the intended situation. KA body specifies the execution steps required to satisfy the KA purpose in terms of primitive functions, subgoals, conditional branches, and so on. The intention structure of KGBot maintains information related to the runtime state of progress made toward the system's top-level or system goals. The UM-PRS interpreter controls the execution of the entire system.

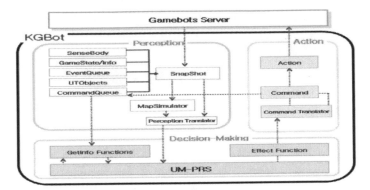

Fig. 3. Architecture of KGBot

KGBot can get some benefits from adopting UM-PRS as its central decision-making part: high reactivity, context specificity, flexibility, ease of development, reusability. Due to the characteristics of UM-PRS, integrating the goal-directed reasoning and reactive behavior, KGBot become more sensitive to the context, and can respond well to dynamic changes of the environment. In most commercial computer games, a program-controlled character – also called non-player character(NPC) – has its all parts implemented directly in a specific programming language(C or C++). In this case, it is not easy to add a new behavior, delete, or update one of the existing behaviors. As for UM-PRS, however, an agent's behaviors can be specified and stored independently of the interpreter. Moreover, most of the agent's behaviors can be specified solely in KA, which is a kind of high-level script or plan. Therefore it is easy to reuse the existing behaviors for defining a new one as well as to modify the behaviors of KGBot without time-consuming C or C++ programming.

Fig. 3 represents the architecture of KGBot, which is a bot client in the Gamebots system. It consists of three major parts: the perception part, the decision-making part, and the action part. The perception part of KGBot extracts useful information about its physical condition(SenseBody), the state of game(GameState), and the state of accessory objects(UTObject) like waypoints, weapons, and other items from sensory data received from the Gamebots server, and then delivers them to the decision-making part. Based on the newly collected information, the decision-making part updates the world model and then determines the best action to execute in consideration of the current goal and plan. The action part of KGBot composes a command message corresponding to the determined action and then sends to the Gamebots server through the network. In other words, both the perception part and the action part of KGBot constitute the interface with the game environment. These two parts of KGBot have been written in Java programming language. On the other hand, the decision-making part has been implemented with JAM, a Java version of UM-PRS. Each part of KGBot executes concurrently with its own independent thread and unique queue. Most KGBot's high-level behaviors have been specified in KA. As a result, the knowledge base of KGBot has included a number of KAs. For the sake of efficient execution, KGBot's behaviors were classified hierarchically into three different layers. Three layers are the reactive layer, the advanced skill layer, and the cooperation layer.

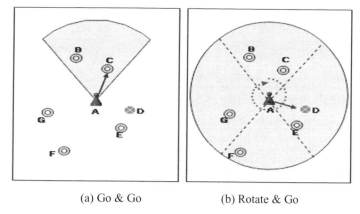

(a) Go & Go   (b) Rotate & Go

Fig. 4. Two Real-Time Search Strategies

```
RTA-RG(x)

/*    x : the current node,
      k(x, x') : the edge cost from x to x'        */

IF the current node x is the goal node, THEN return with success

/* Neighbors Finding */
θ ← 0, V ← { }, N ← { }
WHILE (θ < 360), DO
        V ← VISIBLE-NODES(x)
        N ← N ∪ REACHABLE-NODES(x, V)
        θ ← θ + Δθ
        Rotate right to θ
END

/* Lookahead */
FOR each neighbor x' of x in the set N
        Calculate f(x') = k(x, x') + h(x')
END

/* Consistency maintenance */
Update the value of h(x) to the minimum f(x') value as follows
        h(x) ← min { f(x') } for all neighbors of x

/* Action selection */
Move to neighbor x' that has the minimum f(x') value
x ← x'

Call RTA-RG(x)
```

Fig. 5. A Real-Time Search Algorithm, RTA-RG

4   Path-Planning Behavior

In order to play a domination game well, KGBot have to address the problem of finding the shortest path to one of the hidden domination points in an unknown 3D environment in which it must travel around in the environment to explore unknown waypoints. Problem spaces of path planning problems are commonly represented as
graphs, in which each state is a node and edges represent the possibilities of moving
between the nodes. Heuristic search is known as a fundamental method to deal with
such graph search problems. A* and IDA* are the well-known off-line heuristic search
algorithms which compute an entire solution path before executing the first step in the
path. On the other hand, on-line search algorithms such as RTA* and LRTA* inter-
leave planning for a plausible next move and executing the move. Since our game

world is a real-time environment, KGBot has to use an on-line search algorithm for its path-planning behavior. But most of real-time search algorithms do not consider the limitation of agent's sensing ability. In other words, the existing algorithms assume that an agent standing on a certain node can recognize its all neighboring nodes at once. However, in most first-person game environments, where a character can have neither a complete map of the world nor the unlimited range of view, this assumption fails.

As for its limited view, the agent can choose one of two possible real-time search strategies shown in Fig. 4. The first strategy shown in Fig. 4 (a), *Go & Go*, is to consider only the neighboring nodes within the agent's view at that time. On the other hand, the second strategy shown in Fig. 4 (b) is to find out all neighboring nodes by rotating itself on the current node before jumping to another node. This strategy is named *Rotate & Go*. Fig. 5 represents the real-time search algorithm with *Rotate & Go* strategy, which is denoted as RTA-RG. In a finite problem space with positive edge costs, in which there exists a path from every node to the goal, and starting with non-negative admissible initial heuristic values, RTA-RG is *complete* in the sense that it will eventually reach the goal. KGBot uses this extended real-time search algorithm for planning its paths within an unknown complex environment.

5   Experiments

In order to evaluate the efficiency of the RTA-RG real-time search algorithm and that of the UM-PRS control engine, we conducted several experiments in the Gamebots environment. For the purpose of investigating the efficiency of the RTA-RG algorithm, we compared the RTA-RG algorithm with the RTA-GG algorithm which uses the simple *Go & Go* strategy. On the other hand, as a method of proving the efficiency of the UM-PRS control engine, we compared the UM-PRS engine with a purely reactive engine. For these experiments, we used three 3D maps of different complexity shown in Fig. 6. While the *Dom-Stalwart* map shown in Fig. 6 (a) is the simplest, the *Dom-Leadworks* map shown in Fig. 6 (c) is the most complex. In the experiments for comparison between two search algorithms, we counted the consumed time for searching over each map to find out all three hidden domination points. We tried the experiment ten times with a random starting position on the same map. The limit of search time was set to 600 seconds. Table 1 shows the result of the experiments. Except the case of the simplest map, *Dom-Stalwart*, the RTA-RG algorithm has consumed less time than the RTA-GG algorithm in all cases. The result says the RTA-RG algorithm with *Rotate & Go* strategy is more efficient than the RTA-GG algorithm with *Go & Go* strategy in the complex 3D maps. In order to compare the efficiency between the UM-PRS engine and a purely reactive control engine, we had the UM-PRS agent (KGBot) compete with an agent of purely reactive engine in real UT domination games, and then compared their game scores. The wining score was set to 100. Table 2 shows the result of the experiments. In all cases, the UM-PRS agent defeated the purely reactive agent and won the game. The result illustrates the superiority of the UM-PRS control engine in this domain.

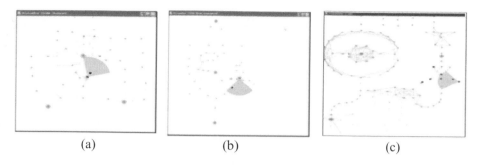

(a)   (b)   (c)

Fig. 6. Three Different Maps

Table 1. Comparison between Two Search Algorithms

Map (number of waypoints)	Search Algorithm	Max. Time (sec.)	Min. Time (sec.)	Ave. Time (sec.)
Dom-Stalwart (39)	RTA-RG	123	76	97
	RTA-GG	75	22	46
Dom-Condomned (51)	RTA-RG	214	137	193
	RTA-GG	>600	>600	>600
Dom-Leadworks (149)	RTA-RG	443	318	387
	RTA-GG	>600	>600	>600

Table 2. Comparison between UM-PRS and a Reactive Engine

Map	Control Engine	Max. Score	Min. Score	Ave. Score
Dom-Stalwart	UM-PRS	100	100	100
	Reactive E.	51	19	26
Dom-Condomned	UM-PRS	100	100	100
	Reactive E.	19	7	12
Dom-Leadworks	UM-PRS	100	100	100
	Reactive E.	22	10	12

6   Conclusions

In this paper, we introduced KGBot which is an intelligent character agent deploying within a 3D virtual environment. It has been implemented as a bot client in the Gamebots system. KGBot adopts a general BDI engine, UM-PRS, as its central decision-making part. KGBot enjoys some benefits from embedding UM-PRS. For planning its paths in a complex world, KGBot uses an efficient real-time search algorithm, RTA-

RG. Through some experiments, we illustrated the efficiency of the UM-PRS engine and that of the RTA-RG algorithm for controlling KGBot in this complex virtual environment.

References

[1]   A. Stentz: Optimal and Efficient Path Planning for Partially Known Environments, Proceedings of ICRA-94 (1994) 3310-3317.

[2]   D. Shapiro: Controlling Gaming Agents via Reactive Programs, Proceedings of the AAAI Spring Symposium on AI and Computer Games (1999) 73-76.

[3]   J. Gerstmann: Unreal Tournament: Action Game of the Year, GameSpot, 1999.

[4]   L. Jaeho, M. J. Huber, E.H. Durfee, and P.G. Kenny: UM-PRS: An Implementation of The Procedural Reasoning System for Multirobot Applications, Proceedings of CIRFFSS-94 (1994) 842-849.

[5]   J.E. Laird, M. Lent: Human-level AI's Killer Application: Interactive Computer Games, Proceedings of AAAI-2000 (2000).

[6]   J. Funge: AI for Games and Animation: A Cognitive Modeling Approach, A.K. Peters (1999).

[7]   K. Knight: Are Many Reactive Agents Better Than a Few Deliberative Ones, Proceedings of IJCAI-93 (1993) 432-437.

[9]   K. Perlin and A. Goldberg: IMPROV : A System for Scripting Interactive Actors in Virtual Worlds, Proceedings of SIGGRAPH-96, (1996) 205-216.

[10]   R. Adobbati, et al: Gamebots: A 3D Virtual World Test-Bed for Multi-Agent Research, Proceedings of Agents-01 (2001).

[11]   R. Korf: Real-Time Heuristic Search, Artificial Intelligence, Vol.42, No.3 (1990) 189-211.

[12]   R. Stern: Optimal Path Search in Unknown Physical Environments, MSc thesis, CS Dept., Bar-Ilan University, Israel (2001).

[13]   S. Rabin: AI Game Programming Wisdom, Charles River Media (2002).

[14]   Y. Kitamura, K. Teranishi, and S. Tatsumi: Organizational Strategies for Multiagent Real-Time Search, Proceedings of ICMAS-96 (1996) 150-156.

Learning Obstacle Avoidance Behavior Using Multi-agent Learning with Fuzzy States

Ming Lin, Jihong Zhu, and Zengqi Sun

Department of Computer Science and Technology
Tsinghua University, Beijing, 100084, P.R.China
Linming99@mails.tsinghua.edu.cn

Abstract. This paper presents a proposal of learning obstacle avoidance behavior in unknown environment. The robot learns this behavior through seeking to collide with possible obstacles. The field of view (FOV) of the robot sensors is partitioned into five neighboring portions, and each is associated with an agent that applies Q-learning with fuzzy states codified in distance notions. The five agents recommend actions independently and a mechanism of arbitration is employed to generate the final action. After hundreds of collision, the robot can achieve collision-free navigation with high successful ratio, through integrating the goal information and the learned obstacle avoidance behavior. Simulation results verify the effectiveness of our proposal.

1 Introduction

The goal of mobile robotics is to build physical systems that can move purposely and without human intervention in known as well as unknown environments. The vital component of a mobile robot is its navigation system that enables it to autonomously navigate to a require destination without colliding with obstacles. The problem of navigating in unknown environments can be called local navigation, focusing on methods of obstacle avoidance. These methods introduce a notion of sensor feedback and transform the navigation into a continuous dynamic process. The robot uses its onboard sensors to find a collision-free path to the goal configuration. An efficient local navigation method is artificial potential field [1]. Although it has been widely used in obstacle avoidance cases, this method has some problems such as local minimum and difficulty of determining the appropriate force coefficients, etc.

Fuzzy logic approach seems quite promising to tackle the problem of obstacle avoidance, as it can deal with various situations without requiring to constructing an analytical model of the environment. Another distinct advantage of this approach is that each fuzzy rule has a physical meaning, which makes it possible to tune the rules through applying expert knowledge. However, in complex environments, it is difficult to consistently construct the rules since there are enormous situations to be handled. A number of learning algorithms, such as evolutionary algorithm [2], supervised learning [3, 4], and reinforcement learning (RL) [5, 6] have been proposed to construct the fuzzy system automatically. Evolutionary learning itself always results in a very long learning process. Supervised learning methods require a substantially

C. Bussler and D. Fensel (Eds.): AIMSA 2004, LNAI 3192, pp. 389–398, 2004.

large set of representative patterns to train the neural networks. Unfortunately, it is difficult to obtain these training patterns that contain no contradictory information. Insufficient training data may result in an incomplete rule base, while the conflicting among the training data may cause incorrect fuzzy rules.

RL only require a scalar reinforcement signal as a performance feedback from the environment, which makes it very attractive in navigation learning problems. However, due to the large dimension of the input space for learning obstacle avoidance, the search space becomes too large to allow efficient learning. This problem has led some researchers to develop hierarchical RL methods that aim to make learning more tractable through the use of varying levels of details [7, 8], and others to use complex statistical methods to speed up learning [9]. Another approach is the use of a function approximation method to approximate the value table [10]. However, this introduces the additional problem of selecting a good approximation method for the task, and does not retain many of the theoretical guarantees known to the tabular reinforcement methods.

In this paper, in order to reduce the dimension of the input space, five agents are defined to associate with the sensor readings in five directions, and Q-learning with fuzzy states is applied in these agents to directly learn obstacle avoidance behavior. The robot chooses a final action employing some kind of arbitration based on the actions recommended by the five agents. After hundreds of collision, the robot can achieve collision-free navigation based on the goal information and the learned obstacle avoidance behavior. This paper is organized as follows. In section 2, the sensors arrangement and robot model is described. The agent design, sensor reading codification, and the algorithm description of learning from collision are presented in section 3. The whole navigation system integrating goal information and obstacle avoidance is expatiated in section 4. The simulation results are given in section 5. And in section 6, we state our conclusions and future work.

2   Sensor Arrangement and Mobile Robot Model

As depicted in Fig. 1, the robot model used is a cylindrical mobile platform with a radius, R_r, of 10cm. The robot is equipped with a set of range sensors, such as ultrasonic ones, via which it can sense the local environment. In this research, 25 sensors arranged radially from the robot center are assumed to give an angular spatial resolution of 9°. Each sensor gives the distance l_i, for i=1 to 25, from the robot center to a possible obstacle that lies within its maximum range of view (60cm).

To reduce the dimension of input space, the sensors of the robot are divided into five sensor groups, SG^i for i=1 to 5, responsible for sensing the environment in the right, front-right, front, front-left, and left direction of the robot, respectively. Each sensor group consists of five neighboring sensors so that its scanning angle is 45°. The distance d^i to a possible obstacle measured by the i-th sensor group is defined as

$$d^i = \min\{l_j | j = 5i-4, 5i-3, 5i-2, 5i-1, 5i\} - R_r, \quad i = 1 \; to \; 5 \tag{1}$$

The whole sensors cover an angle from −112.5° to 112.5° and the scanning angle is 225°. For the j-th sensor, it angle ϕ_j with respect to the robot frame is

$$\phi_j = (j-1) * \frac{225}{(25-1)} - 112.5, \quad j = 1 \, to \, 25 \qquad (2)$$

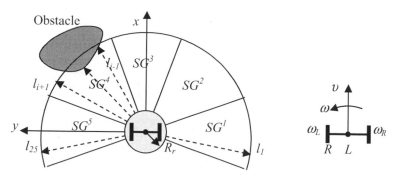

Fig. 1. Sensor arrangement of the mobile robot

We assume that the robot is driven by two active wheels. The x-axis of the robot coordinate frame is aligned with the moving direction of the robot. And the origin of the frame is defined to be the midpoint of the axis linking with the centers of the two wheels. The dynamics of the robot is not considered. The kinematic model of the mobile robot is

$$\begin{bmatrix} \upsilon \\ \omega \end{bmatrix} = \begin{bmatrix} \frac{R}{2} & \frac{R}{2} \\ -\frac{R}{L} & \frac{R}{L} \end{bmatrix} \begin{bmatrix} \omega_L \\ \omega_R \end{bmatrix} \qquad (3)$$

where υ, ω are the translational and rotational velocities of the robot, ω_L, ω_R are rotational velocities of the left and right wheel, R is the wheel radius, $R=1$cm, and L is the distance between the centers of the two wheels, $L=10$cm

The maximum rotational velocity of the robot wheels, ω_{LRmax}, is 10 rad/s. According to equation (3), $|\upsilon|=|\upsilon_{max}|=10$ cm/s, and $\omega=|\omega_{min}|=0$, if $\omega_L=\omega_R=\pm\omega_{LRmax}$. And $\upsilon=|\upsilon_{min}|=0$, and $\omega=|\omega_{max}|=2$ rad/s, if $\omega_L=-\omega_R=\pm\omega_{LRmax}$.

3 Learning from Collision

3.1 Agent Specification

Large dimension of the input space usually leads to heavy learning phase in RL. In our method, we specify five independent agents, agent^i for $i=1 \, to \, 5$, to be associated with the respective sensor groups, SG^i. The agent's FOV is defined to be the FOV of its corresponding sensor group. The remarkable advantage of such a proposal is that it can dramatically reduce the state space of each agent, which is just one portion of the whole space. In our method, each of the five agents has three states and three actions, and the number of state-action pair is 3x3=9, while the dimension of the whole state and state-action space is 3^5 and 3^5x3, if only one agent is employed and its states are the concatenation of the sub-states in the five directions.

3.2   State Codification

For each agent, its environment state is considered as a distance notion between the robot and possible obstacles in respective directions. One proposal is to divide the interval from 0 to the maximum range of the sensors into several subintervals, and each subinterval is classified as a distance notion. However, this kind of division is not consistent with the fact of gradual change of distance. It treats equally all values belonging to the same class, not differentiating the values close to the boundary and those far away from the class boundary. To solve this problem, the notion of fuzzy is employed in the partitioning of distances. Three fuzzy sets are defined to represent the following linguistic concepts, *near*, *medium*, and *far*, as depicted in Fig. 2.

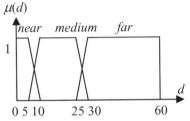
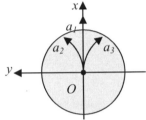

Fig. 2. State codification in distance notions   **Fig. 3.** Alternative actions of the agents

3.3   Action Specification

The movement of the mobile robot is constrained by its kinematic model. The robot gets a 0 rotational and maximum translational velocity if its wheels take the velocity of $[\omega_{max}, \omega_{max}]'$. And when the robot turns "100% left/right", that is, the wheels take a velocity of $[-\omega_{max}, \omega_{max}]'$, the robot gets a largest positive/negative rotational velocity and its translational velocity is 0.

It is obvious that the robot would not collide with any obstacle if it turns 100% left or right, as the position of the robot does not have any change. In order to make learning from collision applicable, three typical actions, a_1, a_2, and a_3, are chosen for the five agents, as depicted in Fig. 3. Action a_1 is "go ahead", an action leading to the maximum translational velocity and 0 rotation. We get action a_1 if the wheels velocity is $[\omega_{max}, \omega_{max}]'$. Action a_2 is "turn 50% left", which means that the rotational velocity of the robot is a half of that of "turn 100% left" and the translational velocity is the largest in this case. Let the wheels velocity be $[0, \omega_{max}]'$, we have action a_2. In a similar way, we get a_3 if the wheel velocity is $[\omega_{max}, 0]'$.

3.4   *Q*-Learning with Fuzzy States

We believe that for a robot, the experience of collision with possible obstacles is very useful. The valuable information exploited from collisions can be used to improve the robot navigator, so that a collision would not happen again in a next time when the robot is in a similar situation. We think the obstacle avoidance behavior could be improved through learning the collisions that the robot experienced. So, in this paper, the robot is programmed to seek to collide with possible obstacles and learns from these collisions to gradually establish the evaluation of possible collision in different states. RL is particularly appropriate for this kind of learning task, as an agent can use it to learn a behavior through trial-and-error interactions with the environment.

In the field of RL, Q-learning is a model-free algorithm based on stochastic dynamic programming and has received the bulks of attention by researchers, most likely for its simplicity and convergence proof. We choose the well-known Q-learning for the five agents to learn from possible collisions. The Q value means the long-run reward of collision. In the point of view of an agent, the higher the $Q(s, a)$, the higher possibility the robot will collide with an obstacle when it is in state s and performs action a. The Q value of the one-step Q-learning algorithm is updated as follows.

$$Q(s,a) \leftarrow Q(s,a) + \alpha \left[r + \gamma \max_{a'} Q(s',a') - Q(s,a) \right] \tag{4}$$

The standard Q-learning algorithm has to be modified to be applicable with fuzzy states. For an agent, the current state s is determined as the fuzzy set to whom the membership degree of the distance to an obstacle, d, is the biggest, depicted in equation (5). As the agent is in a fuzzy state s with a membership degree of μ_s, the new reward, r', is defined in equation (6).

$$s \leftarrow \arg\max_{j} \left\{ \mu_{s_j}(d) \right\}, \quad \mu_s = \max_{j} \left\{ \mu_{s_j}(d) \right\}, \quad j = 1, 2, 3 \tag{5}$$

$$r' = \mu_s \bullet r \tag{6}$$

where s_j for j=1, 2, 3 represents the fuzzy set *near*, *medium*, and *far*, respectively.

To avoid local maximum, ε-greedy policy is used in the action choice.

3.5 Multi-agent Learning

At each time step, each agent determines its state, and recommends an action based on the three action values of the current state. As the agents behave independently, the actions recommended by the agent may be inconsistent. We use a mechanism of arbitration to deal with this problem, depicted in Fig. 4. The arbitrator chooses the final action a with the largest Q value, also employing ε-greedy policy. This final action is the actual taken action for all the five agents. This architecture is the same as behavior-based approach in robotics. The notable point is that each agent corresponds to a behavior and these behaviors can learn to improve themselves.

We define the immediate reward r is 1 with a collision and 0 with no collision. If a collision will happen after the robot performs the action a, then the collision area is estimated and the agents whose FOV has some overlap with that area receive a reward of $r' = \mu_s \bullet r = \mu_s$, and other agents receive 0. If no collision will happen, then all the agents receive a reward of 0. In Fig. 5, the robot initially is centered in O and its heading is aligned with the x-axis. The current states of the five agents are s^i for i=1 *to* 5. After taking an action "turn 50% right", the robot will move to O' and then detects a collision. The collision area is dark-grey-shaped. This area is located in the

FOV of the agent[2] and agent[3], so they receive a reward of μ_{s^2} and μ_{s^3}, while others receive 0. If the robot detects a collision, then it will be reset randomly in the free space after the action values of each agent have been updated. The whole learning algorithm for the five agents is presented in Fig. 6.

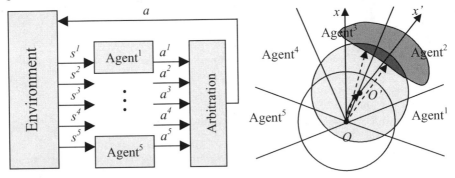

Fig. 4. Learning and arbitration   **Fig. 5.** Collision happens

Initialize $Q^i(s^i, a^i)$ to be 0, **for** all pairs of s, a, i=1 *to* 5
Repeat forever
    Perceive s^i of the agent^i, **for** i=1 *to* 5
    Choose a^i from $A^i\{s^i\}$ with ε_{1}-greedy policy, **for** i=1 *to* 5
    Choose a from $\{a^i\}$ with ε_2-greedy policy
    Perform action a
    Observe the rewards $r^i{}'$, $s^i{}'$
        $r^i{}'$=0, **for** i=1 *to* 5
        $r^i{}' = \mu_{s^i}(d^i)$, **if** COLLISION and (FOV^i ∩ collision area)≠ ø
    $Q^i(s^i, a) \leftarrow Q^i(s^i, a) + \alpha[r^i{}' + \gamma \max_{a^i{}'} Q^i(s^i{}', a^i{}') - Q^i(s^i, a)]$, **for** i=1 *to* 5
    if COLLISION, reset the robot randomly in the free space

Fig. 6. Learning algorithm

4   Collision-Free Navigation

After hundreds of collision, the robot has sufficiently learned the knowledge of collision. This knowledge is the long run reward of collision and larger action value means more possible collision. In navigation, the robot can choose an action with relatively low action value while considering the specified goal direction. In this way, the robot can show a behavior of obstacle avoidance while moving to the goal.

We assume the robot knows the goal direction, δ, and its own heading by means of some sensor. The goal direction is the angle difference of the straight line connecting the robot center and the goal configuration, and the current robot heading. In navigating, δ plays an important role in choosing the final action. If the goal is in front of the robot, then it is better to take action "go ahead". We define goal factor, gf, as the preference of an action based on the goal information. Each action corresponds to a gf. The greater the gf, the more the robot prefers the action considering δ. Fig. 7 depicts the gfs of the three actions.

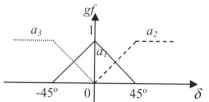

Fig. 7. The gfs of the actions, a_1: "go ahead", a_2: "turn 50% left", and a_3: "turn 50% right"

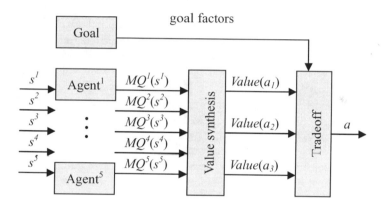

Fig. 8. Action value synthesis and tradeoff between goal information and obstacle avoidance

$$Value(a_i) = \sum_{j=1}^{5} \mu_{s^j} \bullet MQ^j(s^j, a_i), \text{ for } i=1, 2, 3$$

$$Value(a_i) \leftarrow Value(a_i) \Big/ \max_{j}\{Value(a_j)\}, \text{ for } i=1, 2, 3$$

$$Total(a_i) = w_{oa} \bullet [1 - Value(a_i)] + (1 - w_{oa}) \bullet gf(a_i), \text{ for } i=1, 2, 3$$

$$a = \arg\max\{Total(a_i)\}$$

Fig. 9. The algorithm of synthesis and tradeoff

For an agent, the action value means the evaluation of possible collision. At each time step, each agent reports three evaluations corresponding to the three actions. As these evaluations are local and usually inconsistent, the global evaluations of collision associate with the three actions have to be integrated. It has been proven that the action value will converge if the state-action pairs are visited infinitely. As it is impossible to trial infinitely, we just use the mean of the Q values, MQ, over the rear period of collisions to approximate the convergence values in our research. For an action, we simply summate the corresponding MQ values of the five agents to produce the global evaluations of collision of this action. As the robot prefers an action that has a relatively low global collision evaluation, considering obstacle avoidance, and it also prefers an action that is more beneficial for it to move to the goal, so, these two factors have to be compromised to generate the most appropriate action. The diagram and algorithm of the synthesis and the tradeoff between the goal information and obstacle avoidance is depicted in Fig. 8 and 9.

5   Simulation Results

To test its functionality, the proposed algorithm is applied to a simulated mobile robot. It is assumed that the radius of the robot is 10cm and the size of the environment is 500x500cm^2. The maximum measurement range of the sensors is 60cm. The parameters used in the simulations are $\alpha = 0.1$, $\gamma = 0.7$, $\varepsilon_1 = 0.8$, $\varepsilon_2 = 0.8$, in learning phase, and $w_\varphi = 0.5$, $w_{oa} = 0.7$, in navigating phase.

The environment has some randomly distributed obstacles with arbitrarily shapes. In the learning phase, the robot seeks to collide with possible obstacles. At each time step, each of the five agents independently recommends an action, and then the action that is most likely to lead to a collision is chosen to take. Usually the agents receive a reward of 0, except when a collision happens and the corresponding agents receive a reinforcement signal of μ_{s^i}. Then the action values of the agents are updated based on the rewards received. According to our empirical estimation of learning convergence, the learning process is ended after 1000 collisions have happened.

Fig. 10 shows the learning graph of the values of the three actions ("go ahead", "turn 50% left", and "turn 50% right"), depicted as solid, dashed, and dotted lines, in the state "near" and "far", respectively. In (a), the value of "go ahead" is very close to 1, meaning that a collision is very likely to happen if taking this action. In (b), the three action values are relatively low and have no distinct difference, indicating a relatively low possibility of collision. In (c) and (d), the action value of turning 50% right/left is higher than that of turning 50% left/right. This is reasonable because turning 50% right/left" will of course lead to a more possible collision, when an obstacle is near in the front-right/left direction.

The learned knowledge of collision is used in navigation in the way of choosing the action having the least evaluation of collision. Fig. 11 illustrates the robot navigation contrails with different starting configurations. In (a), the robot successfully navigates to the goal from four starting positions. In (b), there are four successful navigations and one failure, which is possibly because of the confined area near the collision position. Nevertheless, the ratio of successful navigation is noticeably high.

6   Conclusions and Future Work

In this paper the proposal of learning obstacle avoidance behavior is presented for a mobile robot that has no prior knowledge of the environment and experience of navigation. The FOV of the robot sensors is partitioned into five portions, right, front-right, front, front-left, and left. And five agents are defined to be associated with these portions. First, the robot seeks to collide with obstacles and Q-learning with fuzzy states is applied in these agents to learn the knowledge of collision. Each agent independently recommends an action and the final action is generated through a mechanism of arbitration. After hundreds of collision learning, the robot can navigate to a specified goal position, with high successful ratio, based on the goal information and the learned obstacle avoidance behavior.

Future work will primarily concern on applying this method with continuous actions and incorporating prior knowledge into these agents.

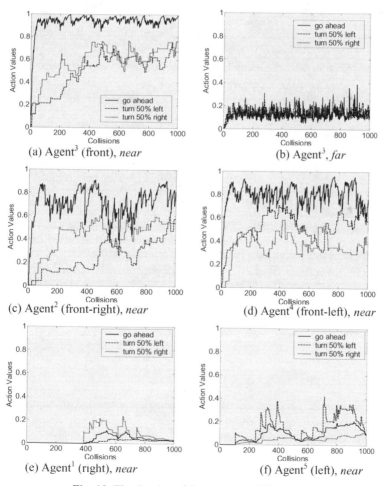

(a) Agent[3] (front), *near*

(b) Agent[3], *far*

(c) Agent[2] (front-right), *near*

(d) Agent[4] (front-left), *near*

(e) Agent[1] (right), *near*

(f) Agent[5] (left), *near*

Fig. 10. The Q value of the agents in different states

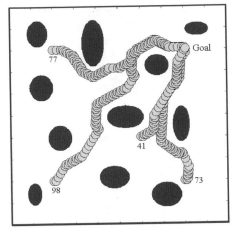 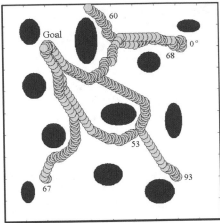

(a) Goal is (400, 400), initial heading is 0°   (b) Goal is (100, 400), initial heading is 180°

Fig. 11. Mobile robot navigation with different goals

References

1. O. Khatib. Real-time obstacle avoidance for manipulators and mobile robots. *The International Journal of Robotics Research*, 5(1): 90-98, 1986.
2. A. Homaifar and E. McCormick. Simultaneous design of membership functions and rule sets for fuzzy controllers using genetic algorithms. *IEEE Transaction on Fuzzy Systems*, vol. 3, pp. 129–139, May 1995.
3. P. K. Pal and A. Kar. Mobile robot navigation using a neural net. *IEEE International Conference on Robotics and Automation*, 1995, pp. 1503–1508.
4. C. Kozakiewwicz and M. Ejiri. Neural network approach to path planning for two dimension robot motion. *IEEE/RSJ International Conference on Intelligent Robots Systems*, 1991, pp. 818–823.
5. H. R. Beom and H. S. Cho. A sensor-based navigation for a mobile robot using fuzzy logic and reinforcement learning. *IEEE Transaction on System, Man, Cybernetics*, vol. 25, pp. 464–477, Mar. 1995.
6. N. H. C. Yung and C. Ye. An intelligent mobile vehicle navigator based on fuzzy logic and reinforcement learning. *IEEE Transaction System, Man, Cybernetics B*, vol. 29, pp. 314–321, Apr. 1999.
7. B. Digney. Learning hierarchical control structures for multiple tasks and changing environments. *Proceedings of the Fifth International Conference on Simulation of Adaptive Behavior*, Zurich, Switzerland, 1998.
8. J. Moren. Dynamic action sequences in reinforcement learning. *Proceedings of the Fifth International Conference on Simulation of Adaptive Behavior*, Zurich, Switzerland, 1998.
9. W. Smart and L. Kaelbling. Practical reinforcement learning in continuous spaces. *Proceedings of the Seventeenth International Conference on Machine Learning*, pp. 903–910, 2000.
10. R. Sutton and A. Barto. *Reinforcement Learning: an Introduction*, The MIT Press, Cambridge, MA, 1998.

Towards Well-Defined Multi-agent Reinforcement Learning*

Rinat Khoussainov

Department of Computer Science, University College Dublin
Belfield, Dublin 4, Ireland
rinat@ucd.ie

Abstract. Multi-agent reinforcement learning (MARL) is an emerging area of research. However, it lacks two important elements: a coherent view on MARL, and a well-defined problem objective. We demonstrate these points by introducing three phenomena, social norms, teaching, and bounded rationality, which are inadequately addressed by the previous research. Based on the ideas of bounded rationality, we define a very broad class of MARL problems that are equivalent to learning in partially observable Markov decision processes (POMDPs). We show that this perspective on MARL accounts for the three missing phenomena, but also provides a well-defined objective for a learner, since POMDPs have a well-defined notion of optimality. We illustrate the concept in an empirical study, and discuss its implications for future research.

1 Introduction

Multi-agent reinforcement learning (MARL) addresses the following question: "How can an agent learn to act optimally in an *a priori* unknown dynamic environment through trial-and-error interaction in the presence of other self-interested and possibly adapting agents?" There are numerous practical application domains for MARL, such as robotic soccer, electronic market places, self-managing computer systems, distributed Web search, or even military/counter-terrorism applications. While single-agent RL has been an active area of research in AI for many years, MARL is a relatively new field.

We do not have sufficient space in this paper to provide a detailed survey of the prior work in MARL, but we can point out two important issues in the current state of research: the lack of a coherent view on MARL; and the lack of a well-defined objective for a MARL algorithm. What behaviour should an agent learn in a multi-agent environment? In single-agent RL, this problem is well-defined, since the agent's performance depends only on its own actions. In a MA environment, the agent's performance may depend on simultaneous actions of others. Thus, a given agent would need to know what to expect from the other agents, and the optimal behaviour may change as the other agents also evolve (adapt) over time.

The question of a clear research agenda has been already emphasised by several RL researchers and is becoming a topic of much ongoing debate in the area [1]. The

---

* Thanks to Nicholas Kushmerick for helpful discussions and valuable comments. This research was supported by grant SFI/01/F.1/C015 from Science Foundation Ireland, and grant N00014-03-1-0274 from the US Office of Naval Research.

contributions of this paper are as follows. We demonstrate the lack of a coherent view on MARL by introducing three phenomena inadequately addressed by the previous research: social norms, teaching, and bounded rationality. While these phenomena are not new to MARL, none of the previous works attempted to systematically account for all three together, and many papers ignore all of them. Based on the ideas of bounded rationality [2], we define a very broad class of "realistic MA learners", and show that MARL in this case is equivalent to learning in partially observable Markov decision processes (POMDPs). Such perspective on MARL accounts for the above phenomena, but also provides a well-defined objective for a learner, since POMDPs have a well-defined notion of optimality. Finally, we illustrate the proposed concept in an empirical study, and discuss its implications for future research.

2   Formal Framework and Definitions

The standard RL model [3] consists of the two main components: a learning agent and a dynamic environment. The agent is connected to its environment via perception and action signals. The interaction with the environment proceeds in steps. At each step, the agent receives as input some indication (observation) of the current state of the environment and then generates an output by choosing some action. The action changes the state of the environment, and the value of this state transition is communicated back to the agent using some scalar reinforcement signal (*reward*, or *payoff*).

In a MA scenario, there may be several agents acting in the same environment, and their actions may affect not only the state transitions, but also the rewards of each other. Formally, a MA environment is well modelled as a *stochastic game* (SG) [4]. A stochastic game is a tuple $\langle I, S, s_0, (A_i)_{i=1}^I, Z, (u_i)_{i=1}^I \rangle$, where I is the number of agents, also called *players* in the game, S is a set of the game states, s_0 is the initial state, and A_i is the set of actions available to player i. If a_i is the action selected by player i at some step, then $a = (a_i)_{i=1}^I$ is an *action profile* (or a *joint action*). A set $A = A_1 \times A_2 \times \ldots \times A_I$ is the set of all possible action profiles. $u_i : S \times A \to \mathbb{R}$ is a payoff function of player i. $Z : S \times A \times S \to [0, 1]$ is a stochastic state transition function, which for given state and action profile returns a probability distribution over the possible next states. That is, $Z(s, a, s')$ gives the probability that after performing joint action a in state s, the next state of the game will be s'.

Stochastic games are a generalisation of Markov decision processes (MDPs) [3] to multiple decision makers. In general, the environment can be non-deterministic, i.e. taking the same joint action in the same state may result in different state transitions and/or reinforcements. However, it is usually assumed that the probabilities of making state transitions or receiving specific rewards do not change over time. A *game history* in a stochastic game is a sequence of tuples $\langle s, a \rangle$, where a is the players' action profile (joint action) at some step of the game and s is the next state.

The goal of the agent is to find a decision rule (a *policy*) that maximises some long-term measure of the reinforcement. From the agent's point of view, there are two types of environments: *fully observable* environments and *partially observable* environments. In fully observable environments, the agent can reliably observe the game history at each step. In partially observable environments, agents have incomplete information about the game. For example, an agent may not be able to distinguish between some states of the environment based on his observations, or he may not be able to observe actions of other players. An *observation function* Ω_i is a mapping from a set of possible elements of the game history to a set O_i of possible observations for player i, $\Omega_i : S \times A \times O_i \rightarrow [0, 1]$. $\Omega_i(s, a, o_i)$ is the probability that player i receives observation o_i when the game state changes to s after agents realise action profile a.

A policy (or strategy) of a player in a stochastic game is a function that maps possible sequences of observations of a player to probability distributions over the player's actions: $\Lambda_i : \mathcal{O}_i \times A_i \rightarrow [0, 1]$, where $\mathcal{O}_i$ is a set of possible observation sequences $\{(o_i(k))_k : o_i(k) \in O_i\}$ of player i. If the mapping is deterministic ($\Lambda_i : \mathcal{O}_i \rightarrow A_i$), then the strategy is called *deterministic*. A strategy of a player in a stochastic game is called *Markov* or *reactive* if it is a function only of the current observation $\Lambda_i : O_i \times A_i \rightarrow [0, 1]$ (i.e. if the player's action at a given step depends only on the current observation of the game at that step).

Let $(r_i(k))_{k=1}^K$ be a sequence of rewards received by the agent i over K steps of interaction with the environment. The *long-term reward* for a given sequence of rewards from separate steps can be calculated as a *discounted sum* $U_i^K = \sum_{k=1}^K \gamma^{k-1} r_i(k)$, where $0 < \gamma \leq 1$ is a discount factor, or as *average reward*: $U_i^K = 1/K \sum_{k=1}^K r_i(k)$. The case when the long-term performance is analysed over infinitely many steps is called the *infinite horizon* model. The long-term payoff in the infinite horizon case is evaluated as a limit for $K \rightarrow \infty$: $U_i^\infty = \lim_{K \to \infty} U_i^K$. The infinite-horizon discounted sum model has received the most attention in RL due to its mathematical tractability.

3   Optimality in Stochastic Games

Unlike in the single-agent case (MDPs), the optimal behaviour in stochastic games is in general opponent-dependent. That is, the long-term payoff of a player's strategy can only be evaluated given the strategies of the other players in the game. Therefore, the notion of optimality has to be replaced with the notion of *best response*. A player's strategy is the best response to a combination of strategies of other players (opponents) in a game, if it maximises the player's payoff for the given strategies of the opponents. Consequently, a strategy is optimal, if it is the best response to the combination of strategies used by other players in the game. A fundamental problem is that a player cannot know what strategies opponents will use, because he has no direct control over their behaviour (all players are independent in selecting their strategies). Moreover, the opponents' strategies may change over time as the opponents adapt their behaviour.

Game theory attempts to resolve this uncertainty using the concept of Nash equilibrium [5]. Nash equilibrium captures a situation in a game in which each player holds the correct expectations about the other players' behaviour and acts the best response to those expectations. Let $\hat{U}_i(\Lambda_1, \Lambda_2, \cdots, \Lambda_I)$ be the expected long-term payoff of player i for the given players' strategies combination $(\Lambda_j)_{j=1}^I$. A strategy combination $(\Lambda_j^*)_{j=1}^I$ is a Nash equilibrium, if $\hat{U}_i(\Lambda_1^*, \cdots, \Lambda_{i-1}^*, \Lambda_i, \Lambda_{i+1}^*, \cdots, \Lambda_I^*) \leq \hat{U}_i((\Lambda_j^*)_{j=1}^I)$, for any strategy Λ_i for all players i. That is, no player can increase its payoff by unilaterally deviating from the equilibrium. The idea behind Nash equilibrium is that if there was a mechanism that correctly predicts for a player what strategies his opponents will use, then the main requirement for such a mechanism would be that it should not be self-defeating (i.e. knowing the predictions of this mechanism players should not have incentives to contradict it). Thus a valid prediction must be a Nash equilibrium.

However, the predictive power of the Nash equilibrium is limited by two problems. The first problem is the possible multiplicity of equilibria. When there are multiple equilibria in a game, players need to reach a coordinated equilibrium outcome to play optimally. The second problem is the assumption that all players in the game have equal reasoning capabilities. If one player can analyse the game to correctly predict the behaviour of other players, then the other players also have these abilities to analyse the game. That is, we assume that all players are equally "clever" (equally rational) and possess the same necessary information about the game to derive their expectations. Generally speaking, this assumption may not always hold in practice.

4   Previous Work

Many learning methods in SGs focused on extending traditional RL algorithms like Q-learning [3] to MA settings. Most of results, however, are for a limited class of single-state SGs, called *repeated games*. Unlike in single-agent RL, the long-term payoff of an action in a SG depends on the strategies of opponents, so the learner has to make some assumptions about the opponents' behaviour. In *Minimax-Q* [6], a player learns to select at each step the action that maximises the reward the player can guarantee. However, this strategy works well only in zero-sum games (two-player games where the sum of players' payoffs at every step is zero). *Nash-Q* [7] extends Minimax-Q to general-sum games by choosing actions that are a part of some Nash equilibrium of the constituent one-step game. Since there may be many Nash equilibria in a game, the analysis is restricted to special cases of games with globally optimal points and saddle points, where equilibrium selection is simplified.

Opponent modellers try to model the opponents' strategies from interaction experience and construct a best-response strategy to those models. Examples of this approach are joint action learners (JALs) [8] and finite automata modellers [9]. These methods can work well when the opponents' strategies are fixed, but are questionable when players learn. *PHC* and *WoLF-PHC* [10] are two algorithms for MARL in fully observable domains based on a policy search approach. PHC is essentially an extension of Q-learning to non-deterministic Markov polices. WoLF PHC uses variable learning rate to encourage convergence of the algorithm to a Nash equilibrium in self-play.

5   Multi-agent Learning Revisited

There are several phenomena that are addressed inadequately in MARL. We subdivide them into social norms, teaching considerations, and bounded rationality. While these issues are not entirely new to MARL, none of the previous approaches provides a complete and systematic coverage of them, and too frequently they are simply ignored.

Social norms. SGs have a rich structure of equilibrium behaviour that may be interpreted in terms of a "social norm" [5]. The idea is that players can sustain mutually desirable outcomes, if their strategies involve "punishing" any player whose behaviour

Table 1. Prisoner's dilemma

	D	C
D	3,3	0,4
C	4,0	1,1

Table 2. The row player prefers to "teach" the column player that her strategy is a

	b	$\bar{b}$
a	1,0	3,1
$\bar{a}$	2,2	4,0

is undesirable. This is regulated by the "folk theorems"[1] originally proposed for single-state SGs, called *repeated games*. Two-player repeated games can be described by a game matrix that specifies the players payoffs for each possible joint action. Consider the example of repeated Prisoner's dilemma (RPD) [5] in Table 1. At each step of the game, players select one of the two possible actions C or D and receive the respective payoffs as specified in the table. At the next step, the same game repeats.

A one-step Prisoner's dilemma has a unique Nash equilibrium where both players choose C. Indeed, no matter what action the opponent selects, the player is always better off choosing C. In the case of RPD however, the outcome (D, D) can also be sustained as equilibrium, if each player punishes the opponent for deviation by also switching to C. If both players follow such strategy, then it is better for them to play (D, D) repeatedly, receiving payoff of 3 at each step, rather than getting the higher deviation payoff of 4 in a single period, but receiving a lower payoff of 1 in all subsequent steps. The formal results below are derived for infinite-horizon average payoff games (called *limit of means games*), though similar results exist for discounted games too.

A vector (x_i) is called a feasible long-term payoff profile in a limit of means SG with initial state s_0, if there is a combination of players' strategies (Λ_i), such that $x_i = \hat{U}_i(s_0, (\Lambda_i)) = \lim_{K \to \infty} 1/K \sum_{k=1}^{K} \hat{r}_i(s_0, (\Lambda_i), k)$, where $\hat{r}_i(s_0, (\Lambda_i), k)$ is the expected payoff of player i at stage k for the given initial state and players' strategies. Let Λ_{-i} denote a strategy profile of all players except i. We define the *minimax payoff* $\mu_i(s_0)$ of player i in a limit of means SG with initial state s_0 as $\mu_i(s_0) = \min_{\Lambda_{-i}} \max_{\Lambda_i} \hat{U}_i(s_0, (\Lambda_i, \Lambda_{-i}))$. Essentially, the strategy profile Λ_{-i} corresponding to the minimax is the most severe punishment that other players can inflict on i for the given initial state. A payoff profile (x_i) is *strictly enforceable* in SG with initial state s_0, if it is feasible and $x_i > \mu_i(s_0)$ for all i. Intuitively, enforceable profiles are the outcomes where each player can be punished, and so threats of punishment can sustain the outcome as an equilibrium.

Proposition 1 (Folk theorem for limit of means stochastic games)
Define the following assumptions: (A1) – *the set of feasible long-term average payoff profiles is independent of the initial state;* (A2) – *the long-term average minimax payoff of each player is independent of the initial state. For a given limit of means stochastic game and assumptions (A1)–(A2), any strictly enforceable long-term average payoff profile is a Nash equilibrium payoff profile of the game [11].*

Informally, assumption (A2) tells us that the punishment is always effective for all players, while assumption (A1) tells that the desired payoff profile can be achieved from any state (hence, it can be achieved after punishment as well). Since repeated games have

---
[1] The term used in the game theory community, since their originator is apparently unknown.

only a single state, and the feasible payoff profiles in a limit of means repeated game are the same as in the constituent one-shot game, any strictly enforceable payoff profile in the constituent one-shot game is a Nash equilibrium payoff profile of the repeated game [12]. An example of such a punishing strategy for RPD is *Tit-for-Tat* [13]. Tit-for-Tat starts by playing D and then plays the same action that the opponent in the previous period. The optimal strategy against Tit-for-Tat is to always play D.

Folk theorems (especially for repeated games) have been known in game theory for a long while. However, they received very little attention in MARL. Implementing punishing strategies requires the players to be able to condition their behaviour on a possibly long game history. At the same time, most MARL algorithms focused on learning only reactive policies which may be inadequate for sustaining social norms.

Teaching. Learning in games has been studied extensively in game theory as well. However, in game theory learning was used as an alternative way to explain the concept of equilibrium as a long-term outcome arising out of a process in which less than fully rational players search for optimality over time. An important point here is that actions of a player influence the learning and, hence, the future play of the opponents. That is, a player is learning himself and simultaneously teaching other players. Thus, in such environments the players ought to consider not only how their opponents may play in the future, but also how players' current behaviour will affect the future play of the opponents. As a result, a player's strategy may become to "teach" the opponents to play a best response to a particular action by playing that action over and over.

Consider an example repeated game from [14] described by Table 2. Since action $\bar{a}$ dominates a for the row player, a row player who ignores considerations of the repeated play will choose $\bar{a}$ as her strategy. Consequently, the column player will eventually learn to play b, because b maximises his payoff for the given strategy of the row player. Hence, the learning process will converge to outcome $(\bar{a}, b)$, where the row player's payoff is 2. However, if the row player is patient and knows that the column player "naively" chooses his strategy to maximise his own payoff given the history of the row player's actions, then the row player can do better by always playing a. This will lead the column player to choose $\bar{b}$ as his strategy, yielding a payoff of 3 to the row player. Essentially, a "sophisticated" and patient player facing a naive opponent can develop a "reputation" leading the learning process to a desired outcome.

Most of game theory, however, ignores these teaching considerations, explicitly or implicitly relying on a model in which the incentive to try to alter the future play of opponents is negligible. One class of such models that make the teaching considerations negligible are *large populations*. In large population models, opponents for each period are chosen from a large population of players making interaction relatively anonymous. Unlike game theory, MARL should take into account the fact that the actions of a given agent influence the learning and, hence, the future behaviour of other agents in the same environment. However, most existing MARL algorithms either ignore these teaching considerations, or use them only implicitly, for example to analyse convergence properties of the learning process in self-play (i.e. when opponents use the same learning algorithm). As shown in [15], teaching can actually allow an agent to exploit his opponents and achieve better individual performance.

Bounded rationality. The type of rationality usually assumed in game theory is perfect, logical, *deductive* rationality. Such deductive rationality presumes that all decision makers possess full knowledge of the game, unlimited abilities to analyse it, and can perform the analysis without mistakes. *Bounded rationality* [2] explicitly assumes that the reasoning capabilities of decision makers are limited, and therefore, they do not necessarily behave optimally in the game-theoretic sense. Bounded rationality proposes *inductive* instead of deductive reasoning.

Theoretical reasons for bounded rationality can be subdivided into knowledge limitations (i.e. players may not have sufficient knowledge of the game to compute an equilibrium) and computational limitations. For example, there is a large body of research on equilibrium selection in game theory using various principles and criteria [16]. However, a generic assumption that players are payoff maximisers is not sufficient to select a unique outcome. Also, it may ultimately require characterising all Nash equilibria of a game. The task is NP-hard even for simple one-shot games and even given complete information about the game [17]. In real world, agents may have physical limitations as well (e.g. faulty acting parts) preventing them from implementing certain strategies.

The main implication of bounded rationality is that even when the deductive game-theoretic reasoning gives an unambiguous answer (e.g. the game has a unique Nash equilibrium), there is still a possibility that opponents will not be able or willing to realise it, and so playing the equilibrium strategy will not be optimal. Though one could expect that machine learning should rely on inductive reasoning, still many MARL algorithms specifically focus on learning some equilibria of a game, resulting in quite limited application scenarios and unclear supporting motivation [1]. Only recently RL researchers have started to recognise and address this issue [10].

6   Learning with Realistic Agents

The discussion in the previous section indicates the lack of two important elements in MARL: a coherent view incorporating the described phenomena, and a well-defined objective (a problem statement) for a learner. What should an agent learn in a MA environment, or what behaviour is optimal? We propose here a novel perspective on MARL that gives a possible answer to these questions.

Multi-agent learning as a partially observable MDP. In general, one can view a reinforcement learner as two interacting components: a behaviour policy that is responsible for action selection, and an update algorithm that uses the learner's past experience to modify the policy so as to improve its long-term performance (see Figure 1). In particular, the update algorithm can use information about game observations, rewards, and actions performed by the agent, as well as the dynamics of the current policy and some prior knowledge of the game (if available).

So far, we have focused on learning a policy that yields the best performance in the given environment. However, Figure 1 clearly illustrates that a reinforcement learner as a whole is nothing but a decision rule mapping observations (including reward observations) onto the agent's actions. That is, learning is simply a special form of acting where actions are conditioned on the learning history. A reinforcement learning algorithm can essentially be viewed as a strategy in a "super" game, where players' actions are possible learning strategies, and payoffs are related to the outcomes of the learning process with a given combination of strategies.

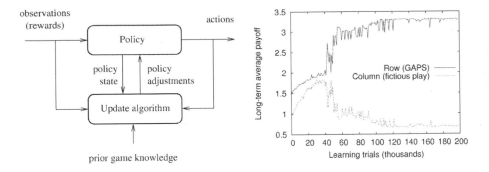

Fig. 1. Inside a reinforcement learner   **Fig. 2.** Learning in the "teaching" game

What assumptions can we make about possible learning strategies? Perhaps the most generic assumption we can make is that strategies should be *computable* (i.e. implementable by a Turing machine). The second assumption we make is that strategies should be implementable by realistic agents. Realistic agents can only have a finite amount of memory available to them (equivalently, the corresponding Turing machines can only have finite tapes). Taking into account that a Turing machine with a finite tape is expressively equivalent to a finite state automaton (FSA), we obtain that realistic learning strategies should be representable by a (possibly non-deterministic) FSA.

It is easy to see that from a single agent's point of view a Markov environment augmented with several FSAs remains Markov, since at each step the immediate reward and the next state of the environment depend only on the agent's action, and the current combined state of the environment and FSAs. Therefore, learning in such environment (i.e. MA learning with realistic agents) becomes equivalent to learning in a *partially observable MDP* (POMDP). The MDP should be partially observable, because it is unlikely that an agent will be able to observe state transitions inside other learners.

Discussion. Treating MARL as learning in POMDPs allows us to systematically account for all three previously discussed phenomena. Indeed, social norms become just a kind of history-dependent behaviour in a POMDP, and it is well known that in POMDPs history-dependent policies can achieve better performance [18]. Getting high rewards in MDPs requires an agent to bring the environment into "well-paying" states. Since now other learners are just a part of the environment from a given agent's point of view, teaching can be viewed as changing the state of other agents to get better rewards. Finally, bounded rationality served as a defining assumption for the realistic learners in our model. The proposed perspective on MARL provides a well-defined objective for a MA learner, because POMDPs have a well-defined notion of optimality

Similar considerations have been proposed in [1], where the authors put forward three research agendas: distributed AI (designing an adaptive procedure for decentralised control of a set of agents); equilibrium agenda (investigating whether given learning strategies are in equilibrium); and AI agenda (finding the best learning strategy against a fixed class of opponents). By defining such a fixed class of opponents as "realistic learners", we have merged these three agendas. Equilibrium strategies and optimal strategies are equivalent in POMDPs. The distributed AI agenda can be viewed as common-payoff games, where all agents have the same payoff functions, and thus it ultimately reduces to finding the best strategy in the corresponding POMDP. The proposed concept does not make MARL easier, but it does provide a coherent view on the previous approaches and possible future directions. From the POMDP perspective, MA learning algorithms that try to take into account the possibility that other agents' strategies may change over time, simply try to account (in somewhat specific ways) for the hidden state of the environment.

Empirical illustration. To illustrate the proposed concept on a concrete example, we used the teaching game in Table 2, where the column player uses the following simple learning algorithm (also known as fictious play in game theory [14]). It assumes that the row player's strategy is a stationary probability distribution over his actions. The learner tries to empirically estimate this distribution and plays the best response to the current estimation. Let $C(x)$ be the number of times the row player selected action x in the past. Then the column player estimates the probability $\Pr(a)$ that the row player selects a as $C(a)/(C(a) + C(\bar{a}))$, and the expected payoff for playing action b as $2\Pr(a)$. Similar calculations are done for the $\bar{b}$ action. Hence, the strategy of the column player is to choose b if $2C(\bar{a}) > C(a)$, and $\bar{b}$ otherwise.

The row player used the GAPS algorithm [19] originally developed for learning in POMDPs. GAPS belongs to the class of policy search algorithms which essentially perform search in a (usually restricted) space of possible policies for the one that gives the highest long-term reward [3]. In GAPS, the learner plays a parameterised strategy represented by a non-deterministic FSA, where the parameters are the probabilities of actions and state transitions. The automaton's inputs are game observations, the outputs are the player's actions. GAPS implements stochastic gradient ascent in the space of policy parameters. After each learning trial, parameters of the policy are updated by following the reward gradient. The advantage of GAPS is that it can learn history-dependent policies, since past observations can be memorised in the FSA state.

Each learning trial consisted of 300 steps, and the GAPS policy had 4 states. The players' observations consisted of the action taken by their opponent at the previous step. We used average payoff to evaluate the long-term performance of the players. As pointed out in Section 5, a clever player can teach the column learner that his strategy is a by repeatedly playing it, and thus encourage the column player to choose $\bar{b}$. This behaviour yields the row player the average payoff of 3 instead of the one-shot Nash equilibrium payoff of 2 for $(\bar{a}, b)$. Figure 2 shows the learning curves for both players.

As we can see, the GAPS learner managed to achieve even higher average payoff close to 3.3. A detailed investigation of the players' behaviour shows that the row player found a strategy that was following a 3-step loop, playing a in two periods and $\bar{a}$ in the third one. Since $C(a) = 2C(\bar{a})$ for such strategy, the column player always selects $\bar{b}$. The row player receives the long-term average payoff of $(3 + 3 + 4)/3 = 3.3\cdots$. Thus, not only GAPS has taught the column player to choose $\bar{b}$, but it also exploited this behaviour to further increase the payoff. However, unlike e.g. PHC-Exploiter in [15], GAPS knew neither the game being played, nor the learning algorithm used by the opponent or whether the opponent was learning at all. Of course, this success was only possible because GAPS learns stateful (non-Markov) policies that could account for the hidden state of the column learner in the resulting POMDP. While this is a very simple example, still it provides a good demonstration for the proposed MA learning concept.

7   Conclusions

In this paper, we used the ideas of bounded rationality to define MARL as learning in a POMDP. Such perspective on MARL allows us to account for many phenomena inadequately addressed by the previous research. Most importantly, the proposed concept gives a well-defined objective for a learner. Unfortunately, POMDPs are intractable in general, so the concept in itself is not a "silver bullet" for the MARL problem. However, it provides a clear structure and direction for future efforts, which in our opinion should focus on learning how to deal with the hidden environment state, rather than explicitly trying to converge to some Nash equilibrium in self-play. For example, it emphasises the importance of learning history-dependent policies, or trying to infer the hidden environment state, e.g. by maintaining beliefs about opponents.

One can imagine that in real world settings, learners may not only change their strategies, but also become more "computationally clever", e.g. by acquiring more memory. Thus, an interesting direction for future work is to investigate such extensions to the proposed framework.

References

1. Shoham, Y., Grenager, T., Powers, R.: Multi-agent reinforcement learning: A critical survey. Tech.rep., Stanford University (2003)
2. Simon, H.: Models of Man. Social and Rational. John Wiley and Sons (1957)
3. Sutton, R., Barto, A.: Reinforcement Learning: An Introduction. MIT Press (1998)
4. Filar, J., Vrieze, K.: Competitive Markov Decision Processes. Springer Verlag (1997)
5. Osborne, M., Rubinstein, A.: A Course in Game Theory. The MIT Press (1999)
6. Littman, M.: Markov games as a framework for multi-agent reinforcement learning. In: Proc. of the 11th Intl. Conf. on Machine Learning. (1994)
7. Hu, J., Wellman, M.P.: Nash Q-learning for general-sum stochastic games. Journal of Machine Learning Research **4** (2003)
8. Claus, C., Boutilier, C.: The dynamics of reinforcement learning in cooperative multiagent systems. In: Proc. of the 15th AAAI Conf. (1998)
9. Carmel, D., Markovitch, S.: Learning models of intelligent agents. In: Proc. of the 13th AAAI Conf. (1996)
10. Bowling, M.: Multiagent Learning in the Presence of Agents with Limitations. PhD thesis, Carnegie Mellon University (2003)
11. Dutta, P.K.: A folk theorem for stochastic games. J. of Economic Theory **66** (1995)
12. Rubinstein, A.: Equilibrium in supergames. In: Essays in Game Theory. Springer-Verlag (1994)
13. Axelrod, R.: The Evolution of Cooperation. Basic Books (1984)
14. Fudenberg, D., Levine, D.K.: The Theory of Learning in Games. The MIT Press (1998)
15. Chang, Y., Kaelbling, L.P.: Playing is believing: The role of beliefs in multi-agent learning. In: Advances in Neural Information Processing Systems. Volume 14., The MIT Press (2001)
16. Harsanyi, J., Selton, R.: A General Theory of Equilibrium Selection in Games. The MIT Press (1988)
17. Conitzer, V., Sandholm, T.: Complexity results about Nash equilibria. In: Proc. of the 18th Intl. Joint Conf. on AI. (2003)
18. Singh, S., Jaakkola, T., Jordan, M.: Learning without state-estimation in partially observable Markovian decision processes. In: Proc. of the 11th Intl. Conf. on Machine Learning. (1994)
19. Peshkin, L., Meuleau, N., Kim, K.E., L.Kaelbling: Learning to cooperate via policy search. In: Proc. of the 16th Conf. on Uncertainty in AI. (2000)

Variant Extensions to Prove MAS Behaviours

Bruno Mermet and Dominique Fournier

LIH, Université du Havre,
BP 540,
76058 Le Havre Cedex {Bruno.Mermet, Dominique.Fournier}@univ-lehavre.fr

Abstract. In this article, it is shown how the behaviour of a multi-agent system can be validated thanks to proof. At first, the method used is briefly presented [10]. Then, the *variant* notion is presented and an extension of this notion to prove MAS is introduced. In the third part, the proof technique is illustrated for the prey-predator problem: the behaviour of the predators can be induced from the failures in the proof process.

Keywords: multi-agent system, proof, variant, prey-predator

1 Introduction

For many years, many researches have dealt with software validation. On one hand, these works lead to methodologies helping to write safe systems and on the other and, to the development of techniques and tools for validation. At first, these techniques were dedicated to *code* validation (test, program proof by methods like Floyd's method). The advantage of such methods is that the target of the validation is the real program. However, there is a major disadvantage : they can only be applied once the code as been written, that is to say at the end of the development process. That's why program proof is nowadays often replaced by specification proof. In this area, there are two kinds of proof : model checking and theorem proof.

- the model checking method consists in an exhaustive test of all the cases. The main advantages is that the implementation of a model-checker is rather simple and that a failure of a test clearly means that there is an error in the specification[1]. However, the problem must be finite or must be able to be converted in a finite one, and the time taken by the process may be very long.
- the theorem proof is a method consisting in using the deduction rules of the first order logic and the sequent calculus to establish the validity of a goal with a set of hypotheses. This mechanism is hard to implement and the undecidability of the first order logic prevents us to deduce from a proof failure that there is a mistake in the specifications. However, with such a method, infinite size problems may often be validated in a short time.

---

[1] if the model-checker works well, of course

C. Bussler and D. Fensel (Eds.): AIMSA 2004, LNAI 3192, pp. 409–419, 2004.
© Springer-Verlag Berlin Heidelberg 2004

For a few years, some works deal with model checking to validate multi-agent systems. In general, these works are illustrated with small systems (less than ten agents) and with limited dynamic possibilities (the population is constant). Moreover, time dedicated to proof is often disappointing [2]. Many other works have dealt with formal specification of multi-agents systems, for instance with the temporal logic [8] or with Z [5], but proofs are not performed on these specifications.

In this article, we show how proof mechanisms allow to validate multi-agent systems, and how a proof-oriented way of specifying helps in determining the behaviours of the agent. In the first part, the method used is briefly reminded to the reader [10]. In the second part, we show how the method and the principles it relies on are extended to prove multi-agent systems. Then, an application of the method on a rather simple concrete problem, the prey-predator problem, is presented. In the fourth section, we show how the proof can also be used to explain emergent phenomena. Finally, we conclude on the process and current and future works are presented.

2   Method

2.1   Motivations

The method we use is summarised here but a full description can be found in [10]. With this method, we aim to provide techniques and tools to design multi-agent systems whose goals are to solve problems.

The method must also allow to build systems with the two following properties : the system may be stopped at any time and as the time goes by, the quality of the solution provided by the system will increase. An important characteristics of our method is that it propose a top-down approach.

The methodology defined here must be used to solve global problems which can be specified by a set of local constraints (LC). A more restrictive usage condition presented in [10] was that this methodology was dedicated to optimisation problems for which a trivial (but bad) solution exists. We will show in the sequel that this restriction has been removed.

Of course, for non NP-hard and non distributed problems for which a sequential algorithm is known, using agents (and so our methodology) is rarely a good solution because communications and synchronisations introduced by MAS make the program less efficient [11].

An example of a target problem for our methodology is the graph colouring problem which consists in colouring a graph with a minimal number of colours in such a way that two connected nodes do not have the same colour. This application was presented in [10].

2.2   Variant Notion

A variant is defined in a well-founded structure.

A *well-founded structure* is a pair (S, R) where S is a set and R is an ordering relation defined on S such that each strictly decreasing sequence of S with the

R ordering relation has a lower bound. An example of such a structure is the set of natural numbers with the relation $<$.

A *variant* is a strictly decreasing sequence defined on a well-founded structure. So, a variant has a lower bound.

Variants are often use to prove temporal properties like liveness properties (<<something good will occur>>), for instance to prove loop termination.

2.3   Principle

The main principle of our method is to define a variant associated to the global goal of the system we aim to develop. The global problem is then divided into local sub-problems. These local problems may be re-organised in order to be as independent as possible between each other. Finally, an agent is associated to solve each sub-problem.

3   Variants

3.1   Global Variant and Local Variants

As it has been explained earlier, a variant, called in the sequel the *global variant* is associated to the global goal of the system (that is to say the problem to solve).

Then a variant, called *local variant* is associated to each local sub-problem.

Then, to show that the decomposition of the global problem into local sub-problems is correct, we just have to prove that when a local variant decreases, the global variant decreases too.

However, variants that are used to prove liveness properties must decrease in a continuous way. This is satisfying to prove sequential processes, but is not well suited to multi-agent systems, where interactions between agents sometimes leads to the impossibility to perform an action at the right time. That is why we introduce the notion of *weak variant*, that weakens the constraint of the continuous and strict decrease of the variant.

3.2   Weak Variants

We call *hard weak variant* a temporal variable V defined on a well-founded structure $(S,<)$ with a lower bound V_0 such that[2] :

$$\Box\Diamond(V \neq V_0 \Rightarrow V' < V)$$

In another way, a hard weak variant does not have to continuously decrease, but must decrease *infinitely often*. Such a variant is more suitable to prove agent behaviours. However, the constraint may be still too strong in some cases. Indeed,

---

[2] in the temporal logic notation, V and V' are the same variable, but if V corresponds to its value at time t, V' corresponds to its value at time $t + 1$.

an agent does not always progress to its goal : it may sometimes perform back-tracking. For instance, this can occur when an eco-agent [7] under attack has to flee.

So, we define a still softer notion, the *soft weak variant*. Such a variant V defined on a well-founded structure $(S, <)$ must check the following property :

$$\Box(V \neq V_0 \wedge V = C \Rightarrow \Diamond(V < C))$$

So the variant may sometimes increase, but must globally decrease.

4   Application to the Prey-Predator Problem

4.1   Presentation of the Problem

The prey-predator problem is a standard example of application for MAS. However, there are multiple versions. That's why we give in this introduction *our* definition of the prey-predator problem used in the sequel.

In our case, agents are on a toric grid. Each cell can not contain more than one agent. There is one *prey* agent, with a move strategy that does not matter, evolving without any resource constraint. Moreover, there are four *predator* agents. These agents do not communicate with a high-level language, and their goal is to capture the prey. They can see the whole grid. Each time an agent acts, it may move from its current cell to one of the fourth neighbour cells (north, east, south or west). The prey is captured when the four cells on which it can move are occupied by predators, as it is shown in figure 1, where the prey is represented by a cross and the predators by circles.

Fig. 1. Prey capture position

Using the method [10], we aim to determine the behaviour of the predators, in order to prove that the prey is always caught.

In the first step, we will consider that the prey is static. Then, we will show how to extend the proof to a mobile prey.

4.2   Variants of the Problem

The global Variant. The aim of the system is to have the predators to catch the prey. In this case, the solution consists of having four predators on the contiguous cells of the prey. On the following, we call $dist(a, b)$, the function that give the infinite norm (also known as Manhattan distance) between the cells where are located the agents a and b. Note that the infinite norm in a two-dimensional space is defined by:

$$||(x_1, y_1), (x_2, y_2)||_\infty = |x_1 - x_2| + |y_1 - y_2|$$

When P_1, P_2, P_3 and P_4 are the four predators and pr is the prey, to solve the problem we must have:

$$\forall i \in [1..4], dist(P_i, pr) = 1$$

Then, for the problem, a global variant V_G, which lower bound is zero is defined as:

$$V_G = max_{i=1..4}(dist(P_i, pr) - 1) \tag{1}$$

Now, we have to demonstrate that V_G is a weak variant and when it has reached its lower bound, the problem is solved:

First, the distance between a predator and the prey is necessarily greater or equal than 1, indeed, at the most there is one agent in a cell. Thus, the lower bound of V_G is 0.

When $V_G = 0$, each distance between a predator and the prey equals one at most. But we have seen that this value is at least equal to 1. Therefore, each of the predators is on a contiguous cell of the prey. Because there is only one agent in a cell, and there are as much predators as the number of cells contiguous to the prey, it involves that the prey is caught and the problem is solved. Hence, V_G is a satisfying variant according to the goal of the problem.

Local variants: In the last section, it is shown that a solution of the problem depends on the distance between each predator and the prey. Nevertheless, considering only one predator, the solution is only bound to its position (as we consider the prey fixed). So, the problem is split into four local sub-problems which consist in having one predator to a contiguous cell of the prey. By the following, such a cell is called *satisfying position* of a predator. As a consequence, we associate a local variant Vl_i (with a lower bound equals to 1) to each local sub-problem:

$$Vl_i = dist(P_i, pr)$$

We have to demonstrate that Vl_i's lower bound is 1 (obvious because it is a distance and there is, at most, one agent in a cell) and that its decrease involves the decrease of the global variant. This last point is now detailed.

According to the definition of V_G (equation 1), It exists an i such as $V_G = Vl_i - 1$. If it does not exist some $j \neq i$ such as $Vl_i = Vl_j$, then for each $j \neq i$, $Vl_i > Vl_j$, hence, the decrease of the local variant Vl_i involves the decrease of the global variant V_G.

Else, the decrease of Vl_i involves the stagnation of the global variant. This is not conflicting with the definition of the weak variant previously seen (section 3.2), but we have to verify that the global variant will eventually decrease.

It is guaranteed if every local variants eventually decrease. Thus, there will be only one local variant Vl_i such as $V_G = Vl_i - 1$ and this variant will decrease, involving the decrease of V_G.

If the local variant Vl_k ($k \neq i$ and therefore $Vl_k < V_G$) decreases, the stagnation of the global variant V_G is also obtained, and this case is similar to the previous one.

Lastly, it remains to demonstrate that when every sub-problems are solved, then the global one is also solved. This is obvious, indeed, if every sub-problems are solved:

$\forall i \in [1..4], Vl_i = 1.$
So: $\forall i \in [1..4], dist(P_i, pr) = 1$
and: $max_{i=1..4}(dist(P_i, pr)) = 1$
moreover: $max_{i=1..4}(dist(P_i, pr) - 1) = 0$
Hence: $V_G = 0$
And the global problem is now solved.

4.3   Deduction and Proof of the Agents' Behaviour

As every sub-problems are bound to independent variables (the predator's position), an agent predator is associated to each of them (as involved by the method [10]).

The basic behaviour of a predator agent is very simple: the agent has to decrease its local variant, so it will try to go nearer of the prey if it is not in a satisfying position.

Thus, the behaviour of a predator agent might look like this is shown on figure 2.

```
if (satisfying position reached)
        do nothing
else
        go to a nearer cell
endif
```

Fig. 2. Behaviour of a predator, version 1

To come up to the prey involves the decrease of the variant of the problem the agent has to solve, indeed, this variant is the distance between the agent and the prey.

However, it is not always possible, particularly when the target cell is held by an other predator. If the target cell is not a satisfying position, the predator holding it will leave. Thus, the cell will be liberated; and the predator has just to wait. If the target cell is a satisfying position, the predator holding it will not leave. So, an other policy is needed.

Two policy are possible: either the agent look for another target cell, or it attacks the obstructing agent to liberate the current target. This behaviour is good from the attacking agent's point of view: its variant do not decrease immediately, but the liberation of the target involves that the attacking predator shall hold it (if a third predator hold this cell before, it will also be attacked, and so on). This new behaviour is presented in figure 3.

```
if (satisfying position reached)
        do nothing
else
        choose a nearer target cell
        if (target cell is free)
                go to target cell
        else
                if (target cell == satisfying position)
                        attack the agent in the target cell
                else
                        do nothing
                endif
        endif
endif
```

Fig. 3. Behaviour of a predator, version 2

We have obtained an agent whose behaviour guarantees that the local variant is a weak variant. Now, we have to study how the attack is taken into account.

The attack occurs only when an agent is in a satisfying position. The fleeing agent will necessarily move away from the prey, involving its variant to increase. It has to be verified that the variant will decrease again and reach again its lower bound. Due to the agent's behaviour, it is obvious that the variant will decrease. Thus, we have a soft weak variant as defined in section 3.2. On the other hand, the same scenario could happen again if the fleeing agent re-attacks the first attacking predator, involving a continuous see-saw motion between the two agents. To avoid this pitfall, a new behaviour is given to the predator when their Euclidean distance from the prey is lower than 1.5. The standard and the flee behaviour of the predators are *oriented* (counterclockwise): they always go on a cell on the right when they are close to the prey, as shown in the figure 4 where the prey is a cross and the white arrows illustrate the fleeing moves.

The behaviour of a predator agent is now detailed in the algorithm 5.

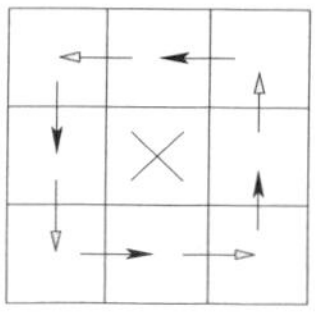

Fig. 4. Predators' moving in the neighbourhood of the prey

```
if (satisfying position reached)
        if (attacked)
                flee on the right
        else
                do nothing
        endif
else
        if (d(Pi, pr) ≥ 1.5)
                choose a nearer target cell
        else
                choose as a target cell the cell on the right
        endif
        if (target cell is free)
                go to the target cell
        else
                if (target cell == satisfying position)
                        attack the agent on this cell
                else
                        do nothing
                endif
        endif
endif
```

Fig. 5. Behaviour of a predator, final version

4.4   When the Prey Moves

Nowadays, the prey was considered static. It allows to simplify the checking of the decrease of the predators' variant. What happen when the prey is mobile? Let assume that, at a moment t_0, the prey hold the position p_0 and a predator hold a position P_0. Then, the variant of the predator is $V_0 = dist(p_0, P_0)$. When the predator comes up to the prey, it moves and decreases its variant (i.e. such as $V_1' = dist(p_0, P_1) < dist(p_0, P_0) = V_0$). But, the real value of the variant is in fact $V_1 = dist(p_1, P_1)$. If we consider the predator is trying to come up to the prey, to have $V_1 < V_0$, the predator has to move faster than the prey. Indeed, in such a case, the predator finally succeeds to come up to the prey. In any kind of prey's move, the predators finally reach the neighbourhood of the prey. At such a point, the proof remains valid.

4.5   Experiments

We have implemented a prey-predator system where the predators behaviour is described in figure 5. In this simulation, the number, the relative speed of the predators and the behaviour of the prey can be modified. The visualisation interface is shown in figure 6.

Indeed, on many trials, we have obtained that if the predators move faster than the prey, then the prey is always caught, even if the prey changes its move

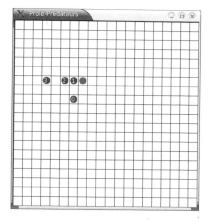

Fig. 6. Simulation Interface

policy. The figure 7 shows the duration to catch the prey, given the relative speed between the prey and the predators.

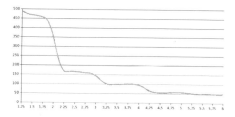

Fig. 7. prey capture speed

5   Discussion

One of the current uses of the multi-agents systems consists in using them to solve complex problems by emergence of a solution [6]. There are many application domains and they can be related either to the pattern recognition [4] or to the scheduling of tasks [3]. In such systems, one seeks to solve problems (for which no effective algorithm is known) using a set of interacting agents. When a multi-agents system is given, this one remains particular to the studied domain. General mechanisms allowing to design such systems were already defined, such as the attack-flee behaviour of the eco-agents [7], but without any associated method. Recently, the AMAS theory [9] gives a first approach to describe multi-agents systems that solve problems by the emergence of a solution. It is based on the resolution of *non-cooperative situations (NCS)*. More recently, a method, ADELFE [1], has been associated to the AMAS theory Nevertheless, there is no proof of the correctness of such systems. The aim of this paper is to fill this gap. Of course, our approach using eco-agents (that attack each others in case of opposed goals) differs from cooperative agents used in AMAS. However, the method gives the behaviour of the agents. There are more constraints to use it than for AMAS because we have to define a variant for the agents' goal, and so we need a progress notion associated to the goal. This is not always possible. Particularly, the variant has to be defined on internal variables of the agent, that is not possible for problems in which the constraints are strongly connected. Some works have to be made to link our method (whose methodology aspects have to be improved) and ADELFE (whose proof aspects are limited).

6   Conclusion and Future Works

In this paper, we have presented a way to use and extend the variant notion in the proof of multi-agents systems. This process is illustrated on the prey-predator example. We have obtained a proof of the convergence of the predators' behaviour. However, the proof is a long and difficult work, and this paper only presents a summary of it. To improve the effectiveness and the validation process, we have to define an automatic method. We are actually systemizing the proof mechanism. To simplify the proof, we are also working on the improve its locality to limit the number of dependencies.

Acknowledgements. We want to acknowledge Gaële Simon and Marianne Flouret for their contribution on connected researches and without which this work would not have been achieved.

References

1. C. Bernon, V. Camps, M.-P. Gleizes, and G. Picard. Deigning agents'behaviours within the framework of adelfe methodology. In *Fourth International Workshop Engineering societies in the agents world*, 2003.
2. R.H. Bordini, M. Fisher, W. Visser, and M. Wooldridge. Verifiable multi-agent programs. In M. Dastani, J. Dix, and A. El Fallah Seghrouchni, editors, *ProMAS*, 2004.
3. T. Daouas, K. Ghedira, and J.-P. Müller. A distributed approach for the flow shop problem. In *3rd Interrnational conference on AI and applications, Le caire (Egypte)*, 1995.
4. Y. Demazeau. La plate-forme paco et ses applications. In PRC-IA, editor, *2ème journée nationale du PRC-IA sur les systèmes multi-agents*, 1993.
5. Mark d'Inverno, David Kinny, Michael Luck, and Michael Wooldridge. A Formal Specification of dMARS. In *Intelligent Agent IV : Proceedings of the Fourth International Workshop on Agent Theories, Architectures and Languages*, pages 155–176. Springer-Verlag, LNAI 1365, 1998.
6. A. Drogoul, N. Ferrand, and J.-P. Müller. Emergence : l'articulation du local au global. *ARAGO*, 29:105–135, 2004.

7. J. Ferber. *Les systèmes multi-agents*. InterEditions, 1995.
8. M. Fisher. A survey of concurrent METATEM – the language and its applications. In D. M. Gabbay and H. J. Ohlbach, editors, *Temporal Logic - Proceedings of the First International Conference (LNAI Volume 827)*, pages 480–505. Springer-Verlag: Heidelberg, Germany, 1994.
9. J.-P. Georgé. The amas theory for complex problem solving based on self-organising cooperative agents. In *First European Workshop on Multi-Agents Systems*, 2003.
10. Gaële Simon, Marianne Flouret, and Bruno Mermet. A methodology to solve optimisation problems with MAS, application to the graph coloring problem. In Donia R. Scott, editor, *Artificial Intelligence : Methodology, Systems, Applications*, volume 2443. LNAI, 2002.
11. Michael Wooldridge and Nicholas R. Jennings. Pitfalls of agent-oriented development. In Katia P. Sycara and Michael Wooldridge, editors, *Proceedings of the 2nd International Conference on Autonomous Agents (Agents'98)*, pages 385–391, New York, 9–13, 1998. ACM Press.

Arabic Words Recognition with Classifiers Combination: An Application to Literal Amounts

Nadir Farah, Labiba Souici, Lotfi Farah, and Mokhtar Sellami

Laboratoire de Recherche en Informatique, Université Badji Mokhtar
Annaba Algerie
{Farahnadir,Souici_labiba

Abstract. The recognition of handwritten bank check literal amount is a problem that humans can solve easily. As a problem in automatic machine reading and interpreting, it presents a challenge and an interesting field of research. An approach for recognizing the legal amount for handwritten Arabic bank check is described in this article. The solution uses multiple information sources to recognize words. The recognition step is preformed in a parallel combination schema using holistic word structural features. The classification stage results are first normalized, and the combination schema is performed, after which using contextual information, the final decision on the candidate words can be done. Using this approach obtained results are more interesting than those obtained with individual classifiers.

Keywords: Multiclassifier system, holistic approach, combiner, syntactic analysis.

1 Introduction

The field of handwriting recognition is a very intensive research domain that led to several works especially for the Latin writing [1], [2], [3]. The current systems tendency is oriented toward the classifiers combination [4], [5], and the integration of multiple information sources.

These last years, a number of papers which analyze the work done on Arabic characters/words recognition have appeared [6], [7], [8]. Some obstacles have played an important role in delaying character/word recognition systems for Arabic language compared to other languages such as Latin and Chinese. Among these obstacles we can find, the special morphology of Arabic writing, and the lack of communication between researchers in this field.

In this article we are interested in off-line handwritten Arabic word recognition, using a limited lexicon. In this direction some works moved toward markov models [9], other toward neural models [10] or toward the neuro - symbolic systems [11].

Our work leads to the realization of handwritten Arabic literal amount recognition system, based on a global approach, using structural high level features (ascenders, descenders, loops, etc). The recognition is performed by a multiclassifiers system

C. Bussler and D. Fensel (Eds.): AIMSA 2004, LNAI 3192, pp. 420–429, 2004.

[12], composed of three modules, a multilayer perceptron, a K nearest neighbor classifier, and a fuzzy K nearest neighbor one.

A combination module is used on the outercome results by classifiers to compensate for individual classifier weaknesses, and a post classification step permits to validate the combiner propositions.

The remainder of this paper is organized as follows. In section 2 Arabic writing characteristics are presented, and then a brief overview of the system architecture is done in section 3. The next sections 4 and 5 present preprocessing and features extraction. The three individual classification systems are described in section 6 and their results in section 7. A combination approach of classifiers is introduced in section 8, then the post classification in section 9. The paper concludes with discussion of the results and an outlook to future work.

2 Arabic Writing Characteristics

The Arabic language is very rich and difficult, by its structure and possibilities. Arabic script is written from right to left. The Arabic alphabet consists of 28 basic characters. The shape of the character is context sensitive, depending on its location within a word. A letter can have four different shapes: isolated, at the beginning, in the middle, at the end. Some Arabic characteristics are particular, we can find for example: 10 of them have one dot (ج,خ,غ,ف,ذ,ظ,ن,ب,ض,ز), 03 of them have two dots (ي,ت,ق), 02 have three dots (ش,ث), several characters present loops (ص,م,ف,ق,ع,ة,و ...).

Most of the characters can be connected from both sides, the right and the left one, however there are six letters that impose a space after (ا,و,ذ,د,ر,ز), they can be connected from only the right side, it's for this reason that Arabic language is said semi cursive. This characteristic implies that each word may be composed of one unit or more (sub-words). Some ligatures involve vertical stacking of characters, this characteristic complicates the problem of segmentation (known as analytic approach) [7], [8]. The considered vocabulary is composed of 48 words that can be written in an Arabic literal check amount (table 1).

Table 1. Arabic literal amounts vocabulary

احد	تسعة	ستون	اربعمائة	ألفا	ملياران
اثنان	عشر	سبعون	خمسمائة	الفان	ملايير
ثلاثة	عشرة	ثمانون	ستمائة	مليون	سنتيم
اربعة	اثنا	تسعون	سبعمائة	ملايين	و
خمسة	عشرون	مائة	ثمانمائة	مليونا	دينار
ستة	ثلاثون	مائتا	تسعمائة	مليونان	دنانير
سبعة	اربعون	مائتان	ألف	مليار	سنتيمات
ثمانية	خمسون	ثلاثمائة	الاف	مليارا	جزائري

3 Proposed System Architecture

The recognition system is constructed around a modular architecture of feature extraction and word classification units.

Preprocessed word image is an input for the structural features extraction module, which transfers the extracted features toward the multiclassifier system (Figure 1). The classification stage is based on three parallel classifiers working on the same set of structural features.

The classifiers results are combined using a statistical decision system. Then the list of candidate words is analyzed by a syntactic module to accept or reject the propositions done by the combiner.

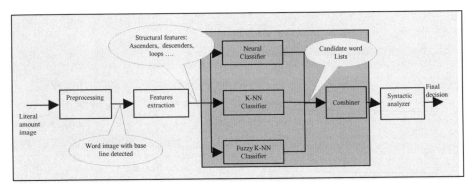

Fig. 1. General diagram of the system

4 Preprocessing

The word image undergoes a set of processing before extracting the structural features. For the extraction of words from the literal amount, we use a vertical projection method in addition to a heuristic (space between words is 1.5 times greater than the spaces between sub-words).

Binarization. It consists in giving from a multilevel gray image, a bimodal one composed with two colors white and black [13].

Smoothing. It is an operation that permits to decrease noises. In our approach we have been inspired by the algorithm presented in [14].

Baseline extraction. We adopted the method of baseline detection proposed in [14]. This method consists in doing the horizontal projections of the image and to consider the densest part as being the median one.

5   Features Extraction

The structural features (figure 2) used in our approach are the structural holistic ones, the number of: Descenders, ascenders, loops, one dot above, two dots above, three dots above, one dot below, two dots below, sub words.

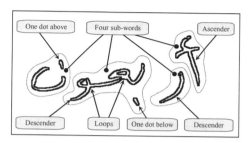

Fig. 2. Word's structural features (forty).

Features used in our system are the global high level ones (holistic) [1], table 2 gives the considered lexicon words features.

Table 2. Part of the lexicon's word with their structural Features

Arabic words	A	D	OD A	DD A	TD A	OD B	DD B	L	SB	Arabic words	A	D	OD A	DD A	TD A	OD B	DD B	L	SW
خمسة			1	1				2	1	سبعمائة	1			1		1		3	2
ستة				2				1	1	تسعمائة	1			2				3	2
سبعة			1		1			2	1	مائتان	2		1	1				1	3
تسعة				2				2	1	ثلاثمائة	3			1	2			2	3
احد	1								2	ثمانمائة	2		1	1	1			3	3
ثلاثة	2			1	2			1	2	اربعمائة	2	1		1		1		3	4
ثمانية	1		1	1	1		1	2	2	ألف	2		1					1	2

A : Ascender, D : Descender, ODA : One Dot Above, DDA : Double Dot Above, TDA : Triple Dot Above, ODB : One Dot Below, DDB : Double Dot Above, L : Loop, SW : Sub-Word.

The image contour extraction serves to describe word's image by using Freeman code chain (figure 3), which represents the image boundaries and topology.

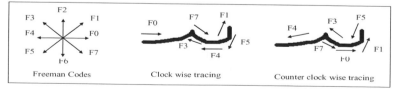

Fig. 3. The eight Freeman codes

To solve the sub-words overlapping problem, a boundary following algorithm has been used inspired of work done in [15]. For the diacritical dots extraction, we use a heuristic that consider the line thickness as it was done by Ameur & al[16]. The diacritical dot's is situated relatively to the baseline.

6   Structural Based Word Recognition

The achieved multiclassifiers system is composed of three different kinds of classifiers, which operate in parallel on the same word's structural features. The three classifiers are: a neural network, a statistical K nearest neighbors system, and a fuzzy K nearest neighbors.

The Neural Network Classifier

The used neural network is a multilayered perceptron, with supervised training. The training is materialized by the neurons weights values optimization; this is done with the presentation of representative examples of the considered problem. From these examples, it performs a generalization for new tested words. This generalization ability makes them interesting for classification and recognition problems [17].

This network has a supervised training stage; we give it two different kinds of information: structural features are inputs while the output is a class among the forty eight classes of the lexicon. The training is done by error correction of connection weights with retro-propagation method [18].

Our Neural system parameters are:
- An input layer formed by 21 neurons, corresponding to 9 structural features according to their possible occurrence numbers in the lexicon (see Figure 2): 3 for ascenders, 2 for descenders, 2 for a one dot above, 2 for two dots above, 2 for three dots above, 1 for one dot below, 2 for two dots below, 3 for the number of loops, 4 for sub words number.
- Number of output neurons: 48 neurons (number of lexicon classes).
- Number of hidden neurons: it is calculated by a heuristic: the square root of (input neurons * output neurons) and then fixed experimentally to 21 neurons
- The activation function has a sigmoid form $f(net_i) = \dfrac{1}{1 + e^{-net_i}}$

The K Nearest Neighbors Classifier (K-NN)

The principle of the K nearest neighbors (K-NN) system consists in searching among the training set (prototype set or reference set), containing the individuals set and their affectation classes, a K number of individuals among the nearest neighbors. We search nearest neighbors in the sense of distance between feature vectors of the tested word and those of the training set. The closeness of a word to another is typically determined by Euclidean distance. The chosen class will be the most represented among the K neighbors. The K-NN classifier conception starts by the creation of the training set, which is constituted of M samples for each of the 48 words of the lexicon, every sample is represented by its 21 features vector. The threshold which permits to reject or to accept the K neighbors under test is the highest value on the representative distances values inter-classes, the representative distance value of a class is the maximal distance value computed between the M samples vectors of the class took by pair.

The Fuzzy K Nearest Neighbor's Classifier (Fuzzy K-NN)

The fuzzy K-NN uses a method different from the one of the crisp K-NN. While the K-NN involves finding the hyper sphere around a word X, which contains K words (independently of their classes), and then assigning X to the class having the largest number of representatives inside the hyper sphere. The fuzzy K-NN method is however based on computing the membership of a test word in different classes.

The introduction of imprecision and the uncertainty generated by the fuzzy notion is very well suited to the handwriting recognition problem, since there is influence of the variability of the manuscript, noises generated by operations on the word, the writing style, make that borders between words classes are overlapping. We begin by searching the K nearest neighbors of the tested word with a crisp nearest neighbor classifier, then we look for memberships (by distance calculation) of each neighbor (noted Yj) with training classes (noted i class), for every training class we have pi prototypes noted Zp, this membership function [19] is given by (1):

$$\mu_i(y_j) = \left[1 + \left(\max_{p=1..pi} d\left(y_j, Z_p\right) / F_d \right)^{Fe} \right]^{-1} \tag{1}$$

This function permits to introduce fuzziness, which allows reclassifying Yj in classes where it presents the highest membership value. When membership value has been tested with the training set, we compute the membership of X noted $\mu_i(X)$ with each of these K nearest neighbors classes, by the formula (2):

$$\mu_i(X) = \left\{ \mu_i(y_j) * \exp(-a * d(X, y_j) / d_m) \right\} \tag{2}$$

dm represents the average distance between words of a same class in the training set. a, Fe, Fd are constants that determine the degree of fuzziness in membership space, they has been fixed experimentally to the following values : a=0,45, Fd=1, Fe=1. We have used a threshold S that has been fixed to 0,5.

7 Classification Results

We have used a database containing 4 800 words where 1 200 have been used for training the different classifier. This basis represents the 48 words of the lexicon written by 100 different writers. The test word set is composed by 3600 words.

For the neural network, we have obtained a recognition rate of 91%.

For K-NN and fuzzy K-NN classifiers purpose, we have constructed four training bases (reference bases), in order to determine the optimal value of the K parameter, and to calculate the corresponding recognition rates. While varying the K value, and training bases, we get results presented in table 3.

Table 3. Word's recognition rates for K-NN and fuzzy K-NN

	Recognition rate					
	K-NN			Fuzzy K-NN		
K	1	3	8	1	3	8
Basis 1 (240 words)	82,00	85,00	36,15	85,00	88,00	87,86
Basis 2 (480 words)	86,52	88,40	40,10	91,16	92,16	82,10
Basis 3 (960 words)	88,56	89,08	45,02	92,16	92,16	90,13
Basis 4 (1200 words)	89,08	89,08	62,00	92,16	92,16	89,47

Several remarks are noted, concerning theses results:
- For K=8, rates lowered distinctly in the K-NN case, it is due to the presence of a majority number of elements from distant classes. - The parameter K value has been fixed to 3, for these two classifiers, that is the one that gave the best results.
- Recognition rates for K-NN and fuzzy K-NN are respectively 89,08% and 92,16%.

8   Decision Combination

Several strategies are possible to achieve combination, we could add or multiply the confidence values or use maximal/minimal values [20], [21]. Furthermore, all these approaches assume a unique interpretation of the confidence values, for instance as a posteriori probabilities P(wi|x) for each tested sample x.

For the K-NN classifier, P(wi|x) is calculated for each class wi appearing in the word's list generated by the classifier [5].

$$P(w_i|x) = \frac{1/d(w_i)}{\sum_{j=1}^{M} 1/d(w_j)}$$

Where d(wi) is the distance between the tested word and the class Cj j=1..48.
For fuzzy K-NN we have:

$$P(w_i/x) = \frac{\mu_i(x)}{\sum_k \mu_k(x)}$$

Where μi(x) is the membership function for the tested word to class i.

For the neural network, each node in the output layer is associated to one class and its output Oi, with [zero to one] range, reflects the response of the network to the corresponding class wi. To facilitate the combination the responses are normalized and used as estimates of the a posteriori probability of each class [22]:

$$P(w_i/x) = \frac{O_i}{\sum_k O_k}$$

In our experiments we used a scheme called score summation [20], each classifier yields as output a list of three candidate words together with their confidence value $P(wi|x)$. The combination consists in merging the three lists of candidates from the three classifiers to produce a new list by confidence values summing. If a candidate is present in the three lists, its new confidence value is simply the sum of the three previous ones. If a word exists in two lists its confidence value is equal to the sum of the two confidence values. Otherwise its confidence value is equal to the old one. This latter sorted list will be used by the syntactic analyzer to generate a syntactically correct literal amount.

9 Syntax Based Post Classification

From a grammar used by the syntactic analyzer (a part is given in table 4), the post classification phase makes a decision and generates a winner word from the set of candidates.

Table 4. Part of the grammatical rules used

```
<Hundreds> ::=
        <Hund>+ و +<Less_Hund> |
        <Hund> |
        <Less_Ten>+ مائة + و +<less_Hund> |
        <Less_Ten>+ مائة
<Hund > ::=
        خمسمائة | اربعمائة | ثلاثمائة | مائتان
        تسعمائة | ثمانمائة | سبعمائة | ستمائة |
< less_Hund > ::=
        < Less_Ten > |
        <Comp_Nbr>
```

When obtaining the candidate words list by the combination stage, we distinguish two cases:

-      If there is a word which confidence value is greater than those of the other, and if this word satisfies the syntactic analysis, it is kept, and will make part of the resulted literal amount. On the other hand if the word doesn't satisfy the syntax, it is rejected and we analyze the second word in the list.

-      If at the head of list we find different words that have the same confidence value, and if the words success the syntax, we retain the one given by the classifier having the greatest recognition rate.

10   Results and Discussion

Let's note that the classification level generates three words lists, a combiner merges them to generate a single ordered list used by the post classification stage to give a syntactically correct sentence.

From errors generated by this system, we can found, the word عشر and و have some missing features, or ill-detected, in the word عشر diacritical dots have not been taken into account, and its first character generates a loop. According to the structural shape of the word, we have therefore in the two cases a loop and a descender, are among the proposed solutions the two words, the analyzer takes decision according to the grammar.

In the case where the recognition produced candidates having the same confidence values and are given by the same classifier, if the syntactic analysis cannot succeed to a decision, it is a syntactic ambiguity case that can be solved only with higher level information. Among examples of words where the ambiguity remains we have:

-   تسعون and سبعون, خمسون
-   تسعة and ستة

When analyzing the results, we find that the recognition rate is raised to 96 % and the remaining 4% are owed to:

10% : bad amounts segmentation, 20% : real mistakes on words, 30% : classification mistakes, 40% : absence of handwritten word's feature.

11   Conclusion and Perspectives

In this work we undertook the recognition of Arabic checks literal handwritten amounts, what implied several processes such as: preprocessing, features extraction, classification and post processing. The obtained rate after the combination stage and post classification one is 96 %, where the recognition rate has been increased by about 4% compared to the average classification one. These results are interesting and experimentally confirm the assumption that the combination of multiple classifiers decision and the integration of contextual information enhance the overall accuracy of a recognition system.

As future perspective for this work, it would be interesting to integrate cooperation with courtesy (numerical) amount recognition. This will permit to solve the majority cases of ambiguousness signaled in the decision phase. Another way to explore is to offer the possibility of feed back (retroaction) toward the different processing phases.

References

1.   Madhvanath, S. Govindaraju, V.:The Role of Holistic Paradigms in Handwritten word Recognition. IEEE Trans. On Pattern Analysis and Machine Intelligence, vol. 23 no.2, February 2001.

2. Steinherz, T. Rivlin, E. Intrator, N. :Off-line cursive script word recognition: A survey. International Journal on Document analysis and Recognition, IJDAR, Vol 2, pp: 90-110, 1999

3. Suen, C.Y. :Réflexions sur la reconnaissance de l'écriture cursive. Actes CIFED'98, 1er Colloque International Francophone sur l'Ecrit et le Document, pp: 1-8, Québec, Canada, Mai 1998.

4. Zouari, H. Heutte, L. Lecourtier, Y. Alimi., A. :Un panorama des méthodes de combinaison de classifieurs en reconnaissance de formes. RFIA2002, 11th Congrès francophone AFRIF-AFIA de Reconnaissance des Formes et Intelligence Artificielle, pp : 499-508, Angers, Janvier 2002.

5. Xu, L. Krzyzak, A. Suen, C. Y.:Methods of combining multiple classifiers and their applications to handwriting recognition. IEEE Transactions on systems. Man, and cybernetics, vol. 22, No 3, May/June 1992.

6. Amin, A. :Off-line Arabic character recognition: The state of the art. Pattern Recognition, vol. 31, N° 5, pp 517-530, 1998.

7. Al Badr, B. Mahmoud, S. A. :Survey and bibliography of Arabic optical text recognition. Signal processing, Vol. 41, pp 49-77, 1995.

8. Essoukhri Ben Amara :Sur la problématique et les orientations en reconnaissance de l'écriture arabe. CIFED 2002, pp 1-8, 2002.

9. Ben Amara, N. Belaid, A. Ellouze, N. :Utilisation des modèles markoviens en reconnaissance de l'écriture arabe: état de l'art. CIFED'2000, France2000, pp. 181-191.

10. Snoussi.Maddouri, S. Amiri, H. Belaid A.and Choisy, C.: Combination of Local and Global Vision Modeling for Arabic Handwritten Word Recognition. International Workshop Frontier in HandWriting IWFHR'02, Canada, 2002.

11. Souici-Meslati, L. Sellami, M. : Reconnaissance de montants littéraux arabes par une approche hybride neuro-symbolique. RFIA'2002, 11th Congrès francophone AFRIF-AFIA de Reconnaissance des Formes et Intelligence Artificielle, Angers, Janvier 2002.

12. Ruta, D. Gabrys, B.: An Overview of Classifier Fusion Methods. Computing and Information Systems 7(1):1-10, University of Paisley, February 2000. http://cis.paisley.ac.uk/ruta-ci0/downloads/paper1.pdf

13. Pavlidis, T. : Algorithms for Graphic and Image Processing. Rockville, MD: Computer science press, 1982.

14. Belaid, A. Belaid, Y. : Reconnaissance des formes: Méthodes et applications. InterEditions, 1992.

15. Sari, T. :Un système de Reconnaissance de mots arabes manuscrits basé segmentation. Mémoire de Magister, Laboratoire LRI, Département Informatique, Université Badji Mokhtar Annaba, Algérie, Février 2000.

16. Ameur, A. Romeo-Pakker, K. Miled, H. Cheriet, M. : Approche globale pour la reconnaissance de mots manuscrits Arabes. Actes CNED'94, 3ème Colloque National sur l'Ecrit et le Document, pp: 151-156, Juillet 1994.

17. Jain, A. K. Mao, J. Mohiuddin, K. : Artificial Neural Networks: A Tutorial. IEEE Computer, Special Issue on Neural computing, Marsh 1996.

18. Jodouin, J. F. : Les réseaux de neurones : principes et définitions. Hermès, 1994.

19. Singh, S. Amin, A. : Fuzzy Recognition of Chinese Characters. Proc. Irish Machine Vision and Image Processing Conference (IMVIP'99), Dublin, 8-9 September, 1999.

20. Duin, R.P.W. : The combining classifier: To train or Not to train?. Proceedings 16th International Conference on Pattern Recognition, Quebec City, Canada, August 11-15, 2002.

21. Anil, J. K. Duin, R.P.W Mao, J. : Statistical pattern recognition: A review', IEEE transactions on pattern analysis and machine intelligence, vol 22, no 1, January 2000.

22. Kittler, J. Hatef, M. Duin, R.P.W. Matas J. : On combining classifiers. IEEE transactions on pattern analysis and machine intelligence, vol 20, no 3, March 1998.

Curved Segmentation Path Construction for Unconstrained Handwritten Hangul Segmentation

Sungho Park[1], Wontaek Seo[2], and Beom-joon Cho[2]

[1]Dept. of Computer Information Communication, Namdo Provincial College, Korea.
shpark@namdo.ac.kr
[2]Dept. of Computer Engineering, Chosun University, 375 Seosuk-dong , Dong-gu,
Gwangju, Korea, wontagi@ai.chosun.ac.kr, bjcho@chosun.ac.kr

Abstract. Up to now, most Korean character recognition has been developed on the assumption that it was segmented into characters perfectly. It is difficult to adapt the method that is used in English, since there are spaces in a character. Because a Korean character, which we call a syllable, is composed of two or more graphemes on 2D plane, and also the characteristic of touch that occurred between character is often occurred between graphemes. In this paper, we propose the method that uses a virtual segmentation path for segmentation of unconstrained handwritten Korean characters. The main property of the proposed method is that not only the curved segmentation path which is using the space between character is used, but also the straight line segmentation path is used. The segmentation process is divided into two steps. In the first step, a straight line segmentation path of a Korean word is determined using pre-processing and vertical projection, and words that are overlapped or touching are passed to the next step. In the second step, feature points are extracted for making a number of virtual curved paths, and then the most suitable path is determined using center of gravity which is marked between three adjacent points.

1 Introduction

Nowadays, we want to save the temporal and economical cost by recoding the amount of data to a computer as information. One useful technology is document recognition, and a correct segmentation has to be performed to the target words of the document for superior document recognition. Most Korean character recognition has been developed on the assumption that it was segmented into characters perfectly, and there has been little concern about that. In this paper, we propose a segmentation technique for unconstrained handwritten Korean characters.

Generally, in case of unconstrained handwritten Korean character recognition, there are some cases that use a device for artificial segmentation in order to minimize the difficulty of segmentation, and despite the structural difference between Korean characters and English, they use a technique which has been developed for English without adapting to the characteristics of Korean characters. For the result, these increase the ambiguity of recognition units, so these become a main cause of declining the system's performance.

Previous segmentation works focused mainly on English[6,7] or digits[4,9], and there was little concern about handwritten Korean characters[1,2,3].

C. Bussler and D. Fensel (Eds.): AIMSA 2004, LNAI 3192, pp. 430–437, 2004.

Berrin[5] proposed the algorithm of using a cost function to produce character segmentation. At the given position and angle, segmentation cost depends on local characteristics which are distance among positions of segment and global characteristics which depend on the writting style such as average width of character and thickness of pen.

Zhao[8] proposed a two stage algorithm for segmentation of unconstrained Chinese characters. In the first stage, called the Coarse stage, it produced a number of proper segment paths using backrground skeleton and vertical projection after preprocessing. In the second stage, called the Fine stage, it decided the final segment path after evaluation for the all possible paths with the Fuzzy decision rule.

Elnagar[4] proposed a segmentation process using spatial characteristics which used a proper template to the handwritten touched numeric characters.

Pal[9] proposed the decision method of optimal segmentation paths based on the characteristic which was obtained from a water reservoir concept to a touched number.

In studies about Korean characters, Gyeonghwan Kim[1] proposed the efficient slant correction algorithm for handwritten Hangul strings using structural properties which are useful for preprocessing and segmentation for recognition units. He also proposed the touched point segmentation method and basic functions for finding the touched point of character using a general writting style and characteristics of two-dimension Korean characters.

Seonhwa Jeong[2] selected the best combination for the segmentation of words by applying the three- way classification method based on the clustering and three distance estimation method, which were already proposed for written English words.

Soonja Hwang[3] proposed the character segmentation algorithm based on the grapheme class recognition. It can detect the grapheme class area using structural properties of Hangul which are obtained from stroke by vertical projection, and it is also based on the organization rule of Hangul and heuristic knowledge.

There are two methods for character segmentation from words, one is the method that produces just one result of high reliability at the segmentation process. The other is the method that decides the final result by passing a number of candidate paths to the recognition process. The former, also known as External Segmentation, takes advantage of processing time regardless of the recognizer, but it has poor ability for finding an exact touched point and can not adjust a wrong segment result. The latter, called Internal Segmentation, has a good recognition rate because it accommodates many segment results, but it takes more time during the recognition process.

This paper proposes a character segmentation method which produces just one segment result of high and efficient reliability.

The main properties of this proposed method are as follows. First, instead of the straight segment path that is used by many segmentation methods, it uses curved paths, which use the space of a Korean character organized by the combination of consonants and vowels. It enhances the reliability in the overlapped case.

Second, the total segmentation time is decreased, obviously, because it divides the segmentation process into two stages. In the first stage, it chooses the section of words needed for more detailed segmentation. In the second stage, it uses minimal feature points and searches the various virtual paths for the chosen section of the word.

The rest of this paper is organized as follows. Section 2 presents the whole process, preprocess and selection process of word section need more detail segmentation using vertical projection. Section 3 presents the process to produce virtual paths to the chosen word section. For the sake of this process, a number of feature points are extracted and virtual paths are produced, and the gravity center is used for a more correct segment path. Finally, it presents the experiment and future work in Section 4.

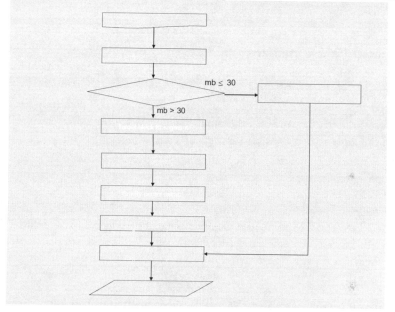

Fig. 1. Segmentation Algorithm

2   Segmentation Algorithm

The entire process of the proposed segmentation algorithm in this paper is presented in Fig. 1, and the process is divided into two steps as follows. In the first step, the word region that needs to take more detailed segmentation is chosen from the whole word, and that a straight line segment path is obtained by vertical projection. In this paper, unconstrained handwritten Korean words that are connected with 2~5 characters where collected from 100 writers, and then a thinning process is performed after input images are converted to gray mode image. With the binary image, vertical projection can find an isolated character which is not overlapped or touched. The characters divided easily by vertical projection are confirmed in the first step, and the remainder is passed to the next stage. We use the average width of the character to confirm whether the block, which is segmented by vertical projection, includes the whole character or not. There are some cases that a block only includes one vowel, owing to the characteristics of Korean characters. In this paper, the average width is 30 pixels from the data collected.

In the second step, the curved segment path, which is searching the virtual path, is obtained from the word region mainly organized with overlapped or touched characters. When the target block is decided by vertical projection, feature points, called nodes, in the case of a network, are considered to make a virtual segment path. We use the delaunay triangle method to make virtual paths. Further, the gravity center of each triangle is also used for a more useful path, and virtual paths are linked from feature point to the gravity center. Finally, using searches from the feature point and the gravity center, the best segment path is obtained so that there is no loss to the original character.

3 Segment Path Construction

3.1 Straight Segment Path

In the first step, the process of decision that chooses the region to be passed to the second step from whole words for the input image is as follow. <Fig. 2(a)> shows the sample word images that consisted of 5 characters. <Fig. 2(b)> shows that '역' and '시' are easily segmented by vertical projection, because they are apart from each other.

This can be easily observed from the result <Fig. 3> of vertical projection. It shows that '人' and ' | ' are divided from each other despite being one character, but since the width of '人' and ' | ' is smaller than average width, they are considered to be one character. Because ' | ' is the vowel in the structural characteristics of Korean, it is connected to the former block. Finally, the straight line of vertical projection results in <Fig. 3> which is the segment path of the first step.

But according to the analysis of collected data, the size, height, and width varies according to the writer, and also varies with the same writer. It is hard to depend on vertical projection, which mainly depends on the width of character. Furthermore, because there are often overlapped and touched characters, straight segment paths cannot be segmented perfectly.

The '광주광' needs to be treated in the second step because the characters are overlapped and touching each other, so it can not make a straight segment line in the first step. In a way, the thinning process is performed to binary image for finding a feature point that used to make a virtual segment path later step.

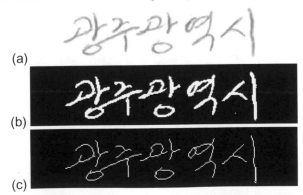

Fig. 2. (a) Original, (b)binary and (c)thinning image

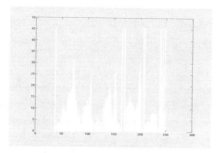

Fig. 3. Vertical projection to Fig. 2(b)

Fig. 4. Target block to segment

3.2   Virtual Segment Path

To generate the virtual segment path, feature points of each character are extracted. The curved type segment path has to go through the space between a character from top to bottom and avoid the foreground image. For the sake of this, end points of each grapheme are considered to be the feature points. Further, the point which is end point of the grapheme and also touching the other grapheme is considered as a feature point.

Next, considered feature points have to be connected to each other in order to create virtual paths. In this paper, the Delaunay triangulation method is used to connect each feature point. By this method, the feature point becomes the vertex of a triangle, and links to be used as virtual paths are created. The gravity center of each triangle is considered as a feature point for creating more detailed virtual segment paths, and more detailed curved segmentation paths will be obtained. The gravity center of each triangle becomes the node like feature point, and the links connected to the node from each vertex of a triangle. <Fig. 5> shows the process of creating the links.

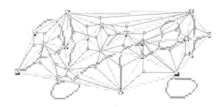

Fig. 5. Feature point extract and virtual path

When the virtual paths are created between characters, virtual paths become a segmented path if the link doesn't go through the foreground image, and this process is iterated until it arrives to the end point.

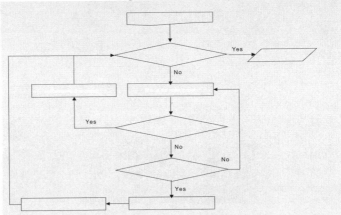

Fig. 6. Segment path searching algorithm

4   Best Segment Path Search

For the best segment path search, the virtual path which goes through the foreground image <Fig. 5> has to be removed from the candidate. To create a path, start and end points have to be considered. In this paper, the top-center point and bottom-center point are used as the start point and end point.

<Fig. 6> shows the segment path search algorithm from the virtual segment path. The α is the connectable feature point set from the start point without crash in the foreground image. The β is the position of the feature point that connects the segment path from the start point to the end point. Among those virtual segment paths, the best segmentation paths are decided by search algorithm which produces the β and searches the paths using a top-down method from them.

<Fig. 7> shows the candidate segment path from the start point to end point and <Fig. 8> shows the best segment path from a candidate path.

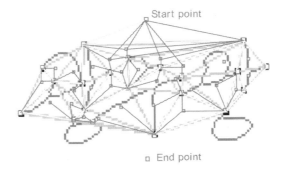

Fig. 7. Candidate segment path

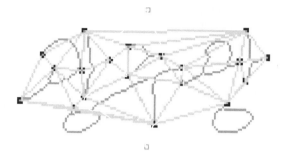

Fig. 8. Best segment path

5 Conclusion

This paper proposes the new segmentation method using a virtual segment path for unconstrained handwritten Korean characters. The main properties of this proposed method are as follows. First, instead of the straight segment path that is used by many segmentation methods, it uses a curved path which uses the space of a Korean character organized by the combination of the consonant and vowel. It especially enhances the reliability of the overlapped case. Second, the total segmentation time is obviously decreased as it divides the segmentation process into two stages.

In the first stage, it chooses the section of the word that needs more detailed segmentation. In the second stage, it uses minimal feature points and search the various virtual paths for the chosen section of the word. Third, it produces a reliable path for touching characters, which is the most difficult problem, by converting the feature point to the background image temporally.

Now, a comparative experiment is being performed using collected handwritten data. Specifically, work to enhance the reliability of touching characters is going on.

Acknowledgement. This study was supported by research funds from Chosun University, 2003

References

1. Gyeonghwan Kim, Jason J Yoon : An Approach to segmentation of address strings of unconstrained handwritten Hangle using Run-length code. Korean Information Science Journal, Vol 28. No.11 (2001) 813-821
2. Seonhwa Jeong, Soohyung Kim : Word segmentation in handwritten Korean text lines based on GAP clustering. Korean Information Science Journal, Vol 27. No.6 (2000) 660-667

3. Soonja Hwang, Moonhyun Kim : Consonant-vowel classification based segmentation technique for handwritten off-line Hangul. Korean Information Processing Journal, Vol 3. No.4 (1996) 1002-1013
4. Ashraf Elnagar, Reda Alhajj : Segmentation of connected handwritten numeral strings. Pattern Recognition, Vol. 36 (2003) 625-634
5. Berrin Yanikoglu, Peter A. Sandon : Segmentation of off-line cursive handwriting using linear programming. Pattern Recognition, Vol. 31 (1998) 1825-1833
6. G. Kim : Architecture for handwritten text recognition systems. Proc. Sixth International Workshop on Frontiers in Handwritten Recognition (1998) 113-122
7. G. Dzuba, A. Filatov and A. Volgunin : Handwritten ZIP code recognition. Proc. Fourth International Conference on Document Analysis and Recognition (1997) 766-770
8. Shuyan Zhao, Zheru Chi, Penfei Shi and Hong Yan : Two-stage segmentation of unconstrained handwritten Chinese characters. Pattern Recognition, Vol. 36 (2001) 145-156
9. U. Pal, A. Belaid and Ch. Choisy : Touching numeral segmentation using water reservoir concept. Pattern Recognition Letters, Vol. 24 (2003) 261-272

Efficient Segmentation Path Generation for Unconstrained Handwritten Hangul Character

Wontaek Seo and Beom-joon Cho

Dept. of Computer Engineering, Chosun University, 375 Seosuk-dong , Dong-gu, Gwangju,
Korea
wontagi@ai.chosun.ac.kr, shpark@namdo.ac.kr,
bjcho@chosun.ac.kr

Abstract. This study suggests background thinning method for segmenting
character unit of handwritten Hangul. Background thinning method conducts
thinning processing using background information between characters and
shows effective performance in segmenting for overlapped and touched
characters. Character segmentation method using background thinning shows
rapid segmentation performance with external segmentation which needs no
judgment of recognition process. This method showed excellent performance in
touched character segmentation as well as in segmentation of overlapped
characters.

1 Introduction

One of the pattern recognition techniques frequently used in daily life is character
recognition technique. Character recognition techniques of Hangul achieved a great
development with researchers' efforts for over ten years. In particular, printed
character recognition is part of an integral recognition rate in applying to real life. On
the other hand, handwritten character recognition is problematic in applying to real
life. Handwritten character recognition is divided into two; on-line and off-line
handwritten recognition. While on-line recognition can obtain a lot of useful
information such as pressure of pen, time information of stroke, etc., off-line
recognition is difficult to recognize because it is done with just spatial information on
input character. Therefore, many researchers perform the research on off-line
handwritten recognition [1][2][3]. An important preprocessing procedures in
recognizing characters is character segmentation to character unit data from word unit
data [4][5][6]. However, research on most character recognitions have been
performed under the assumption that subject characters are segmented perfectly, as a
result, research on character segmentation is imperfect. Although printed character
segmentation can be easily progressed due to uniform shape, size and gap of the
printed characters [5], handwritten character segmentation has a lot of difficulties due
to variety of writing styles and characteristic [6]. In addition, since existing research
on segmentation have not reflected composition principles of Hangul but focused on
English and numerals, research on handwritten character segmentation of Hangul was
insufficient.

C. Bussler and D. Fensel (Eds.): AIMSA 2004, LNAI 3192, pp. 438–446, 2004.

According to related research, Kim Gyeong-Hwan [7] suggested slant compensation algorithm reflecting structural properties of Hangul, reflected characteristics of writers' general writing habit and the two-dimensional structure of Hangul and a presented basic function and a classification method searching for touched point of characters.

Choi Soon-Man [8] segmented touched numbers with segmentation-free method and suggested how to recognize it with neural network. This method can be applied to numbers with recognition of touched numbers as a whole without segmenting individual number, but it cannot be used for character recognition of Hangul with structural complexity. Yoo Dae-Geun [9] presented slant compensation method of handwritten characters based on statistical distribution of strokes reflecting structural properties of Hangul. These methods classified slant distribution of extracted strokes into two groups of vertical and diagonal strokes with the application of K-average grouping and conducted slant compensation with vertical stroke except diagonal stroke through modeling based on the Gaussian distribution.

Segmentation methods can be divided into two types. The first is external segmentation which presents segmentation results of high reliability without help of recognition in the segmentation process. The second is internal segmentation and it selects some candidates in the segmentation process, holds back judgement to recognition process and decides final segmentation in the process. The first method reduces a calculation burden, but is difficult to ensure reliability exactly. The second one increases a calculation burden, but has higher reliability than the first one.

This study suggests the external segmentation method of off-line handwritten Hangul using properties of background composed on outside of character. Chapter 2 explains segmentation process, Chapter 3 states background thinning, Chapter 4 is on experiment and considerations, and lastly chapter 5 is the conclusion.

2   Character Segmentation of Hangul

Most of the research on segmentation of Hangul have not solved touched or overlapped problems frequently found in handwritten Hangul and adopted methods of searching for segmentation point in recognition process under the assumption that the regions follow the six types of Hangul (Fig. 1) uniformed. And recognition has been conducted with candidates of graphemes (Table 1) fixed in each position.

However, there are some cases that are not to be secured in regards to the position of each grapheme group in the case of Hangul without restriction unlike general assumptions. In addition, periodically appeared characters and their gaps are not secured. So forced segmentation with vertical projection may be major causes of producing an incomplete recognition units, increasing the recognition and lowering recognition performance.

The following are factors used for segmenting characters in general.

- Character Width : Horizontal length of character
- Character Height : Vertical length of character
- Character Gap : Length of blank between characters

- Top Base Line : Top base line of region occupied by character
- Bottom Base Line : Bottom base line of region occupied by character
- Lexicon : Gathering of words, used in segmentation by recognition
- Vertical and Horizontal Projection : Values counting number of valid pixels in vertical and horizontal directions

Table 1. Groups of Graphemes in Hangul

First Consonant(FC)	ㄱ,ㄴ,ㄷ,ㄹ,ㅁ,ㅂ,ㅅ,ㅇ,ㅈ,ㅊ,ㅋ,ㅌ,ㅍ,ㅎ,ㄲ,ㄸ,ㅃ,ㅆ,ㅉ
Vertical Vowel(VV)	ㅏ,ㅐ,ㅑ,ㅒ,ㅓ,ㅔ,ㅕ,ㅖ,ㅣ
Horizontal Vowel(HV)	ㅗ,ㅛ,ㅜ,ㅠ,ㅡ
Last Consonant(LC)	ㄱ,ㄴ,ㄷ,ㄹ,ㅁ,ㅂ,ㅅ,ㅇ,ㅈ,ㅊ,ㅋ,ㅌ,ㅍ,ㅎ,ㄲ,ㅆ,ㄳ,ㄵ,ㅀ,ㄺ, ㄻ,ㄼ,ㄽ,ㄾ,ㄿ,ㅀ,ㅄ

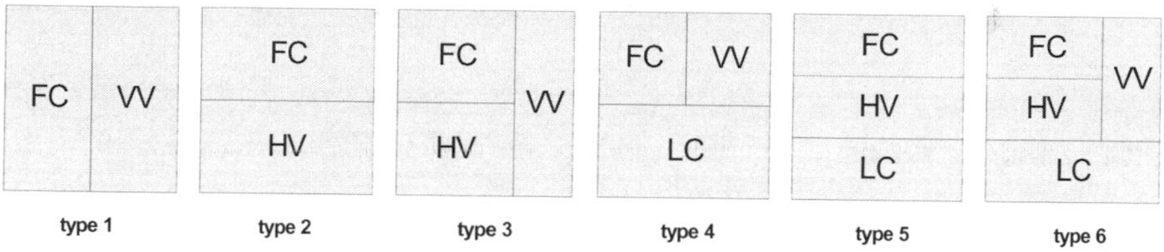

Fig. 1. The Combining Structure of Graphemes in Hangul : Six Types

What is easiest and simplest among these will be vertical and horizontal projections. Well-written or -printed words can be segmented enough with vertical and horizontal projections. So, after first segmenting characters with vertical projection, overlapped or touched points are processed. Overlapped region entered the region of other characters as shown in Fig. 2 and the touched region is attached with two characters as shown in Fig. 2.

Although character segmentation using vertical segmentation was tried, it was divided into three blocks of '광주광', '역' and '시'. If '광주광' was segmented forcefully, it would have a great influence on results of recognition.

In case of handwritten Hangul, it is unreasonable to use vertical projection. Therefore, this study tries to segment character using structural properties of Hangul. Hangul has one sound in one character as phonetic symbols and there is an empty space between the characters. This paper proposes how to segment the characters using this empty space or blank.

3   Character Segmentation Using Background Thinning

This paper employs thinning technique, usually used for recognition process, to background of character image in order to use background information between characters of Hangul. Result of background thinning connects space between character and character not to pass by character and provides how to segment character clearly as confirmed in Fig. 3.

touched   overlapped

(a)

(b)

Fig. 2. Segmentation using vertical projection (a) A case of overlapped and touched handwritten hangul. (b) virtical projection

In this paper, Mophology thinning method is used for thinning background[10]. Mophology thinning uses the calculation as follow.

The thinning of a set A by a structuring element B, denoted A ⊗ B, can be defined in terms of the hit-or-miss transform :

$$A \otimes B = A - (A \oplus B) = A \cap (A * B)^c \qquad (1)$$

A more useful expression for thinning A symmetrically is based on a sequence of structuring elements

$$\{B\} = \{B^1, B^2, B^3, ..., B^n\} \qquad (2)$$

where B^i is a rotated version of B^{i-1}. Using this concept, we now define thinning by a sequence of structuring elements as

$$A \otimes \{B\} = ((...((A \otimes B^1) \otimes B^2)...) \otimes B^n) \qquad (3)$$

In other words, the process is to thin A by one pass with B^i, then thin the result with one pass of B^2, and so on, until A is thinned with one pass of B^n. The entire process is repeated until no further changes occur.

3.1 Segmentation of Normal Character

As shown in Fig. 2, Veritical projection is generally efficient to the characters which is already apart each other. But, in case of Hangul, there is possibility to make error because vertical projection does not reflect the structural properties of Hangul. As shown in Fig. 4, the image which divided by only vertical projection has error because it uses just width of characters. To solve this problem, in this paper, background thinning is adopt to whole characters even though it is sperated well, and uses the structural property of Hangul (Fig. 1).

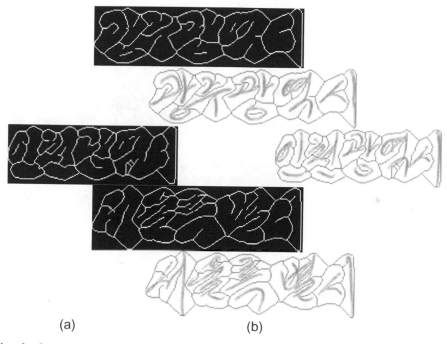

(a)   (b)

Fig. 3. Some results of background thinning. (a) results of background thinning (b) Combination of background thinning result and source image.

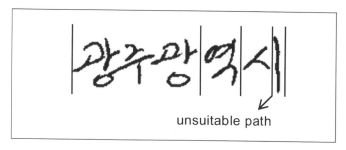

unsuitable path

Fig. 4. A case of error : Segmentation using only vertical projection

First of all, Candidate region is selected by vertical projection, then, by comparing location of regions to composition rules of six types of Hangul , above error can be revised. Figure 5 shows the process of its performance.

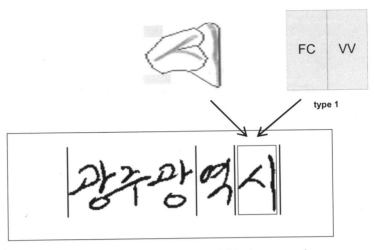

Fig. 5. Segmentation using background thinning : normal case.

3.2 Segmentation of Overlapped Character

In case of overlapped characters, there will be background space in the middle region although it is overlapped between characters. Path should be generated with this space and this background thinning generates path passing through the middle between characters.

After selecting expected segmentation region from vertical projection, we could decide path with results of background thinning and then the following path can be obtained.

Fig. 6. Some case of segmentation path : Overlapped characters.

3.3 Segmentation of Touched Character

Research on the segmentation of touched characters have been seldom, but there are no reliable segmentation methods for Hangul. Most of methods made a lot of candidate point of segmentation and passed them to recognition stage, which results in increasing of burden of recognition and lowering recognition performance. This paper proposes how to search for and segment such a connected region with external segmentation.

In case of touched characters, touched regions formed by background thinning can be easily detected because the region of touched characters has single area in both regions unlike other regions (Fig. 7(a)) and length of the region is longer than mean width of character. Mean width of characters was obtained from collected data. And another candidate region of segmentation between characters can be assumed using vertical projection same with general character. In this study, a decomposition method of handwritten Hangul proposed by Park Jeong-Seon [11] was adopt to finding a segment point in target region where the two candidate region is piled up. In this method, interfaces of curved point or touched point based on observation centering around two features of Hangul pattern, T-interface and B-interface were presented. Fig. 7(b) represents candidate of segmentation point generated by above method. But the candidate of segmentation point which is located in target region will be considered.

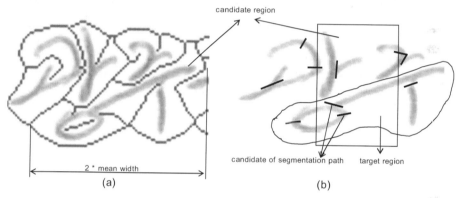

Fig. 7. Candidate region of touched character and segment point. (a) candidate region throughout two regions. (b) candidate of segment point

As it passes through segment point in target region, new path is generated. Fig. 8 shows this process. After generating new border area with opposite point through character region, segment path is set with the same method as overlapped character path.

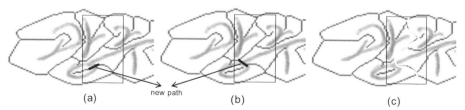

Fig. 8. Segment path between touched character (a) candidate which fails to make path (b) candidate which can make path (c) character segment path is established

4   Experiment and Considerations

This study collected 40 addresses related Hangul words from 150 persons. Each word is composed of 2 ~ 5 characters with pure Hangul without symbol, mark, English or number. Region for writing characters is given, but it is guided to be written freely and natural character type is recommended. Total characters are 19,950 and total cases to be segmented are 13,072. From the collected data, there are 4,471(32%) overlapping cases, and 2,034(14.5%) of single touched cases, 296(2.1%) of multi touched cases. Experiment results of each case are shown in table 2.

Table 2. Experiment results

Type	Cases	Rate(%)	Success Rate
Overlap	4,471	32 %	3,961 (88.5%)
Single touch	2,034	14.5 %	1,692 (83.1%)
Multi touch	296	2.1 %	198 (66.8%)
Total	6,801	48.7 %	5,851 (79.4%)

As shown in table, the segmentation performance of the overlap and single touch is good in 85.5%. But the performance of multi-touch is not so impressive.

5   Conclusion

This study suggested a new method of background thinning for character segmentation of handwritten Hangul. This method could generate a path at an overlapped point between characters using background information and structural properties of Hangul effectively and the segmentation point could be extracted easily from touched points.

Proposed method is significant in that it segmented characters effectively using external segmentation without help of recognition and its performance speed was so fast.

This study can be used in preprocessing part of handwritten Hangul recognizer, and it may be possible that Background thinning method can be used to Hangul grapheme segmentation.

Acknowledgement. This work was done as a part of Information & Communication fundamental Technology Research Program supported by Ministry of Information & Communication in republic of Korea

References

1. Luiz S. Oliveira, R. Sabourin : Automatic Recognition of Handwritten Numerical Strings : A Recognition and Verification Strategy. IEEE PAMI, Vol. 24, No. 11 (2002) 1438-1454
2. Jaehwa Park : An Adaptive Approach to Offline Handwritten Word Recognition. IEEE PAMI, Vol. 24, No. 7 (2002) 920-931
3. S. Zho, Z. Chi, P. Shi, H. Yan : Two-stage segmentation of unconstrained handwritten Chinese characters. Pattern Recognition, Vol. 36, No. 1 (2003) 145-156

446   W. Seo and B.-j. Cho

4. Sung-Bae cho, Jin H. Kim : A Hierarchical Organization of Neural Networks for Printed Hangul Character Recognition. Korea Information Science Journal, Vol.17, No.3 (1990) 306-316
5. Yi Lu : Machine-printed character segmentation. Pattern Recognition, Vol. 28, No. 1 (1995) 67-80
6. Yi Lu, M. Shridhar : Character segmentation in handwritten words-an overview. Pattern Recognition, Vol. 29, No. 1 (1996) 77-96
7. Gyeonghwan Kim, Jason J. Yoon : An Approach to Segmentation of Address Strings of Unconstrained Handwritten Hangul using Run-Length Code. Korea Information Science Journal, Vol, 28, No. 11 (2001) 813-821
8. Soon-Man Choi, Il-Seok Oh : Segmentation-free Recognition of Touching Numeral Pairs. Korea Information Science Journal, Vol, 27, No. 5 (2000) 563-574
9. Daekeun You, Gyeonghwan Kim : An Efficient Slant Correction for Handwritten Hangul Strings using Structural Properties. Korea Information Science Journal, Vol. 30, no. 2 (2003) 93-102
10. Rafael C. Gonzalez, Richard E. Woods : Digital Image Processing. Addison-Wesley Publishing Company (1992)
11. Jeong-Sun Park, Ki-Chun Hong, Il-Seok Oh : Shape Decomposition of Handwritten hangul Characters. Korea Information Science Journal, Vol. 28, no. 7 (2001) 511-523
12. S.-W. Lee and E.-S. Kim : Efficient post processing algorithm for error eorrection in handwritten Hangul address and human name recognition. Pattern Recognition, vol. 27, no. 12 (1994) 1631-1640

Designing Hybrid Cooperations with a Component Language for Solving Optimisation Problems*

Carlos Castro[1] and Eric Monfroy[2]

[1] Universidad Técnica Federico Santa María, Chile
[2] LINA, Université de Nantes, France
Carlos.Castro@inf.utfsm.cl, Eric.Monfroy@lina.univ-nantes.fr

Abstract. In this paper, we use a simple asynchronous coordination language to design some complex hybrid cooperation schemes for solving optimisation problems. The language allows us to specify the interaction between complete and incomplete constraint solvers in a clear and uniform way. Experimental results show the benefits of such hybrid cooperations in terms of efficiency.

1 Introduction

Solving a Constraint Satisfaction Problem (CSP) consists in finding values to a set of variables in such a way that a set of constraints is satisfied [6]. A Constraint Satisfaction Optimisation Problem (CSOP) is an extension of a CSP where we are interested in a solution to the set of constraints that optimises an objective function [10]. CSOPs can be solved using a complete approach, where a global optimum is obtained, or an incomplete approach, obtaining just a local optimum.

The complete approach used by the Constraint Programming community is based on solving a sequence of CSPs. The idea is to get a first solution to the set of constraints and, evaluating the objective function in that solution, set a bound for the objective function. Then, after adding a new constraint using this bound, we solve a new CSP looking for a better solution with respect to the optimisation function. This idea is applied repeatedly and when, after adding such constraints, the problem becomes unsatisfiable, the last possible solution represents the optimal solution [2]. CSPs are solved using general methods based on exhaustive enumeration and local consistency verification. Algorithms, such as *Forward Checking*, *Partial* and *Full Lookahead*, have been developed incorporating consistency verification techniques, that remove values of variables that do not satisfy the constraints, into a systematic exploration of the search space [11].

On the other hand, local search is an incomplete method widely used to solve hard combinatorial optimisation problems. Roughly speaking, a local search algorithm starts off with an initial solution and then repeatedly tries to find better

---

* The authors have been partially supported by the Franco-Chilean INRIA-CONICYT project Cocars.

C. Bussler and D. Fensel (Eds.): AIMSA 2004, LNAI 3192, pp. 447–458, 2004.

solutions by exploring neighbourhoods. A basic version of local search is iterative improvement or Hill-Climbing procedures. Iterative improvement starts with some initial solution that is constructed by some other algorithm, or just generated randomly. Then, it keeps on moving to better neighbours (i.e., improving the objective function), as long as there are some. Finally, it finishes at a locally optimal solution, one that does not have a better neighbour.

The advantages and drawbacks of these techniques are well-known: complete techniques allow one to get global optimum but, when dealing with hard problems, they take too much time and can become useless in practice. Empirically, local search heuristics converge usually rather quickly, within low-order polynomial time. However, they are only able to find near-optimal solutions, i.e., in general, a local optimum might not coincide with a global optimum.

Encouraging results have been obtained by integrating these approaches. A hybrid approach, that sacrifices completeness of backtracking methods to achieve the scalability of local search, has been proposed and results outperform the best local search algorithms [8]. Good results have been also obtained by a hybrid technique where local search performs over partial assignments, instead of complete assignments, and constraint propagation and conflict-based heuristics are used to improve the search [5]. Recently, some schemes of sequential cooperation between Forward Checking and Hill-Climbing have been proposed and results show that these cooperations always outperform a single solver [4].

In this work, we solve CSOPs applying more complex hybrid cooperations that are designed using a simple coordination language [7]. This asynchronous language is composed of interaction components that control external agents (such as solvers) by managing the data flow. A formal definition of our language in terms of concurrent rules can be found in [3]. The motivation for this work is to continue studying the use of control languages to specify elementary constraint solvers as well as the collaboration of solvers in a uniform and flexible way. The goal is also to provide means of designing strategies that are more complex than simple master-slave approaches. The main contribution of this paper is to show the design of new cooperations and their results when solving CSOPs.

To test our approach, we use the Vehicle Routing Problem (VRP). Since we don't focus in improving reported results, but in evaluating different collaboration schemes, we use simplified versions of classical benchmarks. Our problems are based on instances $C101$, $R101$, and $RC101$, belonging to classes $C1$, $R1$, and $RC1$, respectively, defined in [9]. Each class defines a different topology: in $C1$ the location of customers are clustered, in $R1$, the location of customers are generated randomly, and in $RC1$ instances are generated considering clustered groups of randomly generated locations of customers. Without time windows information, fixing the number of vehicles, and considering 25 customers, we obtain Capacity VRP (CVRP) which we named as instances $c1$, $r1$, and $rc1$. Thus, our optimisation problems consist in minimising the total distance driven by a set of vehicles that deliver to all the customers that are visited only once.

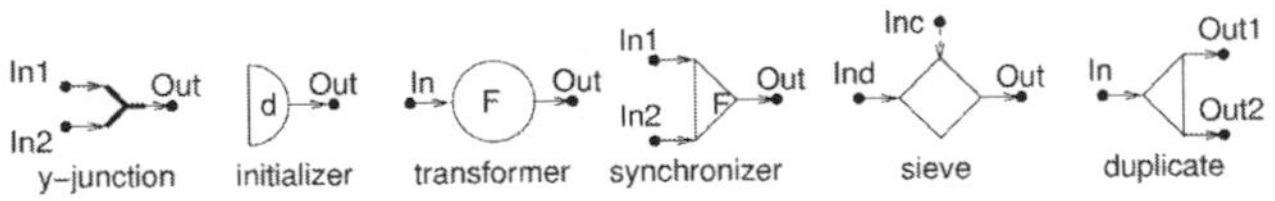

Fig. 1. Graphical description of components

In Section 2, we present our language. In Section 3, we solve a set of problems using both approaches independently. In Section 4, we solve the same problems but making cooperate both approaches. Finally, we conclude in Section 5.

2   A Component Language

Our asynchronous language is a simple coordination language (see e.g., [1]). It is composed of a set of interaction components that asynchronously control execution of external agents, such as solvers, by managing the data flow. An external agent is a computational entity that can be seen as a function with a local memory. The data flow is composed of data messages (such as problems, optimum) and control messages (true or false). A *pattern* is a set of connected components and patterns. Patterns enable one to describe and re-use more complex behaviours. In this paper, they are mainly used to design solver cooperations.

Interaction components (components in short) are entities connected to each other to exchange data and control messages. A component can use some external agents to perform some computations. Components are link by some one to one uni-directional channels. Channels are used as identifiers to exchange data among components, and their name is unique. A channel belongs to two components: it is a First In First Output (FIFO) buffer; one component writes in it, the second one reads in it. A component is represented by a term component_name($[p_1, \ldots, p_n], [a_1, \ldots, a_m]$) where the p_i are the channels of the component, and the a_i are the external agents used by the component (when there is no a_i, the list can be omitted). Both a_i and p_i are variables that must be instantiated when using the component. In the following, upper-case letters represent variables (channels or agents) and lower case letters instances.

A component is sleepy until it receives all the messages it is waiting for. Then, it becomes active: it reads the awaited messages, executes some agents (if needed), and finally sends some messages before becoming sleepy again. Components execute concurrently and cannot be interrupted.

The syntax of each component of our language is:

connect($[In, Out]$)
y($[In_1, In_2, Out]$)   init($[Out], [F]$)   trans($[In, Out], [F]$)
sync($[In_1, In_2, Out], [F]$)   sieve($[In_d, In_c, Out], [F]$)   dup($[In, Out_1, Out_2]$)

Graphical representations of components are given in Figure 1. A solid (resp. dashed) line represents a channel carrying data (resp. control) messages. We now explain informally the operational semantics of the components of our language:

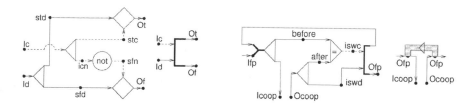

Fig. 2. Switch (left) and fixed point (right) patterns: design and representation

Y-Junctions. As soon as it receives a message either on channel In_1 or In_2, a Y-junction forwards the message on channel Out.

Initializers. An init component sends data d (given by an external agent) on channel Out. These components are used to initialize the data flow.

Transformers. When a trans component receives a message X on channel In, it reads it, and the result of executing the agent F on X is sent on Out.

Synchronizers. These components synchronize two components by the mediating of their messages: they wait for two messages, one on the channel In_1 and one on In_2, then they execute an agent F on the two messages, and finally they put the result of F on the channel Out.

Sieve. A sieve component waits for a data message X on In_d, and for a control message on In_c. If a *true* value is received on In_c, then the data message X is sent on Out; otherwise, X is deleted and not forwarded.

Duplicate. A *duplicate* component duplicates a dataflow: when it gets a message X on In, it forwards a copy of X on both channels Out_1 and Out_2.

A *pattern* is a parameterized piece of program defined by induction: a set of components is a pattern, and a set of patterns is a pattern. Variables that appear in the definition of a pattern are the parameters of this pattern. We consider a re-naming process that uniquely re-names channel names used in more than one pattern or in several instances of the same pattern. We now present two common patterns of interactions that are widely used in solver cooperation: switch and fixed point patterns. Note that a pattern can be given a new graphical representation, e.g., see the switch pattern.

Switch. A *switch* pattern (Figure 2-(left)) synchronizes a data message d received on Id and a control message c received on Ic: if c is *true*, d is forwarded on Ot, otherwise on Of. This pattern is defined by:

$$\mathsf{switch}([Id, Ic, Ot, Of]) = \left\{ \begin{array}{l} \mathsf{dup}([Id, icn, stc]), \;\; \mathsf{trans}([icn, sfn], [not]), \\ \mathsf{dup}([Id, std, sfd]), \;\; \mathsf{sieve}([std, stc, Ot]), \\ \mathsf{sieve}([sfd, sfn, Of]) \end{array} \right\}$$

Fixed Point. A fixed point pattern (Figure 2-(right)) applies repeatedly a pattern $Coop$ (e.g., representing a solver cooperation) until the output of the

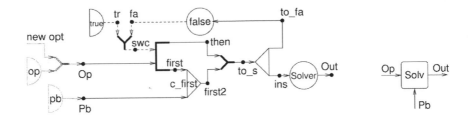

Fig. 3. Solver pattern (implementation and representation)

pattern does not change any more. More precisely, a data message m is received on Ifp (a channel of the fp pattern). m is forwarded to $Coop$ via channel $Icoop$ (an input of $Coop$). The result m' of $Coop$ (received on $Ocoop$) and a copy of m are compared (using an *equal* agent): if $m = m'$, the fixed point is reached and m' is sent on Ofp. Otherwise, the process iterates: m' is sent again on $Icoop$:

$$\mathsf{fp}([Ifp, Ofp, Icoop, Ocoop]) = \left\{ \begin{array}{l} \mathsf{dup}([Ifp, before, Icoop]), \\ \mathsf{sync}([before, after, iswc], [equal]), \\ \mathsf{dup}([Ocoop, after, iswd]), \\ \mathsf{switch}([iswd, iswc, Ofp, Ifp]) \end{array} \right\}$$

3   Complete and Incomplete Constraint Solvers

We consider $fs(t)$, bn, and *start*, three elementary solver agents. Given an optimisation problem and a current best bound for the objective function, $fs(t)$ and bn try to improve the current best bound. These agents have a local memory in which they store the optimisation problem. Thus, the solver agents have to receive only once the optimisation problem with the current best bound in order to improve the bound. Sending only once the problem significantly reduces the data flow. Then, each time they receive a new current best bound, they will try to produce a better bound using the problem they already have in memory. When they cannot improve the bound they return the last bound they received.

$fs(t)$ and bn are encapsulated into transformer components which are themselves used inside a solver pattern (Figure 3) providing the following mechanism: the first time it is used, it combines a problem (from Pb) and a bound (from Op) using the c_first agent; this combination is sent to the solver agent (a parameter of the pattern); the following times, only a new bound (from Op) is forwarded to the solver agent that already stored the problem in its local memory. The bound produced by the solver agent is sent on the Out channel.

$$\mathsf{solver}([Op, Pb, Out], [Solver]) =$$
$$\left\{ \begin{array}{l} \mathsf{init}([tr], [true]), \; \mathsf{y}([fa, tr, swc]), \mathsf{switch}([Op, swc, first, then]), \\ \mathsf{sync}([first, Pb, first2], [c\_first]), \mathsf{y}([first2, then, to\_s]), \\ \mathsf{dup}([to\_s, ins, to\_fa]), \mathsf{trans}([to\_fa, fa], [false]), \mathsf{trans}([ins, Out], [Solver]) \end{array} \right\}$$

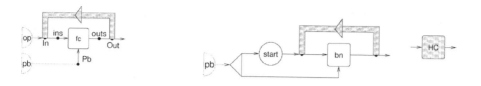

Fig. 4. Forward Checking (left) and Hill-Climbing (right) design and representation

On Figure 3, the components in dotted lines are not part of the pattern: they are used to illustrate a possible initialisation and bound updates.

Start solver: start is a very simple solver agent that given a problem generates a random solution. This agent is only encapsulated into a transformer component.

Forward Checking: fc is a solver based on Forward Checking. This technique specially designed to solve CSP is an interleaving process between local consistency computation (i.e., elimination of values that the variables cannot take in any feasible solution) and variable enumeration (backtracking). This process terminates when an assignment of values to variables satisfying all constraints is found or some variable has an empty domain (i.e., there is no feasible solution to the problem). $fc(t)$ is similar: if it finds a solution in less than t units of time, it returns this solution; otherwise, it returns the bound that it received.

We first test our fc solver to perform a full-search, i.e., exploring all the search space. This strategy (FC) is defined by applying fc iteratively until fc cannot improve the bound anymore (Figure 4-(left)). FC was used to solve problems $c1$, $r1$ and $rc1$ as defined previously. Table 1 presents our results to minimise the objective function z: for each instance, we show all partial solutions found during the execution, the time t (in milliseconds) at which the partial solution was found, and the rounding (computation are performed with 8 digits) of the value of the objective function z evaluated with the partial solution. In the last row of columns t and z for the $r1$ instance, we can see that 375 is the best value obtained for the objective function z after 15 instantiations in 106854 ms. For our experiments we stopped solvers and solver cooperations after 100 minutes. Thus, incomplete methods can sometimes give better results than complete ones.

Hill-Climbing: bn, the best feasible neighbour solver works as follows: given a feasible solution, it generates a set of neighbour solutions using the 2-opt heuristics proposed by Kernighan. After the generation of all neighbours, only the feasible one giving the best value for the objective function is returned ("best improvement" criteria). Repeated applications of *bn* until no better neighbour is found is a Hill-Climbing algorithm. Figure 4-(right) shows this HC cooperation using a random initial point generated by the *start* solver.

We can now compare strategies FC and HC (see Table 1):

– When solving instance $r1$, FC gives a better value for z than HC; it is the opposite in instance $c1$; but in instance $rc1$ the results are very similar.

Table 1. Forward Checking (left) and Hill-Climbing (right)

#	r1 t	r1 z	rc1 t	rc1 z	c1 t	c1 z
1	30	431,39	29803	383	37063	248
2	180	431,38	31545	367	37754	245
3	210	431,16	35200	364	40629	234
4	260	425	109537	359	40719	233
5	270	418	111180	357	40719	231
6	410	414				
7	560	404				
8	560	398				
9	1091	392				
10	38014	391				
11	38014	385				
12	38014	383				
13	51694	377				
14	51694	375				
15	106854	375				

#	r1 t	r1 z	rc1 t	rc1 z	c1 t	c1 z
1	10	988	10	1108	10	648
2	430	816	370	816	380	510
3	831	692	661	583	751	395
4	1231	580	991	486	1131	344
5	1722	470	1311	429	1561	309
6	2213	437	1592	405	1841	290
7	2573	410	1882	395	2122	280
8	2934	398	2173	387	2412	272
9	3294	395	2453	380	2702	259
10	3645	394	2734	373	3043	252
11			3014	368	3413	245
12			3445	366	3724	229
13			3725	360	4004	226
14			4005	356	4285	224
15			4276	355	4565	222
16					4826	220

- FC always runs between 40 and 100 seconds for solving the three instances, but HC only takes between 3 and 5 seconds.
- In general, the time between two consecutive solutions found by FC increases dramatically when approaching the best solution. However, the time between two consecutive solutions found by HC is almost constant, between 300 and 400 milliseconds.

These behaviours are explained by the essence of each search algorithm. FC involves an exhaustive enumeration when no reduction domain is possible. For problems in the phase transition, FC takes a lot of time in obtaining a solution. That is why FC needs more time when the problem becomes harder and has few solutions. HC does not consider the number of solutions to a problem, it just enumerates the neighbour solutions. Thus, between two consecutive solutions, the time remains almost constant. The time needed by HC only depends on the number of constraints to verify and the number of neighbour to evaluate.

4   Hybrid Collaboration of Constraint Solvers

4.1   Fixed Point of fc Followed by HC

The first hybrid cooperation (Figure 5-(left)) we have tried consists in: 1) apply fc to find a first solution, 2) then, apply bn iteratively until it cannot be applied any more, i.e., a local optimum has been reached, 3) iteratively apply 1) and 2) until the problem becomes unsatisfiable or no more change happen.

To verify the effect of applying HC after fc, we try the same cooperation scheme but giving fc the possibility to be applied several times before trying HC (Figure 5-(right)). The idea is to analyse the possibility of improving bounds with FC. Since fc can be too much time consuming to get a new solution, we used $fc(2sec)$. The results of these two cooperations are presented in Table 2:

- Surprisingly, when solving each instance, both cooperation schemes found the same best value.

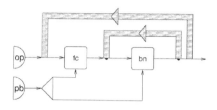 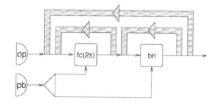

Fig. 5. Fixed point of fc helping HC (left) and fixed point of $fc(2)$ helping HC (right)

Table 2. fc helping HC (left) and fixed point of $fc(2)$ helping HC (right)

#	r1			rc1			c1		
	s	t	z	s	t	z	s	t	z
1	FC	30	431	FC	29803	383	FC	37063	248
2	HC	470	392	HC	30023	341	HC	37344	211
3	HC	820	379	HC	30214	294	HC	37654	197
4	HC	1090	358				HC	38090	194
5	HC	1360	353				HC	38330	191
6							HC	38580	189
7							HC	38810	187

#	r1			rc1			c1		
	s	t	z	s	t	z	s	t	z
1	FC	30	431	FC	29803	383	FC	37063	248
2	FC	180	431	FC	31545	367	FC	37754	245
3	FC	210	431	FC	33200	364	FC	39629	234
4	FC	260	425	HC	35491	294	FC	40719	233
5	FC	270	418				FC	40729	231
6	FC	410	414				HC	43165	197
7	FC	560	404				HC	43465	194
8	FC	560	398				HC	43795	191
9	FC	1091	392				HC	44025	189
10	HC	3803	379				HC	44265	187
11	HC	4083	358				HC	44505	187
12	HC	4374	353						

- The first scheme of cooperation (left table) always takes less time than the second one (right table). In fact, the total time is mainly due to FC.
- In general, applying both cooperations schemes, the results are better in terms of z, than applying either FC isolated or HC isolated.
- In Table 2-(left), when FC returns quickly results (instance $r1$) the performances are better than applying HC; but when FC takes too much time (instances $rc1$ and $c1$) HC isolated gives better results in terms of time.

4.2   Fixed Point of HC Followed by fc

This scheme of cooperation is similar to the first one presented in Section 4.1 but we first start applying iteratively bn (see Figure 6). Thus, the *start* solver in Figure 6 replaces the op initializer that always send $-inf$ or $+inf$ in Figure 5.

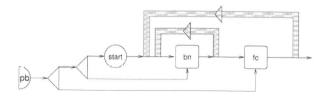

Fig. 6. Cooperation: a fixed point of HC helping fc

Table 3. HC followed by fc (left) and followed by a fixed point of $fc(2sec)$ (right)

#	r1 s	t	z	rc1 s	t	z	c1 s	t	z
1	HC 10	988	HC	10	1108	HC	10	648	
1	HC	10	988	HC	10	1108	HC	10	648
2	HC	430	816	HC	370	816	HC	380	510
3	HC	831	692	HC	661	583	HC	751	395
4	HC	1231	580	HC	991	486	HC	1131	344
5	HC	1722	470	HC	1311	429	HC	1561	309
6	HC	2213	437	HC	1592	405	HC	1841	290
7	HC	2573	410	HC	1882	395	HC	2122	280
8	HC	2934	398	HC	2173	387	HC	2412	272
9	HC	3294	395	HC	2453	380	HC	2702	259
10	HC	3645	394	HC	2734	373	HC	3043	252
11	FC	4646	392	HC	3014	368	HC	3413	245
12	HC	5177	379	HC	3445	366	HC	3724	229
13	HC	5347	358	HC	3725	360	HC	4004	226
14	HC	5618	353	HC	4005	356	HC	4285	224
15				HC	4276	355	HC	4565	222
16							HC	4826	220

#	r1 s	t	z	rc1 s	t	z	c1 s	t	z
1	HC	10	988	HC	10	1108	HC	10	648
2	HC	430	816	HC	370	816	HC	380	510
3	HC	831	692	HC	661	583	HC	751	395
4	HC	1231	580	HC	991	486	HC	1131	344
5	HC	1722	470	HC	1311	429	HC	1561	309
6	HC	2213	437	HC	1592	405	HC	1841	290
7	HC	2573	410	HC	1882	395	HC	2122	280
8	HC	2934	398	HC	2173	387	HC	2412	272
9	HC	3294	395	HC	2453	380	HC	2702	259
10	HC	3645	394	HC	2734	373	HC	3043	252
11	FC	4646	392	HC	3014	368	HC	3413	245
12	HC	7358	379	HC	3445	366	HC	3724	229
13	HC	7638	358	HC	3725	360	HC	4004	226
14	HC	7929	353	HC	4005	356	HC	4285	224
15				HC	4276	355	HC	4565	222
16							HC	4826	220

Table 3 presents results of the cooperations presented in Figure 6-(left) and in Figure 7-(right) for which we consider a fixed point of $fc(2sec)$:

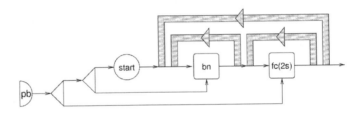

Fig. 7. Cooperation: a fixed point of HC helping a fixed point of $fc(2s)$

- Again, the results of both schemes of cooperation are the same in terms of z. In terms of time, the results are almost the same; the only difference is that when solving instance $r1$ we expend 2 seconds in solution number 12 until $fc(2sec)$ stopped because it could not get a new solution.
- The results of these schemes of cooperation on instances $rc1$ and $c1$ are worse than the results of the first schemes of cooperation (Tables 2) in terms of z; only on instance $r1$ the results are the same.
- In Table 3-(left), we can see that FC helps HC to escape a local optimum: HC can thus continue visiting better solutions, and this cooperation is better than HC alone for instance $r1$. When solving instances $rc1$ and $c1$, FC is not useful to HC and we obtain the same results as applying HC isolated.

Based on these results, we can say that fc gives good initial points to start a search using HC, but when the problem is too hard fc does not help HC.

4.3   Hill-Climbing with Restart

Finally, we analyse the effect of giving a starting point to *bn*, either obtained by *fc* (cooperation of Section 2) or by the *start* solver. We solve the problems applying a fixed point of *bn* but considering four starting points randomly generated by the *start* solver. Note that on Figure 8-(left), the *sel* synchronizer takes as input a problem and an optimum, and returns only the problem: this synchronizer enables *HC* to compute four times in sequence, whereas Figure 8-(right) presents a cooperation in which 4 *HC* computes in parallel with different starting points.

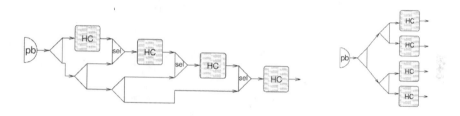

Fig. 8. *HC* with restart (left) and four *HC* in parallel (right)

Table 4 presents the results for instances *r1*, *rc1*, and *c1* of applying in sequence four *HC* with restart:

- For all instances, *HC* with restart gives better solutions than the application of *HC* with just an initial point: the results obtained with the four different initial points are better than the results with the first initial point only (that also corresponds to the results presented in Table 1).
- In general, the results presented in Tables 2 are the best. *fc* gives good initial points to *HC*; *HC* improves quickly the quality of the solutions; and then *FC* continues trying to improve the solution or proving optimality.
- In instances *rc1* and *c1*, the best results obtained by *HC* with restart are better than the results in Tables 3. But for all instances the results obtained by *HC* with restart are worse than the ones obtained by "applying first *fc* and then *HC*".

5   Conclusion

We have solved some optimisation problems using a cooperative approach. We have integrated complete and incomplete techniques in order to profit of the advantages of each one. The cooperation between solvers has been specified using a coordination language which seems to be very suitable for this task. Experimental results show that hybrid algorithms always perform better than isolated solvers. The language used to design the algorithms allows us to specify

Table 4. Hill-Climbing with restart for instances $r1$ (left), $rc1$ (right), and $c1$ (center)

#	r1 t	r1 z	r2 t	r2 z	r3 t	r3 z	r4 t	r4 z
1	10	988	4050	949	8930	915	13472	915
2	430	816	4506	820	9494	693	13930	764
3	831	692	4897	706	9914	570	14351	637
4	1231	580	5288	609	10345	513	14771	562
5	1722	470	5608	529	10785	475	15202	511
6	2213	437	6009	483	11196	445	15552	481
7	2573	410	6409	455	11597	427	15913	455
8	2934	398	6950	431	12228	408	16444	436
9	3294	395	7361	415	12768	381	16984	420
10	3645	394	7771	409	13149	375	17355	400
11			8202	400			17675	378
12			8622	395			18196	376
13							18547	374
14							18957	366

#	r1 t	r1 z	r2 t	r2 z	r3 t	r3 z	r4 t	r4 z
1	10	1108	4643	1084	9562	1069	14250	1000
2	370	816	5018	853	9725	824	14582	760
3	661	583	5329	658	10045	646	14892	596
4	991	486	5629	599	10506	506	15193	520
5	1311	429	5950	556	10827	441	15483	469
6	1592	405	6340	493	11097	429	15794	445
7	1882	395	6691	457	11437	420	16274	426
8	2173	387	7031	398	11778	413	16615	412
9	2453	380	7442	385	12128	406	16965	403
10	2734	373	7752	373	12479	400	17326	394
11	3014	368	8023	367	12829	396	17626	392
12	3445	366	8293	365	13170	368	17907	387
13	3725	360	8563	358	13460	366	18428	357
14	4005	356	8834	357	13741	364	18738	355
15	4276	355	9104	355	14031	355		

#	r1 t	r1 z	r2 t	r2 z	r3 t	r3 z	r4 t	r4 z
1	10	648	5223	654	10124	533	17162	548
2	380	510	5518	518	10405	398	17535	447
3	751	395	5788	418	10675	326	18026	382
4	1131	344	6109	344	10946	309	18456	344
5	1561	309	6479	307	11286	295	18767	304
6	1841	290	6990	286	11637	285	19107	284
7	2122	280	7350	272	11997	278	19478	274
8	2412	272	7711	262	12488	271	19808	265
9	2702	259	8041	259	12798	267	20139	260
10	3043	252	8422	253	13069	263	20529	256
11	3413	245	8783	251	13349	252	20850	251
12	3724	229	9143	249	13599	244	21070	251
13	4004	226	9494	248	13870	241	21361	232
14	4285	224	9834	248	14150	240	21651	224
15	4565	222			14451	239	21951	222
16	4826	220			14781	237	22242	219
17					15052	235	22522	211
18					15392	220	22803	209

concurrent and parallel schemes of cooperations (e.g., see Figure 8-(right)). Thus, from a practical point of view, we are interested in implementing, as further work, these facilities in order to test these cooperation schemes. Concerning the design of the language, we plan to improve it by adding the concept of memories shared by several components. This would simplify the design of cooperations and some patterns, such as the one presented in Figure 3.

References

1. F. Arbab. *Manifold 2.0 Reference Manual*. CWI, The Netherlands, May 1997.
2. A. Bockmayr and T. Kasper. Branch-and-Infer: A unifying framework for integer and finite domain constraint programming. *INFORMS J. Computing*, 10(3):287–300, 1998.
3. C. Castro, E. Monfroy, and C. Ringeissen. A Rule Language for Interaction. In *Recent Advances in Constraints*, volume 3010 of *LNAI*, pages 154–170. Springer Verlag, 2004.
4. C. Castro, M. Moossen, and M. C. Riff. A Cooperative Framework Based on Local Search and Constraint Programming for Solving Discrete Global Optimisation. In *SBIA'04*, LNAI. Springer Verlag, 2004. To appear.
5. N. Jussien and O. Lhomme. Local search with constraint propagation and conflict-based heuristics. *Artificial Intelligence*, 139:21–45, 2002.
6. A. Mackworth. Consistency in Networks of Relations. *AI Journal*, 8:99–118, 1977.
7. E. Monfroy and C. Castro. A Component Language for Hybrid Solver Cooperations. In *ADVIS'04*, LNAI. Springer Verlag, 2004. To appear.

8. S. Prestwich. Combining the scalability of local search with the pruning techniques of systematic search. *Annals of Operations Research*, 115:51–72, 2002.
9. M. Solomon. Algorithms for the vehicle routing and scheduling problem with time window constraints. *Operations Research*, pages 254–365, 1987.
10. E. Tsang. *Foundations of Constraint Satisfaction*. Academic Press, 1993.
11. M. Zahn and W. Hower. Backtracking along with constraint processing and their time complexities. *J. of Exp. and Theor. AI*, 8:63–74, 1996.

Multicriteria Optimization in CSPs : Foundations and Distributed Solving Approach

Inès Ben Jaâfar, Naoufel Khayati, and Khaled Ghédira

UR. SOIE, Stratégies d'Optimisation de l' Information
et de la connaissancE, 41, rue de la Liberté – Cité Bouchoucha,
2000, Le Bardo, Tunis, Tunisia
{ines.benjaafar,naoufel.khayati,khaled.ghedira}@isg.rnu.tn

Abstract. In Constraint Satisfaction and Optimization problems ranging from design engineering to economics, there are often multiple design criteria or cost function that govern the decision whereas, the user needs to be provided with a set of solutions which are the best for all the points of view. In this paper we define a new formalism for multicriteria optimization in constraint satisfaction problems "CSPs" and a multi-agent model solving problems in this setting. This approach separately optimizes different criteria in a distributed way by considering them as cooperative agents trying to reach all the non-dominated solutions. It exploits distributed problems solving together with nogood exchange and negotiation to enhance the overall problem-solving effort. The effectiveness of the approach is discussed on randomly generated examples.

Keywords: multicriteria optimization, constraint satisfaction problem, distributed problem solving, multi-Agent systems, cooperative agents, nogoods exchange.

1   Introduction

The Constraint Satisfaction framework is now widely used for representing and solving various problems, related to the artificial intelligence and operations research (planning, scheduling, diagnosis, design, etc.). It appears that most problems are not pure Constraint Satisfaction Problems "CSPs", but a combination of Constraint Satisfaction and Optimization Problem, "CSOP" [13,14]. A CSP is defined as a triple (X, D, C), where X is a finite set of variables, D is a set of domains, one for each variable, and C is a set of constraints. Each constraint in C restricts the values that one can assign to a set of variables simultaneously. The task is to assign one value per variable, satisfying all the constraints in C[7,8]. A CSOP is a CSP with an associated function that must be optimized.

However, in real life problems, the optimization function is not always well defined and the user needs to optimize more than one criterion at the same time. Some tools consist in aggregating the different points of view into a unique function which must subsequently be optimized[2,11,15]. Unfortunately, this is quite

C. Bussler and D. Fensel (Eds.): AIMSA 2004, LNAI 3192, pp. 459–468, 2004.
© Springer-Verlag Berlin Heidelberg 2004

inadequate, because the criteria are generally incommensurable. They measure different properties that cannot be related to each other directly and cannot be combined into a single function[2,11]. Indeed, such scheme reflects neither real optimization nor the expected result from all criteria points of view[2,11,15]. Hence, when several-often conflicting-criteria must be taken into account, a reasonable approach is to pick the efficient, i.e. Pareto optimal solutions from the set of available choices[15]. Eliminating choices that are not Pareto optimal is a technique which avoids the formation of a scalar measure in the process of optimization and provides the user with the set of all non-dominated points in a CSP.

Since the notion of Multicriteria Optimization in CSP is logically distributed, we propose to explore distributed artificial intelligence and more specifically the multi-agent systems that focus on cooperative and distributed problem-solving techniques [1,5,6].

The main objective of this paper is to introduce a new formalism for Multicriteria Optimization in CSPs, denoted Constraint Satisfaction and Multicriteria Optimization Problem "CSMOP", and a multi-agent model solving problems in this setting. In this model, each agent is responsible for a single criterion and a sub problem from the initial CSP. Thus, the criteria are separately optimized without any "scalarization" form. The entities, called Criterion Agents, cooperate and negotiate in order to find out all non-dominated solutions.

The formalism of Constraint Satisfaction and Multicriteria Optimization Problem "CSMOP" is detailed in the following section. The multi-agent architecture and its global dynamic are presented in the third and fourth sections and experimented in the fifth one. The last section contains concluding remarks and future work.

2   The CSMOP Formalism

The Multicriteria CSP underlying Optimization often involves more than one performance criterion and then requires a formalism more adapted and more suitable than the classical CSOP one. That is why we propose a new formalism called CSMOP inspired from the latter.

A CSMOP is a quadruple (X, D, C, F) defined as following:

- A set of n variables $X = \{x_1, x_2,..., x_n\}$.
- A set of n domains $D = \{D_1, D_2,..., D_n\}$, where each variable x_i has a finite discrete domain of values called D_i.
- A set of m constraint $C = \{C_1, C_2,..., C_m\}$, where each constraint C_i is defined by a sub-set of variables that it constrains, $C_i = \{x_{i1}, x_{i2},..., x_{ini}\}$ and has a relation that defines values.
- A set of i functions, $F = \{f_1, f_2,..., f_i\}$, where f_i is a performance criterion which maps every solution to a numerical value.

We will consider as solution of the CSMOP the set of non dominated feasible assignments.

3   The Multi-agent Architecture

This approach benefits from the multi-agent techniques [1,5,6]that have opened an efficient way to solve diverse problems in terms of cooperation, conflict and concurrence within a society of agents. Each agent is an autonomous entity that is asynchronously able to acquire information from its environment and/or from other agents, to reason on the basis of this information and to act consequently. Within the large domain of multi-agent systems, our model consists of cognitive agents whose number is often limited (here equal to the total number of criteria). The multi-agent architecture consists of Criterion agents cooperating in order to find out all the non-dominated solutions in a CSP. However, this class is not sufficient: an Interface between this society of agents and the user is necessary to detect that the problem is solved. Consequently, a second and last class, called Interface, was created. It contains a single individual.

Each agent has a simple structure: acquaintances (the agents that it knows), a local memory composed of its static and dynamic knowledge, a *mailbox* where it stores the received messages and a behavior. In the proposed model, agents communicate by sending messages. For the transmission between agents, we assume that messages are received in the order they were sent.

3.1   Criterion Agent

Each Criterion agent Cr_i has its own CSP sub-problem. Its criterion to be optimized f_i, the domain of its variables and its associated variables ordering heuristic define its static knowledge. Whereas, its dynamic knowledge consists of its current satisfaction level denoted sl_i (expressing the acceptable utility level for f_i,), its ideal solution valuation denoted id_i (corresponding to the best solution among the Pareto optimal ones according to f_i) and its anti-ideal solution valuation denoted aid_i (which corresponds to the worst solution among the Pareto optimal ones according to f_i). Note that criterion acquaintances consist of the set of all the other Criterion agents denoted Aq_i.

3.2   Interface Agent

The Interface agent has as acquaintances all the Criterion agents. Its static knowledge consists of the whole CSP problem and the set of all the conflicting criteria, whereas its dynamic one consists of the set of Pareto optimal solutions and the final result.

4   The Multi-agent Global Dynamic

The idea of the proposed model is inspired from cooperative problem-solving methods which distribute the search problem and then allow the agents to work cooperatively on their local problems[1,5,6]. It consists in associating with every

Criterion agent a variable ordering heuristic, a criterion f_i to optimize and a sub-problem CSP' resulting from the decomposition of the initial CSP P (X, D, C) into CSP P' (X, D', C) where the variable domains are distributed among agents. Every agent cooperates with its acquaintances in order to generate local solutions to its CSP as soon as possible. This cooperation, is based on the nogoods exchange which their rapid delivery helps the agents to avoid computationally expensive dead-ends[10]. The challenge is in controlling this exchange so that it does not swamp the agents with messages, and so that it efficiently results in convergence to consistent solutions. One way of ensuring systematic exchange and usefulness of the nogoods is to order the agents variables, such that some agents detect nogoods around which others must work and take into account in their future searches[10].

When all local solutions are detected, they are communicated to the Interface agent which will generate all the non-dominated solutions and   achieves the negotiation process whenever the user is left with a huge number of Pareto optimal solutions to choose from.

Before detailing these interactions and the underlying negotiation process, we present the distribution process of the space search and the nogoods exchange based cooperative search.

4.1   Distribution Process of the Space Search

To reduce the space search of the agents and to make them more cooperative, we developed a new distribution process for the CSP where each agent has the most of the variables but a subset of their domains values. This creates potential parallelism by allowing each agent to actively guess his own solutions and to discover different nogoods simultaneously that others cannot detect or they can detect later [10].

The process begins by comparing the number of all the criteria j to be optimized to the size of all the domain variables. Three cases may occur:

- $\exists x_i$ such that $|Dx_i| = j$

In this case, the Interface creates j Criterion agents, decomposes the CSP(X,D,C) into CSP'j such that CSP'j = CSP'(X, D',C) , D'={D_1, D_2, D'x_i,..., D_n}   and D'x_i = {val$j$}. So each Criterion is responsible for only one criterion f_j to optimize.

- $\forall x_i$, $|Dx_i| > j$

The Interface chooses the variable x_i with the smallest domain, creates K Criterion agents $K=1..j$, decomposes the CSP(X,D,C) and each agent is associated with a criterion f_k to be optimized and a CSP'k =CSP'(X, D',C) , D'={D_1, D_2, D'x_i,..., D_n} and D'x_i = {val$_k$, val $_{k+j}$, val $_{k+2j}$,..., val $_{k+mj}$)}   such that m $\leq (|Dx_i|-k)/j$

- $\forall x_i$, $|Dx_i| \neq j$ et il $\exists x_i / |Dx_i| < j$

The Interface chooses the variable x_i with the biggest domain less than j, decomposes the CSP(X,D,C) into $|Dx_i|$ sub-problems   and creates $|Dx_i|$ -1 Criterion agents. Each agent is associated with a criterion f_k and a CSP'k = CSP'(X, D',C) such that D' = {D_1, D_2, D'x_i, ..., D_n} and D'x_i ={val$_k$} for k =1.. $|Dx_i|$ -1. The non associated CSP' obtained from the previous decomposition CSP(X, D'',C) such that D'' = D'={D$_1$, D$_2$, D''x$_i$,..., D$_n$} and D''x$_i$ ={val |Dx$_i$| } and the set of the remained criterion, F' = {f |Dx$_i$|, f |Dx$_i$|+1,...f$_j$} would be recursively distributed following the three cases described previously.

4.2   Nogoods Exchange Based Cooperative Search

The cooperation is considered as the basis of our model functioning and is well known as a concept for improving efficiency and performance of algorithms. The goal of the   cooperation is to share and exchange data between agents to speed-up computation. However, for realizing a cooperative system, we must,
 take into account the following important points [4] :
  - Properties such as correctness, completeness and termination are generally established for a unique solver and must be preserved for a cooperative system.
  - The operational semantics of the cooperation must be specified i.e. we must fix these protocols:
    • Should an agent sends new data as soon as they are deduced, or should it waits until it terminates ?
    • Should an agent integrates new data as soon as they arrived, or should it collects them when the other agent has finished ?

In order to preserve all these properties for the cooperative system we have chosen the NR-FC algorithm which is correct, complete and terminating[10]. Furthermore, it allows the exchange of nogoods. The operational semantics of the cooperation follows this principle : each nogood is emitted to the other agents as early as his detection and is taken into account by the receiver as early as his reception.

The NR-FC is an improved version of the Nogood-Recording algorithm. This enhancement comes from the addition of the "Forward Checking" filtering mechanism. Its principle is as follows : every time that a partial assignment reveals inconsistent, it looks for the assignments of variables, which are responsible for failure before to go back. For this fact, it records the set of the assignments of variables that makes the partial assignment inconsistent (nogood) in order to detect earlier in another branch of the tree the inconsistence of a partial assignment that contains this nogood.

In order to enhance the usefulness and the effectiveness of the systematic nogoods exchange and their influence on the performances of the cooperative search, we have selected some known variables ordering heuristics[3]. Thus, each agent will be assigned a variables ordering heuristic to diversify nogoods production and to identify violations of constraints earlier in the search.

4.3   Negotiation Process

Before detailing the negotiation process, let us recall some useful definitions:

Definition 1 A Multicriteria Optimization Problem is a situation in which, having defined a set A of solutions and a consistent family F of criteria on A, one wishes to:

$$\min_{x \in A} F(x) = [f_1(x), f_2(x),..., f_n(x)] \quad n \geq 2 \quad \text{(MOP)}$$

Where A denotes the feasible set of design alternatives, or the design space[2,15].

Definition 2 The vector $F(\bar{U})$ is said to dominate another vector $F(\check{U})$, denoted $F(\bar{U}) >$ $F(\check{U})$, if and only if $f_i(\bar{U}) \geq f_i(\check{U})$ for all $i \in \{1,2,...n\}$ and $f_j(\bar{U}) < f_j(\check{U})$ for some j in $\{1,2,...n\}$. A point $U^* \in A$ is said to be Pareto optimal or an efficient point for (MOP) if and only if there does not exist $U \in A$ satisfying $F(U) < F(U^*)$. The vector $F(U^*)$ is then called non-dominated or non-inferior.

Definition 3 Let a such that $(1 \leq a \leq n)$, The vector $F(\bar{U})$ is said to a-dominate another vector $F(\check{U})$, if and only if there exist $I_{(n+1-a)} \subseteq I$ such that: $f_k(\bar{U}) \geq f_k(\check{U})$ for all $k \in I_{(n+1-a)}$ and $f_k(\bar{U}) > f_k(\check{U})$ for at least one $k \in I_{(n+1-a)}$.
Note that $I_{(n+1-a)}$ is the index set of a subset of $(n+1-a)$ criteria.

Definition 4 A point $x^* \in A$ is said to be a-efficient for (MOP) if and only if $F(x^*)$ is non a-dominated.

a-Efficiency means that it is not possible to increase anyone's utility without decreasing at least the utility of a criterion[12].

Definition 5 Let $\tilde{o} \in A$, a and $\bar{a} \in \{1,2,...n\}$. If $\tilde{o}$ is a-*efficient* and there does not exist $U \in A$ such that U is $\bar{a}$-*efficient* and $\bar{a} > a$. The point $\tilde{o}$ is then called a_{max}-*efficient*.

When receiving all the locals solutions from the Criterion agents, the Interface agent computes all the Pareto optimal solutions and then uses the notion of *a-efficiency* which provides an intermediate concept of branding some Pareto optimal points as being perhaps superior or more desirable than others[12]. One way to choose the final Pareto optimal point would be to compute progressively the *a-efficient* points and to increase the a value at each step ($a = 1..a_{max}$). When the set of k-efficient solutions is empty, the Interface stops the process and consider the subset of the last founded solutions as the set of the a_{max}-*efficient* solutions denoted E_{amax}. It is clear that a_{max}-efficiency provides alternatives satisfying the strongest requirements and eliminating ones which are inferior. We show now a generic algorithm for generating a_{max}-*efficient* solutions (E_{a-max}):

```
1.    let S_eff be the Pareto optimal solutions set.
2.    let a :=1.
3.    let E_a := S_eff
4.    while E_a ≠Ø
5.        find S ∈ E_a , such that ∀s ∈S, s a-dominate E_a –{S}
6.        a := a+1
7.        E_a := E_a-1 –{S}
8.    end while
9.    E_a-max := E_a
10.   return (E_a-max)
```

Algorithm. 1. Generating a_{max}-*efficient* solutions

The Interface retains the following set of solutions and communicates it to the several Criterion agents as a result of the CSMOP problem.

Often the process of reducing the set of solutions to retain points with the upper order of efficiency may not yield the desired reduction in the number of options. Though a reduced set, the Criterion agent still has to process quite a large number of solutions. The proposed negotiation process will allow us to further reduce the set of solutions in such a case.

At this level, the Interface informs the Criterion agents to start up the negotiation process on the bases of the set of a_{max}-efficient solutions founded earlier. Next we consider separately the properties of the Interface and the Criterion agent behavior.

4.3.1   Criterion Agent Behavior

The Criterion agent behavior is to iteratively computes, both its ideal id_i and anti-ideal aid_i costs as follows:

$aid_i = Min(f_i(x))$ (for maximization), $x \in E_{amax}$, $i \in \{ 1,2,...n\}$,

$id_i = Max(f_i(x))$ (for maximization), $x \in E_{amax}$. $i \in \{ 1,2,...n\}$, and uses these parameters to compute its satisfaction level sl_i, $sl_i = aid_i + (idi - aidi)*\varepsilon$ where ε is an adjustment parameter in $]0,1[$ used to gradually increase sl_i and consequently to set up an order of preference among the set of a_{max}-efficient solutions E_{amax}. In addition to these parameters, the Criterion agent has to separate the E_{amax} set into satisfied solutions $SSol$ and unsatisfied solutions $USol$ subsets such that $SSol = \{ x \in E_{amax}$ / $f_i(x) \geq sl_i\}$ and $USol = \{ x \in E_{amax}$ / $f_i(x) < sl_i\}$. The subset of unsatisfied solutions is considered as the set of solutions that the Criterion agent prefers at least and which he would delete from the E_{amax} whenever most of the other agents have the same agreements. So, he informs everyone about his unsatisfied solutions and asks them to establish their vote. For the other Criterion agent, if any solution is belonging to their unsatisfied solutions they agree to delete it from the E_{amax}.

As the expected answers are received, the Criterion agent sets up for every solution in his unsatisfied subset a vote vector and removes from E_{amax} any solution the majority of the Criterion agents agree to delete. Then informs the Interface about this removal.

4.3.2   Interface Behavior

Under the assumption that all of the Criterion agents agree to remove the least preferred solutions from $E_{amax,}$ the Interface updates this set of solutions and arranges the removed solutions as the first subset of the least preferred a_{max}-efficient solutions. Next, he communicates the modified E_{amax} to all the Criterion agents and asks them to restart a new negotiation process. The process terminates whenever the size of the a_{max}-efficient solutions is equal to one or if after two successive iterations no new solution is removed. The last subset of solutions arranged is considered as the most preferred subset among the various a_{max}- efficient solutions available.

5   Experimental Results

The implementation was developed with Actalk, a concurrent programming language based on Smalltalk 80 environment. In this language framework, an agent is implemented as an actor having the Smalltalk object structure enriched by an ability to send /receive message to / from its acquaintances, buffering the received messages in its own mailbox. The Cooperative search based nogood exchange and the negotiation process based on the distribution process of the space search, which are described above, has been experimented on randomly generated binary CSPs and linear objective functions. Classical parameters were used for generating the problems[9]: number of variables (n), domain size (d), constraint density p (a number between 0 and 100% indicating the ratio between the number of the problem effective constraints to the number of all possible constraints, i.e., a complete constraint graph), constraint tightness q (a number between 0 and 100% indicating the ratio between the number of couples of values forbidden (not allowed) by the constraint to the size of the domain cross product) and the number of performance criterion (ncr).

As numerical values, we use n = 30, d = 15, p=50% and q varying from 20% to 40% by steps of 3% to both keep the solutions number reasonable and to guarantee consistent problems. The Criterion number ncr is varying from 5 to 15.

The first experimentation aims at evaluating the impact of Multi-agents architecture on the nogood exchange based cooperative search. Each Criterion agent is associated with an heuristic and thus to do them cooperate in order to speed up the resolution of the CSP. The effectiveness of the nogoods exchange based cooperative search is assessed through a comparison with the NR-FC algorithm associated with each criterion agent and free of heuristic. The obtained results show a noticeable improvement conveyed by the acceleration of the CSP resolution. This acceleration is due to the reduction of the number of constraint checks and consequently the falling of the CPU time. This can be explained by the fact that, an agent receives a nogood from its acquaintances earlier than it can be generated thanks to the heuristics, which diversify the tree structure, and uses this nogood to cut its search space.

Figure.1 shows the behavior of the nogood exchange based cooperative search compared to the NR-FC algorithm.

Moreover, The application of the distribution process to the space search has reduced the timing results between 36.19% and 42.09%. Figure.2 illustrates a comparison of the cooperative search with the entire CSP for each Criterion agent (MACS) to the cooperative search where the space search is distributed between all the agents (DMACS). Note that this advantage is due to the reduction of the variables domain size.

The next experimentation will try to estimate the effectiveness of the optimization to reduce the set of the final result. Table 1 shows the obtained results for n=10, d=15, p=50%, q=50%. They illustrate that the concept of *a-efficiency* could reduce effectively the final decision. It should be noted that the average portion of the 2-efficient solutions (resp. 3-efficient solutions) represents 25.53% (resp. 6.87%) of the total number of efficient solutions.

6   Conclusion and Future Work

In this paper, we have developed a new formalism for Multicriteria optimization in CSPs and a multi-agent model solving problems in this setting. In this model each agent is responsible for a single criterion. Thus the criteria are separately optimized without any "scalarization" form. They cooperate and negotiate in order to find out and to reach their 'best' Pareto optimal solutions. Using the notion of a-*efficiency* and the negotiation process in succession could help eliminate some alternatives among the multiple non–inferior ones. However, we shall focus on an efficient algorithm for identifying points with a-*efficiency order*. As far as our future work is concerned, other experiments will be performed. In addition, we shall develop an algorithm for dealing with both CSP solving and optimizing in only one stage.

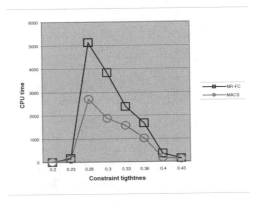

Fig. 1. The Improvements provided by the cooperative search MACS in term of CPU time compared with the NR-FC algorithm.

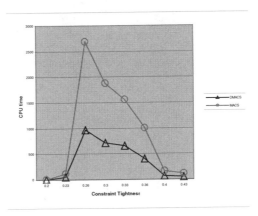

Fig. 2. The effectiveness of the distribution process in term of CPU time compared with the cooperative search MACS.

Table 1. Average number of the obtained solutions

Criterion number	Efficient solutions	2-efficient solutions	3-efficient solutions
5	60	3	0
6	90	7	0
7	179	19	0
8	200	19	3
9	329	55	9
10	400	120	15
11	380	126	30
12	460	160	34
13	433	200	44
14	467	216	100
15	540	245	112

References

[1] S.H.Clearwater, B.A.Huberman and T.Hogg, Cooperative problem Solving, *In Huberman, B., editor, Computation: The Micro and the View*, 1992, p 33-70.

[2] I.Das and J.E.Dennis, Normal boundary intersection, In *WCSMO-2, Proceedings of the Second World Congress of Structural and Multidisciplinary Optimization*, 1997, p 49-54.

[3] D. Frost, "Algorithms and Heuristics for CSPs", A dissertation Submitted in Partial Satisfaction of the Requirements for the Degree Doctor of Philosophy in Information and Computer Science, University of California, Irvine, 1997.

[4] L. Granvilliers, E. Monfroy and F. Benhamou, "Cooperative Solvers in Constraint Programming : a Short Introduction", Workshop on Cooperative Solvers in Constraint Programming at the 7th International Conference on Principles and Practice of Constraint Programming (CP2001), Cyprus, December 2001.

[5] T. Hogg and P.C. Williams, Solving the really hard problems with cooperative search, *In hirsh, H. et al., editors, AAAI Spring symposium on IA and NP-Hard Problems*, 1993, p 78-84.

[6] B.A.Huberman, The performance of cooperative process, *Phisica D*, 1990,p38-47.

[7] A.Mackworth, Consistency in networks of relations, *Artificial Intelligence*, vol.(8), 1977, p 99-118.

[8] U.Montanari, Networks of Constraints: fundamental properties and applications to picture processing, *Information Sciences*, vol.(7), 1974.

[9] D.Sabin and G. Freuder, Contradicting conventional wisdom in Constraint Satisfaction, *In proceeding of ECAI-94*, 1994, p 125-129.

[10] T.Schiex et G. Verfaillie, "Nogood Recording for Static and Dynamic Constraint Satisfaction Problems", International Journal of Artificial Intelligence Tools, p 187-207, 1994.

[11] R.B. Statnikov and J.B. Matusov, Multicriteria Optimisation and Engineering, Chapman and Hall, New York, 1995.

[12] I.Othmani, Optimisation Multicritère; Fondements et Concepts, *PHD- Thesis*, Université Joseph Fourrier, Grenoble 1998.

[13] E.Tsang, Foundations of Constraint Satisfaction, *Academic Press*, 1993.

[14] E.Tsang and C.Voudouris, Constraint Satisfaction in Discrete Optimisation, *Unicom Siminar*, 1998.

[15] P.Vincke, Multicriteria Decision -Aid, JHON WILEY & SONS,1989.

Nonlinear H$_\infty$ State Feedback Control of Rigid Robot Manipulators

Mahdi Jalili-Kharaajoo

Young Researchers Club, Islamic Azad University, Tehran, IRAN
P.O. Box: 14395/1355, Tehran, IRAN

Abstract. In this paper, nonlinear H$_\infty$ control strategy is applied to control of a two-degree-of-freedom rigid robot manipulator. In order to obtain the nonlinear H$_\infty$ control law, some inequalities so-called Hamilton–Jacobi–Isaacs (HJI) should be solved. It is so difficult, if not impossible, to find an explicit solution for HJI inequalities. However, there are some approximate solutions. One of these possible solutions is the use of Taylor Series expansion of nonlinear terms, which will be used in this paper. Using the obtained nonlinear robust controller, the response of the closed-loop system for tracking of fixed point and oscillating reference signals are obtained. Simulation results show better performance for higher order approximated controller than that of lower order one.

1 Introduction

The central target of nonlinear control is to internally stabilize the nonlinear plant while minimizing the effect of disturbances such as measurement noise, input disturbances and other exogenous signals, which invariably occur in most applications because of plant interactions with the environment. However, in deep contrast with linear control methods, which are flexible, efficient and allow solving a broad class of linear control problems, there are few practical methods in nonlinear control, which can handle real engineering problems with similar comfort. A prominent obstacle preventing the use of current techniques is that most of them are based on the Hamilton–Jacobi–Isaacs (HJI) equations to characterize solutions [1-3]. In order to obtain a nonlinear H$_\infty$ controller, one needs to solve the HJI equations. It is very difficult, if not impossible, to find exact explicit solution for the HJI equations. Some successive approximate solution methods are available for this problem [4-7].

Over the past decade, the problem of trajectory tracking for robot manipulators has attracted the attention of many researches, and various algorithms have been proposed for the control of robot manipulators, which consists of a wide range of strategies, such as adaptive controllers and sliding mode control [8-11]. In this paper, nonlinear H$_\infty$ state feedback controller is designed for position control in a two-degree-of freedom rigid robot manipulator. To obtain the approximate solution of the HJI inequality, Taylor Series expansion of the nonlinear terms up to desired order is obtained that result in a nonlinear H$_\infty$ control law. Using the obtained controller, the

C. Bussler and D. Fensel (Eds.): AIMSA 2004, LNAI 3192, pp. 469–479, 2004.

response of the closed-loop system for tracking of fixed point and oscillating reference signals are obtained, which the nonlinear controller results better performance than the linear counter part.

2   Model of the System

We begin with a general analysis of an n-joint rigid robotic manipulator system whose dynamics may be described by the second-order nonlinear vector differential equation:

$$M(q)\ddot{q} + h(q,\dot{q}) = u(t) \tag{1}$$

where $\dot{q}(t)$ is the $n \times 1$ vector of joint angular positions, $M(q)$ is the $n \times n$ symmetric positive definite inertia matrix, $h(q,\dot{q})$ is the $n \times 1$ vector containing Coriolis, centrifugal forces and gravity torques, $u(t)$ is the $n \times 1$ vector of applied joint torques (control inputs). The dynamic equations of the two-link robotic manipulator are expressed in state variable form as $x_1 = q_1, x_2 = \dot{q}_1$, $x_3 = q_2, x_4 = \dot{q}_2$ with $x = [x_1 \ x_2 \ x_3 \ x_4]^T$. The dynamics of this specific system is given by the equations [8-11]

$$\dot{x}_1 = x_2 \tag{2-a}$$

$$\dot{x}_2 = \frac{1}{a_1}[bx_2(x_2 + x_4)\left(1 + \frac{a_2^2}{a_1 a_2 - a_2^2}\right) + \gamma_1 g + u_1 - \frac{a_2}{(a_1 a_2 - a_2^2)^2}(a_1(\gamma_2 g - bx_4 + u_2) - a_1(\gamma_1 g + u_2)))] \tag{2-b}$$

$$\dot{x}_3 = x_4 \tag{2-c}$$

$$\dot{x}_4 = \frac{1}{a_1 a_2 - a_2^2}[a_1(\gamma_2 g - bx_4^2 + u_2) - a_2(bx_2(x_2 + x_4) + \gamma_1 g + u_2)] \tag{2-d}$$

where

$$a_1 = (m_1 + m_2)r_1^2 + m_2 r_2^2 + 2m_2 r_1 r_2 \cos(x_3) + J_1, \ a_2 = m_2 r_2^2 + 2m_2 r_1 r_2 \cos(x_3),$$
$$b = m_2 r_1 r_2 \sin(x_3), \ \gamma_1 = -((m_1 + m_2)r_1 \cos(x_3) + m_2 r_2 \cos(x_1 + x_3)), \ \gamma_1 = -(m_2 r_2 \cos(x_1 + x_3))$$

3   Nonlinear H$_\infty$ Control Design

3.1   Problem Formulation

We consider a system of the form

$$\dot{x} = X(x, w, u), z = Z(x, w, u), y = Y_i(x, w) \tag{3}$$

with x defined   in   a   neighborhood   of   the   origin   in R^n and $w \in R^{m_1}, u \in R^{m_2}, z \in R^{p_1}, y \in R^{p_2}$. It is assumed that X, Z and Y are smooth mapping of class C^k, k being sufficiently large. In addition to smoothness, the following is assumed

A1: System (3) has an equilibrium point at $(x, w, z) = (0,0,0)$.

A2: The matrix $D_{11} = \partial Z(x, w, u) / \partial w\big|_{(0,0,0)}$ satisfies $\bar{\sigma}(D_{11}) < \gamma$ where γ is the bound on L_2 gain of the closed-loop system.

A3: The matrix $D_{12} = \partial Z(x, w, u) / \partial u\big|_{(0,0,0)}$ has full column rank m_2.

A4: The matrix $D_{21} = \partial Y(x, w) / \partial w\big|_{(0,0)}$ has full row rank p_2.

A5: For any bounded trajectory of system (2) with input $w = 0$ $\forall t$
$$Z(x, 0, u) = 0 \ \forall t \quad \Rightarrow \quad \lim_{t \to \infty} x(t) = 0.$$

The controller has to achieve two goals: it must stabilize the closed-loop system and attenuate the influence of the exogenous input signal w on the controlled signal z, i.e., it has to bound its L_2 gain by a given value γ. The disturbance attenuation property can be characterized by dissipativity [3].

3.2 State Feedback Controller

In this section, a feedback law $u = a_2(x)$ is sought which renders the closed-loop system

$$\dot{x} = X(x, w, a_2(x)), \ z = Z(x, w, a_2(x))$$

(locally) dissipative with respect to the supply rate $s(w, z) = \gamma^2 \|w\|^2 - \|z\|^2$. This problem can be define

$$v = \begin{bmatrix} w \\ u \end{bmatrix}$$

with which the system equations read

$$\dot{x} = \tilde{X}(x, v), \ z = \tilde{Z}(x, v) \tag{4}$$

Then,

$$\gamma^2 \|w\|^2 = v^T \begin{bmatrix} \gamma^2 I_{m_1} & 0 \\ 0 & 0 \end{bmatrix} v$$

and the Hamiltonian function for this differential game can be found to be

$$H(x, \lambda, v) = \lambda^T \tilde{X}(x, v) + \|\tilde{Z}(x, v)\|^2 - v^T \begin{bmatrix} \gamma^2 I_{m_1} & 0 \\ 0 & 0 \end{bmatrix} v$$

In a neighborhood of

$$(x,\lambda) = \begin{bmatrix} w_*(x,\lambda) \\ u_*(x,\lambda) \end{bmatrix}$$

satisfying

$$\frac{\partial}{\partial v} H(x,\lambda,v)\Big|_{v=v_*(x,\lambda)} = 0, \ v_*(0,0) = 0. \tag{5}$$

The Hessian of H satisfies

$$\frac{\partial}{\partial v} H(x,\lambda,v)\Big|_{(x,\lambda,v)=(0,0,0)} = 2R = 2 \begin{bmatrix} D_{11}^T D_{11} - \gamma^2 I_{m_1} & D_{11}^T D_{12} \\ D_{12}^T D_{11} & D_{12}^T D_{12} \end{bmatrix}.$$

The matrix R may be factored as $R = N^T MN$ with

$$M = \begin{bmatrix} D_{11}^T D_{11} - \gamma^2 I_{m_1} - D_{11}^T D_{12}(D_{12}^T D_{12})^{-1} D_{12}^T D_{11} & 0 \\ 0 & D_{12}^T D_{12} \end{bmatrix}, \ N = \begin{bmatrix} I_{m_1} & 0 \\ (D_{12}^T D_{12})^{-1} D_{12}^T D_{11} & I_{m_2} \end{bmatrix}.$$

where the upper diagonal element of M is negative definite due to Assumption **A2** and the lower diagonal element is positive definite. Hence, the Hamiltonian function H has a saddle point in (w,u) for each (x,λ) in the neighborhood of $(x,\lambda,w,u) = (0,0,0,0)$:

$$H(x,\lambda,v)\Big|_{v=\begin{bmatrix} w \\ u_*(x,\lambda) \end{bmatrix}} \leq H(x,\lambda,v)\Big|_{v=\begin{bmatrix} w_*(x,\lambda) \\ u_*(x,\lambda) \end{bmatrix}} \leq H(x,\lambda,v)\Big|_{v=\begin{bmatrix} w_*(x,\lambda) \\ u \end{bmatrix}}.$$

Define a smooth, nonnegative function $V : R^n \rightarrow R$ in a neighborhood of $x=0$ such that $V(0)=0$ and the Hamilton-Jacobi-Isaacs inequality

$$H(x,V_x^T(x),v_*(x,V_x^T(x)) \leq 0 \tag{6}$$

holds for each x in a neighborhood of zero. Then,

$$u = u_*(x,V_x^T(x)) \tag{7}$$

yields a closed-loop system satisfying

$$V_x(x)X(x,0,u_*) + \|Z(x,0,u_*)\|^2 - \gamma^2 \|w\|^2 - \gamma^2 \|w\|^2 \leq 0 \tag{8}$$

i.e., a system which has the required dissipativity property in a neighborhood of $(x,w)=(0,0)$, Due to Assumption **A5**, the feedback law (7) locally asymptotically stabilizes the system if $V(x)$ is positive definite. This can be seen by a Lyapunov type of argument. For $w=0$, expression (8) reads

$$V_x(x)X(x,0,u_*) + \|Z(x,0,u_*)\|^2 \leq 0$$

where $Z(x,0,u_*)$ can only be zero for asymptotically stable trajectories of x (Assumption **A5**). Thus, $V(x)$ being positive definite and

$$\frac{d}{dt} V(x) = \frac{d}{dt} V(x) + V_x(x) \frac{\partial x}{\partial t} = V_x(x)X(x,0,u_*)$$

being negative proves asymptotic stability of the closed-loop system.

3.3 Approximated Controller

The HJI inequalities cannot be solved explicitly, in general. However, it is possible to compute an approximated solution based on Taylor Series expansions, which can be used for finding an approximate control law [4,5]. The approximation of lowest order[1] corresponds to the linear problem [5]. The two basic equations (5) and (6), where for the former the equality rather than inequality is considered, may be written as

$$V_x(x)\tilde{X}(x,v_*(x,V_x^T(x))) + \tilde{Z}^T(x,v_*(x,V_x^T(x)))\tilde{Z}(x,v_*(x,V_x^T(x))) \left(\lambda^T\frac{\partial}{\partial v}\tilde{X}(x,v) + \frac{\partial}{\partial v}(\tilde{Z}^T(x,v)\tilde{Z}(x,v)\right. \tag{9}$$

$$\left. - v_*^T(x,V_x^T(x))\begin{bmatrix}\gamma^2 I_{m_1} & 0\\ 0 & 0\end{bmatrix}v_*(x,V_x^T(x)) = 0 \quad\quad -2v^T\begin{bmatrix}\gamma^2 I_{m_1} & 0\\ 0 & 0\end{bmatrix}\right)\bigg|_{\lambda=V_x^T(x),v=v_*(x,V_x^T(x))} = 0$$

Step-by-step approximations of the solutions to these two equations are given in the following subsections.

3.3.1 Lowest Order Approximation: The Linear H$_\infty$ Problem
For the linearized system

$$\begin{aligned}\dot{x} &= Ax + Bv\\ z &= C_1 x + D_{1o}v\end{aligned}\;;\quad \begin{aligned}A &= \frac{\partial}{\partial x}\tilde{X}(x,v)\bigg|_{(0,0)}\\ C1 &= \frac{\partial}{\partial x}\tilde{Z}(x,v)\bigg|_{(0,0)}\end{aligned}\quad \begin{aligned}B &= \frac{\partial}{\partial v}\tilde{X}(x,v)\bigg|_{(0,0)}\\ D_{1o} &= \frac{\partial}{\partial v}\tilde{Z}(x,v)\bigg|_{(0,0)}\end{aligned}\quad,$$

the solution to the H$_\infty$ problem is well known. The storage function $V(x)$ is given by

$$V^{(2)}(x) = x^T K x$$

and the optimum v_* by

$$v_*^{(1)} = -Fx = -R^{-1}(B^T K + D_{1.}^T C_1)x \tag{10}$$

where K is the solution to (8) as

$$2x^T K(A-BF)x + x^T C_1^T C_1 x - 2x^T C_1^T D_{1.}Fx + x^T F^T D_{1.}^T D_{1.}Fx - \gamma^2 x^T F^T\begin{bmatrix}\gamma^2 I_{m_1} & 0\\ 0 & 0\end{bmatrix}Fx = 0 \cdot$$

Since this equality must hold for all x, it can be written as the Riccati equation

$$(A-BR^{-1}D_{1.}^T C_1)^T K + (A-BR^{-1}D_{1.}^T C_1) - KBR^{-1}B^T K + Q = 0 \tag{11}$$

with

$$R = D_{1.}^T D_{1.} - \begin{bmatrix}\gamma^2 I_{m_1} & 0\\ 0 & 0\end{bmatrix} \text{ and } Q = C_1^T C_1 - C_1^T D_{1.}R^{-1}D_{1.}^T C_1 \cdot$$

3.3.2 Higher Order Approximation
With the linearized plant given above, the plant dynamics (4) may be rewritten as

$$\dot{x} = Ax + Bv + f(x,v)$$

with the supply rate $-s(w,z)$

---

[1] The term "order" in connection with approximation does not refer to the dimension of the state vector but rather to the order of the Taylor approximation of each function. Sometimes, we use the expression "approximation order" to clearly distinguish this notion from the order.

$$Z^T Z - v^T \begin{bmatrix} \gamma^2 I_{m_1} & 0 \\ 0 & 0 \end{bmatrix} v = x^T C_1^T C_1 x + 2x^T C_1^T D_1 v + v^T D_1^T D_1 v + g_1(x,v) - v^T \begin{bmatrix} \gamma^2 I_{m_1} & 0 \\ 0 & 0 \end{bmatrix} v$$

$$= x^T C_1^T C_1 x + 2x^T C_1^T D_1 v + v^T R v + g_1(x,v)$$

With these definitions of f and g_1, with the feedback law (10), and with

$$v_*(x) = v_*(x, V_x^T(x))$$

the equations (9) read

$$V_x(x)[(A-BF)x + B(v_*(x)+Fx) + f(x,v_*(x))] + x^T C_1^T C_1 x + 2x^T C_1^T D_1 v_*(x) + v_*^T(x) R v_*(x) + g1(x,v_*(x)) = 0$$

and

$$2x^T C_1^T D_1 + 2v_*^T(x) R + \left. \frac{\partial}{\partial v} g1(x,v) \right)\Big|_{v=v*(x)} + V_x(x) \left(B + \left. \frac{\partial}{\partial v} f(x,v) \right|_{v=v*(x)} \right) = 0$$

Solving the first of these equations for $V_x(x)(A-BF)x$ and the second for v_* yields

$$V_x(x)(A-BF)x = V_x(x)(B(v_*(x)+Fx) + f(x,v_*(x)))$$
$$- x^T C_1^T C_1 x - 2x^T C_1^T D_1 v_*(x) - v_*^T(x) R v_*(x) - g_1(x,v_*(x)) \tag{12}$$

$$V_x(x) = -\frac{1}{2} R^{-1} \left(2D_1^T C_1 x + \left(\left. \frac{\partial}{\partial v} g_1(x,v) \right|_{v=v*(x)} \right)^T + \left(B + \left. \frac{\partial}{\partial v} f(x,v) \right|_{v=v*(x)} \right)^T V_x^T(x) \right) \tag{13}$$

Equation (12) written as a power series of terms up to order m is given by

$$\left(\sum_{d=1}^{m-1} V_x^{(d+1)}(x) \right)(A-BF)x = -\sum_{d=1}^{m-2}\sum_{j=1}^{m-d} V_x^{(d+1)}(x)[B(v_*(x)+Fx) + f(s,v_*(x))]^{(j)} - \sum_{d=1}^{m} g_1^{(d)}(x,v_*(x)) +$$ an

$$- x^T C_1^T C_1 x - 2x^T C_1^T C_1 D_1 \sum_{d=1}^{m-1} v_*^{(d)}(x) - \sum_{d=1}^{m-1}\sum_{j=1}^{m-d} v_*^{T(d)}(x) R v_*^{(j)}(x) \qquad m = 3,4,\ldots$$

d its mth-order term, i.e., the difference between the approximations of order m and $m-1$, by

$$V_x^{(m)}(x)(A-BF)x = -\sum_{d=1}^{m-2} V_x^{(d+1)}(x)[B(v_*(x)+Fx) + f(x,v_*(x))]^{(m-d)} - g_1^{(m)}(x,v_*(x)) + \tag{14}$$

$$- 2x^T C_1^T D_1 v_*^{(m-1)}(x) - \sum_{d=1}^{m-1} v_*^{T(d)}(x) R v_*^{(m-d)}(x) \qquad m = 3,4,\ldots$$

Equation (13) as a power series of terms up to order k is given by

$$\sum_{d=1}^{k} v_*^{(d)}(x) = -\frac{1}{2} R^{-1} \left(2D_1^T C_1 x + \left. \sum_{d=2}^{k} \left(\frac{\partial}{\partial v} g_1(x,v) \right)^{T(d)} \right|_{v=v*(x)} + B^T \left(\sum_{d=1}^{k} (V_x^{(d+1)}(x))^T \right) + \right.$$

$$\left. \sum_{d=1}^{k-1}\sum_{j=1}^{k-d} \left. \left(\frac{\partial}{\partial v} f(x,v) \right)^{T(d)} \right|_{v=v*(x)} (V_x^{(j+1)}(x))^T \right) \qquad k = 2,3,\ldots$$

and its kth-order term

$$v_*^{(k)}(x) = -\frac{1}{2}R^{-1}\left(\left(\frac{\partial}{\partial v}g_1(x,v)\right)^{T(k)}\bigg|_{v=v_*(x)} + B^T(V_x^{(k+1)}(x))^T +\right.$$

$$\left.\sum_{d=1}^{k-1}\left(\frac{\partial}{\partial v}f(x,v)\right)^{T(d)}\bigg|_{v=v_*(x)} (V_x^{(k-d+1)}(x))^T\right) \qquad k=2,3,...$$

(15)

Note that

$$f^{(j)}\left(x,\sum_{d=1}^{\infty}v_*^{(d)}(x)\right) = f^{(j)}\left(x,\sum_{d=1}^{j-1}v_*^{(d)}(x)\right), g_1^{(m)}\left(x,\sum_{d=1}^{\infty}v_*^{(d)}(x)\right) = g_1^{(m)}\left(x,\sum_{d=1}^{m-2}v_*^{(d)}(x)\right)$$ (16)

Since $f(x,v)$ and $g_1(x,v)$ are power series starting with terms in (x,v) of order two and three, respectively (for f, v_* must be of higher order or a multiplication of x and v_* must occur because the linear terms with v_* is already considered in Bv_*). Hence, equation (14) is independent of $v_*^{(m-1)}(x)$, its coefficient being

$$-(V_x^{(2)}(x)B + 2x^TC_1^TD_{1.} + 2v_*^{T(1)}(x)R = -2x^T(KB + C_1^TD_{1.} - F^TR) - 2x^T(KB + C_1^TD_{1.} - (KB + C_1^TD_{1.})R^{-1}R) = 0$$

Thus,

$$V_x^{(m)}(x)(A-BF)x = -\sum_{d=2}^{m-2}V_x^{(d+1)}(x)Bv_*^{(m-d)}(x) - \sum_{d=1}^{m-2}V_x^{(d+1)}(x)Bv_*^{(m-d)}(x) - f^{(m-d)}(x,v_*(x))$$

(17)

$$-g_1^{(m)}(x,v_*(x)) - \sum_{d=2}^{m-2}v_*^{T(d)}(x)Rv_*^{(m-d)}(x) \qquad k=3,4,...$$

where the convention

$$\sum_k^l = 0 \qquad for \quad l<k$$

is adopted.

The right-hand side of (17) depends on the first $(m-2)$ terms of $v_*(x)$ and on the first $(m-1)$ terms of $V(x)$, while the right-hand side of (15) is determined by the first $(k-1)$ terms of $v_*(x)$ and the first $(k+1)$ terms of $V(x)$. Therefore, $V(x)$ and $v_*(x)$ can be approximated by consecutively computing

$$V^{(2)}, v_*^{(1)}, V^{(3)}, v_*^{(2)}, V^{(4)}, v_*^{(3)}, ...$$

This computation does not have to be done in the way its feasibility is derived. Since Taylor approximations have to be computed in every step anyway, the easiest way to compute V is the following:

$$V_x^{(m)}(x)(A-BF)x = [-V_x(x)Bv_*(x) - V_x(x)f(x,v_*(x))$$

$$-g_1(x,v_*(x)) - v_*^T(x)Rv_*(x)]^{(m)} \qquad m=3,4,...$$

(18)

Similarly, for v_*:

$$v_*^{(k)}(x) = -\frac{1}{2} R^{-1} \left(\left(\frac{\partial}{\partial v} g_1(x,v) \right)^T \Bigg|_{v=v_*(x)} + B^T V_x^T(x) + \left(\frac{\partial}{\partial v} f(x,v) \right)^T \Bigg|_{v=v_*(x)} V_x^T(x) \right)^{(k)} \quad k=2,3,\dots \quad (19)$$

For both of these equations, V and v_* on the right-hand sides stand for the sums over all terms already computed.

4   Simulation Results

For simulation, the following parameters are considered
$$r_1 = 1.0m, r_2 = 0.8m, J_1 = 5Kgm, J_2 = 5Kgm$$
$$m_1 = 0.5Kg, m_2 = 1.5kg, g = 9.8Kgm/s^2$$
$$p_1 = 50, p_2 = 50, p_3 = 1, p_4 = 1$$

Using the proposed method the nonlinear optimal control law for u_1 and u_2 can be obtained. Here are the first and third order controllers.
The first order optimal control laws:
$$u_1 = -2.311 x_1 + 10.435 x_2 + 34.788 x_3 + 5.699 x_4$$
$$u_2 = -10.421 x_1 - 8.374 x_2 + 12.545 x_3 + 4.112 x_4$$
The third order optimal control laws:
$$\begin{aligned}
u_1 = &-2.312 x_1 + 10.421 x_2 + 34.784 x_3 + 5.711 x_4 + .231 x_1 x_2 + 1.256 x_1 x_3 - 3.406 x_1 x_4 + .799 x_2 x_3 \\
&- .023 x_2 x_4 - .952 x_3 x_4 - 1.002 x_1^2 x_2 x_3 + .041 x_1^2 x_2 x_4 - 2.239 x_1^2 x_3 x_4 + .007 x_2^2 x_1 x_3 - .442 x_2^2 x_1 x_4 \\
&- .891 x_3^2 x_3 x_4 + .998 x_3^2 x_1 x_2 - .556 x_3^2 x_1 x_4 + 3.221 x_3^2 x_2 x_4 + .945 x_4^2 x_1 x_2 + 1.003 x_4^2 x_1 x_3 - .439 x_4^2 x_2 x_3 \\
&+ 1.203 x_1^2 + .777 x_2^2 - .048 x_3^2 + 3.405 x_4^2 - .287 x_1^3 + .798 x_2^3 + 1.965 x_3^3 + .038 x_4^3
\end{aligned}$$

$$\begin{aligned}
u_2 = &-10.421 x_1 - 8.374 x_2 + 12.545 x_3 + 4.112 x_4 + .456 x_1 x_2 + 2.304 x_1 x_3 + .341 x_1 x_4 - 1.203 x_2 x_3 \\
&- .343 x_2 x_4 - 1.002 x_3 x_4 + .095 x_1^2 x_2 x_3 + .213 x_1^2 x_2 x_4 + .006 x_1^2 x_3 x_4 + .032 x_2^2 x_1 x_3 - .442 x_2^2 x_1 x_4 \\
&+ .211 x_2^2 x_3 x_4 - .0234 x_3^2 x_1 x_2 + .998 x_3^2 x_1 x_4 + 1.201 x_3^2 x_2 x_4 + 3.001 x_4^2 x_1 x_2 - .058 x_4^2 x_1 x_3 - .159 x_4^2 x_2 x_3 \\
&- 1.359 x_1^2 + .034 x_2^2 + .491 x_3^2 + 1.045 x_4^2 + .108 x_1^3 - .426 x_3^3 - .887 x_3^2 + .281 x_4^3
\end{aligned}$$

In this section, the MATLAB based simulations highlight the operation of the manipulator when tracking to a steady state value; q_1 and q_2 converge to 0.85 and 1.25 respectively. The reference signals are
$$q_{r1} = 0.85 - \frac{7}{5} e^{-t} + \frac{7}{20} e^{-4t}$$
$$q_{r2} = 1.25 + e^{-t} - \frac{1}{4} e^{-4t}$$
The initial state values of the system are selected as
$$[x_1 \ x_2 \ x_3 \ x_4]^T = [0.8 \ 0 \ 0.8 \ 0]^T$$
In Fig. 1 the closed-loop system responses using the first order control law (dashed line) and the third order controller (solid line) are depicted. As it is seen, the performance of the system with nonlinear controller is better than the linear one.

In order to investigate further, the effect of nonlinear control action on the performance of the system, the tracking problem of an oscillatory reference signal is considered. Here the desired trajectory reference signals are defined as

$$q_{r1} = 0.175(1 - \cos(2\pi t)) + 0.175$$
$$q_{r2} = 0.22(1 - \cos(2\pi t)) + 0.22$$

The initial state values of the system are selected as

$$[x_1 \quad x_2 \quad x_3 \quad x_4]^T = [0.1 \quad 0.1 \quad 1.3 \quad 0]^T$$

As it can be seen from Fig. 2, the performance of the closed-loop system using the third order controller (solid line) is better than that of the first order one (dashed line) and using the former the system needs less energy to track the reference signal sooner.

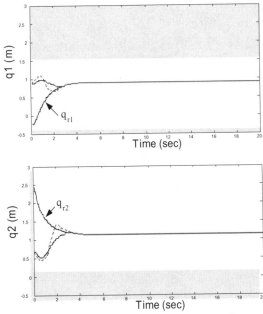

Fig. 1. Closed-loop system responses for tracking a fixed point reference signal using the first order controller (dashed line) and the third order controller (solid line)

5   Conclusions

In this paper, nonlinear H$_\infty$ controller was designed to control of rigid robot manipulators. Because of the nonlinear nature of robot manipulators and this fact that some of the parameters are varying during the operation, the nonlinear H$_\infty$ controller seems to be effective choice. In the design of the controller, we had to solve HJI inequalities but finding an explicit closed solution for these inequalities is too difficult, if not impossible. In this work, we used an approximate solution based on Taylor Series expansion. Using this method, the nonlinear control law with desired order could be obtained. Simulation results showed that the performance of higher order approximated controller is better than that of lower order one.

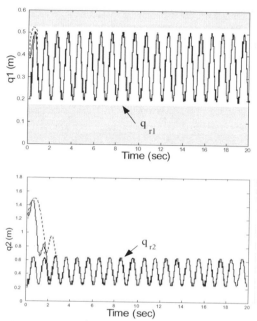

Fig. 2. Closed-loop system responses for tracking a oscillatory reference signal using the first order controller (dashed line) and the third order controller (solid line)

References

1. Isidori, A. and Astolfi, A., Disturbance attenuation and H_∞ control via measurements feedback in nonlinear systems, IEEE Trans. Automatic Control, 37, pp. 1283–1293, 1992.
2. Van der Schaft, A. J., L_2 gain analysis of nonlinear systems and nonlinear state feedback Control, IEEE Trans. Automatic Control, 37, pp. 770–781, 1992.
3. Isidori, A. and Kang, W., H_∞ control via measurement feedback for general nonlinear systems, IEEE Trans. Automatic Control, 40, pp.466-472, 1995.
4. Yazdanpanah, M.J., Khorasani, K. and Patel, P.V., Uncertainly compensation for a flexible link manipulator using nonlinear H_∞ control, INT. J. Control, 6, pp.753-771, 1998.
5. Jalili-Kharaajoo, M. and Yazdanpanah, M.J., Transient control and voltage regulation of power systems using approximate solution of HJB equation, In Proc. European Control Conference (ECC 2003), Oxford, England, 2-4 September, 2003.
6. Lu, Q., et al., Decentralized nonlinear H_∞ excitation control based on regulation linearization, IEE Proc. Gener. Transm. Distri., 147(4), pp.940-946, 2000.
7. Karlsson, N., Dahleh, M. and Hrovat, D., Nonlinear H_∞ control of active suspensions, in Proc. ACC'01, Arlington, VA, pp.3329-3335, 2001.
8. Cai, D. and Dai, Y. A globally convergence robust controller for robot manipulator, Proc. IEEE Int. Conf. Control Application, Mexico City, Mexico, 2001.

9. Zhihong, M. and Yu, X. Adaptive terminal Sliding Mode Tracking Control for Rigid Robotic Manipulators with Uncertain Dynamics. Journal of S. Mechanical Engineering, Series C., Vol. 40, No. 3, 1997.
10. Keleher, P.G. and Stonier, R.J. Adaptive terminal sliding mode control of a rigid robot manipulator with uncertain dynamics incorporating constrain inequalities. J. ANZIAM, 43(E), pp. E102-E157, 2002.
11. Battoliti, S. and Lanari, L. Tracking with disturbance attenuation for rigid robots. Proc. IEEE Int. Con. Robotics and Automation, pp. 1578-1583, 1996.

Qualitative Model of Decision Making

Rafał Graboś

University of Leipzig, Dept. of Computer Science,
Augustus Platz 10/11, 04109 Germany
grabos@informatik.uni-leipzig.de

Abstract. In Classical Decision Theory, preferences and uncertainties of a decision maker (DM) have the quantitative forms of a utility function and a probability distribution. However, a numerical approach for decision making suffers from a knowledge acquisition problem. In this paper a qualitative model for decision making is proposed, where the DM is modeled as the agent with preferences and beliefs about the world. Decision problem is represented by means of Brewka's logic program with ordered disjunction (LPOD) and a decision making process is a constraint satisfaction problem, where a solution is consistent with a knowledge base and maximally consistent with the DM's beliefs and preferences.

Keywords: knowledge representation, logic programming, qualitative decision making

1 Introduction

Classical Decision Theory, formulated by economists von Neumann and Morgenstern in the 1950s [18], relies completely on a numerical representation of a decision process. Preferences of a decision maker (DM) are expressed by means of a utility function and a probability distribution over a set of outcomes represents an uncertainty of a situation under consideration. A rational agent always selects an act which maximizes her expected utility. Savage [16], proposed an axiomatic framework of a theory of subjective expected utility, where acts are modeled by the functions of states and consequences. In this approach only a decision rule (expected utility maximization) has a quantitative nature, while preferences and uncertainties are derived from a total ordering of acts, built by the DM.

However for real life problems, the requirements of numerical preferences and beliefs or, of a total order of acts seem to be still to demanding for the DM. This argument has motivated for various frameworks in AI, proposing partial and imprecise utility functions instead [1], nonstandard utilities and probabilities [13], and a symbolic constraint [12].

The approaches, which rely only on a qualitative representation of decision making are called in AI qualitative decision theories[1]. Some of them, like [8], consider a notion of ordering by means of likelihood and preference relations. Most of them however propose logical-based models of decision making [3], [17], [2], consisting on a

---

[1] Motivations of such theories can be found in [7].

C. Bussler and D. Fensel (Eds.): AIMSA 2004, LNAI 3192, pp. 480–489, 2004.

symbolic representation of a decision process and considering many types of decision rules to select the best decision. They allow formulating the problem in a less abstract way, where knowledge and preferences have a form of human-like expressions. Besides, in contrast to the classical frame, they often investigate a computational complexity of decision making process as well as an expressive power of the representation language.

In the following we propose a qualitative model for decision making by means of logic program with ordered disjunction (LPOD) [4] under answer set semantics [14]. In general, answer set programming has been recognized as a very efficient and expressive knowledge representation and reasoning tool for AI [10], [15]. We generalize and extend the work of Brewka [6], where the idea of a qualitative decision making through LPOD was introduced.

Decision maker is modeled as the agent having beliefs about the likelihood of states of the world (prioritized belief base), and having preferences over the consequences of acts (prioritized goal base). Decision process is a constraint satisfaction problem, and solutions to the problem have forms of answer sets of a LPOD program, and are consistent with a background knowledge (feasible acts) and maximally consistent with a mental state of the Decision Maker (beliefs and preferences).

Section 2 gives some background of qualitative decision theories. In section 3 and 4 a notion of answer set programming (ASP) and logic programming with ordered disjunction (LPOD) is presented respectively, while section 5 studies a possible framework of a qualitative decision model under the LPOD.

2   Qualitative Decision Theories

In AI there are mainly two reasons for the interest of qualitative tools in decision making: knowledge acquisition problem- qualitative information is easier to obtain and computational efficiency- because of simplicity it can be made faster algorithms.

In general, all qualitative frameworks of decision making in AI consider common notions of a qualitative utility and a qualitative probability. For instance in [17] two semi-qualitative rankings are proposed: k(w) ranking as an order-of-magnitude approximation of a probability function P(w), and μ(w) ranking as a form of a utility function, being both the representation of uncertainty and preferences of a DM respectively. The two rankings are compared and the expected utility rule is applied.

In the approach proposed by Boutilier in [3], preferences of a DM are expressed by means of the conditional rules: I(α \ β), to be read as "Ideally, α if β" with the meaning: in the most preferred β-words, α is the case. Probabilities are represented as the default rules of the form: $\gamma \rightarrow \varphi$, interpreted as: in the most normal γ -worlds, φ is the case. A desirable decision is called a goal and is selected among the most preferred from the most normal worlds.

Both systems are referred to decision making under uncertainty (DMUU), where the uncertainty of a DM is modeled by way of an ordering relation over the worlds, being outcomes of possible acts. However there is another way of representation, originally formulated by Savage [16]. If $\mathbf{S} = (s_1,..., s_n)$ is a finite set of a mutually exclusive and complete description of the world, and $\mathbf{C} = (c_1,..., c_n)$ is a finite set of consequences which express the outcomes of acts, then $f: \mathbf{S} \rightarrow \mathbf{C}$ is an act, being a complete mapping from the set of states to the set of consequences. Intuitively, a feasible act is represented by a *vector* of different outcomes contingent on the possible states. Uncertainty means that any of a state in $\mathbf{S}$ may occur but we do not have a certainty, which will hold in fact.

Then, starting with a complete preorder on acts, given by a DM, Savage derived a likelihood relation representing uncertainty on events (subsets of $\mathbf{S}$) in the state space and a preference relation on the consequences, which finally, after satisfying some axioms, can be represented in a quantitative form of the probability distribution p and the utility function u. Then acts can be ranked according to their expected utility:

$$EU(f) = \sum p(s)u(f(s)) \tag{1}$$

In a recent field of AI, a work of Dubois et al. [8] considers a reformulation of Savage's theory, suggesting two orderings: on the set of consequences and on the set of events, instead of a one weak order on acts. As a decision rule, the Likely Dominance Rule of the form:

$$A_1 >_P A_2 \text{ iff } [A_1 >_p A_2] \, _S >_l [A_2 >_p A_1] \, _S \tag{2}$$

is suggested, to be interpreted: an act A_1 is more promising than an act A_2 iff the event formed by the disjunction of states in which A_1 gives better results than A_2 is more likely than the event formed by the disjunction of states in which A_2 gives results better than A_1.

However, the above framework relies still on too demanding requirements for DM. First, both orderings: on states and consequences, are assumed to be complete and transitive relations. It excludes partial and cyclic (conflicting) preferences and beliefs from considerations[2]. Second, it does not investigate conditional preferences, so called state-dependent preferences (or utilities). Third, any procedure to handle with a complete ignorance of the DM about states of the world is not proposed. Besides, as soon as the theory of decision making has only a mathematical form, it does not deal with a problem of representation and reasoning language, which could be efficiently implemented. In contrary, in Boutilier's logic [3] a partial knowledge and defeasible goals[3] as well as different strategies, depending on the level of certainty of the DM, are considered. In [9] a framework based on possibilistic logic was introduced, where default knowledge and many forms of preferences are investigated. However, in first is not possible in general to express complex conditional preferences and a priority to beliefs over preferences in the decision rule is always given[4], while in latter no mechanism to handle with ignorance of the DM is proposed.

It seems that a representation of decision making under uncertainty, proposed by Savage in economy, is too demanding and the expressive power of the language is

---

[2] The latter appear in DMUU, when conditional and defeasible preferences are expressed.

[3] Defeasibility of knowledge can be formally expressed as: given $\alpha \vDash \beta$ (consequence relation) $\alpha \cap \gamma \nvDash \beta$ may hold. This seems to be a feature of preferences, when by adding new preferences or knowledge, previous desirable conclusions become not valid.

[4] Sometimes we want to express situations which are unlikely, but which have a high impact, i.e., an extremely high or low utility and it is not possible in such frameworks.

very limited. Logic-based approaches seem to be more flexible and general, thus useful for qualitative decision tasks, allow to incomplete and defeasible knowledge be expressed and reasoned in a symbolic fashion.

Let us, based on the above remarks, formulate some postulates a qualitative decision making system, based on the symbolic representation (logic), should meet:

- different strategy, depending on levels of certainty of the DM (certainty, uncertainty and ignorance)
- incomplete (partial) preferences and beliefs of the DM
- defeasible knowledge, preferences and beliefs
- general and arbitrary form of preferences (conditional, cyclic)
- priority between degree of beliefs and preferences (extreme utility/likelihood)

Not all of these postulates refer strictly to DMUU; some are more general and are related to decision tasks in general (i.e. cyclic preferences). On the other hand, a few more concrete requirements will be investigated in the next parts of the paper.

3 Answer Set Programming

Answer set programming is a new logic programming paradigm for knowledge representation and problem solving tasks in artificial intelligence [14]. Representation of a problem is purely declarative, suitable for many aspects of commonsense reasoning (diagnosis, configuration, planning etc.). Instead of a query technique (Prolog), it bases upon a notion of possible solution, called *answer set*.

Consider a propositional language L, with atomic symbols called atoms. A literal is an atom or negated atom (by classical negation $\neg$). Symbol *not* is called epistemic negation and the expression *not a* is true, if there is no reason to believe, that a is the case. A rule r is an expression of the form:

$$c \leftarrow a_1, ..., a_m, not\ b_{m+1}, ..., not\ b_n \qquad (3)$$

where $n \geq m \geq 0$, c, a_j, b_i are literals, $Body^-(r) = \{b_{n+1}, ..., b_m\}$, $Body^+(r) = \{a_1, ..., a_n\}$ and $Head(r) = c$. A rule with an empty $Head$ ($\leftarrow Body$) is usually referred to as an integrity constraint. A logic program is a finite set of the rules.

Let assume now, that L is a set of all ground (without variables) literals, being present in the extended logic program P and I is an interpretation of P, $I \subseteq L$. The Gelfond-Lifschitz (GL) transformation of P with respect to I is a positive logic program P' which is obtained in two steps:

- deletion all rules r of P, for which $Body^-(r) \cap I = \varnothing$
- deletion the negative bodies ($Body^-(r)$) from the remaining rules

Then, I is an *answer set* of the logic program P, if I is a minimal model (no proper subset of I is a model of P') of the positive (without *not*) logic program P'.

Example 1. Consider the program $P_1 = \{b \leftarrow not\ a; a \leftarrow not\ b; f \leftarrow a\}$, $L = (a, b, e, f)$, and let $I = \{a, f\}$. The GL reduction of the program P_1 w. r. t. I is the program $P' = \{a \leftarrow; f \leftarrow a\}$. According to the definition, I is an answer set for the program P, if I is a minimal model of P' and in fact $\{a, f\}$ is a minimal model of P', hence I is the answer set of P. The second answer set of the program P is $\{b\}$ and these are the only answer sets for this program.

In general, programs under answer set semantics describe family of intended models. Therefore they encode possible solutions to a problem, being constraint satisfaction problem, and described by the program, where each clause is interpreted as a constraint. By that means many combinatorial, search and constraint satisfaction problems from the field of AI can be represented (diagnosis, configuration, planning etc.) and efficiently solved in implemented systems [10], [15].

4 Logic Programs with Ordered Disjunction

In [11] a notion of disjunctive logic programming under answer set semantics was introduced. A disjunctive rule r is a formula:

$$c_1 \vee \dots \vee c_k \leftarrow a_1, \dots, a_m, \; not \; b_{m+1}, \dots, \; not \; b_n \qquad (4)$$

where $k \geq 0$, $n \geq m \geq 0$, c_i, a_l, b_k are ground literals and the disjunction $\{c_1 \vee \dots \vee c_k\}$ is a *Head*(r) of the rule r. Disjunctive logic program is a finite set of the rules. Intuitively, each of answer sets is allowed to include only one literal from *Head* of any disjunctive rule r, whenever *Body* of that rule is satisfied. Then every model represents a possible solution to the problem. However, the disjunction is not able to capture the idea of a desirable solution among answer sets of a disjunctive logic program.

Consider an extended logic program (with two negations), where the ordered disjunction $\times$ is allowed in the *Head* part of a rule. A logic program with ordered disjunction (LPOD), proposed in [4], consist of rules of the form:

$$c_1 \times \dots \times c_k \leftarrow a_1, \dots, a_m, \; not \; b_{n+1}, \dots, \; not \; b_n \qquad (5)$$

where $k \geq 0$, $n \geq m \geq 0$, c_i, a_l, b_k are literals and the ordered disjunction $\{c_1 \times \dots \times c_k\}$ is a *Head*(r) of the rule r. The rule, let call it the preference rule, is originally to be read: if possible c_1, if c_1 is not possible, then $c_2, \dots$, if all of $c_1 \times \dots \times c_{k-1}$ are not possible, then c_k. The literals c_j are called choices of the rule.

Answer sets of LPOD are ranked according to degrees of satisfaction of ordered disjunctive rules and they are not always minimal models[5]. To distinguish, which answer set is preferred one, a notion of a degree of satisfaction of an ordered disjunctive rule by answer set is introduced.

Let A be an answer set of a LPOD program P. The ordered disjunctive rule r:

$$c_1 \times \dots \times c_k \leftarrow a_1, \dots, a_m, \; not \; b_{m+1}, \dots, \; not \; b_n \qquad (6)$$

is satisfied by A to degree:

- 1, if $a_j \notin A$ for some j or $b_i \in A$, for some i[6]
- k $(0 \leq k \leq n)$, if $a_j \notin A$ for all j, and $b_i \in A$, for all i, and $k = \min \{r \mid c_r \in A\}$.

Note that degrees of satisfaction are treated as penalties, as smaller degree as better answer set is. Moreover, a priority (meta-preferences) between preference rules can be expressed with a meaning: in case of conflict, when it is not possible to satisfy all rules to the highest degree, rules with a higher priority are to be satisfied first.

---

[5] Semantics of LPOD is based on the modified split techniques (for details see [4]).
[6] Sometimes, giving a first degree to unsatisfied preference rule leads to unintuitive results.

Each solution to a problem, represented as an answer set of a LPOD program P, is ranked according to its satisfaction degree of ordered disjunctive rules and one global order is obtained. A following criteria to build this ranking is proposed: *cardinality* optimal criterion- maximizing the number of rules satisfied to the highest degree, *inclusion* optimal criterion, based on set inclusion of the rules satisfied to certain degree and *Pareto* optimal criterion, consisting on a selection of answer set, which satisfies all ordered disjunctive rules not worse then any other answer set does[7].

Example 2. Program $P_4 = \{b \times c \times a; a \times c \times b; \leftarrow a, b; \leftarrow a, c\}$, has one cardinality optimal answer set: $S_1 = \{c, b\}$, which satisfies all rules "the best" (first to degree 1 and second to degree 2). Remaining answer sets: $S_2 = \{a\}$ and $S_3 = \{b\}$, satisfy one rule to 1, and one rule to 3 degree. Pareto and inclusion winners are both S_1 and S_2.

On one hand, it depends on the problem, which of criteria should be used. On the other hand, in case of the decision making task, a crucial is the assumption of comparability of satisfaction degrees of ordered disjunctive rules.

5   Qualitative Model of Decision Making

In section 2, theory of decision under uncertainty was presented, where acts are modeled as functions from a set of states to a set of consequences, preferences of the DM in as the total preorder of consequences and her beliefs as the total preorder of states [8]. Two crucial assumptions are made there: preferences and beliefs are represented as two total orders and they are not comparable to each other. In the light of these assumptions and the postulates, presented at the end part of this section, let us propose a qualitative model of decision making under LPOD. The main purpose is to develop and extend the idea presented in [7] to a more general framework with respect to results and concepts of the classical decision theory.

Decision problem is represented as a logic program consists of three sets of literals: the set **S** represents possible states, the set **A** of decisions and the set **C** of consequences. Rules of the program determine which acts are feasible (hard constraints).

Formally, let $S = (s_1,..., s_n)$ be the set of mutually exclusive states, $C = (c_1,..., c_n)$ be the set of consequences. For every feasible act $a \in A$, the set of rules of the form:

$$\{c_1 \leftarrow s_1, a;...; c_n \leftarrow s_n, a\} \tag{7}$$

for all $s \in S$ and some $c \in C$, is present in the program. Besides, the rule to allow only one consequence to be a result of an act under a given state (cardinality constraint rule) and the rule represents acts literals (disjunctive rule) is added to the program.

Preferences of the DM are expressed twofold: as a prioritized base of positive goals, so the ordered set of disjunctive consequences, which she considers as desirable, and/or as a prioritized base of negative goals, so the ordered set of disjunctive consequences, which are undesirable and she wants to avoid.

For every **S**, **C**, $C \subset C$, $S \subset S$ are represented in LPOD in a disjunctive part of the rule (4) and are interpreted as disjunctions of the same preferred elements. Then:

7   A prototype implementation of LPOD in Smodels system can be found in [5].

- *Positive preference rule r*:

$$C_1 \times ... \times C_k \leftarrow s_m, \; not \; s_{m+1}, ..., \; not \; s_n \qquad (8)$$

to be read: the set of consequences C_1 is the most preferred, next preferred but still reasonable is the set $C_2,...,$ the least desirable but still reasonable is the set C_n.

- *Negative preference rule*:

$$\neg C_1 \times ... \times \neg C_k \leftarrow s_m, \; not \; s_{m+1}, ..., \; not \; s_n \qquad (9)$$

to be read: the set of consequences C_1 is the most unpreferred, next unpreferred is the set $C_2,...,$ the least unpreferred is the set C_n, and for the both rules: $k \geq 1$, $n \geq 0$, $l \geq m \geq 0$, $C_h \subset \mathbf{C}$, and $C_i \cap C_j = \varnothing$ for every i, j; and s_i is a state and c_k a consequence literal respectively[8]. Elements of C_h are interpreted as equally preferred and thus having equal degrees of satisfaction.

DM's beliefs are represented as a prioritized (by means of likelihood's degree), base of likely states (belief rule), which she considers to be possible to occur:

$$S_1 \times ... \times S_k \qquad (10)$$

where $k \geq 1$, $S_h \subset \mathbf{S}$, $S_i \cap S_j = \varnothing$ for every i, j and s_i is a state literal. Elements of S_h are treated as equally likely by means of equal degrees of satisfaction.

To every literal being an element of the ordered disjunction part of LPOD rule, a degree of satisfaction is assigned. Thus, preference and likelihood orders are related to the order of satisfaction degrees of its elements. Answer sets of the form $\{a_i, s_j, c_k\}$ are ranked according to the satisfaction's degree of preference and belief rules.

When a commensurability assumption between degrees of satisfaction of answer sets with respect to states and consequences orderings is not taken, two decision criteria can be used to select the best answer set: a counterpart of the Likely Dominance Rule (LDR), where answer sets are compared by means of containing the most preferred consequences in the most likely states, (priority of the belief rule over the preference rule) and Preference Dominance Rule (PDR), which selects answer set containing an act, which execution leads with the highest degree of likelihood to the most preferred consequence (priority to the preference rule over the belief rule).

A solution to a decision problem is any answer set (thus an act) which is consistent with the knowledge base (feasible acts) and satisfies "the best" the DM's preferences and is maximally consistent with her beliefs[9].

Example 3. (Savage) A DM is in the process of making an omelet. She has already broken five eggs into a bowl and must choose between breaking an egg into a saucer, breaking it into the bowl, or throwing it away. The decision maker is uncertain whether the egg is good or rotten. The consequences of breaking the egg into the saucer are a five-egg omelet or a six-egg omelet and, in either case, a saucer to wash. The consequences of breaking the egg into the bowl are a six-egg omelet or no omelet. The consequences of throwing the egg away are five-egg omelet with one good egg destroyed or a five-egg omelet. Thus: $S = \{rotten, fresh\}$, $C = \{five\text{-}omelet\text{-}one\text{-}egg\text{-}$

---

8   When $m = 1$, it is a conditional preference rule, and for $n \geq 1$, it is a defeasible rule.
9   Preferences and beliefs reflect actual desires and knowledge of a DM; they are not necessary rational, but rather should be interpreted in terms of the willingness to act in a certain way.

destroyed, five-omelet, six-omelet, zero-omelet, six-omelet-wash, five-omelet-wash}
and A = {*throw-away, in-omelet, in-cup*}. The decision problem is the logic program:

five-omelet ← rotten, throw-away.

five-omelet-one-egg-destroyed ← fresh, throw-away.

six-omelet ← fresh, in-omelet.

zero-omelet ← rotten, in-omelet.

six-omelet-wash ← fresh, in-cup.

five-omelet-wash ← rotten, in-cup.

1{*six-omelet, six-omelet-wash, five-omelet, five-omelet-wash, five-omelet-one-egg-destroyed, zero-omelet*} 1.
in-omelet ∨ *in-cup* ∨ *throw-away.*

Let assume now the following preferences and beliefs of the DM, where P and B denote the preference and the belief rule respectively:
P: six-omelet × six-omelet-wash × five-omelet.
B: rotten × fresh.
¬ *zero-omelet.*

The answer sets are: S_1 = {*in-omelet, fresh, six-omelet,* ¬ *zero-omelet*} satisfies P rule to degree **1**, and B rule to degree **2**; S_2 = {*in-cup, fresh, six-omelet-wash,* ¬ *zero-omelet*} satisfies P to degree **2** and B to degree **2** and S_3 = {*throw-away, rotten, five-omelet,* ¬ *zero-omelet*} satisfies P to degree **3** and B to degree **1**. When the commensurability assumption between degrees of satisfaction of both rules is taken, *cardinality* optimal criterion: $S_1 >_p S_3 >_p S_2$ hence the act {*in-omelet*} is the winner. Without this assumption: the LDR criterion leads to: $S_3 >_p S_1 >_p S_2$, hence {*throw-away*} is the winner, and by means of the PDR criterion: $S_1 >_p S_2 >_p S_3$, is obtained and the act {*in-omelet*} is the winner.

The differences between results can be explained by a different attitude of the DM to the risk. In case of the LDR rule, she would rather consider first the most likely state and looks for the act, which gives the best consequences in that state. The PDR centers on the best consequence first and then an act which leads to it with the highest degree of likelihood is selected.

If we consider the DM with the same preferences, but having the belief {*fresh × rotten*}, only one preferred act {*in-omelet*} is the winner because no conflict between the satisfaction of the preference rule and the satisfaction of the belief rule is present.

Let assume now the following agent is given:
P: six-omelet × preference-equality.
B: rotten × fresh.
five-omelet ∨ *six-omelet-wash ← preference-equality.*
where the atom {*preference-equality*} means: {*five-omelet* ∨ *six-omelet-wash*} consequences are the same preferred. Then, by the use of the commensurability assumption (*cardinality* criterion): $S_1 \sim_p S_3 >_p S_2$ hence both acts {*in-omelet*} and {*throw-away*} are the best, while without the assumption, the LDR leads to: $S_3 >_p S_1 >_p S_2$,

hence *{throw-away}* is the winner and the PDR to: $S_1 >_p S_3 >_p S_2$, and *{in-omelet}* is the winner.

There are mainly two difficulties with the approach presented above: what to do with situations, where some answer sets satisfy all preference and belief rules to the same degree and how to handle with a certainty and an ignorance of the DM?

Decision making under certainty in LPOD can be exampled in the following way:

P: six-omelet × six-omelet-wash × five-omelet.

B: rotten.

where *B* is certain. The winner is S_3 = *{throw-away, rotten, five-omelet}*, thus the decision is *{throw-away}*, although it satisfies the preference rule only to **3** degree.

In case of decision under ignorance, it is not reasonable to make a decision based only on information about preferences. Many decision rules were proposed in the literature, which are useful when information about likelihood of states is not present[10]. Consider the example, where two states are equally likely and the preferences are the following:

P: six-omelet × six-omelet-wash × five-omelet × five-omelet-wash × five-omelet-one-egg-destroyed × zero-omelet

B: fresh ∨ rotten

Maxi-max rule (optimistic DM) selects the act which leads to the best among all the most preferred consequences of each act under every state. The answer set *{in-omelet, fresh, six-omelet}* contains the best consequence among all of acts, so *{in-omelet}* is the preferred decision. *Maxi-min rule* (cautious DM) selects the act which leads to the best among the worst consequences of all acts. The answer set *{in-cup, five-omelet-wash, rotten}* is the best according to maxi-min rule and *{in-cup}* is the preferred decision.

The second problem of breaking a tie between equally preferred answer sets can be applied in LPOD in the following way: if some of answer sets (thus acts), satisfy goal and belief bases the same good, acts are compared by means of next preferred answer sets, which encode decision scenarios of these acts under the remaining states of the world. It can be done by adding the same preferred acts as a disjunctive rule to the program, and its consequences as the constraint rules. Then, the same decision rule is applied to the modified program, until the tie is resolved.

6 Conclusions

The main contribution of the paper has been to present a qualitative model of decision making, its representation structure and the reasoning mechanism. A qualitative approach against to a quantitative one seems to be less demanding to the DM ipso facto more natural, allowing a representation of a problem in a more intuitive and a straightforward way. Depending on level of uncertainty of the DM and her attitude towards risk, appropriate strategy to make a decision can be used. Besides, partial and incomplete knowledge can be expressed by means of logic programming techniques. Because of the space restrictions we have not exampled the advantage of LPOD in representing conditional and defeasible preferences and knowledge.

[10] In this case complete or specific information about preferences are required (best or worst).

In the future, problems of collective and qualitative multicriteria decision making in the context of LPOD will be elaborated.

Acknowledgements. The author is very grateful to Gerhard Brewka, Patryk Burek, Asim Ali Shah and anonymous reviewers for useful comments and remarks.

References

1. Aumann, R.: Utility Theory Without the Complet. Axiom. Econometrica **3** (1962) 445-462
2. Bonet, B., Geffner, H.: Arguing for decisions: a qualitative model of decision making. Proc.UAI'96, USA (1996) 98-105
3. Boutilier, C. 1994. Towards a logic for qualitative decision theory. Proc. KR'94, Germany (1994) 75–86
4. Brewka, G.: Logic Programs with Ordered Disjunction. Proc. AAAI, Canada (2002) 100-105
5. Brewka, G.: Implementing Ordered Disjunction Using Answer Set Solvers for Normal Programs. Proc. JELIA'02, Italy (2002) 444-455
6. Brewka, G.: Answer Sets and Qualitative Decision Making, synthesis, to appear 2004
7. Doyle, J.,Thomason,R.: Background to qualitative decision theory. AI Mag. **20** (1997) 55-68
8. Dubois, D., Fargier, H., Prade, H., Patrice, P.: Qualitative Decision Theory: From Savage's Axioms to Nonmonotonic Reasoning. Journal of the ACM **49** (2002) 455-495
9. Dubois, D., Le Berre, D., Prade, D., Sabbadin, R.: Logical representation and computation of optimal decisions in a qualitative setting. Proc. AAAI'98, USA (1998) 588-593
10. Eiter, T., et al.: The KR System dlv. Proc. KR'98, Italy (1998) 406-417
11. Gelfond, M., Lifschitz, V.: Classical Negation in Logic Programs and Disjunctive Databases. New generation computing **9** (1991) 365-385
12. Lang, J.: Conditional desires and utilities: an alternative logical approach to qualitative decision theory. Proc. ECAI'96, Hungary (1996) 318–322
13. Lehman D.: What is qualitative? A framework for quantitative and qualitative decision theory. AAAI Spring Symposium, USA (1997) 65-70
14. Lifschitz, V.: Answer set programming and plan generation. AI **138** (2002) 39-54
15. Niemelä, I., Simons, P.: Smodels-an implementation of the stable model and well-founded semantics for normal logic programs. Proc. LPNMR'97, Germany (1997) 420-429
16. Savage, L.: The Foundations of Statistics. 2nd ed. John Wiley and Sons, NY: Dover (1954)
17. Tan, S. W., Pearl, J.: Qualitative Decision Theory. Proc. AAAI'94, USA (1994) 70–75
18. Von Neumann, J., Morgenstern, O.: Theory of Games and Economic Behavior. 2nd ed. Princeton University Press (1944)

Information Retrieval Model Based on User Profile

Rachid Arezki[1], Pascal Poncelet[1], Gérard Dray[1], and David William Pearson[2]

[1]Centre LGI2P, école des Mines d'Alès, Site EERIE
Parc Scientifique Georges Besse, 30035, Cedex 01, Nîmes, France
{rachid.arezki, pascal.poncelet, gerard.dray}@ema.fr
[2] EURISE, Jean Monnet University of Saint-Etienne 23, rue du Docteur Michelon
42023 Saint-Etienne, France
david.pearson@univ-st-etienne.fr

Abstract. With the development of internet and storage devices, online document servers abound with enormous quantities of documents, so that finding the right and useful information becomes a very difficult task. The end user, generally overloaded by information, can't efficiently perceive such information. It became urgent to propose new information retrieval systems able to apprehend efficiently these enormous quantities of documents. In this paper we present *PQIR* an information retrieval model based on user profile. The originality of our approach is a choice of indexing terms depending on the user request but also on his profile. An empirical study confirms the relevance of our approach.

1 Introduction

With the development of internet and storage devices, online document servers abound with a very large number of documents. The end user, generally overloaded by information, can't efficiently perceive such information. Today, one of the tackled issue is thus to provide the end user with the right and useful information. Indeed, the objective of an information retrieval system is to answer efficiently to a user request often expressed in natural language. Whatever the effectiveness of information retrieval system used, relevant documents can be omitted because the user request does not refer correctly to these documents. Indeed, requests only formulated by key words express badly the user information needs. Of course, these needs depend on the formulated request but also on the knowledge acquired by the user in his search domain. In other words, two users can formulate the same requests for different needs. For example, the results awaited by an expert in Java language formulating the request "Java course" are different from the results awaited by a non expert with the same request. One, solution consists of taking into account the user profile in the information retrieval process in order to increase the relevance of the answered documents. In this paper, we present *PQIR* an information retrieval model based on user profile. The originality of our approach is a choice of indexing terms depending on the user request but also on his profile. That is to say that we consider the need of a user depends on his request but also on his knowledge acquired through time on the

C. Bussler and D. Fensel (Eds.): AIMSA 2004, LNAI 3192, pp. 490–499, 2004.

thematic of his request. The article is organized as follows: Section 2 presents information retrieval in the standard vector space model. Then, Section 3 presents our information retrieval model. Experimental results are presented in Section 4. Section 5 gives an overview of related work. Finally, Section 6 provides some concluding remarks and directions of future research.

2   Information Retrieval Based on Standard Vector Space Model

In the vector space model, each document d is represented by a n-dimensional vector $(w_1,..,w_n)$, where w_i is the weight of the term t_i in the document d. A term can be a word, a stem, a lemma, or a compound. For each pair (u, v) of vectors, a similarity function (or distance function) $s(u,v)$ should be defined. For a given request vector q (a request is also just a text and can be converted into a vector), retrieval is achieved by measuring similarity between a document and request in the underlying vector space. Thus, the most similar documents to the request will be proposed to the user. More formally, the standard vector space model can be presented as a tuple $<X, Q, T, s, f>$, where X represents the set of documents (i.e. document collection), Q stands for the set of requests, T represents the term set indexing, s is a similarity or distance function and f is the term set construction function, with $T=f(X)$.

Term set construction. The indexing term set T is built from the collection X. Its elements are chosen to be as discriminative as possible. Thus, there are various methods: for example the choice of indexing term set can be based on term frequency, where terms that have both high and low frequency within a document are considered to be function words [10][16][18].

Term Weighting. The weight of a term represents the degree of its importance in a document. There are three main factors term weighting: term frequency factor, collection frequency factor and length normalization factor. TF-IDF weighting is one that has been well studied in the information retrieval, where the importance of a term is proportional to the occurrence frequency of this term in each document and inversely proportional to the total number of documents to which this term occurs in a given document collection [16]. More precisely, let TF_i be the frequency of occurrence of term t_i in a document d and let DF_i be the corresponding document frequency. The importance of word i in document d, denoted by w_i, is expressed as follows:

$$w_i = \frac{TF_i}{\sum_j TF_j} \times \log(N/DF_i)$$

where N represents the number of documents in the collection.

Similarity Measure. They are different similarity measures, the most popular one is the cosine coefficient. It measures the angle between a document vector and the request vector. Let d_i and d_j be two documents vectors, the similarity of the *cosine* between these two documents is formulated by:

$$SIM(d_i, d_j) = \frac{d_i \bullet d_j}{|d_i| \times |d_j|}$$

where $/d_i/$ represents the euclidean length of the vector d_i.

3   PQIR Model

PQIR is an extended vector   space model, it can be presented as a tuple
$<X, Q, P, T, s, f>$,   where X represents the set of documents (i.e. document
collection), Q stands for the set of requests, P is the set of user's profiles, T represents
the term set indexing, s is a similarity or distance function and f is the term set
construction function. For a given request q and a profile p we have $T=f(p, q)$.

Our motivation is to integrate effectively the user interests in the information
retrieval process. Thus, the construction of the indexing term set T is done in a
dynamic way and depends both on the user profile p and on the request user q (i.e.
$T=f(p, q)$). For each new user request q, a new term set T is rebuilt. After the
determination of the indexing term set T, the request q and each document of the
collection X are represented by vectors. To better adapt to the user's needs, the initial
request vector q is transformed into q'. The transformation of q to q' requires the
construction of the profile-request matrix (Section 3.3). The algorithm below
describes the information retrieval process associated with a new user request q.

Algorithm 1: Retrieval Algorithm
Input q: user request, p: user profile
Output proposal of documents to the user
Begin
   1. construction of the indexing term set T
   2. calculation of the profile-request matrix M_T
   3. vectorial representation of the request q and of each document of the collection X
   4. calculation of the new request vector q'
   5. calculation of the similarity between q' and the whole documents of the collection X
   6. propose to the user the documents most similar to the request q'
end

3.1   User Profile Representation

A user is defined by a tuple $p=<id, G>$ where id stands for an unique user identifier
and G is a graph representing documents consulted by this user. The general idea is to
analyze the content of the different documents and to store in the graph G the co-
occurrence frequency between various terms of a document, as well as occurrence
frequency of these terms. More formally, $G=<V, E>$ is a labelled graph such as:
   1. $V=\{(t_1, f_{t_1})..(t_n, f_{t_n})\}$ is a set of vertices of G, where each vertex (t_i, f_{t_i}) is
   represented by a term t_i and its frequency f_i.
   2. $E=\{(t_i, t_j, fco(t_i, t_j) / t_i, t_j \in V\}$ is a set of edges of G, where $fco(t_i, t_j)$ reresents
   co-occurrence frequency between the terms t_i and t_j.

The co-occurrence frequency (or co-frequency) between two terms is defined as the frequency of both terms occurring within a given textual unit. A textual unit can be k terms windows, sentences, paragraphs, sections, or whole documents [2][12]. In the framework of our user model, $fco(t_i, t_j)$ represents co-occurrence frequency between the terms t_i and t_j in the set of the documents consulted by the user.

Thus, the user profile is built through the set of the documents consulted by user. For each new consulted document d, a graph of co-occurrence G_d associated to d is built, according to the following steps:

- Identification of terms (lexical segmentation),
- Elimination of the stop words, that is, terms that are not interesting,
- Stemming, that is, the reduction of terms to their root,
- Construction of the graph G_d.

For each new consulted document d, a graph G_d is built, then G_d is added to graph G. User profile is thus represented by the graph G (see Algorithm 2).

Algorithm 2   User Profile Learning Algorithm
Input d: consulted document , $p=<id,G>$ the user profile
Output updated user profile $p=<id,G>$
Begin
  1. construction of the co-occurrence graph G_d
  2. ***for*** each term t_i of G_d ***do***
     if $t_i \in G$ ***then***
$$f_{t_i}^G = f_{t_i}^G + f_{t_i}^{G_d}$$
     else   create a new vertex (t_i, f_{t_i}) in the graph G such as $f_{t_i}^G = f_{t_i}^{G_d}$
  3. ***for*** each edge $(t_i, t_j, fco(t_i, t_j))$ of G_d ***do***
$$fco_G(t_i,t_j) = fco_G(t_i,t_j) + fco_{G_d}(t_i,t_j)$$
end

where $fco_G(t_i,t_j)$ represents the frequency of co-occurrence between the terms (t_i, t_j) in the graph G.

3.2   Indexing Term Set Construction

The choice of the indexing terms takes into account user profile as well as information retrieval request. Our goal is to choose indexing terms reflecting the knowledge of the user in the domain of his search. As shown by the algorithm below, the indexing terms are selected among the terms of the user model which are in co-occurrence with the terms of the initial request.

Algorithm 3   Indexing term set construction
Input q: user request , $p=<id,G>$ the user profile
Output T: indexing term set
Begin
  1. $T \leftarrow$ terms contained in the request q;
  2. ***for*** each term t_i of q ***do***
     for each term t_j of G such as $fco(t_i, t_j)>0$ ***do***

$$\textit{if } \frac{(fco(t_i, t_j))^2}{f_{t_i} \times f_{t_j}} > \beta \quad \textit{then} \quad T = T \cup \{t_j\}$$

End

where β is a constant representing the threshold of term selection.

3.3   Profile-Request Matrix

From the indexing terms obtained previously, we extract from the user profile p, the co-occurrence frequency matrix of the indexing term set T. This matrix represents semantic bonds between the various indexing terms. Let $T_p = \{t_1, .., t_n\}$ be the set of terms contained in the user profile $p = <id, G>$. We call matrix *profile-request*, noted M_T, the square matrix of dimension $|T \times T|$ such as $T \subset T_p$, where each element m_{ij} of M_T is defined by:

$$m_{ij} = fco(t_i, t_j)$$

3.4   Request and Document Representation

The initial request q is indexed on the set of terms T. Then from the matrix profile-request M_T and the initial request q, a new request vector q' is calculated in order to take into account the user profile. This request aims to reflect, as well as possible, the user interest in his search domain.

$$q' = (1 - \alpha) \times \frac{q}{|q|} + \alpha \times \frac{q \times M_T}{|q \times M_T|}$$

$|q|$: Euclidean length of the vector q,

$|q \times M_T|$: Euclidean length of the vector $q \times M_T$

α : threshold such that $0 \leq \alpha \leq 1$, allowing a hybridation between the initial request $\frac{q}{|q|}$ and the enriched one $\frac{q \times M_T}{|q \times M_T|}$, the higher α is the more the user profile is considered.

The documents of a collection are represented in the traditional vector space model [16] and are indexed on the set of terms T. The information retrieval is done by the calculation of similarity between the new request q', and the documents of the collection. To measure the similarity, we use the cosine formula [16] as described in Section 2.

3.5   Example

In order to illustrate our approach, let us consider the following example. Let a user be defined by his profile $p = <id, G>$. Let us consider that this user retrieves a documents on France through the request "France". The Figure 1 shows a part of the user profile graph. The indexing terms are selected among the neighbors of the term "France" in the graph G modeling the user profile. Thus, with for example a threshold $\beta=0.01$, by applying the algorithm of indexing term set construction (Algorithm 3), we obtain:

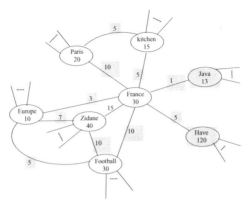

Fig. 1. A part of the user profile graph

$$\frac{fco("france","football")^2}{f_{"france"} \times f_{"football"}} = \frac{10^2}{30 \times 30} = 0.111 > \beta \quad \Rightarrow \quad will \quad be \; selected$$

$$\frac{fco("france","zidane")^2}{f_{"france"} \times f_{"zidane"}} = \frac{15^2}{30 \times 40} = 0.187 > \beta \quad \Rightarrow \quad will \quad be \; selected$$

$$\frac{fco("france","europe")^2}{f_{"france"} \times f_{"europe"}} = \frac{3^2}{30 \times 10} = 0.030 > \beta \quad \Rightarrow \quad will \quad be \; selected$$

$$\frac{fco("france","paris")^2}{f_{"france"} \times f_{"paris"}} = \frac{10^2}{30 \times 20} = 0.166 > \beta \quad \Rightarrow \quad will \quad be \; selected$$

$$\frac{fco("france","kitchen")^2}{f_{"france"} \times f_{"kitchen"}} = \frac{5^2}{30 \times 15} = 0.055 > \beta \quad \Rightarrow \quad will \quad be \; selected$$

$$\frac{fco("france","java")^2}{f_{"france"} \times f_{"java"}} = \frac{1^2}{30 \times 13} = 0.002 < \beta \quad \Rightarrow \quad will \quad be \; rejected$$

$$\frac{fco("france","have")^2}{f_{"france"} \times f_{"have"}} = \frac{5^2}{30 \times 120} = 0.006 < \beta \quad \Rightarrow \quad will \quad be \; rejected$$

The indexing term set selected is:
$$T=\{"france", europe", "kitchen", "paris", "football", "zidane"\}$$

The request vector indexed on the set of term T is: $q=(1, 0, 0 , 0, 0, 0)$
The profile-request matrix will be:

$$M_T = \begin{bmatrix} 0 & 3 & 5 & 10 & 10 & 15 \\ 3 & 0 & 0 & 0 & 5 & 7 \\ 5 & 0 & 0 & 5 & 0 & 0 \\ 10 & 0 & 5 & 0 & 0 & 0 \\ 10 & 5 & 0 & 0 & 0 & 10 \\ 15 & 7 & 0 & 0 & 10 & 0 \end{bmatrix}$$

For example, element $M_T[1][3]$ corresponds to the frequency of co-occurrences between the terms "France" and "kitchen".

Thus, the transformed request becomes:

$$q'=(1-\alpha)\times\frac{q}{|q|}+\alpha\times\frac{q\times M_T}{|q\times M_T|}=(1-\alpha)\times(1,0,0,0,0,0)+\frac{\alpha}{\sqrt{459}}\times(0,3,5,10,10,15)$$

with $\alpha=0.5$, we obtain: $q'=(0.5,\frac{1.5}{\sqrt{459}},\frac{2.5}{\sqrt{459}},\frac{5}{\sqrt{459}},\frac{5}{\sqrt{459}},\frac{7.5}{\sqrt{459}})$

The information retrieval is done by the calculation of similarity between the new request q', and the documents of the collection indexed on the set of terms T. Thus, the most similar documents to q' will be proposed to the user.

4   Experimentation

An evaluation was made to measure the capacity of the *PQIR* model to personalize in a relevant way the information retrieval.

4.1 Method

Data. The documents used for our empirical study are press articles, collected from 5 different online newspapers in different periods. Our collection contains 1200 documents on different thematics (Cinema, Data Processing, Economy, Football, International policy, ..).

Comparison. We have chosen to compare *PQIR* model with the standard vector space model *VS* and with a model similar to the one presented in *DN02* (we call it *PVS*). In *PVS*, user profile has the same structure as a request or a document in the system and is represented by a vector in the vector space, for a given document d, a request q and profile p, a retrieval function $f(q,p,d)$ is defined by:

$$f(q,p,d)=\alpha.s(q,d)+(1-\alpha).s(p,d)$$

where s is the similarity function (we use the the the similarity of the *cosine*).
By varying the value of α, we found that the optimal value is between 0.2 and 0.6, for this experiment α is fixed to 0.5.
The mechanism for updating the user profile in *PVS* is based on a linear adding of vectors (of documents consulted by the user).

Procedure. The evaluation was made on 5 users (real and simulated). We asked each user to formulate request corresponding to its personal interest on the three systems and to evaluate the results provided. Starting with an empty profile, the user consults documents and at each 10 consultations he formulates the same request and evaluates the results obtained. For this experimental study the constants α and β are fixed respectively to 0.3 and 0.01.

Table 1. Precision rate

Consulted documents	PQIR			PVS			VS		
	P(10)	P(20)	P(30)	P(10)	P(20)	P(30)	P(10)	P(20)	P(30)
10	73.33	73.33	68.88	36.66	33.33	27.7	10	11.66	22.2
20	90	81.66	78.88	36.66	30	26.66	10	11.66	22.2
30	90	85	80	40	30	25.55	10	11.66	22.2
40	96.66	90	85.55	40	30	25.55	10	11.66	22.2
50	96.66	91.66	83.33	36.66	31.66	26.66	10	11.66	22.2
60	96.66	85	82.22	33.33	30	28.8	10	11.66	22.2
70	100	91.66	85.55	33.33	31.66	30	10	11.66	22.2
80	100	91.66	86.66	30	26.66	30	10	11.66	22.2
90	100	93.33	87.77	30	26.66	30	10	11.66	22.2
100	100	93.33	87.77	43.33	33.33	32.22	10	11.66	22.2

Results. The evaluation of the IR systems is usually done with the standard measures of precision (P) and recall (R), where:

$$P = \frac{Number\ of\ relevant\ documents\ retrieved}{Total\ number\ of\ documents\ retrieved} \qquad R = \frac{Number\ of\ relevant\ documents\ retrieved}{Total\ number\ of\ relevant\ documents}$$

The table 1 shows the precision of the documents returned by each system *(PQIR, PVS, VS)* according to the number of documents consulted by the user. Thus, P(10), P(20) and P(30) represent successively the relevance of the 10, 20 and 30 first returned documents. These results show significant improvement in the precision score when using the *PQIR* model rather than *VS* or *PVS* model. We also note that more user consults documents more the relevance of the documents returned by *PQIR* increases, and it increase more than *PVS* model.

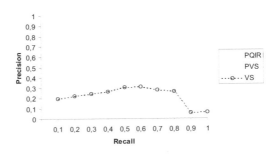

Fig. 2. Precision/Recall of the different systems after 100 documents consulted

In order to illustrate further the comparison between *PQIR* and *PVS* model, Figures 2 presents the precision/recall graph. The results show that the precision of the *PQIR* model is very high (greater than 0.83) for recall values less than 0.6. For high recall values (>0.7) the precision decreases (between 0.13 and 0.6) and these values are however good. We note also that the precision of the *PQIR* model is more important than *PVS* and *VS* for all values of recall.

5   Related Work

In traditional information retrieval systems, users express their needs by formulating requests which are often insufficient to obtain relevant documents. *Blair&Maron* showed that the poor performance of IR systems is mainly due to the incapacity of the users to formulate adequate requests [3]. Indeed, experiments have proved that different users may expect different answers for the same request. Furthermore, the same user, for the same request, may expect different answer in different periods of time [13]. Thus, information retrieval models taking into account user profile were proposed [13,7,5]. Different methods for learning user interests for information filtering and information retrieval were proposed [15,16,4,1,6,19,9,8]. Thus, *Chen* models the user by a multiple TF-IDF vectors [4]. In [14] the authors represent a profile as Boolean features using a Naive Bayesian classifier to determine whether a Web page is relevant or not. In [11,17], the authors use neural networks for learning user profiles. Contrary to the existing information retrieval models, our model integrates semantic information in the representation of the user profile but also in the choice of the indexing terms.

6   Conclusion

In this paper, we proposed a new approach for a personalized information retrieval. The model proposed allows a better consideration of the user's interests in information retrieval process by: (1) A dynamics choice of indexing terms reflecting as well as possible the user knowledge in his search domain, (2) An automatic enrichment of the user request by the matrix of profile-request.

In the information retrieval models where the user is represented by vectors of terms, an iterative process of user profile re-indexing is necessary to take into account of new indexing terms. In our model no re-indexing of user profile is needed. Experimental results confirm the relevance of our approach. One of the prospects for research is the application of the indexing term set construction method in the framework of a standard information retrieval model.

References

1. R. Arezki, A. Mokrane, G. Dray, P. Poncelet, and D. Pearson. LUCI : A Personnalization Documentary System Based on the Analysis of the History of the User's Actions. In Proceedings of the 6th International Conference On Flexible Query Answering Systems (FQAS 2004). LNAI, Springer Verlag, Lyon, France, pages 487–498, 2004.
2. R. Besan,con, M. Rajman, and J.-C. Chappelier. Textual Similarities based on a Distributional Approach. In Proceedings of the Tenth International Workshop on Database And Expert Systems Applications (DEXA99), Firenze, Italy, pages 180–184, 1999.
3. D.C. Blair and M.E. Maron. An Evaluation of Retrieval Effectivness for a Full-Text Document Retrieval System. Communication of the ACM, 28(3):289–299, 1985.

4. L. Chen and K. Sycara. WebMate: Personal Agent for Browsing and Searching. In Proceeding of the Second International Conference on Autonomous Agents, pages 132–139, 1998.

5. P.M. Chen and F.C. Kuo. An Information Retrieval System Based on User Profile. The Journal of Systems and Software, 54:3–8, 2000.

6. C. Danilowicz and H.C. Nguyen. User Profile in Information Retrieval Systems. In Proceedings of the 23rd International Scientific School (ISAT 2001), pages 117–124. PWr Press, 2001.

7. C. Danilowicz and H.C Nguyen. Using User Profiles in Intelligent Information Retrieval. In Proceedings of the 13th International Symposium on Foundations of Intelligent Systems, pages 223–231. Springer-Verlag, 2002.

8. W. Fan, M.D. Gordon, and P. Pathak. Effective Profiling of Consumer Information Retrieval Needs: A Unified Framework and Empirical Comparison. Decision Support Systems, to appear, 2004.

9. H. Lieberman. Letizia: An Agent That Assists Web Browsing. In C. S. Mellish, editor, Proceedings of the Fourteenth International Joint Conference on Artificial Intelligence (IJCAI-95), pages 924–929, Montreal, Quebec, Canada, 1995. Morgan Kaufmann publishers Inc: San Mateo, CA, USA.

10. H.P. Luhn. The automatic creation of literature abstracts. IBM Journal of Research and Development, 2:159–165, 1958.

11. M. McElligot and H. Sorensen. An Evolutionary Connectionist Approach to Personnal Information Filtering. In Proceedings of the Fourth Irish Neural Network Conference, Dublin, Ireland, pages 141–146, 1994.

12. A. Mokrane, R. Arezki, G. Dray, and P. Poncelet. Cartographie Automatique du Contenu d'un Corpus de Documents Textuels. In Proceeding of the 7th international conference on the statistical analysis of textual data JADT, 12-15 mars 2004, Louvain-La-Neuve, Belgique, 2004.

13. S.H. Myaeng and R.R. Korfhage. Integration of user profiles: Models and Experiements in Information Retrieval. Information Processing & Management, 26:719–738, 1990.

14. M. Pazzani and D. Billisus. Learning and Revising User Profiles: The Identification of Interesting Web Sites. Machine Learning Journal, pages 313–331, 1997.

15. J.J. Rocchio. Relevance Feedback in Information Retrieval. In G. Salton, the SMART Retrieval System : Experiments in Automatic Document Processing, pages 313–323, 1971.

16. G. Salton and M.J Mc Gill. Introduction to Modern Information Retrieval. New York: McGraw-Hill, 1983.

17. A. Tan and C. Teo. Learning User Profiles for Personalized Information Dissemination. In Proceedings, 1998 IEEE International Joint Conference on Neural Networks, Alaska, pages 183–188, 1998.

18. C.J. Van Rijsbergen. Information Retrieval, 2nd edition. Dept. of Computer Science, University of Glasgow, 1979.

19. D.H. Widyantoro, T.R. Ioerger, and J. Yen. Learning User Interest Dynamics with a Three-Descriptor Representation. Journal of the American Society of Information Science, 52(3):212–225, 2001.

Schema Matching in GIS

Snezhana Manoah, Omar Boucelma, and Yassine Lassoued

LSIS-CNRS Avenue Escadrille Normandie-Niemen
13397 Marseille, France
{Snezhana.Manoah,Omar.Boucelma,Yassine.Lassoued}@lsis.org

Abstract. With the proliferation of spatial data on the Internet, there is an increasing need for flexible and powerful GIS data integration solutions. Recall that a data integration system provides users with a uniform access to a multitude of (local) data sources. The user poses his query against a virtual (global) schema, which is rewritten into queries against the local sources. A key issue in this context is to provide (semi)automatic schema mappings between schemas. In this paper we describe a machine-learning based approach for GIS schema matching. Our approach extends existing machine-learning approaches for (traditional) data mapping but departs from them due to the nature of geographic data. Our solution reduces the complex mappings by identifying different values of a determining property.

1 Introduction

A data integration system provides uniform access to multiple data sources. The user poses her query against a virtual (*global, mediated*) schema; the query is decomposed into queries that are sent to the *local* sources. The query answer is constructed from responses provided by the local sources. *Wrapper* programs are attached to the local sources in order to provide transformations between the local data models and the global data model. To translate the global query into queries to be posed against local schemas, the data integration system needs to know the correspondences between elements of both schemas. One of the main problems in data integration consists in the construction of semantic mappings between the source schema and the mediated schema.

Non standard domains such as Geographic Information Systems (GIS) need a greater compatibility between the different applications and sources of information, compatibility which could easily supply the user with information of different type and location. Semantic integration of GIS is a hard topic, especially when there is no special hint that helps in choosing the best formalisms and/or integration architectures.

In this paper we describe our approach for GIS schema mapping. Our approach extends existing machine-learning approaches for (traditional) data mapping but departs from them due to the nature of geographic data we are dealing with. We propose a solution which reduces complex mappings by identifying a *determining* property. To improve the performances our approach includes a schema matching algorithm based on geometric criteria.

C. Bussler and D. Fensel (Eds.): AIMSA 2004, LNAI 3192, pp. 500–509, 2004.

2 Motivating Example

2.1 Geographic Data Model

The schema matching problem consists in identifying semantic mappings between local source schemas and the mediated schema. In order to build a data integration system which integrates sources having different data models, we have to choose a unifying data model for the mediated schema. In order to preserve the advantages of the nested structure and to comply with standards advocated by the OpenGIS Consortium [1] we are using GML, the Geography Markup Language [2] as an integration data model.

GML is an XML encoding for geographic data. GML uses XML Schema and offers the possibility to describe different geographic characteristics like coordinate reference systems, geometry, topology, etc. In GML, the world is modeled using concepts such as *features* and *properties*. A GML feature is an abstraction of real world phenomenon that is characterized by a set of properties, where each property can be thought of as a triple {name, type, value}.

2.2 Data Sources

In our example, we will study a subset of two Canadian databases: BDTQ (Base de données topographiques du Québec) and CITS (Centre d'Information Topographique de Sherbrooke) . BDTQ [3] describes a topographic database with 25 geographic features that cover: hydrography, means of transport, buildings, equipment, vegetation, borders, etc. For sake of simplicity we will consider only features for hydrography, means of transport and buildings. BDTQ features have a property denoted Description which indicates the geographic type that may correspond to a given feature instance as illustrated in Table 1.

Table 1. BDTQ Schema

Feature	Signification	Description
Batim_P	Building (point)	Building, Building in construction, Greenhouse
Batim_S_Area	Building (area)	Building, Building in construction, Greenhouse
VComm_P	Means of transport (point)	Bridge
VComm_L	Means of transport (curve)	Road, Street, Tunnel, Bridge, Railway
Hydro_P	Hydrography (point)	Waterfall, Rapid
Hydro_L	Hydrography (curve)	River, Waterfall, Rapid
Hydro_S_Area	Hydrography (area)	River, Lake, Island

Table 2 below represents CITS source schemas. CITS encompasses a bigger zone and contains 196 features that describe the same geographic objects as BDTQ does but in using a different ontology (vocabulary).

Like BDTQ, CITS features contain a property called EntityName that describes the geographic type of a feature instance.

Table 2. CITS Schema

Feature	Signification	EntityName
21E5BUILDID_arc_arc	Building (curve)	Building
21E5BUILDIP_pt_pt	Building (point)	Building
21E5LI_ROAL_arc_arc	Limited-Use Road (curve)	Limited-Use Road
21E5ROADL_arc_arc	Road(curve)	Road
21E5RAILWAL_arc_arc	Railway(curve)	RailWay
21E5WATERBD_arc_arc	Hydrography (curve)	WaterBody
21E5WATERCL_arc_arc	Water Course (curve)	WaterCourse

3   Related Work Limitations

Previous research papers have proposed many techniques and prototypes to achieve a partial automation of schema matching in specific application domains. Among these prototypes are LSD [4], [5], DIKE [6], ARTEMIS [7], SKAT [8] and CUPID [9]. Existing schema matching approaches are mainly based on linguistic techniques and most of them deal only with bijective mappings that map one local schema element into one mediated schema element [10]. This makes them inappropriate to the GIS domain where data has a numeric type and the data structure involves complex mappings.

3.1   Many-to-Many Mappings

Existing schema matching approaches are not appropriate to GIS where in most of them, different features have a different level of classification in terms of geographic types. For instance, suppose that the global (mediated) schema contains two features denoted Road and Railway. According to BDTQ Description property, Road and Railway types have one correspondent Vcomm_L. While in CITS, we have three features that correspond to Road and Railway, these are: 21E5LI_ROAL_arc_arc, 21E5ROADL_arc_arc and 21E5RAILWAL_arc_arc. As a result, bijective mappings are hard to identify when processing mappings between BDTQ schema and the mediated one, because of the different classification granularities that may lead to many-to-many (n:m) complex mappings.

3.2 Nomenclature Problems

Despite of standardization efforts for a geographic nomenclature [11], [12], GIS providers still use different nomenclatures, when they are not using one that may not be significant. This is the case of CITS where names are not very suggestive, and do not help in leveraging of existing matching approaches, which are mostly based on name matching and use word similarities extended with synonymous and homonymous drawn from dictionaries. Hence a non significant nomenclature affects the performance of such approaches.

4 Our Approach

In this section, we briefly describe the key ideas for tackling GIS schema matching.

4.1 Reducing Complex Mappings

As we already explained, the different geographic databases can have different granularity of representation of the geographic objects which engenders complex mappings. When a feature represents different geographic types, in the most of the cases, it contains a determining property which indicates the geographic type of the instances of the feature. In BDTQ such property is the property Description. The solution that we propose is to transform many-to-many complex mappings into many-to-one mappings (n:1) or one-to-one (1:1) with a condition on the determining property values. This property can be found in an automatic way in using name based and constraint based matching algorithms.

4.2 Geography Based Matching

One of the most important characteristics of the geographic data resides on the geographic information that they contain. The different geographic types have often geometric properties that can be used to distinguish them from each other. These properties do not only describe the geometric measures like length, surface, diameter, etc but can include properties concerning the global view of the set of the objects (density, surface density of the objects). For example, when we take a look at the geographic representation of roads we notice that they have relatively regular and lengthened shapes which can distinguish them from other geographic objects (buildings, lakes, etc.). We can also distinguish a street from a highway in using the differences between their lengths and their disposition in an urban zone. Buildings are mainly of regular geometric shape (right angles and a limited number of sides) and their area value varies in certain ranges. Within an urban zone, buildings form groups very close to each other.

While some of these geometric properties are difficult to describe, others may be easily calculated: length, area, lengthening, density, etc. To alleviate name based matching insufficiencies, we suggest to include geometric information in our matching system i.e., to use geometric based matching. For that, we need a set of well-defined discriminating criterions and an appropriated classification algorithm. For each instance of the geographic feature, the matching algorithm or the *learner* will receive parameters like length, area, lengthening, density, etc., and in using a previous learning/training knowledge, the learner should be able to classify the instance in a given geographic category.

5   GIS Matching Design

5.1   Overall Design

The schema matching problem can be viewed as a classification problem. Given a set of mediated schema elements $\{c_1, c_2,..., c_n\}$, our matching algorithms, based on appropriate classification methods, have to classify each local schema element by finding its corresponding element in the mediated set $\{c_1, c_2,..., c_n\}$. The architecture of the schema matching system that we propose is based on a multi-strategy learning approach as suggested in LSD [4], [5]. We use a set of matching algorithms called base learners, each of them is dealing with a single matching criterion. To each pair (l,m), l being a local instance (i.e., an object of a local schema), m being a mediated instance, the base learners assign a score that indicates the probability that l corresponds to m. A composite matching algorithm called meta-learner combines the base learner predictions. The meta-learner assigns for each base learner a set of weights that indicate the relative importance of that learner.

The base learners and the meta-learner provide an instance-based matching. To obtain the final results we generalize the performances on an instances level to the performance on an element level. The base learners that we currently propose are the Name Matcher and the Geo Matcher. A very important characteristic of the schema matching system architecture is its extensibility. We are considering the integration of other kind of base learners that exploit information like, spatial objects location, data types [13], the nested structure of the data, etc. Work performed by the system can be divided in two phases: the training phase and the matching phase, described in the next sections.

5.2   Training Phase

In the training phase the learners are trained to "recognize" the mediated schema elements. The training information is manually prepared using a set of local sources.

First, the system extracts data from a given local source. Second, for each local feature, the system asks the user to specify its determining property (if any). Finally, the system starts training the Name Matcher to recognize the determining property. The training proceeds this way: the system prepares the training examples that contain the name of the determining property for each local feature; these examples may be extended by synonyms before feeding the Name Matcher.

For each feature, the system identifies different values for the determining property. The system refines the features into sub features and asks the user to specify the rules that map a refined local feature to mediated feature. For example, for feature VComm_L, the user will specify:

VComm_L [Description=Street] => Street
VComm_L [Description=Road] => Road
VComm_L [Description=Tunnel] => Tunnel
VComm_L [Description=Railway] => Railway
VComm_L [Description=Bridge] => Bridge

When the refinement level is too high, the mappings are most often of kind n:1. For example, in BDTQ feature Building_in_construction corresponds to the mediated Building; it also corresponds as well to the same Building mediated feature. In this case, learners are trained to classify the refined features. The base learners receive a set of training examples and create their internal classification model. For each instance of a local feature and each base learner, the system prepares a training example that best suits the learner. The Name Matcher, for example, needs the feature names and the value of the determining property, while the Geo Matcher receives a set of previously calculated geometric properties like surface, perimeter, length etc. The meta-learner calculates weights W_{Lj}^{Ci} that indicate the precision level of learner Lj for the mediated element c_i.

5.3   Matching Phase

In the matching phase, firstly, the system extracts the data from the new source. Next, for each feature of the schema, the system distributes to the Name Matcher the needed information for the recognition of the determining property of this feature. The Name Matcher makes its predictions and determines the researched property. Next, the user verifies that the obtained mappings are correct. The system refines the schema features into sub features corresponding to the different values of the determining property. Furthermore, the learners make their predictions on each instance of a given refined feature and then send them to the meta-learner which combines them with appropriate weights. When the system has collected all predictions about the instances of a refined feature, it calculates the average score that generalize the results of the instance-based matching into schema matching. So the result of the system's work is mappings that map the refined feature of the local schema into features of the mediated schema.

6   The Base Learners

Our schema matching system conception includes, for the moment, only two base learners: the Name Matcher and the Geo Matcher. The Name Matcher exploits textual information. It computes the similarity between the names of the elements and their synonyms. The Geo Matcher treats geometric information. It exploits the geometry of the instances that represent concrete geographical objects.

6.1 Name Matcher

The Name Matcher exploits schema elements names. The matcher that we developed is based on the Nearest Neighbour classification algorithm. The Name Matcher has a training phase and matching phase.

In the training phase the Name Matcher receives uses predefined mappings for a set of local sources. It performs pre-treatment operations, like normalization and extraction of synonyms. Normalization consists in removing all characters that are not letters; in doing so we improve the quality of mappings. Extraction of synonyms is done with the help of WordNet [14].

During the matching phase, the matcher receives data from a new local source, performs a pre-treatment on it and then, using the training data and the Nearest Neighbour algorithm, identifies the mappings between the schema of the new source and the mediated schema.

After the pre-treatment process of the training data and the pre-treatment process of the classification data, an element is represented by a bag of tokens, containing the element name, its synonyms (if any) and eventually other keywords. In order to apply the Nearest Neighbour algorithm we need to define a distance between tokens and a distance between bags of tokens. The latter is defined as follows:

$$sim(T_1,T_2)=\sum_{t_1\in T_1}\left[w_{ij}\cdot\max_{t_2\in T_2}sim(t_1,t_2)\right]+\sum_{t_2\in T_2}\left[w_{ij}\cdot\max_{t_1\in T_1}sim(t_1,t_2)\right],$$

where T_1, T_2 are bags of tokens, w_{ij} is a weight that we assign to the similarity between ti and tj, $w_{ij}=1$, if t_i or t_j is not an extracted synonyms and $w_{ij}=0.6$, if t_i and t_j are synonyms.

The similarity between tokens sim(ti, tj) is calculated as a sum of the lengths of common for the tokens substrings, divided by the average length of the two tokens.

The final similarity score between an element eGlobal$_j$ from the mediated schema and an element eLocal$_i$ from the local schema is obtained by the formula:

$$sim(eLocal_i,eGlobal_j)=\frac{sim(Tl_i,Tg_j)^2}{\sum_k sim(Tl_i,Tg_k)},$$

where Tl_i is the bag of tokens corresponding to eLocal$_i$, Tg_j is the bag of tokens corresponding to eGlobal$_j$ and Tg_k is the bag of tokens corresponding to the kth element from the mediated schema.

6.2 Geo Matcher

The Geo Matcher is the new learner we developed a new learner. It uses geometric criterions that can give us a notion of the basic form and size of the object.

Design. For each instance of a geometric feature, the Geo Matcher receives previously calculated parameters like area, length, perimeter, etc. Then, in using an appropriate classification algorithm, it predicts the correspondences between the local instance and the mediated one.

The criterions used by the learners are:

Geometry type: Gives the geometric type of the object i.e. Point; Line, Polygon, MultiPoint, MultiLineString, MultiPolygon.

Area: Gives the total area of the object.

Diameter: It is the longest distance between two points of the object.

Length: The sum of the lengths of all object components

Perimeter: It is the sum of the perimeters of all object components.

Lengthening: It is the ratio of the diameter and the perimeter of the object.

Compacity: It measures the similarity of the object shape with a circle. It is proportional to the ratio of the perimeter and the object area.

Complexity_L: It is ratio of the number of vertexes and the length, for linear objects and the ratio of the number of vertexes and the surface; for the object from a surface type.

Complexity_P: It is the ratio of the number of vertexes and the perimeter of the object.

Implementation, Tests and Results. We developed a Geo Matcher prototype in using IBM's ABLE (Agent Building and Learning Environment) [15], a Java framework for building intelligent agents using machine learning and reasoning. In using ABLE, we have tested different classification algorithms (Neural Networks, Naïve Bayes, k-Nearest Neighbor) with various parameterizations in order to select the most appropriate algorithm for Geo Matcher. The algorithm that showed the best results was surprisingly the simplest i.e., the k-Nearest Neighbor (k-NN) algorithm, a lazy classification algorithm. Before using the k-NN algorithm we filtered the initial data and performed some conversion for discrete attributes.

The performance of the Geo Matcher based on the k-NN algorithm can be explained by the fact that it does not consider similarities among instances of one feature and the same geographic feature. More intelligent algorithms like Neural Networks and Naïve Bayes try to generalize the characteristics of the whole set of instances. But objects from the same geographic type can differ in their size and form. For example, we may have small lakes with a size equal to some building size; but there exist also big lakes with geometric properties rather different from those of the small lakes. When used with a big base of training examples with a variety of instances, k-NN should be able to find as a nearest neighbor an instance of the same geographic type, i.e., it will map a small lake with a small lake.

We tested the Geo Matcher in using BDTQ data, and a mediated schema with 7 geographic features: Street, Road, Building, WaterCourse_L (represents linear watercourses), WaterCourse_S (represents watercourses from type surface), Lake and Island. In order to obtain the training and testing data we divide the source BDTQ into two parts, using the first one for the training process and the second for the matching phase. Splitting BDTQ does not impact the correctness of the results because the data used by the Geo Matcher, i.e. sizes and shapes of geographic objects, is relatively independent of the sources.

The results of the tests show that the accuracy of the Geo Matcher is about 80 %. If we generalize the results for the instances by transforming them into mappings between features, we will find out that it maps 100% correctly the features of the mediated and the source schema. Most of incorrect mappings came from the fact that Geo Matcher was unable to make a difference between a street, a road and a watercourse. That can be easily explained because of similarities (size and in the geometric form) between the geographic types. When the geometric form is not sufficient, we can use as determining criterion the density of distribution of the object. It is clear that in an urban zone, there are more streets than roads and rivers, more buildings than lakes, etc. The density parameter can be represented by the ration n/S, where n is the number of instances of a feature t, that are located in a delimited zone with a fixed size and S is the area of this zone.

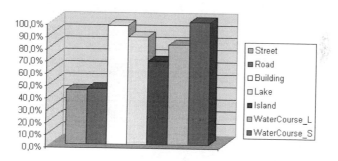

Fig. 1. Geo Matcher Performances.

Table 3 illustrates the results obtained with our Geo Matcher. The first column denotes a feature of the source, the second column represents the number of correct mappings for this feature, and the third column shows the percentage of errors together with the alternate features that has been selected for matching instead of the appropriate one.

Table 3. Detailed Results for the Geo Matcher Tests.

Feature	Rate of correct mappings	Percent of errors	
Street	44.3 %	24.3 %	Road
		31.4 %	WaterCourse_L
Road	45.5 %	45.5 %	Street
		9 %	WaterCourse_L
WaterCourse_L	81.3 %	16.5 %	Street
		2.2 %	Road
Building	97 %	3 %	Lake
Lake	87.9 %	6.6 %	Building
		4.4 %	Island
		1.1 %	WaterCourse_S
Island	68.1 %	31.9 %	Lake
WaterCourse_S	100 %	0%	

7 Conclusion

In this paper we described a machine learning approach for GIS schema matching, an important and crucial issue for GIS data integration. Our approach extends existing schema matching approaches but departs from them due to the particularities of the geographic data. Our approach reduces complex mappings in transforming them into mappings of type one-to-one and many-to-one. It also proposes a novel learner called Geo Matcher that exploits the geometry of objects. The Geo Matching system described in this paper should be included in the GIS data integration platform we are currently developing.

References

1. OpenGIS consortium. URL : http ://www.opengis.org.
2. Ron Lake Simon Cox, Adrian Cuthbert and Richard Martell. Geography Markup Language (GML) 2.0. URL : http ://www.opengis.net/gml/01-029/GML2.html, February 20th 2001
3. Base de données topographiques du Québec (bdtq), July 2001 http//felix.geog.mcgill.ca/heeslib/bdtq_20000.html
4. Pedro Domingos Anhai Doan and Alon Levy. Learning Source Descriptions for Data Integration. In Proceedings of WebDB'2000
5. Pedro Domingos Anhai Doan and Alon Halevy. Reconciling schemas of disparate data sources: A machine-learning approach. In Proc. of ACM SIGMOD, 2001
6. Palopoli L, Sacca D, Terracina G, Ursino D. A unified graph-based framework for deriving nominal interscheme properties, type conflicts and object cluster similarities, IEEE Comput, pp. 34–45, 1999
7. Castano S, De AntonellisV, De Capitani diVemercati S. Global viewing of heterogeneous data sources. IEEE Transactions on Knowledge and Data Engineering 13(2):277–297, 2001
8. Mitra P, Wiederhold G, Jannink J (1999) Semi-automatic integration of knowledge sources. In: Procof Fusion '99, Sunnyvale, USA
9. Madhavan J, Bernstein PA, Rahm E. Generic schema matching with Cupid. In: Proc 27th Int. Conf on Very Large Data Bases, 2001, pp. 49–58
10. E. Rahm and P. A. Bernstein. A survey of approaches to automatic schema matching. VLDB Journal 10(4), 2001
11. Nomenclature d'échange du CNIG associée à la norme Edigéo. http ://www.cnig.fr/cnig/infogeo/france/-Normalisation/nomenclature.cnig.1.fr.html, 1995
12. Ministère de l'Économie de Finances et de l'Industrie. Standard d'échange des objets du plan cadastral informatisé, Décembre 2001
13. Corpus-based Schema Matching, Jayant Madhavan, Philip A. Bernstein, Kuang Chen, Alon Halevy, and Pradeep Shenoy, Workshop on Information Integration on the Web, IJCAI'2003, Acapulco, Mexico
14. WordNet - http://www.cogsci.princeton.edu/~wn/
15. ABLE research project. http://www.alphaworks.ibm.com/tech/able

The Web as an Autobiographical Agent

Maya Dimitrova[1], Emilia Barakova[2], Tino Lourens[3], and Petia Radeva[4]

[1]Institute of Control and System Research, Bulgarian Academy of Sciences
P.O.Box 79, 1113 Sofia, Bulgaria
dimitrova@icsr.bas.bg
[2]Lab. for Dynamics of Emergent Intelligence, RIKEN Brain Science Institute (BSI)
2-1, Hirosawa, Wako-shi, Saitama, 351-0198 Japan
emilia@brain.riken.go.jp
[3]Honda Research Institute Japan, Co., Ltd.
8-1, Honcho, Wako-shi, Saitama, 351-0114 Japan
tino@jp.honda-ri.com
[4]Computer Vision Center, Autonomous University Barcelona,
08193 Bellaterra, Spain
petia@cvc.uab.es

Abstract. The reward-based autobiographical memory approach has been applied to the Web search agent. The approach is based on the analogy between the Web and the environmental exploration by a robot and has branched off from a currently developed method for autonomous agent learning of novel environments and consolidating the learned information for efficient further use. The paper describes a model of an agent with "autobiographical memories", inspired by studies on neurobiology of human memory, the experiments of search path categorisation by the model and its application to Web agent design.

1 Introduction

Autonomous agents have traditionally been built on the grounds of detailed models, focused tasks, or common-sense heuristics, i.e. the top-down approach. Autonomous agents approach is common in Web modelling, soft computing and intelligent robotics among other application fields [1]. In this paper we make a parallel between a robotic and a Web autonomous agent. Intelligent robotics agents have to fulfil various tasks independently and to decide when and what kind of initiative to undertake. Web agents are similar to robots in that they have sensory-perceptual/logical input, the goal to achieve, and they perform within the limits of the implemented algorithms. Recent research, however, has shown that it is technically justified to build intelligent robots on the grounds of neurobiology [2], [3]. It turns out that the neurologically plausible autonomous robots/agents achieve higher behavioural flexibility and goal attainment and are superior to the ones that count on complex, but exact computational heuristics [4], [5], [6]. A higher level of "intelligence" is demonstrated when the robot can efficiently make use of the previously encountered events [6], [7]. This involves not just memory in the

C. Bussler and D. Fensel (Eds.): AIMSA 2004, LNAI 3192, pp. 510–519, 2004.

computational sense, i.e. memory as a stack or storage, but human-like memory, that accounts for concept change, source monitoring, novelty/familiarity detection and goal reformulation [8]. In this paper we hypothesise, that if a Web agent incorporates autobiographical knowledge in terms of "human-like memories" sense, it will be able to interact with the user in a more meaningful way.

Traditionally, cognitive science has produced general models of human cognition, learning and behaviour that, however, lack the diversity of individual user daily experience. The semantics of the interaction of the user with the Web has to be able to convey not just facts, statements, definitions, i.e. the so-called "cold" knowledge, but also "hot" opinions, reviews, intentions, and nuances in user communication within the Web [9]. Moreover, this has to account for user previous Web experience. In trying to build these micro-components of an intelligent Web agent we have turned to cognitive science looking for insights or "smart heuristics" to make them both simple and efficient and perhaps brain-like in their "attitude" to the user [10]. What we have found is abundance of approaches that need to be investigated further. We feel that the Web provides the perfect medium to understand those micro-aspects of cognition and to build Web agents, which are small in size and very adapted, placed on a single server and accessible from any place in the world.

The paper addresses three interrelated research issues we are currently pursuing. The first one is a model of a robot based on episodic/autobiographical memories, inspired by studies on neurobiology of human memory. The second is the interpretation of the autobiographical robot as an intelligent agent similar to Web agents, and the third is an example of a "short-term memory-like" Web agent with its attractive interface features and difficulties in "understanding" the user. We feel the issue of building autonomous/autobiographical agents to account for user experience with the Web is essential to the process of building the new Semantic Web.

2 Agents with and Without Human-Like Memory

At present, intelligent robots are able to perform tasks with different degree of autonomy. Experimental robotics has shown that autonomous systems can be built by simulating, for example, insect-like behaviours. We aim at higher level of intelligent behaviour, which has as a bottom line flexibility - to use its old experiences in novel situations. At present, even higher forms of intelligence, derived from imitation learning, is an object of robotics applications [2], [3], [4]. Since the actual processes underlying this type of behaviour are understood on a very coarse level only, it does not meet our present research objectives.

Computer science and robotics exploit the characteristics of the semantic memory - memory for facts. Actually, memory for events and their relatedness is the way higher organisms build their knowledge; moreover, episodic memory copes naturally with the sensory, perceptual and behavioural character of learning of an embodied agent. In our study novelty is considered a gating factor for forming episodic memories during learning and familiarity - a mechanism for inferential use of episodic memories while behaving in a novel Web environment. The so stated scope puts forward memory-based behaviour, which includes remembering of past events, familiarity detection involved in episodic memory formation and the respective more effective Web behaviour, corresponding to the interests/needs of the user. The basic difficulty, as we will show, is how to reasonably infer future user interests from browsing behaviour. The autobiographical approach is able to predict more consistent future requests than the "straightforward" one.

3 Hypothesis: Episodic and Autobiographical Memory Underlie Intelligent Action

There have been many speculations of what intelligence and intelligent behaviour is. Yet, an exact definition is not available. Instead of elaborating on the subject, we will define the range of intelligent behaviour that is plausible for our study. We aim at a level of intelligence that allows transfer of the previously acquired knowledge into a new task. Therefore, memory is the intrinsic requirement for our intelligent system.

Extensive research in neuroscience [11], [12], [13] has shown that there is a specific brain structure - the hippocampus - that encodes episodic memories (EM). The episodic memories lay the context of the studied task - sensually/perceptually/ emotionally coloured, yet underlying the acquisition of new and restructuring old, declarative knowledge (knowledge for facts and events, not for learning skills). Its characteristic feature is the "when" question   the explicit reference to the exact moment when a given event took place, like learning new knowledge or meeting an old friend, for example. EM has got temporary structure in terms of one-to-several hours. Hence the main difference from the so-called autobiographical memory (AM) where the "when" aspect is often difficult to retrieve.

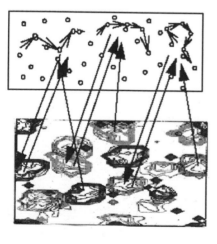

Hippocampal
formation

Neocortical
association areas

Fig. 1. Schematic representation of the interactions between HF and NAA, to support the EM-AM connection

Although AM in general consists of episodes and spans lifetime, the "when" notion is frequently lost and compensated with the "what" notion. And this constant re-categorisation and "renewal" of old memories relates and interrelates to the semantic memory acquisition process, generally taking place in the interaction between the hippocampal and the cortical processes/areas (Fig. 1). Web search has similarities with exploring a new environment and finding one's way in it, this way the environment is constructed of keywords and concepts as analogy to views and itineraries [14].

To connect Web modelling with the episodic memory paradigm and brain-like computing in general, the following hypothesis is made. Web search resembles the exploration and successful information finding processes, as experienced by a navigation activity. During the interaction of a user through a Web engine with the information on the net, the Web agent remembers the successful searches and the most satisfying findings of the user and serves as an optimisation tool for doing new search.

4   Autobiographical Web Agent Concept

The aim of the autobiographical Web agent is to learn the meaningful steps and directions by Web explorations and use them as an optimisation criterion by the next searches. In analogy with a robot exploration task, finding meaningful information is equivalent, for the particular user, to either (sub-) goal or landmark encounter. As an initial step, the encountered useful concepts (keywords) are clustered by an on-line clustering algorithm, in which the characteristic concepts are stored as representatives.

The clustering algorithm uses the following principle. Clusters that often come in a subsequent order get laterally connected, forming episodes. These connections get active by the arrangement of the search results. Let us assume that an episode is formed by three elements: sensing, perception, and evaluation. In formula (1) episode W is a triple,

$$w = (s, p, a), \tag{1}$$

where s, p, a are the sensory, perceptual and evaluational component, respectively. An episode evolves over time under these three influences:

$$\frac{dW}{dt} = f(s + p + a), \tag{2}$$

where f denotes functional dependence.

A search task consists of finding a discrete item of information. Such an item will be further referred to as an event. A Web search episode is a set of n discrete events occurring in temporal order e_t, ($t \in [1,...,n]$), defined by a considerable difference in the event representations. $W = \{w_t\}$, $t \in [1,...,n]$. A single event w_t is defined by the user input s, and p and a, that denote the feedback of the remembered searches (previous searches from the same user) and the evaluational influence. The sensory component s_t refers to the user's current choice and p_t and a_t components are based on previous experience. Here, s_t introduces the influence from the external user and constitutes of feed-forward connections; the perceptual component p_t represents the internal influences and is performed by lateral connections; the reward component a_t represents the influence of the previous actions as brought on the current event. The change from one to another event requires a change in at least one component that is bigger than an internal threshold, indicating the detection of a novel event.

The sensory as well as the reward (evaluational) signals are encoded in unique patterns of activity. These patterns are external-world related. The formation of the internal representations is conceptually motivated by the Piagetian self-supervised paradigm for learning target-oriented behaviour [15]. The essential feature for enabling brain maps to handle this rule is the capacity for topologic organisation, which allows an internal representation of the external space emerge in a coordinate-free way [16]. A good deal of work has been carried out on the ways in which simple, self-organising heuristics can produce such internal representations, from the early work of Kohonen [17] to the recently developed growing self-organising algorithms [18].

Instead of relying on artificial heuristics that perform topological organisation, we have chosen Hebbian learning for episodic encoding. The Hebbian rule most closely simulates the known brain computational mechanisms. The required self-organisation properties can be obtained by lateral inhibition and dominating topological projections between the layers, rather than by artificial computational heuristics. The network is structured as a two-layer lattice of neurons, corresponding to the major hippocampal areas. The lateral inhibition connections enhance the self-organising process.

The actor-critic model [19] most closely resembles the motivational, i.e. reward-related influence. At any discrete moment t, the user-specified keywords result normally in a big variety of options. A particular choice of an option is equivalent to an action on the Web environment. This corresponds to the choices of an actor. If the needed information is not available, the exploration of the chosen link is short, and the user does not branch off for other related links. This information is used as a feedback influence - the critic "criticises" the taken step. The actor-critic mechanism regards the actions of the user that are directed to finding particular targeted information.

The critic also adapts itself in correspondence with the actor. The reinforcement algorithm leads to improved behaviour with time, caused by the learning from the critic. The critic c at a given position l in the search space is as follows:

$$c(l) = \sum_i w_i f_i(l), \tag{3}$$

where w_i is the weight between the current output from the episodic layer and the i-th location in the search space l. The critic learns the value function by updating the weights so that the prediction error that drives learning is reduced:

$$\delta(t) = R(t+1) + \gamma \cdot b(l(t+1)) b(l(t)) \tag{4}$$

where γ is a constant discounting factor, set so that the weight between the output of the episode layer and the i-th location is minimum. R is the reward at moment $t+1$. The error is reduced by so changing the weights to the active locations on the search space to be proportional to:

$$\delta_t f_i(l) \tag{5}$$

In the experiments shown below, the actor makes use of k action cells a_j, $j = 1...k$. At position r, the activity of the each action cell is:

$$a_j(l) = \sum_i v_{ji} f_i(l), \tag{6}$$

where a_j stays for the j-th action cell, and v is the adaptive weight between the action cell and the i-th output of the previous layer. The first step for the movement direction is taken randomly with a probability P_j. The next movement direction is typically chosen in random way. If there is a lateral connection to a related important to the user concept, the possibilities are restricted according to the choices made in the previous movements $P_j(t-1)$, $P_j(t-2)$, so that there is not a random walk, but smoother orbits with eventual sudden turns (Fig. 2).

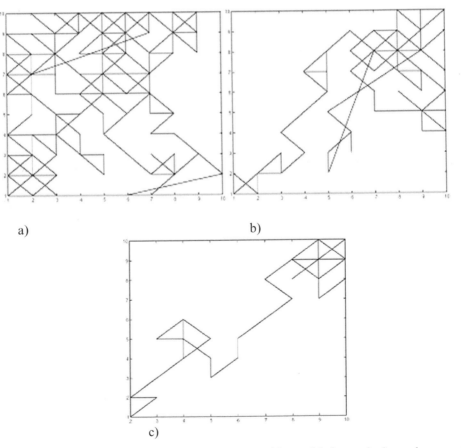

a)

b)

c)

Fig. 2. Learned Web search paths by the actor-critic model for a single goal case; a) performance in the range 1-5 trials; b) performance in the range 75-80 trials; c) performance in the range 190-200 trials

The actor weights are adapted according to:

$$\Delta v_{ij} \propto \delta_t f_i(l_t) g_j(t),\qquad(7)$$

where g reflects the previous-history restrictions on the search path. Fig. 2 depicts the optimisation of a search trajectory, which is only due to the learning of the critic. Finding a more meaningful search path is done by the learned episodes. The optimisation of the search path is guided by the learning of the critic (Fig. 3).

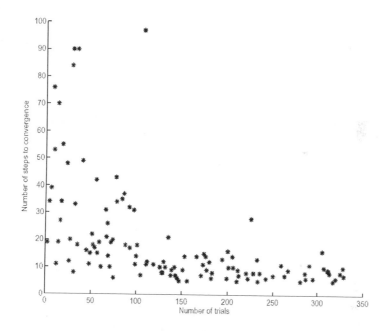

Fig. 3. Convergence rate averaged among 10 sets of 200 experiments

5   Designing Neuro-cognitive Web Interfaces

Among the many ambitious goals of the Web is to build agents/servlets/ applications/ interfaces that are self-explanatory, user-friendly, perceptually salient and conceptually understandable to *every* individual person [20], [21]. This gives confidence in applying the autobiographical agent approach to Web agent design, as at least in robotics, it has given promising and efficient results. In relation to this, an example from Web design is discussed, which is a focused example of the need for "vertical" re-categorisation of the "depth" of the individual user previous-history Web experience. Personalised Web systems [22] often employ "collaborative filtering" or user-similarity based ("horizontal") modelling principles, from the early works [23],

[24] to the numerous recent studies[1]. The cognitive/psychological motivation behind their definition of user interests, however, is vague. The discussed application has attempted to model short-term user interests. The results clearly show that before clustering user preferences based on most recent Web behaviour, the true "persona" has to be defined. The application in focus is called WebPersonae and is aimed to assist the user in browsing the Web [25], [26][2]. The authors have designed a search result reorderer along with the WebPersonae system. The basic goal of the reorderer is to introduce context-sensitivity to search engine results by estimating the user's current Persona and re-ranking the results to a query based on this Persona. As the user moves from page to page, the Personae recognition module identifies the current Persona. When the user runs a search to the Web, the system uses the most similar Persona[3]. to re-rank the received results - the most similar pages are ranked near the top of the list [26]. As the user browses from page to page, the system recalculates Personae similarities. In a sense, this system represents a "hippocampal" (pure "episodic") memory for the previous events/searches.

The evaluation of the search result reorder system has shown the encountered difficulties in user modelling by the autobiographical agent. The straightforward experiment reordered every set of results according to the similarity of each result to the current Persona. The current Persona was itself selected based on the user's recent browsing history. The second set of experiments was aimed at overcoming the 'naivete' of the initial approach. An 'omniscient' version of the system was designed for use with the test data only. This version implements an oracle or look-ahead module that can 'see into the future', i.e. it can look ahead and see which URL a user clicked on, and then select the Persona that *would have given* the best possible up-ranking to that result. This omniscient system is capable of producing a favourable re-ranking for approximately 95% of the search instances in the data-set. This shows that it is possible to give favourable re-rankings most of the time, providing the correct Persona is selected [26]. Being in process of development and evaluation, the WebPersonae system allows to make some conclusions about the nature of the "user-and-the-Web" interaction process as something more sophisticated than simply collections of sequences of events. What is required is a brain-like module, imitating the hippocampal-cortical relations in new knowledge acquisition, i.e. re-categorisation is needed to select the correct Persona. We propose to use our model for finer re-categorisation of user interests and "conceptual reasoning" via, for example, mapping perceptual to semantic cues [27].

The experiments with the interface have shown that the Personae appear intuitive and are adequate for representing different domains of interest. The weak link in the system, according to the authors, is the identification of "when" and "who" to help. The foreseen future improvements are to introduce a thesaurus component for identifying synonyms, and thus cluster based on concepts rather than just words, to employ hierarchical clustering by retaining the hierarchy of interests to represent broad and narrow topics and assist the user when different levels of detail are

---

[1] For example, Google returns 294 000 hits for "collaborative filtering", 30.06.2004
[2] We would like to thank Dr. Nicholas Kushmerick and JP McGowan from University College Dublin for sharing the ideas and the realisation of the WebPersonae interface
[3] TF-cosine similarity

required. The authors emphasize the necessity to create temporary Personae when the user's browsing session does not imply any of their long-term Personae. The temporary Personae can be updated incrementally as the user browses, and used to give short-term context sensitivity. When the user enters another Persona, these temporary ones can be deleted, or if their use continues, they can be made permanent, i.e. long-term [26]. The main aspect of the authors' analysis of the implemented system is the shift from "pure" computer science towards cognitive (neuro-) science approach to personalised Web agent design.

6   Conclusions

Psychological studies show that humans integrate and interpret new experiences on the basis of previous ones [8], [28], [29]. Autobiographical agents attempt similar behaviour on the basis of detailed knowledge of the neuro-cognitive processing mechanisms of new and old episodes in the brain. The paper argues that these mechanisms are needed in artificial/autonomous/intelligent agents to perform better and proposes to set this as an aim in building Web agents. It discusses a neurologically plausible model of episodic/event memory and its application in imitation of user Web behaviour. The autobiographical Web agents are needed to simplify the computational and time-consuming costs and to make the Web friendlier and more meaningful to the individual user.

Acknowledgement. This work is supported in part by TIC2000-1635-C04-04, TIC2000-0399-C02-01 of CICYT, Ministerio de Ciencia y Tecnologia of Spain, a Reseach Grant to Maya Dimitrova by CVC-UAB, 2004, and Contract No 809/98 of the National Research Fund, Bulgarian Ministry of Education and Science.

References

1. Petrie, C.J.: Agent-based engineering, the Web, and intelligence. IEEE Expert, Vol. 11:6, (1996), 24-29
2. Sloman, A., Chrisley, R.: More things than are dreamt of in your biology: Information processing in biologically-inspired robots. Proc. WGW'02 Workshop on Biologically-Inspired Robotics: The Legacy of W. Grey Walter, Hewlett Packard Research Labs, Bristol, August (2002), http://www.cs.bham.ac.uk/~axs/, http://www.cs.bham.ac.uk/~rlc/
3. Sloman, A.: AI's greatest trends and controversies. Edited by Haym Hirsh and Marti A. Hearst, IEEE Intelligent Systems and their Applications, Jan/Feb (2000) 8--17, http://www.computer.org/intelligent/ex2000/pdf/x1008.pdf
4. Triesch, J., Wieghardt, J., von der Malsburg, C., Mae, E.: Towards imitation learning of grasping movements by an autonomous robot. Lect. Notes Artif. Intell, 1739, (1999), 73-84
5. Lourens, T., Wurtz, R.P.: Extraction and matching of symbolic contour graphs, International Journal of Pattern Recognition and Artificial Intelligence, (2003)
6. Barakova, E., Lourens, T.: Novelty gated episodic memory formation for robot exploration. Proc. 2004 2nd IEEE International Conference on Intelligent Systems IS'2004, Varna, Bulgaria, Vol I, (2004), 116-121
7. Verschure, P.F.M.J., Voegtlin, T., Douglas, R.J.: Environmentally mediated synergy between perception and behaviour in mobile robots, Nature, Vol. 425, 9, (2003), 620-624

8.   Conway, M.A.: Sensory-perceptual episodic memory and its context: autobiographical memory. Phil. Trans. R. Soc. Lond. B 356, (2001), 1375-1384

9.   Benga, O., Miclea, M.: New trends in development and cognition. In: O. Benga, M. Miclea (eds.), Development and Cognition. Cluj University Press, Cluj-Napoca, ISBN 973 8095 82 4, (2001), 11-20

10.   Dimitrova, M.: Cognitive modelling and Web search: Some heuristics and insights, Cognition, Brain, Behaviour, vol VII, 3, (2003), 251-258

11.   Wood, E., Dudchenko P., and Eichenbaum, H.: The global record of memory in hippocampal neural activity. Nature, 397, (1999), 613-616

12.   Jensen, O., Lisman, J.E.: Hippocampal CA3 region predicts memory sequences: accounting for the phase precession of place cells. Learning and Memory, 3, (1999), 279-287

13.   Eichenbaum, H., Dudchenko, P., Wood, E., Shapiro, M., and Tanila, H.: The hippocampus, memory, and place cells: Is it spatial memory or a memory space? Neuron. Cell Press, (1999), Vol. 23, 209-226

14.   Barakova E. and Lourens T.: Prediction of rapidly changing environmental dynamics for real time behavior adaptation using visual information. Workshop on Dynamic Perception, Bochum, Germany, Nov. (2002)

15.   Piaget, J.: The Psychology of Intelligence, Routledge, Taylor & Francis, New York, (1950)

16.   Sanger, T. D.: Theoretical considerations for the analysis of population coding in motor cortex. Neural Computation, 6, (1994), 29-37

17.   Kohonen, T.: Self-organizing formation of topologically correct feature maps. Biological Cybernetics, 43, (1982), 59-69

18.   Friske B.: Growing cell structures- a self-organizing network for unsupervised and supervised learning. Neural Networks, 7, (1995) 1441-1460

19.   Sutton, R.S. and Barto, A.G.: Reinforcement Learning: An Introduction MIT Press, Cambridge, MA, (1998)

20.   Lee, Tim Bernards, Fitting it all together, Invited talk at the WWW 2003 Conference, Budapest, Hungary, (2003)

21.   Kushmerick, N., Gleaning answers from the web, Proc. AAAI Spring Symposium on Mining Answers from Texts and Knowledge Bases, Palo Alto, (2002), 43-45

22.   Bonett, M.: Personalization of Web services: Opportunities and challenges, Ariadne, 28, 2001. [http://www.ariadne.ac.uk/issue28/personalization/]

23.   Resnick, P., Iacovou, N., Suchak, M., Bergstrom, Riedl J.: GroupLens: An open architecture for collaborative filtering of netnews. Proceedings of ACM 1994 Conference on Computer Supported Cooperative Work, Chapel Hill, NC: ACM, (1994), 175-186.

24.   Shardanand, U., Maes, P.: Social information filtering: Algorithms for automating "word of mouth". Proceedings of CHI'95 -- Human Factors in Computing Systems, (1995), 210-217

25.   McGowan, J. P., Kushmerick, N., Smyth, B.: Who do you want to be today? Web Personae for personalised information access.   , (2002), 514-517

26.   McGowan, J.P.: A Multiple Model Approach to Personalised Information Access. MSc thesis, University College Dublin, (2002)

27.   Binefa, J., Sánchez, M., Vitrià, J., Radeva, P.: Linking visual cues and semantic terms under specific digital video domains, Journal of Visual Languages and Computing, Vol. 11, 3, (2000), 253-271

28.   Tulving, E., Donaldson, W.: Organization of memory. New York: Academic Press, (1972)

29.   Baddeley, A.D.: Human Memory: Theory and practice. Lawrence Erlbaum Associates, Hove, UK, (1990)

Author Index